*V o l u m e  T wo*

*the*

# INSTITUTES

*of*

# BIBLICAL

# LAW

## *Law and Society*

with a special supplement by
Herbert W. Titus, Professor of Law

# *Rousas John Rushdoony*

ROSS HOUSE BOOKS
VALLECITO, CALIFORNIA 95251

This volume is dedicated to


Dr. Ellsworth McIntyre
and the members of
Nicene Covenant Church
and Grace Community Schools
in great appreciation
for their generous support of
the work of my father.


Rev. Mark R. Rushdoony
President, Chalcedon Foundation

Other titles by
Rousas John Rushdoony

*The Institutes of Biblical Law, Vol. I*
*The Institutes of Biblical Law, Vol. III, The Intent of the Law*
*Systematic Theology (2 volumes)*
*Commentaries on the Pentateuch: Genesis,*
*Exodus, Leviticus, Numbers, Deuteronomy*
*Chariots of Prophetic Fire*
*Sermon on the Mount*
*The Gospel of John*
*Romans & Galatians*
*Hebrews, James, & Jude*
*The Cure of Souls*
*Sovereignty*
*The Death of Meaning*
*Noble Savages*
*Larceny in the Heart*
*To Be As God*
*The Biblical Philosophy of History*
*The Mythology of Science*
*Thy Kingdom Come*
*Foundations of Social Order*
*This Independent Republic*
*The Nature of the American System*
*The "Atheism" of the Early Church*
*The Messianic Character of American Education*
*The Philosophy of the Christian Curriculum*
*Christianity and the State*
*Salvation and Godly Rule*
*God's Plan for Victory*
*Politics of Guilt and Pity*
*Roots of Reconstruction*
*The One and the Many*
*Revolt Against Maturity*
*By What Standard?*
*Law & Liberty*

Chalcedon
PO Box 158 * Vallecito, CA 95251
www.ChalcedonStore.com

# TABLE OF CONTENTS

iii

# INTRODUCTION

The response to *Institutes of Biblical Law* has been a very gratifying one. Few expected so large a study on a subject of so little concern to the churches to succeed. It has, however, met with a very wide approval and response, among students, lawyers, legislators, churchmen, and others.

It has also met with intense hostility at times. It would be well to review the areas of hostility in order to understand some of the key problems of our times. *First,* the comments on homosexuality outraged many. No other aspect led to more intense (if covert) opposition, slander, and sheer venom. Dr. David A. Noebel has observed to me that the church has perhaps been the central area of infiltration by homosexuals. I find this readily believable in terms of my experience. The homosexual clergy are sometimes great champions of love in the pulpit and savage practitioners of hatred on the sly.

*Second,* much hostility has been aroused by my statements with respect to the tithe. Many resent a mandatory tithe in favor of more "spiritual" principles of giving, which they insist lead to more giving than does the tithe. I ask all such to prove to me that their "spiritually minded" giving surpasses the tithe. None have done so. If "spiritual" giving cannot equal the requirements of God's law, it is clearly not the Holy Spirit which is the spirit thereof!

*Third,* a whole series of objections have their roots in the sexual revolution, which has permeated the churches, evangelical and Reformed, far more than appears on the surface. All too many find fornication and adultery justifiable at times, man being himself the judge of the times! A few men, and a surprising number of women, objected to any requirement of the ban on sexual coition during menstruation. Many of these persons felt it was "especially important" to be gratified at that time, which is another way of saying that sin appeals to them.

Obviously, many people are "all for the Lord," provided that He doesn't interfere with their money and their sex life!

A *fourth* general objection has been that the emphasis of *Institutes of Biblical Law* is on law rather than love. But Romans 13:8-10 makes clear that love is the fulfilling of the law, that is, love puts law into action: it respects God's requirements concerning life, property, our neighbor, our enemy, and ourselves. Our Lord makes clear that to love God means to keep the first table of the law, and to love our neighbor means to keep the second table of the law (Matt. 22:34-40; Mark 12:28-34). We do not love our wife or God if we commit adultery, nor do we love God if we are idolaters and take His name in vain. *Love is law in action; hate is lawlessness in action.* Love and hate are more than mere feelings: they are ways of life, either in faith and obedience to God and His law, or in unbelief and disobedience.

An important question we need now to ask is this: Why do we encounter these and similar objections to God's law? Why the sometimes intense reaction even to the point of screamed insults, to an insistence of the binding nature of God's law?

The key is Genesis 3:5. The tempter's key plan is that every man should be his own god, knowing, or determining for himself, what constitutes good and evil. This is original sin; it is the basic sin of man and the underlying factor and foundation of all particular sins. When man tries to be his own god he is saying that he is not a creature, in particular that he is not God's creature.

To be free from God's law means that we are our own law, and this is the heart of antinomianism. It is the denial that God can bind us. We are indeed willing to have God free us from sin, *provided* that we are also freed from bondage to Him and His law! This is the heart of antinomianism, its desire to be free from both sin and God and to become a supposedly free spirit, finding holiness in a spirit-filled life which is disobedient to God's Spirit and word.

To be a creature means that we are created by the triune God and that our redemption and every aspect of our life and society *must* be governed by His law-word. Every word of God is a binding word, because it is God's word. My life must be governed by the word of God. This means that my money, my calling, my family, my sexuality, my political life, my economics, science, art, and all things else must be subject to God's word and its requirements. When I sit at the table and eat, my eating is governed by God's law. When I speak, God's word and Spirit must govern my tongue. When I think and act, I am subject to God's law and must be governed by Him. I have no area of independence from God and His word, and every desire for an independent thought, word, or act is sin.

To be born again means that I, who was once governed by my word and my spirit am now totally to be governed by God's word and Spirit. My failure to be totally under God's word and Spirit is evidence of sin and my imperfect sanctification in this life. I must war against my sinful impulses to independence from God, and, like Paul, regard myself as the enemy whenever and wherever I stray from God's law-word (I Cor. 9:24-27).

The necessity for Biblical law has been underscored of late by the homosexuals themselves. Antinomians have been unable to answer homosexual arguments, because the homosexuals state bluntly that the

Bible gives no grounds for condemning them now that the law is supposedly dead. Thus, in one television interview, homosexuals and their
friends answered objections to homosexuality from the Bible on the
ground that "the Bible banned certain foods, implying that the Bible was
therefore no guide."[1] Again, Howard Erickson, editor of *The Gay
Lutheran,* answered a critic (who failed to stand on Biblical law and lost
the argument), in these words, when the critic cited Leviticus 20:13, to
the effect that homosexuality is an abomination:

> But let's see, doesn't Leviticus also condemn eating shrimp and
> pork?—and having marital relations with one's wife during her
> menstrual period, on penalty of being cut off from God's people?
> Come to think of it, Lev. 20:13 (which you cite), identifying male
> idolatry/abominations, says the penalty for it is death. Is that what
> you have in mind for me, Kaldahl? I hope you're not citing only
> those parts of Leviticus that you personally agree with. This is God's
> Word we're talking about, isn't it?[2]

Indeed, it is God's word, and both parties were using it selectively.
Erickson held:

> Our concern is this: Are gay women and men heartily welcome in the
> house of the Lord?

> In the eyes of our Creator, of course we are, for the Bible assures us
> that God loves every human being, even Paul Kaldahl and even
> Howard Erickson.[3]

If Biblical law be denied, then Erickson is right. Only as we stand clearly
for Biblical law can we avoid a doctrine of universal salvation and a
religion of total tolerance and no condemnation of anything save God
and His law.

But our Lord did *not* set aside the law: He came to *fulfill* it (Matt.
5:17-20). Sandmel points out that "to fulfil" in Rabbinic thought meant
to conform to, to observe faithfully the law of God. Moreover, our Lord
meant not only that the law was in this sense to be brought to fulfilment
but also in the sense of being brought to completion, to its full expression.[4]

> Because the Christian is free *from* sin does not mean that he is free *to*
> sin. Because he is exempt from keeping the law as a means of salva-
> tion does not mean that he is exempt from keeping the law
> altogether. Jesus taught that "No man can serve two masters"
> (Matt. 6:24)—but neither can he serve none. As Throckmorton has

1. Mary Lewis Coakley: *Rated X, The Moral Case Against TV,* p. 36. New Rochelle,
NY: Arlington House, 1977.
2. Howard Erickson, "Homosexual Responds to Heterosexual," in *The Christian
News,* vol. XI, no. 10. March 6, 1978, p. 5.
3. *Idem.*
4. Samuel Sandmel: *Judaism and Christian Beginnings,* p. 356. New York, NY: Oxford
University press, 1978. p. 356.

written, "The Christian who is 'under grace' and not 'under law' must *obey*. He has changed masters, but he is not his own master; he is not, therefore, free to sin if he so wishes." And if he does? Then, although he may believe, he does not have saving faith. For "faith apart from works is dead" (James 2:26). Genuine faith produces a life of disciplined obedience to the moral laws of God—just as a living seed, when properly planted and nurtured, inevitably produces fruit.[5]

The purpose of *Law and Society,* the second of three volumes, is to show how God's law applies to every aspect of our lives and world. There are in God's word specified consequences, curses and blessings, for disobedience and obedience. We cannot understand history apart from that fact.

Moreover, as we look at our world, we need to be encouraged. Its disasters manifest the judgments of God. They make clear that now as always "the wages of sin is death" (Rom. 6:23). If we are unhappy about the disasters and collapses of our time, we may be saying that we regret the failure of sin to prosper, and that we dislike the justice of God in its operations.

There is more to godliness and to righteousness (or, justice) than the mere condemnation of sin. If mere condemnation constituted virtue, then Stalin was most righteous for condemning Hitler, and Hitler was likewise righteous for condemning Stalin! The idea of condemnation as righteousness smacks of pharisaism. Our Lord says, "except your righteousness shall exceed the righteousness of the scribes and Pharisees, ye shall in no case enter into the kingdom of heaven" (Matt. 5:20). Churchmen today are often ready to condemn sin, but where is that righteousness that comes from obedience to God's word? Where is the readiness to teach all nations and to bring all things into captivity to Jesus Christ? (Matt. 28:18-20; II Cor. 10:4-6).

To be creatures means that we are commanded by God the Lord because we are His creation and His re-creation in Jesus Christ. To be a creature means that I know that the Lord is God, my God: "He shall choose our inheritance for us" (Ps. 47:4), and He has done so in Jesus Christ. I can therefore say with David, "My times are in thy hand" (Ps. 31:15), and I can rest, work, and sleep in that confidence (Ps. 4:8).

The purpose of *Institutes of Biblical Law* and *Law and Society* is to point men to God and His word for the government of their lives and our world.

I am grateful, in the writing thereof, for the faithfulness of my Westwood, Los Angeles, group, who, week by week, listened to these

---

5. Joseph Hopkins: *The Armstrong Empire,* p. 126. Grand Rapids, MI: William B. Eerdmand, 1974. The citation is from Burton H. Throckmorton, Jr.: *Study Guide on Romans,* p. 36; New York: Presbyterian Distribution Center, 1961.

developing studies, and to the Pierce brothers, for the use of the Chapel of the Palms. I am grateful also to my publisher, David L. Thoburn and Dolly Thoburn, who kept me supplied with many of the books I needed.

To serve and magnify God is the greatest of privileges and callings, and I am a most privileged man, having been given so happy a calling.

The purpose of the Chalcedon Foundation is the reconstruction of all things in terms of the word of God. This, after all, is the purpose of life, to be conformed to God, and ours is a magnificent task. May God the Lord bless us all therein.

These studies were written from 1973 through 1977.

Rousas John Rushdoony
Chalcedon
Vallecito, California, U. S. A.

## THE SOCIOLOGY OF THE SABBATH

The dictionary defines sociology as, "The science that treats of the origin and history of human society and social phenomena, the progress of civilization, and the laws controlling human intercourse" (Funk & Wagnalls Dictionary). Sociology is a modern science and a product of the past two centuries, but, if we examine the definition carefully, it becomes clear that the word sociology describes, in rather stiff and formal language, the function of the Bible and the prophets of Israel who wrote it. The word *sociology* was coined in 1838 by Auguste Comte to describe his work, and he proceeded to make a religion of humanism out of sociology. His religious ideas were absurd, but his recognition that sociology is a religious discipline was sound.

The prophets of Israel set forth their faith in God as the creator of all things and the determiner thereof. All men and nations had to be governed by God's law, or else face His judgment. The progress of civilization depends on obedience to God's law, and God requires faith in Him to be the controlling factor in society and men. The prophets saw every attempt to work out another concept of society as idolatry, and they would have declared Comte's sociology to be idolatry in essence.

Humanistic sociology arose because the churches had abandoned the faith of the prophets and apostles. By their pietism, they had surrendered the world to the enemy and had retreated to the realm of inner experience almost entirely. This attitude has been commonplace in the church and differences from it are treated as strange doctrine. Thus, Harold Camping, in *Feed My Sheep*, denies that man is restored into kingship and the creation mandate by Jesus Christ. He limits the work of the Christian to evangelism, feeding the sheep. Bittner has called attention to the radical neglect of kingship such a position involves.[1]

One of the great champions of this pietistic approach was John Wesley, along with his brother Charles Wesley. Pietism stressed the ability of man and undercut the sovereignty of God. John Wesley at times championed Pelagius as well as Arminianism.[2] In such a religious position, man, while sometimes *claiming* undue powers for himself, *in*

---

1. Lee P. Bittner III, review of Harold Camping: *Feed My Sheep*, in *Blue Banner Faith and Life,* vol. 28, no. 3, July-September, 1973, p. 134.
2. Bernard Semmel: *The Methodist Revolution,* pp. 81ff., 83, 85f., 194. New York: Basic Books, 1973.

*practice* tends to stress subservience and martyrdom; this view tends to find its crown in suffering rather than in conquest and victory. This was clearly true of John Wesley, whose idea of godliness at times took rather sorry forms. In his late forties, nearing fifty years of age, John Wesley married Mrs. Vazeille, a widow of forty. The sickly nature of this union is summarized by Dobree:

> So, on the understanding that he would preach not one sermon the fewer, nor travel one mile the less, he married Mrs. Vazeille—but this time he did not tell Charles about it; indeed his brother was one of the last to hear of the sad event. And alas, the event did prove sad: for twenty years Mrs. Wesley, who appears to have verged on dementia, harried the life out of her husband. At first she did her best, but she could not bear the constant travelling, the hideous discomfort, the occasional mobbing, and besides, she was sea-sick when they went to Ireland. But why, it may be asked, need she cling to him so burr-like? Ah, Wesley was inordinately attractive to women! And, it must be admitted in extenuation of his wife's behaviour, that he wrote incredibly foolish letters of warmth—purely Christian warmth, no doubt, but it is difficult to distinguish—to many of his tenderer converts. His wife became insanely jealous; she watched all his goings out and his comings in, she rifled his pockets, broke open the drawers of his desk, accused him of making Charles's wife his mistress, would travel a hundred miles to see who was sharing his coach with him, and even, it was reported, pulled him about by his greying hair. "My brother," Charles wrote pungently, "has married a ferret," a phrase echoed by Berridge of Everton. John bore it all with exemplary patience, was unfailing in his care for her; but even he sometimes complained—to his female penitents moreover—that he could not bear "the continually being watched over for evil, the having every word I spoke, every action I did, small and great, watched over with no friendly eye; the hearing of a thousand little, but unkind reflections in return for the kindest words I could advise."[3]

Pietism has elements of neoplatonism and the neoplatonist concept of a divided universe deeply imbedded in its world-view. The material world has to be depreciated as inferior. Thus, Charles Wesley rejoiced when his wife and daughter were hideously pockmarked following smallpox, because, therefore, "they cannot fall heir to sin of vanity." Such a view means that a man's essential attitude towards the world is that it is something to be rescued from rather than something to conquer as God's vicegerunt.

Moreover, pietism, because it makes man primary in salvation (by denying God's sovereignty and predestination), sees all things in terms of man rather than in terms of God. Thus, to cite a specific example, a minister, totally pietistic, saw the meaning of all events in relationship to himself. If a storm upsets his plans, it meant that Satan was trying to

---

3. Bonamy Dobree: *John Wesley* p.114f. New York: Macmillan, 1933.

hinder him. If he foolishly made a costly blunder, it meant that the Lord had brought it to pass to teach him something. The meaning of all events was no larger than himself: the whole universe revolved around frustrating or abetting him. Trains were late, or on time, because the Lord (or Satan in some cases) had a special purpose in it for him.

Such an attitude is not unusual. It has been fostered by generations of preaching. It reduces the sovereign and totally personal God to the level of a witch or warlock playing esoteric games with people. It does not make God personal; it makes God *capricious,* and a capricious God is ultimately impersonal, because He has no inner consistency or nature but merely unconscious drives and impulses.

Moreover, this minister's attitude was really a form of devout humanism, not Christianity. In a Biblical theology, all things have reference to God, and God is totally in control of all things, so that nothing can be understood without reference to Him. In a consistent humanism, all things have reference to man, and nothing has any meaning apart from man. To understand the meaning of anything means then to understand it as it relates to man. Moreover, in a theocentric universe, there is between man and God a whole multiplicity of secondary causes and consequences, so that, although God can act directly, He normally acts through this total work of history, which is totally ordained by Him; even God's miraculous acts within history are a part of that total context the primary meaning of which is primarily determined by Him. In an anthropocentric universe, all things refer to man, and they must be so interpreted. The minister who saw the tardiness or promptness of trains as having a radically personal meaning differed from Sartre only in the form of his existentialism: both derive meaning out of their own being. Pietism thus was a forerunner of modern existentialism.

Let us examine some examples of such pietistic preaching. One common story used in sermons dates from the beginning of the thirteenth century, when Eustache, Abbot of St. Germer-de-Flai, went to England on the orders of Pope Innocent III, to obtain recruits for a crusade. According to this tale,

> A poor Norfolk woman was washing her linen one Saturday afternoon, after three o'clock—the hour the sabbath was deemed to begin—when a divine messenger appeared to her and warned her to desist. She refused, saying she would be in danger of starving if she did not do her usual work. There then appeared a coal-black beast like a sucking-pig, that fastened itself to her left breast and sucked her blood till she died.[4]

This tale is unintentionally important, in that it reveals the persistence of the Hebraic practice with regard to the Sabbath, i.e., the sabbath

---

4. Peter Fryer: *Mrs. Grundy, Studies in English Prudery* p. 89. New York: London House & Maxwell, 1963.

began at sundown of the previous day. The Old Testament concept of time and law thus persisted in spite of the antinomian pietism of the day. The sundown to sundown Sabbath was also kept in New England. For our present purpose, this tale shows a universe which moves in a totally capricious way in that it is governed, not by God's sovereign purpose and law but by man's actions.

Legalism is a code of deeds and observances as a means of justification before God; it substitutes man's acts for God's redeeming act in Christ as the means of justification. When the law is made into a justifying ordinance, it is radically altered by this change. It is atonement which leads to acceptance before God, whereas a false means of atonement leads to judgment rather than to justification. Man's alternatives thus are justification or judgment. The justified grow in grace by means of the law. The unjustified go their way, either to prosper for a time before facing judgment, or to judgment in both time and eternity, as God's laws and purposes decree. The works of the unjustified are irrelevant to the purposes of justification, and, whatever they accomplish, the result is an accrued wealth for the kingdom of God (Isa. 45:14; 49:22, 23).

A false view of justification leads to a belief in immediate judgment and immediate blessing. This idea led later to the concept of poetic justice, a this-wordly reckoning of all scores. In a false view of justification, Sabbath breaking leads to incidents like that of the "poor Norfolk woman." Too often medieval and post-Reformation sabbatarianism followed the same concept of immediacy. In the days of Charles I, such thinking was in evidence:

> The sabbatarians took the offensive with great energy. In various parts of the country they preached that to do any work on a Sunday afternoon was as great a sin as murder or adultery; that to throw a bowl on that day was as great a sin as murder; that to hold a feast or wedding dinner on the sabbath "is as great sinne, as for a Father to take a knife and cutte his childes throate." Even to ring more than one bell to call people to church was accounted as great a sin as murder. Sometimes cited as a good example for Christians was the story of the Jew of Tewkesbury who fell into a large privy one Saturday and, for reverence of his sabbath, would not be pulled out, "choosing rather to dye in that filthie stincking place." Many preachers preferred to make their congregations' flesh creep with awful examples of what happened to sabbath-breakers.[5]

The pharisaism of the "Jew of Tewkesbury" was commended by men who knew full well that our Lord had declared,

> What man shall there be among you, that shall have one sheep, and if it fall into a pit on the sabbath day, will he not lay hold of it, and lift it out? How much then is a man better than a sheep? Wherefore it is lawful to do well on the sabbath days (Matt. 12:11, 12).

---

5. *Ibid.,* p. 96.

Their preaching was anti-Scriptural and in conscious, pharisaic defiance of Christ, although they would have denied such a charge.

Where legalism leads to an undue burden on the law, undue consequences are attributed to every act. Thus, one dean who

> believed that most executed persons blame Sunday pleasure as a first step to their downfall, gave a graphic description of how taking long walks on Sundays led to thirst, and thirst led to drinking, and drinking led to lewd desires, and "when the whore may be had, where the Bottle has raised the inclination to her, and at the very Moment she becomes agreeable; it can hardly be questioned, but that as little Regard will soon be paid to Chastity, as to Sobriety." That was where Sunday travelling led one.[6]

Another error appears in this statement, environmentalism. Legalism ascribes undue powers to man as far as salvation is concerned, and all too little where responsibility is concerned. Adam and Eve claimed that they could be their own gods, in terms of the tempter's plan (Gen. 3:5), but they soon coupled it with an environmentalism and a lack of responsibility. The environment was to be held guilty of their sin, not they themselves (Gen. 3:12-13). The sociology of legalism is thus little different from the sociology of sin.

It is not surprising that the legalists of the seventeenth century were distressed by the fact that Calvin, in the Reformation era, had played bowls on Sunday, and had held that the seventh day's rest could be held on any day. Its transfer to Thursday had been discussed in Geneva.[7]

On the other hand, some men stressed the social significance of the Sabbath, as Hill has shown. Some public officials recognized that Sunday sports and drinking gave rise to social disorders. Hills adds,

> But there was also a strong social case for enforcement of Sunday rest. This has been obscured by historians who repeat contemporary propaganda emphasizing the "killjoy" side of Sabbatarianism. Had there been no administrative action by J.P.s and municipal authorities and no legislation against Sunday work, the competitive pressure on some employers and some of the self-employed poor to work a seven day week for some of the time would have been irresistible.[8]

Sabbatarianism on these grounds was popular with all but those who lived in "unlawful callings or unlawfully in their honest callings," according to John Sprint in 1607.[9]

Calvin, in discussing the Sabbath, saw it as the commemoration of the resurrection, but did not see it as "an invariable adherence" to the

---

6. *Ibid.,* p. 103.
7. Christopher Hill: *Society and Puritanism in Pre-Revolutionary England,* p. 170, 210f. Second edition. New York: Schocken Books (1964) 1967.
8. *Ibid.,* p. 165.
9. *Ibid.,* p. 166.

"septenary number." In discussing the purpose of the sabbath and Lord's Day, Calvin declared,

> Let us sum up the whole in the following manner: As the truth was delivered to the Jews under a figure, so it is given to us without any shadows; first, in order that during our whole life we should meditate on a perpetual rest from our own works, that the Lord may operate within us by his Spirit; secondly, that every man, whenever he has leisure, should diligently exercise himself in private in pious reflections on the works of God, and also that we should at the same time observe the legitimate order of the Church, appointed for the hearing of the word, for the administration of the sacraments, and for public prayer; thirdly, that we should not unkindly oppress those who are subject to us.[10]

Calvin's interpretation is faithful to the declaration of the commandments through Moses:

> Keep the sabbath day to sanctify it, as the LORD thy God hath commanded thee.
> Six days thou shalt labour, and do all thy work:
> But the seventh day is the sabbath of the LORD thy God: in it thou shalt not do any work, thou, nor thy son, nor thy daughter, nor thy manservant, nor thy maidservant, nor thine ox, nor thine ass, nor any of thy cattle, nor thy stranger that is within thy gates; that thy manservant and thy maidservant may rest as well as thou.
> And remember that thou wast a servant in the land of Egypt, and that the LORD thy God brought thee out thence through a mighty hand and by a stretched out arm: therefore the LORD thy God commanded thee to keep the sabbath day (Deut. 5:12-15).

The *first* emphasis of the law is, as Calvin saw, soteriological. We are commanded to rest in order to recognize and celebrate the fact that we are saved, not by our works, but by God's redeeming work in Jesus Christ. The Sabbath thus celebrates salvation; Israel's Sabbath commemorated their deliverance from Egypt, and the Christian Sabbath or Lord's Day the resurrection of Jesus Christ, delivering us from the power of sin and death. Salvation presupposes sovereignty, and our rest is therefore a recognition that it is not we who are sovereign but the triune God. We rest in His sovereign redeeming work and power. We recognize that the world does not depend upon us and our works but upon God and His work. For John Wesley, this faith constituted antinomianism, because for him it was man's work that was all-important. Arminianism and Pelagianism will view Sabbath observance as a good work primarily rather than a rest in God's redemptive work. Much earlier, it had been the Dissenters who stressed Sabbatarianism. In the eighteenth century, one of the first effects of the Methodist influence in Parliament was "an

---

10. John Calvin: *Institutes of the Christian Religion*, Bk. II, ch. VIII, sec. xxiv: I, p. 431f. Philadelphia: Presbyterian Board of Christian Education, 1936.

increased stringency of Sabbatarian legislation."[11]

*Second*, Calvin stressed study and church worship. Church worship is not mentioned in the law, except on feast days (Lev. 23; Deut. 16:8), but it was the requirement of the New Testament (Heb. 10:25). The study of the word and works of God requires continuing growth in the knowledge of God, and worship presupposes a delight in and a gratitude to God. Both of these things, study and worship, are aspects of our rest in God, our faith in His sovereign power and government. Our rest increases as our knowledge and faith increase. Biblical faith is rightly called the religion of the book, in that true faith requires study and a growth in knowledge.

*Third*, Calvin stressed that the Sabbath means "that we should not unkindly oppress those who are subject to us." The law thus not only requires man to rest, but that his servants and animals rest also. Moreover, on Sabbath years, the land also was to rest (Lev. 25). Thus, as man is freed by God's redemptive act, he is to free all those in subjection to him, including the earth itself. The implications of this for the conservation of the earth, and for godly "labor relations," are very great.

These implications were clearly seen in some of the Puritan Sabbatarians. Hill has pointed out that many Puritans saw the aspect of economic oppression in Sabbath-breaking.[12]

> A competitive atomized society was replacing the communities which had to some degree protected their members. In this society it was the Sabbatarians who looked after the interests of the small craftsmen, apprentices and journeymen, who "would be left remediless under such masters as would both oppress them with labour and restrain them from God's service" (R. Baxter). The Massachusetts Bay Company insisted that in the puritan promised land labour should cease at 3.0 p.m. on Saturday. The Rest of the day should be spent in catechizing and preparing for the Sabbath.[13]

The Puritan clergy regarded the Sabbath as "the day for edification, for education."[14]

The Sunday games and recreations attacked by the Puritans were often aspects of fertility cult practices. Hill speaks of "the phallic maypole."[15] John Wesley, in a sermon on I Corinthians 12:31, "The More Excellent Way," spoke of many of the current popular activities as "foul *remains of Gothic barbarity*," i.e., of ancient paganism[16] Thus, while Sabbatarian-

---

11. William Edward Hartpole Lecky: *A History of England in the Eighteenth Century*, vol. II, p. 697. New York: Appleton, 1879.

12. Hill: *Society and Puritanism*, p. 165f.

13. *Ibid.*, p. 166.

14. *Ibid.*, p. 172.

15. *Ibid.*, p. 184.

16. Herbert Welch, editor: *Selections From the Writings of the Rev. John Wesley, M. A.,* p. 102. New York: Methodist Book Concern, (1901) 1918.

ism did become at times legalistic and trivial, its origin in seventeenth-century England was Biblically and sociologically sound. The Sabbath was seen as a means of renewing society, but this aspect was seen all too dimly. Moreover, two strains were confused, the medieval pietistic rules and the Reformation emphasis on rest and worship. Neither of the two strains were wholly free of bias. The medieval era had a strong stratum of law which had been overlaid with legalism. The reformers tended to strike at both legalism and the law. Knappen is correct in declaring that ''Modern English Sabbatarianism is therefore not Reformed or Calvinistic in its origins. So far as it had any theoretical background, it is to be found in the medieval doctrine, which survived in Anglican teaching and legislation, that the day was to be devoted wholly to religious ends.'' [17] Lancelot Andrewes was important in the theological formulation of Sabbatarianism. [18]

One of the central problems of Sabbatarianism appears in Knappen's summation of this belief, namely, ''that the day was to be devoted wholly to religious ends.'' What constitutes *religious* ends? Too often, Sabbatarians define religious as *ecclesiastical*: religion is reduced to the church and to church related activities. Important as the church is, such a definition leads to a deformation of both religion and the church. The advantage of such a definition is that is becomes very much easier then to define valid Sabbath activities. The more general term, *religious ends*, allows some uncertainty. What constitutes a faithful religious observance of the Sabbath? It clearly involves the three aspects Calvin cited, but it can include other things. It must, however, involve these three aspects. Does this lead to vagueness and imprecision?

Legalism leads to a precision which obscures the law rather than clarifying it. The difference is apparent in the contrast between common law, where argument rests on equity as Christian faith and tradition defines it, and statute law, where equity gives way to a matching of offenses with the technical wording or letter of the law. The precision of statute law leads to a breakdown of the idea of law and justice, and the precision of legalism leads to straining out gnats and swallowing camels (Matt. 23:24). Our Lord's most severe indictments were aimed at such pharisaism (Matt. 23:1-39).

We are told that God rested on the seventh day of creation (Gen. 2:2-3). Man having fallen is now restless (Isa. 48:22). The goal of salvation is to reestablish man in dominion, so that he may enter into God's rest spiritually and may establish it materially in all creation (Heb. 4:1-11, 12:12-29). Rest is the renewal of man by God's atoning work in

---

17. M. M. Knappen: *Tudor Puritanism, A Chapter in the History of Ideas.* p. 447. Chicago: University of Chicago Press, 1939.
    18. *Ibid.*, p. 449.

Christ, and the communication of that rest to all of creation.

In Hebrews 4:3, we are told, "For we which have believed do enter into rest, as he said, As I have sworn in my wrath, if they shall enter into my rest: although the works were finished from the foundation of the world." Westcott said of this verse, " 'The rest of God,' the rest which He had provided for His people, is no other in its last form than the rest which He Himself enjoyed. Of this the earthly inheritance was only a symbol."[19] The whole chapter expands on the meaning of this verse. God, in the beginning, rested from His work of creation, and man's rest with Him was planned from the beginning. The rebels are barred from this rest, but those who believe do enter into God's rest.

The typology of that rest cites Joshua (Jesus, in Heb. 4:8) as having given the covenant people a type of that rest and an aspect thereof. The conquest of Canaan and the possession of the land cannot be dismissed as merely a symbol of the ultimate rest, because it is more than that. God rested from His work of creation; man's work is to be a covenant-keeper and to exercise dominion over all things in terms of God's word (Gen. 1:26-28). The conquest of Canaan by men of faith was thus a step into that fulness of rest; it was not in itself rest, but it was a major step in the entering into rest.

Man thus works in faith to conquer and to exercise dominion in order that he might gain that rest. St. Paul makes this clear:

> For he that is entered into his rest, he also hath ceased from his own works, as God did from his.
> Let us labour therefore to enter into that rest, lest any man fall after the same example of unbelief. (Heb. 4:10-11)

Those who have entered into "his" (God's) rest, (for the eternal Sabbath is entirely of God), cease from their own works, as God ceased from His works. "God's rest is not idleness, nor shall ours be when we enter his rest."[20] While the Sabbath means *resting* in God's redemptive act, it also means some kind of labouring: "Let us labour therefore to enter into that rest." What is involved in this labour to rest?

It means the exercise of dominion, and it means the use of dominion to extend God's rest to all things. This is clear in Exodus 23: 9-13:

> Also thou shalt not oppress a stranger: for ye know the heart of a stranger, seeing ye were strangers in the land of Egypt.
> And six years thou shalt sow thy land, and shalt gather in the fruits thereof.
> But the seventh year thou shalt let it rest and lie still; that the poor of thy people may eat and what they leave the beasts of the field shall eat. In like manner thou shalt deal with the vineyard, and with thy

---

19. B. F. Westcott: *The Epistle to the Hebrews,* p. 96. Grand Rapids: Eerdmans, 1952.

20. R. C. H. Lenski: *The Interpretation of the Epistle to the Hebrews and of the Epistle of James,* p. 138. Columbus, Ohio: Wartburg Press, [1937] 1946, p. 138.

oliveyard.

Six days thou shalt do thy work, and on the seventh day thou shalt rest: that thine ox and thine ass may rest, and the son of thy hand-maid, and the stranger, may be refreshed.

And in all things that I have said unto you be circumspect: and make no mention of the name of other gods, neither let it be heard out of thy mouth.

The people of the Sabbath are to be just and God-fearing; they are to bring rest, through their godly social order, even to foreigners in their midst. Animals and the land shall reap the benefit of the peaceful domin-ion established by the covenant race. The goal is to universalize the Sab-bath and its meaning among all nations, and Isaiah declared that this would come to pass, "and from one sabbath to another, shall all flesh come to worship before me" (Isa. 66:23). At the very least, the concept of the Sabbath is associated with victory. Its association with joy is deep in the history of Judaism, despite strains of legalism, which, briefly, in I Macc. 2:31-38, saw the Jews allowing themselves to be killed rather than waging war on the Sabbath.

The partial victory, dominion, peace, and paradise of Joshua's con-quest of Canaan (Heb. 4:8) gives way to the fulness of rest in the new creation. Prior to the end of all things, man will have gained a glorious Sabbath rest on earth, one described over and over again by Isaiah (Isa. 65:17-25, etc.). Micah 4:1-4 describes it thus:

But in the last days it shall come to pass, that the mountain of the house of the LORD shall be established in the top of the mountains, and it shall be exalted above the hills; and people shall flow unto it. And many nations shall come, and say, Come, and let us go up to the mountain of the LORD, and to the house of the God of Jacob; and he will teach us of his ways, and we will walk in his paths: for the law shall go forth of Zion, and the word of the LORD from Jerusalem. And he shall judge among many people, and rebuke strong nations afar off; and they shall beat their swords into plowshares, and their spears into pruninghooks: nation shall not lift up a sword against nation, neither shall they learn war any more.

But they shall sit every man under his vine and under his fig tree; and none shall make them afraid: for the mouth of the LORD of hosts hath spoken it.

The Sabbath rest here described has little to do with the pharisaic rules of modern Sabbatarians.

It is instructive to note how hostile these legalists are towards any association of victory in time with the Sabbath. Calvin, in commenting on Hebrews 4:10, observed, "But though the completion of this rest can-not be attained in this life, yet we ought ever to strive for it."[21] At this

---

21. John Calvin: *Commentaries on the Epistle to the Hebrews*, p. 99. Grand Rapids: Eerdmans, 1949.

point, the translator (in 1853) added this footnote to Calvin's statement: "Many like *Calvin*, have made remarks of this kind, but they are out of place here; for the rest here mentioned is clearly the rest in heaven." Where the Sabbath is not an aspect of God's plan for His vicegerunt, covenant man, to fulfil the creation mandate and to gain the vision of Micah, Isaiah, and all of Scripture, then it is reduced to a day of repression. Micah sees it as the happy and victorious rest of the people of God, "every man under his vine and under his fig tree, and none shall make them afraid: for the mouth of the LORD of hosts hath spoken it."

The Lord's Day, the Christian Sabbath, celebrates the victory of Jesus Christ over sin and death. On that day, we celebrate His victory and ours, and we rest confident in our victories to come in Him. It is a "day of rest and gladness," in Christopher Wordsworth's words (1862), and, in Isaac Watts's words (1719),

> Today he rose and left the dead,
> And Satan's empire fell;
> Today the saints his triumph spread,
> And all his wonders tell.

If the certainty of the spread of that triumph from pole to pole is lacking, the Sabbath becomes a day of retreat, of hermitage rest, of repression and withdrawal. It is then no longer God's Sabbath rest. A false eschatology leads to a false Sabbath.

# 2

## BLESSING AND CULTURAL ADVANCE

The churches, under the influence of pietism, have so spiritualized religion that many central concerns of Scripture are neglected and others have become a source of embarrassment. An example of the problem is Joshua 15:16-19:

> And Caleb said, He that smiteth Kirjath-sepher, and taketh it, to him will I give Achsah my daughter to wife.
> And Othniel the son of Kenaz, the brother of Caleb, took it: and he gave him Achsah his daughter to wife.
> And it came to pass, as she came unto him, that she moved him to ask of her father a field: and she lighted off her ass; and Caleb said unto her, What wouldest thou?
> Who answered, Give me a blessing; for thou hast given me a south land; give me also springs of water. And he gave her the upper springs, and the nether springs.

Caleb, one of the great men of Israel, had, for his reward, asked not for conquered land, but for an unconquered area, by no means the choicest area (Josh. 14:6-15). Now, in trying to subdue that area, one area remained still unconquered. To the men of his clan, Caleb offered his daughter as a prize to the battle leader who took Debir or Kirjath-sepher. To the modern mind, this is offensive. Again, Achsah's efforts, which resulted in added territory for her husband, seem highly "unspiritual" to contemporary Christians.

In Calvin's day, the modern attitudes, fostered by the Renaissance and its humanism, were also prevalent, and Calvin's attitude towards Achsah was colored by them. Normally a perceptive commentator, at this point Calvin was modern rather than Biblical and his attitude towards Achsah was, to say the least, a very harsh one. His comment on vv. 18 and 19 is, to put it mildly, a very brutal judgment on Achsah:

> Although we may conjecture that the damsel Achsah was of excellent morals and well brought up, as marriage with her had been held forth as the special reward of victory, yet perverse cupidity on her part is here disclosed. She knew that by the divine law women were specially excluded from hereditary lands, but she nevertheless covets the possession of them, and stimulates her husband by unjust expostulation. In this way ambitious and covetous wives cease not to molest their husbands until they force them to forget shame, modesty, and equity. For although the avarice of men also is insatiable, yet women are apt to be much more precipitate. The more carefully

ought husbands to be on their guard against being set as it were on flame by the blast of such importunate counsels.

But a greater degree of intemperance is displayed when she acquires additional boldness from the facility of her husband and the indulgence of her father. Not contented with the field given to her, she demands for herself a well-watered district. And thus it is when a person has once overleaped the bounds of rectitude and honesty, the fault is forthwith followed up by impudence. Moreover, her father in refusing her nothing gives proof of his singular affection for her. But it does not therefore follow that the wicked thirst of gain which blinds the mind and perverts right judgment is the less hateful. In regard to Achsah's dismounting from the ass, some interpreters ascribe it to dissimulation and craft, as if she were pretending inability to retain her seat from grief. In this way her dismounting or falling off is made an indication of criminality and defective character. It is more simple, however, to suppose that she placed herself at her father's feet with the view of accosting him as a suppliant. Be this as it may, by her craft and flattery she gained his consent, and in so far this diminished the portion of brothers.[1]

Calvin did not often go so badly astray. Without any warrant from the text, Achsah is found guilty of "perverse cupidity," of being "ambitious and covetous" (and women as a whole are declared to be more avaricious than men, a statement for which there is no evidence); she is declared to be impudent and to have "overleaped the bounds of rectitude and honesty," and to have used craft and flattery to gain her father's consent. At one point, Calvin is accurate: Achsah was obviously a superior woman to qualify as a prize worth risking one's life for. Calvin describes her as obviously "an exquisite and precious recompense."[2]

Other commentators are not much better or are worse. If they try to treat the text favorably, it is by spiritualizing it. Thus, Joseph R. Sizoo can find religion in this text only by calling it "Nourishment from Hidden Springs," and using the upper and nether springs as symbols to declare that, "The roots of life are nourished in the soil of a living faith."[3] Sizoo's statement is true but it is irrelevant to the text and therefore does it an injustice.

Let us examine the text in terms of what it says. *First.* Caleb offered his daughter as a prize to the conqueror of Kirjath-sepher. Was this wrong? From the modern romantic point of view, Caleb's act was a highly offensive one. Scripture sees nothing wrong in it. We will return to this matter later, but, for the present, it is enough to note that the men around Caleb were men of faith, courage, and initiative. Like Caleb,

---

1. John Calvin: *Commentaries on the Book of Joshua*, p. 208f. Grand Rapids: Eerdmans, 1949.
2. Ibid., p. 208n.
3. Joseph R. Sizoo, "Joshua," in *The Interpreter's Bible*, vol. II, p. 631f. New York: Abingdon, 1953.

they were not content with past victories but had an eye to the future, and to the overthrow of existing enemies. Caleb's declaration (Josh. 14:6-12) was clearly their faith also. Not only was Achsah apparently a prize worth risking one's life for, but all the young men involved in the battle were more than worthy husbands, and they were all men of faith. Achsah had a privileged future, a leader of men as her husband.

*Second*, the desire for possessions is not in itself bad and is in fact good when our motives are godly and our purpose is to further our dominion under God. When Achsah asked her husband, Othniel (a cousin, not a forbidden degree of relationship for marriage), to ask for a field as well, there was no harm in this, and much good. A leader of men deserves a position of authority, and Othniel had earned a very good reward.

*Third*, since the land needed water, Achsah went further. She herself asked her father for the upper and the lower springs as an additional gift to give the land (in an arid part of the country) more value. Caleb, a godly man, gave Achsah to Othniel, gave Othniel the land, and gave Achsah the springs, without any hesitation and as a due reward.

*Fourth*, and most important, we cannot understand this text or the Bible without recognizing the import of Achsah's words, "Give me a blessing." The ideas of blessing and cursing are central to Scripture. "Blessings include health, long life, many and enduring progeny, wealth, honor, and victory.... Curses, it follows, are sickness and death, barren-ness in people and cattle, crop failure, poverty, defeat, and disgrace." With God, blessings and cursings are decrees; with man, they are a prayer.[4] Blessing is very closely associated with inheritance, as witness Genesis 27:1-41. Thus, when Achsah declared, "Give me a blessing," she plainly asked for an inheritance. She had brought her father a worthy son and lieutenant, and, as such, she felt that she and Othniel deserved an important inheritance and blessing. Caleb quite obviously agreed, and the presence of this episode in Scripture is a significant one. It is not a critical reference but plainly a good one, set in the context of a heroic and deserving act. Very clearly, Scripture feels that, when we are deserving, we have a right to ask for a good inheritance, both from man and also from God. We are saved by faith and rewarded according to works, and our works do gain us a blessing. It is a sin to deny this fact. Calvin saw Achsah diminishing her brothers' inheritance. Caleb knew his family bet-ter than Calvin or us, and he plainly felt no reluctance about adding to the estate of Othniel and Achsah. Clearly, he felt that they deserved an increased blessing and used their requests to give them an inheritance. He apparently gave more springs than Achsah had asked for. He was blessing

---

4. Herbert C. Brichto, "Blessing and Cursing," in *Encyclopaedia Judaica*, vol. 4, p. 1085. New York: Macmillan, 1971.

those who deserved blessing.

In the blessing by Isaac of Jacob and Esau (Gen. 27:1-41), as well as the blessing by Jacob of his sons (Gen. 49), there is not only the elements of material and spiritual blessing and inheritance but also predictive prophecy. The fact of predictive prophecy in these blessings is used by some to eliminate the relevance of blessing as inheritance. Two ideas are usually used to do this. *First*, we are given an evolutionary perspective. We are told that the Bible shows a development from material to spiritual blessings. (This explanation is far more common in contemporary teaching and preaching than in print.) To see a development from material to spiritual is the mark of neoplatonic and semi-Manichaean influences, which see evil as matter and the good as spirit. Such a perspective is antichristian. For the Bible the whole of reality was created good by God, and all aspects of creation are being redeemed and renewed by Jesus Christ. The resurrection of the body is basic to biblical faith. - *Second*, we are told the element of predictive prophecy makes these early blessings extraordinary ones and hence not applicable to our thinking about blessings.

Scripture, however, makes it clear that the close and necessary tie between blessing and inheritance remains throughout Biblical history. Psalm 37:22 declares,

> For such as be blessed of him shall inherit the earth; and they that be cursed of him shall be cut off.

This is very clear, and the relationship between blessing and inheritance cannot be mistaken. This, some who hold to a divided view of Scripture will say, is the Old Testament. Very well, then, let us examine the New Testament, the beatitudes in particular. Our Lord declared:

> Blessed are the poor in spirit: for theirs is the kingdom of heaven.
> Blessed are they that mourn: for they shall be comforted.
> Blessed are the meek: for they shall inherit the earth.
> Blessed are they which do hunger and thirst after righteousness: for they shall be filled.
> Blessed are the merciful: for they shall obtain mercy.
> Blessed are the pure in heart: for they shall see God.
> Blessed are the peacemakers: for they shall be called the children of God.
> Blessed are they which are persecuted for righteousness' sake: for theirs is the kingdom of heaven.
> Blessed are ye, when men shall revile you, and persecute you, and shall say all manner of evil against you falsely, for my sake.
> Rejoice, and be exceeding glad: for great is your reward in heaven: for so persecuted they the prophets which were before you (Matt. 5:3-12).

"The Kingdom of Heaven" is the same as the Kingdom of God. The Hebraic avoidance of the use of the name of God led to the use of the expression "Kingdom of Heaven." It has reference to God's total kingdom, in this world and the world beyond. The blessings cited by our Lord have both spiritual and material fulfilment, and the inheritance is in time and in eternity. To be blessed means to inherit the earth, and to inherit heaven; it means being comforted and gaining mercy. It means seeing God and having a great reward in heaven. The relationship between blessing and inheritance is inseparable in the beatitudes, and the inheritance cannot be limited to things spiritual. Only the damnable influence of neoplatonism has blinded people to this obvious fact. The same is true of the seven beatitudes of Revelation (Rev. 1:3; 14:13; 16:15; 19:9; 20:6; 22:7; 22:14). To His suffering saints the Lord promises material and spiritual blessings and inheritances.

Let us turn again to Achsah. When she asked her father, "Give me a blessing," she asked for an inheritance. It is false to read our present standards into the mentality of that day. Achsah did not feel upset or unhappy at being a prize of battle. Rather, she had been highly honored, and the ablest of a group of covenant men was now her husband. Achsah had been given a position of honor and glory by her father, and she was now identifying her husband and herself more closely with her father. Caleb was being asked to make Othniel and his children heirs, to regard Othniel as his son as well as son-in-law. The first step towards this had been taken when Othniel asked for and received a field. The second and decisive step was taken by Achsah. The field could be construed as an additional prize for his victory, but, when Achsah prefaced the request for the springs with a plea, "Give me a blessing," she was asking for more than a battle prize: she was asking that she, and Othniel as her husband, be granted full status as heirs of Caleb. Caleb was clearly very happy with this plea and generously granted it. Caleb, as a leader of men, recognized in Othniel a leader of men and made him an heir.

It is of interest to note that this little episode is important enough in Scripture to be repeated. In Judges 1:11-15, the same story is found. Moreover, in Judges 3:8-11, we learn that Othniel became a judge of Israel and delivered the nation from bondage to the King of Mesopotamia. He is called a "deliverer" or "savior" of Israel raised up by the LORD. Caleb's confidence in Othniel was thus rewarded.

This incident points to a neglected aspect of Biblical law. Normally, primogeniture prevailed, i.e., the firstborn gaining a double portion of the estate, assuming a double portion of the debts, and assuming the care of the aged parents (Deut. 21:16-17).[5] Inheritance meant *succession*, as the law makes clear:

> And thou shalt speak unto the children of Israel, saying, If a man
> die, and have no son, then ye shall cause his inheritance to pass unto

---

5. See Samuel Shilo, "Succession," in *Encyclopaedia Judaica*. vol. 15, p. 475ff.

his daughter.
And if he have no daughter, then ye shall give his inheritance unto his brethren.
And if he have no brethren, then ye shall give his inheritance unto his father's brethren.
And if his father have no brethren, then ye shall give his inheritance unto his kinsman that is next to him of his family, and he shall possess it: and it shall be unto the children of Israel a statute of judgment, as the LORD commanded Moses (Num. 27:8-11).

Succession could not be denied to a godly child (Deut. 21:15-17), nor could an ungodly child be allowed the protection of the family (Deut. 21:18-21). The ungodly, according to the law, had to be "cut off," a term used repeatedly in the law to cover excommunication, disinheritance, and capital punishment. Succession thus is godly succession.

Inheritance (and blessing) as succession gives us another perspective on the matter. The Bible is concerned with succession, with continuity, and various laws, such as the levirate (Deut. 25:5-10), are concerned with succession. This emphasis on succession is anti-revolutionary in its implications. It stresses roots, and it looks to the future in terms of the faith.

Succession in much of history has had a reactionary characteristic, in that it has been governed by blood rather than by faith. Blood succession has invited revolution, in that the removal of a stupid and entrenched power has been regarded as impossible without violence. The Biblical stress on godly succession means that a Caleb can regard Achsah and Othniel as his best heirs and strengthen their hand. Othniel became a judge or ruler over Israel and no doubt a joy to the aging Caleb. The inheritance given to Othniel by Caleb meant that not only were Achsah and Othniel blessed thereby but all of Israel. The inheritance enabled Othniel to establish a strong clan which, a few generations later, provided King David with one of the divisional commanders in charge of the twelve monthly relays (I Chron. 27:15; cf. 11:30; II Sam. 23:28-29). Jewish legendary tales give a high place to Othniel as one who restored the knowledge of the law. The Alphabet of Ben Sira spoke of Othniel as one of those who was taken into Paradise alive, thus placing him on the level of Enoch and Elijah. Othniel was the first judge of Israel.

The idea of succession is closely tied to the family. One Hebrew term for the *family* is *bet av*, house of the father (Gen. 24:38; 46:31). To found a family is spoken of as building a house (Neh. 7:4). As a result, when Caleb and Achsah thought of marriage, neither thought in terms of the individual or in terms of romantic feelings. A family was an investment in the future for them; it meant building in terms of today and tomorrow. Thus, a true succession meant a godly heir, and adoption was used as a means of ensuring succession. To reject the idea of adoption and succession was to choose a curse, to prefer being cut off. Even men with children turned to adoption as a means of protecting a godly succession. Jacob adopted his grandsons, Manasseh and Ephriam, as his sons (Gen. 48:5). Caleb himself apparently represented a case of adoption. We have two genealogies given for him, one making him a descendent of Perez, son of Judah (Num. 13:6), and the other a Kenizzite and related to the Edomites (Gen. 36:11, 15, 42) and to an ancient people of the land (Gen. 15:19). Aharoni has said, "It would seem that it was only with the advent of the monarchy that the Calebites were completely integrated into Judah and became one of its major family groups."[6] God Himself speaks of adopting Solomon and ensuring the succession in the Kingdom by means of His adopting grace (II Sam. 7:14).

Adoption was thus a familiar concept to Caleb, in that he, once an outsider, had become a leader and representative of Judah. The name of the clan's Edomite ancestor remained in the family, and Othniel's father's name was Kenaz, the name of the son of Esau from whom they were alike descended. In adopting Othniel, he was thus moving in terms of the principle in terms of which he himself had become chosen.

The family was thus concerned with godly succession. This meant an emphasis on purity of faith and also of genetic inheritance. A talmudic tractate, declares, "A man should not marry into a family which has a recurred history of epilepsy or leprosy."[7] If any unworthy marriage was contracted by a man, all the members of the family performed the ceremony of Kezazah, or cutting off.

The world-view thus of Caleb and Achsah is very different from that of today. In the Biblical perspective, both the one and the many have an equal importance, and both are subordinate to God, the ultimate one and many.[8]

In the modern perspective, either the atomistic individual or the totalitarian one is stressed. In old China, the family system denied the individual in favor of the family. In the modern world, the romantic view of love denies the family in favor of the individual. Thus, from the anarchistic viewpoint of the individual, adultery becomes a virtue.[9] In the Biblical perspective, neither the individual nor the group is primary: God is, and the individual and the group have their place as aspects of God's order.

Those who pass over the marriage of Achsah as a relic of primitive

6. Yohanan Aharoni, "Caleb, Calebites," in *Encyclopaedia Judaica*, vol. 5, p. 42.

7. Louis Isaac Rabinowitz, "Family," in *Ibid.*, vol. 6, p. 1170.

8. See R. J. Rushdoony: *The One and the Many*. Nutley, New Jersey: The Craig Press, 1971.

9. See Magar Edward Magar, Ph.D.: *Adultery and Its Compatability with Marriage*, Monona, Wisconsin: Nefertiti Publishers, 1972.

days have much to learn from Scripture and will not learn it.

At a practical point, Calvin did see the importance of blessings as godly succession. He was once taunted by an enemy as a man obviously accursed of God because he was childless. Calvin's proud answer was the godly one. All Europe, he said, was peopled with his sons.

Basic as the blood family is to Scripture and its view of life, just as clearly godly succession is given priority over it and is stressed as the true succession. British Israel thinking, and premillennialism, stress blood, physical Israel. The Bible, however, makes adoption a central doctrine of faith and supplants blood succession from beginning to end with godly succession. True apostolic succession is similarly to be understood.

**3**

## THE FAITH OF RAHAB

It has distressed many people that the Bible speaks so favorably of Rahab. In some circles, to speak well of Rahab is to invite sharp criticism.[1] Scripture, however, cites Rahab as one of the great examples of faith (Heb. 11:31). James, in fact, sees Abraham and Rahab as the two great examples of true faith (James 2:17-26).

Rahab is a "problem" to many people on two counts. *First*, she was a harlot. Every kind of strained exegesis has been resorted to in order to turn her into an innkeeper instead, but the Scripture is clear: she was a harlot. *Second*, her lie to the king of Jericho's officers is uniformly condemned by the legalists, even though it is specifically cited as a virtue by James. However, the idea that anyone who is about to violate God's law has any right to require the truth of us to further his evil is certainly not Biblical. Dabney saw this clearly.[2]

It is important to realize that the Bible is never academic; it never provides information merely to satisfy our curiosity. In fact, it avoids satisfying our curiosity again and again, because its purpose is rather to instruct and to reshape us ever more closely into conformity to God's word, law, and image. What we are told about Rahab is thus clearly aimed at us, and particularly because she is twice singled out as an example of faith for us to follow, it is necessary for us to know as precisely as possible what we are to emulate in her.

Let us therefore examine the episode narrated in Joshua 2. We are told in Joshua 2:1,

> And Joshua the son of Nun sent out of Shittim two men to spy secretly, saying, Go view the land, even Jericho. And they went, and came into an harlot's house, named Rahab, and lodged there.

The Hebrew word translated *lodged* is literally *lay*. We can see why Rahab has been turned into an innkeeper, both to preserve her reputation and the reputation of the two spies. It is not inconceivable that the two spies went to Rahab for her services as a prostitute, but the evidence is against it. The Bible is not a prissy book; if the spies had gone to

---

1. See R. J. Rushdoony: *The Institutes of Biblical Law*, pp. 542-549. Nutley, New Jersey: The Craig Press, 1973.

2. Robert L. Dabney: *Syllabus and Notes of the Course of Systematic and Polemic Theology*, p. 425f. Richmond, Virginia: Presbyterian Committee on Publication, 1871, 1890. See also Rushdoony, *op.cit.*

Rahab as a harlot, it would have read, "lay with her"; Samson is not spared the truth in this respect, for we are plainly told that he lay with a harlot in Gaza (Judges 16:1-3). Here, we are told that the spies went to Rahab's *house* and *lay* or *lodged* there. The comment of John Bright is of interest:

> That they should have found refuge in *the house of a harlot* is not surprising. The authorities would be used to seeing strange characters going in and out of such a place. Besides, a harlot, because of her very station in life, would not be likely to be a very loyal citizen. There is no need to infer that the men visited her for purposes pertaining to her profession, though this is not impossible.[3]

The trouble with most commentators is a wooden imagination, perhaps because of an inability to see the men of the Bible as real people. Let us look at these two spies thus as real people. On several occasions, I had long conversations with a man who, as a high ranking espionage agent, made numerous trips deep into enemy lines in Europe during World War II. He made it clear that no such venture was ever made in ignorance of where they would go, whom they would contact, and who would be cooperative. They had an extensive dossier on possible people to contact, even though these persons might not know of their existence, because it was the duty of intelligence services to know all possible friends. In this man's case, he was a higher ranking officer than normally undertook such a venture, but, because of his own background in the language and culture of the area, his leadership was imperative. The Book of Jeremiah makes clear that intelligence work was a highly developed profession in antiquity, and Nebuchadnezzar's knowledge of what went on in Jerusalem was very extensive.

It would be naive to suppose that espionage was incompetent in Joshua's day. Three instances are cited as a part of the conquest of Canaan: 1) the sending of twelve spies by Moses from Kadesh-barnea; 2) the instance involving Rahab; 3) the sending of spies to give a report on Ai. We can safely assume that numerous other instances of espionage occured, which it was not relevant for Scripture to report. In terms of standard practice, we can also assume that, before the two spies entered Jericho, they at least knew of Rahab as a person to contact. It is also possible that they were a related people to the men of Jericho, part of the mixed multitude of foreigners who left Egypt with Moses. The agents of the king of Jericho, and the king himself, do not identify the spies as Hebrews, an interesting fact, but as "of the children of Israel," or, as the Berkeley Version reads, "Men have come here this night from the Israelites to spy out the land" (Josh. 2:2). There is thus a possibility that

---

3. John Bright, "Joshua," in *The Interpreter's Bible*, vol. 2, p. 559. New York: Abingdon Press, 1953.

the two spies were religiously of Israel but by blood of a non-Israelite line. Given the situation, it would have been most logical for Joshua to have sent such men.

It may be objected that all of the adult generation, Hebrew and non-Hebrew, which left Egypt were now dead, save Joshua and Caleb. True enough, but their sons would still speak their mother's tongue as well as Hebrew. The espionage agent mentioned previously had been born in England, where his parents found refuge in World War I, and was reared in the U. S., but he spoke English with a trace of an accent, and several Slavic languages like a native.

Turning again to Rahab, it is clear that the spies found in her not only a sympathetic informant but one receptive to their faith:

> And she said unto the men, I know that the LORD hath given you the land, and that your terror is fallen upon us, and that all the inhabitants of the land faint because of you.
> For we have heard how the LORD dried up the water of the Red Sea for you, when ye came out of Egypt; and what ye did unto the two kings of the Amorites, that were on the other side Jordan, Sihon and Og, whom ye utterly destroyed.
> And as soon as we had heard these things, our hearts did melt, neither did there remain any more courage in any man, because of you: for the LORD your God, he is God in heaven above, and in earth beneath.
> Now therefore, I pray you, swear unto me by the LORD, since I have shewed you kindness, that ye will also shew kindness unto my father's house, and give me a true token:
> And that ye will save alive my father, and my mother, and my brethren, and my sisters, and all that they have, and deliver our lives from death.
> And the men answered her, Our life for yours, if ye utter not this our business. And it shall be, when the LORD hath given us the land, that we will deal kindly and truly with thee (Josh. 2:9-14).

The text is not concerned with the data collected by the spies, but certain aspects of it do appear all the same. *First*, the spies, who referred to their dealing with Rahab as "our business," mission, or errand, learned that Jericho was intensely afraid of the Hebrew army. Their reaction was one of "terror" and a loss of initiative. The 1917 Jewish Publication Society translation of the Old Testament renders vs. 11 thus: "And as soon as we had heard it, our hearts did melt, neither did there remain any more spirit in any man, because of you; for the LORD your God, He is God in heaven above, and on earth beneath." The Talmud interprets this to mean that Rahab was saying that "they even lost their virility."[4] In any case, the net result was an inability to act. *Second*, this meant that no attempt had been made to secure the military aid of other city-states.

4. I. Epstein, ed.: *The Babylonian Talmud, Sader Kodashim*, vol. I, "Zebahim," p. 575. London: The Soncino Press, 1948.

Joshua could attack Jericho without any fear of an attack on his rear. This information alone was worth the trip for the spies.

Turning primarily to Rahab's response, we see that, *first*, she is concerned not merely with self-preservation but the preservation of her father's family, and all its members. This strong sense of the family was not always true of Canaanite culture, which had its eras of family decline as well as family strength. It does indicate the closeness of Rahab to her family. Had Rahab been a religious prostitute, a position of some status in pagan antiquity, in some cultures, this would be less surprising. The term used in the Hebrew for harlot is here *zonah*, fornicator or whore, not *quedeshah*, one set apart. The prostitute as such did not have a position of dignity in antiquity, contrary to popular mythology. She was a very much despised person. The examples of dignity and status cited, for example, from ancient Greece, apply only to a limited number of girls, and then only from a limited period of history. The religious harlot had at times a priestly status, but even her status, while a religiously necessary one to the society of that era, was not without penalties and liabilities. Prostitution of all kinds normally meant a divorce from normal society. This was also true of pre-war Japan, where the prostitute, while sold into her life by the family to help support the family, was also thereby radically cut off from it. Thus, while examples which may parallel Rahab's family ties may be found, they are not the normal circumstance for prostitutes. Rahab's concern for her family's welfare and future as a part of her own is thus notable.

*Second*, Rahab, in citing the terror of the Canaanites over the power of Israel, does more than the Canaanites. She attributes this power to the total power of the LORD, who "is God in heaven above, and in earth beneath" (Josh. 2:11). The Canaanites were in terror, because they recognized what Israel had done to all its enemies. The history of Israel from the Red Sea crossing to the present, a forty-year history, was familiar to them. Their recognition of the LORD's role in that series of events was not religious but superstitious. Rahab saw the matter religiously, and she recognized the sovereignty of God and gave herself to His service at the risk of her life. She did not, like the people of Jericho, wait for death to come. Instead, she risked death to help the spies in order to gain life.

Rahab is cited as an example of faith in the New Testament for this very reason. In Hebrews 11, the examples of faith, of whom Rahab is one, were people like Abraham, who "looked for a city which hath foundations, whose builder and maker is God" (Heb. 11:10). Faith is described for us moreover in these terms:

> Now faith is the substance of things hoped for, the evidence of things not seen.

> For by it the elders obtained a good report.
>
> Through faith we understand that the worlds were framed by the word of God, so that things which are seen were not made of things which do appear.
>
> But without faith it is impossible to please him: for he that cometh to God must believe that he is, and that he is a rewarder of them that diligently seek him (Heb. 11:1-3, 6).

We are emphatically told by Scripture that grace and faith are God's gift: "For by grace are ye saved through faith; and that not of yourself: it is the gift of God" (Eph. 2:8). The sovereignty, initiative, and power in salvation originate entirely in God. This does not, however, deny the reality of our own secondary initiative and power in the exercise of grace and faith. It is a *gift,* but it is a gift *to us* and to be exercised by us. It is a gift which is now inseparable from our life, and its use by us brings a reward. Thus, "By faith the harlot Rahab perished not with them that believed not, when she received the spies with peace" (Heb. 11:31). Her faith was manifested in action: she received the spies "with peace," i.e., she protected and defended them out of faith in God and His kingdom.

As James declared, "Likewise also was not Rahab the harlot justified by works, when she had received the messengers, and had sent them out another way?" (James 2:25). James introduces a startling insight into the story. Instead of spies (*Kataskopos*) as in Hebrews 11:31, James uses the word *angelos*, angels or messengers. The word *angelos* is used of John the Baptist in Matt. 11:10, Mark 1:2, Luke 7:27, and of John's messengers, Luke 7:24. It is used of those whom Christ sent before Him in Luke 9:52, and of Paul's thorn in the flesh, called "a messenger of Satan" in II Corinthians 12:7. In what respect were the spies messengers? Is this what Hebrews 13:2 refers to in declaring, "Be not forgetful to entertain strangers: for thereby some have entertained angels unawares." Were the spies symbolically seen as angels of God, bringing the opportunity of life and membership in the covenant people to Rahab? Clearly, as *messengers,* the spies gave life to Rahab and her family as well as receiving life by means of her protection and care.

Rahab and others cited in Hebrews 11, "all, having obtained a good report through faith, received not the promise" (Heb. 11:39). They were links to the future, soldiers in the cause of the kingdom. Still, each gained something, and Rahab's role, among other things, was to be an ancestress of Jesus Christ as well as of David (Matt. 1:5-6).

She is also one who received *messengers, angelos.* Of this Lange said that James selected the word *angelos*

> in allusion to the circumstance that the Gentiles of his time were so ready to receive the messengers of the Gospel...She hospitably received the messengers and sheltered them, she received them forthwith, as the Gentiles received the messengers of the Gospel rejected

and persecuted by the Jews.[5]

This may well be true, but it is at best a subordinate meaning. Let us look again at Hebrews 13:2, entertaining "angels unawares." It is true that in Genesis 18:3, Abraham, and in Genesis 19:2, Lot, actually did entertain angels unawares. However, as Lenski noted,

> The thought of the statement can hardly be that by entertaining strangers we, too, may have the good fortune of sometimes receiving angels into our homes. The Old Testament incidents are too exceptional to admit of such a generalization. It is sufficient to say that, as some were unexpectedly blessed by receiving strangers, so we, too, may be thus blessed. We may go a bit farther: Christ identifies himself with his saints so that what we do for them we do for him, Matt. 25:38,40.[6]

Two men who were spies sent out by Joshua came to Rahab. These men were more than they intended to be: by the providence of God, they were messengers or angels who were opening the door of salvation and freedom for Rahab, and she received them as such. Instead of regarding the men as a threat to her safety, she saw them as an opportunity for life.

Let us look again at the matter of espionage. We have seen that a spy does not go into unfamiliar territory without a contact or contacts. As far as it is possible, the spy is one who speaks the local language like a native or is a native, and he approaches people who are receptive to an approach or have initiated an approach to the other side. It has been shown that there is reason to believe that Rahab was a person at least sympathetic to Israel, and known to be so, and may have sent some word to Joshua of her support. There is a remarkable episode which gives some ground for this opinion:

> And it came to pass, when Joshua was by Jericho, that he lifted up his eyes and looked, and behold, there stood a man over against him with his sword drawn in his hand: and Joshua went unto him, and said unto him, Art thou for us, or for our adversaries?
>
> And he said, Nay; but as a captain of the host of the LORD am I now come. And Joshua fell on his face to the earth, and did worship, and said unto him, What saith my lord unto his servant?
>
> And the captain of the LORD's host said unto Joshua, Loose thy shoe from off thy foot; for the place whereon thou standest is holy. And Joshua did so (Josh. 5:13-15).

In examining this event, let us note *first* that Joshua, in seeing a stranger with a drawn sword did not at once assume him to be an enemy. There had been perhaps one or more secret contacts between the Israelites and

---

5. John Peter Lange: *Commentary on the Holy Scriptures, James-Jude*, p. 76. Grand Rapids: Zondervan (1967).

6. R. C. H. Lenski: *The Interpretation of the Epistle to the Hebrews and of the Epistle of James*, p. 469. Columbus, Ohio: Wartburg Press (1937) 1946.

Rahab's household. Joshua was thus prepared to see an armed stranger as a possible ally. *Second,* the man identified Himself as the "captain" or "prince" of "the host of the LORD," i.e., as God the son, and Joshua worshipped Him as God. *Third,* our natural expectation at this point is that there will be a word-revelation, the impartation of military or religious insight above and beyond the identification. The revelation is simply that He is God, and that Joshua should stand bare-footed, for the place was holy ground. This is the same statement made to Moses at the burning bush (Ex. 3:5). To Moses, a command to deliver God's people was given. Joshua is now to lead them into conquest. *Fourth,* God is present, with sword drawn, because this is His battle. As C. H. Waller noted,

> The war is a Divine enterprise, in which human instruments are employed, but so as to be entirely subordinate to the Divine will. Jehovah is not for Israel, nor for Israel's foes. He fights for His own right hand, and Israel is but a fragment of His army. "The sun stood still," "The Treasures of the hill" were opened, which He had "reserved against the time of trouble, against the day of battle and war."[7]

As a result, God did not allow Israel the glory of the victory over Jericho. It was a supernatural act of God by which Jericho was overthrown, and all things therein were devoted to God (Josh. 6:17-19).

*Fifth,* the ground was holy ground because God was present, and present with drawn sword, as a man of war.

Rahab, in describing to the spies the terror in Jericho and Canaan, distinguished between two powers, the direct power of God and the indirect power of God through Israel. She declared of the first, "we have heard how the LORD dried up the water of the Red Sea for you, when ye came out of Egypt," and, of the second, that they had heard "what ye did unto the two kings of the Amorites...whom ye utterly destroyed" (Josh. 2:10). Rahab was clearly aware of the active presence of God, and she received the spies as the messengers of God and God's cause. The Captain of the Lord's House used these spies to save His elect daughter Rahab. These spies were thus not only Joshua's espionage agents but messengers of God. They were, in this sense, "angels unawares" to themselves and Rahab.

Joshua kept his promise, i.e., the promise made by his agents, the spies, to Rahab. As Bright comments,

> Rahab and her household are escorted to safety *outside the camp of Israel.* The camp of Israel is "holy"; no "unclean" person is to enter it (Deut. 23:14; Num. 5:3; 31:19). Rahab and her family are not only heathen but perhaps are themselves under the *herem* until cleared by the proper ritual. Nevertheless, Rahab was ultimately received into Israel...[8]

---

7. C. H. Waller, "Joshua" in Charles John Ellicott, ed., Ellicott's *Commentary on the Whole Bible,* II, p. 116. Grand Rapids: Zondervan.

8. John Bright, *op. cit.,* II, 582.

From a position of affluence, Rahab came to the position of an outcast stranger, a woman whose past came under the judgment of God's law. She could not have been ignorant of what this meant long before she took the step. The grace, however, which gave her the faith to take this step made her also an honored married woman in Israel. Like Abraham, she had moved forward in faith, and by works of faith, as seeing the invisible. As such, with Abraham, she has the honor of representing true faith, venturesome, active, and mindful in all things of God's sovereign power.

Rahab, the type of faith, is found in the book of Joshua, the book of conquest. Abraham in faith moved as did Moses later, as one who saw Him who is invisible (Heb. 11:27), and Rahab's faith was a type of action to victory. We are prepared, by this indication of the necessary connection among faith, hope, and victory, to see the necessity for a like faith and action on our part. Rahab had acted by faith in God's future, and God made her a part of it.

Abraham and Rahab are the two great types of faith: both were "adopted." Abraham was called out of the mass of humanity, and, by adoption, made God's elect man. It was not the blood of Abraham that gave election but God's sovereign grace, as so clearly is seen in Rahab's case.

Moreover, Joshua, the book of conquest, gives us telling instances of adoption: Rahab, Caleb, and Othniel, to demonstrate that God's premise is not race but grace.

# 4

## SACRILEGE

The word *sacrilege* appears only once in the Bible, in Romans 2:22. The Greek word is *hierosuleo,* to rob a temple, i.e., to rob God, and it is translated as to "commit sacrilege." *Theft* is basic to the word, and sacrilege is theft directed against God. It is apparent from this that the idea of sacrilege is present throughout Scripture. In Malachi 3:7-12, God accuses the people of sacrilege, of robbing Him of His tithes and offerings. The laws of the firstfruits, the tithes, and much else are related to the idea: they forbid sacrilege.

The concept of sacrilege rests on God's sovereignty and the fact that He has an absolute ownership over all things: men and the universe are God's property. The covenant people are *doubly* God's property: *first,* by virtue of His creation, and, *second,* by virtue of His redemption. For this reason, sin is more than personal and more than man-centered. It is a theological offense. As St. Paul wrote of fornication, it is not only a sin against one's own being (and a transgression with another person), it is also a sin against God:

> What? know ye not that your body is the temple of the Holy Ghost which is in you, which ye have of God, and ye are not your own? For ye are bought with a price: therefore glorify God in your body, and in your spirit, which are God's (I Cor. 6:19-20).

This fact is clear in all of Scripture. As Daube noted of the Old Testament, for it "God was the owner and relative of the whole people."[1]

There was a time when sacrilege was regarded by all peoples, Christian and pagan, as the most serious of offenses. The fear of sacrilege was a major restraining force to many a tyrant, not because of any religiosity on their part, but because of their awareness of the observed consequences of sacrilege, obvious and radical judgment.

Because in our time a belief in judgment has waned, and an insistence on love is commonplace, there is a refusal to face up to the consequences of sacrilege. The common use of Malachi 3:7-12 is an instance of this. The text is very plain spoken:

> Even from the days of your fathers ye are gone away from mine ordinances, and have not kept them. Return unto me, and I will return

---

1. David Daube: *Studies in Biblical Law,* p. 47. New York: KTAV Publishing House, (1947), 1969.

unto you, saith the LORD of hosts. But ye said, Wherein shall we return?

Will a man rob God? Yet ye have robbed me. But ye say, Wherein have we robbed thee? In tithes and offerings.

Ye are cursed with a curse: for ye have robbed me, even this whole nation.

Bring ye all the tithes into the storehouse, that there may be meat in mine house, and prove me now herewith, saith the LORD of hosts, if I will not open you the windows of heaven, and pour you out a blessing, that there shall not be room enough to receive it.

And I will rebuke the devourer for your sakes, and he shall not destroy the fruits of your ground; neither shall your vine cast her fruit before the time in the field, saith the LORD of hosts.

And all nations shall call you blessed; for ye shall be a delightsome land, saith the LORD of hosts.

This text has often been used to promote tithing, and rightly so, but the usual emphasis is on *the blessing* which follows tithing and too rarely on *the curse* which marks its absence. But this is not all. What God plainly requires is "tithes *and* offerings." The tithe is His tax; the offering is the evidence of gratitude for His care and mercy. Because God is lord over all things, *all* men owe Him a tithe as the great landlord; His covenant people are also expected to bring Him offerings as evidence of their gratitude.

The absence of tithes and offerings results in God's curse. The curse, as God describes it through Malachi, is a revealing one. Because men do not render God their tithes as God's creation tax, God causes creation to *frustrate* man. Various natural disasters become endemic where man commits sacrilege by denying God His tithe: blights, drought, plagues of locusts, crop failures, and much, much more of like nature.

The curse thus on sacrilege is related to the curse on man at the fall. In the Garden of Eden, all things bore fruit without problem, and man's work was blessed and rewarded. With the fall, matters changed:

And unto Adam he said, Because thou hast hearkened unto the voice of thy wife, and hast eaten of the tree, of which I commanded thee, saying, Thou shalt not eat of it: cursed is the ground for thy sake; in sorrow shalt thou eat of it all the days of thy life; Thorns also and thistles shall it bring forth to thee; and thou shalt eat the herb of the field; In the sweat of thy face shalt thou eat bread, till thou return unto the ground; for out of it wast thou taken: for dust thou art, and unto dust shalt thou return (Gen. 3:17-19).

Failure to tithe aggravates and develops the curse. Whatever our work or calling, it becomes marked by frustration and trouble, because a curse is added to the original curse. The world has seen a marked degeneration from the Garden of Eden to the world before the flood, and from the flood to the present, whenever and wherever man has developed his original sin, his desire to be his own god (Gen. 3:5). Curse is added upon curse to wayward, rebellious man.

On the other hand, the redeemed step out of the curse into redemption, and, to the extent of their sanctification, they move into the world of *blessing*. As they grow in grace, obeying God's law, the blessings of Deuteronomy 28 pursue and overtake them. In Malachi 3:10, the redeemed are assured that God's blessings will *overwhelm* them. The obedience of faith leads to world peace (the elimination of the curse of war), according to Isaiah 2:1-5, and to longevity, as in the earliest days of mankind (Isa. 65:20).

There is thus no neutral ground between the curse and the blessing, nor can a man choose the measure of his obedience and blessing. The essence of original sin is man's usurpation of God's prerogative of absolute lordship: man chooses to govern his own life in terms of what he considers is best. To illustrate, man does not have a choice with respect to the tithe, or to any other law. He cannot say, I do not kill, commit adultery, steal, or bear false witness; therefore, I am free to relax my obedience where the tithe is concerned. Neither can he say, I tithe, and therefore an occasional stretching of the seventh or eighth commandments is excusable in one so faithful as I. The absolute God requires absolute obedience, and our faithful obedience opens blessing upon blessing to us, even as our disobedience opens up curse upon curse.

Sacrilege is robbing God, and it is sacrilege to compromise or limit our obedience to God, or to set our own standards as to what constitutes valid obedience. Malachi 3:7 makes clear that the people were amazed at the idea that God wanted them to "return" unto Him; as far as they were concerned, they were good, faithful worshippers of the Almighty. (Most churchmen today have the same opinion of themselves.) The idea that their limited obedience to the tithes and offerings, and other matters, was an offense to God and had earned a curse was no doubt distasteful to them. They were, after all, the best people God had, and He should be pleased with them! "Wherein shall we return?" Where churches tamper with the law of God, either by disbelieving it, or by limiting the necessary obedience to it, or by releasing men from obedience to the law of God, they commit sacrilege.

The answer of Peter and the other apostles to the council which forbade them to preach was a forthright one: "We ought to obey God rather than man" (Acts 5:29). In the early church this obedience meant that it was declared to be sacrilege if one delivered up his Bible and the sacred utensils of the church to Diocletian's persecutors. The Reformers declared any limitation upon the use of the word of God, the Scriptures, to be sacrilege also, denying to church and state the right to limit God's word and access to it.

*Sacrilege* and blasphemy are closely related offenses; blasphemy is by *word,* and sacrilege by *act,* a crime against God. Leviticus 5:15, 16, and 22:14-16 have reference to sacrilege, or one aspect thereof.

The law requires the covenant nation to punish sacrilege through its courts; hence, the civil enforcement of the tithe in early America. Where no ecclesiastical and civil judgment against sacrilege exists or is possible, God Himself avenges the deed (I Sam. 5:6; Jer. 50:28; 5:11, etc.). The early church was severe in its judgment on sacrilege, and its decrees were in terms of the Mosaic law. Thus, Canon 72 of *The Apostolic Constitutions* declared, in terms of Leviticus 5:16,

> If any one, either of the clergy or laity, takes away from the holy church a honeycomb, or oil, let him be suspended, and let him add the fifth part to that which he took away.[2]

(The use of honey in the church was to signify to the newly baptized that they had now entered the new creation, into a land and life flowing with milk and honey.)

Until the Enlightenment began to replace God's law with man's reason, sacrilege was normally regarded as a very serious matter. Now it is rarely mentioned or taken seriously. God, however, takes it very seriously. In St. Paul, we have an indictment against that nominal faith which is actual sacrilege. "Thou that sayest a man should not commit adultery, dost thou commit adultery? thou that abhorrest idols, dost thou commit sacrilege?" (Rom. 2:22). The Berkeley Version renders it thus: "You who forbid adultery, do you commit adultery? You who detest idols, do you commit sacrilege?" To detest idolatry does not make us godly in and of itself; godliness is more than the avoidance of certain offenses: it is active obedience to God. Certainly to rob God is the epitome of sin, and hence the seriousness of sacrilege.

We have seen that the fall led to the curse, and that the curse develops and increases to the degree that man pursues his independence from God. The fulness of the curse is Hell, total isolation, with every man his own god, universe, and hell. The fulness of the blessing is the new creation, the fulness of communion between man and man, and man and God.

---

2. *The Apostolic Constitutions,* Bk. VIII, xivii, 72, in *Ante-Nicene Christian Library,* vol. XVII, *The Clementine Homilies,* etc., p. 266. Edinburgh: T. & T. Clark, 1870.

# 5

## RESTITUTION

Before continuing further with the subject of sacrilege, it is necessary for us to look briefly at the question of restitution.[1] Justice in the Bible means restitution to a very great degree. Restitution and restoration are the essence of justice. The prison system as an answer to the problem of crime is a modern and anti-Biblical scheme: it does nothing to further either restitution or restoration and accomplishes little other than removing the criminal from society temporarily. It does not remedy the crime, nor does it remedy the criminal, as it purports to do.

In Exodus 22:1ff., we find set forth the elementary principles of Biblical justice. Restitution means returning the item stolen or destroyed, or the equivalent value thereof, plus a fine equal in value to the thing stolen or destroyed. The restitution must be commensurate to the offense, and the penalty must also be commensurate to the offense (Ex. 21: 23-26). In capital offenses, capital punishment is mandatory. False witness means a penalty equal to that of the offense imputed to the innocent man (Deut. 19:16-21).[2]

Our purpose here is to show the interlocking nature of grace and the law, of justification and sanctification. This means that we must begin with the Garden of Eden and God's original creation, which was created good (Gen. 1:31), but, as a result of man's sin, is now fallen (Gen. 3:17-19), but groans and travails, looking for its release in the restoration of man (Rom. 8:18-23). The destruction of God's creation with its original righteousness was the work of man, a destruction which continues as men develop the implications of the curse. The penalty for this offense was set forth in advance: it was the introduction of death into the life of man and the world (Gen. 2:17). God's justice, however, requires restitution and restoration, and, as a result, the promise of this was given immediately after the fall (Gen. 3:15), and declared to be the province of the believer in Christ to effect, after the resurrection of Jesus Christ (Rom. 16:20).

Christ as the second Adam (I Cor. 15:45-47) came to overthrow the work of the tempter by resisting him (Matt. 4:1-11), and by overthrowing

---

1. See R. J. Rushdoony, *The Institutes of Biblical Law,* pp. 525-530, etc. Nutley, New Jersey: The Craig Press, 1973.
2. *Ibid.,* pp. 569-572.

Satan's power (Luke 10:18-19). The end result of His work is the regeneration of all things (Matt. 19:28), and the restoration of all things (Acts 3:21; translated as "restitution" in the A.V., and as "restoration" in the R.V.). The word *apokatastasis* of Acts 3:21 in the papyri means "the restoration of estates to rightful owners, a balancing of accounts."[3] Christ's work is to restore the world, God's estate, to its rightful owner, and to place man and the world back under God's law, and, in the process, to balance all accounts, restoring to God what belongs to God, and casting out of God's presence and realm the reprobate into the Gehenna or dung heap of creation.

Turning now to the definition of sacrilege as given by Spelman, we read:

> Sacrilege is an invading, stealing, or purloining from God, any sacred thing, either belonging to the majesty of His person, or appropriate to the celebration of His divine service.
>
> The etymology of the word implieth the description: for *sacrum* is a holy thing: and *legium a legendo,* is to steal, or pull away.
>
> The definition divides itself apparently into two parts; namely, into Sacrilege committed immediately upon the Person of God, and Sacrilege done upon the things appropriate to His divine service.[4]

The first act of sacrilege was made by Satan, and then followed Adam and Eve. As Spelman noted,

> Thus it appeareth that Sacrilege was the first sin, the master-sin, and the common sin at the beginning of the world, committed in earth by man in corruption, committed in paradise by man in perfection, committed in heaven itself by the angels in glory; against God the Father by arrogating His power, against God the Son by condemning His word, against God the Holy Ghost by profaning things sanctified, and against all of them in general by invading and violating the Deity.[5]

Sacrilege being theft requires restitution and restoration before justice can be satisfied. This due process of justice in God's plan is twofold. *First,* Jesus Christ as the true man and the new Adam makes restitution to God, rendering both perfect obedience and His life in death as our vicarious sacrifice and substitute, dying in our stead. The death penalty is enforced against Him. By His resurrection, He sets forth His power over sin and death and overcomes the enemy for His elect and gives them power over the enemy. He restores men into life and righteousness, regenerating them out of the state of sin and death. *Second,* the redeemed

---

3. W. E. Vine, *An Expository Dictionary of New Testament Words,* vol. III, p. 289. Westwood, New Jersey: Fleming H. Revell, (1940) 1966.

4. Sir Henry Spelman, *The History and Fate of Sacrilege,* p. 1. Samuel J. Eales edition. London: John Hodges, 1888. The original edition of Spelman's work was published in 1698; the Eales edition, with introduction and notes, was published first in 1846.

5. *Ibid.,* p. 3.

man, as the work of sanctification, must further restitution and restoration. Not only must the world be restored to its original glory, but, by virtue of the requirements of restitution, it must, to a double, fourfold and fivefold degree, be developed to the glory of God and His service as man's required restitution. Man must restore to God His due, total lordship over all things, and this restoration, begun by Christ's regenerating act, continued by the Holy Spirit, and made the very life of the redeemed man to further, shall begin to come into its own only when "the earth shall be full of the knowledge of the LORD, as the waters cover the sea" (Isa. 11:9).

Sacrilege must be replaced by restitution and restoration, and the necessary consequences of both sacrilege and of restitution are material, i.e., material curses and material blessings, as Deuteronomy 28 makes very clear. Fallen man and the fallen earth must become restored man and the restored earth.

The function of salvation and sanctification is thus to effect restitution and restoration, and to replace sacrilege with giving God the honor, service, tithes, offerings, obedience, and glory due to His name.

Sacrilege attaches itself to the god and savior of a religion, and to its program of salvation. The Roman idea of salvation clearly reveals its concept of sacrilege. The emperor and Rome are the objects of veneration, and sacrilege is related to them. *The Theodosian Code* preserved many of the older Roman ideas of sacrilege and is thus interesting reading in this connection. For example, we read:

> Valentinian of celestial memory, the ancestor of Our Imperial Divinity, prescribed a fixed rank and merit for each separate dignity. 1. If any person, therefore, should usurp a rank not due to him, he cannot defend himself by any plea of ignorance, and he is clearly guilty of sacrilege in that he has ignored the divine imperial commands.
>
> Interpretation: If any person should usurp a dignity that he has not properly obtained from the Emperor, he shall be held guilty of sacrilege.[6]

Another edict declared that "punishment similar to that for sacrilege shall be inflicted upon any person who fails to accord the proper honor to those who have been deemed worthy to touch Our Purple."[7] Officials could "presume to do nothing contrary to the ancient discipline," for to do so was to be "held guilty of the crime of sacrilege."[8] Violations of the prescribed order or rank and seating was sacrilege.[9] On occasions of

---

6. Clyde Pharr, trans., ed., *The Theodosian Code and Novels and the Sirmondian Constitutions,* 6, 5, 2, p. 127. Princeton. New Jersey: Princeton University Press, 1952.

7. *Ibid.,* 6, 24, 4, p. 136.

8. *Ibid.,* 6, 29, 9, p. 147.

9. *Ibid.,* 6, 35, 13, p. 153.

public rejoicing, no special tax or levy of thanksgiving could be exacted by local officials without sacrilege.[10] Melting down money or transporting it to another area to sell was sacrilege also.[11] In fact, any unauthorized worker, "who, by copying the sacred imperial features and thus assailing the divine countenance, has sacrilegiously coined their venerable images" was guilty of sacrilege.[12] This reminds us of the Biblical ban on graven images representing God. To have an estate rivalling the emperor's was sacrilege.[13] Adultery was sacrilege also, because marriage was a holy institution.[14] There may be remains of ancestor worship in this edict as well as Christian standards. Any new unauthorized public works in Rome, "the Eternal City," constituted sacrilege.[15]

From these edicts and more, it is clear that Rome, both before and after its ostensible adoption of Christianity, still regarded the divinity of the emperor and of Rome as more basic than the deity of Christ. While some Christian ideas of sacrilege had begun to appear in the Theodosian Code, the basic laws had reference to the state. It should be recognized, however, that Christian ideas of sacrilege are clearly apparent in the code: impeding a clergyman in the performance of his office by imposing other duties on him, disturbing worship and affronting the clergy, and neglect and carelessness in the preaching of the word of God to the people, are all defined in chapter 16 of the Code as sacrilege. It is the Roman ideas of sacrilege which are basic to the Code, however.

While the word *sacrilege* has been left out of the modern vocabulary, the idea still remains, in a statist version. The more humanistic the modern state, the more clearly it presents itself as man's lord and savior, and the more serious it regards any crime against itself. Crimes against God are no longer seen as crimes by most modern states; crimes against persons have almost ceased to be capital offenses, although God's word requires capital punishment; crimes against the state, however, have become progressively more important in the eyes of the law and often require death.

True sacrilege, however, is against God: it requires restitution and restoration. Where man does not effect this by his faith and obedience, God exacts it by His judgment.

The rewards and blessings God confers are declared to be a hundredfold (Matt. 19:29). Whereas the restitution God requires is at most fivefold, and this is a necessary restoration required by justice, the restoration God makes for whatever loss we incur for His name's sake, is entirely of grace and is a hundredfold.

---

10. *Ibid.,* 8, 11, 4, p. 212.
11. *Ibid.,* 9, 23, 1, p. 244.
12. *Ibid.,* 9, 38, 6, p. 254.
13. *Ibid.,* 10, 16, p. 276.
14. *Ibid.,* 11, 36, 4, p. 335.
15. *Ibid.,* 12, 1, 27, p. 426.

# 6

## SACRILEGE AND THE CHURCH

We have seen that God acts on a principle of restitution and restoration. Where men rob God of His first-fruits, God robs them of their first-fruits and more as His requirement of restitution. Moreover, He continues to bring judgment until restoration is effected. To rob God is thus to invoke God's curse, and to obey God *and* to work for the restoration of God's order is to invoke His blessing.

Let us now examine sacrilege within the church itself. A dramatic instance of it is reported in I Samuel 2:12-17, 22-36; 3:1-21, and 4:22. The sacrilege was that of Eli's two sons, the priests Hophni and Phinehas, and of Eli himself, the high priest. Eli's sin was that, though a believer, he honored his sons more than God, according to God's charge (I Sam. 2:29), by failing to oust his sons from the priesthood. Eli contented himself with rebukes (I Sam. 2:22-25), as though rebukes were a sufficient discharge of his duty. His sons were radically ungodly and unbelieving. They used their position as priests to practice extortion with worshippers, demanding more than their due share of the sacrifices as a means of gaining wealth by commanding a large supply of meat. Moreover, they placed themselves before God, requiring that they be paid off before God could receive His due sacrifices. They were robbing God, and they were also showing their contempt for God and for the symbolisms of the sacrificial system.

One of the consequences of their unbelief, besides sacrilegious theft, was sexual immorality: "they lay with the women that assembled at the door of the tabernacle of the congregation" (I Sam. 2:22). These women are described in the same words in Exodus 38:8 and were women engaged in the temple or tabernacle service, apparently as a choir. Psalm 68:11 reads, "The Lord gave the word: great was the company of those who published it." According to the Rev. Archdeacon Aglen, this verse is

> Literally, *The Lord gives a word. Of the women who bring the news, the host is great.* The Hebrew for *a word* is poetical, and used especially of a Divine utterance (Pss. xix. 4, lxxvii. 8; Hab. iii. 9). Here it might mean either the *signal* for the conflict, or the *announcement* of victory. But of celebrating a triumph (Ex. xv. 20, 21; Judges v., xi. 34; I Sam. xviii. 6; 2 Sam. i. 20), here evidently alluded to, makes in favour of the latter.[1]

---

1. Aglen, in C. J. Ellicott, ed.: *Ellicott's Commentary on the Whole Bible,* IV, p. 182. Grand Rapids: Zondervan.

Moffatt renders this verse, "When the Lord sent news of victory, the women who told it were a mighty host." Moffatt, however, translates the pertinent words in I Samuel 2:22 as "the women caretakers." In any case, these women had an official function in connection with the sanctuary. Thus, this sin of the two priests had a double evil: it was not only adultery but also sacrilege, in that it robbed God of the holiness which belonged to His sanctuary and to those connected with it. Moreover, as Eli recognized, in his rebuke to his sons, "Ye make the LORD's people to transgress" (I Sam. 2:24). They were corrupting the people by their obvious unbelief and their contemptuous sexuality. The people, seeing no immediate judgment on Hophni and Phinehas, were ready to conclude that there is no God of judgment, and to abandon the law of God for their own sinful advantage. Eli even recognized that his sons' flagrant contempt for God involved a sin beyond forgiveness: "If one man sin against another, the judge shall judge him; but if a man sin against the LORD, who shall intreat for him?" (I Sam. 2:23). In spite of this awareness on Eli's part, he did nothing to remove his sons.

This era is plainly described in Psalm 78:56-64, and the judgment on the sons of Eli, and their death, as well as the capture of the ark of God, clearly set forth:

> Yet they tempted and provoked the most high God, and kept not his testimonies:
> But turned back, and dealt unfaithfully like their fathers: they were turned aside like a deceitful bow.
> For they provoked him to anger with their high places, and moved him to jealousy with their graven images.
> When God heard this, he was wroth, and greatly abhorred Israel:
> So that he forsook the tabernacle of Shiloh, the tent which he placed among men;
> And delivered his strength into captivity, and his glory into the enemy's hand.
> He gave his people over also unto the sword: and was wroth with his inheritance.
> The fire consumed their young men; and their maidens were not given to marriage.
> Their priests fell by the sword; and their widows made no lamentation.

Unbelief had been accompanied by idolatry or will-worship, man's way being enthroned above God's law. This offense against God led Him to deliver them into the hands of the Philistines. God plainly set forth the principle of His judgment by the mouth of an anonymous prophet, through whom He declared to Eli, "them that honour me I will honour, and they that despise me shall be lightly esteemed" (I Sam. 2:30). Since God is the ultimate sovereign and the ultimate source of all law in the universe, the judgment of all things is in terms of Him. The priests, the sons of Eli, had made themselves the ultimate norm and law. The office of priest was merely something to be used, an asset, towards their own advantage and gain. They had, to all practical intent, substituted their sovereignty and ultimacy for God's. Eli had done the same. God had given him high office in Israel's civil and religious history, and he had subordinated these responsibilities to family loyalty. Even after God's rebuke through Samuel and the unnamed prophet, he made no move towards a tardy house-cleaning and reformation.

To identify ultimacy with one's own interests is not limited to Eli and his sons. The church has been guilty repeatedly of this sacrilege. Rome has identified the Church of Christ virtually with itself, and the Kingdom of God with the Church. Protestants have tended to a like error. Indeed, their charges against Rome are today true of them. Whereas Scripture, in speaking of *the church* means more than the visible church, modern usage tends to stress the visible church almost exclusively, and to identify *the church* with a local body or a denomination. Scripture speaks of the local church as "the church of God which is at Corinth" (I Cor. 1:2), and like usage, specifying the church in question as a local instance of the church rather than the church itself. This is an important distinction, in that it is dangerous for a local or a visible body to see itself as *the church* as such rather than a local arm thereof. The followers of Dr. K. Schilder in the Netherlands refuse to speak of their denomination as *a church* but rather as *churches*. In American usage, this would mean speaking, not of the Orthodox Presbyterian Church or the Reformed Presbyterian Church, but rather of the Orthodox Presbyterian Churches, and the Reformed Presbyterian Churches. The reality of both the visible churches and the transcendental nature of the church itself is thereby upheld.

Some of the terms applied to the church have also been too closely identified with the local (or denominational) body. The church is called *the body of Christ*, both the church universal (Eph. 1:23; Col. 1:18), and also the local congregation (I Cor. 12:27). The body of Christ, however, is clearly more than the local instance of a church and cannot be limited to it. The church again is called the temple of the Holy Spirit or of God (I Cor. 3:16; Eph. 2:21, 22), but the usage in Ephesians makes clear also that "the name is applied to the ideal Church of the future, which is the church universal."[2] Moreover, the church is called the Jerusalem that is above, or the new Jerusalem, or the heavenly Jerusalem (Gal. 4:26; Heb. 12:22; Rev. 21:2, 9, 10). The transcendental reference here is very strong. The church is also described as the pillar and the ground of truth in I Timothy 3:15. Berkhof declared,

> It clearly refers to the Church in general, and therefore also applied to every part of it. The figure is expressive of the fact that the Church

---

2. L. Berkhof: *Systematic Theology*, p. 557. Grand Rapids: Eerdmans, 1946.

is the guardian of the truth, the citidel of the truth, and the defender of the truth over against all the enemies of the Kingdom of God.[3]

Calvin, in commenting on I Tim. 3:15, ridiculed the Roman Catholic idea that "all their absurdities ought to be held as oracles of God, because they are 'the pillar of truth,' and therefore cannot err." Calvin went on to declare,

> Hence we may easily conclude in what sense Paul uses these words. The reason why the Church is called the "pillar of truth" is, that she defends and spreads it by her agency....Does she not regenerate them (believers) by the word of God, educate and nourish them through their whole life, strengthen, and bring them at length to absolute perfection? For the same reason, also she is called "the pillar of truth"; because the office of administrating doctrine, which God hath placed in her hands, is the only instrument of preserving the truth, that it may not perish from the remembrance of men.

> Consequently this commendation related to the ministry of the word; for if that be removed, the truth of God will fall to the ground.[4]

The visible churches cannot be identified as *the* pillar and ground of truth, nor can they be separated from that designation: the term "pillar and ground of truth" is both immanent and transcendental in its reference and cannot be limited to either.

Turning again to I Samuel 2:30, God declares that they "that honour *Me* I will honour." Our relationship to all else is conditional upon our relationship to Him who is the author of all things. God is honored by faith and obedience, not by empty words. The churches which refuse to believe God's word or to obey it cannot receive honor from Him. They may flourish for a time, as the unbelieving in heart gather round to rest in contentment at open sacrilege. But God will honor only those who honor Him, and, in His own time, He will manifest his judgment. Those who despise Him He shall lightly esteem. "As a dream when one awaketh; so, O Lord, when thou awakest, thou shalt despise their image" (Ps. 73:20).

The administration of Eli and his sons had led to the official robbery of men. The very source of moral and religious authority, leadership, and teaching had become the corrupter of these things. This was a most flagrant kind of sacrilege. Both God and man were robbed, and that which should have provided the principle of godly order set the pace of pagan corruption.

For the church to be derelict in its duties is thus sacrilege.This need not be obvious theft and adultery as in the case of these two priests. God is

---

3. *Ibid.*, p. 558.
4. John Calvin: *Commentaries on the Epistles to Timothy, Titus, and Philemon*, p. 90. Grand Rapids: Eerdmans, 1959.

robbed and sacrilege is committed where antinomianism is taught and tithing denied, where modernism prevails and a so-called new theology and new morality are preached, where to any degree the churches arrogate to themselves the authority due unto God alone, and wherever authority is used for anything other than lawful, godly ends.

The curse of Eli was that the power of his family would be destroyed, and "there shall not be an old man in thine house" (I Sam. 2:31, 33), i.e., all its men would die young. The Babylonian Talmud has a striking sidelight on this curse:

> But can the final sentence on a community be rescinded? Have we not one text which says, *Wash thy heart from wickedness*, and another which says, *For though thou wash thee with nitre and take thee much soap, yet thine iniquity is marked before me* (Jer. 4:14, 2:22), and does not the one text apply before the final sentence is pronounced, yet there is no contradiction; in the one case the final sentence has been accompanied by an oath, in the other it has not been accompanied by an oath. This accords with the dictum of R. Samuel b. Ammi. For R. Samuel b. Ammi (or, as some say R. Samuel b. Nahmani) said in the name of R. Jonathan: How do we know that a final sentence accompanied by an oath is never rescinded? Because it says, *Therefore I have sworn unto the house of Eli that the iniquity of Eli's house shall not be expiated with sacrifice nor offering.* (I Sam. 3:14). Raba said: With sacrifice and offering it cannot be expiated, but it can be expiated with Torah. Abaye said: With sacrifice and offering it cannot be expiated, but it can be expiated with Torah and charitable deeds. Rabbah and Abaye were of the house of Eli. Rabbah who devoted himself to the Torah lived forty years, Abaye who devoted himself both to the Torah and to charitable deeds lived sixty years.

> The Rabbis taught: There was a family in Jerusalem the members of which used to die at the age of eighteen. They came and told Rabban Johanan b. Zaccai. He said to them, Perhaps you are of the family of Eli, to whom it was said, *and all the increase of thy house shall die young men* (I Sam. 2:33). Go and study the Torah and you may live. They went and studied the Torah and lived, and they used to call that family the family of Rabban Johanan after his name.[5]

Here again we have a very literal fulfilment of a curse manifesting itself centuries later.

---

5. *Rosh Hashanah*, 18a; in *The Babylonian Talmud, Seder Mo'ed*, vol. IV, p. 71f. London: The Soncino Press, 1938.

## 7

## SACRILEGE AND JUDGMENT

According to the law, the first-fruits belong to God, whether of the fruits of the field, in the production of liquors or anything else, or of the sons born to a woman (Ex. 22:29, 30). Like the tithe, the first-fruits belong to God, and to deny them to Him is sacrilege. As a result, when Israel entered Canaan, not only was there a tithe of conquered things, but the first conquered city belonged entirely to God. Jericho was thus set apart in advance as a dedicated city. All its silver and gold, and all its vessels of brass and iron, had to go "into the treasury of the LORD" (Josh. 6:29). However, because of the iniquity of Canaan, God's judgment in full had to fall upon Jericho. They had to destroy utterly "all that was in the city, both man and woman, young and old, and ox, and sheep, and ass, with the edge of the sword," and to burn everything else totally (Josh. 6:21, 24).

Only Rahab and her household were spared, and they too were spared as a part of God's possession. The Prince of the host of the Lord had appeared to Joshua, indicating that Jericho's capture was God's battle, and everything therein, whether kept alive or destroyed, belonged to God alone (Josh. 5:13-15). After the destruction of Jericho, Rahab and her household were kept for a time "without (or outside) the camp of Israel" (Josh. 6:23), until they could meet the ritual purification required of members of the covenant, i.e., circumcision, sacrifice, etc. However, by virtue of their rescue and separation as God's first-fruits, Rahab and her household had an imputed holiness and were, like the gold, silver, and the vessels, sacred and set apart for the Lord. Rahab thus entered Israel with a double status, as an ex-prostitute and also as one with a particular sacredness as God's first-fruit of Canaan.

Sacrilege, however, was committed in the conquest of Jericho:

> But the children of Israel committed a trespass in the accursed thing: for Achan, the son of Carmi, the son of Zabdi, the son of Zerah, of the tribe of Judah, took of the accursed thing: the anger of the LORD was kindled against the children of Israel. (Josh. 7:1).

As a result of this sacrilege, committed by one man while representing the nation, the nation itself felt the impact of God's judgment. As they sought to capture Ai, not an important city, they found themselves unexpectedly defeated. Joshua, like Israel, was ready to blame God for deserting them (Josh. 7:6-9). This was an assertion of causality: God as the ultimate cause was responsible for Israel's defeat. The Lord, in His rejection of Joshua's prayer, asserted causality also; while not denying His ultimate causality but rather affirming it. He emphatically set forth the proximate or immediate cause as responsible: Israel had sinned and had committed sacrilege in the battle of Jericho (Josh. 7:10-15). It was sin to look only at God's ultimate causation: the reality of proximate causes, of human causes, cannot be denied or set aside. God's causality is operative because there is justice. Thus, where God's judgment appears, man must look first to the human factor in order to determine why God has brought judgment to bear on a nation.

The theft by Achan involved considerable wealth: "a goodly Babylonish garment, and two hundred shekels of silver, and a wedge of gold of fifty shekels weight" (Josh. 7:21). The whole family of Achan was involved in his guilt, in that the loot had been buried in the middle of the tent, obviously with the cooperation of all (Josh. 7:21-24). They thus shared in Achan's guilt and judgment.

But this is not all. While settlements sprang up *near* the site of the original Jericho and used the same name, the original Jericho had to remain set apart to God, its ruined ground a witness to God's requirements. We are told,

> And Joshua adjured them at that time, saying, Cursed be the man before the LORD, that riseth up and buildeth this city Jericho: he shall lay the foundation thereof in his firstborn, and in his youngest son shall he set up the gates of it. (Josh. 6:26).

A good many centuries later, in Ahab's day, Jericho was rebuilt:

> In his days did Hiel the Bethelite build Jericho: he laid the foundation thereof in Abiram his firstborn, and set up the gates thereof in his youngest son Segub, according to the word of the LORD, which he spake by Joshua the son of Nun. (I Kings 16:34).

The territory around Jericho belonged to the Tribe of Benjamin and thus properly belonged to the Southern Kingdom, to Judah. The construction was under the auspices of Ahab, indicating that some of Judah's realm was under Ahab's rule, and perhaps all of it somewhat dependent on him. In Joshua's day, the fortress city of Jericho was the eastern guardian of the land of Canaan. With the east bank of the Jordan in Israelite hands, there was now no need of such a fortress in the midst of the realm. The reconstruction of Jericho, militarily, meant a line of division in the land; however, other such fortresses had been built, and both Israel and Judah were at times in open conflict. The religious significance of Jericho was the key issue. The ruined site of Jericho was a continuing witness to God's saving power and God's claim on all the first-fruits of Israel. To rebuild Jericho meant not only to deny God's present claims on Israel but to reach back into past ages and to deny God's first-fruits as Joshua had rendered them. As Bahr commented with respect to Ahab, "As he denied the God of Israel, and placed the Baal of the Canaanites in His stead, so he also denied the great saving act of Jehovah as manifested in the fall and destruction of Jericho."[1]

Is the judgment on sacrilege meted out with regard to Jericho simply "holy history" with no relationship to our everyday history? Is it a supernatural act of Biblical history unrelated to the natural events of our history?

The Bible asserts natural and historical consequences for sacrilege as well as for obedience. When Phinehas killed Zimri and Cosbi, for his faithfulness he was promised a long continuance of his posterity in the priesthood. When Saul committed four sacrilegious acts, he and his family were cut off from their power, even as the sons of Eli had earlier been cut off for their two sacrilegious acts, i.e., misappropriation of what belonged to God, and fornication within the precincts of the tabernacle. Material acts thus have material consequences. If I put my hand into the fire, I have a burned hand, not a burned mind. It is a deformation of reality to transfer the effects from one area to another. Jericho was God's first-fruits in Canaan. When Hiel rebuilt Jericho, he lost his first-born son, and, as the penalty for his offense, his youngest son as well.

Webb and Neale, in applying this fact to history, set forth this thesis:

> Property, consecrated to God in the service of His Church, has generally, when alienated to secular purposes, brought misfortune on its possessors; whether by strange accidents, by violent deaths, by loss of wealth, or, and that chiefly, by failure of heirs male; and such property hardly ever continues long in one family.[2]

Let us survey history briefly in terms of this. When the medieval church used the tithes, offerings, first-fruits and bequests given to Christ prodigally and falsely, it met judgment at the hands of both the various monarchs, first of all, and then the Reformers. Unfortunately, too often both the monarchs, Catholic and Protestant, and on occasion churchmen, added sacrilege to sacrilege. The seizure of church properties by Henry VIII was plainly sacrilege. Granted that there had been some corruption, although probaby far less than Henry VIII claimed, the church buildings, lands, and foundations belonged to Christ, not to Henry. Theft is not reformation: it is sacrilege. Thomas Lever, in a sermon of February 2, 1550, in the days of young Edward VI, declared plainly:

---

1. J. P. Lange: *Commentary on the Holy Scriptures: Kings*, p. 186. Grand Rapids: Zondervan, (1872).

2. Rev. Prebendary Webb and Rev. Dr. J. M. Neale, in "An Introductory Essay" in Sir Henry Spelman: *The History and Fate of Sacrilege*, p. xix, 1846 ed.

> Seeing that impropriations being so evil that no man can allow them,
> be now so employed unto the universities, yea and unto the yearly
> revenues of the king's majesty, that few dare speak against them, ye
> may see that some men, not only by the abuse of riches and authority,
> but also by the abuse of wisdom and policy do much harm, and
> specially those, by whose means this realm is now brought into such
> case that either learning in the university and necessary revenues
> belong to the most high authority is like to decay, or else impropria-
> tions to be maintained, which both be devilish and abominable that
> if either of them come to effect, it will cause the vengenance of God
> utterly to destroy this realm.[3]

Lever said plainly that the old abuses of Rome needed correcting. He was
ready to agree, more than moral grounds permitted, that something of
the church wealth might have accrued to the throne, at the time of the
suppression of the chantries, to take care of expenses, but the commitment
of that wealth was to God's cause, and to charitable causes in Christ's
name, and anything short of that was a betrayal of the Reformation:

> I tell you, at the first the intent was very godly, the pretense won-
> drous goodly, but now the use or rather the abuse and misorder of
> these things is worldly, is wicked, is devilish, is abominable. . . .

> But you which have gotten these goods into your own hands, to
> turn them from evil to worse, and other goods more from good unto
> evil, be ye sure it is even you that have offended God, beguiled the
> king, robbed the rich, spoiled the poor, and brought a common-
> wealth into a common misery. It is even you, that must either be
> plagued with God's vengeance as were the Sodomites, or amend by
> repentance as did the Ninevites. Even you it is that must either make
> restitution and amends speedly, or else feel the vengeance of God
> greviously.[4]

Lever's analysis was an honest one: Church wealth had been turned from
"evil to worse" in some cases, and, in others, "from good unto evil."
The solution was provided by God's law: *restitution*. Without that solution, the nation was degenerating from bad to worse.[5] According to W.
K. Jordan, while Lever's plea did not change the course of the state's
policy, it "had much to contribute towards the rise of the secular
charitable impulse which marks the Edwardian era."[6] The great wave of
Puritan charity and tithing did much to alter England, but the old crime
was not atoned for. However, many, like Lever, felt that in some sense
restitution was being made.

It was in 1536 that Henry VIII began the dissolution of the

---

3. Edward Arber, ed.: *Thomas Lever: Sermons, 1550.* p. 31 (spelling modernized by
RJR). Westminster: Constable, 1901.

4. *Ibid.*, p. 32f.

5. *Ibid.*, p. 37.

6. W. K. Jordan: *Edward VI: The Threshold of Power*, p. 203. Cambridge, Mass.: The
Belknap Press of Harvard University Press, 1970.

monasteries. In 1667, South, in preaching on sacrilege, declared,

> we need not go many nations off, nor many ages back, to see the vengeance of God upon some families, raised upon the ruins of churches, and enriched with the spoils of sacrilege, gilded with the name of reformation. And, for the most part, so unhappy have been the purchasers of church lands, that the world is not now to seek for an argument, from a long experience, to convince it, that though in such purchases, men have usually the cheapest pennyworths, yet they have not always the best bargains; for the holy thing has stuck fast to their sides like a fatal shaft, and the stone has cried out of the consecrated walls they have lived within, for a judgment upon the head of the sacrilegious intruder; and Heaven has heard the cry, and made good the curse. So that when the heir of a blasted family has risen up and promised fair, and perhaps flourished for some time upon the stock of excellent parts and great favour; yet at length a cross event has certainly met and stopped him in the career of his fortunes, so that he has ever after withered and declined, and in the end come to nothing, or to that which is worse. So certainly does that which some call blind superstition, take aim when it shoots a curse at the sacrilegious person. But I shall not engage in the odious task of recounting the families, which this sin has blasted with a curse.[7]

South assumed that the fact of judgment on sacrilege was so obvious in English history between 1536 and 1667 that there was no need to make a case: he only reminded his hearers of a fact apparently obvious to all. To have bought or to own church lands was to be blasted by God's vengeance. Was this popular assumption true?

In 1632, Sir Henry Spelman documented this fact of judgment, and, after his death, his study of sacrilege was published in 1698. He found only fourteen continuing families out of 630 families who had gained church lands, and clear evidence of judgment of 600 families.[8] Webb and Neale carried the study further, and pointed out also that one could not eliminate the data by saying that the extinction of families was common in those days. There was a clear-cut difference between the families guilty of sacrilege and those that were not. According to Webb and Neale,

> statistically, the failure of male heirs in families implicated in Sacrilege is much more frequent than in those which are not so implicated, and further, that church lands change their possessors far more frequently than those which have never been devoted to God.[9]

Hiel for his sacrilege lost both his first-born and youngest sons. Many Englishmen have lost all their male heirs for their greater sacrilege. Moreover, Webb and Neale cited evidences of a continuing and lingering curse with respect to the abbey-lands:

---

7. Robert South: *Sermons Preached Upon Several Occasions*, Vol. I, p. 111. Philadelphia: Sorin & Ball, 1845.

8. Spelman: *History and Fate of Sacrilege*, p. 258.

9. *Ibid.*, p. lviii.

> Now, by purchase, by bequest, by exchange, by marriage, the con-
> tamination has been communicated and recommunicated, till it is
> difficult to say who is absolutely clear. And the case is still more
> complicated with respect to lands.[10]

In one part of England, Henry VIII divided some of the church spoils
among 260 gentlemen; at the same time, Thomas, Duke of Norfolk,
established 20 of his gentlemen out of his own inheritance; not 60 of the
King's 260 donees had a son to inherit, whereas all 20 of the duke's men
had heirs.[11] Webb and Neale give much more precise data substantiating
this fact.[12] Where men have robbed God of His first-fruits, God has
taken their first-fruits and more from them. They concluded,

> We can only lament these things; we cannot correct them. We have
> no reason to think GOD will be reconciled to national sin without
> national restitution; and there is less chance of that every day.[13]

As long as a land has a saving remnant whose works invoke God's blessings, the curse is to that extent limited. Today, however, the saving remnant is everywhere small. Since then, sacrilege has proliferated, not only
with the French and Russian Revolutions, but with the growing statism
in all nations, whereby the state claims the first-fruits. The curse for
rebuilding Jericho was effective 520 years after it was pronounced; there
is no reason to believe that God since then has had lapses of memory
where sacrilege is concerned. Tithes, offerings, lands, and other properties belonging to God cannot be alienated from Him. There are no lapses
of memory with God, and the demand for restitution therefore remains.

What belongs to God cannot be alienated from God. It is His by right,
and He requires it. What has been taken from God must be restored to
God, because every gift given to God is inalienably His, or the full value
thereof. It is not morally possible to hold that, because we are under
grace, we can disregard the laws of sacrilege, restitution, and restoration.
We have been redeemed by God's sovereign grace, not that we should
now aggravate or continue in the sins of unbelief and rebellion, but "that
the righteousness of the law might be fulfilled in us, who walk not after
the flesh, but after the Spirit" (Rom. 8:4).

To disobey God is to invite the curse, and the curse on sacrilege is
especially severe. A time of judgment is also a time of redemption, in
that it delivers the covenant-keepers from the ungodly and enhances their
blessing.

The impropriations in England may seem now to be a dead issue. They
are in fact a very live one in a number of ways. For one thing, impropria-

---

10. *Idem.*
11. *Ibid.*, p. lxi.
12. *Ibid.*, p. lxii
13. *Ibid.*, p. lxxxix

tions constituted a legalized seizure of property, and a precedent for further seizures. Since then, legalized confiscation or theft of property has had a strong precedent, and the properties of the nobility, the middle classes, the lower classes, and of the crown itself have not been immune to the control and/or confiscation of Parliament.

A significant fact too is that sacrilege, once feared by believer and unbeliever alike, is no longer regarded seriously by either. One of the central products of humanistic science has been an undercutting of the idea of causality as too theological a concept. As a result, to consider divine causality is impossible for modern man: he has a mental block against the very possibility of such a concept. However, what man believes or disbelieves does not alter reality. The unrecognized divine causality shall prevail, not humanistic man.

**8**

## THE SACRILEGE OF TIME

In its primary meaning, there is a sacrilege of time when the sabbath or the Lord's Day is abused or profaned. The law, in both Exodus and Deuteronomy, gives particular attention to the interpretation of this law. In the original declaration of the Ten Commandments, it is stated thus:

> Remember the sabbath day, to keep it holy.
> Six days shalt thou labour, and do all thy work:
> But the seventh day is the sabbath of the LORD thy God: in it thou shalt not do any work, thou, nor thy son, nor thy daughter, thy manservant, nor thy maidservant, nor thy cattle, nor thy stranger that is within thy gates:
> For in six days the LORD made heaven and earth, the seas, and all that in them is, and rested the seventh day: wherefore the LORD blessed the sabbath day, and hallowed it. (Ex. 20:8-11).

Rylaarsdam has said, of God's rest on the seventh day, "This rest constituted the creation of the sabbath, which thus expresses God's own nature."[1] The sabbath expresses God's nature because God, being beyond time and necessity, which are aspects of His creation, knows the end from the beginning. His creative work is thus not problematic but totally determined and a fiat expression. God declared the word, "Let there be..."and all things were created. God's rest is thus grounded in the perfection of His work: not a hair nor an atom can go astray or afield in His predestined work of creation, redemption, and re-creation. God's rest is thus an expression of His sovereignty and of the absoluteness of His government. Man cannot govern absolutely any aspect of his life or world, but he can rest in the fact that his God and Savior does govern absolutely and *rests* in His government. Only with such a faith and with such a God can man rest. *Man may worship without such a faith, but he cannot rest.*

In the restatement of the commandment in Moses' farewell restatement of the law to Israel, another aspect of the sabbath is brought out:

> Keep the sabbath day to sanctify it, as the LORD thy God hath commanded thee.
> Six days thou shalt labour, and do all thy work:

---

1. J. Coert Rylaarsdam, "Exodus," in *The Interpreter's Bible*, I, p. 985. New York: Abingdon Press, 1952.

But the seventh day is the sabbath of the LORD thy God: in it thou shalt not do any work, thou, nor thy son, nor thy daughter, nor thy manservant, nor thy maidservant, nor thine ox, nor thine ass, nor any of thy cattle, nor thy stranger that is within thy gates: that thy manservant and thy maidservant may rest as well as thou.

And remember that thou wast a servant in the land of Egypt, and that the LORD thy God brought thee out thence through a mighty hand and by a stretched out arm: therefore the LORD thy God commanded thee to keep the sabbath day. (Deut. 5:12-15).

The sabbath, while commemorating creation in its seventh day pattern, began with the passover in the Old Testament, and with the day of resurrection in the New Testament, in order to celebrate salvation. *Creation is the pattern, salvation the source of our rest.*

Sacrilege of time thus involves, *first*, a denial of the fact of creation, or a contempt thereof. In an evolving universe, man, as the potential god of this "creation" out of a primeval chaos, cannot rest: everything depends on him, and he is not omnipotent nor infallible. The sabbath thus ceases to be rest for him, and becomes instead an opportunity for some other form of activity than work. It means a change of pace, not a total rest.

*Second*, where man denies salvation by Christ, he denies rest and commits the sacrilege of time by making *his* time, work, and activity redemptive. Man creates his own time-table, with the world socialist, humanist utopia at the end, as his man-made sabbath. This sabbath of man will express the finished nature of man, the new god of creation. Until then, there can be no rest, only work to create the workers' paradise.

Before considering a *third* form of the sacrilege of time, it is necessary to examine briefly some aspects of time. Clearly, time is one resource that man, having wasted, can never recover. Time cannot be regained, nor can it be hoarded for future use. There is no way of stock-piling time for future use.

In some cultures, time is made all important, and eternity is despised or denied. Such a culture becomes sensate, totally present-oriented and eager to exploit the moment and its pleasures to the full, in that nothing else is held to be real. Existentialism is the philosophy of such a faith.

On the other hand, some cultures depreciate time for eternity. Only that which is timeless and of enduring value is worthwhile. The academic world, because of its roots in ancient Greece, is deeply imbued with this contempt for time. Its goal is often a post-historical culture, a civilization beyond change and embodying the universals established by autonomous and radically humanistic man. To this end, all effort is exerted, to create the universal world order which will fix civilization and time.

Both the sensate culture and the anti-historical faith lead to a contempt for man. In the one, only the moment matters; in the other, only the new universals have any validity. Man, as a person whose life is thus filled with often trifling concerns, is despised by the man who believes it to be a waste of time to be courteous to anyone, especially non-intellectuals. Buying and selling, and especially salesmanship, are regarded as the epitome of barbarism, because of their deep involvement with time and people. In the dream world of the anti-historical scholars, the sordid world of salesmen and time-involved people will be eliminated. The new eternity of autonomous man will prevail. Some years ago, a professor who was mildly chided by his wife at a university gathering for his boorishness, snarled back, "I have no time for etiquette and small chit-chat." He had no time for *man* as such, only for important people, and his snobbishness, his false philosophy, and his rudeness were justified in his eyes by his self-importance.

The Bible, however, requires us, from the modern viewpoint, to "waste" a great amount of time: one day in seven, one sabbatical year in seven, and the forty-ninth and fiftieth years as a double sabbath because of the jubilee. Added together, this means *more* than one day in seven, because, in addition to this, the sabbatical years greatly increase the time of rest.

But this is not all. A requirement of that rest is a fellowship with the religious and educational leader (the Levite), the foreigner, the widow, and the orphan. We are thus *required* to avoid an aristocratic, snobbish, or class association. The law of the third tithe, rejoicing before the Lord, plainly declares:

> At the end of three years thou shalt bring forth all the tithe of thine increase the same year, and shall lay it up within thy gates:
> And the Levite (because he hath no part nor inheritance with thee,) and the stranger, and the fatherless, and the widow, which are within thy gates, shall come, and shall eat and be satisfied; that the LORD thy God may bless thee in all the work of thine and which thou doest. (Deut. 14:27-28).

This requirement of fellowship and community is a type of that which is expected at all other times. To associate with such poor or unfortunate believers only in the third year, at the time of a festival, was to disobey the spirit of the law.

This law is especially relevant to our time. It is the mark of the age that exclusiveness is sought. The rich want hobbies which will separate them from others; they want to do what nobody else is doing, travel where no one else has yet gone, and to live in separation from others. Those poorer seek to imitate these habits of the wealthy, to be "with it" in being "different." The world of scholarship similarly prides itself on being "different," despises the common man who has neither the time, interest, or ability to master their field of knowledge, and regards it as an imposition to be forced to deal with or be courteous to "ordinary" people. Apart from a sinful pride, there is here also a violation of God's laws of community.

The *third* sacrilege of time is thus not only a denial of the sabbath rest but of the community and fellowship with God *and* man which the sabbath rest requires.

Because God's creation is a seamless garment, we can never over-look or deny the interlocking nature of all things therein. Law and grace, rest and community, man and man, work and sabbath, and all things else are inextricably inter-related.

We cannot define anything therefore purely in terms of itself, but always in the context of God's purpose and His creation.

Thus, the word *government* is today reduced to one aspect of government, the state. Government means first of all the self-government of man, then the family, the church, the school, community, vocation, and society, and also the state. Without the other forms of government, beginning with self-government, the totalitarian state results, and the collapse of the state begins. All forms of government must rest on the prior fact of self-government.

The same is true of *worship*. The idea of worship is today reduced to a church service. If worship is not *primarily* outside the church, it will soon disappear in the church. Worship must first of all exist in man's inner life, in his family and calling, to be alive in the church.

This applies also to the sabbath. If the sabbath as community between God and man, and between man and man in Christ, is not basic, then it becomes an empty form. The sabbath is the joyful rest of men who labor faithfully six days in seven, and can rest on the seventh, knowing that God is Lord over time and all things, and a day in rest together in the Lord is more productive than a millennium of work and rest apart from Him.

Laeuchli has commented, "Because man is saved by God and not by creation, he shares in the reality of eternity and not of time."[2] We must rather say, because man is saved by God and not by himself or the creation around him, he shares in the reality of eternity as well as time, and he knows the priority of God and His eternal decree. He can therefore value time without overvaluing it. He can live in time without being its creature.

The Lord makes this very clear, as He speaks through Isaiah, declaring:

> Therefore thus saith the LORD GOD, Behold, I lay in Zion for a foundation a stone, a tried stone, a precious corner stone, a sure foundation: he that believeth shall not make haste. (Isa. 28:16).

The existentialist *must* make haste, he has *only* time, and not even a time with meaning. He must make haste to establish a meaning and then to develop it, yet always knowing that meaninglessness is ultimate. This

---

2. Samuel Laeuchli: *The Serpent and the Dove, Five Essays on Early Christianity*, p. 78. New York: Abingdon Press, 1966.

reduced man and his attempts to establish meaning to no more than "a futile passion," to use Sartre's phrase. On the other hand, "he that believeth shall not make haste," because the totality of meaning surrounds him; his labor is never in vain in the Lord (I Cor. 15:58), and the future does not depend upon his labor, while requiring it as a service, but on the Lord.

In every age, the existentialist has concluded, "let us eat, drink, and be merry, for tomorrow we die." Such an attitude is a despair of time, a flight from responsibility and reality, and a destruction of hope. It stands in strong contrast to the sabbath rest with others, the sense of community in rejoicing before the Lord. In Deuteronomy 14:27-28 and elsewhere, the call is to eat, drink, and be merry, for the Lord is God, and His sabbath rest is the gift of assured victory to man.

# 9

## SACRILEGE AGAINST THE PERSON

Throughout Scripture, it is clear that those who serve God's sanctuary and proclaim His word have a holiness in God's sight and are to be held in respect by all men. The tribe of Levi was separated by God unto Himself, "to bless in his name" (Deut. 10:8), so that to bless faithful Levi meant to be blessed, and to curse the faithful Levite meant to be accursed. The warning is clear: "Take heed to thyself that thou forsake not the Levite as long as thou livest upon the earth" (Deut. 12:19).

The commandment, however, has a still broader scope. In speaking of God's concern for His covenant people, the psalmist declared (Ps. 105:14-15), of the patriarchs, Abraham, Isaac, and Jacob,

> He suffered no man to do them wrong: yea, he reproved kings for their sakes; Saying, Touch not mine anointed, and do my prophets no harm.

The patriarchs were called "anointed," i.e., inducted into theocratic office as kings of God, and also prophets, men who spoke for God (Gen. 20:7). In terms of this declaration, rulers and prophets (all who are called and set apart to proclaim the word of God) have a privileged status before God, and offenses against them are regarded as sacrilege. The faithful servant of God represents His Lord, and to strike at him is to strike at the God whom he represents.

It is of note that even pagans recognized the seriousness of sacrilege. To strike at the property of the gods or at the person of their representatives was a very dangerous thing and was viewed as a declaration of war against heaven. Spelman observed,

> I must here note, as it cometh in my way, the remarkable justice and piety of Pharaoh towards his idol priests; that when by reason of the famine he had got and bought unto himself all the money, cattle, lands, wealth, and persons of the Egyptians, yet stretched he not forth his thoughts to the lands or persons of his priests; but, commiserating their necessity, allowed them a portion at his own charge, that they might both live and keep their lands. Musculus hereupon infers, "How great a sacrilege is it in our princes, that the good and lawful ministers of holy things are thus neglected?"[1]

To understand the sacrilege of persons, it is important to survey the Biblical doctrine of man. Too often, the view which has prevailed in

---

1. Spelman: *History and Fate of Sacrilege*, p. 10f.

53

Christendom, with respect to sacrilege, has had pagan roots: it assimilated the person of kings and priests into the person of God, and then preserved them from all criticism as a species of divinity.

The Bible does require *respect* for authorities. It does not permit a contempt for authority or a wilful disobedience to it. Jude 8-11 declares emphatically:

> Likewise also these filthy dreamers defile the flesh, despise dominion, and speak evil of dignities.
> Yet Michael the archangel, when contending with the devil he disputed about the body of Moses, durst not bring against him a railing accusation, but said, The Lord rebuke thee.
> But these speak evil of those things which they know not: what they know naturally, as brute beasts, in those things they corrupt themselves.
> Woe unto them! for they have gone in the way of Cain, and ran greedily after the error of Balaam for reward, and perished in the gainsaying of Core.

Two things are clear, among others, in this text. *First*, Michael, the archangel, in his contention with the devil, *did* rebuke him. *Second*, Michael did *not* rebuke the devil on his own authority but rather in terms of the word of God: "The Lord rebuke thee." This is in terms of the Lord's word that we judge not, lest we be judged (Matt. 7:1-5). We are forbidden to judge *if* we judge in terms of arbitrary and personal criteria, *or* if we judge hypocritically, condemning sin in others which we refuse to admit to or condemn in ourselves (John 8:1-11). We are, however, commanded to judge in terms of God's law: "Judge not according to the appearance, but judge righteous judgment" (John 7:24). Michael thus did rebuke the devil in terms of God's word. The sin is in judgment without God's word; apparently this was involved in the devil's claims on Moses.

Judgment must be in terms of God's word because the world and man are creations of God and *cannot* be understood, assessed, or judged apart from Him. If any neighbor were *my* creature, I could use my own fiat will to judge him; since he is God's creature, I can *only* use God's declared word to judge him.

Man, having been created in God's image, cannot be understood apart from God and in particular must be treated with respect. The fact that man is fallen does not eliminate God's image. The image of God in man can be *defaced*, but it cannot be *effaced*; it can be, and, by the fall, is marred, but it cannot be obliterated. The law thus gives particular attention to the relationship of man to man. Our standing with God is manifested by our relationship with men, and our godly relationship with men does further our sanctification. Five of the ten commandments deal specifically with our relationship with other men. To sin against our neighbor is to sin against God. Our relationship with other men, in word, thought, and deed, is totally religious because we are all totally God's creatures and totally under His law. The foundations of all true community are thus in God and His word.

As a result, we are required by the law to respect our neighbor's family, life, property, and name in word, thought, and deed. We can never reduce any man to our personal opinion of him.

Thus, Scripture requires us to obey God's law strictly, to honor God by obeying His word, and to honor all men by observing God's law in relationship to them.

Where the authority of God is at stake, in every area of life, family, state, vocation, and the like, we must give to authorities that honor which is their due (Rom. 13:7). In I Peter 2:17 we are commanded, "Honour all men. Love the brotherhood. Fear God. Honour the king." The word *honor* is here used equally for *all* and for *the king*.

With this in mind, let us turn again to Psalm 105, in order to understand what it teaches us concerning sacrilege. Alexander said, of this psalm,

> This like the Seventy-Eighth, is a historical psalm, recounting God's ancient dealings with his people, especially in Egypt. The practical design of the commemoration is not to bring the people to repentance, as in the case referred to, but to excite their hopes of an analogous deliverance.[2]

It is necessary to understand what that "analogous deliverance" is.

The psalm begins (vss. 1-5) with a summons to praise God, to glory "in his holy name," to "seek the Lord, and his strength," and to "Remember his marvellous works that he hath done; his wonders, and the judgments of his mouth." These "judgments" are then recounted: they are the care and deliverance of the patriarchs, and the plagues of Egypt which freed Israel.

First of all, the goodness of God to the patriarchs is declared (vss. 6-15). God made a covenant and kept faith with His chosen ones. God is *always* faithful to His covenant and mindful of His own. God declared in effect to kings that His covenant people are his anointed ones and His prophets, that in His Son, the new covenant man, they are kings, priests, and prophets. In a more than ordinary sense, the patriarchs were, moreover, God's recipients of revelation and representatives of the great covenant Kingdom of Christ.

Next, the providential care of Joseph (vss. 16, 22) is cited. While Joseph suffered because of his faithfulness, the Lord proved him to be right and established him as lord over Egypt under Pharaoh. Leupold

---

2. Joseph Addison Alexander: *The Psalms, Translated and Explained*, p. 429. Grand Rapids: Zondervan, (1850).

rendered vs. 19 thus: "Until his (Joseph's) word came true; And the word of the Lord proved him to be right."[3] Joseph was vindicated and mightily blessed.

In vss. 23-25, the providential stay of Israel in Egypt is described, not in terms of their later suffering, but primarily in terms of their great strength: "And he increased his people greatly; and made them stronger than their enemies" (vs. 24). The persecution of Israel in Egypt was motivated by fear of their power.

The oppressors, however, were judged by God (vss. 26-36) with a devastating judgment which ranks among the most drastic in all history. Moreover, "apparently the exodus from Egypt took place during the zenith of Egyptian power, prestige and glory."[4] The religious and natural strength of Egypt was met head-on and crushed by God.

From the exodus to the conquest of Canaan (vss. 37-45) God defended and prospered His covenant people with mighty acts. They left Egypt, not as slaves, but as rich men: "He brought them forth also with silver and gold: and there was not one feeble person among their tribes" (vs. 37). The purpose of all this is clearly recognized by Leupold, in his comments, although with an unnecessary apology:

> When one definite divine purpose that lay behind all these gracious favors is now brought to the fore, namely, that "they might observe His statutes and keep His laws," this is not to be faulted as involving an unwholesome emphasis on the use of the law of the Lord but is rather to be approved as being an indication of deeper insight into God's purposes. True gratitude will always express itself by more faithful adherence to the divinely revealed will.[5]

The purpose of God's redemption and His providential care of His covenant people is "That they might observe his statutes, and keep his laws. Praise ye the LORD" (vs. 45).

God created man to observe His statutes and keep His laws in Eden. Man chose his own will as his law and defied God's order, and the result was disaster and death. The covenant people are redeemed to observe the statutes and keep the laws of God in order that this world and the people thereof might become God's Kingdom in the fullest sense of the word.

It was sacrilege for Egypt to lay hands on God's anointed. The demand of God through Moses was, "Let my people go, that they may serve me...." (Ex. 7:16). To lay godless hands on any man by word, thought, or deed is a *sin*. To impede the word, service, and ministry of God is a sacrilege. The sacrilege of persons thus is the violation or abuse

---

3. H. C. Leupold: *Exposition of the Psalms*, p. 737. Columbus, Ohio. The Wartburg Press 1959.

4. John J. Davis: *Moses and the Gods of Egypt*, p. 37. Grand Rapids: Baker Book House, 1971.

5. Leupold, *op. cit.*, p. 741.

of the priests and ministers of God who serve their Lord faithfully and obey His laws. It is also the violation of the covenant man, whatever his calling, when he is persecuted for the Lord's sake. To the degree that one of the least of Christ's brethren is afflicted (or aided) for the Lord's sake, it is done to Him also (Matt. 25:40, 45). "He that receiveth you receiveth me, and he that receiveth me receiveth him that sent me" (Matt. 10:40).

Moreover, sacrilege is not only against persons who are set apart for the Lord's service but is also any violation by a consecrated person against the holiness required of his person and office. Leviticus 21 gives us a list of such forms of sacrilege: the priest committed a sacrilege if he officiated while in mourning, because death, a consequence of sin, is alien to the office which sets forth the resurrection and the life of righteousness. The priest again profaned his office if he married anyone but a virgin, the purity of his office requiring the singleness of devotion by his bride. A blemished, maimed, or crippled man was also barred from the office of priest, since the office represented the unblemished humanity of the new Adam, Jesus Christ.

Aryeh Newman, in summarizing the Biblical doctrine, stated that sacrilege is "the deliberate or inadvertent violation of sacred things."[6] This is a fact of very great importance. Sacrilege is not merely a subjective but an objective offense as well. If I touch a high voltage line, it makes little difference as to the consequence, (i.e., my death), whether I intended to touch it or accidentally touched it; the only difference is as to intent: was my action suicide or stupidity? Similarly, if I commit sacrilege, it involves wilful contempt of God, or, at the very least, an ignorance prompted by an unconcern over what Scripture teaches.

The pastor who is ignorant of the scriptures, or disbelieving, is guilty of sacrilege. His profession of faith does not excuse his ignorance. The rebellion of Korah (Num. 16) represented the wilful arrogation by man of that priestly power which only God can confer. Korah asserted a principle of equality as against the principle of authority, specifically the authority of God's word. The radical judgment on Korah and his followers is a witness to the wrath of God against all sacrilege. The Lord's warning is very plain: "Touch not mine anointed, and do my prophets no harm" (Ps. 105:15).

---

6. Aryeh Newman, "Sacrilege," in *Encyclopaedia Judaica*, vol. 14, p. 615. New York: Macmillan, 1971.

## 10

## SACRILEGE, HOLINESS, AND COMMUNITY

The details of sacrilege can be analyzed at length, i.e., the sacrilege of things, as the ark, the sacrilege of Ananias and Sapphira (Acts 5:6), the sacrilege of holy places (Ex. 3:5), and much more. Our concern, however, is with the meaning of sacrilege for society, its relationship to a law structure and to the fact of community.

Very clearly, the tabernacle and the temple were set apart for their holy function, and any trespass against their precincts was sacrilege. When Uzziah the king usurped the office and function of the priest and trespassed on to priestly ground in the temple, he was smitten with leprosy (II Chron. 26:16ff.). The judgment of God in this case as in others had a grim appropriateness: Uzziah having refused to honor that which was set apart by God was himself set apart by leprosy. His sacrilege was followed by his quarantine.

It would be a serious error to forget these concrete cases of sacrilege. This fact that the commandment forbidding the muzzling of an ox which treadeth out the corn (Deut. 25:4) means in its fullest sense that the laborer is worthy of his hire (I Cor. 9:9; I Tim. 5:18) would never allow us to forget that the ox is also a laborer. The fullest reference is to man, but the reference to the ox is no less clear. It is important to recognize this fact as we come to a central text on sacrilege:

> Know ye not that ye are the temple of God, and that the Spirit of God dwelleth in you?
> If any man defile the temple of God, him shall God destroy; for the temple of God is holy, which temple ye are (I Cor. 3:16-17).
> What? know ye not that your body is the temple of the Holy Ghost, which is in you, which ye have of God, and ye are not your own?
> For ye are bought with a price: therefore glorify God in your body, and in your spirit, which are God's (I Cor. 6:19-20).

The first reference is primarily to the church, the successor to the temple. The penalty for defiling the temple of God, or the tabernacle, by even ritual uncleanness, was death (Lev. 15:36), or excommunication from the congregation (Num. 18:20). As Hodge observed,

> God is not less jealous of his spiritual temple, than he was of the typical temple, built of wood and stone by the hands of men. Ministers injure the souls of men and injure the church when they preach false doctrine, and therefore they defile the temple of God,

58

and will certainly be punished.[1]

The second reference is primarily to the believer's physical being. Here again, Hodge's commentary is excellent:

> There are two things characteristic of a temple. First, it is sacred as a dwelling-place of God, and therefore cannot be profaned with impunity. Second, the proprietorship of a temple is not in man, but in God. Both these things are true of the believer's body. It is a temple because the Holy Ghost dwells in it; and because it is not his own. It belongs to God. As it is a temple of the Holy Ghost, it cannot be profaned without incurring great and peculiar guilt. And as it belongs in a peculiar sense to God, it is not at our own disposal. It can only be used for the purposes for which he designed it.[2]

This law of sacrilege against God's temple takes us from a physical structure of wood and stone to a body of believers, a community of faith which must not be violated, and to the believer's own body. The sins and false divisions of the Corinthian church were sacrilege: they violated the community of faith, and they defiled the body bought by Christ at the price of His blood.

St. Paul declares, in I Corinthians 3, that the church, established on the foundation of Jesus Christ, is being falsely divided in Corinth, not in terms of a separation from heresy or evil, but in terms of "envying and strife" (I Cor. 3:3). Sacrilege here is the sundering of a holy community. Its root is in sin, whether it be the sacrilege against the community, or sacrilege against one's body. The *common factor* in both cases is failure to recognize that God is the only lord of the church and of the redeemed man. The roots of "envying and strife" are in personal ambitions and loyalties rather than in a surrender to God's Kingship; the roots of fornication are in an antinomianism in which man becomes his own god.

The roots of this sacrilegious division are in heresy, tacit or explicit, according to St. Paul. I Corinthians 11:17-19, in the King James and the Berkeley Versions, makes this clear:

> Now in this that I declare unto you I praise you not, that ye come together not for the better, but for the worse.
> For first of all, when ye come together in the church, I hear that there be divisions among you: and I partly believe it.
> For there must be also heresies among you, that they which are approved may be made manifest among you (King James Version).

> I must announce this, however, that I do not approve of your coming together not for your good but to your hurt. For in the first place, I hear that as you meet in church session there are factions among you, and to some extent I believe it. Indeed, there have to be dissensions among you, so that the tried and true may be recognized

---

1. Charles Hodge: *An Exposition of the First Epistle to the Corinthians*, p. 59. Grand Rapids: Eerdmans, 1950.
2. *Ibid.*, p. 106.

among you (Berkeley Version).

Divisions are to be deplored; they are evidence of a lack of community, but they also have a purpose, to separate the heretics and the ungodly from the tried and true believers. Thus, while divisions are rooted in sin, they are also a necessary part of the testing whereby the church is purified and refined, so that the holy community might prosper and be strengthened.

For a few moments, let us turn again to the subject of causality. As noted before, modern man has failed to see the cause and effect factor in God's judgments on sacrilege, whereas unbelievers and pagans once feared sacrilege as a dangerous act from whence judgment overwhelmed man. The reason for modern man's failure is his view of causality. Causality has been depersonalized, and the universe reduced to blind and fortuitous events, so that even man is seen as governed by impersonal forces. Because sacrilege is an offense against a totally personal God with totally personal consequences, it has ceased to be regarded as an offense, or productive of any causal consequences.

This same impersonalism of modern man has led to a decline of community. Where man's view of the entire universe, including man, is in essence an impersonal one, and the universe and man are seen as dominated by impersonal causes and forces, then the person and any community of persons is devalued. Both *sacrilege* and *community* are progressively emptied of meaning as causality is impersonalized.

The "age of reason" which followed the Reformation and Counter-Reformation led to a devaluation of community, in that reason was emphasized as a critical and analytic faculty which had to take precedence over emotional and personal ties. An illustrative instance of this priority of reason was the Dutchwoman of noble origin, Isabella van Tuyll, better known by her pen-name, Zelide. Scott said of her, that

> she appealed at every point from usage to reason: her true eighteenth-century mind could not doubt for a moment that logic was the basis of human happiness. That man was an irrational animal, for whom logic lays a snare; that custom, like the heart, has its own reasons; that folly, as a human attribute, is entitled, if not to veneration, at least to a certain tenderness, she could not conceive.[3]

Because of her rationalism, Zelide idolized Newton and mathematics, and she went so far as to claim,

> I find an hour or two of mathematics gives me a freer mind and a lighter heart; I eat and sleep better when I have grasped an evident and indisputable truth.[4]

---

3. Geoffrey Scott: *The Portrait of Zelide*, p. 7. New York: Charles Scribner's Sons, (1927) 1959.
4. *Ibid.*, p. 9f.

It became a common affectation to dabble in mathematics, the supreme science of reason in those days, as a means of laying claim to membership in the elite circle of pure reason. A very late example of this appears in Millay's sonnet:

> Euclid alone has looked on Beauty bare.
> Let all who prate of Beauty hold their peace,
> And lay them prone upon the earth. . . .[5]

Romanticism is triumphant, however, in Millay, as she summons all lovers of beauty to stretch out "prone upon the earth" in dumb adoration and worship of mathematics. Her poetry is superior, but her imagery negates and debases her point.

In Zelide, the impersonalism and the rationalism are strong and vocal. Her inability to love without rational dominion made her reject suitor after suitor and finally marry a mathematician, to make both herself and him miserable for life. The fact that her mother died did not fill Zelide with *grief* but rather with *horror*, horror over the finality of death.[6] Although closer to her mother than others, Zelide's sterility with regard to love and community made *death* the problem, not the loss of her mother.

With Romanticism, there was no return to community. Instead of community, enforced political socialism and communism became the goal. The egoism of reason was simply replaced with emotional egoism, and the rational elite was replaced with a mystical elite who represented the general will, which they alone could apprehend. Mathematics gave way to biology as the primary science, and Darwin's mythology replaced Euclid as the means to the beatific vision. The hunger for community in the modern era has led to attempts to impose it by force, a contradiction of an extreme sort. The imposed order of communist states leads instead to a radical destruction of community and a distrust. Impersonalism cannot produce community.

Now the antithesis of sacrilege is holiness, and an outcome of holiness is the Kingdom of God, the community of covenant man. Zechariah gives us a vision of this estate of man in 14:20, 21:

> In that day shall there be upon the bells of the horses, HOLINESS UNTO THE LORD: and the pots in the LORD's house shall be like the bowls before the altar.
> Yea, every pot in Jerusalem and in Judah shall be holiness unto the LORD of hosts: and all they that sacrifice shall come and take of them, and seethe therein: and in that day there shall be no more the Canaanite in the house of the LORD of hosts.

---

5. Edna St. Vincent Millay: *Collected Sonnets*, p. 45. New York: Washington Square Press, (1917) 1959.

6. Scott, *op. cit.*, p. 53.

Instead of the sacrilege of Canaanites (the ungodly) in the house of the Lord, all things reveal their devotion to God. Every cooking vessel, the pots and pans, and the ornaments on the reins of horses, shall be like the sacred vessels of the temple, because all men will serve God and will dedicate every aspect of their lives and possessions to Him. In place of sacrilege, there will be universal holiness. Instead of a division between the holy place and the unclean, all things shall be "holiness unto the LORD." As T. V. Moore observed, "When there shall be universal holiness, there shall also be universal happiness."[7] As Moore said also,

> All shall be happy because all shall be holy. Sorrow shall cease because sin shall cease. The groaning earth shall be mantled with joy because the trail of the serpent shall be gone, and the Eden of the future shall make us cease to look back with longing at the Eden of the past. If then a man would have the beginnings of Heaven, it must be by this absolute consecration of everything to God on earth, for precisely as "holiness to the Lord" is upon the "bells of the horses," shall their melody have the ring of the golden harps.[8]

Community in holiness replaces sacrilege.

The impersonalism of the modern world is a product of sin and sacrilege. It leads man away from man, and it leads man away from himself. When influenced by the philosophy of impersonalism, man interprets himself in terms of drives and instincts which depersonalize him and at the same time strip him of responsibility. Modern man talks of *crime* in an impersonal way, as a product of biological and social forces, not of *sin*, which is intensely and plainly personal. As a result, modern man, a prisoner of ideology, talks of his alienation, of communication problems, of conflicts of the mind with the primordial aspects of man's being, and so on. With all this, he destroys the relics of community even further, because community is not a possibility with robots, nor is it an aspect of the beehive. Community is not the animal pack, herd, flock, or hive: it is communion in terms of God, in a common faith and life. It is a product of holiness, of the healing of the rift between God and man, and a product of the law of God obeyed by faith. The laws of community are thus laws of holiness.

Another important fact appears in Zechariah's vision. The glorious realization of Christ's Kingdom is clearly *not* seen in institutional terms. In the medieval era, the great conflict in Christendom was between those who saw Christ's Kingdom in terms of the state, i.e., the Holy Roman Empire, and those who saw it in terms of the church, i.e., the Holy Catholic Church. Their vision of the Kingdom was institutional, and, in either camp, their efforts were directed towards building up their par-

---

7. Thomas V. Moore: *A Commentary on Zechariah*, p. 238. London: Banner of Truth Trust, (1856) 1958.
8. *Ibid.*, p. 236f.

ticular institution. The same division prevails today. Modernism sees the Kingdom in terms of the state, and its gospel is social, or, more accurately, statist. The Kingdom of God will come as the state gains the necessary power to control and remake all of society. Salvation is by means of statist action to remake the world. Conservative Catholics and evangelical and Reformed Protestants tend to the other error, to see the Kingdom of God as the church, and the building of the church as the key to triumph. As a result, their's becomes, not a social or statist gospel, but an ecclesiastical or church gospel, and most of all effort is bent towards developing the church. Now, a measure of truth must be conceded to both parties. *First*, in terms of Scripture, both church and state are *necessary* institutions, not optional ones. To say this does not mean an acceptance of the older classifications of ecclesiology, i.e., of *given* versus *gathered* churches. The *given* churches are held to be God's ordinance, and membership a necessity for man. The *gathered* churches are created by men's free acts, whereby they come together to establish voluntary churches. The church is both given and gathered. Because both predestination and responsibility are essential aspects of Biblical faith, it follows that neither the given nor the gathered aspects of the church can be neglected or under-rated. *Second*, both church and state, while necessary, are secondary and derivative: they are not ultimates. The church of which the New Testament speaks, which is the pillar and ground of truth, had no buildings, a minimum of organization, and was almost more a movement at times than an institution; moreover, it is not the institutional church but the truly ultimate church, which is Christ's mystical body, which is truly and fully the pillar and ground of truth. There is an inseparable link between the true church and the visible and faithful congregation. "the house of God, which is the church of the living God, the pillar and ground of truth" (I Tim. 3:15), but there cannot be an identification. To identify them is to become guilty of institutionalizing God; it is another form of impersonalism. *Third*, it is only as men are established in Christ that there can be a true church and a true state. The decline and moral decay in church and state today is a product of this institutionalism. Only as men are justified by sovereign grace, and sanctified by means of obedience to the law, can either church or state prosper. The vision of Zechariah thus gives us neither the triumph of holiness in the church nor in the state but in the totality of life, in the entire community. Then all things are *Holiness unto the Lord*, and the vision of holiness is a vision of the whole of life and the world consecrated to the Lord. The world is then the Kingdom of God in truth and in power.

# 11

## GRACE AND COMMUNITY

Alexis de Tocqueville, in *Democracy in America*, saw as a major threat to freedom and to community the democratic emphasis on equality. From the French Revolution on, equality became a major and all-important concern to Western man, whereas the importance of community declined. In contrasting freedom and equality, Tocqueville said,

> The advantages which freedom brings are only shown by length of time; and it is always easy to mistake the cause in which they originate. The advantages of equality are instantaneous, and they may constantly be traced from their source.[1]

Modern man, Tocqueville pointed out, is insistent on linking equality with freedom, as though the two are inseparable. More than freedom, equality is idealized as though it constitutes freedom. Tocqueville wrote,

> I think that democratic communities have a natural taste for freedom: left to themselves, they will seek it, cherish it, and view any privation of it with regret. But for equality, their passion is ardent, insatiable, incessant, invincible: they call for equality in freedom; if they cannot obtain that, they still call for equality in slavery. They will endure poverty, servitude, barbarism—but they will not endure aristocracy.
>
> This is true at all times, and especially true in our own. All men and all powers seeking to cope with this irresistible passion, will be overthrown and destroyed by it. In our age, freedom cannot be established without it, and despotism itself cannot reign without its support.[2]

Both totalitarianism and democracy are equalitarian, because equalitarianism is the dominant and commanding faith of the age. Equality can destroy freedom; freedom does not require equality.

An important aspect of the equalitarian mind is its individualism. Individualism is a new spirit in history, but a commanding one in the 19th and 20th centuries. Individualism means the decline of the sense of community; it does not mean that a man was less a person in the eras prior to the rise of individualism but that his person was not set in contrast to the community but in the context thereof. Modern individualism holds that the person is only truly an individual if he cuts his ties to the community

---

1. Alexis de Tocqueville: *Democracy in America*, II, 101. New York: Langley, 1841.
2. *Ibid.*, II p. 102f.

and seeks an independence from it. Thus, George Washington was not an individualist; Thoreau emphatically was. Washington always saw his own goals and wishes in the context of a community; Thoreau felt it imperative to wage war against the community.

Of individualism, Tocqueville wrote:

> Individualism is a mature and calm feeling, which disposes each member of the community to sever himself from the mass of his fellow-creatures, and to draw apart with his family and his friends; so that, after he has there formed a little circle of his own, he willingly leaves society at large to itself. Egotism originates in blind instinct: individualism proceeds from erroneous judgment more than from depraved feelings; it originates as much in the deficiencies of the mind as in the perversity of the heart.

> Egotism blights the germ of all virtue: individualism, at first, only saps the virtue of public life; but, in the long run, it attacks and destroys all others, and is at length absorbed in downright egotism. Egotism is a vice as old as the world, which does not belong to one form of society more than to another: individualism is of democratic origin, and it threatens to spread in the same ratio as the equality of conditions.[3]

In a democracy, because the emphasis is on equality, there is a stress on independence from other people, and an unwillingness to be dependent on them. "Aristocracy has made a chain of all the members of the community, from the peasant to the king: democracy breaks that chain, and severs every link of it."[4] In America, Tocqueville saw, the evil effects of equality and individualism were overcome by a strong Christian faith and by free associations (mainly tithe agencies) which worked to bring people together in godly community.

Modern man, because of his emphasis on individualism and equality, is unable to tolerate faults in other people. Anyone inferior to himself is especially intolerable. The stress on individualism has meant man's unwillingness to live in community with others unless he finds it to his advantage. The modern answer thus to personal problems is not to resolve them but to move on to another group. As a result, very few people maintain ties with their family (unless out of necessity) or with friends over their lifetime. If a problem with another person develops, that person is either cut out of the group, or one or more people leave to find a new association. Clubs, churches, and various associations thus have a continual floating population because of the lack of community. One of the most common remarks in any voluntary orgaization in the modern world is simply this: "Count me out if *blank* is going to be in too," i.e., the unwillingness to put up with anything from "difficult"

---

3. *Ibid.*, II, p. 104.
4. *Ibid.*, II, p. 105.

people. As a result, we *all* become "difficult" people, fixed in our ways and unwilling to live with the faults or failings of other people, which means also our unwillingness to change our own. To deny community to some on our grounds is to insist that community cannot be defined except in terms of virtues, and that we are virtuous to the point of being the standard. Thus, while there are many groupings in the modern world, there is very little community, even within the family. The basic requirement for community among men, who are not perfectly sanctified, is stated in Galatians 6:2, "Bear ye one another's burdens, and so fulfil the law of Christ." The law of Christ is love of the brethren, of the community of faith (John 13:7, I John 3: 23). The *burdens* can be distress or problems, physical, mental, or moral. Our Lord was spoken of as one who bore the physical infirmities of those whom He healed: Matthew 8:17, "He bare our sicknesses." The meaning is that, as very man of very man, He regarded our sicknesses as His own, and ministered to them as such. In this same sense, we are to regard the infirmities of our fellow believers as our own, as members together of Christ, and to work to help one another, even as Christ bore our burdens and redeemed us. Redemptive power is not ours, but sanctifying grace and patience are.

The absence of community gives, in an anarchistic sense, a great deal of freedom. If we cut ourselves off from one another, we then have less and less in the way of restricting ties. The decline of community has also been paralleled by the decline of the family, because both have their origin in a desire for individualistic and anarchistic freedom.

Nisbet has pointed out how the decline of community means also the rise of totalitarianism. In every era of a decline of freedom, there is "the same fatal combination of individualism and political power." The less community there is, the greater the custodial powers of the state. Totalitarianism thus is seen by many as freedom, because the irritating ties of man to man are replaced by the impersonal functionings of a statist bureaucracy.[5]

Practically, what this means is that if we do not enjoy too close a contact with people, and if we break with them readily if they do not suit us, then, whatever our politics, we are helping create a totalitarian regime. Whenever and wherever men's lives are closely enmeshed with the lives of others, and where there is a strong mutual forbearance among people, the basic government is exerted by society. People police one another. Our sensitivity to the standards of our group or community make us more restrained in our behavior. Where there is a strong community influence, there is less anarchistic liberty but more essential freedom.

On the other hand, where men have loose community ties, and little

---

5. Robert A. Nisbet: *Community and Power*, p. 244f. New York: Oxford University Press, Galaxy Books, (1953) 1962.

forbearance one with another, there is a corresponding need for statist action and government to replace what was once effected by the community. A small city in the 1960s began to develop a record number of cases of wife-beating and child-beating. Statistically, therefore, the police records showed a major increase in this type of activity. The statistics were both accurate and misleading. Twenty and forty years before, such arrests were virtually unknown. The reason was that, in the earlier era, the community was more closely knit, and neighborhood, church, and various other institutional ties were very strong. One wife-beater had to move, because public contempt for him was more than he was ready to take. Others like him were intimidated into social conformity. Thus, while both eras had their number of alcoholics and wayward parents, ready to be malicious and abusive, the social situation differed radically. In the 1920s and 1930s, the disapproval of neighbors, friends, and community leaders was vocal. An employer would declare, "Do that again, and you are fired." Then the community involved itself in such an incident; now, it calls the police. In brief, what once the community did, now the state does. People refuse to get involved, are fearful of being regarded as busy-bodies, and yet wonder at the growth of statism. At the same time, the lack of community action has allowed greater freedom to its delinquent and criminal members to indulge their sins, because the police power has been reduced from an entire community to a handful of police officers.

Thus, modern individualism has given greater freedom to the anarchistic person and less freedom to the responsible person, in that the growing power of the state limits his freedom.

One of the startling facts about the United States prior to 1850, and true to a degree for a time thereafter, was the lack of any fixed line of division between business and residential districts, and between rich and poor neighborhoods. Well to do businessmen often lived above, behind, or next to their place of business, and their neighbors could be their workers. Thus, the wealthy owner of a steel mill built a beautiful stone mansion, which still stands, only a short block and a half from his steel mill. There was then less democracy, in that the owner knew his station and enjoyed it, but there was more community, in that he was an active neighbor to all around him. The impersonal universe of Darwinism led to a steady decline of the Christian personalism which had made community life possible. The influence of Darwin has led to the rise of impersonalism and hence of statism.

The Bible, on the other hand, has a radically different perspective from the atomism and impersonalism of modern man. Scientific reductionism leaves men as ciphers, reduced to a numerical level and classified in terms of their wants, aptitudes, achievements, and the like. The more impersonal man is made, the more workable he becomes in terms of scientific socialist planning. For Scripture, man is defined, not on reductionist terms, but as a person created in God's image and unique in his responsibility and calling. Man is man, neither in isolation nor in reduction, but in God, and in community under God. It is impossible for a Christian to regard man except as God's creature, called to serve God. This call to serve God involves life in God's Kingdom or community, and we are told that there is a blessing and an anointing for life in community. David said,

> Behold, how good and how pleasant it is for brethren to dwell together in unity!
> It is like the precious ointment upon the head, that ran down upon the beard, even Aaron's beard: that went down to the skirts of his garments;
> As the dew of Hermon, and as the dew that descended upon the mountains of Zion: for there the LORD commanded the blessing, even life for evermore. (Psalm 133).

Leupold commented on this psalm, "The Spirit's blessings thrive so much more richly when brotherly unity prevails; it is so much more difficult to enjoy these blessings when discord tears men apart and sets them at variance with one another." Of vs. 3, Leupold said in part,

> Just as heavy dews refresh and invigorate plant life, so the blessing of unity descends alike on all those that are within the church, and all godly virtues thrive and flourish. Discord disrupts, destroys, and kills all the finer things that could grow under the blessing of true unity.[6]

"The precious ointment" has reference to the oil with which Aaron was consecrated into the office of high priest; the oil symbolized the Holy Spirit. Unity, community life in faith, is comparable to the oil of anointing: it marks a special consecration and blessing. The Spirit Himself blesses and prospers the holy community.

It should be noted that it is the dwelling together *in unity* that is the godly fact in God's sight. The psalm does not speak of the brethren as dwelling together *in peace* in this world. Within a family, there are differences, tensions, and problems between husband and wife, and between parents and children. The peaceful families are probably the dead ones. It is living *in unity*, in the unity of the faith, that constitutes the blessed fact, and the ground of blessing.

The third verse tells us the context of this promised blessing: the Lord "*commanded* the blessing, even life for evermore," upon "the mountains of Zion," i.e., the promised land. The people of faith, living in the land of promise in terms of the law-word of God, are promised long life

---

6. H. C. Leupold: *Exposition of the Psalms*, p. 919f. Columbus, Ohio: The Wartburg Press, 1959.

for covenantal obedience (Deut. 6:2). If the covenant people "hearken unto the voice of the *LORD*...to keep his commandments and his statutes which are written in this book of the law, and if thou turn unto the LORD thy God with all thine heart, and all thy soul" (Deut. 30:10), then rich blessings follow. "See, I have set before thee this day life and good, and death and evil." (Deut. 30:15). "Therefore choose life, that both thou and thy seed may live" (Deut. 30:19). *Life* in time and eternity, true *life*, in and under God, is the promise for obedience to the law and unity in the Lord.

In vs. 3, there is a reference to Hermon, as well as to the mountains of Zion. In Deuteronomy 4:48, Mount Hermon is made synonymous with Mount Zion, so that the dew of Mount Hermon is the blessing of the Holy Spirit (of the Kingdom of God, the true Zion of God), upon the covenant land and people, the mountains of Zion.

The oil of vs. 2, is "a sign of consecration and of spiritual influences."[7] These "spiritual influences," i.e., the work of the Holy Spirit, fall upon those who live in unity.

This is not the only instance where unity is blessed. In I Peter 3:7, we are told that husbands and wives are to dwell together with unity and forbearance, "and as being heirs together of the grace of life; that your prayers be not hindered." Clearly, Scripture does not associate the out-pouring of the Spirit with the solitary life, so that the ascetic withdrawal from the world is not the way of grace. It is life in community, the covenant community, that inherits the promises of God, and it is the unity of husband and wife, and of covenantal brethren, that receives the blessing of the Holy Spirit.

But life in community involves *problems*. Marriage is spoken of as a *yoke* in Scripture (II Cor. 6:14), and believers are commanded to avoid the unequal yoking with unbelievers. Discipleship is also spoken of as a yoke: "Take my yoke upon you, and learn of me; for I am meek and lowly in heart: and ye shall find rest unto your souls" (Matt. 11:29).

Modern man seeks to avoid the yokes of community life in Christ, and he falls under the heavy yoke of the state. Christ's yoke is easy and His burden is light (Matt. 11:30), because it is a yoke that gives grace, as do all yokes borne in the Lord and in terms of His law-word.

---

7. Joseph Addison Alexander: *The Psalms, Translated and Explained*, p. 527. Grand Rapids: Zondervan.

## 12

## STATE AND COMMUNITY

One of the most obvious facts of Scripture is that on the first Palm Sunday Jesus Christ entered Jerusalem openly declaring Himself to be the Messianic King. His actions were in self-conscious fulfilment of the prophecy of Zechariah 9:9-10, and this was recognized by all. Matthew 21:4 declares, "All this was done, that it might be fulfilled which was spoken by the prophet." We are told that the great multitude joyfully hailed Jesus as the Messianic king, crying out, "Hosanna to the son of David: Blessed is he that cometh in the name of the Lord; Hosanna in the highest" (Matt. 21:9). The children in the temple hailed Jesus also as the promised King of David's line (Matt. 21:15-16). Jesus accepted all this as His due, and cleansed the Temple as its lord (Matt. 21:12-13), and, as a token of the new life of His Kingdom, healed the blind and the lame (Matt. 21:14). All these are obvious and plainly stated facts of Scripture.

Equally obvious is the fact that Jerusalem then and the church today have commonly misunderstood the nature and form of Christ's kingship. Let us examine briefly a few of these errors.

*First,* Israel assumed that the messianic king would be a political ruler and world conqueror, so that it equated the Kingdom of God with an historical state, a greater and world-wide Rome, as it were. The idea of *government* was equated with the *state.* This equation was radically pagan. In pagan antiquity as today, the state was seen as a divine-human order, and as the over-all lord and sovereign. In such a view, all things have their being within the jurisdiction and only with the approval of the sovereign state. Religion, art, family, school, and all things else are departments of state and cannot be allowed to exist in independence of it. The state thus usurps the over-lordship of God and becomes god on earth. No area of freedom can exist outside the state: freedom becomes a privilege granted by the state and subject to its conditions.

Christianity, by asserting the supreme lordship of Christ over Caesar and all other human institutions, reduced the state to its Biblical dimensions, as a ministry of justice (Rom. 13:1-6). With the revival of Hellenic thought, especially Aristotle, the state again began to grow in power. In the thought of Rousseau, the idea of the state again became all-powerful, and the right of society to exist in independence of it was denied. The state was defined as sovereign and omnipotent, so that no area of free associations, independent churches, schools, families, vocations, and communities could exist except within and by the will of the state. Rousseau defined the body politic as Sovereign and by nature and necessity just and beneficent in all its dealings with its subjects:

> Consequently, the sovereign power need give no guarantee to its subjects, since it is impossible that the body should wish to injure all its members, nor, as we shall see later, can it injure any single individual. The Sovereign, by merely existing, is always what it should be. But the same does not hold true of the relation of subject to sovereign. In spite of common interest, there can be no guarantee that the subject will observe his duty to the sovereign unless means are found to ensure his loyalty.[1]

From this perspective, the state is always right, and the citizen or subject always wrong, in any conflict. Not only is *right* thus defined as *what the state does is therefore right*, but freedom is redefined by Rousseau and all modern statists as the necessary constraint of the state, so that Rousseau can speak of compelling men to be free by statist coercion:

> In order, then, that the social compact may not be but a vain formula, it must contain, though unexpressed, the single undertaking which can alone give force to the whole, namely, that whoever shall refuse to obey the general will must be constrained by the whole body of his fellow citizens to do so: which is no more than to say that it may be necessary to compel a man to be free—freedom being that condition which, by giving each citizen to his country, guarantees him from all personal dependence and is the foundation upon which the whole political machine rests, and supplies the power which works it.[2]

Freedom thus means guaranteeing all men freedom from "all personal dependence" on anything but the state. Man is to be "freed" from dependence on the family, the church, or any non-statist associations, and freedom is redefined as independence from these things and dependence on the state. Statist education thus works to "free" man from church and family into total dependence on the state, the political order. Rousseau refused to allow society to exist: it had to be obliterated to make way for the totalitarian state as the freedom of man. Man is only truly man and truly free when he is only governed by the state. In Rousseau's words,

> Each citizen would then be completely independent of all his fellow men, and absolutely dependent upon the state: which operation is always brought by the same means; for it is only by the force of the state that the liberty of its members can be secured.[3]

---

1. Jean-Jacques Rousseau: *The Social Contract, or Principles of Political Right*, in Sir Ernest Barker, ed.: *Social Contract, Essays by Locke, Hume, and Rousseau*, p. 260f. London: Oxford, (1947) 1958.
2. *Ibid.*, p. 261f.
3. Cited by Robert A. Nisbet: *Community and Power*, p. 143. New York: Oxford, 1962.

Man must be made *totally rootless* so that he will have no other power to depend on than the state. This modern education is effectively accomplishing, and modern man is thoroughly cynical about any possible *social action* being successful and thus trusts, if only by default, in *statist action*. Man has been so thoroughly alienated from his fellow man that community or group activity is dying or is regarded cynically. It is commonly said that it is impossible to get any group to work together successfully, and there is a marked hostility to community action. The alternative to community government is statist government. Where the self-government of the Christian man flourishes, there community flourishes. Where atomistic individuals withdraw from one another, there the state grows as the only effectual force. Atomistic man makes perfectionist demands of other people, and he welcomes every evidence of sins and frailties as grounds for withdrawing into his atomistic shell.

Israel, in our Lord's day, was heavily influenced by paganism, and, as a result, its concept of Christ's Kingdom was political or statist. When it became apparent that the Triumphal Entry was not leading to an empire, the multitudes readily shouted, "Crucify him!" Every group today which insists on seeing the Kingdom of God in statist terms is denying Christ afresh.

*Second*, many have assumed that Christ's Kingdom is not *in* this world. This view is a radical misreading of John 18:36, wherein our Lord declares,

> My kingdom is not of this world: if my kingdom were of this world, then would my servants fight, that I should not be delivered to the Jews: but now is my kingdom not from hence.

The Berkeley Version renders it thus:

> My kingdom is not of this world. If My kingdom were of this world, My attendants would have struggled to prevent My being delivered to the Jews. But really the source of My kingdom is not here.

Christ's Kingdom is *not* derived from this world, but is *over* this world; it is "not from hence," for its source is from all eternity, from His godhead as well as from His status as the second Adam.

To deny that Christ's Kingdom is in this world is to alter the faith either to a neoplatonic idealism or a Manichaean dualism. In either case, the world and history are rejected and are handed over to the devil. Not surprisingly, such people who hold this view are insistent on seeing Satan as the prince of the physical universe and become implicit Satanists in the powers they ascribe to Satan. From such a perspective, the church has little to do with history other than to rescue lost souls and then wait for the end (amillennialism and post-tribulation premillennialism) or for the rapture (pre-tribulation premillennialism).

*Third*, many have held that Christ indeed came to establish His

Kingdom, but their interpretation of this Kingdom is humanistic, in that it makes *love* the means to its establishment. A clear statement of this view is to be found in a Roman Catholic devotional guide of the post-Vatican II era:

> The Kingship of Christ, in this age of classless society, seems as relevant as a knight on a white charger patrolling a freeway. Isn't it coincidental that Pilate found the idea equally incredible?
>
> Christ answers present skeptics as He answered Pilate: "My kingdom is not of this world." Those who see triumphalism as essential to Christ's Church err as much as Pilate, who looked for an army at Jesus' side.
>
> Christ is indeed a king—the promised son of David who was to establish the messianic kingdom of God on earth. Enthroned at the right hand of the Father on Ascension day, Jesus began His reign by sending forth the Holy Spirit upon His followers. Supreme in power, Lord of history, assured of final and total victory, He is the gentlest of all rulers. He denounces the sword. He condemns ostentation. He confides in love alone to win His cause.[4]

There is no warrant in Scripture, of course, for the statement that Christ "confides in love alone to win His cause." This is pure humanism. Such a view denies grace; it denies the law of God which requires satisfaction, and therefore it denies the atonement.

*Fourth*, equally invalid is the view of some that the sacrifice or at least the suffering of the saints will bring in the Kingdom. This too is salvation by man. G. B. Caird, in *The Revelation of St. John the Divine* (1966), seems to hold to this view.

Enough has been said to indicate that faulty views of Christ's Kingdom rest on an implicit or explicit humanism and a failure to recognize that Christ's sovereignty precludes any surrender of the world to the enemy.

The world was created by the triune God as His Kingdom. Man was established in the Garden of Eden to rule over God's creation in terms of God's law-word. The tempter offered another idea of the Kingdom, a realm in which every man is his own god and rules in terms of his own law-word concerning good and evil. God's curse fell on man and the world for this rebellion. The ground was cursed for his sake, to prevent man from realizing his hopes on earth, and sin and death became the course of history.

Into this history the incarnate Son of God entered to become the new Adam, to establish a new humanity. As the new Adam, He resisted the tempter, and He kept the law of God perfectly. As elect man's vicarious

---

4. Rev. Melvin L. Farrell, S. S., guest ed. (Rev. Richard Ginder, general ed.): *My Daily Visitor*, vol. 11, October, 1967, no. 9, p. 31. Huntington, Indiana: Our Sunday Visitor, Inc.: 1967.

substitute and representative, He made atonement for man's sin and restored man into fellowship with God, and into his original calling, the creation-mandate (Gen. 1:26-28). This dominion or kingship is *not* to be established by coercion, by political action, nor by love, or by human sacrifices. Its genesis is of an entirely different character.

*First* of all, it is supernatural. Jesus Christ, by His justifying grace, and by His regenerating power, makes us a new creation, so that we die in Him, as He makes atonement for us by His death, and we rise in Him as a new humanity. The key to the Kingdom of God is thus not politics, not the state and its order, but the regenerating power of Jesus Christ.

*Second*, the new man in Christ has a duty to exercise dominion in every realm and to bring all things into captivity to Christ. This means that the state, church, school, family, vocation, and all other areas of life must be Christian; none of these orders can lord it over the others, nor claim jurisdiction over other spheres, but all must equally be under the lordship of Jesus Christ.

*Third*, in the Kingdom of God, the basic government is not by the state but is *the self-government of the covenant man in Christ.* Because the Christian can govern himself, he can govern in the other areas of government, the family, school, church, state or civil government, vocation, and various free associations of men. His ability to govern in any area depends on his faithfulness to Christ and His law-word.

*Fourth*, this means that the basic area of government is *the community.* As the community places itself under God's law-word, it places itself also in a position of necessary obedience to God, and to one another in terms of Scripture. Neither atomism nor collectivism can prevail, because for the Christian man both his self-government and his life in community are mandatory aspects of his faith. As a result, St. Paul made it clear that, between Christians in conflict, first of all the community and then the church must take action (cf. Matt. 18:15-17) and then only, if they are not more than a heathen, as proven by their response, civil action is to be pursued. Brothers or fellow Christians are not to go to court against one another, because this is a confession of a lack of community and an inability to govern within the context of the Christian community and the church (I Cor. 6:1-8). To step outside the community of faith in a conflict with a fellow Christian is to do wrong. This prohibition has to do with differences between Christians, not between a Christian and an unbeliever or one whom the events prove to be a practical or implicit unbeliever by his unwillingness to listen. (If the courts are Christian, then the courts are an aspect not only of the state but of the believing community.)

Our Lord entered Jerusalem in deliberate fulfilment of Zechariah 9:9-10. Briefly, what Zechariah declares concerning Christ and His

Kingdom is that, *first*, He is the King, and He comes, "having salvation." The meaning of this is well expressed by Moore as setting forth

> not simply the reception of a salvation, but its possession as a gift that was capable of being bestowed upon others. The same word occurs in this sense elsewhere, as Deut. 33:19; Ps. 33:16, &c. The meaning then would be that God was with him, in spite of his lowliness, sustaining him in the mighty work he had undertaken, and that this protection was bestowed upon him not as an individual but as a king, a representative of his people, so that he would not only enjoy it himself, but possess the power of bestowing it upon others. Hence, while his inflexible justice might make us tremble in our sin, the fact that he was also endowed with a free salvation, and a salvation which he could bestow as a kingly right, would remove these fears and enable us to rejoice in this coming king.[5]

*Second*, Christ the King will eliminate war from the world. There will be a cessation of all warfare, because Christ is triumphant in His warfare against the power of sin.

*Third*, Christ's Kingdom will be world-wide. He will "speak peace to the nations" (or Gentiles) from "sea to sea," a phrase which in Scripture expressed "absolute universality."[6]

*Fourth*, the covenant people are asked to "rejoice," because their King rules over all things, and His triumph is assured.

Salvation is not the act of man, nor of the church, nor the state. It is the act of God in Christ. It is then manifested in its implications in the Christian community, in church, family, state, school, vocation, and society in its every aspect. Life in the community of grace is an aspect of the redeemed life.

---

5. Thomas V. Moore: *A Commentary on Zechariah*, p. 147. London: Banner of Truth Trust. (1856) 1958.
6. *Ibid.*, p. 150.

# 13

## THE COMMUNITY OF THE ATONEMENT

One of the deadly concepts which crucifies Christ afresh is what can be termed the idea of diminished returns. It is very commonly assumed that God, in the Old Testament era, made accommodations to the crasser and more materialistic ways of supposedly less advanced peoples. Hence, we are told, God gave material blessings as a reward to the patriarchs and Israel, whereas now, being a more advanced people, we gain spiritual rewards in time and in eternity. Basic to this position is an implicit neoplatonism which downgrades the material creation as something lower, degrading, and unworthy, as though the material world, if created by God, was the work of His left hand.

Even Scripture is misused to justify this neoplatonism, and such apostles of diminished returns will piously bleat I Corinthians 2:2, "For I determined not to know any thing among you, save Jesus Christ, and him crucified." They then tell us that the true gospel is supposedly no more than the cross, that true preaching is limited to the cross, and that our life of faith is an endless cross-bearing, because Jesus said, "If any man will come after me, let him deny himself, and take up his cross, and follow me" (Matt. 16:24). Clearly, in a world of sin, a fallen world, life is a battle, and, as St. Paul declared, "we must through much tribulation enter into the kingdom of God" (Acts 14:22). But life is not only tribulation: it is also and supremely life in Christ, who is the victorious King of Kings, the destroyer of the power of sin and death.

Of I Corinthians 2:2, Calvin's comment is a corrective to the modern and ancient neoplatonist misreadings. He wrote,

> ....the substance of the passage amounts to this: "As to my wanting the ornaments of speech, and wanting, too, the more elegant refinements of discourse, the reason of this was, that I did not aspire at them, nay rather, I despised them, because there was one thing only that my heart was set upon—that I might preach Christ with simplicity."

> In adding the word *crucified*, he does not mean that he preached nothing respecting Christ except the cross; but that, with all the abasement of the cross, he nevertheless preached Christ. It is as though he had said: "The ignominy of the cross will not prevent me from looking up to him from whom salvation comes, or make me ashamed to regard all my wisdom as comprehended in him—in him, I say, whom proud men despise and reject on account of the

76

reproach of the cross." Hence the statement must be explained in this way: "No kind of knowledge was in my view of so much importance as to lead me to desire anything but Christ, *crucified though he was*." This little clause is added by way of enlargement with the view of galling so much the more those arrogant masters, by whom Christ was next to despised, as they were eager to gain applause by being renowned for a higher kind of wisdom. Here we have a beautiful passage, from which we learn what it is that faithful ministers ought to teach, what it is that we must, during our whole life, be learning, and in comparison with which everything else must be "counted as dung" (Phil. iii. 8).[1]

Thus, as Calvin saw, what St. Paul was doing was to attack the platonist reductions of Scripture and the platonist horror with respect to the cross. St. Paul was objecting to *any and all dimunition* of Scripture.

In Matthew 16:24, our Lord saw that Peter regarded the cross as the wrong way for the Messiah, and He rebuked Peter, declaring that life is a warfare, and all those who follow him must engage in that warfare. Christ's cross is redemptive; our sufferings at the hands of Christ's enemies are because of our willingness to stand with Christ as His people. We must deny the old Adam in ourselves and voluntarily bear the cross, stand with the new Adam as the old humanity wages war against Him.[2]

The cross cannot limit the gospel, because the cross represents Christ's victory over sin and death. It is the beginning of the new creation, the revocation by the new Adam of the fall, and the establishment of God's Kingdom by the defeat of the enemy. Instead of limiting the gospel by means of the cross, we must hold that the cross opens up all the promises of God.

Because the cross means our atonement, it is necessary to examine the meaning of atonement. A brief survey of atonement in the Old Testament is thus required. Since atonement in the Old Testament was typically foreshadowed in various rites which set forth what Christ was to do, it is obvious that *the meaning of atonement does not diminish from the Old Testament to the New. The meaning, results, and power of atonement must of necessity have grown into their fulness, as the act of atonement moved from symbol to reality.*

*First* of all, the whole of Scripture makes clear the fact that there is a need for atonement, because man has sinned. As Mitton has written,

The Bible as a whole assumes the need for some "atoning action," if man is to be right with God. It is accepted as a fact beyond dispute that man is estranged from God, and is himself wholly to blame for this estrangement. His disobedience to the will of God—i.e., his

---

1. John Calvin: *Commentary on the Epistles of Paul the Apostle to the Corinthians*, vol. I, p. 97. John Pringle translation. Grand Rapids: Eerdmans, 1948.
2. See John Calvin: *Commentary on a Harmony of the Evangelists, Matthew, Mark and Luke*, vol. II, p. 303f. William Pringle Translation. Grand Rapids: Eerdmans, 1957.

sin—has alienated him from God, and this alienation must first be remedied if right relationships are to be restored. The barrier raised by man's past must be removed.[3]

*Second*, as Mitton points out, " 'To atone for' a wrong is to take some action which cancels out the ill effects it has had."[4] Atonement thus wipes out the effects of the fall and restores man to the relationship to God which existed prior to the fall, and to the status and calling which was man's prior to the fall. Thus, it restores man as the image-bearer whose calling it is to exercise dominion and to subdue the earth (Gen. 1:26-28). The extent of the restoration is measured by the extent of our sanctification, our growth in terms of our new status and life.

*Third*, the law of God requires death for man's rebellion, but man's death cannot restore him to the position he enjoyed prior to the fall. Man's death is a consequence of sin; it has no way of removing the barrier of sin but is rather an evidence of it.

*Fourth*, God makes atonement for man by providing an efficacious substitute, whose forfeited life constitutes the ground of reconciliation. Jesus Christ as the new Adam is that substitute, the head of a new creation, and the one who cancels out the effects of sin and death and begins the restoration of God's purposed Kingdom. This vicarious satisfaction is taught in the Old Testament sacrificial system, in Matthew 20:28; I Timothy 2:6; II Corinthians 5:21; Ephesians 5:25; Hebrews 10:14; I Peter 2:24; 3:18; I John 2:2, and other verses.

Now, turning to the Old Testament uses of the word *atonement*, we find that it includes, *first*, the atonement of material objects, such as the altar (Ex. 29:36-37). Aaron was literally asked to "purify the altar by making an atonement for it" so that it might become "an altar most holy" or "holiness of holinesses." This was a seven-day ceremony. Not only men but physical objects are required to have atonement, and the final vision of Zechariah 14:20-21 is of a world made totally holy unto the Lord.

*Second*, in the account of the military census and the head or poll tax (Ex. 30:11-16), we are told that this tax was "atonement money" (Ex. 30:16). It protected the men of Israel from "plague" as they were numbered for military service. The word in Hebrew for plague "comes from a primitive root meaning to push, gore, defeat, slay, smite, put to the worse. This ransom was for the life of the soldier, that he might not be slain in battle." In the battle against Midian (Num. 31:1-54), not a man was lost by Israel in battle.[5] Thus, atonement here plainly means protection from physical harm.

---

3. C. L. Mitton, "Atonement," in *The Interpreter's Dictionary of the Bible, A-D*, p. 310. New York: Abingdon Press, 1962.

4. *Ibid.*, p. 309.

5. Charles Wesley Ewing, "The Soldier's Ransom," in *Faith and Freedom Issue*, p. 4. Royal Oak, Michigan: Faith and Freedom Bible Institute.

*Third*, atonement meant also the annual day of atonement (Ex. 30:10; Lev. 23:27-28; 27:9; Lev. 29:7-11, etc.) wherein God's grace "in forgiveness and redeeming action" was mediated to the nation.[6] There was thus atonement for an entire nation, which, while not redeeming all persons therein, meant that the nation belonged to the Lord and was preserved and prospered by Him. Here again we have a very broad scope for the atonement. Examples of atonement for the nation are many in Scripture, of which Exodus 30:31ff. is perhaps the first. Other examples are I Chronicles 6:49; II Chronicles 29:24; Nehemiah 10:33, etc.

*Fourth*, atonement for persons is also a prominent part of the law (Lev. 1:4; 4:20; 7:7; 8:34, etc.) The sinner is restored into fellowship with God and his calling in the Lord by the act of atonement. The *scope* of atonement thus includes persons and nations, things and people, "body and soul."

The consequences of atonement can be summed up in one word, *salvation*. More specifically, all the breadth of meaning in the word *atonement* is not only apparent in the New Testament but expanded. Instead of *diminished returns*, it is the *fulness of returns* which is stressed. St. John makes this clear, *first*, that *all* the consequences of the fall are being destroyed by Jesus Christ:

> He that committeth sin is of the devil: for the devil sinneth from the beginning. For this purpose the Son of God was manifested, that he might destroy the works of the devil (I John 3:8).

The Greek word for *destroy* here used has the force of dissolving, demolishing, or breaking. Ross commented on this verse that

> In vs. 5 John had given one reason for the manifestation of the Son of God: here he gives another reason. The two verses should be studied together. It is by making atonement for sin that Jesus destroys the works of the devil. The word *destroy* occurs very frequently in the N. T. with the sense of undo, pull to pieces, destroy. The works of the devil are the sins which he causes men to commit: they are the opposite of the works of God (Jn. 9:3) and the same as the works of darkness (Rom. 13:12; Eph. 5:11). The action of the man who makes sin his practice is in direct opposition to *this* purpose of the Incarnation of the Son of God.[7]

"The works of the devil" are still broader, however. They began with his temptation of Eve in the Garden of Eden (nullified by the new Adam in the wilderness temptation, Matt. 4:1-11), and they continued through the fall, which brought in both sin and death (nullified by Christ on the cross). These and all subsequent works of the devil are destroyed,

---

6. J. C. Rylaarsdam, "Atonement, Day of," in *Interpreter's Dictionary of the Bible, A-D*, p. 316.

7. Alexander Ross: *The Epistles of James and John*, p. 184f. Grand Rapids: Eerdmans, 1954.

dissolved, broken up by Christ, in principle and power on the cross, and in fulness when the last enemy, death, is destroyed also (I Cor. 15:26). Christ "must reign, till he hath put all enemies under his feet" (I Cor. 15:25). As a part of that battle against sin, and for the destruction of the works of the devil, the Christian takes up Christ's cross and follows Him. This means that *he engages in the ongoing battle to destroy the works of the devil.* To take up His cross means to engage in His victorious battle. The major casualty in that war is the devil and all his hosts.

*Second*, a consequence of the atonement, according to St. Peter, is our reconciliation with God:

> For Christ also hath once suffered for sins, the just for the unjust, that he might bring us to God, being put to death in the flesh, but quickened by the Spirit. (I Peter 3:18)

Jesus Christ brings us, who were unrighteous, to God by His righteousness ("the just for the unjust"). "We are brought to God when we who are *unrighteous* are by faith in Christ's vicarious expiation justified and *declared righteous.*"[8] We can add, as Scripture often makes clear, that, having been declared righteous, we are also regenerated and commanded to grow in righteousness, i.e., in our obedience to God and to our calling in Him to bring every area of life and thought into captivity to Christ.

*Third*, this means that communion with God has been opened up, "by a new and living way, which he has consecrated for us, through the veil, that is to say, his flesh" (Heb. 10:20). The communion broken in Eden is restored by Christ's atonement, and the fulness of that communion shall be realized in the consummation of the new creation when His servants "shall see his face; and his name shall be in their foreheads," because the curse is entirely gone (Rev. 22:3-4). Christ "died for us, that, whether we wake or sleep, we should live together with him" (I Thess. 5:10).

*Fourth*, the conscience of the believer is cleansed and purified (I Tim. 1:19; 3:9; II Tim. 1:3; Heb. 9:14; 10:2, 22; I Pet. 3:18-22). The believer is called to be holy and is made holy by the workings of the Holy Spirit: "Because it it written, Be ye holy; for I am holy" (I Pet. 1:15).

More can be said about the consequences of the atonement, but it is clear enough from what we have surveyed that the idea of diminished returns is totally false. The atonement of Jesus Christ was vastly greater than typical sacrifices of animals as prescribed in the Old Testament. Christ's atoning sacrifice has as its outcome the resurrection, a total nullification of the work of Satan. The second Adam had resisted the wilderness temptation of Satan, kept the law perfectly, become our

---

8. R. C. H. Lenski: *The Interpretation of the Epistles of St. Peter, St. John and St. Jude*, p. 157. Columbus, Ohio: Wartburg Press, 1945.

vicarious sacrifice, and broken the power of sin and death. The new humanity began with Him who cancelled totally in His person the fall of man, and in His person re-established a new humanity under God. Just as the sacrifices of the Old Testament gave way to the glory of the cross and the resurrection, so in every other area this same fact is to be recognized, that it is not diminished returns, but an enhanced return that Christ's atonement manifests in His person and for us. As the community of the atonement and the resurrection, we are the people of the new creation in Christ, the people to whom "all the promises of God in him are yea, and in him amen, unto the glory of God by us" (II Cor. 1:20). The glory of the new creation, both in time and in eternity, shall surpass the glory of Eden, and the hope set before us is beyond anything the world has yet known. The community of the atonement is the new creation of God, and its end is altogether glorious.

## 14

## COMMUNITY AND CRIME

The totalitarian state, as we have noted, wages war against the community, because the community is a powerful rival government. It works to weaken the community, the family, church, and vocation in order to strengthen its own power.

Every community exercises government and coercion. If a community is hostile to a particular race, the coercion of its hostility and neglect is very real. Of one town in California, a particularly beautiful one in buildings and setting, and made up of the people of a small north European country, one woman, who lived there two or three years, remarked: "It was a miserable place to be. I was an outsider, and they wanted to keep the town set in their old country ways." In a variety of other ways, every community exercises coercion against outsiders and on its members. This coercion can be for healthy reasons, or for narrow-minded causes, but it is still a very real government. The state, as it interferes with the one, also harms the other. By striking at the community's weaknesses, it also limits and undercuts its strength. The state, moreover, is no more immune to sins and shortcomings than the community, but its faults work a more extensive and pervasive harm.

The state lacks a great virtue and strength which the family and the community possess. We *belong* to a family, and we *belong* to a community: we do not *join* it. We are, on the other hand, *citizens* of a state, and we can move from one country to another and change our citizenship by law. *Belonging* is not a matter of law; *joining* is. Thus, as the state weakens every form and aspect of the community, it renders people rootless and atomistic. In the process, people also become more impersonal and more intolerant in fact, however tolerant by state law. People will tolerate in members of their family what they will never tolerate in a fellow citizen, because they belong together. Similarly, in a true community there is mutual forebearance and patience one with another.

Moreover, the more oppressive the state becomes toward a community, the more readily an illicit community arises. This illicit community then begins to govern society. The state having become no more than a band of robbers, to use Augustine's term, the only competing social orders become other and independent criminal bands. In one tyrant, anarchic and/or oppressive state after another, criminal and secret societies have become the effectual governments. The Vehengericht of Germany from the 12th into the 19th century, the Chinese secret societies, the Mafia and other societies are examples of such criminal communities which take over large segments of government. The criminal group recognizes what the state refuses to admit, namely, that *community is life and power on the human level*, and the means to effectual power is the control of the community. The state wishes to *suppress and destroy* the community; the criminal group seeks to *control* the community. As a result, the criminal gains power faster than the state does, because the criminal group seeks to be a parasite on community rather than its destroyer. The criminal community becomes *the effective community* and infiltrates the state as well as society at large. I have heard businessmen say that they prefer to deal with the criminal syndicate rather than with the civil government, because survival is easier with the criminal syndicate.

Because the state works to destroy the family, which is the mainspring of community life, it destroys the peace of the community. It creates a fearful and unstable people. As St. Augustine observed, "If, then, home, the natural refuge from the ills of life, is itself not safe, what shall we say of the city, which, as it is larger, is so much the more filled with lawsuits civil and criminal, and is never free from the fear, if sometimes from the actual outbreak of disturbing and bloody insurrections and civil wars?"[1]

The destruction of community is furthered when revolutionary political groups become criminal groups, robbing banks, bombing buildings and groups, murdering, kidnapping, and creating social disorders to increase social chaos. The criminal society is a parasitic community, one which exists to control and prey on the normal and legitimate community. The revolutionary group is out to destroy the community in order to create a new state, so that its activities, while criminal, have a different function than the activities of purely criminal groups.

The revolutionists and the statists thus have a common cause, to destroy society, to wipe out community. It is important to understand the reasons for this. Men have tried over and over again to establish a community on the basis of *blood*. Modern attempts to do so include the national states, Nazi Germany, the Arab states, and Israel. Others have extended this racist idea of community to include *all* men, a one-world order. All men, it is pointed out, are a common species and hence should live together in community. A widely promoted book of a few years ago was titled *The Family of Man*, a deliberate appeal to the unity of the family in blood as the ground for the same unity of all men as one in

---

1. Saint Augustine: *The City of God*, Bk. XIX, 5, p. 681. New York: Modern Library, 1950.

blood. The result is that not only does this faith seek to incorporate the family tie into the new "family," humanity, but to alter religion into the brotherhood of man, into *the religion of humanity*.

Of this movement Gerardus Van Der Leeuw observed:

> This "religion of humanity," however, has enjoyed scarcely any cult development in our secularized era; all the more powerfully, nonetheless, does the magic of humanity still operate: it is the sole entity worthy of worship that remained to thousands after the fierce conflagration of potencies in the nineteenth century. At one time virtuous, as for the age of enlightment:
>
> > He who delights not in such teachings
> > Deserves not to be a man. (*The Magic Flute*)
>
> At another time, realistically, as in Goethe's sense:
>
> > For all human failings
> > Pure humanity atones:
>
> again, romantically: every mother a Virgin Mary: then as "reverence for life": it has persisted to our time, especially in its woes. And there, at long last, it found cult forms also. Under the *Arc de triomphe de l'Etoile* burns the eternal flame from the grave of the *Unknown Soldier* who, in his anonymity, represents the whole of vast suffering humanity, and before whom the nations bow.
>
> Humanity then is the sole community that can vie with the church in catholicity. But it lacks the Head which constitutes the church a living organism; nor has it any mission. And it is precisely in its mission that the paradoxical character of the church is revealed: the given people, which simultaneously is the spiritual community never existent in fact—the community that both is and is not—that is the church, and it embraces the world. On the other hand, humanity is far too existent: we all belong to it, and for us there remain no possibilities. This is the poverty of humanity as community.[2]

Even more than poverty, however, the fact of the fall divides humanity. Not only are there divisions between criminal and law-abiding groups, but also deep rifts between law-abiding groups which are beyond reconciliation in too many cases. The rationalist holds that all these problems are soluble; in reality, man being more than reason, they are not, and the rationalist only introduces a further division. Thus, however intensely the national state and the one-worlder try to create a unified human community in terms of blood, these attempts are failure. Instead of a unified society, there is a divided one which continues to fractionalize.

The solution then becomes *the abolition of community and its replacement by the state*. Since men on their own cannot create community or maintain it, then society must be abolished. All free associations *and* all natural communities (the family, the tribe, the clan, etc.), as well as all

---

2. Gerardus Van Der Leeuw: *Religion in Essence and Manifestation*, p. 271f. New York: Macmillan, 1938.

supernatural communities (the church and Christian covenantal associations) must be outlawed or suppressed in order to prevent the fractionalizing of humanity. The state then requires conformity; it educates all into a common faith in man (national man or world-man), and it provides unity by means of coercive laws.

Since there is no church in other religions, the revolutionary program of the state and of revolutionists becomes easier to put into effect. The church as the body of Christ, the covenanted community whose life is given by sovereign and electing grace, is both a natural and a supernatural community. It is the instrument of the new Adam, who is the new head of the new natural order and the church is thus a natural institution; it is also supernatural, because it is ordained and called into being by God. Its "destruction" thus is unlike the destruction of tribal groups: its life is beyond the reach of the state.

The death of community, natural and supernatural, is the goal of the state. But to destroy or work to destroy the family, the church, the Christian school, private associations, free vocations, and other aspects of society is a flagrant *injustice*, and for the state to dedicate itself to injustice means that *the state thereby becomes an antinomian body*. In the name of law, it legislates anti-law. It substitutes relativistic laws and bureaucratic fiats for justice, and thus works against law as justice. The courts become organized instruments of injustice, and, instead of becoming the allies of justice and just men, the courts become progressively the instruments of the criminal community. The criminal groups cannot exist without the connivance and cooperation of the state, and the two enter into a working alliance which, despite their mutual distrust, functions very well, because both exist in enmity to justice and godly community. Both have a vested interest in insisting that all men are larcenous at heart, and the only practical way to live is in terms of their theory. The statist holds that men cannot be good unless the state compels them, and goodness is then defined as what the state and its planners ordain. The criminal society insists that all men are crooks at heart, but that their activity is an honest attempt to provide realistically what men desire. Without affirming the doctrine of the fall, and usually denying it, in practice both statists and criminals presuppose the fall. Even more, they assume that there is no remedy for the fall except to live in terms of it. Ultimately, this means that every man becomes his own god, determining good and evil for himself (Gen. 3:5), and the practical consequence is anarchy.

In the community of the atonement, the situation is radically different. In Deuteronomy 21:1-9, we see clearly what such a society implies:

If one be found slain in the land which the LORD thy God giveth thee to possess it, lying in the field, and it be not known who hath

slain him:
Then thy elders and thy judges shall come forth, and they shall measure unto the cities which are round about him that is slain:
And it shall be, that the city which is next unto the slain man, even the elders of that city shall take an heifer, which hath not been wrought with, and which hath not drawn in the yoke;
And the elders of that city shall bring down the heifer unto a rough valley, which is neither eared nor sown, and shall strike off the heifer's neck there in the valley:
And the priests the sons of Levi shall come near; for them the LORD thy God hath chosen to minister unto him, and to bless in the name of the LORD; and by their word shall every controversy and every stroke be tried:
And all the elders of that city, that are next unto the slain man, shall wash their hands over the heifer that is beheaded in the valley:
And they shall answer and say, Our hands have not shed this blood, neither have our eyes seen it.
Be merciful, O LORD, unto thy people Israel, whom thou hast redeemed, and lay not innocent blood unto thy people of Israel's charge. And the blood shall be forgiven them.
So shalt thou put away the guilt of innocent blood from among you, when thou shalt do that which is right in the sight of the Lord.

In the community of the atonement *all* crime must be atoned for. Every crime, every sin, is an offense primarily against God's order, secondarily against man and the natural order. As a result, any crime which is unsolved requires restitution and must be dealt with. Since this is case law, murder is selected as an instance which requires God-ward attention, in a particularly important way, in that life, the creation and gift of God, is that which all sin mars and finally destroys. If in a town or city, that town or city must make atonement for it. If in a field, the nearest town or city is responsible. Restitution must be made by the community where the criminal is unknown, because in every case of crime, there must be restitution. Thus, for the unknown murderer, a substitute is provided, a heifer, to be executed in the murderer's stead. The community provides the heifer, and the community assumes the normal liabilities for restitution as required in Exodus 21. Whether it be theft, murder, or any other crime, the community of the atonement removes from itself the guilt for the offense only by, *first*, apprehending the guilty man and requiring restitution, or, *second*, where the guilty man cannot be apprehended, the community makes restitution.

In either case, a criminal community cannot be allowed to exist. In terms of Biblical law, the habitual criminal must be executed, as well as the incorrigible delinquent (Deut. 21:18-21). The community of the atonement cannot tolerate habitual criminals, nor subsidize them by a prison system.

Similarly, the community of the atonement must be at war with the modern state and its antinomian law. It must declare such a state to be antichristian and lawless. It must work to bring men to the knowledge of the regenerating God and His son, Jesus Christ, and then to establish in every area the power of the godly community.

## 15

## THE COMMUNITY AND THE FAMILY

The state, in its warfare against society, strikes most emphatically against the family, and then the church. If the integrity and the power of the Christian family are destroyed, the church cannot long maintain any strength. The family is the basic community, and thus the primary target of attack, together with Christian faith as such.

It is thus not surprising that a statist educator, in *Escape From Childhood*, proposes "A Children's Bill of Rights" which strikes at the freedom of the family to govern itself. Holt writes,

I have come to feel that the fact of being a "child," of being wholly subservient and dependent, of being seen by older people as a mixture of expensive nuisance, slave, and super-pet, does most young people more harm than good.

I propose instead that the rights, privileges, duties, responsibilities of adult citizens be made available to any young person, of whatever age, who wants to make use of them.

Holt has a different idea of children than do Christians, who do not see children "as a mixture of expensive nuisance, slave, and super-pet." To reduce the family relationship to this caricature and to pathology is indicative not of scholarship, but of the most intense hatred. His catalogue of "rights" for children is in line with this hatred of the family:

The right to financial independence and responsibility—i.e. the right to own, buy, and sell property, to borrow money, establish credit, sign contracts, etc.
The right to direct and manage one's own education.
The right to travel, to live away from home, to choose or make one's own home.
The right to receive from the state whatever minimum income it may guarantee to adult citizens.
The right to make and enter into, on a basis of mutual consent, familial relationships outside one's immediate family—i.e., the right to seek and choose guardians other than one's own parents and to be legally dependent on them.
The right to do, in general, what any adult may legally do.[1]

These "rights" are for children "of whatever age, who want to make use

---

1. John Holt, "The Doomsday Generation," in *Los Angeles Herald-Examiner*, Sunday, May 5, 1974, p. G4.

of them." Implicit in them is the plan to turn all people, adults included, into children and wards of the state, who will, as "Right 9" indicates, all receive some minimum income from the state.

Such ideas are increasingly the goals of more and more statist educators, whose vision of the future would have been familiar to George Orwell, with his vision of *1984*.

This demand for autonomy and independence such as Holt requires for children is also present in women today. Men, of course, first took it upon themselves to be irresponsible and to walk away from responsibilities as they saw fit. Now, women demand the same right. Symptomatic of this is the fact that detective agencies now not only have missing husbands but missing wives to track down. A growing number of wives abandon the home to disappear into a life of irresponsibility. The opinion of Matt Basile of the Brooklyn-based Mutual Investigation Service is that such women have been domineering wives with weak, indulgent husbands:

> Basile counsels that the time to prevent a wife from becoming an eventual dropout is right on the honeymoon. "The most dangerous thing a new husband can say then is 'Whatever you say, dear.' The first few months are critical. Learn early to say, 'This is what I want. This is what I'm giving you,' and your marriage has a better chance of lasting because she'll continue to respect you."
>
> In fact, this is Basile's main advice to men who want to lessen the chances of having a dropout wife: "Learn to say 'no.' It's as important a word in establishing a solid marriage as in raising a child. Love and respect her. Be gentle with her. Ask her advice. But you, the man, should make the decisions. In other words, if you want your marriage to last and be happy, take charge."[2]

This cannot be done by men who cannot discipline themselves or say no to themselves.

Still another factor works against the family, the sexual revolution. Because of the basic nature of the family to true community, revolutionaries have often directed their activities against sexual regulations. This was true of the ancient communistic revolution of the Mazdakites in Persia, true of the French and Russian Revolutions, and especially true of current revolutionary movements. In the Patricia Hearst "kidnapping" of 1974, a revolutionary group used the "kidnapping" not only to propagate its ideas but to reduce a family to impotence and to use Patricia Hearst to attack her father.

This should not surprise us. Marx and Engels made clear their attack on "the Holy Family" as the foundation of their attack on the human family. "Nicolas Calas" (a pen name) set forth the revolutionary credo

---

2. Al Bernsohn, "Will Your Wife Be a Marriage Dropout?" in *True*, vol. 55, no. 444, May, 1974, p. 64.

when he said that "the dominant of the revolutionary complex is to be sadistic. This means that hatred of the father should always be stronger than love of the brother."[3] Implicit in the modern idea of the brotherhood of man, as Kuehnelt-Leddihn shows, is the hatred of the father, i.e., the rejection of all authority in the name of equality. Thus we must say that the motive behind the demand for brotherhood of man is not love but hatred and envy rationalized into a doctrine of equality. In the name of equality, authority is challenged and denied.

The first authority attacked is that of God. Freedom came to be identified, very early in the modern era, with freedom from God and freedom therefore from the church also. It is ironic that the bloody 20th century can speak of the blood shed by the church of earlier centuries, and the most totalitarian of eras can speak of repression by the church. It is important to make slaves or semi-slave citizens believe that they are the freest of people.

The world of literature in particular has been a vocal force for the humanistic assault on community and especially the family. The family in literature has usually been shown in a bad light, as the source of prejudice, ignorance, and reaction. With the birth of the motion picture industry and television, this assault was intensified and popularized. The religious presupposition of films and television is rampant humanism. Freedom is seen as independence from the Christian family and Biblical law with respect to sex. *Freedom and life have been interpreted in terms of sexual experimentation.* This sexual experimentation, moreover, has been geared to violence. Television is geared to action, and its action means violence. The hours of daily exposure to the constant round of violence of television has been discussed by more than a few thinkers. Peregrine Worsthorne of England has in particular summarized very ably the consequences of child education in and out of the modern home, combined with television:

> A contemporary child is pampered and cosseted in the home from the earliest infancy, where his parents slave around him; indulged in the school, where the teachers are forbidden to lay a hand on him and where bullying, once rampant, has been largely eliminated; pandered to in adolescence by a whole commercial structure designed to react enthusiastically to his slightest whim, so that he reaches maturity accustomed to getting his way.... But alongside this protracted training in indiscipline goes a cultural diet that promotes the belief that violence is the highest form of human expression, the

---

3. Cited by Erik von Kuehnelt-Leddihn: *Leftism, From de Sade and Marx to Hitler and Marcuse*, p. 180. New Rochelle, N. Y.: Arlington House, 1974. Kuehnelt-Leddihn cites also the French Catholic philosopher, Jean Lacroix, who "sees in democracy first the revolt against God, resulting in the revolt against all fatherhood." Lacroix wrote, "One could say that to a large extent the present democratic movement is the murder of the father" (p. 454; cf. 517).

quickest and most direct way of getting things done, irresistible to women, the only civilised response to a stinking society, the sharpest instrument of freedom. For every taste and inclination and every level of intelligence a good justification for violence can be supplied pretty well on every bookstall and in most evenings' television entertainment.[4]

Violence has been made respectable by this trend: it is the means to revolution and change; it is a heroic reaction to evil, and is the necessary answer to problems which only cowards shirk. Not surprisingly, in some of the so-called underground press violence has become so respectable that some have argued that it is only religious and middle-class "hang-ups" which lead women to deny that rape is highly enjoyable.

The result of all this exaltation of violence is the cultivation of sadism.[5] Once regarded by all as a perversion and clearly evil, it is today held by many to be a legitimate human expression. Thus, the *National Star* and the *LA Star* carry full page illustrations "by the world master of sadistic art, Eric Stanton."[6]

This exaltation of sexual experimentation and violence has had a brutal effect upon community life and especially upon the family. It has created a rift between generations, in that parental authority is regarded with contempt by the young, and most adults are afraid to exercise it, having a humanistic distaste for it. There is also distrust between man and wife because of the absence of sexual faithfulness.

On a world-wide basis, we are seeing the steady erosion and destruction of natural communities. The family, clan, group and other ties which once held man to man are being dissolved by the forces of revolutionary humanism. The logical outworkings of man's original sin are apparent in all this. The forces of tradition and custom are being swept aside by the modern mood, and the ability of the natural community to resist all this is meager. The resistance is there, as witness the bitter struggle of Tibetans against communism, but the resistance is reactionary and cannot reconstruct, only oppose.

Thus, the only kind of community which is able to survive and grow is the supernatural community. The Christian family, for example, has grown stronger in the 20th century because it has recognized the necessity of battle and has fought intelligently. The Christian school movement has resulted, with far-reaching consequences for the future. The years to come will see a renewal of the church, of vocations, of arts and sciences, and much more. The supernatural community is a product of Christ's

---

4. Peregrine Worsthorne, "Why We Bow to Violence," *Sunday Telegraph*, London, August 13, 1972, cited in John Eppstein: *The Cult of Revolution in the Church*, p. 19f. New Rochelle, NY: Arlington House, 1974.

5. John Eppstein: *The Cult of Revolution in the Church*, p. 23.

6. *Los Angeles Star*, May 10, 1974, vol. III, no. 53, pp. 38-39.

work and an aspect of His new creation. It is both truly natural and of this world and yet an outpost at the same time of the new creation.

The natural community is dying because, apart from Christ, it cannot define itself. It becomes only a phase of evolution and in essence a part of the past rather than the key to the future. For modern evolutionary humanism, the future means change, and thus all present forms of human society, as well as man himself, face possible obsolescence or extinction.

The Christian, on the other hand, together with St. Paul, bows his "knees unto the Father of our Lord Jesus Christ, Of whom the whole family in heaven and earth is named" (Eph. 3:14-15). All things, according to St. Paul, are *named* or called by God. The word *name* in Scripture means *to define*. When the unfallen Adam was asked by God to *name* "every living creature" (Gen. 2:19), this was a scientific task guided by God, the classification of the animal creation. God, in naming Abraham, *defined* Abraham in terms of a divinely ordained calling and future.

Some have sought to limit "the whole family" of Eph. 3:15 to the redeemed, but in vs. 9, St. Paul emphasizes the creation of "all things by Jesus Christ" and then declares, in vs. 11f., as Westcott made clear,

> This marvellous harmony of all parts of creation and life, as tending to one end, now at last made manifest by the coming of the Son of God, answered to an eternal purpose which was thus fulfilled. The same LORD Who is the stay of our faith and hope is also the crown of the whole development of the world.[7]

The whole of creation is defined or named by God, and that "eternal purpose which he purposed in Christ Jesus our Lord" (Eph. 3:11) now becomes apparent in the coming and triumph of Jesus Christ.

In the supernatural community, the definition or naming of all things is in terms of the triune God and His infallible word. In terms of this St. Paul then defines marriage in terms of God. In Eph. 5:22-33, he makes it clear that the relationship of husband and wife is to be understood in terms of the authority structure and unity of life between Christ and His church. The life of the church is defined by Christ: so too marriage is defined by Christ and His word. The unity of marriage is to be as that of Christ and the church; the same pre-eminence must be given in marriage to the authority of the word and its government over man, and by man over his family. The authority of the husband is *named* or defined in terms of Christ, and the husband's faithfulness to Christ and His word.

All things are either *named* or defined by God, because they are His creation, or else they are meaningless brute facts. The authority of the husband and father disintegrates apart from Biblical faith. As the erosive logic of humanism works to its logical end, it destroys all authority and

---

7. Brooke Foss Westcott: *Saint Paul's Epistle to the Ephesians*, p. 49. Grand Rapids: Eerdmans, (1906) 1952.

meaning and leaves every man his own god in an empty world and a meaningless void.

Thus, the humanist begins by defining true sexuality as total sexual experimentation without any restraint of law and ends by "defining" all things as meaningless: he becomes a nihilist. Having denied God, he has denied all meaning.

For those, however, who bow before Him of whom and by whom all things are named, nothing is meaningless, and true community begins with communion with God through Christ. Because nothing is meaningless, we can be confident that, whatever our calling, it is not a disaster nor a tragedy. Whether we are married or single, whether we have children or are childless, we know that God makes *all things* work together for good for those who love Him, for those who are the called according to His purpose (Rom. 8:28).

The ungodly see life only as something farther out on the road of rebellion against God. "You haven't really lived," it is regularly said, unless you have tried one new form of degeneracy or another. The end of this road is the cry of a young man of nineteen, who, with the wealth to do it, tried everything sexual, narcotic, and everything else money and imagination could offer. At nineteen, he thought of suicide, stating, "I've tried everything, and nothing makes sense or is worth living for."

In Christ, however, "we have boldness and access with confidence by the faith of him" (Eph. 3:12). We are then a member of His supernatural community, the new creation, the Kingdom of God, and we have a responsibility to reconstruct every area in terms of His word, His *naming*.

# 16

## COMMUNITY AND ORDER

One of the basic necessities of community is order. Basic to order is peace, so that men can plan and profit from their labors, living in trust with all men and without fear. We are told about Solomon's peaceful reign in these words: "And Judah and Israel dwelt safely, every man under his vine and under his fig tree, from Dan even to Beer-sheba, all the days of Solomon" (II Kings 18:31; Isa. 36:16; Micah 4:4, etc.) to illustrate the peace of the Kingdom of God: to sit safely under one's vine and fig tree has a double meaning: it means safety from attack by enemies, and safety in harvesting one's own fruits.

How does one attain this peaceful order? One of the myths of the modern era, widely spread by some anthropologists, is the idea that the so-called primitive societies are peaceful and have a strong sense of community. Quite the reverse is the case. *First* of all, the basic pressure in such societies is not a sense of community but a sense of envy. So intense is this envy that men dare not advance over other members of the tribe, for to do so means to all that their prosperity is at the cost of someone's welfare. Envy prevents any cohesiveness in society, and it destroys progress by making personal success a criminal offense. As Schoeck observes, "the envious man is, by definition, the negation of the basis of any society. Incurably envious people may, for a certain time, inspire and lead chiliastic, revolutionary movements, but they can never establish a stable society except by compromising their 'ideals' of equality."[1] Envy in the modern world masquerades as virtue and cloaks itself with demands for equality, but the cry for equality is simply a sophistication of the sin of envy. Envy is clearly forbidden in Scripture (Ps. 37:1; Prov. 3:31; 24:1, 19; Rom. 13:17; I Peter 2:1).

*Second*, basic to the false order of "primitive" societies is magic and witchcraft, which are used to strike at people who will not lower themselves to the level of the envious. Magic and witchcraft are thus socially destructive forces whose function it is to strike at the community and to disrupt it. The medieval cults of witches were active in destruction and were aimed at the overthrow of Christian order. Because Scripture recognizes the deadly consequences of witchcraft, it strikes at it sharply

---

1. Helmut Schoeck: *Envy, A Theory of Social Behavior*, p. 26. New York: Harcourt, Brace & World, 1970.

as a murderous force (Ex. 22:18; Lev. 19:26, 31; 20:6, 27; Deut. 18:10; Micah 5:12; Mal. 3:5; Gal. 5:20; Rev. 21:8; 22:15). Witchcraft murders both individuals and cultures and is a deadly and anti-social force. The so-called "primitive" societies are rather degenerate societies in which envy and witchcraft have triumphed. The triumph of these evils in any culture will mark its decline into barbarism.

In the modern era, however, men have an ostensible answer to the problem of social conflict. This answer, law and order, is shared by conservatives and Marxists from differing perspectives. The Marxist feels that the answer to all social problems is a brutal law and order stance. The conservative feels that law and order are the keys to the restoration of society. Granted that law and order are necessities, it must still be said that these perspectives are seriously wrong.

This error can be well illustrated from the papers of Walter H. Page, American ambassador to Great Britain under President Woodrow Wilson. In a *Memorandum* of November, 1913, Page wrote:

> The foregoing I wrote before this Mexican business took its present place. I can't get away from the feeling that the English simply do not and will not believe in any unselfish public action—further than the keeping of order. They have a mania for order, sheer order, order for the sake of order. They can't see how anything can come in any one's thought before order or how anything need come afterward. Even Sir Edward Grey jocularly ran me across our history with questions like this:
>
> "Suppose you have to intervene, what then?"
>
> "Make 'em vote and live by their decisions."
>
> "But suppose they will not so live?"
>
> "We'll go in again and make 'em vote again."
>
> "And keep this up 200 years?" asked he.
>
> "Yes" said I. "The United States will be here two hundred years and it can continue to shoot men for that little space till they learn to vote and to rule themselves."
>
> I have never seen him laugh so heartily. Shooting men into self-government! Shooting them into orderliness—he comprehends that; and that's all right. But that's as far as his habit of mind goes. At Sheffield last night, when I had to make a speech, I explained "Idealism" (they always quote it) in government. They listened attentively and even eagerly. Then they came up and asked if I really meant that Government should concern itself with idealistic things —beyond keeping order. Ought they to do so in India?—I assure you they don't think beyond order. A nigger lynched in Mississippi offends them more than a tyrant in Mexico.[2]

---

2. Burton J. Hendrick: *The Life and Letters of Walter H. Page*, vol. I, p. 188f. Garden City, New York: Doubleday, Page & Company, 1926.

On Nov. 2, 1913, Page wrote to Edward M. House stating that the U. S. must stand firm on its moral principle of government, namely, "the man that rules must govern for the governed."[3] The same principle still governs U. S. policy. In South Viet Nam and elsewhere the demand is for elections as the key to morally tenable government. Law and order are made dependent on elections. As a result, the American influence has been a profoundly ungodly and immoral one. The moral basis of society has been equated with elections: true order has been made equivalent to either a republican form of government with some, or democracy with other American leaders. Other countries have equated true order with the rule of the gun; law and order come out of the barrel of a gun.

On the other hand, others, with a growing influence in various sectors, equate true order with love, trust, and the absence of coercion. These ideas are applied to family and community life as well as to national and international problems.

St. Paul speaks to this issue in Romans 3:20-28:

> Therefore by the deeds of the law there shall no flesh be justified in his sight: for by the law is the knowledge of sin.
> But now the righteousness of God without the law is manifested, being witnessed by the law and the prophets;
> Even the righteousness of God which is by faith of Jesus Christ unto all and upon all them that believe: for there is no difference:
> For all have sinned, and come short of the glory of God:
> Being justified freely by his grace through the redemption that is in Christ Jesus:
> Whom God hath set forth to be a propitiation through faith in his blood, to declare his righteousness for the remission of sins that are past, through the forbearance of God;
> To declare, I say, at this time his righteousness: that he might be just, and the justifier of him which believeth in Jesus.
> Where is boasting then? It is excluded. By what law? of works? Nay: but by the law of faith.
> Therefore we conclude that a man is justified by faith without the deeds of the law.

One of the fallacies of the ecclesiastical approach to this and other texts is that the relevance is limited to the church and to the soul. But the word of God is cosmic in its scope; theology embraces every area of life, and what St. Paul here declares is good for every area of life.

The subject of St. Paul's statements is *justification, a judicial act.* It means, as Hodge pointed out, that "justice does not condemn, but pronounces him just, or declares herself satisfied. This is the uniform meaning of the word, not only in Scripture, but also in ordinary life." Justice and justification are matters of law: they cannot be separated from law. Thus, when St. Paul makes certain statements about the law in terms of

---

3. *Ibid.*, I, 189.

justification, he is making a *legal* pronouncement, a commentary from the law of God, the justice of God, about an aspect of the same law. To abolish the law totally is to abolish justification as well. Hodge stated further:

> We never confound justification with pardon, or with sanctification. It is always used in the sense antithetical to condemnation. To condemn is not merely to punish, but to declare the accused guilty or worthy of punishment; and justification is not merely to remit that punishment, but to declare that punishment cannot be justly inflicted. Much less does *to condemn* mean to render wicked, and therefore neither does *to justify* mean to render good. When we justify God, we declare him to be just; and when God justifies the sinner, he declares him to be just. In both cases the idea is, that there is no ground for condemnation; or that the demands of justice are satisfied.[4]

In all of his preceding argument, St. Paul makes clear that, because all men, Jews and Gentiles both, are fallen and in bondage to sin, they are "incapable of justification on the grounds of their own character or conduct."[5] St. Paul's point is not that obedience to the law cannot justify, because this would amount to saying that obedience is wrong. Rather, he states that, because *all* men are sinners, none can justify themselves by the law, because all men in Adam are anti-law. What the law does is to bring them to a knowledge or realization of sin. The law brings an inward conviction to the sinner; it does not give life to a dead man; rather, it convinces men of their sin.

The righteousness which the law sets forth men cannot attain by works, because, being fallen, their works are evil. It can only be attained by faith, and it is entirely the gift of God. The ground of this imputed righteousness is the propitiation of God's justice by the sacrifice of Jesus Christ on the cross. God's justice is thereby manifested as well as His mercy. Man is humbled, because all boasting and pride are excluded. Moreover, as St. Paul concludes, in Romans 3:31,

> Do we then make void the law through faith? God forbid: yea, we establish the law.

Without agreeing with the substance of Hodge's comment on this verse, we can agree with his statement, "No moral obligation is weakened, no penal sanction disregarded."[6]

Thus St. Paul emphatically vindicates the law while denying that sinful man can find anything other than condemnation through the law. Salvation is the vindication of God's law and the manifestation of His mercy.

---

4. Charles Hodge: *Commentary on the Epistle to the Romans*, p. 126f. New York: A. C. Armstrong and Son, (1882) 1893.
5. *Ibid.*, p. 131.
6. *Ibid.*, p. 158.

The law stands: its penalty falls on Christ. The law is not made void, it is not abolished. Rather, it is vindicated in its indictment of fallen man, and it is established because Christ redeems us from the curse of the law, its death penalty, to place us under the blessing of the law (Deut. 28).

Let us now examine the implications of this for society. Fallen man is incapable of true righteousness, and this incapacity marks him in his person and in his institutions. He is no more able to establish a righteous civil government than he is able to establish his personal righteousness. Here we see the wickedness of those thinkers, Catholic and Protestant, Arminian and Reformed, who imagine that sinful men can, through natural law or the law of nations, establish a just social order. Job was right: "Who can bring a clean thing out of an unclean? not one" (Job 14:4).

It is thus emphatically clear that both personal and social life can only flourish when grounded on the atoning blood of Jesus Christ. The blood of Christ witnesses to the seriousness of God's law, and God does not change. True social order cannot be gained by either guns or butter, nor by the elective process. If every nation were tomorrow to adopt the republican form of civil government, or any other elective and representative form of civil order, the results all over the world would be no different than they are now or would be the same within a year or two. The problem is within man, and it is sin.

Community requires order, but that order can be productive of peace only when it begins with God's order, His redeeming grace and His prospering law. Apart from that, society is continually in disorder because of what W. B. Yeats, in his poem *Byzantium*, called "The fury and the mire of human veins." For the unregenerate, like Yeats, life is frustration, and, on looking back on its results, he asked, in his poem, *Why Should Not Old Men Be Mad?*, why anyone with mature years should expect anything when they know "that no better can be had."

The failures of society are not due to conspiracies; they are due to the unregenerate heart of man.

Basic to the idea of order is *relation*. In true order, all things are related to one another in a significant and basic manner. It is not accidental that the word *order* is used in both botany and zoology to describe a group of families, or a group with related and shared characteristics. This scientific usage touches a fundamental factor in the idea of order. There is neither true community nor order in a prison or in a totalitarian state. Men are brought forcibly together, or are held together by coercion, not by an inner bond or relationship. The botanical and zoological ideas of order pointed to a unity of nature and being which is a part of God's creative order. The Biblical doctrine of social order rests on a unity of nature and being which is a part of God's regenerative order. There is a relationship between men because there is a relationship with God in Christ.

Order is related to peace, but it is more than peace. There can be godly order in a family, and yet conflicts can occur. Again, order is related to organization and structure while being somewhat different, because organization and structure are not necessarily productive of order. The clearest description of true order is the Lord's Prayer (Matt. 6:9-13).

Since order is inseparable from relation, the only possible kind of order, as epistemological self-consciousness develops, is godly order. All other attempts at order are coercive and fail. Where man is related to God by Christ's atonement, he then can be related to others in Christ. He is a member of the redeemed community and is governed by the law of God in his relationships to those in the covenant and outside of it. Those outside of Christ move progressively towards the self-conscious fulfilment of their basic motive, that each man is his own god, determining for himself what constitutes good and evil. The consequence of this faith is radical anarchy, the triumph of envy, and the rise of witchcraft. It is not an accident that both in the late medieval (as well as Roman) era, and in the last days of the modern era, equalitarianism (or envy) and witchcraft have both flourished. Witchcraft in the Middle Ages is well documented. The envious came together with revolutionary, anarchistic, and evil intent, to practice sexual offenses, infanticide, human sacrifices, and cannibalism as a means to power in their murderous assault on society. The witchcraft movement was antinomian and humanistic. "The essence of the magical world view is belief in a homocentric universe.... All things are made for man and on the model of man."[7] Such a perspective is the death of order and community.

7. Jeffrey Burton Russell: *Witchcraft in the Middle Ages*, p. 5. Ithaca, NY: Cornell University Press, 1972.

## 17

## COMMUNITY AND FAITH

The best-selling American book between 1880 and 1935 was a novel by a Topeka, Kansas, minister, Charles M. Sheldon. The book, *In His Steps* (1896), had an important point: a number of Christians in a community, under the leadership of their minister, pledge themselves, as they face their daily tasks, to ask, what would Jesus do?, and then to act accordingly. The book thus represented an important motive, and its popularity was enormous. It is still in print and enjoys a steady sale in fundamentalist circles.

In spite of its success in sales, the book was a failure with regard to its purpose. Because the author had a very weak view of Biblical law at best, his own answer to the question, what would Jesus do? was as a result experiential and sentimental. The goal was to leave people aglow with an experience rather than to accomplish substantial changes. The telling evidence of Sheldon's failure is an episode in the book, in which a good Christian girl takes a drunken prostitute into her home in order to save her. Such an act by a Christian girl, however daring and however much motivated by faith, is still *sentimental.* To house an unregenerate prostitute is hardly good sense, and the religious presupposition, that love will overcome, is sentimental rather than Christian. Thus, the *first* step, taking in a drunken prostitute, is a sentimental rather than a godly act. The *second* step is even worse: the converted prostitute is then allowed to die, and Sheldon thereby avoided the problem of what to do with a redeemed prostitute, how to have her accepted in the church and community, and how to give her any social status. It was easier to ship her off to the next world than to find a place for her in this one. What *In His Steps* reveals is that the distance from Biblical religion to church religion has become a very great one.

Modern liberals find it easy to criticize these and other obvious defects in Sheldon's book.[1] The problem, however, is one common to every segment of modern society, Christian and atheist, almost without exception. The sentimental and bleeding heart motive is ready to reach out to the down trodden, the social outcasts, and the despised, as long as the difference between the sentimental humanitarian and the outcast is an obvious one. When the difference threatens to disappear, trouble ensues.

---

1. See Larzer Ziff: *The American 1890s*, pp. 85-87. New York: The Viking Press, 1966.

To understand this problem, a problem of *community*, we must recognize that these communities have problems including certain people. Every idea of community has a focus or center, and that which is at war with or at least not in harmony with the center is not a part of the community. The closer to the center, the greater the community. To illustrate, in a society of atheists the Christian will be an outcast. In a community of army officers, a pacifist will be regarded with distaste. In the Mafia, an honest police officer is hardly a welcome figure.

On the other hand, if the community is governed by social status, wealth, and prestige, a wealthy prince will be at the center, no matter how irritating his many faults will be, because his status and wealth place him at the center.

Every community has some center of power, a focus in terms of which it is organized, and the departures from it have no place in the community. In Biblical faith, the center of power is God and His word. In terms of His law word, all habitual criminals must be executed. Not only is there no community with them as criminals, but no life allowed to them. In terms of this requirement, a class of professional criminals is an impossibility in a state and community ruled by Biblical law.

The Marxists have recognized the validity of this principle as few others have. For them only the atheistic socialist can exist in their planned society. As a result, they work to destroy, by education, torture, slave-labor camps, and mass murders all other resisting elements in society. By definition, all dissident elements are criminal. Their deadly flaw is that their line of division is anti-justice. Not only does it eliminate the godly element in the population who are the most law-abiding and the best workers, but it also eliminates the communists who lose out in an intra-party struggle. Their idea of community supposedly has a focus in the Marxist faith, but they have as readily tortured and killed fellow communists as anyone else, and the issue has seldom been theoretical. Rather than differences of faith and principles, the reason for the blood-letting has been a power struggle. As a result, because their power center has been power more than the Marxist faith, Marxists have been unable to create a community. They have only a bloody power state.

Community requires a common basis of faith and character, a relationship of man to man in terms of God. A very interesting account of life in a Japanese prisoner of war camp makes clear that, despite the common assumption, and the cases of torture in some camps, "our problems," reported Gilkey, "were created more by our own behavior than by our Japanese captors."[2] The prisoners included too many people of

---

2. Langdon Gilkey: *Shantung Compound, The Story of Men and Women Under Pressure*, p. iv. New York: Harper & Row, 1966. This is an exellent work, much neglected because it points to the problem in man as such, rather than in the enemy.

bad or weak character, and the result was that the internal problems of the camp were constant and were a product of sin. In this situation, a new community arose. Young Catholic priests, in their early and middle twenties, paired off with the daughters of very conservative Protestant missionaries. Although normally opposed on theological grounds, their common faith now brought them together. They could trust one another completely. Their love became very deep but never transgressed their moral standards, and they were a great help to one another, although the parents and Catholic authorities were upset by this relationship. A common faith, despite differences, and common problems in the face of an ungodly camp, brought them together.[3]

Now, to return to the prostitute of *In His Steps*, the problem of community was evaded by Sheldon. *First*, there is no community between a covenant girl and an unredeemed prostitute, although there can be charity, and, *second*, community between the redeemed, the critical point, was evaded by death, by killing off the prostitute. Larzer Ziff rightly found this "solution" a false one, but his concern with "social" rather than moral problems again evades the human problem. By converting human problems into sociological ones, they are depersonalized and also removed from the realm of morality by the depersonalization.

An even greater evasion is that of the modern mind which demands community without faith, without any common standard. An example of this is the bitter indictment of the church by a woman who, during the depression, became a prostitute for a brief time and then operated a brothel for four decades. Her memoirs are an exercise in self-righteousness. She deliberately left the world of the church and of the law-abiding but resented the fact that she paid a penalty for it. "We are no different than the rest of God's children," she argues. "We are subject to the same emotions, the same ambitions, the same despairs, the same pain, the same weaknesses, the same hungers. The only basic difference is that the society from which we come puts us in a different, untouchable category—an ostracized class of 'fallen women' who, if we are lucky and make our fortune, magically are socially cleansed and become respectable once again." Her memoirs indicate that she, as a "madam," had very strict standards for her prostitutes and for her clients. Did she expect the church to have none? Pauline's decision to open a brothel in her home town was a calculated and deliberate one, one made after some planning and investigation. She told both her mother and her pastor that she intended to open a rooming-house, hardly an honest statement. She speaks of having "faith" but gives no evidence of a *Christian* faith. Her hostility to the church is intense and she dates it from an experience, shortly after opening her brothel:

---

3, *Ibid.*, p. 175f.

The most soul-shattering snub came a week or so after I had opened my first house on Smallhouse Road. All my life I had been a faithful churchgoer, from Sunday school classes as a child to adult worship and the teaching of Sunday school. I was a good friend of the minister and his wife, and an admirer of his sermonizing on the need for Christian tolerance and forgiveness. One day I met the pastor and his wife on the street. In view of my new profession, I didn't expect an enthusiastic welcome, but I wished them a pleasant day. They didn't respond. They looked the other way, and scurried across the street as if to avoid contamination. I hurried home and wept bitterly. Since that day I have never been inside a church. I still have my faith, but I cannot tolerate the hypocritical attitudes of so many of the churches and the pastors who rarely practice what they preach.[4]

No doubt, the pastor, as an average more or less antinomian, preached a vaguely humanistic doctrine of "tolerance and forgiveness" and was thus hoist on his own petard. In spite of this, what did Pauline expect? She had lied to the pastor, brought discredit to the church where she had taught Sunday School, and now expected no unhappy reaction? What did she want? An invitation to address the Ladies Aid, or a youth group? A blessing or an avowal of respect whatever she said or did? Actions have consequences, whether we like it or not.

With respect to prostitutes, the Bible warns men against prostituting their daughters (Lev. 19:29); priests were not allowed to marry anyone who had been a prostitute (Lev. 21:7). A priest's daughter who became a prostitute was to be executed for so degrading her family (Lev. 21:9). A prostitute's income could not be used for paying vows, i.e., as a receipt in the Temple (Deut. 23:18). Decrees of expulsion for prostitutes occur in Israels' history (I Kings 14:24; 15:12; 22:47; II Kings 23:7), and toleration of prostitution was declared to be a sign of an approaching judgment and collapse (Hosea 4:14). An elementary knowledge of the Bible makes clear its position on prostitution. "I still have my faith," says Pauline. In what? The Bible, and the God revealed therein? It certainly offers no tolerance for her calculating and self-righteous career as a brothel house operator.

Rahab, we are told, "perished not with them that believed not" because she acted on her faith, i.e., her faith was a living one (Heb. 11:31). Her faith had "works" (James 2:25). She staked her life on her defense of the men of God. As a result, she had a place in God's covenant community. Even then, after she was saved from Jericho, Rahab and her family for a time were left "without the camp of Israel" (Josh. 6:23). They were required to remain there until meeting whatever requirements the leaders of Israel had for formal entrance into the covenant. Then she married well and became an ancestress of Jesus Christ

---

4. Pauline Tabor: *Pauline's*, p. 214f. Louisville, KY: Touchstone Publishing Co., (1971) 1972.

(Matt. 1:5). By faith she had become a member of the covenant people, by faith with works. As an unbeliever, her works had been prostitution. As a believer, she had risked her life for the people of God and had placed her entire trust on the truth of God's word. Her faith moved her from the people of Jericho to the people of God. Her unbelief had given her a unity of life in sin, i.e., a total dedication to sin; her faith gave her a unity of life in terms of God's covenant and had united her to God's people. Community is an act of faith and communion within that faith.

Modern man is hungry for community, but he destroys it by his humanism. Nisbet has called "the longing for community which now exists as perhaps the most menacing fact of the Western world."[5] The hunger for community makes man receptive to the psuedo-community offered by the totalitarian state. Such a hope substitutes envy for community and cynicism for faith and thus furthers the disintegration of community.

All non-Christian attempts to establish community ultimately collapse because of their inability to cope with sin. Sin triumphs in Marxist states as *power*, and Marxists devour Marxists in the struggle for power, which takes priority over *the faith*, the belief in the communist utopia. Any and every faith which cannot answer the problem of sin is destructive of itself and of the hope of community, because *there is a faith implicit in all sin*, which triumphs over its rivals. This faith implicit in all sin is the desire of man to be his own god, determining good and evil for himself (Gen. 3:5). This faith is the antithesis of community, and unless sin is dealt with by atonement and regeneration, it will triumph over every faith.

Sheldon's Arminian views in *In His Steps* undercut the efficacy of the atonement and made *love* more basic.

It is not surprising that, in recent years, because modern man has failed to cope with sin, his strategy is to define it out of existence. It is now argued that prostitution is legitimate, and its prosecution is a violation of the whore's civil rights. In 1974, the first national convention of prostitutes held their meeting in a San Francisco church. *Love* had become *toleration* and finally *acceptance*.

---

5. Robert A. Nisbet: *Community and Power*, p. 246. New York: Oxford University Press, (1953) 1962.

## 18

## COMMUNITY AND MORALITY

A New York doctor, working for the Health Department (Division: Venereal Diseases), had as a patient a 17-year-old girl, in for the second time in five months. As the girl left, to return for the final results of her tests in two weeks, Dr. Yanovsky remarked, "And meanwhile, behave!" For this the doctor received an official reprimand for violating the privacy of the girl by suggesting, however mildly, the necessity for moral behavior. The New Yorker, as the doctor noted, takes "mugging, raping, holdups, blackouts, transportation failures, rotten mail and telephone service, stupid and/or dishonest car mechanics, criminal judges, corrupt assemblymen, senators, and commissioners in his stride," but the slightest moral suggestion is a violation of privacy.[1]

A corrupt nation goes into a frenzy of self-righteous indignation and hatred over the sins of Watergate, but it never stops to consider that it has banned Biblical morality from the schools and courts, and has labored to produce the immorality it professes hypocritically to hate.

The churches, too, hypocritically mourn the loss of morality without considering their guilt in the matter. The modernist churches have favored situation ethics, and the Watergate scandal *is* situation ethics. The evangelical churches have denied the law and yet wonder at the - national moral decline. That wretched pulpiteer, Barnhouse, so widely hailed in the 1940s and 1950s, wrote

> It was a tragic hour when the Reformation churches wrote the Ten Commandments into their creeds and catechisms and sought to bring Gentile believers into bondage to Jewish law, which was never intended either for the Gentile nations or for the church.[2]

Such opinions are very common. One American publication holds that the force of the Ten Commandments was brought to an end by the death of Christ and sees this as freeing "sincere believers in the Redeemer from unwarranted defilement of conscience by them."[3] The law, we are told

---

1. Basile Yanovsky, M. D.: *The Dark Fields' of Venus, From a Doctor's Logbook*, p. 239f. New York: Harcourt Brace Jovanovich, 1973.
2. Cited by S. Lewis Johnson, Jr., in "The Paralysis of Legalism," *Bibliotheca Sacra*, vol. 120, no. 478, April-June, 1963, p. 108, from Donald Grey Barnhouse: *God's Freedom*, p. 134. Johnson adds, "He was right too," joining the ranks of the antinomians.
3. "The Decalogue and the Law the Same," in *The Banner of Truth*, vol. 23, no. 5, June, 1974, Highland, Indiana. This periodical must *not* be confused with the English periodical of the same name.

by many, is *dead*. Not so, according to Scripture. *We* in Christ are dead to the law as an indictment, a death sentence (Rom. 7:4), but alive to it as the righteousness of God to be put into force by God's redeemed people (Rom. 8:4). God's law cannot die or pass away! However, a vast segment of the church is vehemently anti-law, antinomian. Thus, Hal Lindsey writes:

> Now then, what has God done about the law and the believer's relationship to it?
> He has taken us out from under the jurisdiction of the law and placed us under His grace. The law is still there, but we're not under it. . . .
> The law just doesn't speak to us anymore as a basis of operation in the Christian life. When Christ died, was buried, rose, and ascended, we died with Him to the law and its power over us. . . .
> LAW AND GRACE ARE MUTUALLY EXCLUSIVE.
> It is imperative that we realize that law and grace are complete systems in themselves. They are mutually exclusive. To mix these principles robs the law of its bona fide terror and grace of its creative freeness.[4]

The confusion created by such thinking as this is very great. It confuses the law as an indictment against the guilty and the law as the righteousness of God. If I am a criminal, the law is my enemy: it harbors a death penalty against me. If I am by grace a son of the lawgiver, the law is my protection as well as my way of life, in that it expresses my Father's being and my new nature.

Again, there is a confusion between the totally illegitimate use of the law for justification  and its intended use in all of Scripture for sanctification. Implicit in all antinomianism is *dispensationalism*, and a view of a changing God with a changing plan of salvation.

Moreover, as Rev. E. W. Johnson has so ably stated it, not only is antinomianism implicitly Arminian, in that it assumes that man could once justify himself by law rather than be justified by sovereign grace, but also "Arminianism is libertinism."

> If the forgiving grace of God does not lie ultimately in the will of God, but in that of man, what is to keep us from sinning, and then, having said a little prayer, go and sin some more?

> A minister came to us from an Arminian group, having been convinced of Calvinism. He told me how that in his previous connections he had attended trials of ministers accused of adultery, and how these ministers had presented this defense to their official boards. "I told the woman if you are as tempted as I am, why don't we just go ahead and then ask God to forgive us?"

> But the grace of God is not like a water faucet. You cannot turn it on anytime you want to. If you think otherwise, I would recommend

---

4. Hal Lindsey, with C. C. Carlson: *Satan Is Alive and Well on Planet Earth*, p. 164. New York: Bantam Books, (1972) 1974.

that you take another look at the 51st Psalm.[5]

In such a doctrine, forgiveness is reduced to a humanistic feeling, whereas in Scripture it is *legal* or juridical in its frame of reference and means that charges are dropped, because satisfaction is rendered, or, as in Luke 23:34, charges deferred for the time being.

Basic to this false doctrine, among other things, is an erroneous doctrine of man. Pagan dualism governs such a belief, and man's being is divided into two segments, so that thought and action are only loosely related. Socrates, for example, could discourse on virtue while involved in homosexuality; for him, the realm of mind and body were loosely related.

In terms of Scripture, we must hold that, because God is one, and His creation is a unity, man too is a unity. In his fallen estate, man is *totally* depraved, i.e., his depravity extends to every aspect of his being. In his redeemed estate, his justification is total, and his sanctification, while by no means complete in this life, has an inescapable direction. The saints of God can sin (*hamartia*), but they are never guilty of lawlessness (*anomia*).

An example often used of the redemption of a supposedly lawless man is Lot. We forget, however, that the Bible speaks clearly of his righteousness. Because two events of fearful consequences are given great emphasis, we assume that they sum up Lot's life, the move to Sodom, and the consequences of the escape from Sodom. The reason for the move to Sodom was "the well watered" plain of Jordan (Gen. 13:10), and the stricken old Lot was unaware of what his daughters did, so that what we must rather say is that a bad move had disastrous consequences. The plain statement of Scripture is that on the whole Lot was a godly man. He was apparently a city councilman or judge, because he "sat in the gate of Sodom" (Gen. 19:1; cf. 19:9), a term for holding office (Prov. 31:23). According to II Peter 2:7-8, Lot was a "righteous man," and in favor with God in spite of his mistakes and sins.

We must thus distinguish between false prophets who come "in sheep's clothing, but inwardly they are ravening wolves" (Matt. 7:15), and the faithful servants of the word of God. Our Lord emphasized the unity of man:

> Ye shall know them by their fruits. Do men gather grapes of thorns, or figs of thistles?
> Even so every good tree bringeth forth good fruit; but a corrupt tree brings forth evil fruit.
> A good tree cannot bring forth evil fruit, neither can a corrupt tree bring forth good fruit.

---

5. E. W. Johnson, "Arminianism is a Hard Doctrine," in *The Sovereign Grace Message*, vol. V, August, 1974, p. 8.

Every tree that bringeth not forth good fruit is hewn down, and cast into the fire.
Wherefore by their fruits ye shall know them (Matt. 7:16-20).

How then did David commit both adultery and murder? First of all, we cannot use Scripture to contradict Scripture. Our Lord knew full well of David's sin when He insisted on the unity of man. We must simply accept His word, observing only that at times a good tree is affected by blights and its fruit infected, but, when it recovers and bears good fruit again, it is obviously a good tree. Moreover, we must remember the totality of David's life, one of faith and obedience far exceeding that of his critics.

Moreover, our Lord is insistent on the unity of man when He speaks of faith and obedience:

If ye love me, keep my commandments. . . .
He that hath my commandments, and keepeth them, he it is that loveth me: and he that loveth me shall be loved of my Father, and I will love him, and will manifest myself to him.
Judas saith unto him, not Iscariot, Lord how is it that thou wilt manifest thyself unto us, and not unto the world?
Jesus answered and said unto him, If a man love me, he will keep my words: and my Father will love him, and we will come unto him, and make our abode with him.
He that loveth me not keepeth not my sayings: and the word which ye hear is not mine, but the Father's which sent me (John 14:15, 21-24).

The correct reading of vs. 15 is "If ye love me, *ye will* keep my commandments." Our Lord is not *asking* us to keep His commandments: He is declaring that, *if we love Him, we will of necessity* keep His commandments. The word for love here is *agapate*, from *agape*, normally used to describe the sovereign, gracious love of God. "We love him because he first loved us" (I John 4:19). We are only capable of this love because His grace is at work in us. If this grace is operative in us, we will of necessity love God and keep His commandments. If we have faith, we in Christ do "greater works" (John 14:12), i.e., our works have wider spiritual effects in that they bring the whole world under the dominion of Christ. As Westcott notes, "The thought of love follows that of faith (vs. 12). Faith issues in works of power: love in works of devotion. . . . Obedience is the necessary consequence of love."[6] Moreover, Jesus plainly identifies His word with the word of the Father, His commandments with the law of God. The unity of the Father and the Son is also the unity of their law word (vss. 22-24). "To reject His teaching is to reject the teaching of God."[7] In vs. 23, "words" in the original is

---

6. B. F. Westcott: *The Gospel According to St. John*, p. 205. Grand Rapids: Eerdmans, (1881) 1954.
7. *Ibid.*, p. 207.

singular, "word." The whole of Scripture is *one word* although composed of many *words*.

To deny this connection which our Lord declares between the tree and its fruits, and between faith, love, and obedience is to deny Him. But today Christ is denied in the name of Christ. To cite an example of this, one of hundreds I have encountered in my travels: a man, flagrantly guilty of adultery, time without number, is also an alcoholic and an irresponsible, abusive husband. His wife repeatedly "forgave" her husband, on instructions of her pastor, only to have the same pattern repeated. She was told that divorce is wrong (In Scripture it is not wrong but a remedy for evil), and so finally secured a legal separation. Her husband, again, as often before, in an institution for drying out alcoholics, has used a chaplain to tell the wife that, because her husband has "repented," he must be "forgiven" and taken back. To refuse this, she is told, is *sin*. The Lord has taken her husband back, and she must do the same.

Another example: a church officer has repeatedly molested Sunday School children, young girls. After each incident and its discovery, he has "repented" with tears before the church board and been "forgiven." Angry parents have been told that their attitude is unforgiving, ungodly, and sinful.

But *repentance* is not a matter of words: it means a turning around, a change of direction, in the whole life of a man. *It is not a matter of words but of life.* Forgiveness comes when satisfaction, restitution, is made, and the Biblical penalty for adultery is death.

To reduce God's call for repentance to a muttering of words is to offend God. To make forgiveness a matter of words and feelings is to deny God's righteousness and His law. Such an antinomian society will soon crumble. There can be no reconstruction without that sovereign grace which produces faith, love, and obedience. Of this generation it must be said, with respect to most churchmen, what Isaiah said of his (Isa. 29:13), and our Lord of His day, "This people draweth nigh unto me with their mouth, and honoureth me with their lips; but their heart is far from me" (Matt. 15:8).

# 19

## THEOLOGY AND THE STATE

Religion in pagan antiquity was a department of state, and its function was to provide the rationale for the law order of the society and insurance for individuals. The state was seen as the supreme and primary organization of life in developed paganism, so that the essence of religious life was man's relationship to the state, or to its ruler. The gods acted through the state, and all institutions were comprehended in the state and its life.

Biblical religion was a denial of this. When Christianity began its missionary activity, it came into immediate conflict with this belief that the unity of life finds expression in the state rather than in God. The result was a bitter conflict, ending with the recognition of Christianity and its independence. Some emperors sought to reduce the church to an aspect of the life of the state, and some popes sought to reduce the state to an aspect of the life of the church. This struggle was common to the so-called Middle Ages and the Reformation eras. Thus, Jean Morely, sire de Villiers, a Reformed thinker (although attacked by Calvin, Beza, and others), held that "ecclesiastical power and civil administration are two parts of the one true Church of God."[1] Catholics and Protestants alike held that *all* people should be under the jurisdiction of both church and state. In England, for example, this meant that the Church of England was the ecclesiastical organization of England, and the state its civil expression. *All* men were thus in both church and state, although not necessarily in good standing. Power and control were reserved to the ruling powers or leaders and not given to the mixed multitude. To surrender this principle, it was recognized, meant the surrender of the church and state to democracy, to the will of the people, and its consequences would be anarchy. The church then too could be reduced to a small remnant. This belief in a *given* and established church marked the Roman Catholics, Presbyterian and Reformed churches, the Lutherans, Anglicans, and, at the beginning and for some time, the Congregationalists.

On the other hand, the Baptists held to a voluntaristic church, a remnant of faith, governed by democratic processes. It should be noted that

---

1. Robert M. Kingdon: *Geneva and the Consolidation of the French Protestant Movement 1565-1572*, p. 49. Geneva: Librairie Droz, 1967.

early Baptists were almost uniformly Calvinistic in the 17th and 18th centuries. Since the essence of religion in the life of man is *faith*, the Baptists very early held to a voluntaristic church, made up of members who joined on profession of faith.

Clearly, the older position, of Rome and of early Protestantism, found itself in a difficult position: it had to assent to the enactment of legal penalties for dissent and heresy. Instead of a *mission* to the unbelieving in its midst, the church was required to become party to *legal action* against the unbelieving and the dissenting. Because conviction is stronger among dissenters than unbelievers, this meant that the unbelievers could lie low while the dissenters were persecuted.

On the other hand, the Baptistic view meant in practice not only a separation of church and state but a separation of religion and the state. Many Baptists became emphatic in their preference for a secular, humanistic state, and the surrender of the world to the devil was thereby hastened.

Neither side thus answered successfully the relationship of theology to the state, an imperative question for the future of civilization. Since every legal establishment or law structure is an establishment of religion, for Christians to consent to a non-Christian state is to assure their persecution and elimination in the long run. On the other hand, for the church to unite with the state means the persecution of dissent.

Some of the church fathers argued strongly for freedom of worship, in surprisingly modern language. Tertullian thus wrote:

> We are worshippers of one God, of whose existence and character nature teaches all man; at whose lightnings and thunders you tremble, whose benefits minister to your happiness. You think that others, too, are gods, the same we know to be devils. However, it is a fundamental human right, a privilege of nature, that every man should worship according to his own convictions: one man's religion neither harms nor helps another man. It is assuredly no part of religion to compel religion—to which free-will and not force should lead us—the sacrificial victims even being required of a willing mind. You will render no real service to your gods by compelling us to sacrifice. For they can have no desire of offerings from the unwilling, unless they are animated by a spirit of contention, which is a thing altogether undivine. Accordingly the true God bestows His blessings alike on wicked men and on His own elect; upon which account He has appointed an eternal judgment, when both thankful and unthankful will have to stand before His bar.[2]

Tertullian weakened his argument by basing it on natural law rather than Scripture. Moreover, an important question can be raised: criminal law rests on theological, on religious premises. If non-coercion in religion is

---

2. Tertullian, "Ad Scapulam," IV, 2, in *Ante-Nicene Christian Library*, vol. XI, p. 46f. Edinburgh: T & T. Clark, 1872.

so basic, why coerce a murderer, who may kill on religious principle, or a thief whose faith denies private property? Are not heresy and unbelief equally dangerous to society? So runs the ancient argument. It has been more by-passed than answered.

Rome knew that to permit Christianity was to commit suicide, because the Bible required a totally different restructuring of life. More than mere belief was at stake: the life of Rome was the issue, and Rome lost. The issues were the same in the Christian centuries, and they are the same today. The humanistic state, as it becomes more openly humanistic, must either uproot and destroy Christianity or be destroyed. In some areas, the battle is being joined: Christian schools have by law been forbidden to discriminate on the basis of creed, even in hiring teachers. Thus, an atheistic teacher *must* be hired, if he applies, and allowed to teach unbelief, but a Christian teacher in a state school *cannot* teach Christianity. So runs a "civil rights" argument.

The argument of Lactantius for freedom of worship was somewhat different from Tertullian's plea:

> For religion is to be defended, not by putting to death, but by dying; not by cruelty, but by patient endurance; not by guilt, but by good faith: for the former belongs to evils, but the latter to goods; and it is necessary for that which is good to have place in religion, and not that which is evil. For if you wish to defend religion by bloodshed, and by tortures, and by guilt, it will not long be defended, but will be polluted and profaned. For nothing is so much a matter of free-will as religion; in which, if the mind of the worshipper is disinclined to it, religion is at once taken away, and ceases to exist. The right method therefore is, that you defend religion by patient endurance or by death; in which the preservation of the faith is both pleasing to God Himself, and adds authority to religion.[3]

Lactantius' argument falters becaue he is talking about a persecuted church, not a church charged with providing a structure for society. Moreover, in the persecutions, Rome was fighting for its life as surely as the church was for hers. To compel a theology for the state does mean the prosecution of dissent; to make a theology to the state a matter of indifference means the dissolution of law and society and the triumph of another creed, or of anarchy.

We must not assume that men were indifferent to the idea of liberty of conscience prior to the seventeenth and eighteenth centuries. Their problem was this: how can a state have liberty of conscience for all and yet retain a Christian position? With liberty of conscience, will not the state quickly take on an anti-Christian character and begin the prosecution of Christians? This dilemma is a real one. It has not been answered. The

---

3. Lactantius, "The Divine Institutes," V, xx, in *Ante-Nicene Christian Library*, vol. XXI, p. 340.

Baptist Calvinist answer has prevailed by default: a secular, humanistic state with liberty of conscience for all became the order of the day. Now, however, such humanistic states are dropping their Christian legal heritage, and the next step is the prosecution of Christians as an anti-democratic and discriminatory group, because they divide men in terms of Christ.

Theology is inseparable from civil government. Every civil government, every state, represents a theology in action as surely as does every church. Every citizen must thus live under a theology as a member of the body politic. If that theology of state differs from the theology of the church, sooner or later there will be a clash. A society can be pluralistic only within the context of a given framework, within the limits of a given faith. If its limits are expanded beyond that framework, the theology soon collapses.

In the past, some rulers who were not personally Christian still retained and stressed a Christian theology for the state because any other alternative would have destroyed their authority. Today, the temper and faith of the people is humanistic, and civil governments everywhere are becoming more explicitly humanistic. As a result, pornography today has more legal rights and freedom than Christian schools.

Frederick II, whose rule over the empire was hostile to the claims of Pope Innocent III, and whose implicit faith was humanism, still, in his *Liber Augustalis*, established a Christian foundation for the state in terms of medieval thought. *The Prooemium* to the *Liber Augustalis* reads in part, after citing the fact of man's fallen estate:

> Therefore, by this compelling necessity of things and not less by the inspiration of Divine Providence, princes of nations were created through whom the license of crimes might be corrected. And these judges of life and death for mankind might decide, as executors in some way of Divine Providence, how each man should have fortune, estate, and status. The king of kings and prince of princes demands above all from their hands that they have the strength to render account perfectly of the stewardship committed to them so that they do not permit the Holy Church, the mother of the Christian religion, to be defiled by the secret perfidies of slanderers of the faith. They should protect her from attacks of public enemies by power of the secular sword, and they should, if possible, preserve peace and, after the people have been pacified, justice, which embrace each other like two sisters.[4]

This is a very clear statement of an old thesis. Because God rules as a monarch, so a monarch is needed to restrain sinful man, and to protect the church. But a problem remains: the monarch is no more immune to

---

4. James M. Powell, trans., ed. *The Liber Augustalis, or Constitutions of Melfi Promulgated by the Emperor Frederick II for the Kingdom of Sicily in 1231*, p. 4. Syracuse, New York: Syracuse University Press, 1971.

sin than the people, and this was clearly true of Frederick II. The modern hope has been that the people, by their very numbers, will have sufficient diversity to provide checks and balances against one another. This modern hope is now in process of more than a little decay. Moreover, another fallacy appears in the *Prooemium:* the duty of the state is made the defense of *the church* rather than *the faith,* of the institution rather than the theology. The consequences of this misplaced loyalty have been serious.

What does this mean? Does the state have the right to compel the conscience with respect to theology, but not the church? It is clear that, if the theology of the state is *not* propagated, the state will be rapidly altered to conform to another theology. The United States was *assumed* to be a Christian nation by courts and people up to World War I, but, since the state schools taught humanism, explicitly or implicitly, after World War II humanism began to dominate the courts and to *outlaw* Christianity. The extent to which Christianity has been outlawed is by no means as yet total, but the direction is clearly towards a total outlawing of Christianity as incompatible with democracy. John Dewey, James Bryant Conant, and many others have pointed the way: pure humanism and total democracy are not compatible with a faith so divisive as Christianity, with its heaven and hell, the saved and the lost, and good and evil.

In some respect, the theology of the state *must* be taught, or it will perish. Practically, we cannot hope to enforce a Biblical faith through the state. Theologically, we find ourselves at odds with the older views and are hesitant about compelling a man's conscience. In some such sense, we are all Baptists now. We recognize that Deuteronomy 17:18-20 clearly requires the ruler to govern by the word of God, but how shall we compel him to do so?

As Christians, we know that we *cannot* per se deny the validity of compulsion and coercion. Civil government requires compulsion and coercion to survive. Moreover, Proverbs 22:6 clearly declares, "Train up a child in the way he should go: and when he is old, he will not depart from it." The modern world has seen two extremes in this area. Some insist on no coercion for children and adults alike, a totally permissive society. We are living in terms of this anarchy today to a considerable degree. The other extreme is to say that, because most men are children all their lives, they need controlling all their lives. Both alternatives are ungodly. The permissive society treats all as gods, each free to do as he pleases. The coercive society plays god over its citizens. In a Christian social order, God's law *must* govern, and God alone must be God. All our lives we must reckon with some coercion if we depart from the law, and, from our childhood, we have a measure of freedom under God as His creatures and image bearers. We can never become man's creature, nor can we be free *from* our fellow men. We are only free *under* God, and *together with* the people of God, because we are transferred from the slave humanity of the first Adam to the new and free humanity of the last Adam.

On all sides, the *church* answers have failed. The union of church and state has not been successful, and, however we may prefer it, the separation of church and state has not been successful either.

Perhaps, important as the church is, the key is *not* the church. When we examine the covenant with Israel, we see very clearly another emphasis which is strong in the law, the prophets, the psalms, and in Proverbs:

> Behold, I have taught you statutes and judgments, even as the LORD my God commanded me, that ye should do so in the land whither ye go to possess it.
> Keep therefore and do them; for this is your wisdom and your understanding in the sight of the nations, which shall hear all these statutes, and say, Surely this great nation is a wise and understanding people.
> For what nation is there so great, who hath God so nigh unto them, as the LORD our God is in all things that we call upon him for?
> And what nation is there so great, that hath statutes and judgments so righteous as all this law, which I set before you this day?
> Only take heed to thyself, and keep thy soul diligently, lest thou forget the things which thine eyes have seen, and lest they depart from thy heart all the days of thy life: but teach them thy sons, and thy sons' sons;
> Specially the day that thou stoodest before the LORD thy God in Horeb, when the LORD said unto me, Gather me the people together, and I will make them hear my words, that they may learn to fear me all the days that they shall live upon the earth, and that they may teach their children (Deut. 4:5-10).
> Hear, O Israel: the LORD our God is one LORD:
> And thou shalt love the LORD thy God with all thine heart, and with all thy soul, and with all thy might.
> And these words, which I command thee this day, shall be in thine heart:
> And thou shalt teach them diligently unto thy children, and shalt talk of them when thou sittest in thine house, and when thou walkest by the way, and when thou liest down, and when thou risest up (Deut. 6:4-7).

Very plainly, God here does *not* establish the church as the companion institution to the civil government. The function God requires as *the necessary concomitant* to a godly law order is *teaching*. According to Abramsky at the time of the giving of the law, "The Levites were also assigned instructional responsibilities, and it was they who bore the Ark of the Covenant (Deut. 10:8; 31:9).[5] Moses made clear *this teaching*

---

5. Samuel Abramsky, "Levi," in *Encyclopaedia Judaica*, vol. 11, p. 73. New York: Macmillan, 1971.

*function of the Levites*: "They shall teach Jacob thy judgments, and Israel thy law" (Deut. 33:10). The scattering of Levites throughout Israel, *away* from the sanctuary, makes clear the importance of their teaching function over sanctuary duties. Temple duty had dignity and prestige, but teaching was the normal activity of the Levites. Although, like all other groups, the Levites were at times apostate, their teaching function gave them an advantage. Thus, in the days of Hezekiah, we are told that "the Levites were more upright in heart to sanctify themselves than the priests" (II Chron. 29:34).

How important this teaching function of the Levites was appears from the law of the tithe. According to Numbers 18:21-28, the first tithe was paid to the Levites, who then tithed a tenth of this tenth to the priests. Their nine-tenths did provide for temple music and temple duties by the Levites, but the major portion of their nine-tenths was clearly not involved in worship but in instruction, in providing for all the Levites scattered throughout the land to "teach Jacob thy judgments, and Israel thy law" (Deut. 33:10).

Moreover, in Old Testament times, both the excellent Hebrew schools and the synagogues were developments of the Levitical function, as was the church in the New Testament. The Eastern rite churches and Rome continue the priestly and Temple approach to worship, and hence the closeness of the eucharist to the old sacrificial system, whereas some or most aspects of Protestantism normally have been in continuity with the teaching ministry of the synagogue. The Protestant emphasis must thus in essence be educational, and instruction must be the prelude to true worship.

For the Levitical heritage, true worship must be grounded not only in *faith* but in the *true knowledge of the word of God*. Hence, instruction in the word is fundamental to worship. Thus, speaking in foreign tongues was held to be meaningless unless it was to people who could understand, or with an interpreter present (I Cor. 14:1-28). Knowledge is basic to worship.

This does not mean the downgrading of the church. It is Christ's bride, His body, His household, and much more, according to Scripture. *The church, however, cannot be catholic in the sense of including all men in the nation, regenerate and unregenerate, as was once held. The Christian school can be catholic in this sense: it can teach all children.* The great majority of Irishmen in the U. S. are Protestants, not Catholics, because of the work of Christian schools during their early great migration, and this is true of other peoples. The U. S. Catholic parochial schools began as an answer to both the Protestant Christian schools and the state schools.

Deuteronomy makes abundantly clear that God's intended mainstay of the civil function is the teaching function, and that, without teaching, social order will quickly decay. When God gave the laws to Moses, He declared His requirement that Moses "teach them" (Ex. 24:12. cf. Lev. 10:11).

Thus, we are plainly *required* to have Christian schools to teach every covenant child the word of the Lord and to study every area of life and thought in terms of Christian presuppositions. It is also our duty to "*teach* all nations" (Matt. 28:19), and all the inhabitants thereof. The Great Commission is a commission *to teach* and to *baptize*: it has reference to education as well as to worship, to the establishment of schools as well as churches. *Teaching* is cited before *baptizing*. It is *teaching* which alone can create a godly civil government and a faithful church.

Christian schools were dismantled in this country between 1834 and 1870 because of the hostility, *first*, of Unitarianism and socialism to Christian education, and *second*, the militant opposition of Arminian revivalism. The revivalists held that Christian schools gave a "head" knowledge rather than a "heart" knowledge, and, by their Calvinism, made youth immune to revival experiences, the "jerks," falling, and so on. The disastrous consequences of this dual attack are now with us. The church answers, from Catholic to Baptist to Arminian revivalist, have failed. The *primacy* of *teaching* before church worship and national discipleship are asserted by Scripture. The great missionary requirement of the days ahead is Christian schools and institutions. This is in part Chalcedon's function. It must become a central area of activity for all Christians, and for their tithes, in the days ahead. The word of God through Isaiah is this: "for the earth shall be full of the knowledge of the LORD, as the waters shall cover the sea" (Isa. 11:9). This God will accomplish, with or without us. Those who are not a part of God's purpose had better beware of the consequences of being indifferent to His ways.

The state must have a Christian theology. Christian education can best provide it.

**20**

## VOWS AND OATHS

As we have seen, both church and state have claimed too much: they have arrogated to themselves powers reserved either to God or by God to other orders of life. Moreover, they have been guilty of theft, claiming more than is their own. The state's taxing power has become theft: it is not the God-appointed head tax but is now the equivalent of four and a half tithes. The church has claimed the tithe as her own, refusing to admit that the priest's portion is only one-tenth of the basic tithe (Num. 18:21-28).

One of the areas of arrogant claims to power is the vow and the oath. A central problem also is the confusion of these two very distinct things, and more than a little misunderstanding as a result.

*First* of all with respect to *the oath*, Thomson's definition is to the point; "An oath is the invocation of a curse upon one if he breaks his word (I Sam. xix. 6), or if he is not speaking the truth (Mk. xiv. 71)."[1] In *The Institutes of Biblical Law*, we have seen that, where the truth is being extracted from us for evil purposes, for the commission of a crime, we are under no obligation to tell the truth. To tell the truth and help an evil-doer in the commission of a crime is to become an accessory to it.[2] Moreover, another factor appears in our Lord's declaration in Matthew 5:33-37:

> Again, we have heard that it hath been said by them of old time, Thou shalt not forswear thyself, but shalt perform unto the Lord thine oaths:
> But I say unto you, Swear not at all: neither by heaven; for it is God's throne
> Nor by the earth; for it is his footstool: neither by Jerusalem; for it is the city of the great King.
> Neither shalt thou swear by thy head, because thou canst not make one hair white or black.
> But let your communication be, Yea, yea; Nay, nay: for whatsoever is more than these cometh of evil.

Thomson's comment on this is not admissible, since it is dispensational:

---

1. J. G. S. S. Thomson, "Oath," in J. D. Douglas, ed.: *The New Bible Dioctionary*, p. 902. Grand Rapids: Eerdmans (1962) 1973.
2. See R. J. Rushdoony: *The Institutes of Biblical Law*, pp. 542-549, 838-843. Nutley, N. J.: The Craig Press, 1973.

"In the kingdom of God oaths will finally become unnecessary (Matt. 5: 34-37)."[3] There is no warrant in the text for postponing any obedience to our Lord's words. Moreover, in James 5:12, we have this commandment restated: "But above all things, my brethren, swear not, neither by heaven, neither by the earth, neither by any other oath: but let your yea be yea; and your nay, nay; lest ye fall into condemnation." The word *communication* in Matthew 5:37 has reference to a spoken word, to conversation, and hence it is clear that oaths are forbidden insofar as conversation is concerned. They are reserved for formal, legal testimony. Christ Himself testified under oath (Matt. 26:63-64). St. Paul makes a religious use of the oath in his epistles, to confirm his word to the churches (Rom. 1:9; I Cor. 15:31; II Cor. 1:23; Gal. 1:20; Phil. 1:8), to whom he wrote as the apostle of Christ. What is thus clearly forbidden by our Lord is the use of oaths in conversation. Such oaths violate the third commandment: they take the name of the Lord in vain (Ex. 20:7). Vain oaths were condemned by Christ (Matt. 23:16-24):

> Woe unto you, ye blind guides, which say, Whosoever shall swear by the temple, it is nothing; but whosoever shall swear by the gold of the temple, he is a debtor!
> Ye fools and blind: for whether is greater, the gold, or the temple that sanctifieth the gold?
> And, Whosoever shall swear by the altar, it is nothing; but whosoever sweareth by the gift that is upon it, he is guilty.
> Ye fools and blind: for whether is greater, the gift, or the altar that sanctifieth the gift?
> Whoso therefore shall swear by the altar, sweareth by it, and by all things thereon.
> And whoso shall swear by the temple, sweareth by it, and by him that dwelleth therein.
> And he that shall swear by heaven, sweareth by the throne of God, and by him that sitteth thereon.
> Woe unto you, scribes and Pharisees, hypocrites! for ye pay tithe of mint and anise and cummin, and have omitted the weightier matters of the law, judgment, mercy and faith: these ought ye to have done, and not to leave the other undone.
> Ye blind guides, which strain at a gnat, and swallow a camel (Matt. 23:16-24).

Such vain swearing puts the emphasis on man and man's "integrity" rather than on God and the certainty of His curse for false swearing. The emphasis in the examples cited by our Lord of the casuistry of the Pharisees is on *man's gift, not God's rule and realm*: on the gold, not the temple; on the gift brought by man to the altar, rather than the altar itself; on the heavens generally, not God directly, so that God is avoided and an aspect of creation is stressed. The examples of false tithing are

---

3. Thompson, *op. cit.* p. 902.

brought in to illustrate a basic premise in such false swearing. In Deuteronomy 12:17, corn, wine, and oil are specified as subject to the law of the tithe, i.e., the field crops, not the garden products like mint, anise, and cummin. What we have is thus what Ellicott termed "the substitution of the lower for the higher."[4] The result is a false holiness, one which claims great sensitivity because it tithes mint and swears by the gift on the altar, but is in reality only straining at gnats to gain a reputation for sanctity while carelessly swallowing camels, i.e., disregarding the weightier matters of the law.

The legitimate oath thus is to serve godly, not ungodly purposes, is restricted to civil and ecclesiastical purposes, and must be in the name of God. The third commandment clearly requires us to take the oath seriously (Ex. 20:7). Leviticus 19:12 declares, "And ye shall not swear by my name falsely, neither shalt thou profane the name of thy God: I am the LORD." The second half of this statement restates the first half, but not in mere repetition, but by development. A false oath is forbidden where God's name is involved. We should note that the law reads "by my name." The modern oath is godless: the court requires, in many states, that we swear "to tell the truth, the whole truth, and nothing but the truth," merely on our affirmation and the court's demand. Such a court has placed itself and its oaths outside of God, and they are thus lies to begin with. The Christian, in such a court, does swear, whether the court language includes it or not, by God, not by man, because he can recognize no other oath as anything but blasphemy. On the other hand, a godless court which still retains God in its oath is also guilty of taking the Lord's name in vain. An oath is God-centered: if state and/or church depart from God, their use of the oath in any way is profanity. They do not believe in God's judgment or curse, only in man's and their use of the oath is thus false usage.

The godless oath is a personal affirmation in the name of the state. It is swearing by a false god, clearly forbidden in Scripture (Jer. 12:16; Amos 8:14).

Perjury required the same penalty as in the case involved; the penalty against the accused would be the penalty against the false witness for or against him (Deut. 19:16-21).

*Second*, whereas the oath is in the name of God *to an agency* of justice established by God, the vow is directly *to God*. Thus, neither oaths nor vows are to individuals. Our speech to men must be yea, yea, and nay, nay, straightforward and truthful. Because we are servants of God, we cannot be the servants of men. We cannot bind ourselves to men by a careless word. To illustrate: I once urged a man not to get involved in a situtation where trouble between myself and another man was developing.

---

4. C. J. Ellicott, *op. cit.*, VI, 142.

I felt it was none of his concern to make a stand on either side. He promised to stay out, but subsequently changed his mind for reasons best known to himself and stood against me. He was distressed at breaking his word to me and went to great lengths to justify himself. My opinion was that no such self-justification was needed: I had no power to bind him, nor any right to, nor did I ask, nor could I ask, for an unconditional commitment. Only God can require an unconditional commitment from us, and even God puts limitations on our power to commit ourselves by a vow.

In Numbers 30:1-16, this is very clear. We have here case law, cases which illustrate a general premise by applying it to a concrete situation. A vow is a pledge to perform certain things (Gen. 28:20-22), or to abstain from certain things (Ps. 132:2-5), either in return for God's blessing (Num. 21:1-3), or in devotion to God (Ps. 22:25). *First* of all, in making a vow to God, a man "shall not break his word, he shall do according to all that proceedeth out of his mouth" (Num. 30:1-2). This unconditional and binding vow can only be vowed by a free man who is not subject to any authority with power to command him contrary to his vow. This means, *second*, that persons in dependent positions cannot make binding vows if the authority over them disallows the vow. This is illustrated in four cases involving women: a), an unmarried woman, living with her family and thus under her father's authority; b), an unmarried woman who makes a vow but marries before she can keep her vow; c), a widow or a divorced woman; and d), a married woman. The daughter's vow is binding if the father, on hearing it, is silent and does not disallow it; if he disallows the vow, it is not in force. The same applies to the vow of the married woman, if her husband's position is favorable or unfavorable to her vow. When a young woman marries, the husband can allow or disallow her vow made while single, but again only at the time he hears of it, not at a later date. Every vow of a divorced woman or of a widow is binding, because they are not under authority.

Thus, God will not allow a vow to be used to create disunity or an escape from authority within a family.

The vow cannot be a promise to give God what is already His due, such as the tithe (Lev. 27:26). No tax due to God is thus a gift to Him: it is already His rightful possession. Moreover, nothing which is the income of sin can be used to pay a vow: "Thou shalt not bring the hire of a whore, or the price of a dog (a homosexual), into the house of the LORD thy God for any vow: for even both these are abomination unto the LORD thy God" (Deut. 23:18).

Moreover, to give God a substitute and blemished gift for the gift vowed is to incur His curse (Mal. 3: 1-13). No vow can be used to deceive God, nor to make God's law null and void. As our Lord made clear, no vow or gift to God can nullify the requirements of the law:

> He answered and said unto them, Well hath Esaias prophesied of you hypocrites, as it is written, This people honoureth me with their lips, but their heart is far from me.
> Howbeit in vain do they worship me, teaching for doctrines the commandments of men.
> For laying aside the commandment of God, ye hold the tradition of men, as the washing of pots and cups; and many other such like things do ye.
> And he said unto them, Full well ye reject the commandment of God, that ye may keep your own tradition.
> For Moses said, Honour thy father and thy mother; and, Whoso curseth father or mother, let him die the death:
> But ye say, If a man shall say to his father or mother, It is Corban, that is to say, a gift, by whatsoever thou mightest be profited by me; he shall be free.
> And ye suffer him no more to do ought for his father or his mother:
> Making the word of God of none effect through your tradition, which ye have delivered: and many such like things do you (Mark 7:6-13).

For any man to evade his duty to his parents by giving instead to the sanctuary was in God's sight a cursing of his parents and a flagrant denial of God's law. It is thus clearly condemned. Vows do not set aside the law. Marriage vows to God are thus *not* unconditional: they are subject to the law of God, and violations of God's law by one partner frees the other (Deut. 24:1-4; Matt. 19:3-9; I Cor. 7:10-15).

There is no special virtue in vowing, nor in abstaining from vows:

> When thou shalt vow a vow unto the LORD thy God, thou shalt not slack to pay it: for the LORD thy God will surely require it of thee; and it would be sin in thee.
> But if thou shalt forbear to vow, it shall be no sin in thee.
> That which is gone out of thy lips thou shalt keep and perform; even a freewill offering, according as thou hast vowed unto the LORD thy God, which thou hast promised with thy mouth (Deut. 23:21-23).

The vow made by a free person is binding before God and must be paid.

Because oaths are made in the name of God to a God-ordained agency, and because vows are made directly to God, neither church nor state can regard either as in any way binding men to them rather than to God's law. No disobedient and faithless church can regard its clergy and laity as bound to loyalty to the institution, and no lawless state can bind the conscience of man apart from the word of God. The framework of reference in oaths and vows cannot be humanistic.

Clearly, vows are not unconditional, nor are oaths permitted unless they are God-centered. No vow can be turned into a means of evading God's law, or of setting aside God-ordained human authority in its legitimate claims. The oath invokes a curse for breaking one's word or for deceit; the vow also invokes a curse on failure to render unto God what has been promised Him. The essence of a *curse* is that it is a judgment on sin. No oath or vow can thus be used to further a sin, to set aside a godly authority, or to evade a godly responsibility. The purpose of the oath and the vow is to further the Kingdom of God and His righteousness, never to hinder it.

In brief, a man's word must be bigger than a man, i.e., it must have a framework of reference greater than man, marriage, church, or state. Its framework must be the Kingdom of God and His righteousness.

**21**

## THE CURSE

It is necessary now to examine more carefully the meaning of a *curse* in the Bible. The curse is essentially God's act against sin and His judgment concerning it. A valid curse by man is man's invocation of God's written and declared judgment against sin, either against the enemies of God, or against one's own person if he departs from his oath.

God's curse is, *first*, His denunciation of all sin (Deut. 29:19-20; Num. 5:21, 23). Sin is enmity against God, a separation from God and His law, and it therefore incurs God's enmity and anger. *Second*, God's curse is not only His denunciation of sin but His judgment of it, His active condemnation of the person of the sinner (Num. 5:22, 24, 27; Isa. 24:6). *Third*, the man under judgment is himself called a curse (Num. 5:21, 27; Jer. 29:18). The supreme example of this was Jesus Christ, who "hath redeemed us from the curse of the law, being made a curse for us" (Gal. 3:13).

Behind God's curse stands the power of God, so that God's curse is not simply words but the power of His law and judgment at work. Because God's law is life to the faithful (Ezek. 20:11), it is by the same token the separation from life to judgment of the ungodly. Thus, Scripture calls the law *life*, but it also calls it a *curse* (Zech. 5:3). "For as many as are of the works of the law are under the curse: for it is written, Cursed is every one that continueth not in all things which are written in the book of the law to do them" (Gal. 3:10). Thus, those who seek justification by the law are, like all violators of the law, under its curse.

When a man crosses the boundary of Mexico, he is under Mexican law. When a man sins, he crosses the boundary into the world of the curse, and his own words and acts pronounce his own curse. God made this clear to Ahab through a prophet. When Ahab allowed the defeated king of Syria to leave in peace, a case of leniency by one evil man to another, a prophet, pretending to be a soldier who had let a prisoner escape for whom he had pledged his life, appeared before Ahab. Ahab declared him worthy of death. The prophet made clear to Ahab at once that Ahab had pronounced his own judgment, and the cause of it. "Thus saith the LORD, Because thou hast let go out of thy hand a man whom I appointed to utter destruction, therefore thy life shall go for his life, and thy people for his people" (I Kings 20:42). An example of this same self-condemnation is Numbers 5:22. Again, David condemned himself by his own words when the prophet Nathan used the parable of the rich man and poor man to have David judge his own sin (II Sam. 12:1-14).

This judgment of sin, this curse that leaps out against the sinner when he crosses the boundary, is vividly described in Genesis 4:7, God's counsel to Cain: "If thou doest well, shalt thou not be accepted? and if thou doest not well, sin lieth at the door. And unto thee shall be his desire, and thou shalt rule over him." The second half of this verse is a difficult one: it can mean, *first*, sins desire is for you, but you must master sin, or, *second*, if you obey, then his (Abel's) desire and regard will be towards you, and you shall recover your right of primogeniture and rule over him.

It is the first half of the verse which concerns us. If Cain does not obey God, sin lies, crouching like a beast of prey at the door, ready to pounce on him. The framework of reference with regard to the curse is like that of *the hue and cry*, the mandatory pursuit of a criminal by all men within sound of the command. The difference here is that men, in *the hue and cry*, act *after* the fact of the crime. In the curse, it awaits us *before* the commission of sin like a crouched beast at the door. If we sin, it is there to pounce on us; if we believe and obey, instead of the curse, there is a blessing. Moreover, as Deuteronomy 28:2, 15 makes clear, the blessings are irresistible where men believe and obey, and the curses irresistible when men disobey God.[1]

There is still another important aspect. Curses and blessings are spoken of in Scripture as a man's *wages* or *hire*. Scripture is both emphatic in declaring that the reward and blessings we receive from God are all of grace, and yet equally clear that, when the godly obey Him, they receive wages for their services. Thus, in Genesis 15:1, God declares to Abram, "Fear not, Abram: I am thy shield, and thy exceeding great reward." The Hebrew word translated as *reward* is *sakar*, often translated as *wage*. The same word appears in Numbers 18:31 concerning the Levites' portion. It appears also in Psalms 127:3, where children, "the fruit of the womb," are cited as one kind of reward or wage from God. In Isaiah 40:10, we are told, "Behold, the Lord GOD will come with strong hand, and his arm shall rule for him: behold, his reward is with him, and his work before him." Again, in Isaiah 62:11, we have *reward* or *wage* and *salvation* linked together: "Behold, the LORD hath proclaimed unto the end of the world, Say ye to the daughter of Zion, Behold, thy salvation cometh; behold, his reward is with him, and his work before him."

Still another Hebrew word for *wage, maskoreth*, translated as *reward*,

---

1. See R. J. Rushdoony: *Institutes of Biblical Law*, p. 463f. for hue and cry; pp. 660-664 for irresistible curses and blessings.

appears in Ruth 2:12, where Boaz declares, "The LORD recompense thy work, and a full reward be given thee of the LORD God of Israel, under whose wings thou art come to trust."

Many other instances where godly conduct or obedience is spoken of as having a reward or wage from God can be cited. On the other hand, we must at all times see the wage, *not as man's right, but as God's grace.* "So likewise ye, when ye shall have done all those things which are commanded you, say, We are unprofitable servants: we have done that which was our duty to do" (Luke 17:10). On the other hand, the curse is at all times the just and due wage for sin.

Because sin is not only death but separation from God's law, it has its own law, Moloch worship, statism, moral anarchy, and much more. God declared through Ezekiel (20:25), "Wherefore I gave them also statutes that were not good, and judgments whereby they should not live," speaking of their profane society and their idolatrous laws. The law of sin is death. Man cannot live by it. To be under the curse of God is thus to be under humanistic laws by which man cannot live, whereas when men believe and obey God, God's law is a blessing to them: God says of His statutes and judgments, "if a man do, he shall even live in them" (Ezek. 20:13).

## 22

## CAPITALIZATION AND THE TWO BASIC INSTITUTIONS

We find in Scripture two institutions of very great symbolic and typical significance yet with very limited and carefully circumscribed powers. These are church and state. The state is the ministry of justice (Rom. 13:1-7), and it very clearly has thus a very important function. Justice being basic to the Kingdom of God, the state's function is thus an obviously important one. Moreover, the analogy between the state as a realm, dominion, or kingdom and the Kingdom of God is a very obvious one also, although the state can *never* be identified as *the* Kingdom of God, but, like the church, as only an aspect thereof.

God, however, *very severely* limits the powers and the scope of the state by restricting its taxing power to the head or poll tax, whose purpose is the civil covering, atonement, or protection of society (Ex. 30:11-16). Beyond this, apart from possibly some fines, the state has no taxing power and is thus given, as its legitimate area, a severely limited field of activity. The modern state, by exacting, directly and indirectly, taxes on various levels equal to about 45 percent of the citizen's income, is thus illegitimate, lawless, and godless. The state in Scripture thus has an important meaning but a restricted and secondary function.

This is no less true of the church. Whereas the state is the ministry of justice, the church is the ministry of grace. As such, the ministry of the word of grace is its essential function. The response of man to that word of grace is in part *worship*, and worship thus constitutes a central aspect of the life of the church. Worship wanes as the word of grace is adulterated and neglected, because worship is the grateful response of the people of grace. The church is the body of Christ, and its meaning is one of very profound and far-reaching implications, but again, as with the state, Scripture severely restricts its powers and scope.

As we have previously noted, Numbers 18:21-28 makes clear that only one-tenth of the tithe went for worship, to the priests, whereas nine-tenths went to the Levites, whose function was instruction essentially. Only a handful of Levites were engaged in temple service, as against the vast numbers whose work was instruction (Deut. 33:10). At best, the levitical contribution to worship equalled another one-tenth of the tithe, meaning that eight-tenths of the tithe went towards instruction.

Thus, in Scripture church and state both have a severely limited scope of power while an important meaning. In the New Testament, the word of God as it appears in the epistles is addressed often to "the saints," and sometimes to the "church." Clearly, the *saints* includes the church, but it goes beyond the ecclesiastical boundaries. The Corinthian epistles are addressed to "the church of God which is in Corinth" (I Cor. 1:2; II Cor. 1:1), because a church problem is central to St. Paul's concern therein. This is true also of the epistle to the Galatians (Gal. 1:2), but not of Ephesians, Colossians, and other epistles, although the church is in mind in these epistles, as in Philippians 1:1. The Thessalonian epistles are again directly addressed to the church there. The *saints* are the Christian community, inclusive of the church but more than the church.

The activities of these *saints*, the early Christian community, included a wide variety of activities: not only churches in homes, but study groups in homes, a great deal of charity through the church and apart from the church, refuges for abandoned children, hospitality for strangers, hospitals by the end of the fourth century, and much more. While there is no question that the power of the church over these activities grew steadily, it is also apparent that there was earlier a difference, an inter-penetration of activities and institutions rather than a centralized jurisdiction.

The problem in history has been the unhappy sacramentalization of church and state. The Old Testament anointing of king and high priest pointed to their roles as types of Christ, and in the New Testament their ministries in Christ are stressed. The sacrament, however, is *with Christ*, not with the institution. We are "baptized into Jesus Christ" (Rom. 6:3; Gal. 3:27), not into the church; our baptism is administered by the church, but it is into Christ. Similarly, communion sets forth, not that we are *one body* with the church but with Christ and with one another in Christ.

Increasingly, the modern state is a sacramental state: it seeks to make the people one *body* in itself, to bring them together into peace and unity by statist acts of law and coercion. The result is the destruction of the people by the Moloch state.

Similarly, the church sees itself as the sacramental body and preempts Christ's role. Communion is thought of as a church rite rather than Christ's ordinance. In the New Testament, communion is a potluck dinner of people who worked during the day and could meet only late at night. The Lord's Supper was instituted as the true continuation of the Old Testament Passover, the celebration of Israel's redemption by the blood of the lamb. The Passover was and is a family meal, and the Lord's Supper is inclusive of the family of Christ. It is spoken of as a "feast of charity" or "love feast" in Jude 12 and II Peter 2:13. This feast celebrated Christ's redemption of His people by His atoning death and resurrection. Because of Christ, their second Adam and their re-creator, the people of God are one family in Him. There is no true sacrament without "unfeigned love of the brethren" (I Peter 1:22), which is the mark of family members (Rom. 8:29; Heb. 2:11; I John 3:14; Rom. 12:10; I Thess. 4:9; Heb. 13:1; II Peter 1:7, etc.). No one can rightly take communion without a love of Christ and a love of the brethren. Communion celebrates a common life in Christ, and it can never be reduced to a rite, although it cannot be separated from it. As against an empty rite, Christian fellowship in Christ's calling, around a table, is closer to the meaning of the sacrament.

The first Passover, moreover, was also the first Sabbath of Israel, and it celebrated *God's redemptive work*, and the reestablishment of Israel, about to leave for the Promised Land, in God's calling to exercise dominion and to subdue the earth. Shortly thereafter, the law was given to enable them thereby to exercise dominion in God's appointed way. The Sabbath *is inseparable from work*: it celebrates rest in God's efficacious work and our effectual work in Him (I Cor. 15:58). *Wherever the theological meaning of God's work and man's work is diminished, the meaning of the Sabbath diminishes.*

But church and state are not productive agencies. Rather, their essential function lies elsewhere. The state is a protective agency whose function is to maintain a just *order*, to insure *restitution* for civil wrongs, and to *protect* the people from external and internal enemies. The Westminster Confession, ch. XXV, 111, says of the church,

> Unto this catholic visible Church Christ hath given the ministry, oracles, and ordinances of God, for the gathering and perfecting of the saints, in this life, to the end of the world: and doth, by His own presence and Spirit, according to His promise, make them effectual thereunto.

The church's function is *protection and nurture* by means of its ordained ministry. Both church and state thus have important and necessary functions, but they are not *productive* ones.

It will appear to some that an emphasis on *production* is a capitalistic reading of the faith. It must be held, however, that modern capitalism is an apostate version of the creation mandate which, for all its importance, is withering because it has lost its Christian function. Man, set to work by God in a new creation in Adam, and set to work in a fallen creation by Christ, the last Adam, must conquer every aspect of that creation and make it productive in terms of God's purpose. All work, capitalistic, socialistic, and other is under the curse apart from Christ. Only in Christ can work be effectually and permanently productive, with consequences for eternity.

In pagan antiquity, cultures, beyond a certain point, faded rapidly, because their productivity was destroyed by state and temple. Capitalization was wiped out or prevented by the claims of state and temple. The ethnologist Soustelle, in studying the remnants of the Maya in Mexico, describes their religion. "All in all, religion weighs heavily on the daily life of a Lacandon." It is a difficult struggle for him to wrest a living from the jungle, and he lives very meagerly. Yet he must work to take better care of his gods than of himself. "In short, the Indian, who already has so much difficulty in obtaining and producing what is strictly necessary for himself and his family, forces himself to work almost as hard again in order to serve his gods."[1] More cultures than the Mayan have collapsed under the burden of state and temple.

Today, our society is being similarly decapitalized. The state takes about 45 percent of a man's income, and the church claims to be the legitimate repository of the tithe and claims 10 percent or more. With some sects, it runs up to 30 percent. As a result, what remains is usually only sufficient to maintain the family in its living expenses, not to recapitalize the family and society. Whenever and wherever church and state (or temple) reach this point, civilization begins to decapitalize and crumble. God's ordination is a very modest head tax for the state, and a tenth of a tithe, one percent of one's income, for the church. To go beyond this is to begin digging the grave of a civilization.

In Revelation 13, we have the anti-Christian church and state presented as two beasts who are the destroyers of mankind. Anti-Christianity, however, is more than avowed hostility: it includes all departures from God's word, including claims to powers which do not belong to church and state.

Moloch worship is forbidden in Leviticus 18:21 and 20:2-5; Moloch means *king*. Moloch worship divinized the state and made the state man's visible god. When the state required it, children had to be sacrificed to the state, but, under any circumstance, they belonged to the state. Baal worship similarly asserted the lordship of the state. Moloch worhip thus consumed man and society in the blasphemous, idolatrous, and non-productive worship of the state.

In Scripture, centrality of function is given to *the family* and *to instruction*. To the Levites, as we have seen, the major portion of the regular tithe was given, so that instruction was regarded as more important for society than church or state in God's tax laws. The function of instruction is the theological and intellectual capitalization of a society, and there can be no other capitalization if a society is lacking in the capital of sound faith and knowledge. Instruction is thus highly productive. The capture and corruption of schools is a sure means to the decapitalization and destruction of any society. Thus, while *worship* has

---

1. Jacques Soustelle: *The Four Suns*, p. 39f. E. Ross, trans. London: Andre Deutch, 1971.

a very high place in God's plan, priority belongs to *instruction*. The school is more essential to Christian society than the church, although both are necessary institutions.

The family, as we have seen, is the most powerful institution in society, controlling as it does, in terms of Biblical law, the three key areas of society, children, property, and inheritance. It is in addition the major welfare agency of all history with its care of old and young, relatives and friends, and its assistance to members of the "nuclear" family. The family too has its place in the tithe. Waller called attention to a curious fact about the tithes. The first tithe, Numbers 18:21, 26, to the Levites and to the priests, was not considered sacred by the Talmud and Jewish commentators. On the other hand, the tithes of Deuteronomy 14:22-28 and Deuteronomy 26:12-15 were "regarded as a holy thing."[2] The family's rejoicing before the Lord, and its sharing of their bounty in the third and sixth years with the Levites, the fatherless, and the poor, were basic to the holy community, to love of the brethren, and unity in the Lord. Such a tithe was productive not only of rest and refreshing to God's people, to enable them to work more joyfully, but also of godly community. The family is the religious, social, and productive unit; it is also the key institution of sociey. As a result, it must strengthen itself by holy rest and by holy communion with the Levites and the needy, to realize more closely the meaning of the Passover (and communion).

The family and the school thus, with their functions and their portion of the tithes, are instrumental in developing communion and vocation. Society moves forward and is capitalized religiously, intellectually, and materially when the family and instruction are given their due. Where church and state monopolize man's income, there is a radical decapitalization. If today only a segment of the Christian population gave eight percent of their first tithes to instruction, to Christian schools, colleges, educational missions and foundations, and to godly scholarship, the recapitalization of faith and ideas would be considerable. God's legal provisions are not accidental nor haphazard. They have a major function in God's plan for the conquest of men and nations. To neglect them is to surrender the future.

---

2. C. H. Waller, in "Deuteronomy," in Ellicott, *op. cit.*, II 45.

## 23

## COMMUNION AND COMMUNITY

The relation of the Lord's Table to the life of society is badly neglected in our time, because communion has been reduced to a ritual which is too often a parody of its meaning.

To understand communion, we must recognize its Old Testament roots: it is the Christian passover. "Christ our passover is sacrificed for us: Therefore let us keep the feast, not with old leaven, neither with the leaven of malice and wickedness; but with the unleavened bread of sincerity and truth" (I Cor. 5:7-8).

St. Paul speaks of the Christian passover as a "feast"; he then condemns as violations of this feast fornication (I Cor. 5:9). In I Corinthians 10:1-17, he discusses both baptism and communion, and then he cites violations of Christian communion (I Cor. 10:18-33, I Cor. 11:1-34). These violations include idolatry, insubordination by wives and women who seek to assume dominion, disunity among believers, greed and gluttony, and like offenses. These are offenses not only against God, but, in the context cited, *against community*.

The Old Testament passover was a family meal, and the youngest male child who was able to speak asked the question concerning its meaning; the father as priest then declared the meaning of God's redemption (Ex. 13:1-16). The passover was a *family sacrament*. This is very definitely an aspect of the Christian passover: believers are repeatedly spoken of as the family of Christ or in analogous terms. We are, says St. Paul, no more strangers and foreigners but fellow citizens "of the household of God" (Eph. 2:19). We are commanded to "do good unto all men, especially unto them who are of the household of faith" (Gal. 6:10).

What does this involve? In the law, the family has very far-reaching responsibilities: care of the young, care of the old, relief to its needy relatives, hospitality to one's kin, instruction, i.e., teaching one's children both a trade and the law, and much more. Everything in the New Testament points to the fact that these same obligations are *binding* on both the Christian family *and* the Christian community, the larger family of faith. From its very inception, the church in Jerusalem assumed these responsibilities, and one of its first problems was the complaint of "Grecians against the Hebrews, because their widows were neglected in the daily ministration" (Acts 6:1). The result was the creation of an order of deacons to supervise this task, so that the twelve apostles could "give ourselves continually to prayer, and to the ministry of the word" (Acts 6:4). As the Christian community grew across the empire, its family activities also grew, and they were no longer limited to the deacons but started to be the responsibility of all. The community cared for its sick, needy, and imprisoned members (Matt. 25:34-40); it was forbidden to help the shiftless: "if any would not work, neither should he eat" (II Thess. 3:10).

In the ancient Near East, a concern for the protection of widows and orphans against injustice and their care was regarded as *a royal virtue*.[1] Widows, for example, were to be honored and relieved, according to the Old Testament (Ex. 22:22; Deut. 14:29; 24:17; Job 29:13; Isa. 1:17; Jer. 7:6, etc.). These same texts refer also to the care of the fatherless. The people of God were to be a royal people (Rev. 1:6), a point implicit in all of Scripture. In the New Testament, we find that Dorcas was "full of good works and almsdeeds," and this included the care of many widows (Acts 9:36, 39); Dorcas did this, not under church direction, but as one member of Christ's family aiding another. St. Paul's words are emphatic: "Honour widows that are widows indeed" (I Tim. 5:3). The Greek word for "honour" is *time*, value, pay a price or sum. This means in I Timothy 5:17 that presbyters who rule well should receive "double honour" or pay; here it means that widows without children or nephews in the faith to support them (I Tim. 5:4) are to be supported by the Christian community. In fact, James says, "Pure religion and undefiled before God and the Father is this, To visit the fatherless and widows in their affliction, and to keep himself unspotted from the world" (James 1:27). The word *visit* in Greek is a form of *episkopeo*, and it means to visit with help, to care for, to exercise oversight.

Turning now to St. Paul's account of reprobate communion-taking, what he cites as instances thereof are violations of community. People came together to worship on the *evening* of the first day of the week; Sunday was then a work-day for all. They brought their evening meals with them. Instead of a sharing, there was often a greedy hoarding of one's food from those who had less. There were "divisions" among the members (I Cor. 11:18). Paul then, as he gives the words of institution of the Lord's Supper (I Cor. 11:23-26), goes on to declare:

> Wherefore whosoever shall eat this bread, and drink this cup of the Lord, unworthily, shall be guilty of the body and blood of the Lord.
> But let a man examine himself, and so let him eat of that bread, and drink of that cup.
> For he that eateth and drinketh unworthily, eateth and drinketh damnation to himself, not discerning the Lord's body.

1. Helmer Ringgren: *Religions of the Ancient Near East*, p. 39. Philadelphia: Westminster Press, 1973.

For this cause many are weak and sickly among you, and many sleep.
For if we would judge ourselves, we should not be judged.
But when we are judged, we are chastened of the Lord, that we
should not be condemned with the world.
Wherefore, my brethren, when ye come together to eat, tarry one for
another.
And if any man hunger, let him eat at home; that ye come not
together unto condemnation. And the rest will I set in order when I
come (I Cor. 11:27-34).

"Not discerning the Lord's body" can refer to theological heresy, failure
to follow the Biblical doctrines concerning our Lord's life, work, atoning
death, and resurrection. St. Paul does refer to "heresy" in I Corinthians
11:19. All heresy is a refusal to discern the Lord's body, but this refusal
can be both theological and practical; it can be with respect to doctrine
and also community. Clearly, St. Paul here has this failure with respect
to community essentially in mind: they are not a family. They do not see
Christ's body as inclusive of all true believers and hence reject others and
refuse to share their bounty with them (I Cor. 11:21). Thus, *where the
church fails to be a community, and where any member thereof is
negligent of his family responsibilities to other Christians, there the body
of Christ is not discerned, and communion is taken unto damnation.*

A concrete instance will illustrate this fact: in a denomination, far
more faithful than most, a ministerial candidate, in his regular report to
his church and presbytery, wrote of his serious problems; his wife was ill,
their funds low from medical and other bills, and their infant child had
died. Neither help nor a single letter of sympathy were forthcoming.
However, when he returned as a young minister, theological knives were
sharpened on this theologically orthodox youth by men anxious to prove
their righteousness and orthodoxy by means of a nasty examination. Can
such people partake of communion, or serve it, except blasphemously?
They refuse to discern *the Lord's body.* Theologically, they claim to
know the *Lord* as few others; *the Lord's body,* His people, they refuse to
discern. They stand in danger of hearing the Lord declare,

Then shall he say also unto them on the left hand, Depart from me,
ye cursed, into everlasting fire, prepared for the devil and his angels:
For I was an hungred, and ye gave me no meat: I was thirsty, and ye
gave me no drink:
I was a stranger, and ye took me not in: naked, and ye clothed me
not: sick, and in prison, and ye visited me not.
Then shall they also answer him, saying, Lord, when saw we thee an
hungred, or athirst, or a stranger, or naked, or sick, or in prison, and
did not minister unto thee?
Then shall he answer them, saying, Verily I say unto you, Inasmuch
as ye did it not to one of the least of these, ye did it not to me.
And these shall go away into everlasting punishment: but the
righteous into life eternal (Matt. 25:41-46).

In the parable, no strictly doctrinal error is charged against the reprobate: they are outwardly orthodox. Their failure to discern the Lord's body, however, means also their failure to discern the Lord.

Today, in one Christian group after another, there are sick and elderly people who are neglected. Their shopping and housecleaning need to be done: there is a practical way of discerning the Lord's body which goes daily neglected.

In Calvin's last communion, his prayer of invocation balances forgiveness of sins with Christian action:

Thus make us true partakers of the new and everlasting testament, which is the covenant of grace. And thus assure us of thy willingness ever to be our gracious Father; *not imputing unto us our sins, but that we may magnify thy name by our words and works,* providing us as thy beloved children and heirs with all things necessary for our good.[2]

Forgiveness of sins has as its positive result the fruit of godly words and works, godly action.

In the exhortation after the words of institution, I Corinthians 11:23-30, Calvin declared in part:

We have heard, brethren, in what manner our LORD celebrated the Supper among his disciples; whence we see that strangers, who are not of the company of the faithful, may not approach it. Wherefore, in obedience to this rule, and in the name and by the authority of our Lord JESUS CHRIST, I excommunicate all idolaters, blasphemers, despisers of GOD, heretics, and all who form sects apart, to break the unity of the Church; all perjurers, all who are rebellious against fathers and mothers, and other superiors, all who are seditious, contentious, quarrelsome, injurious, adulterers, fornicators, thieves, misers, ravishers, drunkards, gluttons, and all others who lead scandalous lives; warning them that they abstain from this Table, lest they pollute and contaminate the sacred food which our Lord JESUS CHRIST giveth only to his faithful servants.

Therefore, according to the exhortation of St. Paul, let each of you examine and prove his own conscience, to know whether he have true repentance of his sins, and sorrow for them; desiring henceforth to lead a holy and godly life; *above all, whether he putteth his whole trust in GOD's mercy, and seeketh his whole salvation in JESUS CHRIST; and renouncing all enmity and malice, doth truly and honestly purpose to live in harmony and brotherly love with his neighbour.*[3]

In the service of Holy Communion in *The Book of Common Prayer* (which shows the influence of Bertram of Corbie on the English reformers), the sentences preceding the deacon's offering strongly

2. Charles W. Baird: *The Presbyterian Liturgies*, p. 51. Grand Rapids, Mich.: Baker Book House, 1957.
3. *Ibid.*, p. 53f.

emphasize the requirement of help to fellow members of the Lord's body. Such verses as Galatians 6:10; Hebrews 6:10; 13:16; I John 3:17; Matthew 25:40, and others are cited for use at this time.

The issues were stated more theologically by Aelfric, before the Norman Conquest, in his Paschal Homily:

> We oughte also to consyder diligently how that the holy housell is both Christes body, and the body of all faythfull men, after ghostly mystere. As the wyse Augustine sayeth of it: Yf ye will understand of Christes body, heare the apostle Paule thuse speaking: Ye truly be Christes body and his members. Nowe is your mysterye sett on Godes table; and ye receyve your mysterye to that whiche ye your sulves be. Be that whiche ye see on the alter, and receive that whiche ye your selves be. Agayn, the Apostle Paule sayth by it: we manye be one bread, and one bodye. Understand nowe, and rejoyce; many be one bread, and one body in Christ. He is our head, and we be his limmes.[4]

Aelfric's latter reference is to I Corinthians 10:16-17:

> The cup of blessing which we bless, is it not the communion of the blood of Christ? The bread which we break, is it not the communion of the body of Christ?
> For we being many are one bread, and one body: for we are all partakers of that one bread.

Calvin said of this that it meant that "we are united to Christ in such a way, that we are flesh of his flesh, and bone of his bones (Eph. 5:30). For we must first of all be incorporated (so to speak) into Christ, that we may be united to each other."[5]

On this aspect, Aelfric said further:

> Christ hallowed on hys table the mysterye of our peace, and of our unytye: he whyche receyveth the mysterye of unytye, and kepeth not the bond of true peace, he receyveth not a mysterye for hym selfe, but a witnesse agaynst hym selfe.[6]

Going back to an earlier era, we find a like exposition in Bertram's *De Corpore et Sanguine Domini* (A. D. 840), a work which profoundly influenced the English reformers in their stand against transubstantiation. According to Bertram,

> LXXIII. It is also to be considered that in that bread, not only the body of Christ, but also the body of the faithful, is represented as in a figure; for it is made of many grains, even as the body of the faithful is increased by individual believers through the word of God.

---

4. E. Thomson, ed.: *Select Monuments of the Doctrine and Worship of the Catholic Church in England Before the Norman Conquest*, p. 36f. London: John Russell Smith, 1875.

5. John Calvin: *Commentary on the Epistles of Paul the Apostle to the Corinthians*, I, p. 335. Rev. John Pringle translation. Grand Rapids, Mich.: Eerdmans, 1948.

6. Thomson, *op. cit.*, p. 39f.

LXXIV. Wherefore as in a mystery that bread is taken to be the body of Christ, so also in a mystery are the faithful in Christ signified. And even as not corporally but spiritually, that bread is said to be the body of the faithful, so also it is necessary that the body of Christ be not corporally but spiritually understood.[7]

The point is sufficiently clear. To be a member of Jesus Christ is to be a member of His new humanity, and to meet one's responsibilities to the members thereof, for "Inasmuch as ye have done it unto one of the least of these my brethren, ye have done it unto me" (Matt. 25:40). Failure to discern "the Lord's body" means that God's purposes for and through the new humanity are rejected: "For he that eateth and drinketh unworthily, eateth and drinketh damnation to himself, not discerning the Lord's body" (I Cor. 11:29).

Why have we had so strange a development in the doctrine of communion? Is it not a deeply entrenched neoplatonism, which has led the ostensibly orthodox and evangelical churches to downgrade the material realm? Is it not also an implicit monophysitism, whereby the humanity of Christ is absorbed into His deity? (The other face of neoplatonism, which appears in modernism, is adoptionism; the material is transcended and is divinized, or is deity in process.) It is not surprising that such theologies have been unable to create a Christian culture: their presuppositions deny its possibility.

---

7. W. F. Taylor, ed., trans.: *The Book of Bertram, Monk of Corbie, A. D. 840, on the Body and Blood of the Lord*, p. 48f. London: Simpkin Marshall, 1880.

## 24

## COMMUNION AND CULTURE

Heretical doctrines of communion assume that the believer, on partaking of the bread and wine, is mystically made one with God the Son, i.e., that the recipient becomes one with the divinity. Late medieval mystics made much of this "fact," and it has remained as an aspect of the Roman Catholic and Protestant doctrines. While not so baldly stated as in the mystic's versions, all the same it is held that there is somehow a union of some sort with God the Son.

Scripture teaches something somewhat different. According to I Corinthians 10:16-17,

> The cup of blessing which we bless, is it not the communion of the blood of Christ? The bread which we break, is it not the communion of the body of Christ?
> For we being many are one bread, and one body: for we are all partakers of that one bread.

We are here told, *first*, that our communion is "the communion of the blood of Christ." We stand together as a new creation through the atoning blood of the Redeemer. Our communion and community are a product of His nullification of the Fall and His regeneration of His elect people. We are thus a new humanity in Him. There is no implication here of any mystical union with the deity of Christ. The meaning is that the incarnate one has redeemed us by His atoning blood.

*Second*, the cup we partake of, the communion wine, is therefore "the cup of blessing" because we thereby commemorate and celebrate our new creation by His grace in our atonement. We take the cup as the cup of blessing, rejoicing that in Christ we are a blessed people, and we bless that cup in joyful gratitude and praise. We should not therefore fall into idolatry, St. Paul warns us, as we interpret baptism and communion. "Wherefore, my dearly beloved, flee from idolatry. I speak as to wise men; judge ye what I say" (I Cor. 10:14-15). The prevailing views of communion involve idolatry, and idolatry is in essence the worship of the creature and ultimately self-worship.

*Third*, the bread of communion commemorates the broken or crucified body of Christ, again reminding us of His atonement, but it is not that alone. It is "the communion of the body of Christ," His redeemed people. Not the dead body, three days in the grave, but the living body of His elect people is in mind. Our minds are turned to the present. By becoming partakers of that atonement, the shed blood and the crucified or broken body of Jesus Christ, "we being many are one bread, and one body." We are the new humanity of the new Adam, Jesus Christ.

*Fourth,* idolatrous communion is "fellowship with devils" (I Cor. 10:20). The Greek word here is *koinonos,* communion, fellowship, sharing in common. Our common life, and the things we share and have fellowship in, are with the Lord's people, not with the ungodly. The same word is translated in I Corinthians 10:18 and 20 as "partakers." To share in common the Lord's table means to share in common a faith and a new life in Christ.

Very early, however, another interpretation came in, under pagan influences. The sacrament was seen as an aspect of the deification of the believer. The roots of transubstantiation are in this belief. Very many church fathers declared that God became man that men might become gods.

Gregory of Nyssa declared that "in no other way was it possible for our body to become immortal, but by participating in incorruption through its fellowship with that immortal Body." Gregory declared further,

> The question was, how can that one Body of Christ vivify the whole of mankind, all, that is, in whomsoever there is Faith, and yet, though divided amongst all, be itself not diminished? . . .
>
> Rightly then, do we believe that now also the bread which is consecrated by the Word of God is changed into the Body of God the Word. . . .
>
> Since, then, that God-containing flesh partook for its substance and support of this particular nourishment also, and since the God who was manifested infused Himself into perishable humanity for this purpose, viz. that by this communion with Deity mankind might at the same time be deified, for this end it is that, by dispensation of His grace, He disseminates Himself in every believer through that flesh, whose substance comes from bread and wine, blending Himself with the bodies of believers, to secure that, by this union with the immortal, man, too, may be a sharer in incorruption.[1]

Especially in the Eastern Church, where Greek and Far Eastern ideas were influential, such ideas flourished. Chrysostom, in his *Epistle to Caesarius,* shows similar tendencies. In his commentary on I Corinthians 11:29, Chrysostom showed the evidences of a non-Biblical interpretation of the body of Christ, writing,

---

1. Gregory of Nyssa, "The Great Catechism," ch. XXXVII, in *Nicene and Post-Nicene Fathers of the Christian Church,* Second Series, vol. V, 505f. Grand Rapids: Eerdmans.

But why doth he eat judgment to himself? "Not discerning the Lord's body:" i.e., not searching, not bearing in mind, as he ought, the greatness of the things set before him; not estimating the weight of the gift. For if thou shouldest come to know accurately Who it is that lies before thee, and Who He is that gives Himself, and to whom, thou wilt need no other argument, but this is enough for thee to use all vigilance; unless thou shouldest be altogether fallen.[2]

Because of this development, we can understand why the bishops, having alien ideas about communion, worked to suppress the agape feasts, or communions, of the early church, and forbad the clergy to attend them. We have too long accepted their propaganda concerning them. The communion service of the early church was very early seen in part as a continuation of the feast of rejoicing before the Lord with one's tithe, in terms of Deuteronomy 14:22-29. Deuteronomy 14:29 requires the feeding of the Levite, the stranger, the fatherless, and the widow, and very early both the church and the Christian community held agape feasts to invite the widows and the poor. The Council of Gangra (c. 325-381), in Canon XI, condemned critics of the love feasts, declaring,

If anyone shall despise those who out of faith make love-feasts and invite the brethren in honour of the Lord, and is not willing to accept these invitations because he despises what is done, let him be anathema.[3]

An African Code of 419, however, sharply separated communion from the love-feasts, and it required in Canon XLI, that only men who fasted be allowed to celebrate "the sacrifices."[4] The Synod of Laodicea, in c. 343-381, Canon XXVIII, forbad love feasts "in the Lord's Houses, or Churches."[5] Quinisext, in 692, ordered excommunication for those who persisted in holding love-feasts in churches.[6] It is clear that it was not disorders but rather hostility to the practice in principle which led to the abolition of the love-feasts. (A few groups have revived the love-feasts in modern times, notably the Mennonites, the Dunkards, and the German Baptists of the Anglo-American type.)

While the service of communion and the love-feasts are not identical, one having its roots in the passover, the other in the tithe feast, they do coincide in practice in I Corinthians 11, in New Testament practice. It is clear that this was a coincidence of necessity and expediency, not a requirement of faith. However in intent and meaning the two are very closely related.

---

2. St. Chrysostom, "Homilies on First Corinthians," Homily XXVIII, in *Nicene and Post Nicene Fathers*, First Series, vol. XII, p. 164.
3. *Ibid.*, Second Series, vol. XIV, p. 96.
4. *Ibid.*, p. 461.
5. *Ibid.*, p. 148.
6. *Ibid.*, p. 398.

Neoplatonism and Aristotelianism both favored the development of transubstantiationism, and, in Aquinas, we see the consequences clearly. In Aquinas' sermon before Pope Urban IV, c. 1264, he declared:

O Marvellous sacrament in which God lies concealed, and our Jesus, like another Moses, cloaks His face under the creatures He has made! May all generations praise Him! Wonderful is this sacrament in which, in virtue of the words of institution, charged with the Divine power, the symbolic species are changed into flesh and blood; in which accidents subsist without a subject; and in which, without violation of nature's law, by consecration the single and whole Christ self-identically exists in different places—as a voice is heard and exists in many places—continuing unchanged, remaining inviolable when partaken, nor suffering any diminution; nay, He is whole and entire and perfect in each and every fragment of the host, as visual appearances are multipled in a hundred mirrors.[7]

In another context, Aquinas held

The Only-begotten Son of God, being pleased to make us "partakers of the Divine nature," took our nature upon Him being Himself made Man that He might make men gods.[8]

For Luther too the "accidents" of bread and wine concealed the actual flesh and blood of Christ as their "substance." The reason for this, Luther held, was that

He (Christ) did not want to give us His divinity unconcealed; this was impossible. For God said (Ex. 33:20): "Man shall not see Me and live." Therefore it was necessary for God to hide, cover, and conceal Himself, thus enabling us to touch and apprehend Him. He must disguise Himself in flesh and blood, in the Word, in the external ministry, in Baptism, in the Sacrament and Lord's Supper, where He gives us His body in the bread and His blood in the wine, to eat and to drink. He must conceal Himself in forms to which He adds His Word, in order that we may recognize Him.[9]

In his Small Catechism, Luther taught:

What is the Sacrament of the Altar?
It is the true body and blood of our Lord Jesus Christ under the bread and wine, for us Christians to eat and to drink instituted by Christ Himself.[10]

Van Til has called attention to the error in Lutheran theology which makes such views of the sacrament possible. It is a disregard for Chalcedon's formula.

---

7. M. C. D'Arcy, ed.: *Thomas Aquinas, Selected Writings*, p. 25f. London: J. M. Dent, 1939.

8. *Ibid.*, p. 38.

9. Jaroslav Pelikan and Daniel E. Poellot, eds.: *Luther's Works, vol. 23, Sermons on the Gospel of St. John, Chapters 6-8*, p. 123. St. Louis, Mo.: Concordia, 1959.

10. Martin Luther: *Small Catechism*, p. 20. St. Louis: Concordia, 1943.

With all the refinements of the terminology employed as, e.g., that Christ is present, not in the natural mode, but in a supernatural mode, it remains a fact that according to the Lutheran position the *human can become the divine*. And that is the crux of the matter. That is a distinctly dangerous doctrine. That is antitheistic in origin and tendency. It not only involves, but is, an open avowal of the intermingling of the eternal and the temporal. It is once more in line with the Greek idea of the independent existence of the temporal.

In consonance with this eternizing of the temporal, Schneckenburger speaks of a *temporizing of the eternal* on the part of Lutheranism. He brings this out in his discussion of the perseverance of the saints. Lutheranism does not believe in the perseverance of the saints, he says. It holds to certainty for the moment, but believes that it is quite possible for a man to be actually saved at one time and actually lost at some later date. This position of Lutheranism he then traces back to its conception of the relation of time and eternity in general....

Here Schneckenburger, who himself favors the Lutheran position, asserts that according to Lutheranism, the eternal can be temporized and the temporal can be eternized. The infinite enters into the heart of the believer, he is happy and rejoices, but when the infinite withdraws, the salvation has also disappeared and joy is no more. Thus we find that instead of eradicating the leaven of paganism, Lutheranism once more returns with longing eyes to the fleshpots of Egypt. If there was need of anything, there was need of an emphasis upon the absolute distinction between the eternal and the temporal if the difficulties of Platonic reasoning were to be avoided. And exactly there we are disappointed in Lutheranism.[11]

Very early in church history these tendencies were apparent. In Monophysite thought, the human is absorbed into the divine. In Nestorian thought, the human, by an act of will, can unite itself with the divine and become divine. In either case, there is the confusion of the human (the created) and the divine (the uncreated). The Definition of Chalcedon, A. D. 451, denied the validity of all such thought. Only in the incarnation of Jesus Christ is there a union of the divine and of the human, of God and of man, but even here "in two natures, without confusion, without change, without division, without separation."[12]

Monophysitism cannot create a Christian culture. It involves an abandonment of history in its ultimate consequences in favor of an eternalizing of the temporal. The temporal thus loses meaning unless it transcends itself. Time becomes important only as it seeks to become eternal.

In Nestorianism, the reverse is true. Eternity is temporalized. Eternity gains meaning only if it is a dimension or a potentiality of time. Nestorianism thus creates a humanistic culture which it divinizes.

---

11. Cornelius Van Til: *In Defense of the Faith, vol. II, A Survey of Christian Epistemology*, p. 70f. Den Dulk Foundation, 1969.

12. See R. J. Rushdoony: *The Foundations of Social Order, Studies in the Creeds and Councils of the Early Church*. Nutley, N. J.: Presbyterian & Reformed, 1968.

The communion services in modernist churches can be characterized as implicit Nestorianism, whereas evangelical and orthodox churches observe an essentially Monophysite communion. Although transubstantiation has been dropped by them, *Its framework is retained.* The communion service has substantially the same meaning, except that the elements are not mystically changed in their substance. One might say that they still partake of the real body of Christ in the sense of His flesh, except that it is mystically rather than substantially understood. This is unhappily true of the Westminster Confession of Faith, ch. XXIX, section v, which reads:

> The outward elements in this sacrament, duly set apart to the uses ordained by Christ, have such relation to Him crucified, as that, truly, yet sacramentally only, they are sometimes called by the name of the things they represent, to wit, the body and blood of Christ; albeit, in substance and nature, they still remain truly and only bread and wine, as they were before.

As authority, the Confession cites Matthew 26:26-27, and the parallel passages in Mark and Luke. There is, however, a difference between the Gospel accounts and St. Paul's statements of the meaning of communion. *First* of all, the Gospel accounts are *before the event* set forth in the communion, the atonement, and St. Paul writes *after the event.* The one speaks of a sacrifice about to take place, the other, of one that has taken place, and is observed in "remembrance" (Luke 22:19) of the event, as Christ required. There is a difference, and a vast one, between an atoning death, and a "remembrance" of that death. Thus, when our Lord, before the event, spoke of His body and blood as set forth in the elements of bread and wine, they symbolized what was soon to be the reality of the new covenant in His vicarious sacrifice. *If we retain the original meaning, we are logically celebrating the perpetual sacrifice of the mass*, and Rome's position is logical, if such be the case.

*Second*, while there is a backward look in St. Paul's account, and "this do in remembrance of me" is stated twice, for both the wine and bread (I Cor. 11:24, 25), there is the forward look also in "till he come"(I Cor. 11:26), and the present and future are both in mind with respect to the people or body of Christ. This is also apparent in the original, the Last Supper itself, in at least the reference to the "new" drinking:

> But I say unto you, I will not drink henceforth of this fruit of the vine, until that day when I drink it new with you in my Father's kingdom (Matt. 26:29).
> For I say unto you, I will not drink of the fruit of the vine, until the Kingdom of God shall come (Luke 22:18).
> Verily I say unto you, I will drink no more of the fruit of the vine, until that day that I drink it new in the kingdom of God (Mark 14:25).

The commentaries do not give us a satisfactory interpretation of this statement. Clearly, however, it is intended to give an insight into the meaning of the wine of communion. Here our Lord does not speak of it as "blood," and in Matthew it is "this fruit of the vine," meaning the wine used in the Last Supper.

Because the commentators discuss the Synoptic Gospels (Matthew, Mark, Luke) without reference to John, they fail to make any connection with our Lord's own commentary *after* the Supper (John 13:2) on what He had done. Having declared the significance of the *wine,* and having spoken of the fruit of the *vine,* can it be an unconnected symbolism that He should then speak of *the vine*? Should we not look to that statement for the meaning of the Lord's Table? Jesus declared:

> I am the true vine, and my Father is the husbandman.
> Every branch in me that beareth not fruit he taketh away: and every branch that beareth fruit, he purgeth it, that it may bring forth more fruit.
> Now ye are clean through the word which I have spoken unto you. Abide in me, and I in you. As the branch cannot bear fruit of itself, except it abide in the vine, no more can ye, except ye abide in me.
> I am the vine, ye are the branches: He that abideth in me, and I in him, the same bringeth forth much fruit: for without me ye can do nothing.
> If a man abide not in me, he is cast forth as a branch, and is withered; and men gather them, and cast them into the fire, and they are burned.
> If ye abide in me, and my words abide in you, ye shall ask what ye will, and it shall be done unto you.
> Herein is my Father glorified, that ye bear much fruit: so shall ye be my disciples.
> As the Father hath loved me, so have I loved you: continue ye in my love.
> If ye keep my commandments, ye shall abide in my love; even as I have kept my Father's commandments, and abide in his love.
> These things have I spoken unto you, that my joy might remain in you, and that your joy might be full.
> This is my commandment, That ye love one another, as I have loved you.
> Greater love hath no man than this, that a man lay down his life for his friends.
> Ye are my friends, if ye do whatsoever I command you.
> Henceforth I call you not servants; for the servant knoweth not what his lord doeth: but I have called you friends; for all things that I have heard of my Father I have made known unto you.
> Ye have not chosen me, but I have chosen you, and ordained you, that ye should go and bring forth fruit, and that your fruit should remain: that whatsoever ye shall ask of the Father in my name, he may give it you.
> These things I command you, that ye love one another (John 15:1-17).

The disciples could recognize the symbolism immediately. In the Old Testament Israel was the "noble vine" of the Lord (Jer. 2:21). Hosea, however, declared, "Israel is an empty vine, he bringeth forth fruit unto himself" (Hosea 10:1). Now, it was clear that Jesus Christ is the true Israel ("Out of Egypt have I called my son," Matt. 2:15), and also "the true vine." Jesus called His disciples also the "new wine" which required new wineskins, a new culture, to be free to expand and realize its being (Matt. 9:14-17). The disciples thus saw the old Passover succeeded at the Last Supper by the new Passover, and the old vine replaced by "the true vine." The body and blood of the physical Jesus would within hours bring atonement for His elect people. Freed from the Fall's consequences, from the power of sin and death, they would now be the new wine, breaking the old world's wineskins and bearing to every area of the world the joy of the new wine.

They were also "the branches" of "the true vine," required to bear fruit. If they failed to do so, they would be cast out and burned as false or untrue branches. A central aspect of that fruit-bearing is to love one another. This is emphatically restated. Thus, the Passover, celebrating redemption, is linked closely with the tithe of rejoicing with the Levites, the poor, the lonely, and the needy (Deut. 14:22-29) as an aspect of the true observance of the Lord's Table. By their love, and by their expansive force as the perpetually new wine, they are to create a godly society, to establish the Kingdom of God.

*Third,* St. Paul makes clear in I Corinthians 10:16 that the cup is not *the blood of Christ* but "the communion of the blood of Christ," and the bread, not His *flesh,* but "the communion of the body of Christ." Both thus celebrate a fellowship or communion, because "The many of us are one bread, one body, since we all participate in the one bread" (I Cor. 10:17, Berkeley Version), and Phillips renders I Corinthians 10:17-18 thus: "Because there is one loaf, we, many as we are, are one body; for it is one loaf of which we all partake. *Look at the Jewish people. Are not those who partake in the sacrificial meal sharers in the altar?*" Each faith, St. Paul says, has its own fellowship in terms of its own doctrine of salvation, and our fellowship is in Christ's atonement. If we are truly redeemed by Christ, then our fellowship, in terms of "discerning the Lord's body" (I Cor. 11:29) by love and mutual help and charity, is ever active and alive.

Such a teaching is not the occultism of the mystery religions of antiquity. It is the purpose of the living God, as set forth in the creation mandate, in the law, and through His only begotten Son required of those who are made the people of God by His grace through the atonement.

Communion in this sense is in the faith of all the Scriptures, and in conformity to the Biblical doctrine of the incarnation as defended by the

definition of Chalcedon. The communion elements are not another incarnation. They are not a mystical absorption into or union with the
divinity of Christ. Communion celebrates our redemption and sets forth
the requirements of Christian community; it summons the branches to
bear fruit in obedience to the word of God, and, as the new wine borne
by "the true vine," to break all the old wineskins of a fallen world.

## 25

## COMMUNITY AND CULTURE

More than a few thinkers seem to presuppose a philosophy which ranges from neoplatonism to a Manichaean dualism as a necessity to any advanced culture. For them, culture in such a sense is a product of tension between two kinds of being or two aspects of being. In addition, it is *sin,* although rarely so labelled, that adds color and meaning to life and culture for all too many thinkers. Leo Tolstoy began *Anna Karenina* with this sentence: "Happy families are all alike; every unhappy family is unhappy in its own way." As a student, I recall hearing this sentence cited again and again as a fundamental truth. Virtue and happiness, it would appear, are boring; sin and unhappiness are exciting. But Tolstoy's sentence can as easily read, "Unhappy families are all alike; every happy family is happy in its own way." In either case, it does not say much about life, but it says much about the writer.

The tension idolized by such neoManichaeans does not create cultures: it destroys them. It confuses issues and leads to a flight from basic issues and conflicts to imagined ones. It can also lead to a surrender, if flesh or matter is divided from mind or spirit, in that one aspect can be surrendered as incapable of resisting the power of the other. It can also lead to quietism, as one surrenders hope of victory in favor of a withdrawal from conflict into spiritual exercises.

Much of evangelicalism is today incapable of creating a culture. It either surrenders to the world, or flees from it, or both. In the 1950s, I spoke to a group of evangelical students at a major university. The meeting actually began and continued, until I spoke, with the singing of childish preschool choruses, such as "This little light of mine." After I spoke (I had been suggested as a speaker, and none knew me), the group, unwilling to recognize the division between a Christian view of education, science, and culture, and fully committed to accepting the rank humanism and atheism of their studies and ignoring all conflict, happily revived itself by singing more choruses. Such people can build large neo-evangelical churches, but they cannot establish a Christian culture.

We have also the opinion of W. H. Auden that Christianity as such *cannot* establish a culture:

> I sometimes wonder if there is not something a bit questionable, from a Christian point of view, about all works of art which make

overt Christian references. They seem to assert that there is such a thing as a Christian culture, which there cannot be. Culture is one of Caesar's things. One cannot help noticing that the great period of "religious" painting coincided with the period when the Church was a great temporal power.[1]

Auden has impeccable credentials as a Yahoo. *First* of all, he identifies culture with various art forms, such as painting, a true mark of the parasite and the collector, who can only see some manifestations of a culture, never the culture itself, and identify the fruit as the roots. *Second,* Auden manifests his rootless, anti-cultural bent in a homosexual poem.[2]

Culture is not a product of artistic activities but of ideas and faith; it is the social and material consequences of religion. The reason why many peoples in the early centuries chose Christianity as their religion was a pragmatic one: Christianity could provide a workable social order. Because of the law-nature of Biblical faith, order is inherent to it, and this was recognized by the barbarians.

Much later, in the Icelandic saga of Burnt Njal, this same pragmatic preference appears:

> The Christian men set up their booths, and Gizur the White and Hjallti were in the booths of the men from Mossfell. The day after both sides went to the Hill of Laws, and each, the Christian men as well as the heathen, took witness, and declared themselves out of the other's laws, and then there was such an uproar on the Hill of Laws that no man could hear the other's voices.
>
> After that men went away, and all thought things looked like the greatest entanglement. The Christian men chose as their Speaker Hall of the Side, but Hall went to Thorgeir, the priest of Lightwater, who was the old Speaker of the law, and gave him three marks of silver (This was no bribe, but his lawful fee) to utter what the law should be, but still that was most hazardous counsel, since he was an heathen.
>
> Thorgeir lay all that day on the ground, and spread a cloak over his head, so that no man spoke with him; but the day after men went to the Hill of Laws, and then Thorgeir bade them be silent and listen, and spoke thus: "It seems to me as though our matters were come to a dead lock, if we are not all to have one and the same law; for if there be a sundering of the laws, then there will be a sundering of the peace, and we shall never be able to live in the land. Now, I will ask both Christian men and heathen whether they will hold to those laws which I utter?"
>
> They all said they would.
>
> He said he wished to take an oath of them, and pledges that they would hold to them, and they all said "yea" to that, and so he took pledges from them.

---

1. W. H. Auden: *The Dyer's Hand, and other essays,* p. 458. New York: Random House, 1962.

2. W. H. Auden, "A Day for a Lay," in *Avant Garde,* no. 11, March, 1970, p. 46f.

"This is the beginning of our laws," he said, "that all men shall be Christians here in the land, and believe in one God, the Father, the Son, and the Holy Ghost, but leave off all idol worship, not expose children to perish, and not eat horseflesh. It shall be outlawry if such things are proved openly against any man; but if these things are done by stealth, then it shall be blameless."

By all this heathendom was all done away with within a few years' space, so that those things were not allowed to be done either by stealth or openly.

Thorgeir then uttered the law as to keeping the Lord's day and fast days, Yuletide and Easter, and all the greatest highdays and holidays.[3]

The saga has reference to the meeting of the Althing in A.D. 1000. It was preceded by some conflict, including some aggressive acts by Christian leaders. After the very strongly Christian settlement, paganism continued in Iceland, despite the official Christianity. Why then, here and elsewhere, the surprising shift in religion? In some cases, the Christians were easily massacred and eliminated, but in other cases, despite the deeply imbedded and continuing paganism, Christianity was adopted when it could have been suppressed.

The force of the new religion as a law-power was clearly recognized by the pagans. Just as the American Indian recognized the superior value and power of the white man's gun and was quick to adopt it, so the barbarians recognized the power of the Christian faith and were ready to utilize it for pragmatic reasons. In the 1940s, I was told by American Indians that the white man was superior because of the Bible religion, but they were unwilling to adopt it because they recognized that the white man was abandoning it for evolution, which must mean greater power. Superior power is readily desired, and Christianity's cultural force has been a major missionary factor, in that various peoples have been attracted to the faith because of its ability to order and motivate society.

Christian faith has material and social consequences when it is true faith, when it obeys God's words. This is the repeated statement of Scripture, as witness not only all of Deuteronomy 28 but also Leviticus 26. In Leviticus 26:3-21, we are told

If ye walk in my statutes, and keep my commandments, and do them:
Then I will give you rain in due season, and the land shall yield her increase, and the trees of the field shall yield their fruit.
And your threshing shall reach unto the vintage, and the vintage shall reach unto the sowing time; and ye shall eat your bread to the full, and dwell in your land safely
And I will give you peace in the land, and ye shall lie down, and none

---

3. George Webe Dasent, trans.: *The Story of Burnt Njal,* p. 184f. London: J. M. Dent and Sons, (1911) 1944.

shall make you afraid: and I will rid evil beasts out of the land, neither shall the sword go through your land.

And ye shall chase your enemies, and they shall fall before you by the sword.

And five of you shall chase a hundred, and an hundred of you shall put ten thousand to flight: and your enemies shall fall before you by the sword.

For I will have respect unto you, and make you fruitful, and multiply you, and establish my covenant with you.

And ye shall eat old store, and bring forth the old because of the new.

And I will set my tabernacle among you: and my soul shall not abhor you.

And I will walk among you, and will be your God, and ye shall be my people.

I am the LORD your God, which brought you forth out of the land of Egypt, that ye shall not be their bondmen; and I have broken the bands of your yoke, and made you go upright.

But if ye will not hearken unto me, and will not do all these commandments;

And if ye shall despise my statutes, or if your soul abhor my judgments, so that ye will not do all my commandments, but that ye break my covenant:

I also will do this unto you; I will even appoint over you terror, consumption, and the burning ague, that shall consume the eyes, and cause sorrow of heart: and ye shall sow your seed in vain, for your enemies shall eat it.

And I will set my face against you, and ye shall be slain before your enemies: they that hate you shall reign over you; and ye shall flee when none pursueth you.

And if ye will not yet for all this hearken unto me, then I will punish you seven times more for your sins.

And I will break the pride of your power; and I will make your heaven as iron, and your earth as brass:

And your strength shall be spent in vain: for your land shall not yield her increase, neither shall the trees of the land yield their fruits.

And if ye walk contrary unto me, and will not hearken unto me; I will bring seven times more plagues upon you according to your sins (Lev. 26:3-21).

Certain things stand out very clearly in this declaration. *First,* God declares that He will capitalize the people that obey Him. This capitalization will include a variety of things, natural and social. He will bless His people with peace and safety, both necessary ingredients to the prospering of a culture. Their enemies will be scattered and defeated; internally, they will be free of problems from criminals and from the depradations of wild animals. Rain shall be abundant and helpful, and the harvests very rich and bountiful. Above all else, God will Himself tabernacle among them and make them His people.

*Second,* God declares that He will decapitalize a disobedient people.

By bad weather, poor crops, wild animals, enemy nations, drought and much else, He will strip them of "the pride of your power" and leave them weak and impotent in the face of their problems. Clearly, such judgments radically decapitalize a country and shatter its culture.

Culture is an act of faith and the application of standards and ideas to the disciplines of life and to life itself. When a culture denies its faith, it also negates its life and practice. Unless it adopts another and a viable faith, it commits suicide. The humanism adopted by modern culture has had the capital of Christian civilization, but this capital is rapidly disappearing. Modern civilization is as a result in crisis.

*Third,* the basic capital of any society is in the realm of faith and ideas, and, inescapably, because man is a unit, his faith and ideas have very practical consequences: they create a culture. God declares that this premise of all stable culture is to "walk in my statutes, and keep my commandments" (Lev. 26:3). When men deny God, they thereby deny themselves also, and finally have nothing, because apart from God all things collapse into meaninglessness and void. In the 19th century, the poet Edward Rowland Sill saw the collapse of faith as the "Infirmity," In a poem by that name, he wrote:

> What is the truth to believe,
> > What is the right to be done?
> Caught in the webs I weave
> > I halt from sun to sun.

> The bright wind flows along,
> > Calm nature's streaming law,
> And its stroke is soft and strong
> > As a leopard's velvet claw.

> Free of the doubting mind,
> > Full of the olden power,
> Are the tree, and the bee, and the wind,
> > And the wren, and the brave may-flower.

> Man was the last to appear,
> > A flow at the close of the day;
> Slow clambering now in fear
> > He gropes his slackened way.

> All the up-thrust is gone,
> > Force that came from of old,
> Up through the fish, and the swan,
> > And the sleak king's mighty mould.

> The youth of the world is fled,
> > There are omens in the sky,
> Spheres that are chilled and dead,
> > And the close of an age is nigh.

> The time is too short to grieve,
> > Or to choose, for the end is one:

And what is truth to believe,
And what is the right to be done?[4]

Because the faith that established truth and right and wrong was gone,
Sill felt that "the close of an age is nigh."

*Fourth,* while God declares that *a strict causality,* in the form of
rewards and punishments, will prevail with respect to His law, there is
also more than that, *the personal factor,* His covenant: God declares, "I
will...establish my covenant with you... And I will set my tabernacle
among you" (Lev. 26:9, 11). It is always the totally personal God with
whom we have to reckon. Culture is not a product of causality and the
world of animals. Ants, baboons, and bees all have very interesting and
divinely ordered lines; their worlds manifest the order which is God's
handiwork. Progress, history, and culture are, however, beyond them,
nor can they establish civilizations. These are products of persons created
in the image of God and products of their relationship, explicit and implicit, with the sovereign and omnipotent God. Behind the basic capital
of faith and ideas are persons, and, supremely, the personal and triune
God.

Any philosophy or theology which tends to depersonalize the world
and man will to that extent inhibit and destroy the development of
culture and civilization. Materialism, naturalism, idealism,
neoplatonism, Manichaeanism, Monophysitism, Arianism, and other
like ideas tend either to depersonalize or divide reality, or both in some
cases, and, to that degree, there is an inhibition on the growth of culture.
Only as we see the unity of creation under God, and recognize that
behind all causes is the totally personal cause, the sovereign and triune
God, can culture, the expression of personality in practical and immediate forms, flourish and express man's cultural mandate. A false or
deformed doctrine of communion means a deformed community and
culture.

---

4. *The Poetical Words of Edward Rowland Sill,* p. 362f. Boston: Houghton, Mifflin,
(1867) 1906.

## 26

## FORTUNE-TELLING, WITCHCRAFT, LAW, AND THE FUTURE

According to Leviticus 19:26,

Ye shall not eat any thing with the blood: neither shall ye use enchantment, nor observe times.

The Berkeley Version renders it thus:

Eat nothing that contains the blood. Make use of neither fortune telling nor witchcraft practice.

The ban on eating blood is closely related to what follows. Blood is equated with life, "For the life of the flesh is in the blood" (Lev. 17:11). Eating blood was often used as a means of gaining life and power from other creatures, and, among the ancient Zabii, the blood of sacrifices was offered to demons in order to please them by this gift of life, and to fraternize with them.[1]

Our concern, however, is with the aspect of this law which prohibits fortune-telling and witchcraft. Fortune-telling is closely associated with gypsies, and it is very revealing to know that gypsies themselves will have nothing to do with having their fortunes told: it is something done for outsiders only. Fortune-telling is done exclusively by gypsy women, never the men. It is done both because it pays very well, and because it provides good information about whatever community they are in at the moment, and its moods during their current visit. Jan Yoors gives us a summary of the comments of a young gypsy woman on fortune-telling:

In essence Keja said that the avidity for fortune-telling came from an inability to cope with one's anxieties. Instead of satisfying, it created a self-perpetuating greed for prophecy, akin to compulsive gambling, only more harmful since one lost not money but insight. It blinded one to the causes of one's problems, and this was "madness." It was a vain and self-defeating search for expedient solutions to problems of moral integrity, and was caused by an unwillingness to face life as it was. Most people consulted fortune-tellers primarily to seek the confirmation of their fears, more often than of their hopes. Fears could become father to a wish, for many subconsciously wanted to have happen that which they said they fear most. Keja said that fear impoverished, while the acceptance of sorrow could enrich. The Lowara said, "Without wood the fire would die," disclaiming guilt. Seen from a practical point of view, the

---

1. C. D. Ginsburg, "Leviticus," in Ellicott, I, p. 427.

153

tangible substance of fortune telling was the ability to listen with endless patience to every human folly. To this they added some vague generalities into which specific and personal meanings could be read. Keja talked for a long time and with great openness.

She told me about a country squire in Serbia, long ago, who imagined that he had a dreaded, incurable disease. He consulted a physician in Sarajevo who reassured him and emphatically denied his fears. The squire rushed to see other physicians, all of whom agreed with the first doctor. He went to Nish and to Belgrade and to Sofia in Bulgaria. In despair, he went to see a soothsayer, who immediately confirmed his fears, proving the medical authorities wrong in the eyes of the squire. After a protracted and costly treatment he managed to save the squire—from an imaginary illness![2]

Whereas fortune-telling is a desire to know the future, and is a self-defeating, self-fulfilling desire, witchcraft, equally lawless and ungodly, is a desire to force the future to conform to man's will by means not allowed by God's word. Witchcraft has a long history of association with murder, and some have held that the meaning of *witch* in the Bible is *poisoner*. In essence, the attempt of witchcraft is to play god and to force man's lawless will on to man, God, and nature.

Both fortune-telling and witchcraft are thus attempts to by-pass God's law. According to the law, as summed up in Deuteronomy 28 and Leviticus 26, *man can know the future and predict and establish it only by obedience to God's law*. The Lord declared to Ezekiel, "And I gave them my statutes, and shewed them my judgments, which if a man do, he shall even live in them" (Ezek. 20:11). All other attempts to establish or to know the future are illegitimate. Man, created to have dominion by means of righteousness, holiness, and knowledge, can study, act, and develop in terms of a command of ideas and things which will enable him to determine and to govern the future under God. All such legitimate activities capitalize man and society. Fortune-telling and witchcraft decapitalize a society radically.

Both these lawless activities, instead of seeking godly knowledge and power, seek an ungodly and destructive knowledge and power. Yoor's report on gypsy views of fortune-telling makes clear the essentially *suicidal* nature of such an interest. To probe into the future in such a way is to separate the future from man's will. It is determinism or fatalism, an external ordination of man's life, whereas predestination asserts the coincidence of God's determination and man's determination. God's eternal decree is the primary determination, but man's secondary determination, while a secondary cause, is no less real. When Saul went to the witch of Endor to seek knowledge of the future by necromancy (I Sam. 28),

---

2. Jan Yoors: *The Gypsies,* p. 55f. New York: Simon and Schuster, (1967) 1969.

he was at the same time refusing to repent or to change. He was in effect saying that his wretched plight was not his own doing but an imposition on him, and he was inquiring as to what further vicious events would be imposed on him. Saul was both indicting God and declaring implicitly that he was an unfortunate and much imposed upon man.

Those who seek lawless and unsanctified knowledge about the future are both masochistic and environmentalistic. They invite disaster and judgment and relegate their sins and stupidity to the environment. By their abdication of the *requirement* to exercise dominion by means of God's law and godly knowledge, they decapitalize themselves and society.

The devotees of witchcraft want to dominate the future lawlessly. Russell's study of medieval witchcraft makes clear how closely allied witchcraft is to lawlessness and antinomianism.[3] The use of poison and ritual murders to gain magical powers is an essential part of witchcraft, despite frequent denials.

Here again, we have a decapitalization of society, an even more radical one. Whereas fortune telling is a masochistic and suicidal activity, witchcraft is a sadistic and murderous one. The society which gives itself to these activities soon ceases to be a society. Its intellectual, religious, social, and material capital is laid waste, and there is a sundering of all ties and standards.

According to Buckland, "Behind the magic of witchcraft is a belief that 'power' comes from the human body,"[4] It ascribes the possibility of ultimacy to individual man, and the capture of this ultimacy and power mean warfare against God and man. A witch is a witch by "self-proclamation. Essentially a witch is a witch if he says he's a witch."[5]

Ironically, however, both fortune-telling and witchcraft are quests for *power*. Fortune-telling seeks power by means of an illegitimate peek into the future, but it is a self-defeating power because it is a self-fulfilling prophecy that is gained. Witchcraft seeks power by lawless control, which is again self-defeating, in that it destroys society. It is like being a captain on a sinking ship, a position of importance indeed, but hardly an enviable one. Witches can only command society by destroying it.

In a very real sense both fortune-telling and witchcraft involve an eating or drinking of blood, one's own and society's. They are forms of social cannibalism.

The essential fact remains: society can be capitalized only as it obeys God's law.

---

3. Jeffrey Burton Russell, *Witchcraft in the Middle Ages.* Ithaca, New York: Cornell University Press, 1972.

4. Ray Buckland, *Ancient and Modern Witchcraft,* p. 144. New York: H. C. Publishers, 1970. Buckland is a "high priest" of a witch coven; see Brad Steiger, *Sex and the Supernatural,* p. 164; New York: Lancer Books, 1968.

5. Martin Ebon, *Witchcraft Today,* p. 142. New York: Signet, 1971.

## OCCULTISM AND EXPERIENTIALISM

According to Moses, the nations of his day were dedicated to an evil and ugly quest for power through a variety of occult practices. These things represented a hostility to God and were gaining the judgment of God. Therefore,

> When thou art come into the land which the LORD thy God giveth thee, thou shalt not learn to do after the abominations of those nations.
> There shall not be found among you any one that maketh his son or his daughter to pass through the fire, or that useth divination, or an observer of times, or an enchanter, or a witch,
> Or a charmer, or a consulter with familiar spirits, or a wizard, or a necromancer.
> For all that do these things are an abomination unto the LORD: and because of these abominations the LORD thy God doth drive them out from before thee.
> Thou shalt be perfect with the LORD thy God.
> For these nations, which thou shalt possess, hearkened unto observers of times, and unto diviners: but as for thee, the LORD thy God hath not suffered thee so to do (Deut. 18:9-14).

The summary statement of this is Exodus 22:18, "Thou shalt not suffer a witch (or sorceress) to live." The word translated as witch or sorceress appears in the Septuagint version of Exodus 22:18 and other passages, as well as in the New Testament as *pharmakos* (English pharmacy), and had reference to the use of drugs and thus poisoning.

Haim Hermann Cohn, justice of the Supreme Court of Israel and a professor of law at the Hebrew University of Jerusalem, has observed, with respect to the Biblical law against sorcery and related practices, that, according to the law,

> It was to be the characteristic of Judaism that nothing would be achieved by magic, but everything by the will and spirit of God: hence the confrontations of Joseph and the magicians of Egypt (Gen. 41), of Moses and Aaron and Egyptian sorcerers (Ex. 7), of Daniel and the Babylonian astrologers (Dan. 2), etc., and hence also the classification of crimes of sorcery as tantamount to idolatrous crimes of human sacrifices (Deut. 18:10) and to idolatrous sacrifices in general (Ex. 22:19) and its visitation, just as idolatry itself, with death by stoning (Lev. 20:27). In a God-fearing Israel, there is no room for augury and sorcery (Num. 23:23; Isa. 8:19), and the

presence of astrologers (Isa. 47:13) and fortune tellers is an indication of godlessness (Nah. 3:4; Ezek. 13:20-23 et al.).[1]

One of the forms of occultism condemned in Deuteronomy 18:9-14 is divination, or various practices used to foretell the future; divination is closely associated with witchcraft or sorcery. In Acts 16:16-19 it is clear that divination and soothsaying are associated with demonic possession.

At the end of the Middle Ages and in the early years of the modern era, a widespread outbreak and revival of pagan and anti-Christian occultism was responsible for a massive assault on Christianity, an attack on tithing, the mainstay of Christian society, a sexual revolution aimed at destroying the family, and a revival of cannibalism, human sacrifice, and related acts.[2]

Subsequently, these occult practices returned as an ostensible Christian revival, in both Catholic and Protestant circles. Let us consider briefly the American aspect of this development. The witchcraft problem in Salem Village in 1691 began with the experimentation of youth, mainly girls, in occult practices. The origin of these practices was a new minister's slave, one acquainted with West Indian voodoo faith and practice, who found a willing circle of followers in adolescent girls, including the Rev. Samuel Parris' daughters. These experimentations became a major concern and passion to the girls, who met regularly.[3] The results, however, were soon frightening rather than entertaining. "The magic they had tried to harness was beginning, instead, to ride them: visibly, dramatically, ominously."[4] The Rev. Samuel Parris, father of two of the girls and uncle of another, called in Dr. William Gripps, who saw no normal, natural cause for the affliction and suggested some sort of possession.

Instead of the girls being blamed, however, they were allowed to blame others for bewitching them. With this development, what had been an unpleasant affliction for the girls became an exhilarating and happy development, and accusations became, one later admitted, a matter of sport for them.[5]

Another development was also in evidence. The girls at times seemed to claim a divine rather than demonic source for their "fits" and spasms. Spectral evidence began to be regarded as valid, and the lines of evidence shifted from godly to occultist grounds.[6] The girls were also accusing

---

1. Haim Hermann Cohn, "Sorcery," in *Encyclopaedia Judaica*, vol. 15, p. 163. New York: Macmillan, 1971.
2. See J. B. Russell: *Witchcraft in the Middle Ages.*
3. Payl Boyer and Stephen Nissenbaum: *Salem Possessed, The Social Origins of Witchcraft*, pp. 1f., 23f., 181, 199. Cambridge, Massachusetts: Harvard University Press, 1974.
4. *Ibid.*, p. 1f.
5. *Ibid.*, pp. 9, 23f.
6. *Ibid.*, pp. 27f., 148, 150f.

others of the very occult practices they themselves were guilty of.[7] The girls were also claiming now to have angelic messengers and glorious visions.[8]

While these latter claims did not receive full acceptance, the way was prepared for such an acceptance when like phenomena appeared among youth in the Great Awakening. From that time on, these kinds of "charismatic" manifestations were less and less regarded as demonic and more and more as godly.

The result of this invasion of Christianity by "charismatic" manifestations was the assault from within the church on basic doctrines. The sovereignty of God gave way to the sovereignty of man. The place of law in sanctification gave way to antinomianism, and the Great Awakening saw militant free-love preaching as a part of the "revival," and as "proof" of salvation and freedom from the law.[9] Although the main body of the clergy suppressed this antinomianism, it remained endemic to revivalism and led later to J. H. Noyes's sexual communism and to various contemporary practices. Perfectionism and premillennialism also flourished as a result of these developments, as did "charismatic" manifestations as "proof" of conversion.

In the nineteenth century, such "charismatic" manifestations became virtual evidence of the Holy Spirit. Loud did not exaggerate when he wrote:

> Involuntary twitchings, known as the "jerks," would rack the body. The head would twist from side to side faster and faster till it spun the rest of the palsied frame. Rending cries burst from the lips of the "jerkers," screams of anguish, shrieks of terror. Some howled and some, down on all fours, even barked like dogs. They leaped as if jabbed. They whirled like dervishes, rolled, wormed, hopped like frogs. And finally they plunged headlong, grovelling on the ground till they collapsed in cataleptic rigidity.[10]

Revivals, instead of leading to good results, were followed both by an increase in illegitimacy, and, as even C. G. Finney admitted, by a bitter, fault-finding, and denunciatory spirit. The Bible was put aside during revivals, because men wanted experience, not truth.[11] Rampant humanism led not only to exalting man's pretended sovereignty as against God's, but to exalting man to ridiculous dimensions. Finney's perfectionism led him, as Warfield has shown, to exalt the idiot, whose obligation, being limited by his ability, is perfect, doing nothing.

---

7. *Ibid.*, p. 211f.

8. *Ibid.*, p. 30.

9. See C. C. Goen: *Revivalism and Separatism in New England, 1740-1800*, pp, 200ff. New Haven, Conn.: Yale University Press, 1962.

10. Grover C. Loud: *Evangelized America*, p. 102. New York: The Dial Press, 1928.

11. See B. B. Warfield: *Perfectionism*, vol. II, p. 25. New York: Oxford University Press, 1931.

The moral idiot—Finney does not hesitate to say it—is as perfect as God is: being a moral idiot, he has no moral obligation; when he has done nothing at all he has done all that he ought to do: he is perfect. God Himself cannot do more than He ought to do; and when He has done all He ought to do, He is no more perfect than the moral idiot is—although what He has done is to fulfil all that is ideally righteous and the moral idiot has done nothing.[12]

For Finney, self-gratification became virtue, because of his man-centered orientation.[13]

Throughout the history of American revivalism, many godly pastors were at work in the revivals, but their efforts were, like those of Aquinas, who tried to put Aristotle to a holy use, a contradiction in terms. Even their successes thus were aspects of a real but diminished faith.

It is not surprising that such a background leads to a strand in the charismatic movement of the twentieth century, with its antinomianism and its emphasis on experimentialism. The moral character of such charismatics is emphatically bad; where some moral character is in evidence, there is a background of mainline Protestant church upbringing. Pentecostal and non-Christian backgrounds give little evidence of moral stability.

Such charismatics misinterpret the gift of the Spirit, which in John 20:21-23 is clearly the commission to go forth and evangelize with the authority of Christ's inscriptured word, with its binding and releasing power. The experience at Pentecost came as an aspect of this calling, as a witness to the continuing power of the risen Christ, but as temporary gifts which passed away, whereas the gift of the Spirit remains.

However, for these charismatics, not faith and obedience, saving grace and its moral character, are normative, but speaking in tongues. Moreover, the experience of tongues is made so beyond understanding by all others that even the witness of many tape recordings that actual languages are never spoken is set aside as worthless: "Linguists sampled tape recordings, and *excathedra* assured all and sundry that *glossolalia* is not really language."[14] Ervin later assures us that languages are spoken; are we to suppose that they cannot be taped?[15] If it be said that the many, many hours of taping by Christian scholars simply missed an occasion when an actual language was spoken, then it follows that the great majority of tongues speakings are frauds, a conclusion Ervin would not like.

---

12. *Ibid.*, II, 69f.
13. *Ibid.*, II, 189f.
14. Howard M. Ervin: *"These Are Not Drunken, As Ye Suppose,"* p. 2. Plainfield, New Jersey: Logos International, 1968. Ervin is a professor at Oral Roberts University and sees no problem apparently in Roberts' disregard for sound theology and easy affiliation with modernism. The "test" for charismatics is experience, not Scripture.
15. *Ibid.*, p. 127f.

The mindless, meaningless babble of such worship is common to paganism, ancient and modern, where it is often associated with spiritistic possession. It is in any form alien to the Biblical faith. It is a form of the "abominations" condemned by Biblical law. It is not found with any faithful and consistent affirmation of the sovereignty of God and a full trust in the atoning blood of Christ.

The essence of false faith, St. Paul declares, is that false apostles transform "themselves into the apostles of Christ. And no marvel; for Satan himself is transformed into an angel of light" (II Cor. 11:13-14).

Moses' condemnation of occult practices is a part of a longer statement, Deuteronomy 18:9-22, which, after defining all the false means of controlling or knowing the future, declares that only a prophet who speaks from God can declare the future. The prophets were proclaimers and interpreters of God's law, who declared what God decreed specifically in various instances in terms of His already established law. God's word remained always one word, to which men could neither add or diminish (Deut. 4:2).

This passage, moreover, is a part of one which also speaks of the priests (Deut. 18:1-8), so that Moses established as the God-given ministries the Levites and the prophets and excludes all other means of ascertaining the future, or of gaining power and insight. True authority is inseparable from God and His word. The rise of man-centered norms has been the decline also of Christian faith and power.

A contributory cause to the rise of experiential revivalism was the rise at the same time of modern science with its emphasis on experimentalism. Experimental or experiential religion, in terms of this new thought (and America was early in its vanguard, being close to the new scientific thought rather than to the Enlightenment), was true and evidential religion. Conversion was expected thus to have a dramatic physical effect.

There were strong elements of spiritualism in the Salem Village episode, and modern spiritualism had its birth in the claims of the daughters of John D. Fox, in 1848, when Margaret (1834-93) and Kate (1836-92) practiced supposed but fraudulent "spirit-rappings." The excitement and interest they created was phenomenal. Close by, at Palmyra, New York, Joseph Smith had begun preaching Mormonism. The area had been heavily infected by the virus of experiential revivalism and became fertile ground for other aberrations.

Without agreeing with tongues, we can say that among God-centered charismatics, there are important movements astir. No doctrine of Scripture is more neglected than that of the Holy Spirit. Our emphasis, however, must be God-centered, not man-centered. All humanism is occultistic. The development of faith and life among theocentric charismatics is one of the most promising aspects of 20th century Christianity. Its potentialities are very great.

## 28

## REBELLION AND OCCULTISM

As we have seen, witchcraft in the Bible means the use of drugs to control or to kill people, and it is one aspect of occultism, which is condemned in its every form.

We see still another facet of the meaning of occultism in I Samuel 15:23, "for rebellion is as the sin of witchcraft, and stubborness is as iniquity and idolatry." The word rendered as *witchcraft* can be better translated as *soothsaying* or *divination*. Keil and Delitzsch translated the verse thus: "rebellion is the sin of soothsaying, and opposition is heathenism and idolatry" and commented:

> Opposition to God is compared by Samuel to soothsaying and oracles, because idolatry was manifested in both of them. All conscious disobedience is actually idolatry, because it makes self-will, the human I, into a god. So that all manifest opposition to the word and commandment of God is, like idolatry, a rejection of the true God.[1]

Very clearly, the text says that rebellion *is* the sin of witchcraft or divination, and stubbornness, intractableness, or opposition *is* heathenism and idolatry.

Central to all occultism is man's desire to be his own god; practically, this takes the form of trying to seize control over men and the universe by lawless and ungodly means. Occultism in its every form is thus rebellion against God and therefore against every godly authority.

Now basic to all such rebellion is self-righteousness and Phariseeism. When Satan and then Adam and Eve rebelled against God, they did not thereby say that they planned to be sinners. Far from it. Rather, they saw themselves as *freedom-fighters*, as heroic champions of freedom against a tyrannical and arbitrary God. For them, sin was in the picture only as an attribute of God who had supposedly concealed from them their own claim to divinity and had lied about the consequences of freedom from God. "Ye shall not surely die"; God has lied. The purpose of His lie was to prevent man from realizing himself: "For God doth know that in the day ye eat thereof, then your eyes shall be opened, and ye shall be as gods, knowing good and evil" (Gen. 3:4-5).

---

1. C. F. Keil and F. Delitzsch: *Biblical Commentary on the Books of Samuel*, p. 157. Grand Rapids: Eerdmans, 1950.

Since then rebellion has been the principle of freedom and self-realization, self-development, for fallen man. Men have rebelled against God and chosen freedom from responsibility as their ideal. *Playboy*, one of the most successful magazines in history, sees man, not in the image of God, but in the image of a bunny, an aging child's version of the rabbit, a carefree, non-productive, non-working, copulator. Women have rebelled against men, and, in a world with a sky-rocketing amount of rape, only a small fraction of which is reported, women seek less protection and more exposure as the answer to all problems. Children are encouraged to see themselves as the equal of adults, with equal bargaining powers and rights, when the basic right of the child is to obey godly authorities which will lead him into godly maturity. It is a right of the child to have godly authority in home, church, school, state, and community, because it is that godly authority which will best equip him for maturity, responsibility, and authority. Our Lord said, "Whoso shall offend one of these little ones which believe in me, it were better for him that a millstone were hanged about his neck, and that he were drowned in the depths of the sea" (Matt. 18:6). The word for *offend* means to put a snare or a stumbling block in their pathway, i.e., to frustrate their godly growth in faith, obedience, and responsibility.

Why is rebellion comparable to occultism, to fortune-telling, witchcraft, and every form of such illicit practice? To seek the occultist route to the future is to say that the future is determined apart from God, either by a dark and sinister fate, or else by an ostensibly autonomous man. In any case, the future is determined, and man is capitalized, by means other than those of God's ordination. For Scripture, it is faith, work, and obedience to the law of God that capitalized man and society spiritually and materially. For occultism, the future can be capitalized only by rebellion against God and against all godly authority.

Revolutionary movements have commonly had a background of atheism, free-masonry, and other occultist beliefs. The very idea of revolution is a belief that destruction, chaos, disobedience, and lawlessness can capitalize a society, and such a belief is basic to occultism. Hence, "rebellion is the sin of soothsaying, and opposition is the sin of heathenism and idolatry." Such attitudes decapitalize man and society and foster anarchy in every area.

Turning again to Matthew 18:6, the reference to execution by drowning, with a millstone around one's neck, was a Greek form of execution (Diod. Sic. xvi. 35), and, according to Suetonius, was used by Augustus for especially infamous offenses. Christ cites a particularly severe pagan penalty as preferable to the judgment God would execute on any who become a stumbling-block to "one of these little ones." The millstone cited was the larger, ass-drawn stone used for milling; no doubt, useless, worn, or broken millstones were used for execution purposes.

The rabbis regarded Jeroboam, the son of Nebat, as the greatest sinner because by his leadership all Israel was drawn into sin (I Kings 14:16). It is in this same spirit that Christ condemns all who cause little ones to stumble or fall into sin. Teachers, parents, pastors, and all others who incite or encourage rebellion in children thus fall under this severe indictment and classification.

Rebellion thus and all incitement to rebellion is a form or manifestation of occultism. The occult is that which is deliberately concealed from observation or knowledge; it is so concealed because it is antinomian; it is at war with law because it is lawless. It creates an opposition which is in essence idolatry, the enthronement of man's will as against the word of God.

The rise of occultism thus will foster rebellion in every area of society, and the rise of rebellion will likewise foster occultism. The two are linked and have their common origin in man's rebellion against God.

St. Paul, in citing the works of men who are not in the Spirit of God but are under the indictment or death penalty of the law, lists the related manifestations of such an unregenerate person:

> Now the works of the flesh are in evidence, such as adultery, unchastity, impurity, lewdness, idolatry, magic (KJV, witchcraft), animosities, hatred, jealousy, bad temper, dissensions, a factional spirit, heresies, envy, drunkenness, carousings and everything of the kind, of which I warn you as I did previously, that those who practice such things shall not inherit the kingdom of God (Gal. 5:19-21, Berkeley Version).

Rebellion is thus not an isolated fact; it is a part of a much larger pattern. In the history of revolutions and of cultural collapse, the occult plays a significant role. It is an evidence of radical decay and a major influence for destruction.

## 29

## INFUSION VS. IMPUTATION

Earlier (in chap. 24), Gregory of Nyssa's "Great Catechism" is cited, to the effect that "the God who was manifested infused Himself into perishable humanity for this purpose, viz., that by this communion with Deity mankind might at the same time be deified."

As against this heretical opinion, let us examine the statement of the Westminster Confession of Faith, chapter XI, "Of Justification," section I:

> Those whom God effectually calleth, He also freely justifieth: not by infusing righteousness into them, but by pardoning their sins, and by accounting and accepting their persons as righteous; not for any thing wrought in them, or done by them, but for Christ's sake alone; nor by imputing faith itself, the act of believing, or any other evangelical obedience to them, as their righteousness; but by imputing the obedience and satisfaction of Christ unto them, they receiving and resting on Him and His righteousness by faith; which faith they have not of themselves, it is the gift of God.

Infusion is pagan to the core, and means spirit-possession, or the infusion of divine gifts and attributes, sometimes induced by wine or by drugs. Thus, in the cults of Bacchus, the women were by means of systematically induced frenzy and ecstasy, whipped up into a supernormal and savage kind of activity. Bacchus was not only the god of wine, but, for the Egyptians, one of the rulers of the underworld, according to Herodotus.[1] The rites of Bacchus (or Dionysus) were marked by wild dances, drunkenness, and ecstasy. An aspect of the worship of Bacchus or Dionysus was the killing of a live goat by rending it in pieces and devouring it raw. Since the goat was a form assumed by Dionysus, the cult members apparently believed that they ate thereby the body and blood of their god. Thus, there was an infusion of the god by drinking wine, by ecstasy, and by eating the goat's body and blood. At every step, infusion meant the act of man, whereby an attribute, spirit, or power of utterance of the god was seized by man.

Imputation, on the other hand, is entirely the act of God's sovereign grace, whereby the righteousness of Christ, His obedience to and satisfaction of God's justice and law, is imputed to the elect. Imputation is a legal fact; infusion is a human experience. The elect are righteous in

---

1. *Herodotus*, II, 123; p. 144. New York: Harper, 1879.

their justification only by imputation, not by any experience or infusion. Romans 4:6-7; 5:18-19; II Corinthians 5:21, and other texts make this abundantly clear.

The regeneration of the elect is not by infusion but their recreation, their transference from the death of sin into the new humanity of Jesus Christ. Sanctification is not by infusion but by growth in obedience to the law of God.

Pagan oracles represent very good examples of infusion. Whether in ancient Greece or old Hawaii, the god or spirit supposedly entered the priest and created convulsions and frenzy, a rolling on the ground, foaming at the mouth, and a meaningless babbling at times, all of which was often induced by drugs, food, or by music, fumes, and similar means.[2]

The line thus between *infusion* and *possession* is a thin one, and possession often accompanies infusion.

In the pagan practices, a god or spirit spoke through the person. In the phrygian movement within the church, there is an implicit and sometimes explicit new canon, apart from Scripture, in the various utterances. Some of the consequences are both ludicrous and disruptive. Such people will at times declare that God's Spirit has ordered through them that John Smith marry Jane Jones! They will declare that certain acts are ordered, or countermanded, and normal obligations, duties, and debts are set aside. Infallibility is claimed for these utterances. These become thus a new canon, but not a Christian one.

---

2. Sir James George Frazer, edited by T. H. Gaster: *The New Golden Bough*, p. 63f. New York: Criterion Books, 1959.

## 30

## DEBT AND DECAPITALIZATION

It is inevitable that occultism should decapitalize man and society, both materially and spiritually. Occultism is an intensive application of the Satanic principle that every man is his own god, choosing, knowing, or establishing what constitutes good and evil for himself (Gen. 3:5). The fall of man meant not only that man was now his own god but also his own heaven and hell, his own universe. As his own universe, man could not therefore tolerate another man, and it is not surprising thus that Cain killed Abel (Gen. 4:8), and Lamech early in history celebrated his autonomy from all men by boasting of his freedom and power to kill other men at will (Gen. 4:23-24).

God's heaven and hell being denied, it becomes necessary for man to create his own heaven and hell. But, because man cannot, being a sinner, create a heaven, but only a hell which is a projection of his own nature, fallen man, aiming at paradise, creates ever-proliferating hell on earth.

A consequence of this is that man, in his social development, while an unbeliever in God, becomes in some fashion a believer in the devil. The only real world fallen man will acknowledge has to be, in terms of the implied logic of his position, in some sense demonic. The result is the kind of perspective set forth in the fall of 1968 by Mick Jagger and the Rolling Stones, a "rock-music" group, in a composition called "Sympathy for the Devil." In the song, the Devil, as the singer, says we know him better than we think. He is present in all violence, good and bad, in revolution in all its horrors, and we cannot choose only the "good" side of the violence our efforts engender but must accept our world as our creation.

The acceptance of violence as a new faith appeared in another Jagger song about rape, in which "Jagger brilliantly mimed the acts of rape and murder. As he twisted himself voluptuously around his unseen victim, teenage girls leapt up on the stage and threw themselves hysterically at his feet—'Do it to me!' I heard one yell"[1]

The principle of this Faustian "sympathy for the devil" is the belief that "it is only by virtue of 'everything you call sin, destruction, evil' that any sort of creation can go on."[2] The conclusion therefore is, "Accept

---

1. Marshall Berman, "Sympathy for the Devil: Faust, the 60s and the Tragedy of Development," in Theodore Solotaroff, ed.: *American Review 19*, January, 1974, p. 34. New York: Bantam Books, 1974.
2. *Ibid.*, p. 47.

your destructiveness as part of your divine creativity, and you can throw off your guilt and leave your closet."[3] In terms of this world-view, The Doors, another "song" group, sing "We want the world, and we want it—NOW!" But as Berman recognizes, he and his fellow radicals of the 1960s, who were out to destroy in order to create, were no different from the Establishment they were opposing, for President Johnson too "wanted the world even more than we did, and who was bombing it—for the sake of its future developement, of course—even as we marched and sang."[4]

Departure from God means the affirmation of regeneration by violence and destruction, hell as the means of building heaven. It means not only sympathy for the devil but that *all* sides of the humanistic spectrum are now in principle demonic, communists and conservatives, anarchists and socialists, fascists and republicans, *all alike embrace variations of a common principle of autonomy from God and a self-definition of ends and means.* In every area, therefore, their activity becomes destructive. Hatred remains, but the ability to make valid moral judgments disintegrates.

The society of fallen man's dreams is one which is an imitation of his ideas of heaven. Because God neither grows old, develops, or changes (Mal. 3:6), being absolute and perfect, the imagined society has like attributes. Future consequences are not properly envisioned, in that their "eternal" order should supposedly embody both will and potentiality in its creation.

Let us examine the implications of this for the economic organization of society, particularly in the area of *interest*. More than a few societies in the past have been bitterly hostile to the taking of interest, or, to use the older term, *usury*. Usury is a recognition of problems, or shortages, needs, and crises. A man or a business needs money desperately, to survive a crisis or to effect a necessary growth, and a loan with interest becomes their resort. Such loans can be effected either directly to a person or business, or indirectly through a bank. All depositors in banks are lenders, and the bank serves as their lending agency and shares the proceeds or interest with them. Those who affirmed an eternal social order, here and now, dislike the idea of interest because it means problems, change, and development.

In ancient Greece, the horror for usury was based on a realistic recognition that continuous interest had led to a concentration of power in the hands of moneylenders, so that most Athenians, for example, who were nominal freemen were actual slaves to a small plutocracy. The consequence was debt repudiation under Solon (594 B. C.).

---

3. *Ibid.*, p. 48.
4. *Ibid.*, p. 69.

Ancient Rome tried to regulate interest by setting a maximum rate, but again the result was failure. A maximum rate denies the significance of supply and demand; those who decried the high rates resented even more the unavailability of any loans at a required low rate. In Rome, the small free farmers, caught in the pressures of war, taxes, and interest, were either wiped out and reduced to slavery, or continued as virtual slaves. When Julius Caesar instituted debt repudiation, the middle classes were already destroyed.

Because of these and like experiences, the ancient world, and its thinkers, men such as Aristotle, Cato, and Cicero, regarded usury or interest as evil, and Cato held it to be as destructive as murder. On the other hand, neither they nor the medieval opponents of usury could eliminate it: in a non-eternal world, societies required it for development. Moreover, as societies grew, the commercial use of interest began to outweigh by far the use of loans for necessities and disasters. In modern society industrial development is heavily dependent on commercial loans, so that now far more loans are made to wealthy individuals and corporations than to poor and needy persons. As a result, the old hostility to usury is regarded in most quarters as a matter of historical interest only. (This situation can change drastically in an economic crisis.)

The classical view opposed usury because it was not only a recognition of problems, shortages, needs, and crises, but also a factor which aggravated what it was supposed to solve. Ancient pagan societies were in some sense all divine societies, representations of the order desired by the gods, and usury was a standing insult to the integrity of that order. Plato's *Republic* is an extreme statement of social order, but it is also very representative of the ancient, classical idea of a fixed, unchanging state. Interest or usury is a most effective instrument of change, and its wise or unwise use alike alter the nature of man's economic status and the social order he lives in. Interest or usury was thus a principle of revolution within society and hence a menace to a supposedly fixed social order. Whenever the old pagan dream of a fixed and permanent order is revived, as under Marxism, the free functioning of interest is arrested or abolished, because it is recognized as a revolutionary (or counter-revolutionary) force.

In the modern era, together with the humanistic doctrine of progress, the idea of the free market for interst has been precisely this, a revolutionary force, and the result has been a radical and continuing change in every social order which becomes modern. Interest has been seen as freedom to grow, and the early champions of interest in the seventeenth century wrote of it with almost religious fervor. In the 1960s, a major industrialist, an orthodox Christian, told me that, at this point, Biblical law was invalid, because interest was essential to the growth of modern technology.

Howard E. Kershner saw the fallacy of the modern perspective to a degree, in his analysis of the falacy of long-term, compound interest: "At 5 percent compounded annually, money doubles in a little less than 15 years, or about seven times in a century." As a result, Kershner points out, had one million dollars been loaned at five percent compounded annually from the day that Columbus discovered America, there would today not be enough money in all the world to repay the loan. "Obviously, long, continued compound interest is a fallacy and any government dedicated to maintaining it will bankrupt itself."

Society, Kershner states, has devised three methods over the centuries to correct this error. The *first*, which he does not consider seriously, is the Biblical law of the sabbath years and the Jubilee, and the limitation of loans to six years.

*Second*, the private enterprise system provides correction through bankruptcies, so that only the unwise are penalized, Kershner states. This does not prevent the process of concentration common to Greece, Rome, and modern societies, so that, while Kershner prefers this alternative, it is no long-range answer. As he recognizes, "The people of this country are now paying out one-sixth or more of their income for interest on various kinds of debts."

*Third*, in socialist countries "monetary reform" is used to solve the matter. On a given day, all old rubles, for example, are exchanged for new ones, so that 100 old ones become replaced by 10 new ones. Inflation is thereby halted, but the essential evil of the creation of new money, by long-term compound interest and by credit and state creation, is not eliminated. The same process is soon repeated.[5]

The answer of Biblical law to the problem of debt needs urgent attention in our time. In Deuteronomy 15:1-7, we have a central statement of this law:

> At the end of every seven years, there must be a cancelling of debts, and this shall be the way of the cancelling: Every creditor shall cancel the loan he made to his neighbor or to his brother; he shall make no demand for repayment, because the LORD'S release has been proclaimed. A foreigner you may press for payment, but whatever of yours was due from a brother you shall cancel.
> However, there should be no poor among you, for the LORD your God will abundantly bless you in the land He will give you to possess as a heritage, if you listen to the LORD your God and rightly observe all these commandments which today I am enjoining upon you. When the LORD your God blesses you as He promised you, then you shall lend to many nations, but not borrow; you shall rule many nations, but they shall not rule over you.
> When there is among you a poor man, a brother of yours, in one of

---

5. See Howard E. Kershner, "Why the Socialist State Will Inevitably Bankrupt Itself," in *Through to Victory*, vol. X, no. 3, March, 1970, pp. 1, 3-5.

the towns which the LORD will be granting you, you shall not
harden your heart or close your hand for your poor brother, refusing
him a loan; no, you shall open wide your hand for him and lend him
liberally to meet his need amply (Berkeley Version).

Basic to this law are several principles. *First*, for free men in a free society,
the only godly principle is short-term debt, six years only, no more. No
man has a right to mortgage his future: he belongs to God. Since debt is
slavery, the godly man cannot enslave himself by means of debt for "the
borrower is slave to the lender" (Prov. 22:7, Berkeley Version). *Second*,
since the ungodly are slaves to sin, they are in principle slaves and cannot
be prevented from manifesting their bondage. Long-term loans are permissible to them, nor is there any cancellation of debts on the sabbatical
year. *Third*, loans to a needy brother, charitable loans, are to be without
interest (Ex. 22:25-27; Lev. 25:35-38; Deut. 23:19-20). Charity and
business are two separate things and are not to be confused. However, a
loan to a brother is *not* a gift: it is a loan. *Fourth*, the ungodly are excluded
both from the charitable loan and from the cancellation of debt. They
cannot have the privileges of faith without faith.

*Fifth*, during the six years of debt, there is no limited liability, as in
modern society.[6] There is unlimited liability, but a limited term to debt
and interest.

*Sixth*, in a society in which men are believers who obey God's law,
there will be no poor, according to God's declaration. Obedience to this
law would prevent the polarization of society into the rich and poor.
Debts would be restricted; the pernicious and inflationary effects of debt
and interest would be curtailed, and a greater degree of freedom and
responsibility would prevail.

*Seventh*, the modern form of long-term debt with compound interest
on notes and loans, plus the limited-liability laws, make possible a rapid
and inflationary growth followed by a radical and revolutionary
decapitalization and destruction of society. This the Biblical law
prevents.

---

6. On limited liability, see R. J. Rushdoony: *Politics of Guilt and Pity*, pp. 252, 254-262.
Nutley, N. J.: Craig Press, 1970. See also R. J. Rushdoony: *Institutes of Biblical Law*, pp.
104-106, 273f., 463-467, 664-669, Nutley, N. J.: Craig Press, 1973.

## 31

## THE LAWS OF INHERITANCE

The *occult* is the hidden, the veiled, the underground, and the word *occult* comes from the Latin *occultus*, past participle of *occulo*, hide. In an occultist society, if such a thing were possible, all assets, power, and activity would be hidden. To the degree that occultism flourishes in any society, to that degree, through fear of envy, confiscation, and assault, wealth is hidden and signs of prosperity carefully concealed. Leadership is avoided, because it invites hidden malice and attack, and no one wants to appear more active and industrious than others, for fear of ostracism and veiled retaliation. Occultism is closely tied to envy and hatred, and to levelling and equalitarian demands. Occultism *uproots* the open, stable orders of society by its insistence on the priority and fulfilment of hidden demands and impulses.

As a result occultism and equalitarianism have a common hostility to freedom of inheritance, to successions, because such succession establishes a continuing, orderly, and stable basis to society. If the hidden order is to succeed, the visible order must be dismantled. By arresting succession, the future is decapitalized, equalitarianism promoted, and the hidden, underground forces given a great advantage. An open, inherited order needs freedom and visibility to develop; an occultist order must destroy such freedom in favor of underground forces and hostilities which will paralyze capitalization and growth.

It is important therefore to understand the Biblical law of inheritance and its function. The order of succession is summarized as follows:

And thou shalt speak unto the children of Israel, saying, if a man die, and have no son, then ye shall cause his inheritance to pass unto his daughter.
And if he have no daughter, then ye shall give his inheritance unto his brethren.
And if he have no brethren, then ye shall give his inheritance unto his father's brethren.
And if his father have no brethren, then ye shall give his inheritance unto his kinsman that is next to him of his family, and he shall possess it: and it shall be unto the children of Israel a statute of judgment, as the LORD commanded Moses (Num. 27:8-11).

It is a parental duty to provide an inheritance to godly children as far as one's means will allow (II Cor. 12:14). A godly child could not be set

171

aside for reasons of a personal sort, i.e., a dislike for the mother and a preference for a second wife (Deut. 21:15-17). Unless set aside for moral reasons, as in the case of Reuben and others, the first-born sons gained a double portion (Deut. 21:16-17), which meant the responsibility for the care of the parents, and a double portion of responsibility for their debts. Although the inheritance of one tribe of Israel could not be transferred to another (Num. 36:1-12), meaning that land could not pass into outside control, a slave could inherit (Gen. 15:1-4), since he was a member of the family. Confiscation or seizure of property by the state is prohibited in Biblical law (Ezek. 46:18)[1]

The Biblical law of inheritance is religious and theological. Its basis is in the doctrine of the fatherhood of God over His chosen or elect people. God redeemed Israel as a Father, according to Exodus 4:22-23:

> And thou shalt say unto Pharaoh, Thus saith the LORD, Israel is my son, even my firstborn:
> And I say unto thee, Let my son go, that he may serve me; and if thou refuse to let him go, behold, I will slay thy son, even thy firstborn.

*First*, it is clear that God declares Himself to be the Father of Israel by grace, and, as Father, He will redeem His captive son. The *fatherhood* God speaks of is not simply hyperbole or imagery: it is *a legal fact*. Israel as God's son by grace has a legal relationship which means *heirship*, and God has no intention of allowing His heir to be destroyed. *Second*, God declares, "Let my son go, that he may serve me." The realm to be inherited by the son requires work and development. The father builds up an estate so that his son may continue therein, and he requires service of the son towards the holy purposes of the family, subduing the earth and exercising dominion over it. Inheritance means successions and service in a common task. Heirship means responsibility and service. Thus, heirship is not only a legal fact, but it is also a question of work and succession. The element of necessary succession makes clear why a slave could inherit but not a relative in another tribe; the slave, while not a blood relative, would be in the succession of faith and purpose, an important fact. *Third*, God takes His fatherhood so seriously that He declares, "if thou refuse to let him (My son) go, behold, I will slay thy son, even thy firstborn." The death of the firstborn of Egypt was the result. In every age, God strikes at the power and the firstborn of the world to deliver His chosen sons into His service. *We have every reason to expect the same today, and we must also serve God as He requires us to do.*

God not only declares Himself to be His people's creator (as of all men), and their friend (Isa. 43:1; Jer. 30:10-11), but also the more

---

1. See R. J. Rushdoony: *The Institutes of Biblical Law*, p. 180f. Nutley, N. J.: The Craig Press, (1973) 1974.

faithful Father than their fathers after the flesh.

> Doubtless thou art our father, though Abraham be ignorant of us, and Israel acknowledge us not: thou O LORD, art our father, our redeemer; thy name is from everlasting (Isa. 63:16).

As Daube has pointed out, for Scripture "God was the owner and relative of the whole people."[2]

As the redeeming Father, God requires absolute obedience to His law (Ex. 20:2; Lev. 25: 38, etc.). His right to command obedience and to establish all is thus based not only on His role as creator of all things, but also on His role as the redeemer, the next of kin who is in fact the Father. As lawgiver, God establishes laws for every area of life, including land and inheritance.

Of the land laws and inheritance thereof, Leggett writes:

> Basic to the laws of land tenure in the Old Testament is the conviction that Yahweh is the true owner of the land. "The land shall not be sold in perpetuity, for the land is mine, for you are strangers and sojourners with me" (Lev. 25:23). Because the land was conceived of as belonging to Yahweh, religious and moral considerations were involved in questions of land ownership and transfer. One of the outworkings of this idea of God's ownership of the land was that no Israelite could lose his property permanently.[3]

Important though Leggett's study is, it misses the point to a degree, because the emphasis in the land laws and inheritance is God-centered, not man-centered. Israelites did lose their land, and it was God who dispossessed them by His judgment. To understand God's meaning in Leviticus 25:23, let us examine it closely: "The land shall not be sold for ever: for the land is mine; for ye are strangers and sojourners with me." The land cannot be sold "for ever" or "beyond recovery," and, in Leviticus 25:24, it is added, "And in all the land of your possession, ye shall grant a redemption for the land," or "a right of redemption shall ye give to the land" (Rotherham). *First*, it is clear that the emphasis is not on man's tenure but on God's ownership. In fact, vs. 24, in speaking of redemption emphasizes the right of *the land* to be redeemed, not man's tenure. Because the earth is the Lord's, the land is reserved to God for His purposes, not man's, nor the state's. The redemption of the land is *to the Lord*, "for the land is mine." *Second*, God says to the Israelite possessors, "for ye are strangers and sojourners with me." C. D. Ginsburg made clear the meaning of this in his comment:

> God has not only helped the Israelites to conquer the land of Canaan, but has selected it as His own dwelling-place, and erected

---

2. David Daube: *Studies in Biblical Law*, p. 47.
3. Donald A. Leggett: *The Levirate and Goel Institutions in the Old Testament, with Special Attention to the Book of Ruth*, p. 84. Cherry Hill: Mack Publishing Company, 1974.

His sanctuary in the midst of it (Ex. xv. 13; Num. xxxv. 34). He therefore is enthroned in it as Lord of the soil, and the Israelites are simply His tenants at will (chapts. xiv. 34, xx. 24, xxiii. 10; Num. xiii. 1, xv. 2), and as such will have to quit it if they disobey His commandments (chapts. xviii. 28, xx. 22, xxvi. 33: Deut. xxviii 63). For this reason they are accounted as strangers and sojourners, and hence have no right absolutely to sell that which is not theirs.[4]

God remains, and the land remains. The people are tenants whose tenure depends on God's mercy and on their obedience. They are accounted as aliens and pilgrims, even though they are God's people, because they perish, but the land remains. The people's perspective thus cannot be in terms of their own life span, or that of their blood heirs, but only in terms of God the Father and His creation purpose. The more they are aware of their transient nature, the more permanent their roots in God and His land become, because they then align themselves with God rather than their brief span. The psalm of Moses, Psalm 90, sets forth the godly attitude, whereas our Lord's parable of the rich fool (Luke 12:16-21) gives us that attitude which leads to dispossession. *Third*, because the earth is the Lord's, man's possession thereof must be in terms of godly heirship in the Lord and in terms of His purpose. The point of the law of land tenure and inheritance was not to establish an Israelite *blood* line in possession but an Israelite *faith* line. Anything other, God declared (Deut. 28) He would dispossess. The temple land of the Lord had to be surrounded by the people of the Lord who would pass on a succession of faith and land in terms of God's law and creation mandate. To fix land tenure in the hands of the ungodly is not God's purpose: He works to dispossess all such men. It is His purpose that "the meek shall inherit the earth; and shall delight themselves in the abundance of peace" (Ps. 38:11). This is emphatically restated by our Lord: "Blessed are the meek: for they shall inherit the earth" (Matt. 5:5). Again, in both cases, the word *inherit* is used in its literal, legal sense: as heirs of the Father, the blessed meek, the redeemed, the tamed of God, shall inherit the earth and shall serve the Father. The godly tenure of productive land is thus a necessary and Biblical requirement, but the inheritance thereof must be essentially a theological rather than a genealogical fact.

Leggett is very right in seeing the Biblical relationship between *property and person*. Property is an essential instrument of dominion; the creation mandate requires, among other things, the development of property and power in and through property as an instrument of dominion. The purpose of the levirate was to perpetuate a godly inheritance and to develop its particular function in God's Kingdom.

Thus, instead of a hidden, occult strand, we have an emphatic require-

---

4. C. D. Ginsburg, "Leviticus," in Ellicott, I. 456.

ment in Scripture of an open, godly succession. According to Proverbs 13:22, "A good man leaveth an inheritance to his children's children: and the wealth of the sinner is laid up for the just." God's purpose in history works towards the dispossession of the false sons, who seized the earth after the Fall, and its repossession and succession in the hands of His sons of grace. Moses in his song on the Red Sea shore declared of Israel, "Thou shalt bring them in, and plant them in the mountain of thine inheritance, in the place, O LORD, which thou hast made for thee to dwell in, in the Sanctuary, O LORD, which thy hands have established" because it is so ordained in the counsel of God. The "planting" of God's elect people is in relationship to God's Sanctuary, in relation to God's being and purpose.

The psalmist declares, "The LORD is the portion of mine inheritance and of my cup: thou maintainest my lot" (Ps. 16:5). The reference here is to the tribe of Levi, whose inheritance is the Lord Himself rather than a specific place (Deut. 10:9; 18:1, 2). As the Lord's Kingdom prospers, so through tithes and offerings Levi prospers. This is ultimately true of all God's people: like the Levites, they depend on the prosperity of God's Kingdom.

Every attempt to undermine God's Kingdom and God's laws of inheritance is an attempt also to destroy the foundations of orderly life and is suicidal. There is indeed an apparent correlation beween occultism and suicide, a will to death.

A psalm of David deals with the problems of those whose life and inheritance is threatened by those who are destroying the foundations of society. David's answer to their doubts and fears is to call attention to the certainty of God's inheritance for His people, and the inheritance of judgment for the wicked. According to Psalm 11:

> In the LORD put I my trust: how say ye to my soul, Flee as a bird to your mountain?
> For, lo, the wicked bend their bow, they make ready their arrow upon the string, that they may privily shoot at the upright in heart.
> If the foundations be destroyed, what can the righteous do?
> The LORD is in his holy temple, the LORD'S throne is in heaven: his eyes behold, his eyelids try, the children of men.
> The LORD trieth the righteous: but the wicked and him that loveth violence his soul hateth.
> Upon the wicked he shall rain snares, fire and brimstone, and an horrible tempest: this shall be the portion of their cup.
> For the righteous LORD loveth righteousness; his countenance doth behold the upright.

Fearful men raise the question: when the foundations of society are being destroyed, what can the righteous do? David's answer is that God's inheritance is justice, and therefore the position of His people must not be flight but confidence in His redeeming power and their possession of a goodly inheritance in it, whereas the portion of the wicked is radical judgment.

Because the inheritance God gives His people is both temporal and eternal, His law governs the earth and eternity; it governs the inheritance of property and the gift of salvation. Property is not a secular or a humanistic concern for those who believe God's word: it is a theological trust, and a God-centered fact. Property cannot replace God in our lives, but neither can it be regarded as irrelevant to God and to matters of faith.

Children, like property, are an inheritance from the Lord (Ps. 127:3), and both are alike means of exercising and extending dominion over the earth. Children, like property, are weapons in the hands of godly men, and a means of subduing the enemy (Ps. 127:4-5). The people of God, "the flock," are "God's heritage" (I Peter 5:3), and their properties and children are aspects of God's heritage. Psalm 61:5 speaks of "the heritage of those that fear thy name," meaning thereby "the honours and privileges of the chosen people."[5] Inheritance is a theological fact in Scripture, and a legal fact. To by-pass the laws of inheritance as somehow "worldly," "purely civil", and irrelevant is to miss the point of Biblical faith and to diminish our understanding of the heritage of those who fear His name.

---

5. J. A. Alexander: *The Psalms, Translated and Explained*, p. 268. Grand Rapids: Zondervan (1850), reprint.

# 32

## INHERITANCE AND DOMINION

As we have seen, in Biblical law the firstborn gains a double portion of the estate but also assumes a like share of the debts as well as the care of the parents and family leadership.

The modern state has in effect declared itself to be the firstborn of every family and claims by means of inheritance taxes the right to often far more than a double portion, a prior right to the inheritance, and, by means of welfarism, it assumes support of the parents, if the survivor is needy. (The state does not assume any of the family's debt.) The state thus claims to be *the family of man* to a greater degree than the medieval church once asserted.

In the family under God, the eldest son (unless disinherited) receives, as we have noted, a double portion, and all other sons (unless disinherited) receive equal portions. There is thus a principle of *equality* for all godly sons. The state, as the firstborn, increasingly asserts its absolute priority as an heir to every estate and declares that a rigid principle of *equality* must apply to *all* members of "the family of man." The premise of such statist thinking is a modern equalitarian philosophy which has been well expressed by Josiah Wedgwood, in *The Economics of Inheritance*. The philosophy of this work, first published in 1929, is basic to the great decline of Britain. According to Wedgwood, in his Introduction to the 1938 edition,

in the new age of uncharitable faiths, the liberal economic method remains dispassionate and agnostic—agnostic in all but one respect. Those who employ that method need not affirm a wholesale belief in utilitarian philosophy; but they must not throw away the baby with the bath water. They must accept (in theory at least) the idea, inherent in all the great philosophies and not least in the ethics of Christianity, that the welfare of all human beings, irrespective of race, class, creed, or colour, is of equal importance in the sight of God and should be in the minds of men. Ten years ago it was not absurd optimism to assume that that belief formed a common basis underlying free discussion of social problems. An age seems to have passed since then. But anyone who takes the trouble to do any research on social and economic questions must still try to believe with Plato and the Stoics that "no soul wilfully misses truth."[1]

1. Josiah Wedgwood: *The Economics of Inheritance*, p. 7. Port Washington, N. Y.: Kennikat Press, (1929) 1971.

Despite his statement, Wedgwood is anything but "dispassionate" and emphatically *not* an "agnostic" with respect to statist humanism. Moreover, the Bible does *not* affirm his ideas of equality; Wedgwood knows full well that "the ethics of Christianity" mean the Bible and its law, and Biblical ideas of inheritance *cannot* be equated with his passionate equalitarianism. Again, to believe with Plato and the Stoics that "no soul wilfully misses the truth" is an amazing faith as well as a denial of man's depravity and sin. Wedgwood has wilfully missed the truth about the Bible and about himself.

Biblical law requires us to deal differently with (1) our family, (2) our brethren in the faith, and (3) the rest of men. All are to be dealt with in that love which is the fulfilling of the law, but we *cannot* love our neighbor's wife as we do our own without sin. Love does not mean equality, and godly law does not mean the equality of good and evil. It is intellectual suicide to reduce all things to equality or to insist on equality as the common denominator with either God or man. God, after all, is the maker of both heaven and hell.

Wedgwood cited Edwin Cannan against any correlation of income with work or service, and in favor of an equality of income based upon *need*. According to Cannan,

> Income according to service is almost obviously a hopelessly rotten ideal, since it means nothing for those who, temporarily or permanently, cannot serve at all, and these, in many cases, are the very people whose needs are greatest.... I have never swerved from the advocacy of the nearest possible approximation to distribution according to need, and have always looked on distribution according to service as a chimera, and an undersirable chimera.[2]

This is, of course, the Marxist principle, but it is common in varying forms to all humanists. The equality of the new godhead, mankind, is thereby asserted, and, in any theology, humanist or Biblical, the equal ultimacy of all persons in the godhead is a theological and philosophical necessity. The state as the firstborn has the prerogative of enforcing this equality on all so that society can be freed from subordinationism.

Practically, this means moving against the inheritance of wealth by gifts, succession, and marriage.[3] Wedgwood is aware "that all men are not born equal, and that they have inborn differences which are determined by differences in their ancestry."[4] However, what nature or God has done, he is determined to undo and mend by statist action. The goal is an equalitarian society.

---

2. From a letter to Dr. Scott Nearing, republished in *An Economist's Protest* (1927), and cited by Wedgwood, p. 52n.
3. *Ibid.*, pp. 76f. 240f.
4. *Ibid.*, p. 89.

Now Scripture gives no justification for an equalitarian order, and it also gives no ground whatsoever for an elitist order. Only a godly order, established in terms of Biblical law, is tenable in terms of Scripture. Elitism and equalitarianism are alike humanistic; they move in terms of man and man's hopes. The Bible is heedless of either philosophy. Scripture requires a God-centered society, one in which God's law militates against equalitarian and elitist goals. Both equalitarianism and elitism are in essence contemptuous of man in the name of man. The elitist despises the majority of men, and the equalitarian despises all able and independent men, but, in essence, both despise all men as men and love rather their *idea* of men, not man himself in the singular.

*Inheritance* in the Bible is theocentric. A word frequently used in Hebrew for inheritance is *chelek*, a portion or a providential bestowment. An inheritance is in essence from God and to be governed by His law. God as the creator designed the earth for the use of His people. Man is to hold land, cultivate it, and enjoy it (Gen. 1:28f.; Ps. 105: 16; Eccles. 5:9). This is God's avowed purpose. Man having fallen into sin, God began to plan the dispossession of the earth by fallen man in favor of covenant man. As a result, God promised a portion of the earth, Canaan, for Abraham's seed. When the Hebrews became numerous, God gave them Canaan as their portion. To prevent the return of God's earth to ungodly hands, God forbad the alienation of farm land by sale. The earth being the Lord's, it could not be transferred to any but covenantal kin. If Israel became apostate, God declared that He Himself would dispossess them (Deut. 28:63-68). The purpose of the non-transferrence law was thus to safeguard the land in the hands of covenant man, who would himself train up a godly seed to continue the use of the earth in the hands of God's agent. The goal was and is the possession of all things by covenant men. In Canaan, however, being surrounded by covenant breakers outside the land, and Canaanites within, as well as covenant-breaking Israelites, godly men were restricted in the disposition of the earth.

How seriously Scripture requires godliness to take priority over all other considerations in inheritance appears in a strongly stressed case, that of Othniel and his wife Achsah, daughter of Caleb. Caleb passed over his sons to make his daughter Achsah, and his son-in-law Othniel, his central heir (Josh. 15:16-19; Judges 1:13-15). Caleb and Othniel were in the covenant people by faith rather than by blood, and the priority of faith was set forth over blood and sex.

An inheritance could be divided during the lifetime of the father, and the prodigal son so requested it, and it was accordingly given to him. At the time, his prodigality was not yet apparent (Luke 15:12). The *purpose* of an inheritance is a *portion* or a *providential blessing*, which will enable the godly to extend their dominion over the earth.

There is thus of necessity a required inequality of inheritance, because there is a required moral division among men, and a religious division. God's law requires that the godly seed be blessed, and the ungodly set aside. Rebekah was thus religiously and righteously concerned when her husband Isaac showed every intention of making an heir, and the central heir, of an ungodly son, Esau, who despised the inheritance of faith and was casual about the material inheritance. The essential alienation of an inheritance is its transmissions to ungodly or to irresponsible hands. A *portion*, or a providential bestowment, should be the lot only of the righteous. It is thus unrighteousness to transmit an inheritance to the ungodly, whether blood kin or not.

Scripture gives us some very revealing usages of the word *chelek*, or providential bestowment. In Psalm 16:5, David declares, "The LORD is the portion of mine inheritance and of my cup: thou maintainest my lot." In Psalm 73:26, Asaph declares, "My flesh and my heart faileth: but God is the strength of my heart, and my portion for ever." More than land and gold, our greatest and essential portion or inheritance is the Lord.

In the Song of Moses, however, this same word is used in a startling sense: "For the LORD'S portion is his people; Jacob is the lot of his inheritance" (Deut. 32:9). The meaning is clearly set forth by C. H. Waller: "He chose Israel for His own portion, that through them He might inherit the world."[5] God's people are His inheritance, through whom He purposes to recapture the world and to exercise direct and full dominion according to His law. No inheritance can be separated from this purpose without sin.

It is clear too why statist intervention into matters of inheritance is so demonic. Such intervention enthrones the disinheritance of God into law. It strikes at the whole purpose of succession and dominion, and, as Cannan so malevolently affirmed, it sets aside service in favor of need, need as humanistically defined. Inheritance taxes are in essence anti-Christian, and every legitimate means should be used to avoid them.

The goal of occultism, atheism, and unbelief is the inheritance and possession of the earth and power without God and in defiance of Him. The goal of covenant man is the inheritance and possession of the earth and power and dominion over the earth under God and according to His law.

When God struck down the firstborn of Egypt in the tenth plague, He thereby destroyed the heirship of apostate man. By declaring Israel to be His firstborn, to be delivered from Egypt, He affirmed the heirship of covenant man to the earth. A godly law order will work to disinherit, execute, and supplant the ungodly and to confirm the godly in their inheritance. For Christians to work for anything less is to deny God.

---

5. C. H. Waller, "Deuteronomy," in Ellicott II, 88.

# 33

## INHERITANCE AND POSSESSION

God's fatherhood is not a matter of imagery or typology but is *a legal fact*. By the adoption of grace, we have been made "Abraham's seed, and heirs according to the promise" (Gal. 3:29). The promises to Abraham's seed are for those who are faithful to the covenant with Abraham, i.e., those who are by faith sons of Abraham. Those who meet this "spiritual" requirement are promised far-reaching *material* blessings (Gen. 17:1-9). If we are sons of God by faith, we are "then an heir of God through Christ" (Gal. 4:7). We are "heirs of God, and joint-heirs with Christ; if so be that we suffer with him, that we may be also glorified together" (Rom. 8:17). The work of Christ makes us His joint-heirs; our readiness to stand with Him and to suffer for His name's sake marks us as true heirs. The inheritance is real because Christ's work is real, and our membership in Him is real. Every aspect of the equation is real: to spiritualize away a part is to erode all.

Because God's fatherhood is a legal fact, our heirship is a legal fact, and we have by virtue of it been called to serve God and to reclaim our lost inheritance. The fulness of the inheritance is in the new creation, but it cannot be deferred entirely to the end of time. Proverbs 13:22 declares, "A good man leaveth an inheritance to his children's children: and the wealth of the sinner is laid up for the just." Scott comments, "This seems to mean that only the just can leave an inheritance, and they also inherit from the wicked."[1] When the just stand fully and clearly on the whole word of God, they are indeed heirs of all things, *but they cannot deny the law of God and be heirs under that law.* We are commanded to seek "first the Kingdom of God and his righteousness; and all these things shall be added to you" (Matt. 6:33). To place priority on gaining wealth invites judgment: "An inheritance (or, estate) may be gotten hastily at the beginning; but the end thereof shall not be blessed" (Prov. 20:21).

The inheritance of believers is a total one: The Kingdom of God (Matt. 25:34; I Cor. 6:9, 10; 15:50; Gal. 5:21; Eph. 5:5; James 2:2). They inherit the earth (Ps. 37:29; Matt. 5:5). They are heirs of salvation (Heb. 1:14), or a blessing (I Peter 3:9), of glory (Rom. 8:17-18), and of incorruption (I Cor. 15:50).

---

1. R. B. Y. Scott: *The Anchor Bible: Proverbs, Ecclesiastes*, p. 95. Garden City, New York: Doubleday, (1965) 1974.

To understand the meaning of inheritance, it is necessary to recognize that, in the Biblical law structure, *land and property belong to the family, not to the individual*. There were thus no wills: the estate remained in the family, and the only question was thus whether or not the firstborn was to be passed over, as with Ishmael and Esau, because of unbelief or rebellion, and whether any others were to be cut off for the same reason. Excommunication was from the faith *and* the family.

Because property belongs to the family, to be with the father meant to hold the property. As our Lord declares, in the parable of the Prodigal Son, the father reminds the elder son, "Son, thou art ever with me, and all that I have is thine" (Luke 15:31). To be with the father is to be a possessor here and now. This is a theological and legal fact.

To have a godly son was to have an inheritance from the Lord (Ps. 127:3), and God uses the same language concerning His sons: Ephesians 1:18 speaks of the saints as God's inheritance. However important the later expanded inheritance, the fact of possession is an important one here and now. The Lord God has His covenant people as an inheritance, and the covenant people have the Lord and all the earth as an inheritance here and now. According to R. E. Nixon, "In the Old Testament there are two basic roots for inheritance, nahal and yaras. In each case the emphasis was much more upon possession generally than upon the process of succession, though this is not altogether absent."[2] However, it must be added that there is possession because there is a succession of faith, a covenantal succession.

God's covenant requires *faith and obedience*, and the inheritance is conditional upon faith and obedience. This is clear throughout Scripture. Thus, in Leviticus 18:24-30, we read:

> Defile not ye yourselves in any of these things: for in all these the nations are defiled which I cast out before you:
> And the land is defiled: therefore I do visit the iniquity thereof upon it, and the land itself vomiteth out her inhabitants.
> Ye shall therefore keep my statutes and my judgments, and shall not commit any of these abominations: neither any of your own nation, nor any stranger that sojourneth among you:
> (For all these abominations have the men of the land done, which were before you, and the land is defiled;)
> That the land spue not you out also, when ye defile it, as it spued out the nations that were before you.
> For whosoever shall commit any of these abominations, even the souls that commit them shall be cut off from among their people.
> Therefore shall ye keep mine ordinance, that ye commit not any one of these abominable customs, which were committed before you, and that ye defile not yourselves therein: I am the LORD your God.

2. R. E. Nixon, "Inheritance," in J. D. Douglas, ed.: *The New Bible Dictionary*, p. 562. Grand Rapids, Mich.: Eerdmans, (1962) 1973.

*First*, it is clear that the defilement of sin is both personal and national. Both are alike made reprobate in the sight of God by the practice of loathsome offenses. Although these verses follow a catalogue of sexual offenses, the same judgment is pronounced on all sins. *Second*, the disinheritance is both personal and national. The timing of the judgment is in God's hands, and His patience sometimes exceeds man's comprehension. His patience too is in terms of His plans, and the judgment on Canaan was thus delayed until Israel was a numerous people and ready to utilize that land. *Third*, the disinheritance and judgment are both of God and of the earth itself, because of His providence and law. God speaks of casting out the Canaanites in His anger, and of their defilement. Sin defiles both the people and the land: "the land is defiled." Creation, although fallen, is still God's handiwork, and it rejects as alien all sin: it means a malfunctioning and a breakdown, and, even as the body works to heal and to cast out an infection, so the universe works to cast out sin. This is no less true of man: because man is not his own maker, his being is not only, in its fallen estate, in rebellion against God, but it is also in rebellion against his own sin. When we sin against God, we also sin against ourselves, and we are at cross purposes with our own being. *Fourth*, sin not only disinherits us but also renders us unclean. Uncleanness in Scripture is ceremonial, moral, and religious defilement, and it means both pollution and ultimately death. Most scholars fail to recognize the moral and religious aspects of uncleanness because they are under the influence of neoplatonism and cannot see that for Scripture the material and the spiritual are essentially identical. For the same reason, our inheritance from the Lord cannot be separated into the material and the spiritual. The idea that the Old Testament brought forth material promises and blessings, and the New Testament offers spiritual promises and blessings is invalid and is a false division of Scripture; it rests in part on an evolutionary perspective, so that some openly affirm that the more "primitive" Old Testament saints needed material encouragement to be holy, whereas now believers live on "a higher plane."

Some will deny the validity of material inheritance by pointing to the persecution of the early church by the Roman Empire. The early church, while not without its sins and shortcomings, was still richly blessed. One of the reasons for the savage hostility of Rome was precisely the rapid growth and success of the church, the prosperity of its members, and their prominence. The church was seen as a threat to Rome even when some described its faith as the silly superstitions of the ignorant. It is false history to read the history of the early church thus as one of persecution only: it was also a history of remarkable growth and prosperity.

To deny the unity of the material and spiritual is to deny the reality of God's creation and also to deny history. The growing irrelevance of the churches is grounded in part on this fact. Evangelical churches downgrade the material, and modernist churches downgrade the spiritual, and the result is for both of them a failure to cope with reality, let alone command it.

*Fifth*, inheritance means dominion, because it means that the blessing of God follows obedience (Deut. 28), and all true heirs obey the Father. Antinomianism thus is a mark of the disinherited. To believe and obey means that, despite the struggle with an evil generation, we are blessed with the prospering hand of God. *We cannot be sons and not heirs*. The sons therefore pray to the Father, their *legal* Father and Guardian, in the confidence that their common estate, power, and dominion will be used, in the Father's discretion and wisdom, to prosper His Kingdom.

# 34

## INHERITANCE, LOT, AND LAND

An essential insight into the Biblical doctrine of inheritance is found in Psalm 16:5. "The LORD is the portion of mine inheritance and of my cup: thou maintainest my lot." We have seen that *portion* is related to inheritance and means a providential bestowment, more specifically, the providential bestowment of God's justice, overriding man's sin and injustice. Thus, in Psalm 11:5-6, it is said that "the LORD trieth the righteous: but the wicked and him that loveth violence his soul hateth. Upon the wicked he shall rain snares, fire and brimstone, and an horrible tempest: this shall be the portion of their cup." Psalm 23 has this in mind also when it declares, in verse 5, "my cup runneth over"; in the presence of his enemies, David is richly provided for by God's redeeming justice.

Leupold translates Psalm 16:5 thus: "The Lord is my choice portion and my cup; thou wilt make my portion of land broad."[1] Because the land, at the time of Joshua's conquest of Canaan, was divided by lot, the land itself came to be called by this term, as in Joshua 15:1; 17:14ff.; Judges 1:3; Isaiah 57:6, etc. Hence, observed Whitehouse, "we frequently find this term metaphorically applied to express the destiny which is awarded by God, whether favorable or the reverse (Ps. 16:5; Is. 17:14; 34:17; Jer. 13:25; Deut. 12:12)."[2]

Psalm 16:6 seems to bear out Leupold's interpretation: "The lines are fallen unto me in pleasant places; yea, I have a goodly heritage." Leupold renders it, "The allotted piece of field has fallen to my lot in pleasant places; Yea, I have a goodly heritage." By his rendering, "*allotted* piece of field" and "*my* lot," Leupold brings together the double meaning of *lot*, providential appointment or inheritance, and land, the land inherited from the Lord.

The word *lot* has reference to the Biblical practice, terminated at Pentecost, of making a choice by casting lots. Such a decision took the matter out of man's hands and stressed a total reliance on God's predestination. By separating man, himself an aspect of God's predestination, from the decision, the direct decree of God was stressed.

---

1. H. C. Leupold: *Exposition of the Psalms*, p. 147, Columbus, Ohio: The Wartburg Press, 1959.
2. Owen C. Whitehouse, "Lots," in James Hastings, ed.: *A Dictionary of the Bible*, III, p. 153. New York: Charles Scribner's Sons, 1919.

After Pentecost, the Spirit working through the people of God effected the same results.

Thus the word *portion* stresses an inheritance from God by means of His providential bestowment, and the word *lot* makes the same doctrine more emphatic by underscoring the predestinating counsel of God in our *portion*. Our *portion* and our *lot* include our total inheritance of all things and experiences, material and spiritual, but the association of *lot* with *land* makes impossible its separation from the material. Just as the supreme fact of history is the incarnation, so the requirement of history is the materialization of our *lot*. The people of faith must become the people of the land, because "The earth is the LORD'S, and the fulness thereof; the world, and they that dwell therein" (Ps. 24:1). Therefore, "the meek shall inherit the earth; and shall delight themselves in the abundance of peace" (Ps. 37:11).

This association of *lot* with our *inheritance of land* is apparent in Psalm 125:

> They that trust in the LORD shall be as mount Zion, which cannot be removed, but abideth for ever.
> As the mountains are round about Jerusalem, so the LORD is round about his people from henceforth even for ever.
> For the rod of the wicked shall not rest upon the lot of the righteous; lest the righteous put forth their hands unto iniquity.
> Do good, O LORD, unto those that be good, and to them that are upright in their hearts.
> As for such as turn aside unto their crooked ways, the LORD shall lead them forth with the workers of iniquity: but peace shall be upon Israel.

This is hymn of trust, declaring that the Lord is the protector of His people. It deals with the menace of evil men to a godly people; the material and spiritual aspects cannot be isolated from each other. Thus, verse 3 deals with the protection of the righteous from marauding and murderous enemies. Leupold holds that "the lot of the righteous" refers to the land divided to the covenant people from the time of the conquest of Canaan.[3] Such an interpretation makes the whole psalm clearer in meaning, for "the rod of the wicked" or "sceptre of wickedness" (Leupold) clearly refers to an oppressive and menacing foreign power which threatens the covenant nation. A covenant nation which trusts in the Lord will not have its "lot," its land, subject to the tyranny and depradation of the ungodly nations.

*The significance of the land to the covenant* appears in Psalm 105. God, having established His covenant with Abraham, "confirmed the same unto Jacob for a law, and to Israel for an everlasting covenant: Saying, Unto thee will I give the land of Canaan, the lot of your

---

3. Leupold, *op. cit.*, p. 885.

inheritance" (Ps. 105:10-11). In gaining Canaan, "they inherited the labour of the people" (Ps. 105:44). The covenant people are promised a land, and the land is a sign of the covenant, and the place where God's law is obeyed, enforced, and made the way of life, or sanctification, for the redeemed people. The covenant of redemption has the law as its way of life, and the law requires the land for its application and for the fruits or results of obedience. The ungodly nations are disinherited, and the covenant nations inherit their labors.

The last use of lots is in Acts 1:26, when the lot was used to replace Judas with Matthias, to restore the number of apostles to twelve. Why the necessity for twelve? Why the symbolic use of this number? Others besides the twelve apostles functioned equally well and ably as proclaimers of the gospel. In fact, more than a few are better known for their ministry than are many of the twelve, as witness Paul, Silas, Barnabus, Timothy, Titus, and others. Why were twelve men retained in a special status?

The answer clearly is that the twelve apostles represent the true succession to the twelve sons of Jacob, as the new Israel of God. There was thus no need to maintain a continuing body of twelve apostles; like the twelve sons of Jacob, they represent the beginning of a new nation, a new kingdom of kings and priests unto God (Rev. 1:6), and the new heirs of the promised land, now the whole earth (Rev. 21:1). It was therefore imperative that the apostles confront Israel and the world as the twelve men of Christ's Israel, whose lot it was to divide the world for their inheritance, a task still under mandate to all in the apostolic succession of faith.

The preaching of the gospel to "the whole world" was clearly in our Lord's mind (Matt. 26:13). Once the apostles and disciples began their missionary work outside Judea, they began to go aggressively into the whole world, to bring all powers and principalities into captivity to Christ. It is not hyperbole when St. Paul speaks of "the whole world" hearing the gospel in his day (Rom. 1:8; 10:18). We know that St. Thomas, who may have made two missionary journeys into China, died in India.

The *lots* were thus used for the selection of the twelfth apostle, Matthias, to indicate that the new conquest, greater than Canaan, belongs to the people of the renewed covenant, who shall inherit the earth, their lot, and establish Christ's Kingdom in righteousness and truth.

Inheritance in Scripture thus means that by the adoption of grace we are the legal sons of God, and our inheritance is the land or earth. The means to the possession of our inheritance is faith *and* the application of the covenant law.

## 35

## INHERITANCE AND WORK

One of the many sorry aspects of the neoplatonic influence is its contempt for physical work. Because neoplatonism sees the material world as the realm of bondage, manual labor is regarded as degrading and enslaving. The Talmud gives evidence of similar ideas having infiltrated Hebrew thought. Thus, R. Neborai declared, "I abandon every trade in the world and teach my son Torah (law) only."[1] R. Huna b. Idi held, "Once a man is appointed head of a community, he may not do (manual) labour in the presence of three."[2] The more common and prevailing rabbinic teaching was more Scriptural and held:

> The father is bound in respect of his son, to circumcise, redeem (if the son is a firstborn), teach him Torah, take a wife for him, and teach him a craft. Some say, to teach him to swim too. R. Judah said: He who does not teach his son a craft, teaches him brigandage.[3]

The contempt for work gained power with the Renaissance and Enlightenment, and it led to the degradation of the worker throughout Europe. The worker's status in medieval Europe was low enough, but there was at least theologically some vindication of his position. Humanism undid this advantage. The Victorian era, from whence came Darwin and Marx, was notable also for its contempt for physical work. A gentleman was a man who did not work but lived off an inherited income. The middle class merchants and industrialists who earned fortunes often struggled then to rid themselves and their sons of the taint of work. A gentlewoman of the period was even more radically removed from all physical labor. As Dawes notes,

> Women of the Victorian and Edwardian middle classes regarded a life of complete idleness as being essential to maintaining their position in life. If they put a piece of coal on the fire, lifted a duster or answered a doorbell, they were "letting their husbands down." Or worse, depriving a needy person of employment. So, during the Great Age of Servants, a whole class of women was reared that was incapable of performing even the simplest domestic services for itself. These gentle mistresses never had to make a pot of tea, wash a

---

1. *The Babylonian Talmud, Kiddushin*, 82a; p. 423 of The Soncino Press, London, 1936 edition.
2. *Ibid.*, *Kid*. 70a, p. 355.
3. *Ibid.*, *Kid*. 29a, p. 137f.

cup, darn a sock, post a letter, or even brush their own hair.[4]

Because of its Puritan background, the United States has been least subject to this contempt for physical work, and much of its leadership in productivity has been due to this fact. In recent years, the Europeanization of American intellectuals has led to a growing contempt for work together with a patronizing "defense" of the working man. This "defense" rests on the intellectuals' premise that all physical work has implicit in it some form of exploitation, an idea common also to Marx.

We cannot begin to understand the Biblical doctrine of work unless we approach it theologically, unless we begin with God. According to Moshe Greenberg, in the Bible

> Labor was considered so much a part of the cosmic order that God Himself is depicted as a worker. He "founded" the earth, and the heavens are his "Handi-(or "finger-") work" (Ps. 8:4; 102:26); He is the "fashioner" (yozer) of everything (Jer. 10:16); man is clay and God the potter (yozer; Isa. 64:7, based on Gen. 2:7). He worked six days at creating the world.... [5]

In all the creation outside of heaven, only God and man work as an aspect of their being. Domestic animals are made to work by man. Some animals, like squirrels, collect and store food, but work beyond the requirement of survival is an attribute only of God's image-bearer, man. Work which looks beyond survival to long-term purposes in terms of dominion and the Kingdom of God is a characteristic of man alone in this universe.

In a remarkable passage, Isaiah speaks about the love of God in judgment. God's judgments upon His chosen people are compared to the faithful work of a good farmer for his soil: he breaks it up to plant it and make it fruitful unto himself. According to Isaiah 28:23-29,

> Give ye ear, and hear my voice; hearken, and hear my speech.
> Doth the plowman plow all day to sow? doth he open and break the clods of his ground?
> When he hath made plain the face thereof, doth he not cast abroad the fitches, and scatter the cummin, and cast in the principal wheat and the appointed barley and the rie in their place?
> For his God doth instruct him to discretion, and doth teach him.
> For the fitches are not threshed with a threshing instrument, neither is a cart wheel turned upon the cummin; but the fitches are beaten out with a staff, and the cummin with a rod.
> Bread corn is bruised; because he will not ever be threshing it, nor break it with the wheel of his cart, nor bruise it with his horsemen.
> This also cometh forth from the LORD of hosts, which is wonderful in counsel, and excellent in working.

4. Frank Dawes: *Not in Front of the Servants, A True Portrait of English Upstairs/Downstairs Life*, p. 22. New York: Taplinger Publishing Company, 1974.
5. Moshe Greenberg, "Labor," in *Encyclopaedia Judaica*, 10, p. 1319.

The farmer, Isaiah points out, is not haphazard. He has a careful method in plowing, planting, and threshing, and his timing and method varies from crop to crop. God similarly is "purposeful, orderly, and discriminating." Moreover, "like the farmer, God is working out a long-term plan and adapts his methods to its successful stages and to different stages."⁶ God's purpose is the ultimate salvation of His covenant people, and thus there is always more to the moment's work than the considerations of the moment.

In the course of this statement, Isaiah makes some very important statements concerning work. In verse 26, it is clearly stated that God teaches and corrects the farmer. This is not by special revelation but by the image of God in men, so that man's ability to work purposely is an aspect of his being and the creative gift of God. As he examines this ability of man to work with foresight, Isaiah in verse 29 expresses his amazement. He uses language earlier applied to the Messiah (Isa. 9:6), declaring of God, that He "is wonderful in counsel, and excellent in working" as He reveals Himself in man's work.⁷

Work was thus God's purpose for men. The fall affected work; it is *not* work that is a curse, as some have wrongly assumed, but fallen man's work that is under a curse (Gen. 3:17-19). Work, whereby man was to exercise dominion and subdue the earth (Gen. 1:26-28), now became, no longer the means to dominion but a frustration. Thus, the curse placed upon work, man's great privilege, was a *first* consequence of man's revolt against God. *Second*, death was the inevitable consequence of sin (Gen. 2:17). *Third*, because man had made himself, rather than God, the arbiter and judge of good and evil, he was separated from the good, from the tree of life, and cast out of Eden (Gen. 3:22-24). However, as H. D. McDonald noted, "In redemption, work is again transformed into a means of blessing."⁸

Because work is an aspect of the image of God in man, the application of knowledge, righteousness, holiness, and dominion to actual problems and situations, work can in the long run only prosper when it is done in obedience to His word. "Except the LORD build the house, they labour in vain that build it: except the LORD keep the city, the watchman waketh but in vain" (Ps. 127:1). As a result, the Biblical greeting to godly workers is, "The blessing of the LORD be upon you: we bless you in the name of the LORD" (Ps. 128:8; cf. Judges 6:12; Ruth 2:4).

On the other hand, according to Proverbs 18:9, "He also that is slothful in his work is brother to him that is a great waster (or destroyer)."

---

6. R. B. Y. Scott, "Isaiah," in *The Interpreter's Bible*, V. 321. New York: Abingdon, 1956.
7. E. J. Young: *The Book of Isaiah*, II. p. 301. Grand Rapids: Eerdmans, 1969.
8. H. D. McDonald, "Work" in J. D. Douglas, *The New Bible Dictionary*, p. 1337.

*Work*, the ability to work productively and with foresight, is an aspect of our natural inheritance as men created in the image of God. Because in fallen man this ability is afflicted by the curse, it is a supernatural inheritance when with our redemption and obedience work is again under a blessing. Work then becomes a blessing which inherits blessings (Deut. 28:1-14). The meek, those who are broken into God's harness and work in and under Him, "shall inherit the earth; and shall delight themselves in the abundance of peace" (Ps. 37:11).

Inheritance in Scripture is a theological fact. It rests in our nature, in the image of God in man, and in our redeemed status as legal sons of God by adoption, called into His service (Ex. 4:22-23).

# 36

## PRESUMPTION

Like sacrilege, *presumption* is a sin rarely mentioned in our time; not even Biblical and theological works mention it, and it is necessary to turn to older works to find any mention of it. Scripture does speak of it often, as witness these verses:

> But if a man come presumptuously upon his neighbour, to slay him with guile; thou shalt take him from mine altar, that he may die (Ex. 21:4).

> And the man that will do presumptuously, and will not hearken unto the priest that standeth to minister there before the LORD thy God, or unto the judge, even that man shall die; and thou shalt put away the evil from Israel. And all the people shall hear, and fear, and do no more presumptuously (Deut. 17:12-13).

> Keep back thy servant also from presumptuous sins; let them not have dominion over me; then shall I be upright, and I shall be innocent from the great transgression (Ps. 19:13).

> The Lord knoweth how to deliver the godly out of temptations, and to reserve the unjust unto the day of judgment to be punished: But chiefly them that walk after the flesh in the lust of uncleanness, and despise government. Presumptuous are they, self-willed, they are not afraid to speak evil of dignities (II Peter 2:9-10).

Very clearly, presumption is a particularly fearful form of injustice. It leads men to despise authority or government, and to speak libelously of their superiors.

An understanding of the meaning of presumption can be had by examining its definition by a popular divine of an earlier era, The Rev. Charles Buck (1771-1815). According to Buck,

> PRESUMPTION, as it relates to the mind, is a supposition formed before examination. As it relates to the conduct or moral action, it implies arrogance and irreverence. As it relates to religion in general, it is a bold and daring confidence in the goodness of God, without obedience to his will. *Presumptuous sins* must be distinguished from sins of infirmity, or those failings peculiar to human nature, Ecc. vii. 20, I John i, 8, 9; from sins done through ignorance, Luke xii, 48; and from sins into which men are hurried by sudden and violent temptation, Gal. vi. 1. The ingredients which render sin presumptuous are, knowledge, John xv.22; deliberation and contrivance, Prov. vi. 14, Psal. xxxvi, 4; obstinacy, Jer. xliv. 16; Deut. i. 13; inattention to the remonstrances of conscience, Acts vii. 51; opposition

to the dispensations of Providence, 2 Chron. xxviii. 22; and repeated commission of the same sin, Psal. lxxvii. 17. Presumptuous sins are numerous; such as profane swearing, perjury, theft, adultery, drunkenness, sabbath-breaking, &c. These may be more particularly considered as presumptuous sins, because they are generally committed against a known law and so often repeated. Such sins are most heinous in their nature, and most pernicious in their effects. They are said to be a reproach to the Lord, Numb. xv. 3; they harden the heart, I Tim. iv. 2; draw down judgments from heaven, Numb. xv. 31; even when repented of, are seldom pardoned without some visible testimony of God's displeasure, 2 Sam. xii. 10. As it respects professors of religion, as one observes, they sin presumptuously, 1. when they take up a profession of religion without principle; 2. when they profess to ask the blessing of God, and yet go on in forbidden courses; 3. when they do not take religion as they find it in Scriptures; 4. when they make their feelings the test of their religion, without considering the difference between animal passions and the operations of the Spirit of God; 5. when they run into temptation; 6. when they indulge in self-confidence and self-complacency; 7. when they bring the spirit of the world into the church; 8. when they form apologies for that in some which they condemn in others; 9. when professing to believe in the doctrines of the Gospel, they live licentiously; 10. when they create, magnify, and pervert their troubles; 11. when they arraign the conduct of God as unkind and unjust.[1]

This definition rather thoroughly includes most Christians of our day under the classification of presumptuous sinners.

Delaney defined presumption as that sin which relies on God's mercy and power while manifesting no works in conformity to the profession of faith. It is closely linked, he pointed out, to "a Pelagian frame of mind," and in some cases will even presume to ask for God's assistance in doing evil as though baptism and an outward profession had made God a necessary ally.[2]

The God-ward aspects of presumption are by now apparent. However, Buck's excellent definition makes it clear that presumption has manward and personal implications: "it is a bold and daring confidence in the goodness of God, without obedience to his will."

To give an example of the social aspects of presumption, let us examine an instance from 1911, when Lloyd George brought in the National Insurance Bill, which requires employers "to contribute 3 c. a week each (rather less than 1½p)" to insure their servants against illness. Every attempt was made by employers to compel opposition to the bill by their servants.

---

1. "Presumption," in Charles Buck: *A Theological Dictionary*, p. 490. Philadelphia: Joseph J. Woodward, 1826.
2. "Presumption," by Joseph F. Delaney, in *The Catholic Encyclopedia*, XII, 403. New York: The Encyclopedia Press, (1911) 1913.

Petitions were got up, which were signed by employers and their servants, many no doubt under duress. One young servant girl who
refused to sign such a petition recalls the vicar calling to ask her to
change her mind, and when she refused, telling her she was a *very
wicked girl.* "I had plenty of black looks from the mistress and
master."[3]

Attempts by employers to compel or control the minds of employees
where their opinions are irrelevant to the discharge of their duties is
presumption. Man has no right to play god in the lives of those under
him. He has a right to expect the faithful discharge of stated duties, not a
compliance to his will and whim.

On the other hand it is presumption for employees to try to instruct,
correct, or dictate to their employers. They have the freedom to leave,
but not to control, their place of work. Similarly, children have no right to
criticize parents, teachers, pastors, or their elders; to do so is presumption.

These are examples drawn from normal human affairs, but in all a
theological principle of authority governs. It is God's order, not man's,
which must be maintained. But this is not all: the principle of obedience
must be God-centered, because our lives must be so. To be other than
God-centered is presumption.

To cite another example, to illustrate this fact, a wealthy man had two
sons, who, together with their wives, were earnest and professing Christians. Although no open conflict had developed, and outwardly, there
was peace and harmony, the sons and their wives resented the fact that
the father made no effort to help them financially, to finance home purchases, or to assist in various ways, despite his super-abundant means.
The father, on the other hand, knew of the children's expectations and
resented it. While they shared his faith, they lacked his prudence. Both
sons had very good incomes, but neither they nor their wives saved
anything, nor felt any need to, in view of the prospects of an inheritance
to enjoy.

The attitude of the sons and their wives was *presumption.* Their view
of an inheritance was entirely personal, man-centered, rather than
theological and God-centered. Despite their profession of faith, they
were humanists at heart. They not only used all the fruits of their labors,
but wanted the fruits of their father's labors without any awareness of
the Biblical meaning of inheritance.

Presumption also means a denial of God's wisdom and providence in
His dealings with us. When Israel in the wilderness said, "Let us make us
a captain, and let us return into Egypt" (Num. 14:4), they were guilty of
presumption. The rebellion of Israel when the spies made their report,

---

3. Frank Dawes: *Not in Front of the Servants, A True Portrait of English
Upstairs/Downstairs Life,* p. 117. New York: Taplinger Publishing Company, 1973.

and their subsequent attempt to undo their sin by attacking the Amorites, is called a presumptuous sin by Moses (Deut. 1:43). A prophet or preacher who speaks a word which God has not commanded, or speaks in the name of other gods, has spoken presumptuously (Deut. 18:20-22). The builders of Babel (Gen. 11) and Korah (Num. 16) were presumptuous. The men of Beth-shemesh who had looked presumptuously into the ark (I Sam. 6:19) were smitten by God. Other examples of presumption are Uzzah (II Sam. 6:6), Uzziah (II Chron. 26:16), and the Jewish exorcists of Acts 19:13-16.

Perhaps our clearest insight into the meaning of the sin of presumption is in Psalm 19:7-14. In verses 7-10, the psalmist speaks of the glory of the law, and by the law or Torah he means the law as given to Moses and the whole of God's written word. He declares the law to be *perfect*, in that it covers every aspect of life and is a shield for man against evil. It is a *sure* word, because it comes from the omnipotent God, and it makes us wise. It is a *right* word, because it is more fitting and clearer than anything man can devise or imagine. It is a *pure* word which cleanses and enlightens the eyes. The law is a word which inspires a *clean* and wholesome *fear* which is a permanent guide for man. The law is also *judgments* or *verdicts* which are totally *true* and *righteous altogether*. Moreover, the law of God is more precious than *gold* and sweeter than *honey*.

After speaking with such joyful eloquence of the excellence of the law, the psalmist related the law to himself in verses 11-14. The law is a warning to us, and it is also a source of "great reward" when we obey it. The law thus is condemnation to the sinner and a source of great reward to the righteous.

To avoid the condemnation of the law, the psalmist now asks for grace to overcome two kinds of sins. *First*, in verse 12, there are the "hidden faults," the weaknesses often unknown to ourselves, which, under stress, appear. *Second*, there are the presumptuous sins, those committed in open defiance or in casual heedlessness of God. Presumptuous sins readily rule over us, because they are not sins of weakness but of headstrong and independent action. We sin presumptuously when we calculate God out of His tithe, or deliberately neglect His word at any point, or waive obedience to His law at some detail because we feel so satisfied with our general compliance.

We sin presumptuously when we use our God-given authority beyond its prescribed limits. Many men sin presumptuously when they assume that their God-given authority means that a woman has no authority at all. Many pastors and elders similarly demand an obedience which only God can require. It is likewise presumptuous for people to attempt to rule over their superiors in authority, or to correct them as though they were their teachers.

Our modern world is, of course, a presumptuous culture, as indeed every culture of fallen man is. The nature of original sin is man's presumption that he can be his own god, and as a result presumption is deeply imbedded in all sin. Modern politics, for example, is the politics of presumption, and much of modern science, especially in its motivation, is presumption.

Presumption decapitalizes a culture religiously, morally, and materially, because presumption acts as though it represents the covenant God while in radical defiance of His will. Contemporary antinomian "evangelicalism," and the supposedly reformed churches with their implicit antinomianism, as well as other church bodies, represent clearly the sin of presumption. As a result, while more than one contemporary nation, such as the United States, has an ostensibly large Christian population, it is being rapidly decapitalized because of the sin of presumption. To decapitalize a culture is to destroy it, and, where Christians are guilty in this manner, they are in the Lord's eyes salt which "is thenceforth good for nothing, but to be cast out, and to be trodden under foot of men" (Matt. 5:13).

An inheritance, material and spiritual, must not be depleted or ended with us without great transgression. Rather, it must be developed and advanced, because it is not we who are the goal of history but Christ and His Kingdom. In God's plan, nothing ends with us. We are to be workers and transmitters. Failure to see our responsibilities to the future is presumption.

In the presumptuous culture of our time, man at every turn emphasizes his presumptive will as a virtue. One major church in 1975 refused a young man ordination because he could not in good conscience participate in the ordination of a woman. A spokesman for the church made it clear that unbelief in Scripture's infallibility, in Christ's deity, the virgin birth, the resurrection, and more, was acceptable to the church, because no man was hurt by unbelief, whereas objections to the ordination of women could hurt a human being. The test for him was clearly man.

More than a few presumptuous Bills of Rights for children have been issued. One youth issued a statement containing the following:

> 1. I have the right to be my own judge and take the responsibility for my own actions.
> 2. I have the right to offer no reasons or excuses to justify my behavior.
> 3. I have the right to decide if I am obligated to report on other people's behavior.
> 10. I have the right to say, "I don't care."[4]

---

4. From Ann Landers, "Author of Children's Bill of Rights Isn't Kidding," in the *Los Angeles Herald Examiner*, Sunday, June 15, 1975, p. F-5.

Another example of presumption is the attitude of welfare recipients. According to reports, welfare recipients in more than one city regard welfare as their right. Even more, they regard any denial of additional demands as intolerable, and they readily attack and razor-slash welfare workers, even though the welfare office staffs operate generally on the premise that the welfare client is always right.[5]

Such things should not surprise us. When the church no longer treats presumption as a sin, and is itself presumptuous, we should not be surprised that on all sides men act presumptuously.

---

5. Victor Riesel, "Welfare Toll is Written in Blood," in the *Los Angeles Herald-Examiner*, Sunday, June 15, 1975, p. A-15.

## 37

## INHERITANCE AND THE LARGER FAMILY

The pattern of Biblical law with regard to inheritance is by now clear. *First*, the covenant people are by the adoption of grace the firstborn of God in Christ, and they have been called to serve God. "Thus saith the LORD, Israel is my son, even my firstborn: And I say unto thee, Let my son go, that he may serve me, and if thou refuse to let him go, behold, I will slay thy son, even thy firstborn" (Ex. 4:22-23). The function of our inheritance is our capitalization in the service of the Father, towards establishing the dominion of His Kingdom.

*Second*, the blood family in the faith is a colonizing agency: while required to marry within the faith, it extends the ties and the discipline of the covenant and its law to a new household. It works to bring all associated with it into the faith. The covenant family, because it increases and multiplies (Gen. 9:1), is a form of family imperialism for the faith. "Therefore shall a man leave his father and his mother, and shall cleave unto his wife: and they shall be one flesh" (Gen. 2:24). The family of faith, the covenant people, whether organized as a church, state, school, or any other agency, is also a colonizing agency, in that the command in the Great Commission is *by no means* limited to the church. It is to every covenant man in his every capacity. Our Lord declared, "All power is given unto me in heaven and in earth. Go ye therefore, and teach all nations, baptizing them in the name of the Father, and of the Son, and of the Holy Ghost: Teaching them to observe all things whatsoever I have commanded you: and, lo, I am with you alway, even unto the end of the world. Amen" (Matt. 28:18-20). We inherit in order that we might conquer in Christ's name, extending *His dominion over all the earth and over every sphere of life and thought.*

*Third*, the scattering of the ungodly, as at Babel (Gen. 11:1-9), is to prevent them from realizing their hopes of an anti-God order. The scattering of the faithful is a systematic plan of conquest and dominion. The wealth of the ungodly shall flow into the hands of the covenant people, and every tongue shall ultimately swear by the covenant God (Isa. 45:14, 23).

In this plan, *the stranger* has an important place. The word *stranger* (foreigner, alien, sojourner) is a common one in Scripture, especially in the law. Covenant man's relationship to the stranger is very strictly governed.

198

In summarizing some of the laws with respect to strangers, it is necessary to note, *first* of all, that the term stranger has reference to someone residing within the country who is from another tribe, nation, or race. The reference is not to travellers passing through; the reception of such men is governed by the laws of hospitality. Permanent or temporary residents who are aliens are meant by the usual references to *strangers*.

*Second*, there are laws *requiring* discrimination against strangers, but *the principle of discrimination is religious, not personal, racial, or national.* In terms of their religious and moral background, they are to be judged fit for entrance into "the congregation of the LORD," i.e., as ruling members of the commonwealth of faith, only after three generations in some cases, and ten generations in others (Deut. 23:3-8). They *can* be believers, but they cannot vote or rule until some generations of steadfast faith and cultural growth are in evidence. This does *not* mean social discrimination in the interim. Moreover, this exclusion did not apply to strangers only; thus, the descendants of bastards were barred to the tenth generation also (Deut. 23:2). Thus, Phares, the son of Judah by Tamar, was a bastard; it was only with the tenth generation, David, that rulership was legally possible. This did not prevent the intervening generations (Phares, Esrom, Aram, Aminadab, Naason, Salmon the husband of Rahab, Matt. 1:5, Boaz, Obed, Jesse, Luke 3:32-33) from being important and prosperous men, highly regarded in the community. The discrimination was with respect to religious and civil authority and rule; it was religious and principled, *not personal*.

*Third*, with regard to the *person* of the stranger, the law is emphatic in requiring his protection. Because the stranger is God's creature also, he too must be subject to God's law (Ex. 20:10; 23:12; Lev. 16:29; 18:26; 20:2; 24:16; Num. 9:14; 15:14-16; 15:30; 19:10; 35:15). Moreover, he is singled out, together with widows and orphans, as requiring especial care in the form of protection from injustice. "Thou shalt neither vex a stranger, nor oppress him: for ye were strangers in the land of Egypt" (Ex. 22:21; cf. Deut. 27:19). This is again stressed in Exodus 23:9. In Leviticus 23:22 and 19:10 and Deuteronomy 24:19-22 the law of gleaning requires the inclusion of strangers in our charity. The alien believer has the same religious obligations as any other believer (Lev. 17:8-13; 22:18). The first statement of love of neighbor is stated with respect to aliens (Lev. 19:33-34). The principle is, "Ye shall have one manner of law, as well for the stranger, as for one of your own country: for I am the LORD your God" (Lev. 24:22; cf. Num. 9:15-16). Justice thus must be the principle of life with one's brother as well as with an alien (Lev. 25:35, 47; Deut. 1:16; 24:17-18).

The stranger in Israel was a propertyless man, usually a day-laborer or an artisan, and sometimes a merchant in the city. All the land belonged to Israelites, and, as a result, the majority of foreigners were thus of a lower social status and of humbler means. A few did acquire wealth (Lev. 25:47), but the majority were clearly of a humble status.

These aliens were of three classes: believers who fully kept the law; believers who accepted the whole of the Torah except the dietary laws; and a few who accepted nothing. Deuteronomy 14:21 has reference to the latter two classes; those who had no objection to eating animals which died a natural death could be sold such animals, but none others.

We have seen that the commandment to love our neighbor is stated with specific reference to foreigners. This commandment comes out of a theological fact: God declares His love of the stranger, the man who dwells in peace amongst the covenant people and who needs their justice and help.

> Only the LORD had a delight in thy fathers to love them, and he chose their seed after them, even you above all people, as it is this day.
> Circumcise therefore the foreskin of your heart, and be no more stiffnecked.
> For the LORD your God is a God of gods, and Lord of lords, a great God, a mighty, and a terrible, which regardeth not persons, nor taketh reward:
> He doth execute the judgment of the fatherless and widow, and loveth the stranger, in giving him food and raiment.
> Love ye therefore the stranger: for ye were strangers in the land of Egypt (Deut. 10:15-19)

What is called for here is not a humanistic love which equalizes all men but a missionary love, a manifestation of grace. Moreover, these words had an intensely personal meaning for all of Israel, in that they deliberately echoed Jacob's vow at Bethel, words familiar to every Israelite from his youth:

> And Jacob vowed a vow, saying, If God will be with me, and will keep me in this way that I go, and will give me bread to eat, and raiment to put on,
> So that I come again to my father's house in peace; then shall the LORD be my God (Gen. 28:20-21).

Jacob's elementary need in his flight was food and raiment; God now declares that He "loveth the stranger, in giving him food and raiment." The foreigner is placed in the position of another Jacob, being readied to become the Israel of God. This is a missionary love, an act of grace. Again, this same kind of love is referred to by our Lord: "I was a stranger, and ye took (or, gathered) me in" (Matt. 25:35).

"I was a stranger," said our Lord, in need of visitation, food, clothing, and the necessities of life and also of brotherly love (Matt.

25:35-36, 42-43). These are very obvious references to the laws concerning strangers, and to "the food and raiment" of Deuteronomy 10:18. Our Lord thus makes a test of faith, not mere belief, for the devils in hell believe and tremble (James 2:19), but our treatment of the stranger. "Inasmuch as ye have done it (or, did it not) to one of the least of these my brethren, ye have done it (or, ye did it not) unto me" (Matt. 25:40, 45).

Today, the world-wide movements of peoples place many strangers in our midst, and we are confronted by a God-given opportunity and requirement, a test of our faith.

Not only does the Lord require charity towards the needy stranger (Deut. 14:29; 16:11), but He also specifies that the stranger is to be given a position of respect together with the Levite, the orphan, and the widow (Deut. 26:11-13). "The Levite, the stranger, the fatherless, and the widow" are linked as alike under the special care of the Lord, and hence of necessity under the special care of covenant man.

Thus, while there were religious restrictions on some kinds of foreigners, and none could be priests (Num. 16:40), or a king (Deut. 17:15), they were also an object of particular love from God as a people on the threshold of the covenant.

Jacob or Israel gained not only food and raiment but the promised land as well. Since it is the destiny of covenant man to conquer the earth and to exercise dominion over it, every opportunity to bring other men into the Kingdom of God is to be welcomed. The stranger in our midst is thus God's opportunity to us, an inheritance to be welcomed and converted.

Christ as King of Kings is emperor over all, and Christianity is an imperial religion, a colonizing religion. To withdraw from the stanger is to withdraw from the Lord. The law insistently compels us to think of the Levite, the stranger, the fatherless, and the widow. We are required to open our home to them from time to time, and to share our bounty with them. Failure to do so incurs God's judgment. Failure to give them justice incurs a curse (Deut. 27:19).

As a result, the tithe of rejoicing before the Lord requires that these people share in the bounty of our house (Deut. 26:10-13). Our rejoicing before the Lord must include therefore more than our blood family. It must include those whom God specifies as deserving of our reward, such as the Levites, or in need of our help and love, such as the widow and orphan, or in need of our missionary love, such as the stranger.

# 38

## THE LAWS OF POSSESSION

One of the most remarkable facts about the law goes unnoticed because we read history backwards. The Hebrews who first heard Moses pronounce the Ten Commandments were only a few weeks before a slave people. They required supernatural deliverance to free them from Egypt's power and supernatural power to sustain them for decades thereafter. Their first sabbath had been celebrated as the Passover, as a slave people soon to abandon homes and land, and their possessions now at Sinai were limited and meager.

Notice, however, how *the law assumes their wealthy estate*:

> Six days shalt thou labour, and do all thy work:
> But the seventh day is the sabbath of the LORD thy God: in it thou shalt not do any work, thou, nor thy son, nor thy daughter, thy manservant, nor thy maidservant, nor thy cattle, nor thy stranger that is within thy gates:
> For in six days the LORD made heaven and earth, the sea, and all that in them is, and rested the seventh day: wherefore the LORD blessed the sabbath day, and hallowed it. . . .
> Thou shalt not covet thy neighbour's house, thou shalt not covet thy neighbour's wife, nor his manservant, nor his maidservant, nor his ox, nor his ass, nor anything that is thy neighbour's (Ex. 20:9, 11, 17).

It can no doubt be said that the law so speaks because it covers all contingencies, but this is not a sufficient explanation. The law presupposes as a necessary consequence that an obedient people will be a strong, wealthy, and dominant people. This is the point of Deuteronomy 28 and many another part of Scripture, and it is the presupposition of all of it. The Puritans recognized this fact and acted on it. In 1643, in New England's *First-Fruits*, it was plainly affirmed: "Now where sin is punished and judgment executed, God is wont to bless that place and protect it, Psal. 106:30; Jer. 5:1; Jos. 7:25, with 8:1, *e contra* Esa. 20:21."[1]

Deuteronomy 8:18 speaks more plainly:

> But thou shalt remember the LORD thy God: for it is he that giveth thee power to get wealth, that he may establish his covenant which he sware unto thy fathers, as it is this day.

---

1. Alden T. Vaughan, ed.: *The Puritan Tradition in America, 1620-1730*, p. 68. New York: Harper & Row, 1972.

God gives power to get wealth in order to establish His covenant, in order to further man's dominion over the earth in terms of God's law. Obedience to the covenant law gives wealth, and wealth in turn furthers the establishment of the covenant law order and peace. The goal is the government of the world by the covenant people. As St. Paul reminds the Corinthians, "Do ye not know that the saints shall judge (or, govern) the world?" (I Cor. 6:2).

There is an essential relationship between this promise of dominion and wealth and the sabbath, and it is not accidental that it is first of all in the Sabbath law that a slave people was told that they would have great possessions. It is basic to the understanding of the Sabbath to see this relationship.

Scholars such as Hill have pointed out that the Puritan Sabbath had two essential functions: it gave an opportunity for rest *from* labor and *for* education or instruction.[2] The Puritan Sabbath also meant the protection of the workingman from the exploitation of unceasing work.[3] These things are important products of the Sabbath: its meanings lie elsewhere. The Sabbath requires us to rest *in the Lord*, because it is He who has redeemed us, and it is He who gives us "power to get wealth." Psalm 127:2 states it thus: "It is vain for you to rise up early, to sit up late, to eat the bread of sorrows: for so he giveth his beloved sleep." Moffatt's rendering of the last clause clarifies the point: "God's gifts come to his loved ones as they sleep." The results of covenant faithfulness and work are greater than their sum total of labor. Solomon expresses the fulness of this blessing thus: "The blessing of the LORD, it maketh rich, and he addeth no sorrow with it" (Prov. 10:22).

The Sabbath rest is thus far more than the do-nothing observances of modern Sabbatarians. Their failure to recognize what God means and does with the Sabbath is almost blasphemous. The true Sabbath means that, because the universe is God's creation, and all its laws are totally His, He acts therein in such a way that *the sum is always greater than its parts for His covenant people, and less for covenant breakers*. This is very clearly and plainly set forth in the law of the Sabbath of the land:

> And if ye shall say, What shall we eat the seventh year? behold we shall not sow, neither gather in our increase:
> Then I will command my blessing upon you in the sixth year, and it shall bring forth fruit for three years (Lev. 25:20-21).

No naturalistic explanation of this is possible. It is true, as farmers in various parts of the United States have verified, that land allowed to lie fallow for a year is far more productive in the years following, far more

---

2. Christopher Hill: *Society and Puritanism in Pre-Revolutionary England*, p. 213. New York: Schocken Books, (1964) 1967.
3. *Ibid.*, p. 166.

so than the use of fertilizers would have made it. Rest revitalizes the soil as well as man. But this law declares that, where men have by faith kept God's law, then God, in *advance* of their next land sabbath, gives them a three years harvest in one. Clearly, the sum is greater than its parts.

This is true of all man's history, and hence modern historiography is profoundly and radically in error in its insistence that history is only and exclusively the sum total of its parts. This is the denial of Biblical history, of course. In recent years, because the historian Egon Friedell gave mild expression to such a faith in the transcendental aspects of history, he has been despised, called a "romantic," and his readers damned as uncritical and unscholarly.

The fact remains, however, that the Sabbath is in effect denied if Leviticus 25:20-21 is denied or avoided. The first Sabbath law told ex-slaves that they would be lords of estates through faith and obedience. Possessions are an aspect of our covenantal inheritance. We *rest* on the Sabbath in order to be instructed by the Lord and to be taught that our results in Him are far greater than the sum total of our labors and our planning.

The Sabbath rest is thus the confident rest of heirs who know that their calling and inheritance in the Lord are assured and certain. They know that mankind's history and their own personal history can never be reduced to what man alone does without a reduction to *less* than man's labors because of God's judgment. God speaks plainly of this through Micah:

> Are there yet the treasures of wickedness in the house of the wicked, and the scant measure that is abominable?
> Shall I count them pure with the wicked balances, and with the bag of deceitful weights?
> For the rich men thereof are full of violence, and the inhabitants thereof have spoken lies, and their tongue is deceitful in their mouth.
> Therefore also will I make thee sick in smiting thee, in making thee desolate because of thy sins.
> Thou shalt eat, but not be satisfied; and thy casting down shall be in the midst of thee; and thou shalt take hold, but shalt not deliver; and that which thou deliverest will I give up to the sword.
> Thou shalt sow, but thou shalt not reap; thou shalt tread the olives, but thou shalt not anoint thee with oil; and sweet wine, but shalt not drink wine (Micah 6:10-15).

Again, in Haggai we read:

> Now therefore thus saith the LORD of hosts; Consider your ways. Ye have sown much, and bring in little; ye eat, but ye have not enough; ye drink, but ye are not filled with drink; ye clothe you, but there is none warm; and he that earneth wages earneth wages to put it into a bag with holes (Hag. 1:5-6).

Much, much more in the same vein can be cited from Scripture, but, for the present, let us add one more verse:

"And he gave them their request; but sent leanness into their souls" (Ps. 106:15).

The reduction of history to its parts is the denial of God and of history.

Thus, the whole of the law is a law of possession; it is the means whereby man can subdue, possess, and exercise dominion over the earth. Obedience to these laws of possession presupposes faith. How else can a man approach Leviticus 25:20-21? How else can he believe that, in advance of the Sabbath of the land, God will bless His covenant-keeping man with a three years' harvest in one? It is thus an absurdity to separate faith and the law. Each is meaningless without the other. True obedience presupposes faith, and "faith without works is dead" (James 2:26).

## 39

## THE INHERITANCE OF FREEDOM

A common sinful viewpoint is our disposition to regard as an inheritance only what we have not yet received. We forget that those whose heirs we are have already given us much. Our parents, for example, have given us life, nurture, education, discipline, and much else, things which we must regard as the richest part of our inheritance.

The same is true with reference to God. As His heirs, we are born rich, because we have, in our covenant wealth, *grace* and *the law*. By means of the *grace* of God in Jesus Christ, we have freedom from sin and death. We are delivered entirely from sin as *anomia*, "lawlessness," and are assured victory over sin finally in the world to come, i.e., sin as *hamartia*, "falling short," or missing the mark. By means of the *law*, we have an inheritance of *freedom and dominion under God*.

Freedom as the humanist defines it is freedom from law, as with anarchism, or freedom over law, freedom to be the ultimate lawmaker, as with statism. For Biblical faith, freedom is under law, God's law, and the means to freedom is the law of God.

Obedience to the law as the means to freedom and dominion is repeatedly declared in Scripture, as in Deuteronomy 28 and Leviticus 26. Obedience, the obedience of faith, means freedom from drought (Lev. 26:4), and freedom from want (Lev. 26:5); it means peace in the land, and victory over our enemies (Lev. 26:6-8); it means fertility, and abundance (Lev. 26:9-10), and it means the tabernacling presence of God the Lord (Lev. 26:11-13).

The law thus must not be viewed as a burden or an oppression or limitation.

The tithe, for example, is not only God's tax, but His appointed means toward blessing and dominion (Mal. 3:8-12). Tithing is plainly set forth as a means of power, whereby the people of God can be assured the outpourings of God's prospering hand. The tithe provides the means materially for godly reconstruction, and it makes possible the development and application of Biblical faith to the basic problems of life. To deny the tithe is to affirm slavery. It means choosing statism as against God's order. It is basic to Christian faith, and essential to any Christian order. No man can honestly hunger and thirst for a righteous order and fail to tithe, for to fail to tithe is to ask for statist slave-masters to rule over us.

Restitution likewise is God's law for society and a key to freedom and order. Restitution restores God's appointed order to society and makes certain that sin is not rewarded, and that crime does not pay. By requiring the community to make restitution where the criminal is not caught, a premium is placed upon law enforcement, so that the seriousness of crime without restitution is underscored.

Restitution is God's appointed way of justice. Our sin against God required restitution, the atoning death of Jesus Christ. Only God the Son can make restitution for us God-ward, but we are required to apply this principle of restitution, basic to God's righteousness, to our relationships man-ward. In effect, we deny the cross of Christ if we fail to see how essential restitution is to all of life. Man can never make restitution to God; this only God the son can do and has done. Man can and must make restitution to man.

*The way of holiness* again is the law. As Deuteronomy 28:9 declares: "The LORD shall establish thee an holy people unto himself, as he hath sworn unto thee, if thou shalt keep the commandments of the LORD thy God and walk in his ways." The stress clearly is that we are established, when we obey the law, as "an holy people unto himself," i.e., the Lord. We are separated unto the Lord by obedience to His law, and this is the specified and only legitimate means to holiness. Pretended holiness by means of man-made spiritual exercises leads only to frustration and a false religiosity. The law is the way of sanctification, and only by sanctification can we draw near to God. Where there is no holiness, there is no faith, nor salvation, nor real knowledge of God, for "faith without works" is plainly declared to be dead (James 2:20; Matt. 7:16-20). The requirement, "Ye shall be holy: for I the LORD your God am holy" (Lev. 19:2), is prefixed to a catalogue of very material laws and cannot be separated from them. Holiness is the rigorous and faithful application of God's laws to our lives and our society, and its consequences are the liberation of God's blessings on man and his world.

According to Scripture, there is an essential and necessary relationship between man's obedience and the natural order (Lev. 26:3-6). This relationship is stressed by Paul in Romans 8:19-22. The Biblical position is thus in a real sense the opposite of astrology and all other forms of environmentalism: instead of being determined by the environment, our level of sanctification, the nature of our obedience to the law of God, determines the environment. The means of this determination is the law, the instrument of holiness and dominion.

The holiness of God is His separateness and sovereignty, and man's holiness establishes him in a separateness, as a peculiar or privileged people in the Lord, and as a people possessing dominion.

Heirship in Christ is not simply a future fact but a present reality. It is inseparable from the law, which is given to the covenant people as a privilege and power. To the ungodly, it is a sentence of death. To the redeemed, it is a plan for dominion and blessing.

*If the law is done away with, then freedom too is abolished*, because the law imposes restraints on the demands which can be made on man by church, state, or any other institution, or by any man. Thus, the tithe is a limit on the required giving which can be asked of man, even as the poll tax is a limitation. Antinomianism demands more than a tithe and troubles the conscience with its claims. Thus, modernists often leave their listeners feeling guilty because they have more food, clothing, and money than some poor unfortunates elsewhere, as though the lowest common denominator were the test of conscience. Their implied inference is that we must give all our substance to be truly religious. The fundamentalists imply that true holiness means a disdain of all things material, and giving to the point of impoverishment. Both antinomian groups trouble the conscience with demands in excess of God's law, and neither places any real limit on what can be demanded of man. The result is spiritual bondage.

The same protection is provided by the law of restitution. Man's conscience cannot be held in continuing bondage for offenses where God's law of restitution is enforced. The conscience is freed, and order, material and spiritual, is restored by means of restitution. In one area after another, the law provides freedom by delivering man from bondage to man's law and by liberating the conscience. *Without God's law, neither man nor his conscience can be free.* The "higher way" of holiness espoused by antinomians is in fact the way of enslavement.

# 40

## THE INHERITANCE OF LIFE

The Bible gives many dramatic examples of the intensity of grief among the Hebrews on the death of a friend, relative, or leader. These demonstrations include a rending of the garment (Gen. 37:29, 34; Josh. 7:6; II Kings 19:1; Isa. 37:1; Esther 30:12; Lam. 2:10), or special mourning robes (Ezek. 26:16; 7:26; II Sam. 14:2), sometimes nakedness perhaps (Micah 1:8), placing dust on the head (Josh. 7:6; II Sam. 13:19; Jer. 6:26; 25:34; Ezek. 27:20; Lam. 2:10, etc.), refraining from wearing ornaments (Ex. 33:4), abstaining from anointing and washing (II Sam. 12:20), fasting (II Sam. 3:35; Esther 4:3; Ezra 10:6; Neh. 1:4), a beating of breasts (Isa. 32:12) and wailing (I Kings 13:30; Micah 1:8). The tonsure was also common to mourning (Isa. 22:12; Jer. 16:6; Ezek. 7:18; Amos 8:10; Job 1:20; Deut. 21:12). The use of gashes cut into the flesh was also common (Jer. 16:6; 41:5). All these were means of witnessing to the deep sense of personal loss, a participation in the death, and a sense of having lost a part of one's own life and blood.

Ironically, these practices are at the least of very dubious moral and legal status. Deuteronomy 21:10 includes a shaving of the head as a mark of the humiliation of a captive woman, but, having required a mark of humiliation to express what her status has become, the law then protects her from abuse, sale, or divorce (Deut. 21:14). Thus, the shaving of the head upon capture compelled the captor to recognize that he had humiliated his captive, and that her status was thenceforth to be no more humiliation but a mandatory protection. Again, in Leviticus 13:45, the leper, a term which may refer to a contagious disease or diseases now unknown to us, had to rend his garments, shave his head, and wear a mask over his upper lip, to avoid contagion by breathing. The shaved head acted as a bar to further infection, as did the ventilated clothing.

The common marks of mourning, as well as tatoos in general, are forbidden to all in Leviticus 19:27-28 and Deuteronomy 14:1-2:

> Ye shall not round the corners of your heads, neither shalt thou mar the corners of thy beard.
> Ye shall not make any cuttings in your flesh for the dead, nor print any marks upon you: I am the LORD (Lev. 19:27-28).
>
> Ye are the children of the LORD your God: Ye shall not cut yourselves, nor make any baldness between your eyes for the dead.

209

For thou art an holy people unto the LORD thy God, and the LORD hath chosen thee to be a peculiar people unto himself, above all the nations that are upon the earth (Deut. 14:1-2).

Holiness means life, and a separation from sin and death. To go into mourning in any degree is a defilement, but this is permitted within degrees if it is not attended by any ritual disfigurement. Priests can within limits mourn and thus defile themselves, but not the high priest:

And the LORD said unto Moses, Speak unto the priests the sons of Aaron, and say unto them, There shall none be defiled for the dead among his people:
But for his kin, that is near unto him, that is, for his mother, and for his father, and for his son, and for his daughter, and for his brother.
And for his sister a virgin, that is nigh unto him, which hath had no husband; for her may he be defiled.
But he shall not defile himself, being a chief man among his people, to profane himself.
They shall not make baldness upon their heads, neither shall they shave off the corners of their beard, nor make any cuttings in their flesh.
They shall be holy unto their God, and not profane the name of their God: for the offerings of the LORD made by fire, and the bread of their God, they do offer: therefore they shall be holy. . . .

And he that is the high priest among his brethren, upon whose head the anointing oil was poured, and that is consecrated to put on the garments, shall not uncover his head, nor rend his clothes;
Neither shall he go in to any dead body, nor defile himself for his father, or for his mother;
Neither shall he go out of the sanctuary, nor profane the sanctuary of his God; for the crown of the anointing oil of his God is upon him: I am the LORD (Lev. 21:1-6; 10-12).

Our grief, however real, cannot mark or rule us, because we are heirs of life, not death.

In a dramatic instance, our Lord confirmed these laws and summarized them:

And another of his disciples said unto him, Lord, suffer me first to go and bury my father.
But Jesus said unto him, Follow me; and let the dead bury their dead (Matt. 8:21-22; cf. Luke 9:59-60).

Matthew makes clear that the question was raised by a disciple. Our Lord thus placed the disciples on the same level as the high priest, in that they had to separate themselves from death. In this dramatic manner, He brought home to them their high estate and calling. The implications of this could not have been lost on either the disciples or the leaders of the nation.

Again, during His stay on earth, the Lord forbad fasting, a mark of mourning among other things, on the grounds that His presence made mourning impossible.

> Then came to him the disciples of John, saying, Why do we and the Pharisees fast oft, but thy disciples fast not?
> And Jesus said unto them, Can the children of the bride-chamber mourn, as long as the bridegroom is with them? but the days will come, when the bridegroom shall be taken from them, and then shall they fast. (Matt. 9:14-15)

A number of pagan religions stressed ascetic practices and used the tonsure as a means of evidencing a contempt for this world and a mourning over the burden or impediment of flesh. Acording to Bingham, the early church had no such customs.

> Which is still more evident from what St. Jerom says upon those words of Ezekiel xliv. 20, "Neither shall they shave their heads, nor suffer their locks to grow long; they shall only poll their heads." This, says he, evidently demonstrates, that we ought neither to have our heads shaved, as the priests and votaries of Isis and Serapis; nor yet to suffer our hair to grow long, after the luxurious manner of barbarians and soldiers; but the priest should appear with a venerable and grave countenance: neither are they to make themselves bald with a razor, nor poll their heads so close, that they make look as if they were shaven; but they are to let their hair grow so long, that it may cover their skin. It is impossible now for any rational man to imagine, that Christian priests had shaven crowns in the time of St. Jerom, when he so expressly says they had not, and that none but the priests of Isis and Serapis had so.[1]

Shaving is in the Bible associated with mourning (Job 1:20), although it is the partial shaving, between the head and the cheeks (the sidelocks) that is forbidden in Leviticus 19:27; and 21:5.[2] Shaving was a sign of mourning and loss because to be beardless was for a man a mark of humiliation and degradation. In certain cases, shaving was a part of a ritual of purification: for a leper examined and found clean or healed (Lev. 14:8); for a man who has undergone ritual defilement while performing a vow (Num. 6:9); and for Levites preparing themselves for separation to their duties (Num. 8:7). In each of these three cases, the beard was immediately regrown. "The priests, the Levites, the sons of Zadok," were not permitted either to shave their heads or to let their hair grow long (Ezek. 44:15, 20).

The inheritance of life through the covenant of redemption thus means a separation from death, even in its symbolic forms. It means thus too a separation from the diminution of manhood through long, effeminate hair.

---

1. Joseph Bingham: *The Antiquities of the Christian Church*, vol. I, Bk. VI, ch. iv, sect. 16: p. 229. London: Henry G. Boyn, 1850.
2. Ze'ev Yeivin, "Beard and Shaving," in *Encyclopaedia Judaica*, vol. 4, p. 357. New York: Macmillan, 1971.

These symbolic forms require us to give even more attention to larger facts. *Tragedy* is thus a non-Christian form of literature. Tragedy sees an essentially perverse universe and an inherent frustration to life. In true tragedy, there is a strong element of necessity, of a perverse kind of predestination which makes disaster inevitable. In Shakespeare's tragedies, the Christian background is sufficiently strong to make the disaster a product usually of sin. In modern tragedies, it is seen rather as an aspect of a cosmic hostility to innocence, truth, and justice. Such tragedies rest on an anti-Christian premise.

The interest in such anti-Christian tragedies and tales of horror is a religious interest. Witness, for example, the great interest on the part of moderns with horror films, tragedies, and disaster stories. Some of this is disguised as social concern for downtrodden minority groups and the like, but it is in essence an exercise in religious devotion. The horror story depicts *the passion of man*, who, in a perverse universe, is the perpetual victim of God. Even more than victory, justification is at stake, and the viewer of these modern passion plays sees the story as the passion of innocent man, ever the victim of the cruel and anonymous God.

If inordinate grief is barred to the Christian, then how much more so the triumphing in misery as a means of self-justification? In a time of persecution and troubles, St. John wrote: "For whatsoever is born of God overcometh the world, even our faith" (I John 5:4). In the totality of our lives, we must manifest that we have been called to victory.

There is still another aspect to the limits on mourning which is perhaps most important of all. The Lord knows the reality of our griefs and sorrows, so that it is not hardness of heart that leads to this law. Surely the disciple's grief at the death of his father was felt by Christ, who was mindful of His mother even on the cross. The answer is to be found in what has since been formulated as the idea of sunk costs. This concept simply affirms that the past is the past, and attempts to retrieve past losses by a further commitment to a failing enterprise lead only to a further loss. The idea of sunk costs is a product of a Christian, and, in particular, Puritan, perspective. It is best stated in our Lord's words, "Let the dead bury their dead" (Matt. 8:22).

The limits on undue mourning prohibit us from being unduly attached to the past or grieving over what cannot be mended. It requires a future-oriented perspective.

A telling example of its application is to be found on the American frontier. Families moving westward often found that their wagons or oxen could no longer make headway on the difficult trails and mountain passes because of their heavy loads. As against tools, food, seeds, and tree-plantings, families regularly and with more than a little heartache discarded heirloom furniture and wedding presents by the roadside. This was the making of a true pioneer. Those who could not part with the past did not leave, or, if they left, turned back or perished on the way.

By contrast, a refugee who suffered in the 1940s from both Nazi and communist oppression reported to me that many or most Jews and conservatives were the easiest victims because of the inability to break with the past. The wise course, he said, on occupation of a country by a totalitarian power is to walk out of the house as if on a stroll, carrying nothing. Tickets are then purchased for short trips only, repeated ones, until near a border where escape is possible. Those who tried to leave with suitcases, or even a briefcase (full of money) or a padded coat, were quickly and easily picked up. Only those who left all behind them, shut the door on their house as though planning to step out for ten minutes only, normally escaped. The ability to escape required an awareness of sunk costs, leaving the dead to bury the dead.

Instead of heeding our Lord's words, too many people today are trying to resurrect the dead. This man cannot do. We must remember that our Lord's declaration, "Let the dead bury their dead" (Matt. 8:22), is a summation and confirmation of God's law. In fact, this law and principle is stated twice by our Lord in very well-known and proverbial form:

> And he said unto another, Follow me. But he said, Lord suffer me first to go and bury my father.
> Jesus said unto him, Let the dead bury their dead: but go thou and preach the kingdom of God.
> And another also said, Lord I will follow thee; but let me go first and bid them farewell, which are at home at my house.
> And Jesus said unto him, No man, having put his hand to the plow, and looking back, is fit for the kingdom of God (Luke 9:59-62).

Very simply, the backward look is forbidden to the covenant people. The modern mood, with its nostalgia for a dead past, belongs to the world of the dead.

## 41

## THE MEANING OF HEIRSHIP

Inheritance in the Bible is a religious principle whose purpose is godly dominion, so that the Kingdom of God is its essential orientation. Its concern is with the family of faith and blood. The function of the individual heir is both social and private. What has been inherited is something which must be transmitted to the future, or used to develop the life and prosperity of the family as a continuing power.

Some aspects of a wife's property were purely private, i.e., exempt from her husband's control or interference, when such property was a gift from her family for her personal uses. This could include slaves or handmaidens, as witness Hagar, Bilhah, and Zilpah, who were exclusively under the control of their particular mistresses.

Property was not seen as an impersonal fact but as an aspect of a person's life and as a highly personal thing. Bond servants and concubines could and regularly did inherit property as gifts, so that control of them sometimes meant control of property. The marriage by sons to a father's concubine was thus forbidden, but it did occur at times in violation of the law (Lev. 18:8), as a means of consolidating family wealth (I Chron. 2:21-24; Ezek. 22:10). Denying children their due rights, as Laban did Leah and Rachel, was regarded as injustice and theft (Gen. 31:14-16). For the state or any outsider to tamper with matters of ''heritage'' or inheritance is oppression and evil (Micah 2:2; Ezek. 46:18).

The purpose of inheritance, as we have seen, is *godly dominion*. As a result, a godly servant is a better chief heir (or eldest son by adoption) than a foolish son and should rule over him. This is clearly set forth in Proverbs 17:2.

> A wise servant shall have rule over a son that causeth shame, and shall have part of the inheritance among the brethren.

Similarly, Scripture repeatedly declares that the wealth of the ungodly nations shall flow to the godly (Rev. 21:24, 26; Isa. 46:18; 60:3, 5, 11; 66:12, etc.).

To be an *heir* in the Bible is to be a possessor. The Greek word in the New Testament is *kleronomea*, one receiving a lot or a portion, and, in the Old, the Hebrew word, *yarash*, means to possess, occupy, or succeed. *Heirship is thus possession*, in part now, in fulness in the life to come. The great Heir is Jesus Christ, ''who is the image of the invisible

God, the firstborn of every creature" (Col. 1:15). Christ as the firstborn is ruler over the household. If we are Christ's, "then are ye Abraham's seed, and heirs according to the promise" (Gal. 3:29). This heirship is by faith:

> For the promise, that he should be the heir of the world, was not to Abraham, or to his seed, through the law, but through the righteousness of faith.
> For if they which are of the law be heirs, faith is made void, and the promise made of none effect (Romans 5:13-14).

It is not, St. Paul makes clear, by any law of blood inheritance, but is by "the righteousness of Christ" and thus neither a self-righteousness through a Pharisaic use of the law for justification, nor by a blood inheritance from Abraham. The estate involved in this heirship is to "be the heir of the world."

Christ is "heir of all things" (Heb. 1:2), i.e., their possessor. Our inheritance in Christ is an immutable one (Heb. 6:17). It is a "promise" (James 2:5) and also a possession. It is an heirship or possession of this world and of the world to come. It is co-extensive with sanctification and the spread of the gospel. Christ, in His letters to the churches in Revelation 2 and 3, makes clear this aspect of heirship. The saints are summoned to strong faith and obedience in order to gain their inheritance:

> To him that overcometh will I give to eat of the tree of life, which is in the midst of the paradise of God (Rev. 2:7).

> He that overcometh shall not be hurt of the second death (Rev. 2:11).

> Be thou faithful unto death, and I will give thee a crown of life (Rev. 2:10).

> To him that overcometh will I give to eat of the hidden manna, and will give him a white stone, and in the stone a new name written, which no man knoweth saving he that receiveth it (Rev. 2:17).

> And he that overcometh, and keepeth my words unto the end, to him will I give power over the nations:
> And he shall rule them with a rod of iron; as the vessels of a potter shall they be broken to shivers: even as I received of my Father.
> And I will give him the morning star (Rev. 2:26-28).

> He that overcometh, the same shall be clothed in white raiment; and I will not blot out his name out of the book of life, but I will confess his name before my Father, and before his angels (Rev. 3:3-5).

> Behold, I come quickly: hold that fast which thou hast, that no man take thy crown.
> Him that overcometh will I make a pillar in the temple of my God, and he shall go no more out: and I will write upon him the name of my God, and the name of the city of my God, which is new Jerusalem, which cometh down out of heaven from my God: and I will write upon him my new name (Rev. 3:11-12).

Behold, I stand at the door, and knock; if any man hear my voice, and open the door, I will come in to him, and will sup with him, and he with me.
To him that overcometh will I grant to sit with me in my throne, even as I also overcame, and am set down with my Father in his throne (Rev. 3:20-21).

Our first concern here is not with the details of these statements but their general nature. *First*, as we have already noted, heirship is possession, but also progression in possession. *Second*, it involves "power over the nation" and also victory over death. It means communion with God in Christ, and communion in the City of God. It is righteousness in Christ and sustenance in Him, and more. *Third*, here as elsewhere in Scripture the line between heaven and earth is nowhere sharply drawn. Modern Christians draw it sharply; in the great ages of faith, it was not as sharply drawn. There is no depreciation of this world, nor any downgrading of it as a lower realm. We ourselves do not make sharp distinctions between one part of our house and another; we do not call one our main house, and another our sometime or future house. It is all one. In like manner, Christ views heaven and earth as alike His realm and alike under His absolute power and authority (Matt. 28:18). Nothing happens, exists, moves, or acts apart from the determination of the sovereign Lord of all creation (Matt. 10:28-31). Nothing under the sun is distant from God, and all things in heaven and earth are equidistant from the throne and totally present before it and under it. Our Lord thus makes no break between heirship here and in the world to come: He views them as essentially one while different in time and place.

*Fourth*, no abstract, individualistic spirituality is set forth in these promises of heirship. Our sanctification involves, not a quest for a personal holiness in abstraction from our world, but an obedience to the calling and commandments of our Lord. The Christians and the churches are thus summoned to an uncompromising stand on the whole of God's word and action in terms of it.

*Fifth*, our calling and our election makes us heirs, so that, to deny the full and clear meaning of heirship is to deny our calling. "For the promise is unto you, and to your children, and to all that are afar off, even as many as the Lord our God shall call" (Acts 2:39). We are not told that the promise *shall* be to us, but that it *is* to us.

*Sixth*, heirship is also power. "But as many as received him, to them gave he power to become the sons of God, even to them that believe on his name: Which were born, not of blood, nor of the will of the flesh, nor of the will of man, but of God" (John 1:12-13). "Power to become the sons of God" means not only power to become regenerate men by the Spirit of God, but power to serve and obey Him. Some will object that it does not say much for power when Christians have often been persecuted and put to death. But no man, unless he is a fool, seeks to persecute the dead, or the impotent. The enemy strikes at the areas of strength. Heirship is inseparable from power, because regeneration is rebirth from sin and death into life and the power of life.

Our Lord, when He sent forth His disciples with the Great Commission, declared, "All power is given unto me in heaven and in earth. Go ye therefore, and teach all nations, baptizing them in the name of the Father, and of the Son, and of the Holy Ghost: Teaching them to observe all things whatsoever I have commanded you: and, lo, I am with you alway, even unto the end of the world. Amen" (Matt. 28:18-20). *All power* belongs to Christ, and because He is *always* with His fellow-heirs, His power is with them also. This means the hatred of His enemies is directed against us also; it means battle, certainly, but it means, above all else, power and victory in Christ as joint-heirs with Him.

## 42

## COMMUNITY AND HEIRSHIP

We have seen the relationship of communion to community, and of inheritance to redemption, and the relationship of both to God's law. In the name of the law, and in the name of obedience to God, men have regularly destroyed community and inheritance, and have made rebellion against God a virtue. An illustration of this from the rabbinical tradition is most explicit:

> Rabbinical enactments were prohibitions called *gezerot* (decrees) and regulations of a positive character called *takkanot* (ordinances). With respect to *gezerot* one of the maxims of the Men of the Great Assembly was: "Make a fence for the Torah" (*A vot* I, 1) i.e.: Protect the laws by a hedge of prohibitions more stringent than the letter. A warrant for this was found in Lev. 18:30 interpreted as "Make an injunction additional to my injunction" (*Mo'ed Katon* 5a; *Sifra, Ahare* f. 86d, ed. Weiss; II *Dor.* 247). The explicit prohibition of Deut. 4:2: "Ye shall not add unto the word which I command you, nor shall ye take aught from it" was easily got over by reliance upon Deut. 17:8-11,... where implicit confidence in the courts of each generation and obedience to them are prescribed. Thus, paradoxical as it may seem the Rabbis believed that it was their right and duty to make changes in the Biblical law if imperatively required, while maintaining, nevertheless, that the commands of the Torah were unchangeable and might not be added to or diminished.
>
> "When the exigencies of the time seemed to demand it the Rabbis in council or individually did not hesitate to suspend or set aside laws in the Pentateuch on their own authority, without exigetical subterfuges or pretense of Mosaic tradition. Where justification was offered for extraordinary liberties of this kind, Ps. 119:126 was frequently quoted with a peculiar interpretaion. Instead of 'it is time for the Lord to do something; they have made void thy Torah' the verse was taken to signify 'It is time to do something for the Lord, so make void thy Torah' i.e. there are times when to abrogate a law is to do something for the law as a whole. There are rabbinical enactments from all periods which are more or less at variance with the plain letter and intent of Scripture (cf. I Dor. 50-52)."[1]

Judaism has been more honest than Christianity in its pragmatism and in its departures from Scripture. The churches have been less faithful to the law, or as unfaithful, but also less honest about it.

---

1. George Horowitz: *The Spirit of Jewish Law*, p. 94f. Foreword by Dr. David de Sola Pool. New York: Central Book Company, (1953) 1963.

The rabbinical "right" to set aside the law "when the exigencies of the time seemed to demand" was in essence the old pagan pragmatic principle. Rome expressed it thus: "The health of the people is the highest law." Such a principle is the triumph of humanism. Antinomian churches deny God's law while claiming salvation in terms of this same humanism; it means securing "benefits" from God without any obedience to Him. Man's salvation, "the health of the people," is made the true and only law.

Sin is thus rebelling or revolution against God. It is an affirmation of man's right as against God's right, and man's law as against God's law. *By means of sin, man seeks to bless himself apart from God's law.* The goal of sin is to further man's claim to be his own god, to establish his own dominion and sovereignty, and to bless himself according to his own counsel of predestination. *By means of sin, man seeks to make himself his own heir.* By dishonest means, he seeks wealth; by lawless sexuality, he seeks to heighten his sexual pleasure and sensations; by false witness, he seeks to promote his own welfare, and so on. By every sin, he hopes to bless himself.

What is true of the individual is also true of society and the state. The state has instituted a number of godless forms of taxation: the property tax, the inheritance tax, the income tax, and so on and on. Statist taxation is revolution against God: its purpose is to supplant God's order with man's order. The function of God's tax, the tithe, and God's ordained civil tax, the poll tax (and limited fines), is to establish God's order.

Statist taxation is revolution against God, but this does not justify a tax revolt, which only compounds humanism. Neither Christ nor the apostles, faced as they were with the exactions of Judea and Rome, both far worse than modern states in their godless policies, ever gave any ground for a tax revolt against Herod, Nero, or anyone else. God's Kingdom is not established nor furthered by lawlessness but by God's law and obedience thereto. It is rare to find a tax revolt advocate who tithes. Tithing creates a new order. The tax revolt adds anarchy to existing evils.

How is God's order to be established, if not by faith and obedience? To praise God requires obeying Him. This is clear in Psalm 146:

> Praise ye the LORD. Praise the LORD, O my soul.
> While I live will I praise the LORD: I will sing praises unto my God while I have any being.
> Put not your trust in princes, nor in the son of man, in whom there is no help.
> His breath goeth forth, he returneth to his earth; in that very day his thoughts perish.
> Happy is he that hath the god of Jacob for his help, whose hope is in

the LORD his God:
Which made heaven, and earth, the sea, and all that therein is: which keepeth truth for ever:
Which executeth judgment for the oppressed: which giveth food to the hungry. The LORD looseth the prisoners:
The LORD openeth the eyes of the blind: the LORD raiseth them that are bowed down: the LORD loveth the righteous.
The LORD preserveth the strangers; he relieveth the fatherless and widow: but the way of the wicked he turneth upside down.
The LORD shall reign for ever, even thy God, O Zion, unto all generations. Praise ye the LORD.

Commentators, who often manifest all the marks of a eunuch, tend to see this psalm as so much holy burbling, and they miss its relevance to man's everyday duties.

The psalmist, *first*, stirs himself and others to the praise of God, and this praise means faith and obedience, trust and service. Men are prone to trust that which is immediate and obvious, namely, the state, or princes (vss. 1-4). They look to the state for help; they praise and serve the state with their mind and substance. There is neither safety nor help in man, who is both sinful and mortal. He is a creature of God, made from the earth and destined to return to it. Our trust rather should be in the Lord who made heaven and earth and all things which are in them. The government of all things is in His hands, and absolute power (vss. 5-6).

*Second*, the government of God is then specified in its concern for the unjustly oppressed, the unjustly imprisoned, the hungry and needy, those who are in spiritual and physical blindness or darkness, the bowed down, the aliens, the widows and orphans, and all who cry for justice. The purpose of God is to *relieve*, or, better, *restore* these people to their rightful estate and to deflect and frustrate the plans of the wicked (vss. 7-10).

*Third*, how does God do these things? Do men sit back and say of the oppressed, "It is no concern of mine; God will work a miracle for them"? Or does not God work a miracle of redemption in us so that we might apply His law to every aspect of life? It does not seem to occur to commentators that we have here a series of references to God's law, to His requirements of us in our societies. Let us cite *some* of these laws:

1.  Relief for the oppressed: Jeremiah 22:17; Micah 2:2, 8f.; Habakkuk 2:6, 9; Acts 20:33; Ephesians 5:3; Colossians 3:5; Hebrews 13:5; Galatians 5:21; Jeremiah 5:27; Ezekiel 22: 12, 29; Isaiah 33:1; Exodus 20:17; Deuteronomy 5:21; Proverbs 22:22; Leviticus 19:14; Deuteronomy 27:18; Psalms 94:20; Ezekiel 45:8; Proverbs 16:12, etc.

2.  Relief for the hungry: Leviticus 19:17, 18, 32-37; Proverbs 25:21; Isaiah 58:7-10; Jeremiah 22:16; Zechariah 7:9; Exodus 23:6, 7; Leviticus 19:9-10; Leviticus 25:35-43.

3. Relief for prisoners: Leviticus 19:15; Matthew 25:35-36; (Psalms 79:11; 102:20).

4. Relief for the blind: Leviticus 19:14; Deuteronomy 27:18; Job 29:15; Isaiah 9:2.

5. Relief for the strangers: Exodus 22:21-24; 23:9; Leviticus 19:33-34; Exodus 12:49; Leviticus 24:22; Numbers 9:14; 15:15, 16; Acts 10:34; Romans 2:11; Ephesians 6:9; Colossians 3:25; I Peter 1:17; Ezekiel 22:7, 29; Zechariah 7:19; Malachi 3:5.

6. Relief for widows and orphans: Exodus 22:21-24; Leviticus 19:33-34; Malachi 3:5; Isaiah 1:17; James 1:27; Zechariah 7:10; Ezekiel 22:7; I Timothy 5:3, 4, 16.

God is to be praised *because* His Kingdom and law order are concerned with the needy and the oppressed of the earth, and God is to be praised *by* ministering to these whom God commands us to care for as a necessary part of our obedience to and praise of Him.

The tax revolt advocates forget that God makes all things work together for good in terms of His purpose (Rom. 8:28). Even the iniquitous income tax of the United States has an important function in God's sight. At a time when antinomianism has undermined the tithe, the income tax deductions granted to religious and charitable gifts have kept untold millions of dollars flowing into godly agencies to keep Christian work alive. There is no questioning the impact of this legal situation: shortly before the tax year ends, and people face tax payments, gifts to such agencies abound. In a time of indifference and antinomianism, God has used an ungodly tax to further incentives towards the support of His Kingdom!

To read Psalm 146 without an awareness of what it means to praise God is evil. To praise man, princes, or the state means to administer a statist program for the relief of human need by means of dishonest taxation which is in principle revolution against God. A fat and corrupt welfare bureaucracy is created, and an evil mob of welfare recipients, because from start to finish there is a necessary consistency: an evil tree bears evil fruit (Matt. 7:17).

Psalm 146 makes clear that the praise of God requires obedience to His law. It means inheriting responsibilities under God, and also receiving blessings. To follow the contrary course of the welfare state is to disinherit ourselves from God and to make ourselves heirs of man, heirs of the state.

The state, however, is not God; it cannot create, nor, in any sovereign sense, govern. As a result, to maintain its power, it must, like Kronus (or Saturn) of old, devour its children or heirs continually. To be heirs of the state is to be heirs of destruction, but to be heirs of God in Christ is to be heirs of regeneration, life, and the glories of all creation.

To be heirs here and now involves, very clearly a concern for the people of God, for the strangers, the needy, and the oppressed, in terms of God's requirements in His law. Inheritance should not isolate us: it should establish us more fully in Christ's Kingdom and community.

## 43

## COMMUNITY IN CHRIST

The word fellowship in the New Testament is a translation of *koinonia*, which means communion, community, fellowship, or sharing in common. The idea of community involves not only a communion or fellowship but a sharing in common. Unless there is something in common, there is no community.

The basis of the Christian community is set forth by St. John in I John 1:1-7:

That which was from the beginning, which we have heard, which we have seen with our eyes, which we have looked upon, and our hands have handled, of the Word of life;
(For the life was manifested, and we have seen it, and bear witness, and shew unto you that eternal life, which was with the Father, and was manifested unto us;)
That which we have seen and heard declare we unto you, that ye also may have fellowship with us: and truly our fellowship is with the Father, and with his Son Jesus Christ.
And these things write we unto you, that your joy may be full.
This is the message which we have heard of him, and declare unto you, that God is light, and in him is no darkness at all.
If we say that we have fellowship with him, and walk in darkness, we lie, and do not the truth:
But if we walk in the light, as he is in the light, we have fellowship one with another, and the blood of Jesus Christ his Son cleanseth us from all sin.

This passage declares, *first*, that the basis of the Christian community is theological. It rests on a prior communion with the Father and the Son. We can only have community on the human level if we first of all have it on the theological level. *Second*, the evidences of membership in this community are the works of faith, obedience to the laws of the Kingdom of God., i.e., walking in the light. This term, walking in the light, is a familiar Hebrew expression for walking in obedience to the Torah. It appears in Scripture repeatedly, and Psalm 119 echoes it, as in Psalm 119:105-106. God's "word," "commandments," "law," or "judgments," are a light or lamp unto man's feet, and to walk in the light means to walk in terms of God's law-word. *Third*, if we walk in the light, we then have fellowship one with another, and the blood of Jesus Christ, which is our redemption, is also a perpetual cleansing to us from all sin.

Communion is a *religious* principle, but only in Scripture is it a *theological* principle. In other forms, communion and community are commonly humanistic. In many religions and cultures communion is essentially a political concept, as in ancient Rome and also in Islam. In other cases, it is racial. The most recent examples of this are Nazi socialism, with its emphasis on Nordic blood, and internationalism, with its emphasis on the human race as a whole.

The modern state is hostile to the idea of community, because it creates a society or fellowship in independence from the state and with its own separate standards and effectual laws of social behavior. As a result, the state works to undermine communities in the name of a higher loyalty. The Soviet Union pays lip service to the idea of national communities by means of its constituent "republics," but it works to destroy the identity of these groups at the same time. In the United States the purpose of integration is not as much to overcome racial evils but to eliminate independent communities. In Boston, for example, Irish and Negro areas lead to organized minority powers with a political influence which is utterly lacking in integrated areas. The destruction of "ghettos" and the integration of schools means a loosening of electoral power over the state, in that an integrated area is not a solid but an unstable political entity.

Community, however, cannot be eradicated. Racial and nationalistic communities persist, but, more basic to the modern era now are what Boorstin has brilliantly analyzed as *consumption communities.*[1] In a consumption community, people gather together in terms of common standards of consumption. People do not choose a home, for example, in terms of proximity to other Christians, or in terms of their racial background (this kind of community persists among immigrants for a generation or two, sometimes more), but in terms of a common income. It seems strange to the twentieth-century American that, in the Old South, mansions could be built next to Negro huts of poor, free blacks, or that, in the Old North, a very wealthy steel manufacturer would build a stone mansion near his steel plant. Our perspectives have changed. Men now want to live in homes, shop in stores, and dine in restaurants in a little above their income level. Consumption snobbery is the ruling motive. The neighbors and their children may be unpleasant people, but men are more "comfortable" among unpleasant people who are their economic equals or slight superiors than among agreeable Christians of lower economic standards.

The *test* of a Christian community is credal: it is *orthodoxy*. The test of a consumption community is socio-economic: it is *snobbery*. Churches today are very commonly organized, not as a credal community, but

---

1. Daniel J. Boorstin: *The Decline of Radicalism: Reflections on America Today*, pp. 20-39. New York: Random House, 1969.

as a consumption community. The religious and theological standards may be there, but they are secondary to consumption standards. As a result, the church is highly effective as a social organization and ineffective as a theological one.

Our standard, instead of being Christian man, is economic man. When capitalism began to abandon the sovereignty of God, free market economics became totalitarian and deadly. It is common for libertarians to insist that the idea of the free market *must* be applied to non-economic realms. Thus, there must be, it is often avowed, a free market for monogamous marriage, prostitution, homosexuality, bigamy, polyandry, or what you will. These same free market totalitarians tell me proudly that they give their children a subscription to *Playboy* and tell them that all sexual options are equally valid.

As a result of free market totalitarianism, everything has been made subject to the market place and to the price mechanism. The final test thus becomes a monetary or economic one. The result is that economic conservatives are often the worst snobs of all. They idolize money; they give only to what is successful; they worship size, numbers, and success; and they exceed all others in despising "the day of small things" (Zech. 4:10). When twentieth-century man is called *economic man*, and his era the age of economic man, it means that his mind is dominated by an economic totalitarianism. For him to see his future except in terms of the same or better consumption community is for him disaster. He would in most cases rather die in the right neighborhood in a burning city than live happily in godly communion on a humbler level.

However, this is not only the age of economic man, but it is also the time of his death, as Peter F. Drucker demonstrated in *The End of Economic Man* (1939). Every idea of community which humanism has offered is bankrupt, and the bankruptcy of economic man is destroying civilization. The need is for a restoration of Christian community.

The calling of Abraham began with a requirement to break with a successful and prosperous community in Ur, to break with blood relatives, and to journey into a strange country, looking "for a city which hath foundations, whose builder and maker is God" (Heb. 11:10). The same requirement rests upon twentieth-century man, a break with all existing ideas of community and a spiritual pilgrimage towards the Kingdom of God, the true community.

St. John, as he writes of the community or fellowship in Christ, declares, "And these things write we unto you, that your joy may be full" (I John 1:4). This emphasis is noteworthy. The Christian community is not presented as an easy one, but it is declared to be the joyful one. The consumption community produces, not joy, but melancholy. The 1970s have been called the age of melancholy. The deeply rooted unhappiness of modern man is not grounded in a lack of things: "It is not the 'negative' aspects of a person's life that makes him unhappy, it was discovered, so much as a lack of 'positive' aspects," Phyllis Battelle reports. People feel a lack of closeness to one another and an isolation.

> The trouble, in our swift-moving crime-harrassed society, is that Americans don't seem to have as many friends and relatives to relate to as did Americans in other eras. Close friendships, which may be the best solution to melancholy, are a luxury many citizens do not possess. . . .
>
> With no enforced guidelines to follow, people flounder about—and often take self-defeating actions.[2]

The consumption community, like Sodom, is perishing. Those who return or look back, like Lot's wife, perish with it.

Modern man is often more aware of the growing decay of the consumption community than is the ostensibly Christian man. Modern, humanistic man is ready to call the consumption community a Sodom and to flee from it, or to tear it down. His alternative is even deadlier, however. He wants to create an equalitarian community and to level and deny all differences, to eliminate rich and poor, good and evil (all criminals being redefined as victims), and high and low. As a result, the social destructiveness inherent in the economic or consumption community is only intensified. Every man must be reduced to the lowest common denominator, a depth not yet plumbed.

---

2. Phyllis Battelle, "1970's Are the Age of Melancholy," in *Los Angeles Herald-Examiner*, Thursday, July 10, 1975, p. A-14.

# 44

## SANCTIFICATION AND HISTORY

Sanctification can be variously viewed, depending on one's presupposition. For a neoplatonist, sanctification is the renunciation of material things for things spiritual, and it requires a progressive indifference to the world. For Biblical faith, sanctification is the destruction of the power of sin and death over man and the world by means of the effectual calling of the regenerated man, who, as a new creation, exercises righteousness, holiness, knowledge, and dominion over all things and brings all things into submission to God through Christ; the way of sanctification is the law of God.

Too often, what has passed for the Biblical doctrine has been in fact neoplatonism. Neoplatonism can exist where the formal philosophical aspects of that faith are lacking, if the material world is neglected, and undue emphasis given to spirituality without regard for the mundane requirements of the law. Thus, William Gurnall is regarded as a Puritan who remained in the Church of England. He was, however, close to the Cambridge Platonists, and, while technically separate from them was, in reality a member of that school. His beautifully written *The Christian in Complete Armour* (1665) is closer by far to the spirit of medieval monasticism than to the Reformation. From start to finish, the way of sanctification is essentially an inner struggle, so that we never see a redeemed man effectually in action, exercising dominion over the world, but an almost Manichaean man, who, to his dying breath, is engaged in a bitter life and death struggle with the devil.

Gurnall's text is Ephesians 6:11-20. St. Paul in that epistle, as in all his letters, speaks very specifically of the relationships of man in marriage, man in society, man in the church, and much, much more. Gurnall's concern is more "spiritual," and his use of St. Paul neglects the practicality and material relevance of the apostle. Gurnall emphasizes prayer and spiritual devotions with a medieval intensity. He is not unaware of the relevance of the law. In passing, he writes, "Apocryphal holiness is no true holiness. We cannot write in religion a right line without a rule, or by a false one. And all are false rules beside the word—'to the law, and to the testimony; if they speak not according to this word, it is because there is no light in them' Is. viii. 20."[1] Doctrinally, Gurnall is

---

1. William Gurnall: *The Christian in Complete Armour*, vol. I, p. 410. Edinburgh: The Banner of Truth Trust, 1974.

sound; in emphasis, he downgrades the material world. His emphasis on the practical aspects of sanctification constitute a minor part of more than 1100 pages of writing. The book is so heavy in its emphasis on prayer as against the obedience of faith to the law that it is in spirit closer to the medieval convent than to Puritan England. Of all the intense and practical battles of his day, Gurnall gives us no hint. Of the relevance to sanctification of a stand in terms of his times, Gurnall is oblivious. Like a true neoplatonist, he rises above mundane matters.

Coming closer to our day, the same kind of abstraction from the law is to be found in George Muller, one of the winsome figures of nineteenth-century peity. A basic motive in Muller's perspective was his anti-postmillennialism. (He was a premillennialist.)[2] Muller bypassed the law for a new standard of holiness, a dependence on faith and prayer for his support. The widespread publicity his stand attracted very early gave him a strong basis of support. At a time when a few hundred dollars a year was a good income, his income as early as 1856 to 1865 amounted to "over $50,000 a year." He returned most of this to his missionary works.[3] He was against giving by God's law. "With regard to the amount to be given, no rule can be laid down, because what we ought to do should not be done in a legal spirit, but from love and gratitude to the Blessed One, Who died for us."[4] We have here the typical antinomian attitude that obedience to God's law lacks love and gratitude. Muller opposed debt, not because of the Old Testament law, but because of the New Testament injunction.[5] He opposed planning, and hence savings of any kind.[6]

For Gurnall and Muller, the future as history was irrelevant. Man's function was for them not dominion under God, but, for Gurnall, inner victory and peace in the spiritual struggle against Satan; for Muller, it was soul-saving, through his orphanages and through evangelism. Both men are good examples of the Protestant monastic spirit, an abstraction from history and an unconcern with it. They are very remote from the prophetic and apostolic concerns with the very material realms of personal and world history.

In examining Gurnall's book, we see another characteristic of neoplatonic writing, namely, its *timelessness*. Gurnall's work cannot be dated from any internal evidence. St. Augustine, Calvin, Luther, Dabney, and others are readily dated because their writings are so rich in their contemporary context, in sometimes very long digressions on

---

2. Basil Miller: *George Muller, Man of Faith and Miracles*, p. 37. Minneapolis, Minnesota: Dimension Books, Bethany Fellowship, 1941.
3. *Ibid.*, p. 125.
4. *Ibid.*, p. 128.
5. *Ibid.*, p. 30, 38.
6. *Ibid.*, pp. 31, 131.

current problems. It is of the essence of Biblical revelation, and of Biblical religion, that, while it speaks the eternal word of God, it speaks that word in time and in the full context of the moment. The word comes from beyond time, but it is more relevant to the moment than any other word can be. Compared to neoplatonic writings, the Bible is very pedestrian in its dated word. It is also full of "begats" and other mundane details, which are very much a part of the infallible word. Thus, the book of Amos begins,

> The words of Amos, who was among the herdmen of Tekoa, which he saw concerning Israel in the days of Uzziah king of Judah, and in the days of Jeroboam the son of Joash king of Israel, two years before the earthquake (Amos 1:1).

On Tuesday, February 9, 1971, at about 6 a.m., a damaging earthquake struck a portion of Los Angeles County in California, centering in the Newhall area. Naturally, the earthquake was a topic of local interest and conversation for some time thereafter. Much later, I learned that one "spiritually minded" pastor had rebuked such interest and concern as "worldly-mindedness." He held that earthquakes should remind us how fragile life and earthly things are and therefore lead us to forsake the things which pass away for those things which are eternal. His sermon was well buttressed by Scripture, but it had all been put to an essentially neoplatonic use.

According to Scripture, man's "spirit" is also a frail creation of God, who formed it (Zech. 12:1). Man's spirit is literally breath or wind (Gen. 2:7), not an immortal substance, for, in the strict sense, God alone has an inherent immortality (I Tim. 6:16). The frailty of man's being does not render him unimportant. Indeed, "all flesh is grass" (Isa. 40:6), but our Father is mindful of the humblest grass and flowers of the field (Matt. 6:28-30), the very hairs of our head, and the sparrows (Matt. 10:29-31), so that our value is not determined by mutability or the lack of eternity, but by the purpose and plan of God.

God dates His word through Amos by an earthquake, because, as absolute Lord, the earthquake is a part of His purpose, and culminates in good (Rom. 8:28). Only if God is not the creator of all things can we eliminate from relevance an aspect of creation. Only if matter is alien to God can we deny its relevance and seek religion in spirituality.

The word to Amos is *a dated word*, an historical word, with a particular relevance to the people who lived in the context of the reigns of two kings, one a reprobate, the other a somewhat good king. The word to Amos is relevant to us precisely because it is a dated word. God having made all things, His law abides as *the constant word* and factor in all things, yet fully relevant because it always speaks to a creation formed and totally governed by God's sovereign word. Of necessity, God's word is *both eternal and dated*. It is the word before creation, and it is the word at every moment most relevant to creation.

My word too is a dated word, but never as dated and relevant as God's word, because I have not created the situation or the history, do not know its full meaning more than remotely, and thus speak God's eternal word to the historical moment with limited vision and knowledge. God's word has absolute universality and particularity.

For this reason, God's law comes to history as grace and freedom for the redeemed, whereas it is judgment and death for the ungodly. For the regenerate, it signifies that God has given us His ordained means for governing history and exercising dominion therein. The people of God can thus speak of "the grace of law," to use a Puritan term.

A dated word is thus a living word, because it speaks to history. Existentialism is humanistic man's attempt to establish a dated word, but it involves a denial of all history in favor of the inner world. The existential word means a denial of all outer influences and forces in favor of the biological inner urge of the moment. Like neoplatonism, of which it is an heir, it surrenders history in favor of the spirit of man. Its dated word is in essence neoplatonic timelessness and a denial of history. Moreover, neoplatonic timelessness is not eternity: it is rather a withdrawal from both time and eternity, from history and eternity, into the imagination of man. It is antinomianism, and it is suicide.

It is not surprising, therefore, that an existential age cannot live in *the moment* it so passionately affirms. It takes flight in narcotics, liquor, and nostalgia, anything to escape the moment and history. Existentialism in practice does not affirm the moment: it denies it in favor of a flight from time and history. To affirm time means to affirm continuity, to affirm past, present, and future time, and existentialism in practice can affirm none of these.

## 45

## LAW AND COMMUNITY

In a central and basic text on the meaning of the law, God declares

Because thou servedst not the LORD thy God with joyfulness, and with gladness of heart, for the abundance of all things: Therefore shalt thou serve thine enemies which the LORD shall send against thee, in hunger, and in thirst, and in nakedness, and in want of all things: and he shall put a yoke of iron upon thy neck, until he have destroyed thee (Deut. 28:47-48).

Clearly it is not enough that there be conformity to the law in any formal sense. God must be served "with joyfulness, and with gladness of heart," or else there is no true obedience at all. Formal obedience is merely the prelude to actual disobedience. This stress on true obedience, on a joyful and heartfelt pursuit of the law's purpose and order, is basic to an understanding of Psalm 119. The psalmist by faith obeys, and his delight is in the law of the Lord. His only liberty is under law. The law is his mainstay against evil, and his guide and light on his daily path. Life for the psalmist means God's law.

This is a radically different view of the law than that promulgated by antinomians, but it is a view which is basic to Scripture, and therefore basic to civilization. When men seek freedom from law they seek freedom from civilization. Boorstin has observed

Our new opportunities and our new temptations to overcommunicate require a new and harder self-discipline among citizens, one of the most difficult forms of discipline to enforce. It illustrates the wisdom of the English judge who said, "Civilization must be measured by the extent of obedience to the unenforceable." In a world of overcommunication, the survival of a decent society may depend on our willingness to accept this truth.[1]

In earlier eras, almost all law was enforced by the family, clan, religion, or by some person whose authority undergirded and required obedience. Humanism, as it has come to epistemological self-consciousness, has eroded all such authorities in the name of the autonomy of man. The belief is inceasingly commonplace that valid law requires man's consent, which in essence means that every man is his own law. The democratic theory of law is thus the death of humanistic law.

---

1. Daniel J. Boorstin: *Democracy and its Discontents, Reflections on Everyday America*, p. 10f. New York: Random House, 1974.

The democratic theory of law also means the erosion of community. The heart of all law is unenforceable, because law and obedience thereto require faith in the lawgiver and a surrender of autonomy to the lawgiver. If the lawgiver is God, this means that man obeys God as sovereign and recognizes that departure from God's law, and violations thereof, are forms of apostasy and rebellion. If the lawgiver is autonomous, anarchistic man, then man is the sovereign, and man cannot then obey any external law to which he has not given consent without denying himself. If the lawgiver is the humanistic state, then the state is sovereign, and no law nor obedience can exist apart from the will of the state.

Let us now illustrate what modern, self-conscious humanism is doing to law.

Among the Paiute and Shoshone Indians of the 1940s and early 1950s, when I was a missionary among them, there were no homeless children, even though in more than a few cases both parents had died. The children were taken into the homes of relatives, or sometimes neighbors, and, despite the fact that this meant a family of eight or ten in a small cabin, no one was unhappy. Indian society was exercising a function not yet seized by the state.

The same situation existed in 1975 among Alabama's rural Negroes. As Bernice Robertson wrote,

> A Tuskegee Institute professor has completed a two-year study of one of the most fascinating aspects of life in Alabama's Black Belt—informal adoptions.
>
> Dr. Lewis W. Jones, director of the Center for Rural Development, found that black families have, by tradition, bypassed legal red tape in providing homes for children whose parents have separated or died, or those who have been born out of wedlock.
>
> In Lowndes and Wilcox counties, 28 per cent of the black families have kinfolks other than their own offspring living with them. By contrast, only four per cent of the white families were included in this category.
>
> "I chose these two counties because they are almost 100 per cent rural." he said. Life hasn't changed much here over the years. They have not had customs disturbed by social change."
>
> In most cases, he found, the substitute guardian was a grandmother or aunt, likely over 50 years old, with an income of less than $250 a month.
>
> "In many of these cases," he added, "the family could very well lose custody of the children they are keeping if they filed for adoption. They would not meet minimal standards as far as income and the like."
>
> Be that as it may, he noted, most of the children he encountered were content, well fed, and shared in the closeness of family living.

"In fact," he added, "this phenomenon of informal adoption has woven a tight kinship network within black families.

"This practice has been going on for generations. It goes back more than 100 years. No black child in this area goes without a home."

Even though some of the families may not meet standards set for legal adoption, Dr. Jones does not fear an invasion into the Black Belt by officials bearing legal requirements for adoption.

"The idea of adoption is to find good homes for children. The people here have done it without any help from the courts."

Last year in Alabama, of the 319 children placed for adoption, only 48 were black. Most of these were in urban areas.

Finding homes for black children has long been a problem for social agencies. . . .[2]

Such family responsibility cannot be enforced successfully by civil law; it can, however, be destroyed when civil law intervenes and arrogates to itself a power over the family in such matters. This does not mean that the older system of family responsibility, with church orphanages as emergency agencies, was by any means perfect, or that it lacked its problems and evils, but it does mean that, in a sinful world, where nothing can be expected to be perfect, that which stresses God-ordained authorities will best meet social problems and crises. The modern era has indeed had serious problems with children in its urban centers, because it has undermined and usurped the authority of the family, the church, and society.

Basic to the health of any society is obedience to that area of law which is unenforceable. This means that the obedience of men to the authority behind the law must come from a faith in the lawgiver and his purposes for society. For the Christian, this means a trust in God as the omnipotent and all-wise Lord and Redeemer whose law is man's freedom, prosperity, and strength. For the older pagan societies, this meant an obedience to the authority of the lawgiver as the necessary and dread power of the social order. As these older, pagan forms of humanism erode, social collapse becomes a growing factor on the world scene. The communist nations replace the older authorities with total terror as a means of maintaining law, but the results are increasingly failure. Basic to law enforcement is the commitment of the people to the law as not only the way of life but as life itself: it is this which is the major factor in law enforcement, but it is unenforceable by the state. It requires *faith*.

Community therefore begins as an act of faith in a sovereign power whose law is accepted as the life of the community and of the individual. This is repeatedly stressed in all of Scripture, not only in Deuteronomy

---

2. Bernice Robertson, "Custom is Successful. Bypassing legal adoption studies," in *The Birmingham News*, Birmingham, AL, Monday, August 4, 1975, p. 2.

28:47. Thus, in Deuteronomy 6:6-7, Moses declares:

> And these words, which I command thee this day, shall be in thine heart:
> And thou shalt teach them diligently unto thy children, and shalt talk of them when thou sittest in thine house, and when thou walkest by the way, and when thou liest down, and when thou risest up.

The sin occasioned in part by "the abundance of all things" (Deut. 28:47) is in reality an expression of man's original sin, his desire to be his own god. Man readily turns back to his own claim to sovereignty and replaces God's law with his own will. The requirement is to *remember* and to *consider in thine heart* the sovereignty and grace of God (Deut. 8:5-20).

Not only is *faith* basic to law and obedience to law, but love as well. Our Lord declared, "If ye love me, keep my commandments" (John 14:15). Obedience is an expression of faith and love, so that at heart all law rests on a vast ocean of unenforceable aspects in order to have any realm of enforcement.

Humanism and antinomianism both undermine the foundations of law.

## 46

## GOD AND THE CITY

Abraham, we are told, "looked for a city which hath foundations, whose builder and maker is God" (Heb. 11:10). This city, we are commonly told, is not in this world, because we are plainly informed that it is "an heavenly" city (Heb. 11:16), i.e., it is in heaven. Such an interpretation reduces the text to nonsense. *First*, if Abraham was looking only to a city in heaven, then why was he called out to go to "a place which he should after receive for an inheritance" (Heb. 11:8), and why should he regard this as a beginning for that City of God? *Second*, why then is the place of sojourn called "the land of promise" (Heb. 11:9), if somehow it was unrelated in a physical sense to the City of God? If the city were only in heaven, Abraham could have sought it equally as well in Ur. *Third*, the word translated "heavenly" is in Greek literally *epouranios*, "in heaven," but it must be read in view of Hebrews 11:14, "they seek a country." *Country* in Greek is *patris*, "fatherland." The city is heavenly because its "builder and maker is God" (Heb. 11:10); it is covenant man's fatherland, but it is a fatherland which is to *come* on earth. The Lord's Prayer is emphatic here: "Thy will be done in earth, as it is in heaven" (Matt. 6:10). Abraham was in Canaan to lay the groundwork for that city, and the coming of Christ opened up the way for its construction on a large scale. *Fourth*, in Revelation 21:2, the City of God is shown as "coming down from God out of heaven." This means an historical realization as well as an eternal order. To limit the city to eternity is to destroy Scripture. The first manifestation of that city was the Garden of Eden. Man's sin barred him from that city, and Cain then created a false city, the City of Man. In the New Jerusalem, which is both Garden and City in one, the City of God returns. It is "the bride, the Lamb's wife" (Rev. 21:9), i.e., it is the church, the kingdom, the covenant people and community, the totality of the redeemed world of Christ. *Fifth*, in its eternal perfection, the City of God is marked by perfect sanctification, perfect lawkeeping, so that "there shall in no wise enter into it any thing that defileth, neither whatsoever worketh abomination, or maketh a lie: but they which are written in the Lamb's book of life" (Rev. 21:27). It is the community of the justified and sanctified. It is a city, the city.

Just as the essence of law, and the major part of law, is unenforceable, because it rests on faith, so the city requires a common faith to be a city. Without this common faith, the city disintegrates. The city is designed to be a community, which means life in common, and life close together. We want to be in proximity to loved ones and friends; we want nearness to people of a like mind and faith. Earlier, the city was a walled area, keeping out enemies and ensuring that those within could preserve and develop their community.

Cain tried to create a community without God (Gen. 4:17), based on the principle of the fall, Genesis 3:5, that every man is his own god, but the anarchy inherent in his position became apparent in his descendent Lamech. Lamech asserted his autonomous right to kill anyone who offended him (Gen. 4:23-24). Such a position makes community impossible. A city requires a common faith, law, and life. Lamech's position made all three impossible.

As humanism reaches its logical development, as epistemological self-consciousness sets in, city life becomes progressively impossible. Rusher has observed,

> But most of the large cities of America have experienced their share of deterioration in recent years, and several in the East— Philadelphia, Cleveland and Detroit all spring to mind—are right up there with New York in the percentage of their area that has become an urban wasteland.
>
> In the South Bronx and upper Manhattan (of New York City), and corresponding regions of other major cities, mile after mile of residential buildings have been abandoned to the criminals who made them uninhabitable; the whole area has a "bombed-out" look —and no wonder.
>
> Concurrently, of course, we have seen the flowering of the suburbs: the green belt, where children can still play and go to school in reasonable safety.[1]

But the suburbs now see the same rise of crime. According to the police, 52 per cent of the crimes in suburbs in 1975 were committed by youth living in the neighborhood. Smaller cities and towns are also seeing a rapid rise in crime. As the infection of humanism spreads, anarchy and lawlessness increase, and community collapses. The result is an unusual trend, the flight from the city to the countryside in order to live and work in peace.

In the Bible, the city is the place of justice, where justice is administered at *the gate*. Because *the gate* was the place for town council meetings, court sessions, public hearings, and all necessary administrations of justice, *the gate* was an important symbol to the Hebrews. C. C.

---

1. William A. Rusher, "The Deterioration of American Cities," in the *Los Angeles Herald-Examiner*, Sunday, November 9, 1975, p. A-12.

McCown was right when he stated, "'gate' stood for 'justice.'"[2] When Eliphaz speaks of men being "crushed in the gate," he speaks of the horror of injustice (Job 5:4). In Nehemiah, the beginning of the rededication of Jerusalem to community life was the public reading of the law at the gate and its acceptance by the people (Neh. 8:1-18). Without God's law, the city was and is a place of evil and, before long, not a community but a place of court warfare between opposing forces.

The triumphal arches at the gates of Rome were placed in terms of this background. *The gate*, as the place of justice, was the place where victory over the enemies of the community was celebrated.

Basic to citizenship in the ancient city was atonement. Whether pagan or Biblical, the city knew that law and community require a common faith, that the foundation of city life is a common faith. The humanisms of pagan antiquity, not having the epistemological clarity of modern humanism, did not disintegrate urban life as the modern form of humanism does.

It is apparent now what Psalm 127:1 means when it declares, "Except the LORD build the house, they labour in vain that build it: except the LORD keep the city, the watchmen waketh but in vain." As Leupold comments, "The unseen but all-important factor is that God must bless what man does. Stated more drastically: He Himself must build the house and guard the city."[3] On the human side, this means that the foundation of family and city life is faith and the law, justification and sanctification.

A revealing insight into the centrality of the discipline of law in the life of man is Proverbs 25:28, "He that hath no rule over his spirit is like a city that is broken down, and without walls." The discipline of God's law is the protection of a man and of a city. We cannot read "rule over his spirit" in terms of modern humanistic ideas of self-discipline: it means the submission of our being to the law of God. "Seest thou a man wise in his own conceit? there is more hope of a fool than of him" (Prov. 26:12). The fool is not anarchistic in principle as the man is who is wise in his own conceit.

Where God's law is the basis of civil government, as the messianic Psalm 72 declares, and where Christ is King, "they of the city shall flourish like grass of the earth" (Ps. 72:16). According to Leupold, "the cities are thought of as being the very acme of prosperity and success, men thriving in them and growing in thick profusion as does the grass of the field."[4]

It is not surprising that it is in Christendom that capital formation,

---

2. C. C. McCown, "City," in *The Interpreter's Dictionary of the Bible*, vol. I, p. 636. New York: Abingdon Press, 1962.

3. H. C. Leupold: *Exposition of the Psalms*, p. 892. Columbus, Ohio: The Wartburg Press, 1959.

4. *Ibid.*, p. 521.

industry, and technology have flourished. Where there is no law, there is no community. As a result, a major part of a man's capital goes then to protection against crime, and progress becomes difficult. A recent article on a man in a foreign country whose annual gross income in 1974 was over $4 million stated that his personal profit, over and above normal expenses, was modest because of the necessity to bribe civil officials in order to function with any freedom or at all. Moreover, in a pagan society, accumulated wealth does not lead to social production as much as to personal power and pleasure. It becomes non-productive wealth.

The Hebrew word *city* means an enclosed space, a protected area, a walled place. The English word *city* comes from the Latin *cititas*, which is akin to the Greek *keitai*, he lies, or is recumbent. Both the Greek and Hebrew meanings clearly imply *safety*. The safety of the city was its common faith and law. Where that common faith and law are eroded or denied, there is no safety. The safe place becomes then the dangerous place, because the enemy is now entrenched within the city. The modern city is thus in crisis. The liberals seek to make further concessions to evil as a means of reclaiming it. The conservatives want a return to strict enforcement, assuming that the fruits of the law are possible without the roots. The enforcement of the law begins with an act of faith and then continues with the application of the law of that faith. Apart from this vital relationship law is unenforceable, and the city is a nightmare.

## 47

## "THE LAW SHALL GO FORTH"

As the prophet Micah began to announce the coming in God's time of the Messiah-King, he set forth the glory which was to develop after His coming, "in the last days," as the period from the first to the second coming is termed in Scripture. He declared

> But in the last days it shall come to pass, that the mountain of the house of the LORD shall be established in the top of the mountains, and it shall be exalted above the hills; and people shall flow unto it. And many nations shall come, and say, Come, and let us go up to the mountain of the LORD, and to the house of the God of Jacob; and he will teach us of his ways, and we will walk in his paths; for the law shall go forth of Zion, and the word of the LORD from Jerusalem. And he shall judge among many people, and rebuke strong nations afar off; and they shall beat their swords into plowshares, and their spears into pruninghooks: nation shall not lift up a sword against nation, neither shall they learn war any more.
> But they shall sit every man under his vine and under his fig tree; and none shall make them afraid: for the mouth of the LORD of hosts hath spoken it.
> For all people will walk every one in the name of his god, and we will walk in the name of the LORD our God for ever and ever (Micah 4:1-5).

*First* of all, we are told "it shall come to pass," a phrase which means not only an absolute certainty of fulfilment because God has ordained it, but also *historical* fulfilment. The glory described by Micah is not an aspect of eternity but a prospect of time, of the temporal process: "it shall come to pass."

*Second*, "the mountain of the house of the LORD" shall be exalted, and all people shall flow into it. The "mountain" here signifies God's Kingdom, His rule, authority, and word. Since the prophecy is messianic, it means that the rule of the Messiah's Kingdom shall prevail over all the earth.

*Third*, there is a double passage with respect to the Kingdom. On the one hand, the people flow into it, and, on the other, the law goes out from the Kingdom, and the word of grace from its members. The statement that "the law shall go forth of Zion" means that God's law will be the law of the nations, the basis of the courts and of judgments, and the prevailing authority among the nations.

*Fourth*, this function of the law is made more specific when we are told that "he shall judge among many people." When the law goes forth and is enforced, the judgment then is not man's but the Lord's. The consequence of the worldwide enforcement of God's law is world peace. Even the arts of war are forgotten, and armament is reduced to scrap to make implements of agriculture. The law of God requires restitution: crime then does not pay. The law executes all incorrigible criminals and thus eliminates all habitual and professional criminals. As a result, men live in peace and safety, "and none shall make them afraid." This is a very literal prediction of peace, safety, and prosperity, and it is a prediction concerning history, not heaven.

*Fifth*, in Micah 4:5 we are told how all this comes to pass, and we are given a yardstick whereby we can understand history: "For all people will walk every one in the name of his god, and we will walk in the name of the LORD our God for ever and ever." Hengstenberg very succinctly summarizes the meaning of this verse in these words: "The lot of every people corresponds to the nature of their God."[1]

There is a very close link between this verse and such statements as our Lord's in Matthew 9:29, wherein He declares to the blind men, as *He* healed them, "According to your faith be it unto you." This is not the power of positive thinking, which relies on man's own supposed inherent powers. Rather, it is according to our faith in the Lord and our obedience to His law.

Thus, as we re-read Micah in terms of this declaration, we see that, because the covenant people are by faith the redeemed people of their Messiah-King, and because they obey His law, they gain a power in the world which makes peoples and nations move in their orbit. History flows into their hands.

Moreover, the Messiah is called "The Prince of Peace" in Isaiah 9:6 because He is the lawgiver whose law establishes peace. The government is upon His shoulder, and "Of the increase of his government and peace there shall be no end" (Isa. 9:6-7). The law of the Messiah destroys the wicked, and the grace of the Messiah makes His people flourish and prosper.

The incarnation thus means that history cannot escape from the justice of God. God the Son becomes flesh, redeems His covenant people by His atoning blood, and creates a law-people out of whom His word, grace, and law are to go forth to bring all things into captivity to Him as their King. If, however, the church has a false theology, it will have a false god, and it will walk, in Micah's words, in the name of its false and limited god. It may present this false god in the name of Christ, but not

---

1. E. W. Hengstenberg: *Christology of the Old Testament*, vol. I, p. 450. Grand Rapids, Mich.: Kregel Publications, 1956.

in His power. It may be full of sweetness and kindliness, but it will not have the power of God unto salvation, nor the power of God unto the throwing down of all citadels of rebellion and apostasy.

As Abba has noted, in Hebrew "name is inextricably bound up with existence."[2] The *name* of God is revelational. "The name of God means primarily his revealed nature and character—the Savior God as he has manifest himself and desires to be known by man."[3] To walk in the name of the Lord is to walk in the reality of His existence, power, grace, and law. It is to walk in terms of the basic and ultimate reality which determines all things. It means therefore to walk in truth and power, not in terms of illusion and impotence. To walk in His name necessarily leads to personal and world peace and safety, and it is a strength which causes all nations ultimately to turn to Christ's covenant people, knowing that the only true law which can govern the world goes forth from Zion.

To walk in the name of other gods is to walk in slavery to sin and to illusion. Despite the modern pretensions, the ungodly choose a course of enslavement because they are at heart slaves. Few are ready to be as honest as the people of Barcelona who in 1814 hailed the return of that sorry ruler, Fernando VII, shouting, "Long Live the Absolute King," "Long Live the Inquisition," "Down with Liberty," and even "Long Live Our Chains."[4] Such honesty sinners are rarely capable of, but, in any case, their chosen destiny is bondage in some form.

The Biblical meaning of *name* appears in older English usage, in such expressions as "Open in the name (i.e., the power and authority) of the law."

But, most important, Jesus Christ, possessor of *all* power and authority "in heaven and in earth," commissions His followers to go, teach, disciple, and baptize *"all* nations," requiring them to obey *all* of Christ's commandments. This commission is "in the *name* of the Father, and of the Son, and of the Holy Ghost" (Matt. 28:18-20). No higher authority can be given us.

---

2. R. Abba, "Name," in *The Interpreter's Dictionary of the Bible*, K-Q, p. 501.
3. *Ibid.*, p. 502.
4. John D. Bergamini: *The Spanish Bourbons*, p. 165. New York: G. P. Putman's Sons, 1974.

## 48

## INDICTMENT AND COMMUNITY

Our reading of Scripture is so consistently pietistic that we consistently miss the full meaning of a passage, in particular its social and legal aspects. An example of this is Hosea 4:1-5.

Hear the word of the LORD, ye children of Israel: for the LORD hath a controversy with the inhabitants of the land, because there is no truth, nor mercy, nor knowledge of God in the land.

By swearing, and lying, and killing, and stealing, and committing adultery, they break out, and blood toucheth blood.

Therefore shall the land mourn, and every one that dwelleth therein shall languish, with the beasts of the field, and with the fowls of heaven; yea, the fishes of the sea also shall be taken away.

Yet let no man strive, nor reprove another: for thy people are as they that strive with the priest.

Therefore shalt thou fall in the day, and the prophet also shall fall with thee in the night, and I will destroy thy mother.

The word *controversy* in verse 1 is used in the sense common in English at the time of the translation of the King James Version, i.e., a *lawsuit*. This same usage of *controversy* appears in the U. S. Constitution, Article III, Section II, par. 1; this meaning, i.e., *civil actions or suits*, is still common to law. The Berkeley Version translates "controversy" as "charge," as does Moffatt. Such translations do convey a little better the meaning of the original Hebrew in this context. Similar usage appears in Hosea 12:2, Micah 6:2, and Isaiah 34:8.

Our problem today is that words too often are taken at their minimal meaning, and this is true of "controversy." This should not surprise us. Cheap people cheapen words as well as almost all else they handle. Modern versions commonly cheapen words by their translation, and words like atonement, reconciliation, imputation, justification, and controversy are reduced in meaning. Wherever there is a juridical reference, and the Bible is set in a juridical framework, modern man reduces the meaning to a non-juridical one. But not only is *controversy* a legal term, but *grace* also is one. God's *grace* is the sovereign mercy of the Judge of all creation who provides a satisfaction to His justice and Himself fulfils the requirements of the law in the person of God the Son, incarnated as Jesus Christ, in order to express His mercy and reestablish a covenant people under His law.

The word controversy thus appears in the context of God's law, His covenant people, and their departure from His law and contempt for His mercy.

In this judicial suit, God is both plaintiff and judge. He indicts Israel because there is no truth, love, nor knowledge of God in the land. "Blood toucheth blood," or murder is added to murder, and justice is not done. "Therefore shall the land mourn" because of the famine of judgment. In such an evil time, God's counsel is "let no man strive, nor reprove another," for it is too late for warnings; let judgment take its course. The reason is that "thy people are as they that strive with the priest." This has reference to the refusal of people to pay attention to the law of God as taught by the priests, and refers specifically to Deuteronomy 17:12-13:

> And the man that will do presumptuously, and will not hearken unto the priest that standeth to minister there before the LORD thy God, or unto the judge, even that man shall die: and thou shalt put away the evil from Israel.
> And all the people shall hear, and fear, and do no more presumptuously.

A presumptuous people is not to be reproved: it is marked for destruction. Its false priests and prophets, and its "mother," the nation, will be destroyed.

The absence of any "knowledge of God in the land" means the ignorance of God's law. As John Mauchline noted, "That is indeed meant, and also something more, viz., the disregard of God's law and the refusal to honor the obligations of it, an attitude of wilful neglect."[1]

It should be noted, *first*, that God's *controversy* against Israel is a total charge, criminal and civil. Israel is charged with a breach of the covenant, i.e., a lack of regard for God's law and person, and also with particular breaches of the covenant law. We violate the covenant when we neglect the covenant law and are without truth and love. Before there is a specific breach of the covenant law there is a prior disregard for the covenant and the covenant God. But Israel had gone further. It had been guilty of false swearing, lying or bearing false witness, theft, adultery, and murder; the whole of the "second table" of the law had been flagrantly violated.

*Second*, the violations of God's law have destroyed Israel as a community. Where the violations enumerated exist, there is neither community, family, nor religious life of any tenable sort possible. As a result, the state of the nation is depicted to Hosea, and in his own private life, as comparable to marriage to a whore. Such a marriage is no marriage at all

---

1. John Mauchline, "Hosea," in *The Interpreter's Bible*, vol. 6, p. 600f. New York: Abingdon, 1956.

but a continuous hell and an agony of suffering and hurt. The violation
of God's covenant is comparable to adultery, and it must be seen as
equally repulsive and requiring a divorce and judgment. Moreover, the
adulterous nation can have no peace within itself. Its denial of God's law
is adultery; it is a breach of community in favor of lawlessness and moral
anarchism. The result will be mourning and alienation from the earth
and its bounty, for God will use the natural world to curse an apostate
people.

*Third*, the consequence is destruction. As Hosea 4:6 declares,

> My people are destroyed for lack of knowledge: because thou hast
> rejected knowledge, I will also reject thee, that thou shalt be no
> priest to me: seeing thou hast forgotten the law of thy God, I will
> also forget thy children.

The ground for destruction is forgetting the law of God; God in turn
forgets their children, for they are not His. Because they reject the
knowledge of God's law, God rejects parents and children alike and gives
them over to destruction. They shall no more be a priestly people unto
God. Their destruction is their own doing, brought about by their
faithlessness and their neglect of God's law.

*Fourth*, another consequence is shame. Hosea 4:7 declares,

> As they were increased so they sinned against me: therefore will I
> change their glory into shame.

> Berkeley Version: The more they multiplied, the more they sinned
> against Me; I will turn their glory into shame.

To be shamed means to be put to confusion, confounded, and thereby
isolated. Shame is an isolating emotion. Adam and Eve, in their sin and
shame, hid themselves from God (Gen. 3:8). Shame isolates man from
his fellow men also, and shame turns a man's vision away from the
present and future into the past. Shame leads to endless self-
recrimination and self-justification, to futile attempts to relive the past.
Shame is a consequence of lawlessness, and God therein turns man from
the glory to which man is called by His creation and by His grace into an
inwardly sick, self-torturing bundle of self-hatred and self-disgust.
Shame is an aspect of hell and a result of lawlessness.

Over and over again, the Bible not only states God's law but also
God's indictment against the lawless. Isaiah begins with a bill of indictment against Judah and Jerusalem. The message of all the prophets is
related to the law, and their words are indictments against all the nations
for their violations of God's law. The prophets assert the certainty of
judgment from the hands of the supreme judge of the universe, God
Himself. An "underground" writer in Communist Russia has written in
our time of that inexorable judgment: "The Court is in session, it is in

session throughout the world. . . all of us, however many we may be, are being daily, nightly, tried and questioned. This is called history."[2]

The consequence of sin is the loss of community with God and man and the indictment and judgment of God. Moreover, it means also a loss of true knowledge. Hosea 4:6 as well as 4:1 make clear that "knowledge" as used by the Lord means knowledge of "the law of thy God." However, it is not without significance that *knowledge* is used there in a generalized sense, because the heart of valid knowledge is an understanding of God's law. Solomon declares, "The fear of the LORD is the beginning of knowledge: but fools despise wisdom and instruction" (Prov. 1:7). The fear of the LORD means fear of transgressing His covenant law, and Proverbs is a commentary on the law. Knowledge, wisdom, learning, and instruction are all in terms of the law of God. They are not abstract concepts, as with humanism, but specific and concrete, having reference to the law of God.

To apply now the significance of these things, and to see their implications, let us examine a specific situation. Before beginning this paragraph, I was interrupted by a young man and his serious problem. He travelled from the Atlantic area to California to work for a prominent "Christian" organization. In thirteen weeks of work, he has been paid for only five weeks. The organization just raised $102,000 to satisfy all outstanding debts ($90,000), but he and others are still unpaid. Money raised to provide for specific projects has been used for unknown items. One other employee, until recently a night club performer, observed that he had been treated with more honesty and respect by the ungodly employers of his previous work. Pages would be required to cite the specific examples of lies, breaches of contract, misrepresentation, and much, much more that this prominent "evangelical" organization is guilty of. This situation is routine and commonplace in antinomian pseudo-Christianity. As a result, such religion is anathema even to the ungodly; it is productive of savage dissension under the sugar-coated pietism, and there is less community there than even in the ugly, narcotics-ridden world of secular humanism. It lacks all sense of true community, and it is without knowledge. Its idea of "knowing the Lord" is an emotional binge.

Such a world, being antinomian, is also by necessity anti-community, for no valid community in any but an artificial, hypocritical sense is possible apart from God's law. To observe God's law means to live in community. To be an antinomian is to be under indictment.

---

2. "Abram Tertz": *The Trial Begins*, p. 59. New York: Pantheon, 1960.

**49**

## THE ROYAL VIRTUE

In the ancient Near East, every king of any consequence issued or reaffirmed laws protecting the helpless members of society, widows and orphans in particular. Thus, in Sumeria, we are told that when the god Ningirsu gave the throne of Lagash to Urukagina, Urukagina "made a covenant with Ningirsu that a man of power must not commit an injustice against an orphan or widow."[1] It is apparent, *first*, that in antiquity many pagan religions still retained, as a part of the original general revelation of God to mankind, the idea of a covenant between God and man. *Second*, basic to the covenant was the requirement that God's way become man's way. A law therefore is a part of every covenant. *Third*, this concern for the lowly in society, widows and orphans in particular, came to be regarded as "a royal virtue in all the Ancient Near East."[2]

It is a royal virtue because it manifests grace and is not a self-seeking act. The weak and lowly in society are easily taken advantage of, easily pushed aside and forgotten, and easily regarded as beneath one's interest and attention. The royal virtue in this case must be the divine virtue, *grace*. The grace which God manifests to anyone, including the king, must be manifested to others. God condescends, or, with paganism, a god condescends, to choose the king and make him great. To mark his faithfulness to God, the king or man of power must then manifest a like grace to all those below him.

Snobbery and exploitation are thus both marks of the upstart and parvenu who lack grace and therefore cannot manifest it. Thus, the way to manifest that God's hand is upon one, and responsible for his blessings and success, is to bless those around and beneath him. Those who receive grace manifest grace. Those who have gained their power and wealth undeservedly cannot bear to associate with those of a lower estate lest people see their own low nature. As a result, they avoid close contact with all of a lower class.

The result of grace is *community*. The royal virtue reaches to others even as God's divine virtue has reached out to the person possessing it. Grace thus creates community, binding high and low, whereas snobbery creates isolation and class warfare.

---

1. Helmer Ringgren: *Religions of the Ancient Near East*, p. 39. John Sturdy, trans. Philadelphia, Pa.: The Westminster Press, 1973.
2. *Idem.*

Scripture makes clear that the covenant people, who are repeatedly ordered to manifest grace, friendship, and community with the lowly, are a royal people. "Ye shall be unto me a kingdom of priests, and an holy nation" (Ex. 19:6). "But ye are a chosen generation, a royal priesthood, an holy nation, a peculiar people; that ye should shew forth the praises of him who hath called you out of darkness into his marvellous light" (I Peter 2:9). Christ "hath made us kings and priests unto God and his Father; to him be glory and dominion for ever and ever. Amen" (Rev. 1:6). The Lamb "hast made us unto our God kings and priests: and we shall reign on the earth" (Rev. 5:10).

We must therefore manifest the royal virtue. In rejoicing before the Lord, we are to invite not only the Levite, who had religious prestige, but the fatherless, the widow, and the foreigner to eat with us, "that the LORD thy God may bless thee in all the work of thine hand which thou doest" (Deut. 14:29). In the Jewish *Sayings of the Fathers*, this same fact is stressed: "Let thy house be open wide; let the poor be members of thy household." (I, 5). Dr. Joseph H. Hertz commented, "Hospitality to the homeless has always been one of the conspicuous virtues of the Jewish life (Gen. 18). 'In the Middle Ages the treatment of poor Jewish travellers was considerate beyond description. Nothing might be done to put the poor guest to shame' (Abraham)."[3]

The royal person does not need to establish his separateness nor his royalty, his kingly nature. It is essential to his being. He does not demean himself by his concern for the lowly and distressed; rather, he manifests his royal nature. It is a part of his exercise of dominion to open his house, bounty, time, and concern to others. It is a privilege and function of royalty. Thus Christians, as a royal people, are told that, if they are of the faith, they manifest the royal virtue:

> Distributing to the necessity of the saints; given to hospitality (Rom. 12:13). (For a bishop must be) a lover of hospitality, a lover of good men, sober, just, holy, temperate (Titus 1:3).

> Be not forgetful to entertain strangers: for thereby some have entertained angels unawares. Remember them that are in bonds, as bound with them; and them which suffer adversity, as being yourselves also in the body (Heb. 13:2-3).

> Use hospitality one to another without grudging (I Peter 4:9).

> Beloved, thou doest faithfully whatsoever thou doest to the brethren, and to strangers (III John 5).

Much more could be cited, but these verses will suffice to illustrate the fact that God's royal people manifest the royal virtue.

On the other hand, the snob dislikes associating with the lowly lest his

---

3. Joseph H. Hertz, trans., ed.: *Sayings of the Fathers*, or Pirke Aboth, p. 16f. New York: Behrman House, 1945.

own very low nature be revealed thereby. Some years ago, a man with a trace of Negro ancestry, who was in appearance "white" and had passed as such for years, wrote that he disliked intensely being in the company of Negroes lest some kinship be thereby detected between himself and them. This is the same spirit which marks the snob: he rejects his common humanity, his inner nature, and any association beneath him; he insists on associating upwards only, on social climbing. The snob is fearful of being found out. The royal virtue marks those who know that it is the grace of God which has ennobled them, and they manifest that same grace unto others. The snob lives in a private world, the royal priesthood of Christ in God's universe.

The word repeatedly used in Scripture to describe the royal virtue is *hospitality, philoxenia,* literally, the love of strangers. It means the manifestation of God's grace, as the New Testament uses it, to those in need or in less favored circumstances. It is not a promiscuous openness: Paul, in laying down the requirements of leadership, says that a bishop must be "a lover of hospitality, a lover of good men" (Titus 1:3). While we cannot examine every situation, neither can we by our caution withhold mercy and hospitality.

Hospitality is not the same as routine friendliness to our circle. To entertain friends is well and good, but, by its Biblical meaning, hospitality means something more, the grace of God extended to strangers in terms of physical help to their needs, and this done with grace and "without grudging" (I Peter 4:9).

The royal virtue thereby extends the domain of the royal household. A king by his exercise of the royal virtue extends for the time his protection to the guests, and he makes them members of his household by giving them food from his table. One of the supreme privileges of the ancient world was the invitation to eat at the king's table. Nothing could equal this opportunity: it meant inclusion in the royal household.

For the Christian, as one invited and called to the wedding feast of the King, his privilege, as an adopted son by the grace of God, means the necessity to extend the royal grace and bounty to others. He either manifests the royal virtue or manifests his base-born nature.

# 50

## THE ROYAL VIRTUE AND THE FAMILY

The royal virtue means an open table to the widows, orphans, strangers, and the needy. That open table is a *family* table. The passover was a family rite, and its imagery is derived from the family meal and table.

The family is basic to the royal virtue. It is into the home, the family's heart, that the stranger comes. It is the family as an institution which is basic to Biblical law and charity.

The family today is regarded as a "private" domain, and charity has been largely transferred to the "public" domain, the state. To be *private* has been equated with being outside the jurisdiction of civil and moral law, and to be *public* means to be subject to total law. This distinction between public and private is born of humanism and ascribes to autonomous man, in his privacy, a jurisdiction outside all law and government other than his own.

However in the Bible, the family is the most public of all institutions, and adultery, treason against the family, is punishable by death, whereas treason against the state is not mentioned. Sexual relations are thus strictly regulated by the Bible, because they are crucial aspects of the most social and "public" of all institutions. The idea that whatever two consenting adults may choose to do is irrelevant to other men and to society is anti-Biblical and revolutionary. As Brian Wicker observes, with respect to sexual revolutionaries,

> It is at this point that the Christian concept of sex—based upon a lifelong, unconditional, and willingly undergone self-exposure by one person to the dense and intricate reality of another—needs to be recognized as a genuinely revolutionary model of social relationships. The true Christian insight into sex is that there can be no genuine sexual encounter without a profound revolution on the part of both partners. To be united in this sense is to be faced with just that kind of identity crisis which the process of initiation itself demands. Indeed, the two are part of the same thing. Marriage, like birth and adolescence, is a new world entered only through a kind of personal death and resurrection.[1]

We *cannot* understand what Scripture has to say about marriage without

---

1. Brian Wicker, "Ritual and Culture: Some Dimensions of the Problem Today," in James D. Shaughnessy, ed.: *The Roots of Ritual*, p. 31f. Grand Rapids, Michigan: William B. Eerdmans Publishing Company. 1973.

an appreciation of *the theological dimensions* of marriage. This is set forth in Ephesians 5:21-33. The key is submission "in the fear of God," and this duty of submission applies to husbands as to wives. The husband cannot expect submission "as unto the Lord" (Eph. 5:22) unless he himself is subject to the Lord. His authority is at all times conditioned by the word of God and by his prior obedience to the word of God. His authority is not an abstract fact: it is headship in a union which makes of the two one flesh (Eph. 5:31-32), and is patterned after the unity between Christ and the true church.

An insight into the significance of this relationship can be had by looking briefly at the varying natures of men and women. The differences between them are such that a single cell from a human body is identifiable as to its sex. Feminists hold that sexual differences are a product of social conditioning; feminism is a form of radical environmentalism. The fact is that the differences are basic and have nothing to do with superiority or inferiority. In fact, on the average, "women equal or surpass men in all test areas not related to aggression and abstract reasoning."[2] As Christians, we would term what anthropologists classify as *aggression* as *dominion*. Man's concern is with dominion, and hence with status. Man insists on striving for dominion and on giving dominion status to what he does. A woman is a cook, a man a chef. A woman is called a scrubwoman, the man calls his work a position as sanitary engineer, and so on. When men dominated the home, being a housewife had status; when men turned outward and left the home and children to women, being a housewife became demeaning, and women began to revolt against their status. The areas of life and activity abandoned by men to women's dominion quickly lose status for men and women alike. Status is acquired by masculine dominion, and this fact governs every area.

On the other hand, in the providence of God, women have been given excellence in areas other than dominion and abstract thought so that they might be able associates or help-meets to man. A man's thinking is abstract and wooden: he needs a woman's broader scope of intelligence and abilities to flesh out his perspective, which tends to be too abstract and too much geared to dominion to be always realistic. As a result, only a very stupid husband exercises dominion without the counsel of his wife.

It is this unity of action as one flesh, as a life in common, which gives power to the family as the central public institution. The man who acts as though his wife were only created to obey him denies the "one flesh" aspect of marriage and assumes the role of a bachelor exercising sexual

---

2. Steven Goldberg: *The Inevitability of Patriarchy*, p. 209. New York: William Morrow, 1973.

and self-serving demands over a resident woman. Instead of a marriage, there is then simply cohabitation. It is the man's will, not God's public purpose concerning the family, which is then put into force.

On the other hand, there cannot be a divided dominion. If the husband rules at his job, and the wife at home, dominion is shattered, the man has abdicated, and his abdication will soon be apparent at work as well.

The purpose of Christ concerning the church is redemptive dominion (Eph. 5:25-27). Since mixed marriages are forbidden, man's marriage cannot have redemption in mind, but together the man and wife can have as a family a central task in God's plan of redemption and sanctification. The church is one body with Christ, a community of life with Him, "for we are members of his body, of his flesh, and of his bones" (Eph. 5:30). Therefore, St. Paul declares, "*For this cause* shall a man leave his father and mother and shall be joined unto his wife, and they two shall be one flesh" (Eph. 5:31). Because we are members of Christ's body, we must in marriage become one body together and in obedience to Him and in union with Him. This "great mystery" of the redemptive grace of God in Christ is thereby institutionalized in the public fact of marriage and the family. The family is thus not a domain of private affairs but the central area of social action and concern, the basic church, state, school, and vocation of man. By virtue of the family's centrality in the control of children, property, and inheritance, it is the nursery of the future.

The sexual revolutionaries thus are people who prefer irresponsibility to a future. *Irresponsibility* rather than pleasure is their key note. First there is true pleasure only in God's appointed way, and, second, sexual revolutionaries are frenetic and pleasureless people whose basic motivation is a hatred of God, man, and of responsibility. *Responsibility* is not a private matter; it is always to someone or something; it is a social fact. Man's basic and ultimate responsibility is always to God. By attempting to convert sexuality into a private, non-legal concern, the sexual revolutionary is trying thereby to remove sex from the area of responsibility. By so doing, he absolves himself from the charge of irresponsibility. He then transfers responsibility to the state and loudly proclaims himself a highly responsible citizen by clamoring for socialist action in one area after another.

The royal virtue means an open *family* table and responsibility. It means that the Biblical family is a royal estate. In the Armenian wedding rite, bride and groom are crowned as a part of their induction into their new estate. They are now king and queen in Christ, called to exercise dominion, and, as God's household, the royal virtue, grace to the needy. The man's headship is one exercised in community with his wife, as one flesh with her. The grace of that community is expressed not only to the children but in the exercise of the royal virtue to strangers.

## 51

## THE FUNCTION OF THE ROYAL VIRTUE

There has been much talk in the U. S. about "the silent majority" which is ostensibly against the current political trend, against socialism, against revolution, pornography, and much more. If such a majority exists, we must call it the sinful rather than the silent majority, because it is largely guilty of inaction. Why?

The evidence clearly indicates that a very small minority in the Soviet Union are Marxists. The great majority of people detest Marx and communism. This is true also of the Russian intelligentsia, and some of its leadership. Then why is nothing done? According to Solzhenitsyn,

> Everyone waits bewitched for something to happen *of its own accord*. But that something will not happen.[1]

This is the heart of the matter. Man wants things to happen of their own accord. The ungodly will justify inaction by saying, "It will change. Things go in cycles." This is paganism. The cyclical view of history is a deadly fallacy and an excuse for a retreat from historical action. Churchmen, on the other hand, are all too often no better. They excuse their inaction by declaring that the rapture is near, or the end of the world is approaching, or else by bleating piously, "Well, it's in the Lord's hands."

But man was created in God's image, regenerated into that image, and established by the adoption of grace as a child of God in order that he might through the law of God establish God's dominion over the earth. He cannot without sin wait for things to happen of their own accord. It is his duty to *make* them happen. Christian schools do not just happen of their own accord: they represent faith, hard work, and patient dedication. The same is true of Christian homes, churches, states, institutions, and all things else.

Hence we see the significance of the royal virtue. Its function is that it does not leave things to happen of their own accord: it makes them happen. Hence too in the parable of judgment, when Christ as Judge confronts His church, He tests its membership in Him by asking, when I was hungry, thirsty, a stranger, naked, sick, or in bonds, were you mindful of Me? "Verily I say unto you, Inasmuch as ye have done it unto one of the

---

1. Alexandr I. Solzhenitsyn: *Letter to the Soviet Leaders*, p. viii. New York: Harper & Row, Perennial Library, (1974) 1975.

252

least of these my brethren, ye have done it unto me" (Matt. 25:40). As St. James declares, " For as the body without the spirit (or, breath) is dead, so faith without works is dead also" (James 2:26). We are, says St. Paul, "members one of another" (Rom. 12:5), although with differing gifts and offices.

We can understand therefore why it is that the world is in its present sorry plight. Churchmen have joined the pagans in waiting for things to happen of their own accord. As a result, where the grace of God is not in action in history, the fall of man and his depravity are active and command the field. We are told by St. Peter to "be diligent" (II Peter 3:14). Our Lord declares,

> But if I with the finger of God cast out devils, no doubt the kingdom of God is come upon you.
> When a strong man armed keepeth his palace, his goods are in peace: But when a stronger than he shall come upon him, and overcome him, he taketh from him all his armour wherein he trusted, and divideth his spoil (Luke 11:20-22).

Christ has come and is that stronger man, and we in Him are stronger than the powers of darkness. Thus, to apply the royal virtue and the whole of God's law to our world is to apply God's grace and power and to overcome the enemy.

Gunther Rosenberg has observed,

> Rebellion is popular today and Satanism is total rebellion against everything that is considered good, holy, and decent in the world. It is the ultimate trip of evil.[2]

If rebellion is "the ultimate trip of evil," it is even more clear that *obedience* to the law of God is the alpha and the omega of *faith*. Christians were not called into being by Christ's regenerating power in order to be impotent but to be world conquerors. The Great Commission is emphatic about the power and authority of Jesus Christ: "All power is given unto me in heaven and in earth" (Matt. 28:18). It is because Christ is the omnipotent King that He gives His sovereign order that we are to occupy and possess all nations in His name, "teaching them to observe all things whatsoever I have commanded you" (Matt. 28:20). We cannot properly teach the observance of what we ourselves have not obeyed. Hence the significance of the royal virtue. It brings obedience into the most personal realm.

Moreover, James Jordan has shown that the communion meal or love feast of the New Testament (I Cor. 11:20-34) combined the Christian Passover with the feast of rejoicing before the Lord with the needy brethren (Deut. 14:28-29). The mark of true communion is community.

---

2. Cited in Brad Steiger and Warren Smith: *Satan's Assassins*, p. 47. New York: Magnum Books, Lancer Books, 1971.

Community is the natural and open relationship between people of a common faith. It means a ready response to need as members one of another. St. Paul states it thus:

> Let brotherly love continue.
> Be not forgetful to entertain strangers: for thereby some have entertained angels unawares.
> Remember them that are in bonds, as bound with them: and them which suffer adversity, as being yourselves also in the body.
> Marriage is honourable in all, and the bed undefiled: but whoremongers and adulterers God will judge.
> Let your conversation be without covetousness: and be content with such things as ye have: for he hath said, I will never leave thee, nor forsake thee.
> So that we may boldly say, the Lord is my helper, and I will not fear what man shall do unto me.
> Remember them which have the rule over you, who have spoken unto you the word of God: whose faith follow, considering the end of their conversation.
> Jesus Christ the same yesterday, and today, and for ever (Heb. 13:1-8).

The *first* premise and fact of this declaration is that Jesus Christ is the unchanging and total Lord, now and forever. It is inescapable that His word is law, and that it is a fixed and unchanging law-word. St. Paul can speak with assurance that God's infallible word rests in an infallible and unchanging authority and Person. *Second*, because this word has authority, those who faithfully proclaim the word of God must be "remembered" in support and obedience, and their faith followed. *Third*, because God is not an arbitrary or capricious Lord, we have the assurance of His presence and His help. Whatever man may do to us, it is the Lord's purposes for us which will prevail. He is ever gracious to His own. *Fourth*, the grace we have received we manifest in brotherly love, and in hospitality to strangers. Having received grace, we give grace to others. *Fifth*, this grace manifests itself in our own behavior in the form of contentment and an absence of covetousness. We gain things, not by malice, envy, or covetousness, but by godly labor. *Sixth*, this grace is manifested in our sexual lives, which in honorable marriage, is marked by purity, peace, and joy, because no aspect of our being is outside the province of grace, whereas apart from grace, we are always under judgment.

Clearly, things do not happen of their own accord. This is *not* a mechanical universe but a personal one, the creation of the personal God and the domain of man, the creature God fashioned in His own image. In a personal world, things happen, not of their own accord, in terms of a dialectical materialism, but in terms of human action under God and in His grace.

Marxism believes that historical inevitability is a materialistic fact built into the very atomic structure of the universe. For Marxism, things will inevitably happen of their own accord. Such a faith finally leads to fatalism and death. For the Christian, things happen by God's ordination and man's obedience to God's word. God is the primary cause, and man the secondary. Things happen by the accord of God and man and under the sovereign decree of the Lord of creation.

## 52

## CULTURE AND THE ROYAL VIRTUE

In *Escape From Evil*, Ernest Becker, a social scientist, attempted to describe man's problem with evil. Civilization from its earliest origins has been tormented by the fact of evil and humanism has been unable to cope with it. The goal of humanists, and no less of Becker, is "to bring in the humanistic millennium."[1] Becker saw the continuing goal of humanistic man clearly. "Primitive society was a formal organization for the apotheosis of man."[2] Despite humanism's exaltation of man, it is *the idea of man*, a future ideal man, that is exalted, or an elite man of ostensible superiority. Man as he exists is mortal and fallible. *Man's culture is thus an attempt to transcend the limitations of man in the name and by the power of man.* Following Otto Rank, Becker held,

> Culture *means* that which is super*natural*; all culture has the basic mandate to transcend the physical, to permanently transcend it. All human ideologies, then, are affairs that deal directly with the *sacredness of the individual or the group life*, whether it seems that way or not, whether they admit it or not, whether the person knows it himself or not.[3]

It is not the supernatural in any Christian sense which is the goal, but the supernatural in a humanistic sense, man as superman recreating himself, his culture, and his world into a new order which transcends all the known limitations of nature. Otto Rank, in *Beyond Psychology* (1941), declared:

> All our human problems, with their intolerable sufferings, arise from man's ceaseless attempts to make this material world into a man-made reality...aiming to achieve on earth a "perfection" which is only to be found in the beyond...thereby hopelessly confusing the values of both spheres.[4]

Becker affirmed the principle of the fall, man's desire to be his own god, determining good and evil in terms of his self-righteousness, as the basic fact in man. This is an important fact: for Becker, man is not God's creation whose desire for apotheosis is sin and a product of the fall but

---

1. Ernest Becker: *Escape from Evil*, p. 1551 New York: The Free Press, A division of Macmillan, 1975.
2. *Ibid.*, p. 16.
3. *Ibid.*, p. 64.
4. Cited from Rank, *Beyond Psychology*, p. 58f. in Becker, p. 91.

rather man is a being whose nature is the drive to become god, and whose basic drive simply needs direction and understanding in order to achieve the humanistic millennium. Man is unfree because of his own nature, Becker declared, "He carries *within him* the bondage that he needs in order to continue to live."[5]

> Evil is caused by all the things we have outlined, plus the one thing they have left out, the driving impetus that underlies them all: *man's hunger for righteous self-expansion and perpetuation.* No wonder it has taken us so long to pull all the fragmentary insights together, to join the view of both sides on the nature of man. The greatest cause of evil included all human motives in one giant paradox. Good and bad were so inextricably mixed that we couldn't make them out; bad seemed to lead to good, and good motives led to bad. The paradox is that *evil comes from man's urge to heroic victory over evil.* The evil that troubles man is his vulnerability; he seems impotent to guarantee the absolute meaning of his life, its significance in the cosmos. He assures a plenitude of evil, then, by trying to make closure on his cosmic heroism *in this life and this world.*[6]

Meanwhile the fact of guilt is real and cannot be explained away. Man needs both "power and expiation." The question then is, "to whom does one expiate?"[7] Becker hoped that social scientists would write in seeking answers to this question, although he cited in passing William James, one of whose last thoughts was that "when all is said and done there is no advice to be given."[8] The thought of Marxism's "great things" in Russia left Becker more hopeful.[9]

It is evident on all sides that humanism is radically dissatisfied with man and is in essence anti-human. It is well expressed in Nietzsche's desire to replace man, a hated thing, with superman, a new being who is anti-man. The goal is not to redeem but to replace man. The doctrinaire humanist dislikes people in the flesh and prefers his idea of man, man remade in his own image. As a result, he views most of mankind as a stubborn roadblock to utopia.

In the Biblical perspective, man is a sinner whose sin is his rebellion against God and his desire to be his own god. Man's sin is not the ultimate or basic reality of man, because man is a creature created in God's image. Sin is a deadly and fatal cancer which only the miracle of God's grace can remove. Sin is a moral not a metaphysical fact. For Becker, it is man's "health," his good nature, which leads to sin. For the Bible, sin is not the basic fact: it is God's creation which is. As a result, for the Bible man's hope is not the creation of a superman, man

---

5. Becker, p. 43.
6. *Ibid.,* p. 135f.
7. *Ibid.,* p. 162.
8. *Ibid.,* p. 169.
9. *Ibid.,* p. 170.

transcended, but man regenerated and restored into the image of God by God's sovereign grace in Jesus Christ.

Each perspective on man has its own sociology. For the humanist, man must be reeducated into total humanism so that he can transcend himself. Man must be placed in the custody of totally humanistic agencies, and all institutions must be remade in terms of humanism. For man's culture to be "super*natural*" in Becker's sense, an omnipotent or at least very powerful humanist agency, man or the state, must take full control of man's life, nature, and destiny. This control is an *impersonal* one. The non-Biblical world view is of an evolving and blind impersonal universe. Personality has no meaning, and life is an accident. The best "handle" in coping with a natural order which is mindless is an impersonal one, in that it approximates the reality of things more clearly than a personal one. The key to the understanding of man is not God but the naturalistic and primordial past of man. *Meaning* is imposition by man onto reality, and all such impositions must be a blending of science and reason whereby an objective and workable plan of order is developed.

For the Bible, on the other hand, man's salvation and sanctification are not products of science and reason nor are they impersonal. The personal God by His sovereign grace redeems man through the atoning work of Jesus Christ. Man's response to salvation is thoroughly personal. It means on the one hand the personal worship of and devotion to the triune God. On the other hand, it means a personal extension of the life of grace to other persons by our behavior.

Our Lord declared, "Thou shalt love thy neighbour as thyself" (Matt. 19:19). Love is the fulfilling, or putting into force, of the law (Rom. 13:8), because God's law is His personal law for people, to be used to create a society or culture of love, whereas humanistic law is impersonal and creates a statist order. Statist ideas of love mean statist action; the Biblical doctrine means that we manifest our concern for others by putting God's law into effect.

St. Paul, in writing to the Thessalonians in I Thessalonians 4:1-12, declares:

> Furthermore then we beseech you, brethren, and exhort you by the Lord Jesus, that as ye have received of us how ye ought to walk and to please God, so ye would abound more and more.
> For ye know what commandments we gave you by the Lord Jesus.
> For this is the will of God, even your sanctification, that ye should abstain from fornication:
> That every one of you should know how to possess his vessel in sanctification and honour:
> Not in the lust of concupiscence, even as the Gentiles which know not God:
> That no man go beyond and defraud his brother in any matter: because that the Lord is the avenger of all such, as we also have

forewarned you and testified.

For God hath not called us unto uncleanness, but unto holiness.

He therefore that despiseth, despiseth not man, but God, who hath also given unto us his holy Spirit.

But as touching brotherly love ye need not that I write unto you: for ye yourselves are taught of God to love one another.

And indeed ye do it toward all the brethen which are in all Macedonia; but we beseech you, brethren, that ye increase more and more;

And that ye study to be quiet, and to do your own business, and to work with your own hands, as we commanded you;

That ye may walk honestly toward them that are without, and that ye may have lack of nothing.

*First,* of all, St. Paul makes clear that the law is communicated by God through him, and "to please God" means to obey His commandments. *Second,* sexuality is an area of law, and any sexual sin is a sin against God and defrauds or cheats our fellowmen. It is thus totally personal. *Third,* brotherly love, with its requirements for hospitality and the care of the needy brethren, is also cited, and the Thessalonians are commended for their love to the Macedonians, among whom their work was an example, as also in Achaia and beyond (I Thess. 1:7-8). *Fourth,* towards unbelievers, their witness should include a reputation for honesty and for a spirit of independence. St. Paul makes clear that the eyes of God are on believers, and also the eyes of men, and that the rule of life for believers must be the word of God. This means obedience to His law, and this obedience reveals itself in *purity, love, and hard work.*

We can see thus why the poor tithe, and hospitality to the brethren, and to the needy is so important. It is grace manifested and extended, and it makes clear that our God is a person, and that our faith restores the person of man. We who have been restored, restore others; we who have been blessed, bless others. The royal virtue of God the King becomes our virtue. It is Christian culture thus which is alone truly natural and supernatural.

## 53

## THE ROOTS OF THE ROYAL LAW

It is now important that we examine even more closely the roots of the royal virtue. This is clearly stated for us by our Lord in answer to a Pharisee:

Then one of them, which was a lawyer, asked him a question, tempting him, and saying,
Master, which is the great commandment in the law?
Jesus said unto him, Thou shalt love the Lord thy God with all thy heart, and will all thy soul, and with all thy mind.
This is the first and great commandment.
And the second is like unto it, Thou shalt love thy neighbor as thyself.
On these two commandments hang all the law and the prophets (Matt. 22:35-40).

*First,* in order to understand what this means, it must be recognized that our Lord's concern here is faith in action. "By their fruits ye shall know them" (Matt. 5:20), He declares, and basic to the fruits or manifestations of faith is the kind of love He here describes. *Second,* he is here stating what the law is, what the commandments of God mean, and He declares it is love. It is the fulfilling of the law (Rom. 13:8). *Third,* the whole of the law and the prophets "hangs" or *depends on* these two commandments. *Fourth* our Lord, in the parable of the Good Samaritan (Luke 10:25-37), then told the lawyer, on this occasion, that our neighbor must be understood in terms of the royal virtue, i.e., as the stranger in need. The great commandments thus sum up the imperative of *personal action.*

With this in mind, let us examine these two commandments. *First,* our Lord does not permit us to indulge in the pagan disunity of man which separates faith, law, obedience, and love. He is giving us the two *great commandments* "in the law"; He requires obedience to them, and He terms that obedience love. In the pagan view, man has a nature of two, three, or more substances, each of which is capable of a different impetus. In the Biblical perspective, man is one, entirely a created being, totally depraved in all his being by the fall, but also regenerate in all his being by virtue of Christ's redemption. The conflict in man is not between spirit and body but between sin and obedience. However fallen the sinner, the fact of his creation by God makes inescapable the witness in him to the law of God and his required obedience. However holy the redeemed man, he is not yet wholly freed from the fact of sin in this life, so his struggle too is between sin and obedience. The spirit-body conflict is neo-platonic and pagan.

*Second,* our Lord requires a totality of obedience. It is obedience with all our being, "with all thy heart, and with all thy soul, and with all thy mind." The whole of our being and of our lives must be involved in active obedience to God, because obedience is a total being. We are either obedient or disobedient.

Within the realm of man this obedience means to love our neighbor as ourselves. It has often been observed that we cannot truly love another if we do not love ourselves, and this is true. This is why fallen man, despite all his professions of love, is a potentially dangerous man. By his sin, he seeks to be his own god. He affirms self-love. Since his being is God-created, fallen man finds that his self-love involves also a deep self-hatred, since, in rebelling against God, he is also rebelling against God's image-bearer, himself. In the words of Wisdom, "he that sinneth against me wrongeth his own soul: all they that hate me love death" (Prov. 8:36).

On the other hand, he who loves himself is always and continuously mindful of himself, so that he is never forgetful of his needs. This means, *third,* that a totality of obedience means a continuous and abiding love.

We can understand the meaning of this requirement of love by examining tithing. Many who profess to love God do not tithe; for them, this is pushing love too far. They call tithing legalistic, although it is God's requirement, and profess to manifest love instead. This is like a husband professing to love his wife and children when he is guilty of non-support. On the other hand, there are legalistic tithers, who tithe with exactitude because they recognize that it is God's law. But, having tithed, they feel they are quits with God, and no more demands can be made on them. The tithe for them is a painful duty and a way of purchasing a clean bill of health from God. The Biblical tither does so because the support of God's work is as necessary and natural as his care of himself and his family; it is a part of life, and a good part.

To illustrate further: I love good food, and a good, hot shower; I want them when I want them. To be forced to shower, or to eat, hour after hour, all day long, would be punishment and hateful. But this is precisely how some people want to love God, their neighbor, and their family, to have them on tap, like a shower, to use or to enjoy when desired, and then to turn off. This is, in fact, one reason for the failure of many families and marriages. People marry and have children in order to have love on tap. Their attitude is, when I want love, give me love; when I don't want it, don't bother me. While the first cause of delinquency in youth is personal sin, a frequent *aggravating factor* is the attitude of parents who give love on tap, which is no love at all. God and man, His image-bearer, are not things, like faucets, to be turned on and off, but persons. When we treat people like faucets, we do not love them, and we do aggravate them. This is no less true of God, who certainly finds aggravating the indifference of men to Him except in time of need. A person who is good, thoughtful, and loving to us only when he wants something from us does not love us at all. We are not deceived by their fraudulent love, nor is God by ours. Our Lord says, "Ye are my friends, if ye do whatsoever I command you" (John 15:14). "If ye love me, keep my commandments" (John 14:15). "He that hath my commandments, and keepeth them, he it is that loveth me" (John 14:21). His commandments "hang" on or depend on this totality of obedient love, of continuous and abiding love.

It is one of the disasters of our time that the meaning of love has been altered to mean a profession of emotion rather than the Biblical meaning, which sees love as putting the law into force in an abiding obedience to God and as the manifestation in action of grace to man. Love today is a word for an emotional statement without action, or else with statist action on an impersonal plane.

The roots of the royal virtue are in faith, and true faith reveals itself continuously. "All the law and the prophets" depends on this meaning of love, and without it the gospel is denied and man's world depersonalized.

# 54

## TAXATION AND THE ROYAL VIRTUE

In the *Institutes of Biblical Law,* we saw that forgiveness, which means that the claims of the law against us are dropped because satisfaction has been rendered, is both *civil* and *theological. Civil forgiveness* means that we have made restitution to man for our offenses in terms of God's requirements. To use an older expression, a relic of Christian law, "our debt to society is paid," and we are free. *Theological forgiveness* means that, with respect to our restitution to God, Jesus Christ has, by His atoning death, paid the penalty for our transgressions as our legal representative and our Redeemer, our next of kin. The fact of theological forgiveness does not eliminate God's requirement for civil forgiveness. To use the atonement to eliminate the law is antinomianism. A murderer may and can find theological forgiveness; he can become a child of God by the adoption of grace through the work of Jesus Christ; the law as an indictment, a death penalty against him, is then set aside, because there is no longer a *theological indictment of the law* against him. This does not mean, however, that God's civil law against murder is set aside; here, the death penalty still applies. Unless we recognize the difference between civil forgiveness and theological forgiveness, we fall into antinomianism and have severe problems in trying to make sense of the Scriptures. Although the terms civil and theological forgiveness are not found in the Bible, nor the term Trinity, these words sum up basic aspects of the Biblical revelation.

Similarly, we must distinguish between *civil atonement* and *theological atonement.* The word atonement, like forgiveness, is related to legal process. Forgiveness means that charges are dropped, because satisfaction has been rendered, or, as in Luke 23:34, charges deferred for the time being. Atonement means a covering, a clothing or protection. Christ, by His atoning sacrifice, clothes us in His righteousness and covers us by His sovereign grace, so that we are delivered from judgment and protected from the enemy by His grace. This is theological atonement. Civil atonement gives us a protection and a covering in the world of men from the attacks of evil men and the works of Satan among men. Hence the throne or temple tax of Exodus 30:11-16 was delivered to the seat of God's government, the Holy Place, as a covering for the souls or lives of the people. God's civil government, the theocracy, provides a

263

*Law and Society*

covering to the covenant people, and the head or poll tax is the legitimate tax, and the only tax, for this purpose. I Samuel 8:1-22 makes clear that any more taxation than this is a usurpation by man of God's prerogative. St. Paul makes clear in Romans 13:1-8 that the function of all civil government is to provide a covering to good works and to be a terror to the evil, and, even when rulers usurp God's prerogatives, we are to render tribute and obedience, because this is God's requirement of us. The reconstruction of society comes not by tax revolts or any kind of revolution but by regeneration.

Moreover, men cannot complain about the state's usurpations when they themselves are usurpers by withholding their full tithes and offerings from God. The route to national and personal prosperity is not by revolt but by obedience to God's law of the tithe. Disobedience means cursing as surely as obedience means blessings (Mal. 3:7-12).

Isaiah declares of Jesus Christ, as he looks ahead to His coming, that "the government shall be upon his shoulder" (Isa. 9:6), a fact confirmed by our Lord in the Great Commission (Matt. 28:18), and by St. Paul in I Corinthians 15:25.

Very early in U.S. history, the U.S. Supreme Court recognized that "the power to tax is the power to destroy." This is not a power which God in His law confers upon the state. He Himself limits His tax to a tithe. Moreover, by means of the tithe and by offerings over the tithe, God places in man's power the ability to reconstruct society in terms of the word of God.

Thus, the relationship of the royal virtue to tithes and offerings begins to emerge. Both church and state seek to institutionalize reform; they impersonalize it by channelling it through agencies and commissions, so that personal responsibility is diluted at all points. The royal virtue requires us to manifest a personal concern and relationship to the needs of all, in particular of God's covenant people, and the tithe is ours to administer to groups and persons as we see their validity in terms of God's calling. The word of God remembers the man from Baal-shalisha, who, in a time of dearth, chose to give his firstfruits to Elisha and his school rather than to an apostate or cowardly clergy (II Kings 4:42).

"The *government,*" says Isaiah, shall be upon His shoulder; government means *rule,* the rule of the King's law. We govern where our word is law, and where our law prevails.

Christ as King therefore declares His sovereignty "All power is given unto me in heaven and in earth" (Matt. 28:18). The totality of the government of all things is now focused by the triune God in the person of Christ. In Him, the *religious atonement* is manifested, and in His government and law alone is there any true *civil atonement.* Apart from the justice and law of God, civil governments degenerate, as St. Augustine saw, into bands of robbers. The citizens cannot legitimately complain, because they too are also no more than robbers. No thief likes to be robbed, but being robbed makes no man righteous. Men who begin by robbing God (Mal. 3:7-12) will soon be robbing one another. God does not vindicate them until they first honor Him.

Christ as the incarnate Son of God, very God of very God, and very man of very man, is alone able to provide religious atonement. As the sovereign King and Lawgiver, whose law alone is true law, He alone is able to provide civil atonement. As the psalmist declares, "Except the LORD build the house, they labour in vain that build it: except the LORD keep the city, the watchman waketh but in vain" (Ps. 127:1). The covering is provided by the Lord. Christ, as the new Adam and the covenant man, is under the covering of God, so that the angels watch over Him as He enters into His ministry; we as His covenant people are covered also in Him (Ps. 91). In this antinomian era, it is not surprising that the Lordship of Christ is denied by many. By denying Christ's Kingship and His law, however, they undercut His work as Savior. To deny Christ's Kingship is to deny His sovereignty and His law, and if God has no law, there is then no need for either civil or religious atonement. If the law is rendered dead when we are saved, it means that by "accepting Christ" we have dethroned Him! This is the logic of antinomianism and Arminianism.

*Because* Christ is Lord, He commands us to go forth into the world and to conquer it it in His name. The Lord commanded Joshua, saying:

Moses my servant is dead: now therefore arise, go over this Jordan, thou, and all this people, unto the land which I do give to them, even to the children of Israel.

Every place that the sole of your foot shall tread upon, that have I given unto you, as I said unto Moses.

From the wilderness and this Lebanon even unto the great river, the river Euphrates, all the land of the Hittites, and unto the great sea toward the going down of the sun, shall be your coast.

There shall not any man be able to stand before thee all the days of thy life: for as I was with Moses, so I will be with thee: I will not fail thee, nor forsake thee.

Be strong and of a good courage: for unto this people shalt thou divide for an inheritance the land, which I swore unto their fathers to give them.

Only be thou strong and very courageous, that thou mayest observe to do according to the law, which Moses my servant commanded thee: turn not from it to the right hand or to the left, that thou mayest prosper withersoever thou goest.

This book of the law shall not depart out of thy mouth; but thou shalt meditate therein day and night, that thou mayest observe to do according to all that is written therein: for then thou shalt make thy way prosperous, and then thou shalt have good success.

Have not I commanded thee? Be strong and of a good courage;

be not afraid, neither be thou dismayed; for the LORD thy God is with thee whithersoever thou goest. (Joshua 1:2-9)

There is a very definite and close parallel between the Commission to Joshua and the Great Commission. *First,* Joshua is given the assurance that the Twelve Tribes of Israel shall possess the promised land because the omnipotent God is with them and will not forsake them. Christ assures His disciples of His absolute power and similarly commissions them to advance. *Second,* the disciples were aware of the parallel between themselves and Joshua, and between Christ and Joshua. Jesus and Joshua are the same names. The one, Joshua, receives a commission, the other, Jesus, gives a commission. The twelve disciples set forth the creation of a new covenant people to replace the Twelve Tribes of Israel. Hence a restatement of the commission follows, with this difference: Now it is the whole world which the covenant people are to possess. The twelve disciples and their followers are commissioned to teach all nations and to baptize them in the name of the Trinity. Thus, the whole world is to be brought into the covenant Kingdom. *Third,* just as Joshua is ordered to be faithful to God's law as the condition of blessing, so the disciples are required to teach all nations "to observe all things whatsoever I have commanded you" (Matt. 28:20). This means the whole word of God. As our Lord declared, "it is easier for heaven and earth to pass than one tittle of the law to fail" (Luke 16:17; cf. Matt. 5:17-20). *Fourth,* Joshua is told, "I will be with thee: I will not fail thee, nor forsake thee" (Josh. 1:5), and, again, "Have not I commanded thee? Be strong and of a good courage; be not afraid, neither be thou dismayed: for the LORD thy God is with thee whithersoever thou goest" (Josh. 5:9). Jesus, the Great Joshua, declares, "lo, I am with you alway, even unto the end of the world. Amen" (Matt. 28:20). Not surprisingly, the early church saw itself as God's new Israel, commissioned to conquer and occupy the world Canaan.

This conquest means civil atonement and religious atonement. It requires godly taxation. It calls for the exercise of the royal virtue, and of the tithe.

## 55

## EXPIATION AND POWER

Because God is not divided, nor does He share His sovereignty with any other, His government is total, and His law covers every aspect of creation. To restrict the Bible, and the language of the Bible, to the church, and to assume that its scope is limited thereto, is to deny God and His word. We have seen, in *The Politics of Guilt and Pity,* that atonement is an inescapable human necessity. We either have self-atonement, as masochism or sadism, or we have atonement through Jesus Christ. We have further seen that God's plan for atonement covers all of life: it is civil and theological, as is the case with forgiveness also.

Earlier, in observing the perspective of the humanist Ernest Becker, in *Escape from Evil,* we saw that he held that man needs both "power and expiation." He raised the question, however, "to whom does one expiate?" For the humanist the sin of man is against man, and therefore expiation is to man. The problem then is to affix guilt, so that expiation can occur. Are the capitalists guilty, or are the downtrodden masses themselves responsible for their plight? Are parents responsible for the sins of their children, or are the children themselves responsible? Is it heredity, or is it environment? If man needs both power and expiation, he is in trouble. Without expiation, he is guilt-ridden and tainted in his use of power, and progressively rendered impotent by his guilt. But if he makes expiation, it is still meaningless, because it does not necessarily alter the offended. The U. S. foreign aid program in the era after World War II was in part a form of expiation, but, while technologically it has been helpful, and militarily also, in any basic sense it has been impotent. It has done as much damage as good, and it has perhaps done more to convince other peoples of America's guilt than of their own shortcomings. Man's expiation rests on man's definition of the problem as well as providing man's answer. As a result, it begins and ends in a fallacy. Instead of expiation leading to power and peace, it leads to problems and impotence.

In considering the nature of expiation, let us examine, *first,* David's confession, which is a revelation of the nature of sin.

> For I acknowledge my transgressions: and my sin is ever before me. Against thee, thee only, have I sinned, and done this evil in thy sight: that thou mightest be justified when thou speakest, and be clear when thou judgest. (Ps. 51:3-4)

267

David was fully aware of the fact that he had sinned against Bathsheba, against Uriah, against the army whom he used at the cost of human life, and against Israel, whose king he was. His adultery and murder involved a vast network of human relationships. David, however, without discounting or denying the human aspects of sin, states its theological meaning: *sin is an act against God and His law.* When I sin against my neighbor, or my spouse, against anyone, I am essentially sinning against God; I am rebelling against His law and my duty to Him. Hence the clarity of judgment: God, as David acknowledges, is "justified when thou speakest, and... clear when thou judgest." Not so with man. Taken humanistically, the sin of David becomes dissolved and diluted. Many questions can be raised. Was not Bathsheba agreeable to the adultery? Did it not mean a great advancement for her? Bathsheba was married to a foreigner; were there problems between them? Was Uriah a good husband? Had he been involved in adultery on the side? As for the nation, did it not reveal its disloyalty and ingratitude at the first opportunity, with Absalom? On the human side, all sin is easily discounted. So much evil exists, that David's sin and ours seem at their worst to be trifles as against the sins of the world. David's whole life was a moral plus for himself and the nation, and so on. A humanistic reading of sin and crime readily collapses into permissiveness on the one hand and tyrannical vengeance on the other.

Only where the essentially God-centered perspective is upheld can we retain a valid doctrine of expiation, i.e., atonement in relationship to God and man. This expiation requires restitution to man and society *because* God's law requires it. We are not permitted by God's law to compare and evaluate sins humanistically, nor to excuse them because the victims are equally involved in sin. We are not allowed to rob a thief, or steal because we have been robbed, nor because someone we love commits adultery are we thereby justified in committing adultery. If sins were essentially an offense against us, we could then determine the penalty and our legitimate action. Sin, however, is always essentially and radically an offense against God, and His law stands untampered by our own involvements and justifications.

David thus said what he did precisely because he saw the meaning of his sin so clearly, and without any self-justification.

*Second,* in Leviticus 4, we have an account of sin offerings and the sacrifices necessary for forgiveness. It is significant that forms of offerings are separately specified for priests, rulers, and the people. These make clear that, *the greater the responsibility, the greater the culpability and guilt before God. The greater the power, the greater is the need and nature of expiation.* The sins of religious and civil leaders are more fearful and offensive in God's sight. Moreover, the separate specification of forms of expiation for men in church and state calls attention to the fact that they are as much under the word of God as other people, and more so because of their office.

This is an important fact, in that rulers in church and state tend to see themselves as above God's law because of their role as administrators. The poet, Robert Burns, described this mentality for us in "Holy Willie," an actual person; we have more Holy Willies than ever now, in church and state. In the church, for example, most disciplining is in terms of man-made rules, church law. Men are rebuked, excommunicated, and savagely condemned, in modernist, evangelical, and Calvinist churches, for failure to meet man's law, whereas God's law is regularly flouted by these same men. After the publication of my *Institutes of Biblical Law,* I received letters and long-distance telephone calls from ministers who regarded my references to the death penalty for adultery and homosexuality as anti-Christian and hard-hearted. In a few cases, where I knew these men, or learned something about them, I found them to be savagely censorious churchmen where church rules are concerned. This is the mark of Phariseeism and Sadduceeism.

Leviticus 4 does not permit such an attitude. It stresses the seriousness of the ministry of grace (the church) and the ministry of justice (the state). But what the Pharisees and Sadducees are implicitly saying is that *expiation is to the church, or to the state.* Church and state both say, Keep your peace with me and my rules, or suffer the consequences; pay up, and obey us.

*To whom the essential expiation is made, total power is rendered,* because it acknowledges their implicit role as the ultimate authority and law. For the church to demand that men take its law so seriously when it treats the law of God casually means, however much churchmen may deny it, the deification of the church. The same is true of the state. In both cases, power is enhanced by means of denying the theological nature of sin; the state does this openly, the church covertly.

The result is the enslavement of man. Man becomes the creature of the institution to whom he makes expiation, and he becomes progressively its slave.

True expiation means freedom and power. True expiation renders to God the things which belong to God, and it knows forgiveness, a release from all criminal charges before God, and the power of the sons of God. Most men today are sons of the church, and, more often, sons of the state, and both institutions make eunuchs out of their sons, and therefore slaves, because they are jealous of their power and authority. The purpose of God, however, is to restore His sons into power and dominion. David recognized that God's grace meant restoration to cleanness, joy, and gladness, and the ability to rule, teach, and convert:

Restore unto me the joy of thy salvation: and uphold me with thy free spirit.

Then will I teach transgressors thy ways; and sinners shall be converted unto thee.

Deliver me from bloodguiltiness, O God, thou God of my salvation: and my tongue shall sing aloud of thy righteousness. (Ps. 51:12-14)

The illegitimate taxing power of the state, therefore, robs the people not only of their money and property, but also of freedom and power.

## 56

## TAXATION AND THEFT

When the law declares, "Thou shalt not covet thy neighbour's house, thou shalt not covet thy neighbour's wife, nor his manservant, nor his maidservant, nor his ox, nor his ass, nor any thing that is thy neighbor's" (Ex. 20:17), it means by *covet* to envy and defraud. Our Lord makes this clear, saying:

> Thou knowest the commandments, Do not commit adultery, Do not kill, Do not steal, Do not bear false witness, Defraud not, Honour thy father and mother. (Mark. 10:19)

Today, however, to covet and to envy are regarded as normal and are vindicated by most political theorists. Fraud is only condemned if it is illegal in terms of statute law, not moral law.

Thus, writers Bruce Goldman, Robert Franklin, and Kenneth Pepper in *"Your Check is in the Mail," How to Stay Legally and Profitably in Debt,* advocate a policy of debt in direct and open contradiction to the Bible. Commenting on Exodus 22:24, they aver, "In the years since then, mankind has made a tremendous moral progress—to the point where usury is considered a virtue and only inability to pay a sin."[1] Their book is dedicated to "John Maynard Keynes, the father of deficit spending," and the first chapter is titled, "John Calvin Died in 1654. Unfortunately, His Ethics Didn't." This chapter concludes by declaring that "slow payment... is neither immoral nor illegal." It is the practice of the U.S. government, of industry, and of many smart people. Will this practice of deficit spending finally lead to ruin? The authors answer this by quoting Keynes: "In the long run, we shall be dead."[2] They are not ignorant of the consequences of what they suggest: "According to Dun & Bradstreet, some 918 companies went out of business in 1972 apparently because they couldn't collect on their receivables."[3]

It is an aspect of envy, and of all sin, that it takes a limited view of things; it's perspective is simply, "What's in it for me?" As a result, it cares little about the broader and social consequences.

It is not surprising that the authors cite Keynes as their authority.

---

1. Bruce Goldman, Robert Franklin, Kenneth Pepper: *"Your Check is in the Mail,"* p. 18. New York: Warner Books, (1974) 1976.
2. *Ibid.,* p. 31.
3. *Ibid.,* p. 22f.

Theirs is the ethics of exploitation, as indeed all forms of socialism must be. Moreover, in a society in which envy has been institutionalized by the state, and fraud made into a system of taxation, the standards of Scripture represent retrogression. In the modern world, the state has systematized envy and theft into a system of taxation. Instead of the limited head or poll tax of Scripture, the modern state has a vast array of taxes whereby wealth and property are expropriated and confiscated.

Early in U. S. history, the U. S. Supreme Court, in a statement we must keep in mind, said that the power to tax is the power to destroy. Since then, however, the policies of every modern state equate the power to tax with the power to create social progress. This is a faith emphatically held by modern man, for whom the state is redemptive and constructive. Nisbet has said of the 19th and 20th century radicalism that it manifested a faith in

> the redemptive possibilities which lie in political power: its capture, its purification, and its unlimited, even terroristic, use in the rehabilitation of man and institutions. Coupled with power is almost limitless faith in reason in the fashioning of a new social order.[4]

The state was thus to be the creator of a new social order, even as earlier it was held that this was the role of the church.

*But the command of God to exercise dominion and to subdue the earth (Gen. 1:26-28) is not given to institutions but to man himself.* Man, by means of God's law, and by the exercise of his calling under God, by work, thrift, and the tithe, is called to establish God's Kingdom in every area of life and thought. For an institution to assume this responsibility, rather than to be a tool of man therein, is a dangerous step. The church, by arrogating the tithe to itself, says that the tithe is a church tax, not God's tax. The state, by its system of taxation apart from Scripture, assumes a like independence from God. Both church and state implicitly declare that the kingdom is theirs, and that they are God on earth, able to command the things of God apart from God's word. Taxation then, whether it is the arrogation of the tithe by the church, or of a non-Biblical form of taxation by the state, becomes theft. This theft becomes possible because the people have first of all become thieves, because they neglect or despise God's word and are governed by envy and covetousness. Taxation then becomes their instrument whereby they rob those whom they envy. Having institutionalized theft, they cannot legitimately complain when the state uses theft against them. God will not hear nor vindicate their complaint (I Sam. 8:18), because it is not self-interest, grief over theft, or human misery which moves God to action, but repentance (II Chron. 7:14).

---

4. Robert A. Nisbet: *The Sociological Tradition,* p. 10. New York: Basic Books, 1966.

Taxation is a means whereby man seeks to create a false Kingdom of God, in reality the Kingdom of Man, by means of expropriation or theft. The answer to this evil is not a tax revolt, because it evades the basic theological issue. Rather, it is a revolt to tithing, to work, thrift, and, essentially, to faith and obedience. God does not honor man's way, whether it be taxation or a tax revolt.

The purpose of taxation is social reconstruction, schools, hospitals, welfare, the arts and sciences, and much, much more. Taxation as it exists today has that purpose which God requires us to fulfil through the tithe. To abandon the tithe and to adopt the modern tax system thus involves a double theft. *First,* God is robbed of His tax (Mal. 3:7-12), the tithe. It is amazing how many church members today will insist that the tithe is legalistic, and is done away with, whereas they will declare that Scripture requires us to pay our taxes to the state. There can be no denying that Scripture requires us to meet both taxes, God's and the state's, and there is also no question as to which tax God specifies in His law. *Second,* the modern tax system involves a continual theft by the state from the people. It is a system thus of double theft: it robs everyone it can possibly rob.

Modern taxation is deliberately *profane,* outside of God's temple, word, and purpose. It is profane because the goal of modern man, and of fallen man in every era, is *profanity,* life apart from and outside the jurisdiction of God. Profanity in this sense is sin, not reality. It is impossible for man ever to escape from God (Ps. 139:7-12). The totality of our lives is at all times comprehended by Him, and there is no escaping from His government. As a result, the basic theft which God sees is not the theft of man from man, and of the state from man, but of man from God.

Because man, as a consequence of the fall, sees himself as god (Gen. 3:5), he sees evil in relationship to himself. He will casually rob God and say, "God doesn't need my little tithe," but if he himself is robbed, whether or not he needs that which was stolen, man is indignant and outraged. The theft is a trespass against himself. It is the same with God: *every* sin, in particular those sins which deal directly with Him, such as the tithe, is a trespass against His person. The profane state's system of taxation is a trespass against God; the citizen is simply another thief in the sight of God, trespassing against God, if he does not tithe, and God will not treat him as a victim but as a criminal. His judgment will be against the state *and* the people. As the Lord told Samuel, "they have not rejected thee, but they have rejected me, that I should not reign over them" (I Sam. 8:7).

# 57

## THE BASIS FOR CITIZENSHIP

In various passages, the law gives us God's requirements for citizenship, notably in Deuteronomy 23:1-3:

He that is wounded in the stones, or hath his privy member cut off, shall not enter into the congregation of the LORD.
A bastard shall not enter into the congregation of the LORD: even to his tenth generation shall he not enter into the congregation of the LORD.
An Ammonite or Moabite shall not enter into the congregation of the LORD; even to their tenth generation shall they not enter into the congregation of the LORD for ever.

The term "congregation of the LORD" applies both to Israel as a nation and Israel as a church. The requirement of membership in both covenant nation and "church" were the same: faith, and obedience to the covenant law. Non-citizens could be believers, but, only after the required conditions were met, could they become members, with governmental powers, in the congregation. Eunuchs were barred; a whole man, and a free man, alone could be a member. Because the family is the basic unit in God's plan, anything departing from the legitimate family is barred. The Biblical standard is the monogamous family, but the Bible regards polygamy as still family oriented and hence tolerable in a way that adultery and bastardy are not. The line of David was a notable one, from Judah to Jesse, but, because of the bastard ancestor, Judah's son by Tamar, only with David, the tenth generation, was covenant membership and office possible. Perverse or morally low peoples had to have three generations of faith and obedience, as with the Edomites (Deut. 23:7-8), or ten, as with Ammonites and Moabites (Deut. 23:3), in order to enter into covenant membership and power.

This fact of covenant citizenship is one of the most far-reaching facts of history, in that it involved a radical break with all other ideas of citizenship. The city-state and the nation-state of antiquity had a religious character, in that the political order was the basic religious unit. This religion, however, was not a personal faith in essence but a social arrangement, a political alliance between a god and a political order. Very often, the political community was also an ethnic community; Rome was a notable exception here. The focal point of the religion was *not* worship but political order. There was no contact with the god apart from the

274

political order. David's ancestors, however, were men of faith, as far as can be determined.

In Israel, citizenship was not racial nor political but covenantal. The basic unit thus was not the political order but covenant man. The requirement of covenant citizenship was faithfulness, i.e., faith in the God of the covenant and an obedience to His covenant law. To violate the law meant separation or excommunication from the covenant in all its aspects. This fact was retained by Christendom: excommunication meant the loss of civil and ecclesiastical status both for the medieval church and for most Protestant churches later on. The loss of citizenship in the United States on conviction of criminal charges is a survival of this fact. Ironically, while criminal offenses still mean a loss of civil citizenship, the antinomian churches do not regard it as requiring a loss of church membership or citizenship.

Christianity very early had to deal with the question of citizenship. The question was best resolved in the Western church with the emphasis on the credal formula, *I believe.* In the Eastern churches, the creed sometimes began with *We believe.* The emphasis is not on the personal faith of covenant man but on the profession of the community; the individual can thus repeat a creed he does not believe but affirm thereby his part in the community and his assent to the community. The Western tradition stresses covenant man, the believing person. The consequence has been a greater vitality in the Western churches.

In the middle ages, citizenship was determined by participation in the mass. The city was thus an association of individuals who participated in the mass; non-participants were thus non-citizens, such as the Jews. This fact meant a radical break with the group oriented societies of paganism and stresses the individual and his centrality. The sociologist Max Weber pointed out two important consequences of this new view of citizenship. *First,* the individual was now legally disengaged from racial, clan, and kinship groups and made more individual while at the same time given a greater, more personal and intense communality. *Second,* this gave to the individual an autonomy which aided in the development of capitalism and modern secular rationality.[1]

This is not surprising. Without the link of the covenant between God and man, the person becomes an atom. Atomistic individualism then breaks down, and people began to demand the reign of the group, pagan fashion. Socialism and fascism in the 20th century witness to modern man's inability to face up to individualism apart from God and His covenant.

The medieval view, however, was defective. The church mediated the

---

1. Robert A. Nisbet: *The Sociological Tradition,* p. 81f. New York: Basic Books, 1966.

citizenship via the mass. Not covenant faithfulness but the mass, not faith and obedience to God's covenant law, but participation in a church sacrament, became the ground of citizenship. Earlier, Biblical law was basic to communion, but, gradually, church rules began to accumulate and to dominate. The key to citizenship came to be relationship and obedience to the church. Biblical law includes obedience to church, state, family, etc., but its focal point is covenant obedience to God.

Protestantism adopted the medieval view, although the Puritans in America moved towards re-instating the centrality of Biblical law. As a result, Orthodox Jews very early were able to vote in America because of their adherence to common law.

Meanwhile, however, another trend was in evidence in the Western world, one which began with a Biblical orientation and soon departed from it.

Biblical faith has a strong orientation to the land and to property. Two of the commandments ("Thou shalt not steal" and "Thou shalt not covet...") are directly concerned with property. Another refers to "the land" as a blessing ("Honour thy father and thy mother...that it may go well with thee in the land which the LORD thy God giveth thee"), while still another refers to work ("Six days thou shalt labour..."). (Deut. 5:13-22). The covenant blessing clearly includes prosperity and property.

Not surprisingly, very early property became an aspect of the qualification for citizenship. This has deep roots in the Biblical view of *land*.[2] It was, however, converted into an aristocratic doctrine and an economic concept, so that citizenship meant a landed aristocracy rather than a covenant people. The results were ugly, in that the Christian community was subverted and a large element of the population depressed. The collapse of Cromwell's regime meant also repression for the common people. One of the results was the development of a savage law code, which had roots in the Renaissance era and earlier, and the ready execution of individuals for minor offenses against property. In America, these views were very early established in Virginia, again with savage overtones, such as the death penalty for killing a chicken or stealing an ear of corn.

The democratic movement led to a moderation in legal penalties, but its influence on equality has meant that the criminal and the citizen have tended to be equalized. Many advocate the abandonment of laws requiring a loss of citizenship on criminal conviction. As a result, savage penalties are increasingly in evidence for law-abiding citizens as lawlessness begins to dominate the scene.

---

2. See W. D. Davies: *The Gospel and the Land, Early Christianity and Jewish Territorial Doctrine,* Berkeley, California: University of California Press, 1974.

The Biblical basis seems to many hard-hearted. The idea of penalizing bastards is especially cited these days as an instance of unfair legislation. Such penalties are, however, designed to protect the integrity of the family, its property, inheritance, and legitimacy. Where these penalties are taken seriously, less bastardy will occur, and society will be more stable. To establish *any* kind of order, someone must be penalized, because *order cannot exist, unless disorder is outlawed. To legalize disorder means in the end to penalize order.*

## 58

## THE PRINCES OF GOD

For Israel, in our Lord's day, God's true vine was Abraham, the princes of God's Kingdom were the twelve sons of Jacob. The blood of Abraham was holy blood, saving blood, so that the Pharisees denied that they were slaves of sin, saying, "We be Abraham's seed, and were never in bondage to any man" (John 8:33). Abrahamic blood was salvific, and hence they resisted our Lord's summons. They conveniently overlooked the fact that, in Abraham's day, the covenant people was very slightly Abrahamic. *All* of Abraham's household were in the covenant (Gen. 17:13), and *all* the males were circumcised and entered into the covenant, whether slave or free. Since Abraham fielded 318 fighting men against the kings of the east (Gen. 14:14), this means that Abraham was a ruler of a powerful household. Elderly slaves would have been left behind, as well as male children, so that a fair count of the males in the household would be 800 to 1,000. Those who wonder at the count of about two million Israelites at the time of the Exodus forget that, while the *blood* line of Abraham numbered 315 in Canaan when Jacob entered Egypt to join Joseph, the *covenant* line now numbered many thousands, and hence the necessity of assigning the land of Goshen to this great company. No doubt, by the time of the Exodus, *all,* through inter-marriage, had some Abrahamic blood, but the covenant was grounded, not on God's preference for Abrahamic blood, but on sovereign grace. In Amos 9:7, God makes clear to Israel that they are "as children of the Ethiopians unto me," i.e., *of themselves* they have no more standing before God than the Ethiopians; their covenant status is of God's sovereign grace.

To renew the covenant broken by Israel's apostasy and unbelief, our Lord chose twelve disciples to signify that the New Israel of God was being established. At the Last Supper, He declared, "I am the true vine, and my Father is the husbandman. Every branch in me that beareth not fruit, he taketh away" (John 15:1-2). To remain in Christ the Vine the disciples must obey their Lord's commandments (John 15:7-12). Then our Lord makes a most important declaration: "Ye are my friends, if ye do whatsoever I command you" (John 15:14).

Some years ago, Dr. Adolf Deissmann pointed out that the title *friend (philos)* was used at the court of the Ptolemies for the highest royal officials or princes, so that *philos* or *friend* means, in the context used by our Lord, *princes*. The Septuagint reading for Esther 2:18 is *philos*, rendered *princes* by the King James Version.

All this throws a clear light on John 15:14, which thus can read also, "Ye are my princes; if ye do whatsoever I command of you." Our Lord had spoken previously of their princely role (Matt. 19:28; Mark 19:29-30; Luke 22:28-30). His cousins, the sons of Zebedee, James and John, had sought princely status, and Christ made clear the terms (Matt. 20:20-23).

To be a *prince of grace*, i.e., to be made a friend of the king and thereby a prince, meant *incorporation* into the royal family. A king made men princely by his friendship, i.e., by inviting them to the communion of his royal table, and by giving them gifts of clothing. Our Lord, in the parable of the wedding feast, declares that the true guests to His banquet table wear the garments provided by Himself (His atonement and righteousness), and eat at the King's table (Matt. 22:1-14). The King's family, i.e., the princes of the realm, His Household, is made up, not of blood, but "whosoever shall do the will of my Father which is in heaven, the same is my brother, and sister, and mother" (Matt. 12:50).

It is at the Last Supper, the Passover, a *family* rite, that our Lord, as the host, provides the meal and declares the princely status of His family, and the conditions thereof: "Ye are my friends (my princes) if ye do whatsoever I command you (John 15:14).

Princely status in the Kingdom of God is in terms of *faith* and *obedience*. The parable of the talents (Matt. 25:14-30) makes clear that, the greater the faithfulness, the greater the princely status and rule. Faithfulness means power as a prince, as Dominion Man.

Our Lord precedes His statement of John 15:14 with the words, "Greater love hath no man than this, that a man lay down his life for his friends" (John 15:13). Again, the word for *friends* is *philos*.

When we turn to the Old Testament, we find that a key word is *hesed,* which refers to a covenant relationship and means *loyal kindness.*[1] It implies grace and suggests love.

In Genesis 20:13, Abraham asks Sarah for this "thy kindness which thou shalt shew unto me; at every place whither we shall come, say of me, He is my brother." This is to save Abraham from being murdered by men desiring to possess Sarah (Gen. 20:11). Abraham's servant asks Abraham's kinsmen to "deal kindly and truly with my master" (Gen. 24:49). Naomi praises God for His kindness (Ruth 2:20), and again the word is *hesed,* as in Boaz's praise of Ruth's kindness in Ruth 3:10.

According to Glueck, the *hesed*-relationship exists between relatives by

---

1. Nelson Glueck: *Hesed in the Bible,* p. 2ff. Cincinnati, Ohio: The Hebrew Union College Press, 1967.

blood or marriage, related clans and related tribes, host and guest, allies and their relatives, friends, ruler and subject, and "those who have gained merit by rendering aid, and the parties thereby put under obligation."[2] According to Glueck, Ruth, a foreigner, made herself a covenant member by her faithfulness and her loyal kindness:

> She was as free as Naomi's other daughter-in-law to return to her own people. Yet, in faithful love she followed her mother-in-law. In true religiosity she complied with Jewish custom. Ruth took it upon herself to practice *hesed* in order to fulfill the obligations of a Jewish widow.[3]

Rahab uses the same word in Joshua 2:12, 14 to describe the mutual obligation between herself and the spies to deliver one another. She asks them to swear to her by the Lord to save her and her family as she had them. Their response was, "our life for your's" (Joshua 2:14). *Hesed* is a mutual covenantal relationship; there is both *obligation and loyalty* in the relationship. The spirit is one of *faithfulness* in terms of a covenant and its law. The concepts of "loyalty, justice, righteousness, and honesty. . . are embraced in its meaning." This is its significance as it pertains to human relationships. "God's *hesed* can only be understood as Yahweh's covenantal relationship toward his followers."[4] It is grounded upon His grace. Covenant man can ask, as did Nehemiah, that God manifest this relationship of *hesed* to man as man is faithful to God. Nehemiah prays, "Remember me, O my God, concerning this, and wipe not out my good deeds that I may have done for the house of my God, and for the offices thereof." Grounding his faithfulness to the Lord on the Lord's faithfulness to him, Nehemiah asks for continued and open faithfulness.

*Hesed* presupposes covenantal kinship, i.e., an established relationship which, between God and man, rests entirely on grace. This covenantal kinship establishes the covenant man with a princely status. This status, however, depends on a covenantal loyalty and faithfulness. Ye are my friends, my princes, my Dominion men, Jesus says, if ye keep my commandments.

*Because* they are now friends, kinsmen, princes, they can go forth in the King's power and in His Name: "All power is given unto me in heaven and in earth. Go ye therefore, and teach all nations, baptizing them in the name of the Father, and of the Son, and of the Holy Ghost: Teaching them to observe all things whatsoever I have commanded you: and lo, I am with you alway, even unto the end of the world. Amen" (Matt. 28:18-20). Royal agents have always gone forth on a royal

---

2. *Ibid.,* p. 37.
3. *Ibid.,* p. 41.
4. *Ibid.,* p. 102.

commission with special powers, dignity, and authority. A king's commission makes a commoner into a lord pro tempore, for the time being; upon faithlessness, or lack of diligence, he is degraded. So we too are friends, princes of the King of Kings, if we obey His law. Hence too St. Paul's concern that, if he failed to retain mastery, he would become a castaway (I Cor. 9:27). The friends or princes of the king must ever be faithful to the work of the king.

## 59

## "THE JUST SHALL LIVE BY FAITH"

Words often change their meaning and gain new frames of reference as a culture changes. Because Hebrew is a language of a very ancient and long history, meanings have often changed, and words gained new perspectives. The same is true, to a lesser degree, of New Testament Greek. Thus, each Testament, and the Septuagint, throws light on the other, and contemporary documents, as Deissmann showed, throw light on both. We have seen how Ptolemaic usage, and the Septuagint version of the Old Testament, make clear the meaning of *friends* in John 15:17. The usage of *bastards* in Hebrews 12:8 clarifies the meaning of Deuteronomy 23:2, and so on.

The same is true of the word *faith,* the central usage of which in the New Testament is in Romans 1:16-17:

> For I am not ashamed of the gospel of Christ: for it is the power of God unto salvation to every one that believeth; to the Jew first, and also to the Greek.
> For therein is the righteousness of God revealed from faith to faith: as it is written, The just shall live by faith.

Paul is quoting God's word to the prophet Habakkuk. The prophet was deeply concerned over the attack by the Chaldeans, and he could foresee the dangers ahead for Judea. It was easy, in such a situation, to feel *hopeless* and despairing. As a prophet, Habakkuk faced the despair of the people and their questioning of God. He was fully aware of the nation's sin and of the necessity for judgment, but the evil nature of the Chaldeans distressed him. He asks God for an explanation, not in doubt, but in order to understand. God's answer thus is addressed to the problem of *hopelessness and despair:*

> I will stand upon my watch, and set me upon the tower, and will watch to see what he will say unto me, and what I shall answer when I am reproved.
> And the LORD answered me, and said, Write the vision, and make it plain upon the tables, that he may run that readeth it.
> For the vision is yet for an appointed time, but at the end it shall speak, and not lie: though it tarry, wait for it; because it will surely come, it will not tarry.
> Behold, his soul which is lifted up is not upright in him: but the just shall live by his faith (Hab. 2:1-4)

The meaning of faith is here set forth, and St. Paul cites it in full awareness of its implications. *First* of all, men read events in relation to themselves rather than to God. Men feel their grief and hurt, and they easily give it priority. God, however, cites as basic to any understanding of history "the vision," or prophecy. Because the meaning of history is not from man but from the Lord, "the vision" or prophecy is essential to any understanding of history.

*Second,* the *vision* or prophetic goal of history is the redeemer. As Laetsch most tellingly comments on Habakkuk 2:3,

> This era of visions has its "appointed," divinely determined time. God could have fulfilled immediately His Eden promise of sending the Redeemer. Eve and Lamech had hoped He would (Gen. 4:1, 5:29). Yet it had pleased the I AM THAT I AM to choose together with the person of the Redeemer also the time of His appearance. The long interval between the first promise and its final fulfillment was to serve the purpose of keeping His people watchful, hopeful, ever alert for the advent of the Woman's Seed. At Habakkuk's time the believers had waited, hoped, prayed for more than thirty-three centuries, and God tells the prophet, "Vision is yet for an appointed time." Not because God had forgotten His promise or was no longer willing or able to fulfill it. He was still Jehovah, the eternal, the almighty God. Only His appointed time had not yet arrived. "But at the end it shall speak!" The Hebrew is still more forceful and impressive: "It gasps toward the end." [1]

God is not unmindful of His covenant people, but His concern for them is in terms of His covenant goal, the Redeemer.

*Third,* God declares that "the just shall live by his faith." Men who live in trust and obedience, in *covenant faithfulness,* to the vision, to the goal of God in history, are justified and defended by the Lord in terms of that faith. The just *live* by this faith: they live in faithfulness to the covenant, its law, and its goal, the new Adam, Jesus Christ, the coming Messiah. We *cannot* drop the word *live* from Habakkuk and Paul without distorting the meaning. Faith then is reduced to belief only, whereas Scripture makes clear that it is belief and life in terms of the covenant and all that the covenant means, its law and its promise.

*Fourth, faith* is contrasted to hopelessness and despair. Faith means a life in terms of the covenant God, His law, and the goal of the covenant, the Kingdom of the Messiah. Thus, hopelessness and despair is the antithesis of faith and a denial thereof.

Now, turning to St. Paul, the meaning of Romans 1:16-17 becomes clearer. Paul writes as another Habakkuk; the little church, like little Judea, faces a hostile world. St. Paul shows on the one hand the radical depravity of the unredeemed world and on the other the sovereign majesty

---

1. Theo Laetsch: *The Minor Prophets,* p. 330. St. Louis, MO: Concordia, 1956.

of the predestinating, covenant-keeping God. The Lord is mindful of His own. He is the potter, and men are the vessels of His creation, moving in terms of His sovereign decree. Thus, He makes all things work together for good to them that are His own, and all things serve Him. The landless new Israel of God can therefore live by faith more confident in the vision or prophecy than old Israel. Hence, St. Paul begins, in Romans 1:16-17, *first,* by affirming his confidence. He is "not ashamed of the gospel of Christ." It will not put him to confusion, nor will he be confounded. He glories in the gospel, because it alone is the ground of salvation and victory.

*Second,* the gospel "is the power of God unto salvation." Paul discounts the seeming impotence of the Christian. God's plan and strategy are at work, and, in due time, the vision will become total reality. Christ has come; He is the first-fruits of the new creation (I Cor. 15:20-23). The full triumph of His covenant and Kingdom in time and eternity lies ahead, having the seal of His coming.

*Third,* this "power of God unto salvation" is "to every one that believeth; to the Jew first, and also to the Greek." The condition of entrance into the power and the covenant is *faith;* historically, the first opportunity was to the Jew, then to the "Greek," or the world and culture beyond Israel. It is to *everyone* that believes; the covenant is to include all peoples, tribes, tongues, and nations. Israel tried to restrict the covenant to blood, to make it humanistic; the restriction is not in terms of man but of God, and the restricting condition is *grace.* "The everlasting gospel" is preached, not to a race, but "unto them that dwell on the earth, and to every nation, and kindred, and tongue, and people" (Rev. 14:6). Those who are redeemed by the blood of the Lamb are "out of every kindred, and tongue, and people, and nation" (Rev. 5:9).

*Fourth,* it is in the gospel of Christ that "the righteousness of God" is revealed "from faith to faith." The righteousness of God includes His person, His law as an indictment and death sentence against covenant-breaking man, Christ as the atonement provided for man's redemption, the law as God's righteousness and the charter of the Kingdom, the certainty of God's government, grace, mercy, and justice, and much more.

*Fifth,* St. Paul sums it up by citing Habakkuk: "the just shall live by faith." The just are the justified. They are the redeemed of God in Christ. They *live* by faith: theirs is the vision of Christ's triumph and Kingdom. They know by faith that history is not a farce, nor man's hopes destined to be confounded. Their hope is from God, as is their faith. They are covenant-keepers. They move in the power of Christ's first coming and His resurrection as the first-fruits of the new creation. They themselves are by their regeneration members of that new creation. They look therefore in the confidence of faith to the spread of Christ's Kingdom and its world-triumph, and to His coming again in power.

They know the vision or prophecy, and they believe that God's word is *truth*.

Therefore, as the *friends* or *princes* of the King of Kings, they keep His commandments, knowing that they shall reign with Him and in Him (Rev. 5:10), and are even now "kings and priests unto God and his Father" (Rev. 1:6). They do not retreat from the world: they conquer it. They are marked by *covenant faithfulness:* they *live* by faith; they believe and obey.

# 60

## THE WORD OF THE KING

Psalm 24 presents us with God the King in His throne room, in the temple (or tabernacle), with the covenant people approaching Him. As King and Judge of all creation, His entry is marked by a demand for silence. In our courts today, when the judge enters, the cry of the court officer is, "Silence in the Court." The judge alone speaks, or those to whom he grants permission to speak. Habakkuk 2:20 has this in mind when it declares, "the LORD is in his holy temple: let all the earth keep silence before him."

The earth must keep silence, because the Supreme Judge speaks. It is of the essence of kingship that it declares the law; it guides, comforts, defends, rebukes, and judges. The earth must be silent before the Great King because His word is law; His word is omnipotent and binding, and there is none other who can speak to man's condition.

As men approach the presence of the Great King, they are reminded of His judgment on the world before the Flood. The foundation of God's government over the world and all they that dwell therein is His righteousness, and the judgment of the world by means of the Flood means that the world has no foundation in and of itself. It has the insecurity of historical process, which manifests God's judgment. History is firmly anchored in the fact of the Flood and all floods of judgment; men and nations are founded upon the seas of history.

The earth is reminded of all this as it approaches the throne. Plumer commented on this fact:

> *The earth is the Lord's.* This clause contains the truth on which the rest of the Psalm is founded. The message is to the inhabitants of the earth, and the first thing said to them is, The very earth on which you walk is Jehovah's, not yours. Here God has rights of ownership and rights of sovereignty, undeniable and inalienable. He is the proprietor to the exclusion of all others. Satan is the God of this world in no other sense than as a usurper, supported by the wicked, who are his children. The gods of the heathen are vanities and lies. They can neither see, nor save, nor hear, nor help. They and the devil have no rights here. The earth is the Lord's, *and the fulness thereof.*[1]

Only those can approach the throne who are faithful to the King.

---

1. William S. Plumer: *Psalms,* p. 321f. Edinburgh, Scotland: Banner of Truth Trust, (1867) 1975.

*Faithfulness* means faith and obedience, both "clean hands, and a pure heart." It means one who "hath not lifted up his soul unto vanity, nor sworn deceitfully."

The favor and blessing of God the King is manifested to all such: "He shall receive the blessing from the LORD, and righteousness from the God of his salvation." The King's favorites are those who obey Him and who manifest His Spirit. Such people are "the generation of them that seek him, that seek thy face, O Jacob," or, the Berkeley Version reads, "who seek Thy face, like Jacob." J. A. Alexander rendered it: This is the generation seeking him: the seekers of thy face (are) Jacob, i.e., the true Jacob, the true Israel. The true Jacob is Israel, a prince before God.

Psalm 24, apparently celebrating the investiture of Jerusalem, was written to be sung when the ark of the Lord was brought to the recently captured Jebusite city, Jerusalem. Now to be the capital city of the Davidic realm, it is therefore, since Israel is a covenant nation, to be the throne city of God the universal King. In verses 1-6, the majesty of God the King is celebrated, and the conditions of approach to God. Three months earlier, Uzzah had perished (II Sam. 6:6-11) for his casual and lawless approach to God. God's requirements are binding in their every detail, and Uzzah had regarded his practical considerations as more important than God's order.

As the procession approached Jerusalem it halted before the city's closed gates to demand their submission. "The name of the incoming king (cf. II Sam. vi 2b) is declared to be the Lord mighty in battle."[2] The Lord had recently given David victory in all his battles. This, however, is an insufficient description of God the King. His reign is more than national, and the grounds of His kingship are more than the success of Israel. He is the King of the universe, King of all creation, and not only the ancient doors of Jerusalem must open to Him, but all doors and gates of time and eternity.

> This designation alone was insufficient to warrant the opening of the gates, and the call to provide access to the city is repeated (9). The Lord's presence and pre-eminence in Zion is based on grounds other than His intervention in Israel's historic battles. The Lord is king of all in His own right, possessing powers and qualities which transcend earth and time. The King of glory is *the Lord of hosts* (10; cf. I Ki. xxii. 19). This high concept of God has been foreshadowed in the Psalm's opening words, whose meaning extends far beyond the temporal and national outlook of Israel.[3]

The implications of all this are immediately obvious. *First,* at the moment of Israel's triumph and joy, the fact is strongly stressed that God

---

2. Leslie S. M'Caw, "Psalms" in F. Davidson, A. M. Stibbs, E. F. Kevan, eds.: *The New Bible Commentary,* p. 430. Grand Rapids, Michigan: Eerdmans, 1953.
3. *Idem.*

the King is Lord of all nations, and Israel cannot receive Him except on the recognition of this fact. The gates of Jerusalem are, in a true sense, closed to the King if they see Him only as their King. Isaiah 57:7 says of the strangers or foreigners who are brought to the covenant faith, "Even them will I bring to my holy mountain, and make them joyful in my house of prayer: their burnt offerings and their sacrifices shall be accepted upon mine altar; for mine house shall be called an house of prayer for all nations." The great indictment of the religious leaders of Jerusalem by our Lord cites this fact: "It is written, My house shall be called the house of prayer; but ye have made it a den of thieves" (Matt. 21:13).

*Second,* because God is King of all creation, His reign is at all times universal. Every event in history is the manifestation of His plan, purpose, justice, punishment, or blessing. "The earth is the Lord's and the fulness thereof." The gates of any city or people, and the gates of our hearts, are in effect closed if we limit God to ourselves, or if we deny His total concern. God's government, care, and concern extend to the very sparrows (Matt. 10:29-31). Everything has a place in His plan and care, although we who are redeemed by Him "are of more value than many sparrows" (Matt. 10:31).

*Third,* because God is the universal King, all creation is under His law. Isaiah declares of the Messiah:

> Behold my servant, whom I uphold; mine elect, in whom my soul delighteth; I have put my spirit upon him: he shall bring forth judgment to the Gentiles.
> He shall not fail nor be discouraged, till he have set judgment in the earth: and the isles shall wait for his law. (Isa. 42:1, 4)

In vs. 3 we are also told, "He shall bring forth judgment unto truth," on which Fitch comments, "The idea is that He shall fully and faithfully set forth the law and thereby vindicate His righteous cause."[4] All nations, including the remote islands, shall joyfully await the law or justice of the King.

*Fourth,* it is the purpose of God to unite all nations in obedience to His law and in covenant faithfulness. Isaiah 42:4-7 sets this forth powerfully:

> Thus saith God the LORD, he that created the heavens, and stretched them out; he that spread forth the earth, and that which cometh out of it; he that giveth breath unto the people upon it, and spirit to them that walk therein:
> I the LORD have called thee in righteousness, and will hold thine hand, and will keep thee, and give thee for a covenant of the people, for a light of the Gentiles;
> To open the blind eyes, to bring out the prisoners from the prison, and them that sit in darkness out of the prison house.

---

4. W. Fitch, "Isaiah," in Davidson, Stibbs, Kevan, *op. cit.,* p. 591f.

The Messiah is given "for a covenant of the people," i.e., the Gentiles, so that all nations may be brought into covenant faithfulness.

*Fifth,* the Messiah, His covenant, and His covenant law, come to the nations and isles as freedom, as release from blindness and from prison. The covenant in its totality means that God is Lord and Creator, that God as King in His mercy redeems the peoples and gives them His Servant, the Messiah, to release them from captivity and to give them the freedom of His government and law.

In terms of all this, we can understand Habakkuk 2:20; "The LORD is in his holy temple: let all the earth keep silence before him." The Great King speaks: His word is the saving word, the law word, and the absolutely governing word. His word is a total word: it is grace, justice, mercy, peace, and law, and it is also reprobation and warfare against all who keep not silence before Him but insist on declaring their own word.

## 61

## THE KINGSHIP OF CHRIST

In a remarkable passage, St. Paul ties together the implications of the incarnation, the death, the resurrection, and the ascension of Jesus Christ for His Kingship and Kingdom. The focal point of all this is *the cross* and the victory gained there over sin and death. But this is not all. Sin and death are more than abstractions. They are the consequences of an alien kingdom, the Kingdom of Man, and they are the outworkings of a government in contradiction to itself. The purpose of the tempter's program in Genesis 3:5 was to give man eternal life by means of self-righteousness, with every man his own god and law. The consequence of this plan was instead sin and death. It gave to every man an anarchic principle of operation which was hostile to all community and at war with God and man. Whereas St. Paul in Ephesians 4:7 declares, "But unto every one of us is given grace according to the measure of the gift of Christ," the tempter in Gen. 3:5 gave to every man a suicidal principle of government and a program of total war against God and man.

St. Paul goes on to say:

> Wherefore he saith, When he ascended up on high, he led captivity captive, and gave gifts unto men.
> (Now that he ascended, what is it but that he also descended first into the lower parts of the earth?
> He that descended is the same also that ascended up far above all heavens, that he might fill all things.) (Eph. 4:8-10)

Christ is here declared to be the conquering King of Creation who has overthrown the power, authority, and government of the enemy. To do this, He descended to earth in His incarnation, lived in perfect obedience to the law as the sinless new Adam, made atonement on the cross for His people, began His ascension into power by His obedience to the law, His triumph over sin and death with the resurrection, and continued His ascent into power by His physical ascension into heaven. The high point of His ascension into power is His imperial largess, whereby He showers His grace and gifts upon His people. This is the mark of the triumphant and wealthy king. He uses His power and substance to bless His people. The results of the government of darkness are "unfruitful works" (Eph. 5:11); it is a government for disaster.

The cross thus is presented here and elsewhere as the turning-point in history with respect to *government and judgment*. Government is, after all, judgment and law. All government is in terms of law, and judgment is premised on a concept of law. The government of the world, of the Kingdom of Man, is in terms of the law of sin and death, because man as his own god means sin and death. *The crucifixion is the culminating and central act of judgment in all of history.* It is the judgment of the fallen world on Christ. The world cries out, "Crucify Him! We will not have this man to rule over us." The justice of fallen man was never more clearly shown than in its verdict on Christ. For all its show of toleration or of piety, this judgment still remains. It is daily re-enacted against the faithful people of Christ in persecution, envy, malice, slander, or resentment. We cannot expect non-Christian men and civil governments to establish and maintain just social orders when their supreme act of "justice" was to crucify Jesus Christ.

On the other hand, in the wisdom of God, the cross of Christ is also a revelation of God's justice. It is a death sentence to sin and death and to the government of this world. Significantly, that judgment meant the shaking of all nations before Christ's coming, and a greater shaking now that He has come (Heb. 12:25-29). It meant the fall of Jerusalem, the greatest disaster of all of history (Matt. 24:21-22), because it represented man's justice and government against God.

The cross reveals God's justice, His sentence of death against sin, and His plan for the obliteration of sin and death from His Kingdom (I Cor. 15:53-57). The people of God are given gifts by the victorious King in order that they may carry out the implications and manifestations of His victory into every corner of the world. It is the King's purpose to "fill all things," to occupy all things and bring them into their fulfillment in His Kingdom; it means putting His government into force in every aspect of the world, and in a totality of power.

Because the cross is God's judgment on the world's law, judgment, and government, it rendered *null and void* all of man's governments, although "for conscience sake" it requires our obedience to them and they continue in power by the ordination of God because all nations are not yet made disciples of their true King (Rom. 13:1-5; Matt. 28:18-20). *To obey "for conscience sake" means out of obedience to God rather than to the civil authorities. It means that the authority to require obedience is transferred from the governments of this world to God.* God always was and is the source of all authority, but with the triumph of Christ the issue is totally clear: *He alone can command us in any independent and absolute sense.*

Moreover, God requires us to be obedient to the powers that be not only because thereby He declares that it is His decree by which alone all powers rule, but also because all the governments of the fallen world are by their nature anti-government. The principle of the fall, that every man is his own god and law, is hostile to the possibility of community and to any government by or over a community. Carried to its logical conclusion, then every man does that which is right in his own eyes, because Kingship of God is denied (Judges 21:25).

A civil order rests, as far as law and order are concerned, *less* on the state and more on the faith and conscience of the people. A civil order will nearly collapse if *one percent* of its people are systematic law breakers. Consider what one car in a hundred can do to tie up traffic and bring it to a stand-still if it acts anarchistically, if it tries going the wrong way in the wrong lane, and so on. One percent of the population of the United States means more than two million people; two million law-breakers, making theft, murder, adultery, or false witness a way of life can bring the entire 200 million to the point of anarchy and collapse if the 200 million have no sound principle of law whereby they can punish and execute the two million. A law enforcement man tells me that my figures are too high; 200,000 hard-core criminals could paralyze the police and reduce the country to near chaos.

Moreover, the major part of all government rests on non-statist institutions, the family, church, school, vocations, social pressures, friends and relatives, traditions, and much more. The successful state, whether democracy, republic, monarchy, or dictatorship, rests primarily on these non-statist agencies. Not too many years ago, a large percentage of Americans could live and die without ever seeing a statist official, a sheriff or his deputies, a judge, or any like statist officer. Crime was remote, and local non-statist institutions blanketed man with their government. In tribal life in many parts of the world, all government, for better or for worse, is by non-statist agencies.

The modern humanistic state, applying the logic of the fall, works to dissolve all traditional forms of government in favor of its own. The state seeks to represent humanistic man's reason applied to the problems of man and society. The older forms of government are seen as irrational and hence to be replaced by the state. According to *Time,*

> From the founding of the nation and well into the 20th century the family was seen as the keystone to both personal and social well-being. Writes sociologist Sheila M. Rothman of the Center for Polity Research in New York: "The fundamental assumption was that the good order of society depended finally on the good order of the family, its ability to instill discipline and regularity in its members. Success in this mission augured well for the safety of the republic. Failure jeopardized the experiment that was democracy."
> But that view has changed. What Rothman calls the "discovery of personhood" leads often to the notion that happiness rests not with the family unit but, perhaps, in opposition to it. The rapidly changing sense of women's proper roles, the uncertainty over children's

rights, doubts about the very worth of having and rearing children, the ever-loosening legal bonds of marriage—all these have brought into question, in Rothman's phrase, "the legitimacy of the family."[1]

As the humanistic state destroys the family, it will itself collapse. Successful civil governments rest on the foundation of *other* forms of government. Communist China has the background of old China's family government and discipline and ancestor worship. The Soviet Union has the background of Russian Orthodoxy; Nazi Germany had the background of Lutheran and Catholic discipline, and so on. *A state of any kind, let alone a dictatorship, is impossible if it cannot rest on the backs of non-statist forms of government. The destruction of these is the destruction of the state.*

In the Kingdom of God, the source of rule is in the regenerated man, who is governed by the infallible word of God. The conscience and self-government of this regenerate man are informed by the word of God which has the Holy Spirit to bear witness to it and enlighten it. Every regenerate man has received the grace of God unto salvation, and he receives gifts as well, so that, by his calling, he may work "for the perfecting of the saints, for the work of the ministry, for the edifying of the body of Christ" (Eph. 4:12). By God's grace and regenerating power, His covenant people become "members one of another" (Eph. 4:25), having in Christ a community the state cannot create.

Jesus Christ is the firstfruits and the beginning of the new creation of God (I Cor. 15:23; Rev. 3:14). *Only* as His government over and in us grows will all other governments, (church, state, family, school, vocation, etc.), grow and flourish. His triumph over death and sin in His resurrection therefore sets forth the only possible ground for any true government. It marks His ascension to royal power: He takes "captivity captive." He is exalted, because He is victorious. Possessing all things as King of Kings, He can give gifts freely to His covenant people. As Creator of all things (John 1:3), His power is inexhaustible.

His dominion as King is total, and extends over all things created, including Satan. As Stevenson wrote,

> Our Lord's dominion over Satan proceeds upon the ground of his legal conquest as a priest...Satan's dominion over mankind is, on his part, usurped; but, on God's part, judicial. Man having yielded to Satan as a tempter, God judicially delivered him over to his power as a tormentor, until the claims of the law should be satisfied. Satan, therefore, is secured in his dominion by the curse of the law. But when our Lord as a priest redeemed his people from that curse, by submitting to be made a curse for them, he obtained a legal triumph over Satan, inasmuch as he bereaved him of his dominion, so far as it was secured to him by the penal sentence of the law, and procured

---

1. "The Family," *Time*, April 12, 1976, p. 29.

for himself a right to enter Satan's territories, and to rescue his redeemed people. Hence, when Christ was to have his heel bruised by Satan's agents in the world, he was to bruise Satan's head. Gen. iii. 15. Hence also, he is said by death to have destroyed him who had the power of death; and to have spoiled principalities and powers, triumphing over them in his cross. Heb. ii. 14; Col. ii. 15.[2]

God the Father says to God the Son, established as King of Creation,

Ask of me, and I shall give thee the heathen for thine inheritance, and the uttermost parts of the earth for thy possession.
Thou shalt break them with a rod of iron; thou shalt dash them in pieces like a potter's vessel. (Ps. 2:8-9)

Because of Christ's descent and ascent, because of His victory over sin and death in His resurrection, the whole earth is His inheritance. He will rule all men either as their gracious Lord or their sovereign Judge.

The Apostle's Creed therefore rightly comprehends within one sentence the whole of Christ's life, from His birth to His coming again. The totality is His descent and ascent, His physical ascent followed by the empowering descent of the Holy Ghost.

We live today in the decay of the Kingdom of Man. It is a desperately flailing and failing form of government. It is, in fact, an anti-government force, destructive of law and community. Men who fear the power of the state should remember that the more the state succeeds, the closer it comes to destroying itself. When the Christians of the early church, like Tertullian, told the emperors of Rome that they were Rome's most obedient citizens, they were right. No state can survive long without a very large body, a preponderant body, of principled and self-governing people. The power of the modern state, as well as the ancient state, is a luxury created by a host of non-statist institutions and loyalties whose network of government, law, order, and obedience creates the myth of state power. The state in its insane power works to undermine this network, and statist education is a powerful agency for this destruction. By so doing, the state undermines itself. Its police and army cannot function against massive lawlessness and only reflect it. Rome was not overthrown: it collapsed. The modern state seeks total power and therefore total collapse.

Thus, when St. Paul speaks of Christ and "the power of his resurrection" (Phil. 3:10), he is speaking of the only power that can rule the world. There is no other power nor government than Christ's: all else is in principle anti-government. The resurrection thus marks the beginning of a new creation; it is the ascension of man out of the darkness of sin and death into life and righteousness. It is the open manifestation of the Kingship of Christ.

---

2. George Stevenson: *A Treatise on the Offices of Christ,* p. 259f. Philadelphia: William S. Martien, 1838.

## 62

## "THE GOVERNMENT SHALL BE UPON HIS SHOULDER"

Mrs. K. L. (Ellen) Myers, a faithful friend of Chalcedon, has been a frequent speaker for a Right to Life Organization. In a letter of April 9, 1976, she wrote:

I spoke to a high school home economics class near Wichita April 8. Part of the program consists in a show of color slides on prenatal development, and abortion and its effect on the baby.

In the discussion period directly following the slides, an obviously *for* "abortion on demand" girl stated: "1 would rather know it (the baby) was dead, instead of having it adopted by people who might not treat it right, and whom I did not know. I want to know what would happen to it, so I'd rather have an abortion."

Proverbs 8:36b in action!

This very revealing incident highlights an important facet of fallen man's nature. His will to be god means the determination to govern reality and to transfer predestination from the hand of God to the hand of man. This demand for total control involves a readiness to kill a lover or family member rather than to allow them to have any independence. We are all familiar with the unhappily too common murder by someone of an ex-spouse and sometimes the children also; even more common than such murders are the number of people who toy with such ideas. Love is not the motivation in such crimes. Rather, it is the unwillingness to allow anyone to escape their domination and determination and to have an independent life.

In one of Isaiah's prophecies concerning the coming of the Messiah, we are told

For unto us a child is born, unto us a son is given: and the government shall be upon his shoulder: and his name shall be called Wonderful, Counsellor, The Mighty God, The Everlasting Father, the Prince of Peace.

Of the increase of his government and peace there shall be no end, upon the throne of David, and upon his kingdom to order it, and to establish it with judgment and with justice from henceforth even for ever. The zeal of the LORD of hosts will perform this. (Isa. 9:6-7)

Emphatically, the government and determination of all things is on Christ's shoulders, and His government and Kingdom shall prevail and shall cover the earth. The beginning of that open conquest of the world is

295

the resurrection, which marked Christ's ascension into royal power.

Two ideas of government are thus in conflict, that of the Kingdom of Man, and that of the Kingdom of God. In the Kingdom of Man, true government means self-determination in an autonomous rather than responsible sense. Responsibility means accountability to someone; the self-determination desired by autonomous man is an irresponsible one; it involves a denial of responsibility because man is his own god, accountable ostensibly to no one. The goal of the Kingdom of Man is a world of total self-predestination in which all controlling institutions, including the state, shall disappear, and man will be what he wishes to be when he desires it. Gary North, in *Marx's Religion of Revolution,* has described Karl Marx's dream of a world where a man can be, for example, a brain surgeon in the morning, a concert violinist at night, and a skilled worker in a totally alien field the next day. There are many versions of this dream, most more sophisticated, but all essentially the same. Man will live without any external compulsion in a new kind of paradise.

This dream clearly echoes Biblical strains of thought. In the Garden of Eden, there was no external compulsion; man, created good, delighted himself in serving God. His troubles began when he attempted to seize the government in an attempted but insane coup d'etat. Of the coming Messiah, it is said that the government shall be upon His shoulder, so that we realize finally the inner directed government of Eden. Christ declares, "Lo, I come (in the volume of the book it is written of me,) to do thy will, O God" (Heb. 10:7[9]). The people of Christ, as they grow in Him, progressively become more and more willing to echo Christ's readiness to do the will of God. The result, in the fulness of time, is the gloriously harmonious world described in Isaiah 2:1-5.

The goal of anarchistic man is a world in which each man is totally his own law. The goal of Christ's Kingdom is a society in which every man freely serves God's law, not as coercion, but as the expression of his own heart, on which now the law is also engraved:

> But this shall be the covenant that I will make with the house of Israel: After those days, saith the LORD, I will put my law in their inward parts, and write it in their hearts; and will be their God, and they shall be my people.
> And they shall teach no more every man his neighbour, and every man his brother, saying, Know the LORD: for they shall all know me, from the least of them unto the greatest of them, saith the LORD: for I will forgive their iniquity, and I will remember their sin no more. (Jer. 31:33-34 cf. II Cor. 3:3)

The goal of the fallen, anarchistic man is self-determination and a world free from all coercion. From his perspective, the ultimate source of coercion, and the worst, is God. He dreams, therefore, of a world without coercion, and with "rational" solutions to all problems.

An amusing example of this, published in 1928, is a prediction concerning 1975. According to Pitkin, rational arbitration would replace the courts:

My guess is that, by 1975, our courts and our legal system will have been reformed by the simple method of wholesale desertion. Nobody in his senses will take his case before an American judge. The civil courts will follow the Protestant church into peaceful oblivion. Intelligent people will simply lose all interest in it because it has nothing of value to offer them. But there will still remain plenty of profitable work for superior men in our proposed legal corporations. For, no matter what methods men use to settle their quarrels, some expert will always be needed to analyze and present the facts and underlying principles of justice.[1]

Of course, since 1928 the courts have become more clogged than ever, less just, and more arrogant. Instead of Pitkin's rational arbitrations, more coercion prevails in the world at large. This should not surprise us. Anarchism is the father of statism and totalitarianism, and this is as true today as in Greece, Rome, and the Renaissance. *Anarchism, by exalting the ultimacy of every man, and the independence and autonomy of every man, leaves no common ground between men except coercion.* The result is a war of the gods, or would-be gods. In a world of autonomous men, the only contact between man and man is coercion, imperialism. Self-determination in the anarchic sense of autonomous man means that the only common or general will among men is the imposed will of one.

Just as the man whose wife and children have left him decides they must die rather than be independent, so the consequences of political humanism are also coercive and destructive. People are *forced* to love one another, forced to integrate or segregate, forced to study certain things, forced and forced at every turn, because the only possible common ground for autonomous man is coercive government.

Law is a form of predestination and prediction. Law determines the nature of a society and rewards and punishments therein. The law of God has consequences for time and eternity. So too humanistic law seeks to predestine and predict the course of history. Humanistic law, however, is pure coercion. It has no real place in man's heart: it is arbitrary and pragmatic.

God's law, on the other hand, is so basic to all His creation that it is written into every atom of creation, so that it witnesses to God's truth even though the ungodly hold down or supress the truth in unrighteousness (Rom. 1:18-20). It has an inescapable and ineradicable place in man's being. With regeneration, this witness of man's being is unleashed and says Amen to God's enscriptured word. As man grows in sanctifica-

---

1. Walter B. Pitkin: *The Twilight of the American Mind*, p. 167. New York: Simon and Schuster, 1928.

tion, so too his ready and willing obedience to God's law flourishes, and the role of the state declines, although, in this life, it never disappears because our sanctification is never perfect. However, the more we submit to that government which is of Christ, the less human coercion there will exist.

At one time, as E. A. Powell has observed, policemen walked a beat with crime a rarity, and the prison population very small. As faith has receded, and coercion increased, it has increasingly become difficult for the police in many urban areas to walk alone, and a major aspect of police training and activity is given over to protecting one another. A police force, one of whose major tasks is to protect and defend itself, has proportionately less and less time to protect others. This is an inevitable consequence when man takes the government upon his own shoulders. He may talk of brotherhood, but he has instead inaugurated an age of force and of the gun. The humanistic idea of love means brotherhood out of a gun-barrel. It means too that you murder an unborn baby rather than allow it an independent life under God.

# 63

## "IN THE NAME OF THE LORD"

One of the more common phrases of the New Testament makes use of "the name of the Lord," or "the name of Jesus Christ." In Acts 10:48, we read of St. Peter, "And he commanded them to be baptized in the name of the Lord." Peter in Acts 3:6 declares to the lame beggar, "In the name of Jesus Christ of Nazareth rise up and walk." At Pentecost, Peter declares, "Repent, and be baptized every one of you in the name of Jesus Christ for the remission of sins, and ye shall receive the gift of the Holy Ghost" (Acts 2:38). This usage is a common one.

Moreover, this usage of *the name* was common outside Christian circles. For example, when slaves were bought to serve a pagan temple, they were spoken of as being bought "into the name" of that god, which meant that they belonged to that god and served and obeyed him. When Roman authorities commanded men in the name of Caesar, it meant that Caesar's law and authority had priority over all else and could exert eminent domain over man and his property at will. The modern phrase, "Open, in the name of the law," means that the law of the state commands us and takes priority over our wishes in the matter. Thus, the phrases which cite *the name* are spoken in terms of a common and important practice.

Very early, the believers were called by *the name*. Acts 11:26 tells us that "the disciples were called Christians first in Antioch." By this *name*, Christian, they were marked as the property of Jesus Christ, their God, and under His law. Thus, by keeping Christ's commandments, the disciples are at one and the same time His servants or slaves, and also His friends or princes (John 15:14). Paul, for example, repeatedly speaks of himself as "a servant of Jesus Christ" (Romans 1:1; Titus 1:1; Phil. 1:1). James describes himself as "a servant of God and of the Lord Jesus Christ" (James 1:1). Peter says he is "a servant and an apostle of Jesus Christ" (II Peter 1:1), and Jude calls himself "the servant of Jesus Christ" (Jude 1). The Greek word used in each case is *doulos*, slave. These men called themselves not only *slaves* but *apostles* (Paul is insistent on this). The Greek word *apostolos* means one who is sent; its meaning is passive; the apostle is an emissary or a colonist who goes out under orders. Thus, the meaning is in line with the word *slave* or *servant*, *doulos*. The apostles go out in the name of Jesus Christ; all that they do, they do in His name. There is no element of autonomy in their mission. At the same time, their rank as slave-apostles makes them princes in Christ's Kingdom. This is in line with Oriental imperial practice. Daniel and his friends were captives and slaves, yet they and other young slaves were chosen to become the rulers and princes of Persia and themselves the owners of slaves.

Jesus said to the disciples,

> Greater love hath no man than this, that a man lay down his life for his friends.
> Ye are my friends, if ye do whatsoever I command you.
> Henceforth I call you not servants; for the servant knoweth not what his lord doeth: but I have called you friends; for all things that I have heard of my Father I have made known unto you. (John 15:13-15)

To understand this, we must realize that in antiquity the slave was more than property; he was a subordinate member of the family, an organic member thereof, adopting its name and religion, and capable of being made an heir (Gen. 15:2-3). Thus, even blood children were in a sense legally in the same status as a slave and in some cultures could be sold if the father regarded them as unworthy. To the modern mind, this is an ugly fact, but in the ancient world it meant that the family was too important to be trifled with; therefore, the great honor was to be a member of an important family, whether slave or free, and the great dishonor, to be cast out as unworthy. To be invited to break bread with a family at their table also meant a degree of incorporation into their life and protection. Thus, the apostles as princes are still ready to call themselves slaves; it is a mark of their dignity and the adoption of grace. Moreover, as they invite Israel, and then summon the Gentiles to the Lord's household of faith and to His table, they are inviting them into a similar status, protection, and office. If their role as slave-apostles is passive in relation to Christ, so too the role of converts is passive. They come by the adoption of grace.

Immediately after declaring their status as friends, Christ tells the disciples,

> Ye have not chosen me, but I have chosen you, and ordained you, that ye should go and bring forth fruit, and that your fruit should remain: that whatsoever ye shall ask of the Father in my name, he may give it you. (John 15:16)

Again, the passive note is stressed: The Lord's predestinating will is declared. The *friends* or *princes* were once *slaves* of sin; they have been redeemed, purchased by Jesus Christ, and they are now *His slaves*, made friends and *princes, sons of God*, by the adoption of grace. They are active in relation to the world, manifesting the power, authority, and government of Christ *in His name*, but passive in relation to Him, totally obedient to His word, if faithful.

This means that to live *in the name of Jesus Christ*, and to pray *in Jesus' name*, is to live as His slave, ever obedient to His law. To live by faith in Him and in His name is to live in obedience to His law.

The hireling (John 10:12-13) is not a member of the family. He works for wages. Thus the attitude of the hireling towards the law or word of the lord is that he obeys the lord's law in order to gain his wages and be rid or free of the lord. The goal of his obedience to the law, or of his works, is an independence from the lord. The attitude of Phariseeism towards the law was that of a hireling. Theirs was a works religion, aimed at obedience to gain independence. For the hireling, the law of the lord is something external, a burden and a coercion. For the slave-disciple, it is the law of his family and of his life, something internal as well as external, written on the tables of his heart as well as on tables of stone and in the Scriptures. The hireling gives a grudging obedience to the law in order to be rid of the lord and his law. For the servant, the law is his life.

For the thief or enemy, the law of the Lord is something to despise or break. He is hostile to the law; he is anti-law, or antinomian to the core. He wants the wealth of goods of the Lord but no obedience to the Lord. He indeed *believes* in the wealth of the Lord, as the devils believe in God (James 2:19), but he despises the Lord's law. He wants to gain whatever advantage the Lord has to offer, but without responsibility to Him.

Let us now examine two cases, in order to understand what we face in the religious world of our day.

Mrs. Arlene Gollnick, Chalcedon's secretary, attended a meeting which turned out to be one conducted by a charismatic woman. The Bible "study" was a talk on prayer. We should not report cases of theft, she declared. We should turn to the Lord in prayer and tell Him that what the thief took we donate to Him. For this, she declared, the Lord will repay us all that we lost. She also declared that *everything* (she was emphatic when questioned) she had asked the Lord for in prayer, she had received. This woman was heretical in her views on a woman's place. She was a liar in declaring that *all* her prayer requests had been granted. She was an enemy of God in setting aside His law and denying the need for restitution. To call her a Christian is to despise God.

The Rev. Norman R. Jones, a Reformed pastor, spoke to a group of supposedly Calvinistic ministers. One of them, the hyper-orthodox grandson of a theologian regarded by some as the greatest of this century, refused to be even concerned about abortion. He was totally unconcerned and regarded as irrelevant the cultural power of the gospel, Pastor Jones wrote. "He remarked that he would vote for (President) Ford because he met him once and thought 'he was a nice guy.' He also said that the *kind of society* he lived in made no difference to him." This man was an amillennialist as well. Besides having an eschatology of irrelevance, this man's basic unconcern with the cultural mandate, and his implicit antinomianism, mark him at the least as a hireling, if not worse.

Christ's slave-princes are obedient to the Lord. They do whatsoever He commands them (John 15:14). They know that "the servant is not greater than his lord" (John 15:20), and they who are the Lord's servants know that, when the Lord speaks, His word is to be obeyed, not dissected and judged. Christ is God Incarnate. The Old Testament speaks of "the day of thĕ Lord," and the New Testament identifies this as "the day of our Lord Jesus Christ." In Romans 10:17, St. Paul cites Joel 2:32 and makes clear that Christ is meant: "For whosoever shall call upon the name of the Lord shall be saved." In Isaiah 45:23 God declares, "Unto me every knee shall bow, every tongue shall swear." Philippians 2:10-11 declares that this Person is Jesus "at the name of Jesus every knee shall bow, of things in heaven, and things in earth, and things under the earth; And that every tongue should confess that Jesus Christ is Lord, to the glory of God the Father."

The word of the Lord is one word: He commands, and we must obey Him, or else we are not the people of the Name, but His enemies.

# 64

## "RICH FRUIT"

In the past week, a letter from one of Chalcedon's friends, Mr. C., included a letter to him from the chief of police of a major American city. Mr. C. had given the chief some of our Chalcedon Reports and a tape of one of these studies. The reaction of the chief, a dispensational, premillennial fundamentalist, was strong. He wrote:

He (RJR) is *not correct* that Christ is king of this world (otherwise we should not be experiencing all the problems. Satan is God of this world. Believers are a heavenly people, not earthly.) Therefore we will not change the terrible conditions ahead (the Tribulation). Rightly dividing the word, means understanding dispensational differences between orders to the Jew and marching orders for the Christian under the age of Grace (the current time). God's earthly people, (the Jews) were to show his blessing if they obeyed, and his wrath if they didn't, to the rest of the world. We *are* to lead Godly lives but I do not believe in social action programs since my bible says they will fail. God himself will bring in the Kingdom Age after the great tribulation. Until that time, this world will never know justice, peace or righteousness. (Letter of 4-15-76)

The 40-50 or more million Americans who share this chief's antinomianism and dispensationalism constitute a very major roadblock to any Christian action which will further "justice, peace or righteousness." More than once we have found that very many of these people will actually say, being more blunt in speech than in print, that to affirm Christ's Lordship or Kingship now and to apply His law is a Satanic work and delusion. Gary North's article, "Backward, Christian Soldiers," has very ably pin-pointed the evil of this hostility to righteousness.

What are the roots of this faith in Satan's kingship? The radical humanism it manifests is apparent in the police chief's comment, "He is *not correct* that Christ is king of this world (otherwise we would not be experiencing all the problems....).'' The test of kingship, whether it be Christ's or Satan's, is made *man's experience*. If Christ be King, He must spare me *all* my problems. Since evil prevails in my life and experience, then Satan must be god of this world. The logic of this position then requires us to say, then worship Satan. The chief evades this logic by declaring Christians to be an exclusively heavenly people, and hence not

responsible for this world in this age or dispensation, since it is not yet
Christ's Kingdom. He pays no attention to all the Scriptures which
declare Jesus to be *Lord* (or God-King) and Savior. Indeed, the chief
even uses without thought Jesus' royal title Christ, even while he denies
Him. Such a faith is humanism; it makes the test of Christ's kingship
man's experience read in a totally man-centered way.

But this is not all. Any extended contact with such men as this chief
makes clear that what Roger Price has to say about "the Roob" applies
to them. The Roob is the new urban barbarian whose weapon is his purchasing power and whose one over-riding need and standard is the need
for Self-Gratification. His great yardstick, Price says, is "I don't like
it." Moreover, "believing in nothing, he is prepared to believe in
everything."[1] The sophisticated Avant Roob turns his lack of standards,
as do all Roobs, into a self-righteous virtue:

> The Avant *believes* in Injustice, because in an unjust world he cannot
> be held responsible for his own failure as a person. To justify this
> belief, he is able to define almost every circumstance of life accord-
> ing to his own needs as inequitable.
> And, Hallelujah, with each new proof of man's incorporated and
> overwhelming inhumanity to man, he is Redeemed.[2]

In an essentially unjust world, God's law is futile because it is not
applicable. Satan's law is alone applicable if he be "God of this world,"
as the chief holds. Then we are excused from any responsible and strong
action for "justice, peace or righteousness." We can maintain a formal
righteousness by affirming these things in the abstract, or as an ideal,
while avoiding God's law which requires them of us as a daily necessity.
To turn the law into an ideal is to deny its reality, for the law declares
what is in reality the nature of things. Man and creation were created
wholly good by God (Gen. 1:31), and God's law is the health of that
creation. Sin is the deadly cancer, whose end is death, which has beset
creation; it is not the nature of things but the disease of things. To turn
the law into an ideal is to imply that the disease is the norm, and health
an ideal hope which goes against the nature of things.

The chief's test of this world and of God is his condition. Because, he
says, we are "experiencing all the problems," Christ is obviously not
Lord or King. He manifests the same man-centered standard which God
rebukes in the Book of Job. To make man the standard is to work out the
principle of the fall, of Satan's temptation, in terms of which man is his
own god, deciding in terms of himself and his experience what constitutes good and evil. Original sin is the denial of God and the affirmation of man, explicitly or implicitly. It is idolatry. Idolatry is present

1. Roger Price: *The Great Roob Revolution*, p. 13. New York: Random House, 1970.
2. *Ibid.*, p. 63.

wherever man repudiates God, explicitly or implicitly, in any manner, mode, or form, and affirms his word, law, will, and vision instead.

Christ declared, "Ye are my friends (my princes, my slave-princes by the adoption of grace), if ye do whatsoever I command you" (John 15:14). Just previously, He said,

> Herein is my Father glorified, that ye bear much fruit; so shall ye be my disciples.
> As the Father hath loved me, so have I loved you: continue ye in my love.
> If ye keep my commandments, ye shall abide in my love; even as I have kept my Father's commandments, and abide in his love.
> These things have I spoken unto you, that my joy might remain in you, and that your joy might be full.
> This is my commandment, that ye love one another, as I have loved you. (John 15:8-12)

We have here the perfect juxtaposition of God's law and God's love: they are not in contradiction. To isolate one from the other is to deny both. Man's world is not a unity, because, whatever his pretensions, man is not god; as a result, he must oppose aspects of reality one to another and maintain an imperialism of action, whereas the God of Scripture maintains a unity of ownership and lordship. In God's world, law, love, hate, justice, peace, righteousness, condemnation, election, reprobation, and all things else have a common source, the perfect being of God. God is not schizophrenic as man often seems to be.

As a result, we see the necessity of the unity of law and love in Christ's declaration. We abide in His love if we keep His law even as He kept the law in relationship to God the Father. We are His disciples only if we bear "much fruit," or, in the Berkeley Version, "rich fruit." We are not permitted a modest or passive obedience, in other words, the kind of obedience which comes from passive conformity to law as the line of least resistance. We are required to be productive, to bear rich fruit, to obey actively, strongly, and faithfully: "so shall ye be my disciples."

*Then* we abide in His love, even as Christ, by keeping God's commandments, abides in His love. Christ's joy in us, and His love for us, and our love for one another, rests on our faithfulness to His law, to our bearing rich fruit.

To illustrate, a man who is adulterous does not love his wife, for "love worketh no ill to his neighbour: therefore love is the fulfilling of the law" (Rom. 13:10). Such a man loves himself, not his wife; he may at times be pleased with his wife, because she is an advantage or a pleasure to him, but he does not love her, because "love is the fulfilling of the law." However, mere physical faithfulness is not love. The husband may be faithful because he is afraid of his wife, or of social pressures and scandal, or out of fear of disease, or some such reason. Faithfulness fulfills the law by a thorough cleaving to his wife, by having community of life with her, by manifesting a patience with frailties and a delight in fellowship, so that it is a rich relationship.

The same is true with God. Idolatry, the Bible repeatedly declares, is to go "a whoring" after other gods. A mere outward faithfulness and profession of faith and obedience, however, is not what God calls faithfulness. Such a profession is playing safe; a man then is looking after his own best interests, and is conforming to God pragmatically. As one fundamentalist foreign missionary once declared to my wife and myself, "Look at it this way: if you believe, and are right, then at death you gain everything. If not, you haven't lost much and have been on the whole better off for believing." This is idolatry and unbelief. We are required to bear "rich fruit" unto our King.

If He is not our King, then we will obey another king and enthrone Satan as god of this world. To enthrone Satan means to enthrone ourselves, to be our own god (Gen. 3:5). This means a world of injustice, war, and evil, but for all too many men this is a small price to pay for the right to be their own god. If, on top of this, the old God and Christ can be told that their Kingdom will arrive in another dispensation, and the dispensationalist will have the best of both worlds, then indeed we have a religion after man's own heart, but not God's.

To believe in injustice is to vindicate, as Price saw, one's own failure, or, better, unbelief and disobedience. It is to vindicate man as against God. Such a faith bears fruit, but not unto God. The dispensationalists *are* bearing fruit, but to a false god.

# 65

## PROPERTY

Christ the King sees *all* men in relationship to Himself, never in abstraction from His crown rights, His law, and His total right of government. Men are thus of three classes. *First*, there are the slaves, whom He makes His friends and princes. All in this category, whether their office or service be great or small, are the King's by the adoption of grace. They are thus His family and His sons and daughters of grace. *Second*, there are hirelings, who keep the King's law in order to be free from the King. This is Phariseeism and works religion. Whereas the family member sees the King's law as His life, the hireling sees it as an alien burden to be obeyed as a means to escaping from the King into freedom. *Third*, the thief or enemy despises and breaks the King's law but seeks the King's wealth.

No man can exist except by the creative decree of the triune God, and thus no man can escape from a relationship to Christ the King as either a family member, a hireling, or an enemy. Similarly, no *thing, fact,* or *event* can exist apart from Christ or be understood apart from Him. Thus, in any analysis of any area of life and thought, our thinking must be Biblical and therefore God-centered, and by *God* we must always mean the Trinity.

As we examine the fact of *property* we must realize therefore that man-centered thinking is not in order. Humanism views property in terms of man: it either asserts the individual's "sovereign" powers over property, or, if socialist, the state's or the community's title to property. While the concept of the private ownership of property is outwardly in conformity to Biblical law, it does involve a major error in that it is man-centered rather than God-centered in its idea of property.

Let us survey briefly some of the Biblical land laws in order to understand what Biblical law presupposes and requires. *First*, because Canaan was to become for a time the throne area of God the King, the land was sacred and a divine inheritance which could not be alienated. The sale of land to aliens was out of the question, and even transfers from one tribe to another were prevented. The land could not be sold in perpetuity because ownership rested with God: "The land shall not be sold for ever: for the land is mine; for ye are strangers and sojourners with me" (Lev. 25:23). Urban property could be sold (Lev. 25:29-31). Although in dispersion (in non-throne land), Israel did not keep this law, the principle of God's ownership of *all* the earth is repeatedly stated. It is, in fact, declared to Pharoah in Egypt (Ex. 9:29) and is the premise of the plagues. As "strangers and sojourners" on God's earth, *all* men are required to obey His law or suffer its consequences, and *all* men must acknowledge Him as Lord of the land. In the eternal Kingdom of God, there will be no alienation of the land, and there will be no shadow of questioning God's total lordship thereof.

*Second*, in Davies' summary, "For as the land belonged to Yahweh so rightfully did all the produce. His ownership was symbolically acknowledged through the offering of first fruits. The same concept governed the custom of gleaning."[1] The tithe belongs to God because it is His rent for our use of the earth and its resources. Because we too are the Lord's, the law of the firstlings (Ex. 22:28) makes clear His title to us. The use of the earth is thus governed by God; the produce of the earth is also subject to the claims of God; the human producer, moreover, is himself subject to God's total government and ownership.

*Third*, not only do God's rights cover property and persons, but also relationships, i.e., marital, communal, commercial, etc. As a result, laws govern usury, and the relationship of debtor and creditor. Since *all* men are God's creatures, whether servant-slaves, hirelings, or enemies, *none* can be dealt with apart from God. Weights and measures thus are also governed by God's law, because they are an essential aspect of relationships. The criminal law is still another aspect of God's property rights as creator and governor of His domain.

*Fourth*, the Sabbath laws again are an assertion of God's property rights. While the Sabbath has a very great human value in the rest which it provides to man, this is secondary to the fact that it provides for the better care of God's creation, man, domestic animals, and land alike. Important as man's rest is to man, even more important it is to God that *all* His creation rest in Him. The Sabbath is "unto the LORD." We cannot in any aspect place ourselves or our family above God and His law. *Right* is what God declares it to be. With respect to the land, God requires that it be given a Sabbath. As Davies states, "The land's rest recalls the seventh-day rest of the Lord himself after the creation, and came to symbolize Yahweh's creation and ownership of the land."[2] The land rest every seventh year is set forth in Leviticus 25:2, 4. Humanistic sabbatarianism exalts the seventh-day rest for man and conveniently forgets all else. This is a denial of God's ownership of the land.

*Fifth*, because the land of Canaan was God's throne-place and throne-land (faintly comparable to Washington, D. C., or Versailles under

---

1. W. D. Davies: *The Gospel and the Land*, p. 28. Berkeley, California: University of California Press, 1974.
2. *Ibid.*, p. 29.

Louis XIV), Numbers 35:34 declares, "Defile not therefore the land which ye shall inhabit, wherein I dwell: for I the LORD dwell among the children of Israel." It is not the land which is holy, but the Lord God who dwells therein. While Canaan is no longer a throne-land, because all the earth is the Lord's, and in the Great Commission (Matt. 28:18-20) all of it is declared an area of impending conquest, the laws of holiness are applicable to all the earth. All nations were subject to this in some sense before Christ; thus, the people of Canaan were judged by the law because Canaan was to be God's throne-land (Lev. 18:24-30). Since all the earth is the Lord's and is to know Christ's Kingship, all the earth is under His law.

Although *all* violations of God's law pollute the land, certain offenses are singled out as especially polluting. For these offenses, men make themselves *abominable* to the Lord and provoke the earth itself in a violent way. *First* among these offenses are *dietary* violations, the eating of unclean beasts (Lev. 20:22-26). The language of Scripture here is strong and emphatic. Phariseeism turned the dietary laws into a means of justification, against which the church took a stand. St. Paul rebuked Peter for following the Judaizer's Pharisaic standard (Gal. 2:11-16), which, it should be noted, included extra-Biblical requirements and aspects. Paul kept the law, not as a way of justification, nor to separate himself from men he sought to convert, but as the way of sanctification. James and the elders of Jerusalem could say to Paul, and he assented to it, that "thou thyself also walkest orderly, and keepest the law" (Acts 21:24). It was a false charge by the Judaizers that St. Paul taught "all the Jews which are among the Gentiles to forsake Moses, saying that they ought not to circumcise their children, neither to walk after the customs" (Acts 21:21). Paul opposed rather any and every effort to make salvation contingent or dependent on these things, on any aspect of the law or the totality of the law. He did not allow the table practices of the Gentiles, i.e., their uses of vessels, etc., in a non-kosher manner, to keep him from their table. Except for one or two items, the Greek and Roman diet with respect to meats was close to the Mosaic law. There is no real evidence that unclean meats, which God declared an abomination, ceased to be such. St. Peter's vision (Acts 10:9-48) had reference *to people, not meats*; it is people who cannot be judged as racially or nationally unclean and a perpetual abomination to the Lord; hence, Cornelius is received on confession of faith, not by becoming a Jew.

*Second*, Leviticus 19:29 declares, "Do not prostitute thy daughter, to cause her to be a whore; lest the land fall to whoredom, and the land become full of wickedness." The *land* here certainly means in part *the people thereof*, but it clearly means the land as well. Leviticus 18:25 says that, because of the sexual sins of the Canaanites, and of any imitating their sins, "the land is defiled: therefore I do visit the iniquity thereof upon it, and the land itself vomiteth out her inhabitants." Sexual sins pollute not only a people but the earth itself.

*Third*, murder pollutes the earth also, according to Numbers 35:29-34, Deuteronomy 21:6-9, Psalm 106:38-39, and especially Genesis 4:10.

*Fourth*, although the land is not mentioned but rather God the Lord's disgust with uncleanness, it is forbidden to even soldiers to defecate without covering "that which cometh from thee" (Deut. 23:12-14). God the Lord regards the pollution of His land as offensive to His purposes.

*Fifth*, it defiles the land if a condemned man is allowed to hang from a tree overnight (Deut. 21:22-23). Because the earth is the Lord's, it must manifest His holiness. The judgment on the criminal is required by His holiness, but the flaunting of death is not compatible with His domain.

*Sixth*, remarriage with a previously divorced and remarried wife is an abomination to the Lord and brings guilt and defilement to the land (Deut. 24:1-4; Jer. 3:1).

*Seventh*, to mingle seeds and to produce hybrids, or to make a garment of mingled materials defiles the land: it denies boundaries God has established (Lev. 19:19, 22:5, 9, 10, 11).

*Eighth*, *all* sin, and every attempt to deny the division between the sacred and the profane (Lev. 22:5-16), defiles the land, because God's earth and His creatures must be holy as He is holy (Lev. 19:1-2).

The premise of all this is God's total property right in all His creation. It means that we are not our own (I Cor. 6:19-20), and therefore we can never think of ourselves or of our property in abstract terms, i.e., abstracted from God's absolute ownership. We are at all times stewards, never lords, over our possessions, and we must render an accounting. That accounting is to Christ the King, and it is the premise and meaning of the Last Judgment.

# 66

## THE WILDERNESS

*All* the earth is the Lord's, but from the very beginning, God has set a difference between various parts of it. Although Genesis 1 makes clear that all things were created good by God, a distinction was made between the Garden of Eden and the rest of the world *before* the Fall. Eden was created as a place apart, a planned and planted garden made in terms of a perfect plan (Gen. 2:8-15). Outside of the Garden of Eden the world was a vast wilderness, a wilderness of an unfallen and perfect character, but still a wilderness, whereas the Garden was a fenced and protected area. Man was placed in paradise to enhance that fencing and protection by tilling, cultivating, pruning, and tending it.

Thus, in a real sense, while the rest of the world was entirely good, it was not yet perfect in the Biblical sense, i.e., it was not yet brought to its mature potential. What man did in the Garden, with the impetus of a planned beginning by God, he was later to do in all of creation, because the creation mandate was specifically not limited to Eden but covered the entire earth (Gen. 1:26-28). Eden was the pattern established by God which man was to apply to all the earth, its development into its full potential as the Kingdom of God. Man was restored into this task by the regenerating power of Jesus Christ, who commanded men to seek first the Kingdom of God and His righteousness (Matt. 6:33).

Davies says, with respect to the wilderness, "By 'the wilderness' the Old Testament generally denotes unsown land: it stands over against the sown land... which was inhabited (Gen. 2:5; 47:23; II Sam. 9:10).... Outside the sown land the curse prevails.... However, no geographic line clearly separates the desert-land from the land of man: the former can insidiously invade the latter and is always a threat to it:... sin can reduce the land of man to desert-land."[1] When Cain complained to God against the judgment passed against him, he said, "My punishment is greater than I can bear. Behold, thou hast driven me this day away from the earth" (Gen. 4:13), and by *earth* is here meant in Hebrew the sown ground.

Thus, the cultivation, utilization, and development of the earth is a necessary aspect of the creation mandate. Fallen man, however, seeks to exploit the earth for the Kingdom of Man. As a result, his development is

---

1. Davies, *op. cit.*, p. 86f.

thus an extension of the curse, wherever he goes.

The attitude of the Kingdom of Man, or of Humanism, is thus an ambivalent one. *First*, the humanist seeks to develop the earth and create a paradise without God. He builds cities, subjugates the wilderness, and exploits the earth in order to realize his Kingdom. His program of exploitation has as its goal the full subjection of all of earth's resources to man's dominion and use. However, instead of achieving his goal, he brings destruction not only to the earth but upon his own works, his cities and his farms, by his self-destructive wars and conflicts. Being at war with God, humanistic man is at war with himself, his neighbor, and the earth itself.

*Second*, because sin is suicidal, all who hate God love death (Prov. 8:36). This love of death manifests itself as a self-hatred, which means a hatred of man also, and of all man's works. The humanist then professes a love of the wilderness, not because he loves the wilderness but because he hates man and all the works of man. The wilderness, being untouched by man, is therefore good. Man's *order* is despised in favor of the *disorder* of the wilderness. A very significant aspect of the lives of current ecology advocates is their deliberate pollution of forest and river areas. Paper, beer cans, feces and more mark their visitations to the wilderness areas. If asked to be clean and orderly, they mock at such a request as evidence of a Puritan hangover. *Disorder* is with them a principle, in their lives and in the world. Hence, their persons, vehicles, and surroundings are marked by a *deliberate disorder*. The devastation which humanistic man brings by his planned development is as a result only increased very often by his ideas of perpetuating the wilderness. *Humanism ends up as anti-humanism.*

The Biblical view of the wilderness is very different. It is apparent in many passages, such as Isaiah 35:1-10, and 41:18-20. *First* of all, it declares God's purpose to be the extension of godly man's dominion over every part of the earth. The wilderness is to become an area under the government of the redeemed man. *Second*, as man moves out from under the curse into God's blessing, God will cause the very wilderness to change, so that springs and rivers will break out in the mountains and streams in the desert. The desert will see lumber trees flourish, and producing trees grow. Lakes and pools will appear where there are none. "The wilderness and the solitary place shall be glad for them; and the desert shall rejoice, and blossom as the rose" (Isa. 35:1). *Third*, the distinction between country-side and city will diminish, because, instead of the earlier distinction between the walled city and unsafe and unfenced areas, all areas will now be governed by man under God, and all areas will be safe. The "ravenous beast" will not threaten man anywhere. *Fourth*, the earth moves back and forth between a wilderness and a fruitful land in terms of its relationship to God, who sends rains and droughts as blessings and cursings. This is very thoroughly set forth in Deuteronomy 28, and summarized in Psalm 107:33-34. It is not an imaginary entity called "Nature" which governs the earth and its weather but the God of Scripture. *Fifth*, the wilderness is thus a symbol and evidence of judgment, or, at the least, an area man has not yet developed in terms of its function in the Kingdom of God. However, it is not the wilderness which is evil but man the sinner, by whose sins the earth is cursed. The contrast is sharply and humorously set forth in Proverbs 21:19: "It is better to dwell in the wilderness, than with a contentious and an angry woman." *Sixth*, the world outside of Christ is a wilderness, and John the Baptist came as the voice crying out in the world-wilderness, "Prepare ye the way of the LORD, make straight in the desert a highway for our God" (Isa. 40:3; Matt. 3:3). In that world-wilderness, Christ, the last Adam, was tempted by Satan, and He overcame the tempter. As a result, He was with the wild beasts in peace, as Adam in Eden, and "angels ministered unto him" (Mark 1:13). *Seventh*, the whole of Zion, i.e., the Kingdom of God, shall be like the Garden of Eden. "For the LORD shall comfort Zion: he will comfort all her waste places; and he will make her wilderness like Eden, and her desert like the garden of the LORD; joy and gladness shall be found therein, thanksgiving, and the voice of melody" (Isa. 51:3).

Thus, the purpose of redeemed man must not be either the ruthless exploitation of the wilderness or its protection, as though its perpetuation were necessary, but rather the careful development of all things under God. As the regenerate man obeys God and furthers His Kingdom, God blesses both man and the earth. In fact, the *pouring out* of the Holy Spirit on man and the *pouring out* of refreshing rains on the earth are spoken of as part of a common blessing by God in Isaiah 44:1-5:

> Yet now hear, O Jacob, my servant; and Israel, whom I have chosen:
> Thus saith the LORD that made thee, and formed thee from the womb, which will help thee; Fear not, O Jacob, my servant; and thou, Jesurun, whom I have chosen.
> For I will pour water upon him that is thirsty, and floods upon the dry ground: I will pour my spirit upon thy seed, and my blessing upon thine offspring:
> And they shall spring up as among the grass, as willows by the water courses.
> One shall say, I am the LORD'S; and another shall call himself by the name of Jacob; and another shall subscribe with his hand unto the LORD, and surname himself by the name of Israel.

It is of a similar *pouring out* that Joel speaks. On the one hand, for sin there is a plague of locusts, military disaster, invasion, and personal griefs and disasters, and, on the other, a *pouring out* of the Holy Spirit and of material blessings (Joel 2:21-29). Very clearly, the rebellious have judgment and drought. Psalm 68:6 declares, ''God setteth the solitary in families: he bringeth out those which are bound with chains: but the rebellious dwell in a dry land.''

The ultimate wilderness is hell. The ultimate cultivated and dominion-land is heaven.

## 67

## THE EARTH AND THE COVENANT

The humanist, in terms of the doctrine of evolution, holds that an organic relationship exists between man and the earth because man evolved out of an inorganic matter, through the spectrum of animal life, into his present condition. The Christian, however, must declare that man's organic relationship with the earth and its creatures is due to the fact of a common creator, the triune God. The humanist holds that the primary factor of influence is the biological conditioning of man by his evolutionary past, i.e., by the world around him. The Christian holds, if he is Scripturally sound, that the primary factor of influence works in the other direction, the influence of man upon the earth.

This influence might perhaps be compared to that of a ship's captain upon his ship; the captain's dereliction affects the ship. This comparison, however, proves too much. *First*, the relationship between a captain and his ship is mechanical in operation, and, *second*, it involves a very different kind of command than man exercises over nature. Man strives for dominion over the earth; he does not simply command it. The relationship of man to the earth is not mechanical; it is *religious*. Because God created man in His image to exercise dominion over the earth and to subdue it (Gen. 1:26-28), God gave to man a relationship to the earth similar to His own relationship to His total creation. If God did not sustain creation, it would collapse into nothingness. "By the word of the LORD were the heavens made: and all the host of them by the breath of his mouth" (Ps. 33:6). Man's relationship to the earth is subject to the absolute Kingship of God, but, in a secondary sense, it is one of dependence: the earth depends upon man. Man's moral incompetence means the disorder of the world. Because man sinned, the earth also fell. The ground is cursed because of man's sin (Gen. 3:17). The earth flourishes and is blessed as man is holy and obedient to the Lord; it is cursed and profane when man is disobedient (Deut. 28). This is clearly set forth also in Isaiah 24:

> The earth also is defiled under the inhabitants thereof: because they have transgressed the laws, changed the ordinance, broken the everlasting covenant.
> Therefore hath the curse devoured the earth, and they that dwell therein are desolate: therefore the inhabitants of the earth are burned, and few men left....

315

And it shall come to pass, that he who fleeth from the noise of the fear shall fall into the pit; and he that cometh up out of the midst of the pit shall be taken in the snare; for the windows from on high are open, and the foundations of the earth do shake.
The earth is utterly broken down, the earth is clean dissolved, the earth is moved exceedingly.
The earth shall reel to and fro like a drunkard, and shall be removed like a cottage; and the transgression thereof shall be heavy upon it; and it shall fall, and not rise again.
And it shall come to pass in that day, that the LORD shall punish the host of the high ones that are on high, and the kings of the earth upon the earth.

Some of the things clearly set forth here are, *first*, that the earth is defiled or profane because the people thereof are profane. Man is called to be holy, because God is holy (Lev. 19:1-2). When man is holy, the earth and all things therein become "holiness unto the LORD" (Zech. 14:20-21), because the dominion and holiness of God, prevailing over man, prevails thereby also over man's dominion. When, however, man is profane, i.e., outside of God and His temple, then not only is man profane but the earth also. There is a created and necessary connection between man and the earth. *The federal headship of Adam was not only over mankind but over the earth as well.*

*Second*, the radical apostasy and profanity of man led to the Flood, and the radical judgment of the Flood is echoed in these verses. The judgment here spoken of is largely by earthquakes, so that the earth is spoken of as staggering like a drunkard. To modern man, the idea of earthquakes being subject to a religious rather than a "mechanical" cause is repugnant. However, without denying the "mechanical" factors, we must assert the priority of the religious. This is repeatedly stated in Scripture, and to attempt to read such passages symbolically or other than a literal assertion of the priority of the religious or theocentric cause is to do violence to all of Scripture. The enemies of the faith here are more honest with the Biblical facts than are the neo-evangelicals and others.

*Third*, the root cause of the profanity which provokes God's judgment on man and the earth is plainly stated: "they have transgressed the laws, changed the ordinances, broken the everlasting covenant" (Isa. 24:5). The covenant of God is with *all* of mankind in Adam; the Fall released no man from the creation mandate. Fallen man has changed the focus of that mandate and made the covenant have as its goal the Kingdom of Man rather than the Kingdom of God. This is the ultimate transgression of the covenant law. "Christian" man is thus doubly a sinner when he is antinomian and despises God's law: he has denied the law in Adam, and now, with consummate profanity, he denies it in the name of Christ. He thus doubly denies the everlasting covenant, and doubly transgresses the laws.

*Fourth,* when man forsakes his required dominion over the earth, the earth then gains a dominion of judgment over man. The earth is pictured as pursuing man vengefully as God's agent of destruction (Isa. 24:18). The cause of this is the Lord, who uses the earth as a means of judgment against man. The latter part of Isaiah 24:18, in the Berkeley Version, reads, "for the sluices on high are opened, and earth's foundations tremble." Flood and earthquake strike the earth, and the earth becomes a desolation to man. The Berkeley Version renders Isaiah 24:5 thus: "The land lies polluted by its inhabitants, because they have transgressed the Law, violated the statutes, and broken the everlasting covenant." The earth is profaned, defiled, and polluted by man's sin, and it becomes as untrustworthy as a drunken man. A drunkard is undependable; so too is a profaned earth: flood and drought, earthquake and hurricane, locusts and plagues, and much else infest the profaned earth.

On the other hand, where God is on earth, the earth is holy ground (Ex. 3:5). Holiness is not inherent in the earth but is derived from the Lord, or through man from the Lord. When Christ was transfigured, Peter was ready to declare the mount of transfiguration holy ground (Matt. 17:1-5), but it was Christ who was holy, and the earth holy only because of His presence. Palestine is not the Holy Land now, because it rejected Christ and was long under the curse of Islam. Man is called to be holy (Lev. 19:1-2), and to make all things under his dominion holiness to the Lord (Zech. 14:20-21). Man, however, cannot be holy apart from regeneration, which means being made a new creation, a member of the new covenant humanity of the greater Adam (I Cor. 15:45-47), and by obedience to the law of that covenant. That law is the same from one end of Scripture to the other. The purpose of that law is the fulfilment of the creation mandate. Scripture gives us one Lord, one covenant, one plan of salvation, and one law. The members of that one covenant live and die; the covenant is renewed and continues. The old Israel gives way to the new, but the covenant continues. It is an everlasting covenant. It governs man, and it governs the earth.

## 68

## SIN AND THE EARTH

The Bible very plainly declares that there is a relationship between man's faithfulness and the earth's fertility. If men are lawless, the earth will by God's providence exact a judgment from man. As Theodor H. Gaster has noted,

> It was believed that the fertility of the earth could be affected by the misconduct of men. It was then said to be "polluted" (Heb. *hanefah*; Isa. 24:5). As a result of Adam's sin, the earth yields grain only when man puts heavy labor into it (Gen. 3:17-19), and for receiving the blood of Abel it was forbidden to "yield its strength" to Cain under any circumstances (Gen. 4:11-13). The idea that the land could be rendered infertile by having innocent blood shed upon it is widespread in other cultures, and probably stems from the notion that "the blood is the life" and, therefore represents the outraged spirit of the murdered man who exacts vengeance until the crime is redressed or expiated. Bloodshed could likewise cause lack of rainfall (II Sam. 1:21).[1]

All things having been created by God therefore serve His purposes alone. The very wrath of man shall praise God and serve His purpose (Ps. 76:10). In the supreme act of sin and man's most arrogant assault on God, the condemnation of Jesus, we are told that the high priest spoke as a prophet, fulfilling God's purpose (John 11:47-53). God's law and justice are so basic to all of creation, that all things will serve Him, whether they intend to or not. In history man either serves the Kingdom of God or works out his own condemnation, because the law of his being is the handiwork of the Almighty; the sovereign decree which governs his life is the decree of God, not of man. The governing factor in all events is the will of God; the controlling purpose in every atom of creation is the decree of the triune God, never of man. The necessity in all events is God's necessity, whose government is such "That no unnecessary burden shall be laid upon us, that even a dog cannot bark against us without permission."[2]

In the counsels and governments of man, law and justice are commonly two different things, and the law is all too often organized injustice. In

---

1. Theodor H. Gaster, "Earth," in *Encyclopaedia Judaica*, vol. 6, p. 339.
2. Rev. D. Beaton, ed.: *Diary and Sermons of the Rev. Alexander Macleod*, p. 51. Inverness: Robert Carruthers & Sons, 1925.

Scripture, law and justice (*mishpat*, translated judgment, ordinance, etc.) are synonyms, because *God's law is justice.* Any departure from God's law is injustice. When we ourselves depart from God's law, then our whole being cries out against us; we are at war with ourselves, because God has made us for His glory and pleasure, and when we serve any other purpose we sin against God and do violence to ourselves. "The LORD hath made all things for himself: yea, even the wicked for the day of evil" (Prov. 16:4). As a result, all things, including ourselves, are at war with us when we are at war with God, at odds with His law, or unwilling to serve Him with our whole heart, mind, and being. We are told that "the stars in their courses fought against Sisera" (Judges 4:20).

In terms of this, God pronounced a curse on Cain:

> And the LORD said unto Cain, Where is Abel thy brother? And he said, I know not: Am I my brother's keeper?
> And he said, What hast thou done? the voice of thy brother's blood crieth unto me from the ground.
> And now art thou cursed from the earth, which hath opened her mouth to receive thy brother's blood from thy hand;
> When thou tillest the ground, it shall not henceforth yield unto thee her strength; a fugitive and a vagabond shalt thou be in the earth. (Gen. 4:9-12)

The church's eunuchs, being antinomian, interpret this *only* in terms of Cain: they fail to see its relevance to all times and all men.

Some things which must be said about these verses in reference to our present concern include, *first*, the fact that sin makes Cain and all sinners fugitives and vagabonds in the earth. Whether or not they stay in one place, or, like Cain, in a fortified city, they are still the same, fugitives and vagabonds. The earth is no longer their home but a hostile place, so that, even in one settled place, they are homeless. Because the earth is the Lord's, it cannot give peace or security to His enemies. God's people, however, are spoken of as pilgrims (Heb. 11:13); they are "strangers" or aliens to a fallen world; their pilgrimage is to the Kingdom of God, and they thus buy lands, settle down like Abraham, and work to make this earth the Lord's. Their pilgrimage is from Adam's fallen earth to Christ's Kingdom, and it is their calling and commission to make disciples of all nations to that end (Matt. 28:18-20). The covenant man is never a fugitive and a vagabond in the earth in this sense; he is a dominion man, and his pilgrimage has dominion as its calling.

*Second*, Abel's blood cries out unto God from the ground. This blood-cry is for vengeance.[3] Leupold's comment is very much to the point:

> That a voice should be attributed to blood is not strange inasmuch as the soul is regarded as lodged in the blood of man (Lev. 17:11), and

3. R. Payne Smith, "Genesis," in Ellicott, *op. cit.*, I, 29.

the death of God's saints is precious in His sight (Ps. 116:15). That God requires blood, that is, seeks out and avenges all instances of unjust shedding of blood, appears from Job 16:18; Gen. 9:5; Ezek. 3:18; 24:7, 8; 33:6; and Ps. 9:12. Men may esteem souls or blood lightly. Not so God.[4]

This blood cry for vengeance is a call for restitution and restoration: God's order has been violated, and God's order is to be restored by exacting the penalty of God's law against the offender. (Cain was not executed, because the death penalty is the one major power withheld from the family, and, at that time, only family government existed.)

*Third*, Cain, like many men and nations since, did not receive his due retribution at that time. However, to all such, and to all who tolerate injustice, the earth reduces its fertility and increases the work required to gain anything from it (Gen. 3:17-19). As a result, we must insist that Scripture throughout declares that there is a necessary relationship between sin and the natural disasters of the earth, drought, flood, infertility, and the like. God exacts His justice through the earth where men despise His law and disregard justice. To limit such a relationship to Biblical history alone is to deny the validity of God's revelation, government, and law for our time.

Not only is the earth hostile to the sinner, but *fourth*, the sinner is weakened by his sin, because it is the beginning of his death. Cain, in calling himself a man whose "punishment is greater than I can bear," is literally saying that his *iniquity* is greater than he can bear. Not only so, but the Lord, in describing Cain as "a fugitive and a wanderer" is literally declaring Cain to be a "totterer and wanderer."[5] His sin and the burden thereof make Cain a "totterer."

*Fifth*, Cain's sin separates him from God and therefore from the earth. Leupold renders the first portion of verse 11, "And now cursed shalt thou be, driven away from the ground...."[6] It is the sown land that Cain is driven away from, and the meaning is more than geographical. Wherever the sinner attempts to subdue the earth and develop it, there, because of his sin, there is a separation between himself and the earth. The earth will not yield its strength to him.

On the other hand, the earth yields its strength and fertility to God's people to the degree that they abound in obedience and service. Deuteronomy 28 gives an eloquent statement of this. The whole of creation serves God's purpose. God, who is patient, will for a season send His rain upon the just and the unjust (Matt. 5:45), but, when they continue in sin and defile the earth (Isa. 24:5), then the heavens become as

---

4. H. C. Leupold: *Exposition of Genesis*, p. 205. Columbus, Ohio: Wartburg Press, 1942.
5. E. A. Speiser: *Genesis*, p. 31. The Anchor Bible. Garden City, NY: Doubleday, 1964.
6. Leupold, *op. cit.*, p. 206.

brass, and the earth as iron to those who despise the Lord and His law (Deut. 28:23-24).

The earth was created to be the Kingdom of God. The cornerstone of that Kingdom is justice. Those who deny God's law will have the earth itself against them. Christ, who as King of the new creation, gave His life in satisfaction of God's justice, cannot be used to set aside the law of God. To set aside the law of God is to deny the cross and to say that murder can now prosper, and the earth yield her strength readily and freely, to the enemies of God. It is tantamount to saying that the purpose of the King's coming and atonement is to give freedom for sin.

**69**

# LAND, HOLINESS, AND DOMINION

Comedians in our time have a habit of spouting philosophy, almost always a variety of humanism. George Jessel is no exception. He concludes his autobiography with comments:

> My advice to you. . . is to have the best possible time. Enjoy your cup to the brim, but always be sure to hurt nobody but yourself. You've got a right to do that, if you want to. You don't belong to the state; you belong to you. . . .
>
> As for religion, pick any one you like. The room you enter, be it windowed with stained glass or not, is a place of worship, if in it you can think kindly of your fellow man and his brother.[1]

Jessel says we belong to ourselves and can therefore do as we please with ourselves. The Bible says, however, "The earth is the LORD'S and the fulness thereof: the world and they that dwell therein" (Ps. 24:1). Again, Leviticus 25:23 declares, "The land shall not be sold for ever: for the land is mine: for ye are strangers and sojourners with me."

Man is God's creature, God's property, and God's servant or slave. The earth is the Lord's, and all of creation. The only law which can properly govern man and the earth is God's law. The premise of the law is set forth in Exodus 19:5: "all the earth is mine." When *any* nation, Canaanite, Israelite, or otherwise, despises God's law, in His time He brings judgment on them, and the land "vomiteth out her inhabitants" (Lev. 18:25). Possession of the earth is a privilege of God's grace, and is revoked by lawlessness. God's law in its totality has reference to the land, to man's dominion by means of the law over the earth, which is the locale for His Kingdom in history. As Joseph Ploger has observed, the land "is the proper milieu for the fulfilment of the law."[2] Of the system of laws set forth in the Old Testament and practiced by Israel, Freemantle said, "Their land law was the basis of the system; and this rested distinctly on a religious sanction."[3] The land law is basic because it is the earth which must be subdued and made into God's Kingdom, and it is on earth that

---

1. George Jessel: *So Help Me*, p. 226. Cleveland: World Publishing Co. (1944) 1946.

2. Magnus Ottoson, "erets," in G. Johannes Botterweck and Helmer Ringgren, eds.: *Theological Dictionary of the Old Testament*, p. 404. John T. Willis, trans. Grand Rapids, Michigan: Eerdmans, 1974.

3. W. H. Freemantle: *The World as the Subject of Redemption*, p. 47. New York: Longmans, Green, (1895) 1907.

God's will must be done. The Lord's Prayer sets this forth: "Thy kingdom come. Thy will be done in earth, as it is in heaven" (Matt. 6:10).

The Bible makes clear that God is present in His providential government wherever there is *faithfulness*, faith in Him as Lord and Savior, and obedience to His laws. To be in an area where God's law is disregarded is to be in a godless land, cut off from God's providential care to a considerable degree. David saw separation by banishment from a land under God's law into a land without God's law as in effect an order to serve other gods. He makes this clear to King Saul, saying:

> Now therefore, I pray thee, let my lord the king hear the words of his servant. If the LORD have stirred thee up against me, let him accept an offering: but if they be the children of men, cursed be they before the LORD: for they have driven me out this day from abiding in the inheritance of the LORD, saying, Go, serve other gods. (I Sam. 26:19)

Where the law of the land does not serve the triune God and is not His law, there we serve other gods. David did so reluctantly, and under protest. Now churchmen do it as a mark of virtue. The implication of David's statement is far-reaching. The primary law of the Ten Commandments, and its essence, is, "Thou shalt have no other gods before me" (Ex. 20:3). David makes clear that *other laws* means *other gods*.

We cannot begin to understand any religion, least of all Biblical faith, unless we realize every religion has an idea of ultimacy, its god, a plan of salvation, deliverance, or release, and a law system setting forth the nature of its god or ultimacy. A religion without law is an impossibility. Where we have a profession of antinomianism, as with many churchmen, it is because the God of Scripture is rejected in favor of another god, usually nowadays existentialist man. In any system of thought law is the prescription of a sovereign, so that the source of law in any society is the working god of that society. Law is *torah*, the instruction, guidance, and direction of God, He Who Is, the eternal one. Law is *covenant* law: it declares the basis of man's covenant relationship with God. Man *cannot* be in covenant with God except in obedience to the law of that covenant. Man's obedience is his witness to his faith in and loyalty to the covenant God.

The covenant God declares, "Ye shall be holy: for I the LORD your God am holy" (Lev. 19:2). When St. Peter restates this requirement, he declares that they are called to be "obedient children" (I Peter 1:14), called to forsake their lawlessness and lusts.

> But as he which hath called you is holy, so be ye holy in all manner of conversation;
> Because it is written, Be ye holy: for I am holy (I Peter 1:15-16)

Holiness means separation to God; profanity means separation from

God. To be holy means to be a regenerate covenant man obeying the law of God. It means re-establishment in the covenant calling and Kingdom task of dominion. Thus, without holiness, there is no dominion, and without dominion, there is no holiness. Holiness means dominion over our lives, over our calling, and over our work. The holy man is a dominion man. To be separated to God means to manifest the righteousness or law of God, and to manifest the righteousness or law of God means to exercise dominion.

David thus, when banished to a land where God's law was not in force, recognized its implication. Where the law of another god is in force, a rival plan of dominion to that of the God of Scripture prevails. The law of the land thus in effect requires a man to serve other gods. In such a land, David would have to be either an outlaw, against the law of the land, or a pagan, serving another god. As a temporary recourse, David feigned madness (I Sam. 21:10-15) and used deception (I Sam. 27:8-12) to cover his actual outlaw status while among the Philistines. Anything other than a choice between God and His covenant law, or Philistine law, was a stop-gap solution.

When Israel was faithless to the covenant God and His law, the result for Israel was the Babylonian Captivity. The covenant God gave them over into captivity to other gods, because in practice they were the worshippers of other gods (Ezek. 8:1-18). The Glory of God departed from Israel (Ezek. 10:22-23), because of the apostasy of the people.

The central problem of our time is that men, in the name of the Lord, are serving other gods while denying that this is the case. Because of their apostasy, humanistic law is increasingly prevalent all over the world. Every law system is a way of holiness, but for God all these other holiness codes are forms of blasphemy, and His law alone is the way of holiness.

Peter declares of Jesus Christ, "Neither is there salvation in any other: for there is none other name under heaven given among men, whereby we must be saved" (Acts 4:12). Jesus Christ is alone our Savior. To be in fact his covenant people, we must manifest His righteousness, His law. We must be holy, because He is holy. Holiness means the law of God. It means that the earth must be separated and devoted to God, and God's law made the governing rule of land, life, and thought. Holiness means dominion under God, over ourselves, our callings, and the earth. The holy man is a Dominion Man.

## 70

## THE NAZIRITE VOW

One of the neglected episodes of the Book of Acts is the role of St. Paul as Nazirite (Acts 21:18-35).

The law of the Nazirites is in Numbers 6:1-21: other laws which governed him (and others) in relationship to his vow and his holiness are Numbers 19:11ff.; Leviticus 5:7; 12:8; 14:30f.; 15:14f.; 29f.; Leviticus 4:2ff.; Numbers 15:22ff.; etc. These covered the defilement of a Nazirite and the forms of purification. The Nazirite was a man (or woman) who consecrated himself to the Lord for a time for the fulfilment of a vow to the Lord. At the end of that time, he went through a prescribed ritual to mark his return to ordinary life. The Nazirite was not an ascetic; his vow required active fulfilment of some service to God. However, in the course of this service, he was, *first*, to abstain from wine and strong drink, from vinegar, and from raisins. He was to be governed only by the word and Spirit of the Lord. We do not know why raisins (or, dried fruit) were included in the prohibitions, and the various guesses by scholars are unsatisfactory.

*Second*, his hair was to be uncut during the time of the vow; this included the beard. Normally, the hair on a man's head was cut regularly. Now he was a *nazir*, an unpruned vine, and his hair was the equivalent of the high priest's mitre and a mark of his consecration.[1] *Third*, like the high priest, the Nazirite must not go near a dead body, even of a near relative. As one especially dedicated to the living God, he could have no contact with death.

Nazirites clearly existed in the early church. While the influence of Manichaeanism and Platonism on the monastic movement is marked, there is also evidence of the Nazirite vow in their celibacy (Matt. 19:12). Asceticism, however, is not a part of the Nazirite calling.

When St. Paul returned to Jerusalem, four men in the church were ending their Nazirite vows and service. The advice given to St. Paul by St. James and the elders was that he join these four men and undertake the cost of their terminating rituals at the Temple. The reasons advanced are, *first*, that many Jews had erroneously been told that St. Paul was hostile to the Law (Acts 21:21). *Second*, the fact is clearly stated of St.

---

1. D. Eaton, "Nazirite," in James Hastings, ed.: *A Dictionary of the Bible*, III, 499. Edinburgh: T. & T. Clark, (1900). 1909.

Paul by James and the elders, "thou thyself also walkest orderly, and keepest the law" (Acts 21:24). Thus, for St. Paul to take part in such a ritual would be in keeping with his avowed principles. It would give a public disavowal of the false reputation promulgated by the Judaizers that St. Paul was an antinomian.

St. Paul complied. The reasons given for his compliance are regularly insulting to St. Paul. *First*, it is said that he complied on the grounds of expedience, and I Corinthians 9:19ff. is misused to justify this. St. Paul believed in being "all things to all men," not in the sense of compromise, but in terms of a readiness to give priority to the Gospel over all things else. He was unwilling to compromise, as Galatians 2:11-21 makes clear; the law could not be used as a means of justification, and he was uncompromising on this point and others. No dietary laws could thus keep him from meeting Gentiles on their level; this does not mean that he despised such laws.

A *second* reason is that, because the Temple rituals now meant nothing to St. Paul, he could observe them, because they were meaningless. But this again makes Paul a pragmatist and unprincipled. The assumption of James and the elders is that the ritual meant something to the four Christians, to themselves, and to St. Paul.

A *third* reason advanced is that St. Paul was ready to be purified from the sojourn in Gentile lands on his return to the Holy Land. But Jerusalem was the city which crucified Christ: it would not be a holy place to St. Paul by any means. It was rather a place he believed to be under judgment. If St. Peter could declare that judgment would begin at the house of God (I Peter 4:17), can we believe that St. Paul had a more tolerant view of Jerusalem and its future?

What is overlooked is this fact: the four Christians were to undergo *the end* of their specific vow and service. St. Paul not only financed the ritual, he joined them in terminating his own specific time of service and vow. St. Paul's missionary journey had been in part or whole a time of avowed srvice. His return to Jerusalem, to James and the elders, was to report, not as a subject but as a co-worker, a fellow apostle, on his discharge of this particular vow and service.

This faithfulness to the law and to his role as a Nazirite is noted and commended by James and the elders. The only difference introduced is thus: St. Paul was terminating this period of avowed service before the church; he was asked to do the same in the Temple, and with an observance of the Temple forms and ritual, exactly as the four other Christians. St. Paul readily complied.

St. Paul complied because he saw his mission to the Gentiles as a fulfilment of the meaning of the Nazirite role in its best sense. More notable is the fact that the Temple priests, who certainly knew who St. Paul was, made no objection as he entered the Temple and, for almost a week, faithfully observed the ritual. For St. Paul, all that the Temple represented, and all that the Nazirite vow stood for, had their truest fulfilment in Christ, and in St. Paul's own ministry as an apostle of Christ.

It was the Jews of Asia, i.e., from the mission fields St. Paul had worked in, who, when the seven days were almost ended, created the opposition. They declared that St. Paul was "against the people (Israel), and the law, and this place (the Temple)" (Acts 21:27-28).

The men who denounced Paul were probably Ephesians, because they recognized Trophimus, an Ephesian, as a companion of Paul, having seen them together in the city (Acts 21:29). St. Paul's declaration in Ephesians 2:11-22 is that Christ's purpose is to reconcile men to Himself and to one another, and to bring Jews and Gentiles together as one people in God. This had no doubt been Paul's teaching in Ephesus and elsewhere. The hostility aroused by the Ephesians in the Temple was directed against this. *As against the exclusiveness of the physical Israel, St. Paul taught the exclusiveness of Jesus Christ.* Paul's Nazirite vow was related to this. As against Israel as the way to God, he preached "Christ crucified" (I Cor. 1:23). In I Corinthians 2:2, he declares, "For I determined not to know any thing among you, save Jesus Christ, and him crucified." The word translated *determined* is *krino*, which means *separated* or *to separate*. Paul had separated himself, dedicated himself, as a Christian Nazirite to one purpose, the proclamation of Jesus Christ as Lord and Savior. The crucifixion was for Paul Christ's destruction of the power of sin and death and the creation of a new humanity. Acts 18:18 tells us that Paul had made a vow on his missionary journey, so that Acts 21:24 follows logically.

The Nazirite vow was thus clearly a part of the life of the early church. When the break with the Judean past developed, the vow remained, although it was not called Nazirite. The vow took forms forbidden by St. Paul (I Tim. 4:1-5), but the vow as such persisted, although without the ritual aspects of the Old Testament. The vow stressed the calling of all men in the covenant; it gave to every person a symbolic role, comparable to that of the high priest, in God's service. The Nazirite vow stressed the primacy of Scripture and its requirements in the life of man, and the calling open to all to serve God above and beyond their daily calling.

Without the forms of the old, St. Paul kept to the function and life of a Nazirite. To comply to the forms was entirely agreeable to him. What the elders and James recognized, and the Temple priests did not object to, was St. Pauls's own form of obedience to the life of separation and service required of a Nazirite. This in itself is a most noteworthy fact.

The failure of commentators to note the significance of Paul's role as a

Nazirite is due to their modernism. Modernism reads the past in terms of the present: it disbelieves what is irrelevant to its present-oriented philosophy. Open modernism denies therefore the historicity of much of Scripture. Implicit modernism may profess a belief in all of Scripture while discarding much of it because its only focus is the present. If we try at all to see the Scriptures through the eyes of its participants, St. Paul plainly emerges as a Nazirite. This puts a distance between us only if we insist on the priority of our modernity.

# 71

## PSYCHOLOGY AND ASSURANCE

The deeply rooted humanism of Western culture in several ways infiltrated and destroyed Puritanism and Reformation thought, and, at the same time, took over the Counter-Reformation. Neo-platonism was one such factor.[1] Psychology was another. In the name of spiritual self-examination, psychology took precedence over theology and ethics. In every theological tradition, we see a growing pre-occupation after 1600 with self-examination to the point of morbid dissection. Puritan literature, for example, became so inner directed in terms of self-examination that a world-conquering faith rapidly lost interest in the world. Larzer Ziff observes, of early American Puritan developments, "Psychology took precedent over ethics as the science of the salvation experience. If one objected that a tree is known by its fruits, the obvious answer was that the tree does not know itself by its fruits but by its roots."[2] The consequences of this change continue in American life and letters. Conscience, Austin Warren observed, in writing of Hawthorne, turns into consciousness.[3]

Practically, this meant that psychology became more important than morality, and the self and its consciousness took priority over law. Morality and the law, it has been increasingly asserted, cannot hinder or fetter the free expression of man's experience and his consciousness or awareness of every avenue of life.

This primacy of psychology and experience generates a rebellion against the "chains" of laws and institutions which would fetter the freedom to experience. The priority of experientialism means that sexuality and the free experience of every form of sexuality is more important than marriage and the law. As a result, we have the prevalence of the sex revolution and a marked hostility to marriage and the family.

This freedom to experience requires a freedom from stability. Both law and marriage provide stability and security, and this in itself is sufficient to condemn them in the eyes of many. I recall as a student hearing a radical professor heap what to him was the ultimate insult upon the

---

1. See R. J. Rushdoony: *The Flight From Humanity.* Nutley, New Jersey: The Craig Press, 1973.
2. Larzer Ziff: *Puritanism in America*, p. 60. New York: The Viking Press, 1973.
3. *Ibid.*, p. 306.

Christian middle class: they were contented with their homes, their children, and with "missionary" sex! To be contented was a sign of not being really and truly alive. This same professor found the psychological chaos and self-torment of a then popular dramatist, Eugene O'Neill, whom he seemed to know, a mark of greatness. He assured us that, if we knew the facts of Shakespeare's life, we would find it to be somewhat similar.

In the world of experientialism, assurance is thus an evil, because it is a bar to psychological self-examination. It closes the door to a psychological openness to experience, and it makes unnecessary any endless self-examination. Thomas Aquinas (*Summa*, pt. ii, 1, quest. 112, art. 5) and Alexander of Hales began the formulation of the doctrine of assurances in Scholasticism. Calvin gave it a clear statement, as did the Augsburg Confession and the Westminster Confession. Not even Wesley abandoned it. In our time, however, while formally held, the doctrine is generally sterile. Where psychology is dominant over theology, the very doctrine of assurances becomes a means of psychological self-testing rather than a reliance on the objective work of Jesus Christ.

Here is the key to the problem. Christ's objective work is His atoning and vicarious sacrifice on the cross, and His triumph over sin and death by His death and resurrection. The death penalty against the covenant people was enforced against Jesus Christ who, as the new Adam, reopens to His people God's new creation. That new creation begins with their regeneration; it continues with their dominion over the earth, and it culminates with Christ's Second Advent and the fulness of the new creation. The penalty of death is removed by Christ's obedience to the law: as our sin-bearer, and as the perfect and obedient Adam, He frees us from sin and death into life and righteousness. The law ends as a death penalty against us and becomes our charter of life and dominion, our way of life and conquest.

Experientialism replaces both grace and law with the experience of man. Not by their fruits, their obedience and faithfulness to their Lord, but by their experience, are such men determining their status. This becomes an exercise in self-determination and self-election, and a downgrading of grace and law.

The self-probings and psychologizing of the modern mind rest upon a false doctrine of man. If man is tripartite in nature, or dualistic, this means that there are two or three mutually exclusive or contradictory aspects to man's being. Neo-platonic man and Manichaean man are in a perpetual state of civil war, internal war, because their souls and bodies have very diverse impulses. Such a man has as it were two or three lives. Neo-platonic man, for example, has a physical life and a spiritual life, and each has its own history and destiny. Not so with Biblical man. He has one being, a created being. The *whole* of that being is involved in the Fall; the entirety of his being is redeemed, and both "body" and "soul" are resurrected. The conflict which St. Paul describes in Romans 7 is not a neo-platonic nor a psychological condition but rather a conflict between Paul the whole man and the witness of God in his being. It is a theological and moral, not a psychological, conflict; it is psychological only in the sense that Paul's mind is involved. The root problem is the relationship of Paul to God; the problem and the solution are alike theological, not psychological.

When St. Paul asks that we examine ourselves, and that we judge ourselves (I Cor. 11:28, 31), it is in terms of God's word: in this case, our readiness to share with others at the love-feasts. Our Lord's test, based again on the unity of man's being is that by men's fruits we know them (Matt. 7:15-20).

The Bible thus declares that *faithfulness* to the covenant God and His law, and *gratitude*, are the marks of the covenant man. The expression of gratitude is faithfulness. This is clearly set forth in the ritual of the presentation of the first-fruits. The covenant man, in presenting the first-fruits, acknowledged God's Lordship and His sovereign right to all. He presented himself as God's slave, rejoicing in that privilege of salvation. In Deuteronomy 26:1-11, the believer confesses that "Yahweh is both lord of history and lord of nature, and blesses Israel through both."[4] He acknowledges that "he and his people owed their existence and welfare to the grace of God, manifested in the miraculous redemption of Israel out of the oppression of Egypt and their guidance into Canaan."[5] The covenant man's gratitude was thus, *first* of all, more than personal. He rejoiced, not simply for the salvation of his soul, but for God's redemption and care for a covenant people, of which he was one. It is personal gratitude, but it is not egocentric gratitude. His joy is at one and the same time personal and communal, or covenantal.

*Second*, he has "an inheritance" from the Lord by the adoption of grace, and he acknowledges the living God who has redeemed him, made him an heir, and blessed him in that inheritance.

*Third*, he acknowledges that adoption by bringing his first-fruits and tithes (Deut. 26:12-15) to the Lord. As a part of that tithe, and in gratitude to the Lord, he gives to the Levite, the stranger, the fatherless, and the widow, "according to all thy commandments."

*Fourth*, as covenant men, by their faithfulness, avouch the Lord to be their God, so God avouches them to be His people (Deut. 26:16-19). If

---

4. Anthony Phillips: *Deuteronomy*, p. 174. The Cambridge Bible Commentary, Cambridge: The University Press, 1973.
5. C. F. Keil and F. Delitzsch: *Biblical Commentary on the Old Testament, The Pentateuch*, vol. III, p. 426. Grand Rapids, Michigan: Eerdmans, 1949.

they are obedient, He makes them high above all nations, and they know His blessings when they obey His law.

There is here no psychological self-examination nor endless self-probing. Are they *faithful*? Do they believe and obey? Do they confess and obey the Lord? Instead of psychology, there is theology and morality in action.

## 72

## THE KEYS OF THE KINGDOM

Several years ago, I had an amazing conversation with a man who professed to be an "evangelical Christian," believing the Bible from cover to cover, supposedly. He said that it was quite often very difficult to know the will of God. I told him that, on the contrary, it was very easy, because His will for us is clearly stated in His law. The man objected: we are under grace, not law. Why?, I asked. The Lord, he said, has given us a higher and simpler way, and has delivered us from the fearful burden of the law and obedience to it. How, I asked, can it be simpler, if now you find it difficult to know the will of God? He said it was clear that I did not understand Scripture! Such was the gist of our conversation.

I was reminded of it in listening to a radio broadcast by an "evangelical" pastor. He read a letter from a man in prison. The convict has "accepted Christ," would soon be released, obviously knew many Bible verses by heart, and said that he wanted prayers so that the Lord would reveal His will and show him what was right so that he would not be back in prison again. It was to me a startling letter. How could a man with a Bible not know what is right? How can there be any doubt as to what is good and what is evil in God's sight?

And yet, in the past two years, I was denied a pulpit in a "Bible-believing" church because I affirmed capital punishment. I can cite at length other like incidents too many to honor by record.

Why this antinomianism in the church? Why the problem in identifying good and evil in God's sight? *Moreover, why is the church so vehement in denying God's law?*

Our Lord tells us why. The scribes and Pharisees, He said, made "the commandment of God of none effect" by their "tradition" (Matt. 15:9). They replaced God's law with man's law; this gave them power; this made them the working gods of their social system.

The term "keys of the kingdom" was a name for the interpretation of God's law. God's law is the key to God's kingdom. To possess the keys is to have the privilege of expounding and interpreting God's law. To render a false interpretation, or to substitute man's law for God's law, is to close God's Kingdom to men and to substitute *another* kingdom for God's, i.e., the Kingdom of Man. Our Lord condemns this, saying, "But woe unto you, scribes and Pharisees, hypocrites! for ye shut up the kingdom of heaven against men; for ye neither go in yourselves, neither suffer ye them that are entering to go in" (Matt. 23:13).

The true man of God binds what God's law binds, and looses what God in His grace commands to be loosed (Matt. 16:19).

It is clear, *first*, that where the church faithfully expounds the word, it is God's power, law, justice, grace, and mercy which are exalted. The true exercise of the power of the keys opens the door into the Kingdom of God for men. It enables men to become Dominion Men.

*Second*, failure to use the power of the keys properly means anti-nomianism. It denies God's law, although like Phariseeism, it can replace it with another law claiming to be God's. Antinomianism always comes "in the name of the Lord," but is antichristian to the core.

*Third*, when the church is antinomian, it is anti-God's law, not anti-law per se. It still affirms a law, but it is now man's law. Its canon or rule is not God's law but the church's law. Whenever antinomianism abounds in history, the church's power is vastly enhanced. The church becomes the law-source and the god of that law system. The church then has a passionate interest at stake in defending its antinomianism and in disarming God of His law.

*Fourth*, the church then begins to stress the Holy Spirit in a non-Biblical, anarchistic fashion. The charismatic movement is one aspect of this emphasis. The Spirit is used to vindicate antinomianism as a "higher" and more spiritual way.

*Fifth*, meanwhile man is enslaved and bound to the church, which, as the new source of law, controls man's conscience (Matt. 23:4). Man cannot live without law: if it is not God's law, it will be man's law that he lives by. Both church and state enhance their powers whenever and wherever God's law is undercut or denied.

*Sixth*, today both church and state follow the scribes and Pharisees and "shut up the kingdom of heaven against men" (Matt. 23:13). We cannot begin to grasp the nature and dimension of our present crisis if we fail to see this fact. The cure is not revolution or rebellion but regeneration, and a full and ready use of the keys of the Kingdom by all Christians. We must affirm that it is God who is sovereign, God who reigns, God who is the lawgiver, and God alone who is our Savior. We can know the will of God: he has revealed it to us in His word. Our problem is not a question of knowledge: it is a question of obedience, i.e., of faith and the morality of our faith.

# 73

## THE CHURCH

One of the most confusing aspects of any study of Scripture is the misuse of the word *church*. The English word *church* comes from the Greek adjective *kyriakos* "as used in some such phrase as *kyriakon doma* or *kyriake oikia*, meaning 'the Lord's house,' i.e., a Christian place of worship."[1] The New Testament word, *ecclesia*, does not refer either to a building, or to an institution. Present day usage has church meaning a physical bulding, or an institution, such as the Roman Catholic Church, the Southern Baptist Church, the Presbyterian Church of America, and the like.

The Old Testament has two words to designate the covenant people: *'edhah* (congregation) and *qahal* (assembly). The Greek word *ecclesia* conveys both meanings. As Alfred Plummer noted, "The name 'Church' is in itself strong evidence of the connexion between the Old Covenant and the New."[2] S. C. Gayford said, "*Ecclesia* is used in NT of a single community of Christians, or of the sum of the single communities, the whole body of Christians."[3] Moshe Weinfeld has written of the Old Testament usage of *congregation*, that it refers to "the people of Israel" in their "social, military, and sacral capacity."[4] A careful reading of the Old Testament makes clear that *congregation* includes "church," "state," army, and more.

Rather early, however, *church* came to mean the institution and the building, although this meaning only became fixed in the later "medieval" period. The equation of the institution with the church led to the growth of Rome's power in an institutional sense. The reading of Scripture made clear how broad the scope of the church is, but the institution claimed the scope and the power of the church. The Reformation did not alter matters; theology changed, but ecclesiology was less altered, and Milton was able to observe rightly, "New presbyter is but old priest writ large." Subsequent history has not altered that course.

---

1. D. W. B. Robinson, "Church" in J. D. Douglas, ed.: *The New Bible Dictionary*, p. 228. Grand Rapids, Michigan: Eerdmans, (1962) 1973.
2. Alfred Plummer, "Church," in James Hastings, ed.: *Dictionary of the Apostolic Church*, I, p. 204. New York: Charles Scribner's Sons, (1916) 1919.
3. S. C. Gayford, "Church," in James Hastings, ed.: *A Dictionary of the Bible*, vol. I, p. 425. New York: Charles Scribner's Sons, (1898) 1919.
4. Moshe Weinfeld, "Congregation," in *Encyclopaedia Judaica*, V. 894.

Baptists broke with this tradition, but they retained the use of the word *church* for the local congregation and building and thus read Scripture on the *church* in terms of a local institution. Thus the institutional frame was still retained.

Some English theologians came up with still another answer. They recognized the broad and inclusive nature of the word *church*. Plainly, it included people, church, state, school, and more. These men sought to restore the more catholic meaning of the word *church*, but, as opposed to the late medieval inclusion of all spheres and powers under the institution for worship, they included all under the monarch. The nation was to be a covenant nation, both church and state, and it was to be a restoration of the lost unity which Christendom was seeking. Freemantle described the English settlement thus:

> It recognizes that the will of Christ resides, not in the ministers of public worship acting separately, but in the whole brotherhood, to which alone we can apply the words, 'His body, the fullness of Him who filleth all in all.' And this is consonant with the most ancient opinion and usage of the Church....
>
> We may sum up the Reformation settlement, then, in these terms. The whole body of citizens, which was called by one collective term. 'This Church and Realm' (a single word followed by a verb in the singular number), moved together under its sovereign ruler.[5]

Since the days of Archbishop Laud, the opinion has been fostered that the Church of England is nearest to Rome, and half-way between the Reformation churches and Rome. This is only true if we look at vestments and the like. In its concept of the church, the Church of England is furthest removed and is diametrically opposite to the Church of Rome. Only a few of the most radical Anabaptists held to a like view of the unity of church and state under the civil order.

We must, however, recognize that Rome, the Baptists, and the Church of England have each in their way called attention to an important aspect of the Biblical doctrine. Rome has stressed the catholicity of the meaning of the *church* but identified it too closely with the institution. The Baptists have recognized the local nature of the worshipping group and the primacy of faith. The Church of England has seen the relationship of the entire people and their institutions to the church of Scripture but has reduced the church to the nation. Finally, the Reformed Churches have recognized the centrality of the covenant, but they have reduced the covenant to the community of institutionalized worshippers.

In Hebrews 12:22-24 we meet with a declaration concerning the church which throws much light on the breadth of its meaning:

---

5. W. H. Freemantle: *The World as the Subject of Redemption*, pp. 215, 216. New York: Longmans, Green. (1895) 1907.

But ye are come unto Mount Sion, and unto the city of the living God, the heavenly Jerusalem, and to an innumerable company of angels.
To the general assembly and church of the firstborn, which are written in heaven, and to God the Judge of all, and to the spirits of just men made perfect,
And to Jesus the mediator of the new covenant, and to the blood of sprinkling, that speaketh better things than that of Abel.

*First* of all, the church is clearly linked to the Old Testament covenant people. It is one body with them. *Zion* and *Jerusalem* are terms now applied to *the church*. What the old was, the new now is. It is not Mount Sinai that we approach but Zion, the established place of God's people. We are not in the wilderness; in Christ we have entered into the promised land, and we are now to exercise dominion in it.

*Second, the church is the City or Kingdom of God.* It is thus more than any church (as we call it) or state can be. The boundaries of God's church include every "church," state, school, family, individual, institution, etc. which is under Christ's royal law and rule. But it includes far, far more. In the church are also the wholly sanctified saints in heaven, "an innumerable company of angels," Christ our Redeemer and King, and God our Judge and Creator. Buchanan notes, of the term "heavenly Jerusalem," that

"Heavenly Jerusalem" was not used to mislead the reader into thinking Mount Zion was in heaven, although Jews and Christians believed there was a Jerusalem in heaven as well, but to affirm its divine origin.[6]

*Third*, entrance into the church is by regeneration. It is the "church of the firstborn." Jesus Christ is the firstborn of God, the heir of all things, and we are, by the adoption of grace, sons of God and firstborn heirs in Christ. The firstborn of God is the heir of the Kingdom of God (Matt. 21:38, 43). The covenant people are thus required in Christ to possess God's earth which the false husbandmen have seized (Matt. 21:33-46).

*Fourth*, the church is "the general assembly...of the firstborn," or, we can say, the *entire* assembly. The New English Bible renders it "the full concourse and assembly." Since it includes angels, it is not limited to men.

Very clearly, the church in Scripture means the Kingdom of God, not merely the worshipping institution or building. In includes all who are in covenant with God, who believe in Christ and obey His law. It includes all regenerate men, the redeemed in heaven and earth, the angels, true "churches," Christian states, families, schools, callings, and more. It includes godly men and their possessions, and the earth they subdue in the name of the Lord. The church is very clearly a worshipping local

---

6. George Wesley Buchanan: *To the Hebrews*, p. 222. The Anchor Bible. Garden City, New York: Doubleday, 1972.

congregation, or a larger group of congregations, but it is far, far more, and we cannot restrict its meaning to an institution nor limit its cosmic scope.

To confound the church of Scripture with the church of history, the institutional church, means that an absorption with the institution rather than the faith ensues. Worship and the growth of an institution takes precedence over the application of the faith to every realm and sphere of life.

The result is a radical warping of the entire life of the Christian. His life is then off center, and his daily walk becomes radically different from that required by Scripture.

## 74

## CHURCH IMPERIALISM

One of the key texts used over the centuries to justify ecclesiastical imperialism has been Ephesians 1:23. St. Paul writes of the manifestation of God's power,

> Which he wrought in Christ, when he raised him from the dead, and set him at his own right hand in the heavenly places,
> Far above all principality, and power, and might, and dominion, and every name that is named, not only in this world, but also in that which is to come:
> And hath put all things under his feet, and gave him to be the head over all things to the church,
> Which is his body, the fulness of him that filleth all in all (Eph. 1:20-23).

As we have seen, the modern church, a building or an institution, is not the *church* of Scripture, but rather one aspect of the Kingdom of God or church. In the New Testament church, the members saw themselves, nor merely as members of an institution, but as citizens of the new creation under Christ the King. That new creation was variously titled: the New Jerusalem, the heavenly Jerusalem, the Jerusalem which is from above, the Israel of God, the City of the living God, the general assembly and church of the firstborn, the church, the Kingdom of God, and much more. Each of these expressions include all men, institutions, groups, callings, and those areas of the earth which are under Christ and His dominion men. None of these terms can be limited to the institutional "church," nor to the state and monarch as in England, nor to the Holy Roman Empire as in some strata of early European thought. The *church* of Scripture is far, far more.

Because the members of the early church saw the church as Christ's Kingdom and new creation, and themselves as citizens thereof, an early problem was this: how can we obey an alien lord, an earthly ruler? The result is precisely a strong stress on such obedience throughout the New Testament, because Christ's Kingdom depends, not on revolution but on regeneration, and disobedience is a revolutionary act. In Romans 13:1-14, St. Paul makes clear that God uses all rulers as His ministers, despite themselves, and He requires His covenant people to walk in *subjection* to these rulers, but in obedience to God's law, to which Paul gives some attention, summarizing the law and its every-day implications.

Although Stoeckhardt does not clarify the meaning of the *church*, he is correct up to a point in commenting on Ephesians 1:23 that it sets forth the omnipresence of Christ: "This divine omnipresence which is an attribute of the man Christ, is not quiescent, *nuda adessentia*, but an active, energetic dwelling within the entire created universe, in virtue of which Christ gives life and breath to everything and all things and 'all things consist by Him,' Colossians 1:17."[1] While we must dissent with Stoeckhardt's anti-Chalcedonian confusion of the two natures of Christ, we can assent to the statement that Christ's omnipresence is declared. However, much more is declared by St. Paul: he is not speaking merely of omnipresence, but of Christ's cosmic *dominion*. As Simpson has noted, "The dominion here ascribed to the ascended Saviour accords with His own testimony: 'Behooved it not the Christ to suffer these things and to enter into his glory?' (Luke 24:26)"[2]

Very early, however, the "church," or institution began to identify itself with the church of Scripture, or the Kingdom of God. Cyprian held that, because the bishop was elected by the people, he was their embodiment. The bishop is the member of the people in councils. The bishop is in the church, and the church is in the bishop. Since the church is Christ's body, the bishop also represents Christ. The bishop is thus the embodiment of both Christ and of the people. Cyprian drew the logical implications:

> The episcopate is one, each part of which is held by each one for the whole.[3]

> He can no longer have God for his Father, who has not the church for his mother.[4]

> He cannot possess the garment of Christ who parts and divides the church of Christ.[5]

> Let none think that the good can depart from the church.[6]

> He cannot be a martyr who is not in the church; he cannot attain unto the kingdom who forsakes that which shall reign there.[7]

> Does he think that he has Christ, who acts in opposition to Christ's priests, who separates himself from the company of His clergy and people? He bears arms against the church, he contends against God's appointment. An enemy of the altar, a rebel against Christ's sacrifice, for the faith faithless, for religion profane, a disobedient

---

1. George Stoeckhardt: *Commentary of St. Paul's Letter to the Ephesians*, p. 117. St. Louis, Missouri: Concordia, 1952.

2. E. K. Simpson, in E. K. Simpson and F. F. Bruce: *Commentary on the Epistle to the Ephesians and to the Colossians*, p. 42. The New International Commentary. Grand Rapids, Michigan: Eerdmans, 1957.

3. Cyprian, "On the Unity of the Church," in *Ante-Nicene Christian Library*, vol. VIII, *The Writings of Cyprian*, I, p. 381, para. 5. Edinburgh: T. & T. Clark, 1868.

4. *Ibid.*, p. 382, para. 6.

5. *Ibid.*, p. 383, para. 7.

6. *Ibid.*, p. 385, para. 9.

7. *Ibid.*, p. 388, para. 14

servant, an impious son, a hostile brother, despising the bishops, and forsaking God's priests, he dares to set up another altar, to make another prayer with unauthorized words, to profane the truth of the Lord's offering by false sacrifices, and not to know that he who strives against the appointment of God, is punished on account of the daring of his temerity by divine visitation.[8]

God is one, and Christ is one, and His church is one, and the faith is one, and the people is joined into a substantial unity of body by the cement of concord.[9]

It is easy to see from this equation of Christ with churchmen and the institution with the church of Scripture how ecclesiastical totalitarianism developed in one church after another, and is implicit today in both Protestantism and Catholicism as well as in the Eastern Churches. Once the equation is accepted, and the institution equated itself with the church of Scripture, it sees itself as the totality of the Kingdom of God, and it acts on this premise.

The origins of this equation are deeply rooted in the pagan idea of the divine-human state. Let us examine some Western forms of this church or Kingdom concept:

1. a. The bishop must represent and is the vicar of Christ.
   b. The bishop represents the people.
   c. The bishop is the church.

2. a. The king (or emperor) is the vicar or representative of Christ or God the Father.
   b. The king (or emperor) represents the people.
   c. The king is the state (and sometimes the church as well)

3. a. The presbytery, conference, or local congregation is the church.
   b. The church therefore is present in that body.
   c. The center of man's life must be that institutional body.

4. a. Democracies represent the people.
   b. The voice of the people is the voice of God.
   c. Democratic rulers are the voice of God.

5. a. The dialectical process is the only truth.
   b. The dialectical process incarnates the general will of history in the dictatorship of the proletariat.
   c. The dictatorship is the infallible voice of history.

In pagan thought, the gods are inseparable from their appearances or theophanies. Because the gods cannot transcend history, they pass away and are replaced by time. Their inability to transcend history means that they are exhaustively present in history. They can neither transcend nor escape time. They can have a future, good or bad, but they are still subject to time and history.

---

8. *Ibid.*, p. 392, para. 17.
9. *Ibid.*, p. 396, para. 23.

The God of Scripture *has* no future: the future of all things is His creation. He created time, history, and the universe, and totally governs all things therein. Christ as Lord of history transcends history. His rule, government, and Kingdom are the *church*, the gathering, the area of rule. To limit this *church* to an institution or to history is to limit Christ's Kingship.

The church *includes* the institution of worship, but it also includes the godly state, the godly family, and all things else which are under Christ's rule. Clement of Alexandria wrote (in *Stromata*, III, 10) "Our Lord said that where two or three were gathered in His name, there was the true Church. Who are these two or three, but the father, the mother, and the child...?" The same is true of any Christian group or activity. The church thus is more than the clergy and the religious institution. *Clericalism*, the exaltation of the church institution and its clergy, is a product of the identification of the institution for worship with the church of Scripture. This identification is a product of premillennialism and amillennialism, both of which limit God's redemptive and sanctifying workings in history to the institution. The result is clericalism. Here Freemantle is right:

> By clericalism I understand the system which unduly exalts the clerical office, and the function of public worship, so as to draw away the sense of divine agency and appointment from other offices and other functions. This tendency... is not really one which exalts the Church. It exalts the clergy alone; it dwarfs and emasculates the Church.[10]

Clericalism will arise where postmillennialism is denied, whether it be a Roman Catholic, Baptist, Presbyterian, or Congregationalist context. Only when the work of the church is seen as one of broad implications for dominion in every realm under Christ can clericalism be avoided.

It is hardly likely, that after centuries of erroneous usage, we can readily return to the Biblical usage which saw local congregations as outposts of Christ's Kingdom, as the church or kingdom in Ephesus, and so on, but only by a postmillennial perspective is any such usage at all possible. Today, as the world more openly embraces humanism, our religious institutions, schools, families, and callings must see themselves as outposts of Christ's Kingdom, local gatherings of the citizens of the new creation. In the building for worship, the true church in a local community gathers to hear the word of God, whereby they are to go forth and exercise dominion.

---

10. Freemantle, *op.cit.*, p. 315.

## 75

## KINGDOM COURTS

It should be clear to us now that, while government is a basic concern of Scripture, church and state as we know them barely exist in Scripture. It is the Kingdom of God which is basic, and we are commanded to seek first the Kingdom of God and His righteousness (Matt. 6:33). It is the doctrine of Satan that God is trying to repress and coerce man out of his supposed right and freedom to be a god, but it is the City of Man, Satan's hope for the world, which is in reality coercive. The method used by the City of Man to reach its goal is the creation of coercive institutions to compel man to be "free" from God. In the name of warring against God's supposed coercion, it establishes total coercion as a way of life. Raging against God's non-coercive predestination, the humanist creates a plan of predestination by the sovereign state which means total coercion.

In the Kingdom of God, the family is in history the basic institution. Beyond the family, the religious institutions for worship and for justice have very limited powers and jurisdiction. A network of voluntary associations, whose strength lies in the mandatory tithe which sustains them, provides the basic government beyond the family.

In a more basic sense than Davies meant it, his observation is true that "Christianity is a protest *against* Judaism in favour of the Old Testament."[1] Unfortunately, it has since been changed into a protest against Judaism *and* the Old Testament, and the result is a radically warped view of the Bible.

In terms of this, let us examine I Corinthians 6:1-8, Paul's comments concerning recourse to pagan courts:

> Dare any of you, having a matter against another, go to law before the unjust, and not before the saints?
> Do ye not know that the saints shall judge the world? and if the world shall be judged by you, are ye unworthy to judge the smallest matters?
> Know ye not that we shall judge angels? how much more things that pertain to this life?
> If then ye have judgments of things pertaining to this life, set them to judge who are least esteemed in the church.
> I speak to your shame. Is it so, that there is not a wise man among you? no, not one that shall be able to judge between his brethren?

---

1. Davies: *The Gospel and the Land*, p. 377.

But brother goeth to law with brother, and that before the unbelievers.
Now therefore there is utterly a fault among you, because ye go to law one with another. Why do ye not rather take wrong? why do ye not rather suffer yourselves to be defrauded?
Nay, ye do wrong, and defraud, and that your brethren.

*First* of all, this passage is incomprehensible apart from the privilege of the Jews in the Roman Empire in applying their own laws to all cases involving Jews. The Jews, in terms of Old Testament faith, held that to be under an alien law was to be under another god. Hence, they insisted on the right to maintain their own courts and their own law. The survival of the Jews through the centuries has been due to this insistence. Many Jews feared, in the nineteenth century, that liberalism and the abolition of the ghetto would destroy their people. This opinion seems well grounded, in view of the rapid losses and intermarriages since World War II especially.

The Talmud, in terms of the Old Testament principle, spoke strongly against the trying of any case between Jews before a non-Jewish court and called it a profanation, a departing from God and His law.[2]

*Second*, we miss the point of St. Paul's statement if we fail to see that Paul is declaring that Christians must maintain the same separateness with respect to law and courts as did the Jews. Christians can only appear before a Christian court in any controversy with Christians. Not only was this insistence made a part of the life of the early church, but it persisted throughout the middle ages. The church maintained separate courts from the state. When the states became Christian, the church persisted in this separateness, partly at first because of the barbaric nature of the state, and then to retain its power over its own clergy.

When a state or its laws are godly, its courts are legitimate and can be used. The state then, despite its sins and shortcomings, is an aspect of the Kingdom of God. Present civil law is in process of becoming radically humanistic, but its framework is still to a large degree Biblical. It is the duty of Christians, not to withdraw from civil law (i.e., the law of the state), but to make it Biblical.

*Third*, in terms of this goal, the conquest of the civil order for the Kingdom of God, St. Paul reminds them that Christians are to *judge* or govern the world. This government is in time and in eternity. They are to govern angels, and "how much more things that pertain to this life?" (I Cor. 6:3). A basic goal thus must be preparation for world rule by their conduct in the early days of faith and trial. They must resolve their conflicts within their Kingdom courts, and, if their situation be too feeble or

---

2. George Horowitz: *The Spirit of Jewish Law*, p. 650f. New York: Central Books, (1963) 1973.

undeveloped for such courts, to suffer wrong rather than to go to ungodly judges. Their own courts are not ecclesiastical in the modern sense, but Kingdom courts in the Old Testament sense, where elders ruled the life of the people and judged them.

*Fourth,* pagan courts were rightly held in low esteem. Hodge rightly renders verse 4, "If then ye have judgments of things pertaining to this life, those despised by the church,—those do ye set to judge?"[3] Those who are despised by the church are the pagan judges. A judge or court whose premise is other than the law of God is an untrustworthy administrator of justice. Justice is not impossible with such a man, but it is not to be expected.

*Fifth,* just as they give more worth to pagan courts than they deserve so they give more worth to their own contentions than they deserve. They claim to be defrauded by a brother, but, "Nay, ye do wrong, and defraud, and that your brethren" (I Cor. 6:8). St. Paul is writing about specific cases of Corinthians who have gone to court; he is not generalizing about every possible case, as commentators imply. He is not condemning resort to godly courts. He is declaring that these men are doubly sinful: they have gone to an ungodly court, and they have gone with a fraudulent case, perhaps hoping that an ungodly judge would favor them. St. Paul is commenting thus on specific cases and persons brought to his attention. His point is not, "Never go to court," but that God's law must be sought in God's appointed courts, and to go to an ungodly court is an ungodly act, and the men so doing are men with ungodly motives, seeking to defraud their brethren. Nothing else makes sense of the context.

*Sixth,* "two terms are used for believers: *brothers* and saints. . . . They are in contrast to the *unrighteous.*"[4] As *saints,* they are separated from the world and constituted as a family in Christ; hence, they are *brothers.* The strength of family government is that the godly family, while having numerous problems and disputes, settles these within its own circle. The family is the institution of strength. To go outside the family is to deny the family and to break it up. When a husband and wife, or parents and children, or brother against brother, go to an outside court, the family life and government is in most cases dissolved or at least shattered. The state is then declared a greater agency, and the family denies its own power and the basis of its existence. So too the Christian denies the reality and power of the Kingdom of God if he seeks justice outside the Kingdom. The only real Kingdom for him is then this other agency.

*Seventh,* the Corinthians had been boasting about their wisdom (I

3. Charles Hodge: *An Exposition of the First Epistle of the Corinthians,* p. 96. Grand Rapids, Michigan: Eerdmans, 1950.
4. Clarence T. Craig: "I Corinthians," in *The Interpreter's Bible,* vol. X, p. 69.

Cor. 1:20-25; 2:6-7; 4:10; 6:5, etc.). They had claimed to be "wise in Christ" (I Cor. 4:10), but Paul shows them that their behavior is instead sin and folly. He does this by turning to the practice of courts and law from Old Testament times.

# 76

## THIS IS GOD'S WORLD

It should be apparent by now that the Biblical perspective gives no ground whatsoever for a church-oriented (i.e., institution oriented) view of the world, nor for a state-oriented view. Moreover, basic as the family is to the Bible, we cannot fall into the trap of making the world family-centered. Such a perspective has been the curse of the Far East, where too often the family functions as god over man.

Neither can we fall into the sexual trap of seeing this as a man's world. This illusion is strongly believed in by many men as well as by feminists, who want to convert it, in some cases, to a woman's world, and, in others, to a world which is equally the property of men and women. An example, amusing and pathetic in its illusions, of the male viewpoint is Richard Alan's *The Complete Male Chauvinist. How to Make the Women of the World Your Loving Slaves* (1974). Alan agrees with Henry Miller that, "from the moment of birth, women's main duty is to satisfy his (a man's) needs."[1] Alan gives an amateurish and childish guide to the sexual exploitation of women (without marriage), one which will no doubt be effective among fools. The amazing and naive extent of the book's self-righteous self-deception is the solemn advice to the seducers, "You must not only ACT sincere, but you must BE sincere."[2] The gist of the book is this: it's a man's world; enjoy it, enjoy the women, but don't fall into the marriage trap.

The book, of course, is fantasy and lacks any sense of reality, because, contrary to its fundamental assumption, this is not a man's world: it is God's world. "The earth is the LORD'S, and the fulness thereof; the world, and they that dwell therein" (Ps. 24:1). Anyone who thinks this is a man's world has taken leave of his senses, is out of touch with reality, and is suicidal.

In dealing with "Church Imperialism," we have seen some of the implications of Ephesians 1:20-23. To continue further, *first*, Christ is made to sit at the right hand of God (Ps. 110:1): he is exalted after the resurrection into total authority and power, so that all creation is subject to Him. All power is delegated to Him. Our Lord spoke of this before

---

1. Richard Alan: *The Complete Male Chauvinist*, p. 92. Los Angeles, California: Scientific Research Services, 1974.
2. *Ibid.*, p. 260.

His ascension: "All power is given unto me in heaven and in earth" (Matt. 28:18).

*Second*, he is therefore above every principality, power, might, and dominion, earthly or heavenly, good or evil, "and every name that is named," i.e., any other authority or power that anyone can imagine. He is "far above" them all, for "All things were made by him; and without him was not any thing made that was made" (John 1:3).

*Third*, this authority is not only in this world and era, but "also in that which is to come," i.e., throughout all time and eternity. His power and His authority are beyond all conditions and all time.

*Fourth*, God "hath put all things under his feet." Every area of life, and every aspect of creation, is totally under Christ. Hence it is that St. Paul, in Ephesians 5:21-33, goes on to discuss marriage, and the relationship of man and wife, in terms of Christ's authority and government over "the church," i.e., the Kingdom of God. Man's authority exists in that context, because it is not man's world, but God's world, under Christ the King.

"The Complete Male Chauvinist" is the complete fool and idiot, because he imagines himself to be the goal and purpose of creaton. The meaning of life is reduced to his will and pleasure, and all things must serve him, and he feels it only right that "the women of the world" should be his "loving slaves." This is the world of Richard Alan, *Playboy, Penthouse*, and others, and it is a world of insanity and self-delusion.

The declaration, that God "hath put all things under his (Christ's) feet," echoes Psalm 2:12, "Kiss the Son, lest he be angry, and ye perish from the way, when his wrath is kindled but a little." This means to be abased at the feet of the world emperor, in total submission and service. Our relationship to Christ cannot be as it is to a great national hero. With a hero, we periodically honor him, declare our indebtedness to his accomplishment in history, acknowledge how basic his work is to our present advantages, and then we pass on. All we owe him is honor and respect. Having given this, we go our own way. Not so with Christ the King. His work did not end with His atoning death and resurrection. We sin if we look only to His past work. He is the absolute Lord of all things, and absolute governor over all our todays and tomorrows. This is His world, and we are His creation and property. We have no right, nor any life and existence apart from Him. We cannot separate ourselves, nor any institutions we create, from his sovereign government and law without penalty of death. Precisely because of this, the law of God is our mandatory plan of submission and allegiance, and the plan for our dominion under God.

We can honor a national hero, but he does not command our lives.

The Lord does. His Kingdom and law, His "church" or congregation, His new humanity and new creation, is His "fulness, the fulness of him that filleth all in all." His Kingdom, His royal rule, law, and government, will fill all creation and bring all things to their true purpose.

We have here then an emphatic declaration that this is God's world and Kingdom. He made it for His own purpose and glory, and it is to man's glory to give himself entirely over to his Lord and Maker. Thus, men who regard their work, family, wife, and this world as things to be used for their own advantage are living in violation of the purpose of their being. The chief end of man is to glorify God and to enjoy Him forever, according to the Westminister Shorter Catechism. This is only possible when man believes and obeys God in every area of life and thought.

It is paganism, therefore, to believe that God can be worshipped on one day of the week, obeyed in certain areas of morality, and then abandoned in the rest of our lives. We have no right to devise a do-it-yourself philosophy for politics, church life, the family and sexual relationships, economics, the sciences, the arts, or anything else. A man-made plan in any area of life is a denial of the sovereignty of God and His total claims over us.

This is God's world, and we had better recognize it to be so.

Thus, as we look at godly reconstruction, we must recognize God's total claims, and no area of life can be exempted from God's sovereign claims. The pretensions of man in every realm must be recognized for what they are, challenged and broken.

Moreover, we must remember that Christ did not create a new institution to be the cornerstone of the new humanity. He alone is that. He does create a renewed man, whose duty it is to bring every area of life and thought into captivity to Jesus Christ.

# 77

## "BRING NOT BLOOD UPON THINE HOUSE"

According to Deuteronomy 22:8, "When thou buildest a new house, then thou shalt make a battlement for thy roof, that thou bring not blood upon thine house, if any man fall from thence." Flat roofs were then commonplace, and, in the heat of summer, the roof-top was a convenient living area in the evenings. A parapet is required around the edge of the roof, to avoid "blood" or *blood-guilt* from an accident.

It has been quite rightly seen that we have here a case law with respect to liability and responsibility. It was so understood in Israel and in rabbinic interpretations. In fact, a parapet of about forty inches, or over three feet, became mandatory, and it had to be strong enough to take human pressure.[1] The general principle was that no dangerous condition which could be a hazard to life and health should be allowed to remain around the premises. The same prohibition extended to animals, such as a goring ox (Ex. 21:28-32), or an uncovered pit (Ex. 21:33-34). If an ox gored a person, it had to be killed; if the ox had been guilty of such behavior in the past and had not been killed, and it now killed someone, then both the ox and its owner had to die. However, if the owner kept a dangerous ox penned up, then the person who became gored in an instance of trespass was himself the guilty party. An excavation should be covered or fenced to eliminate liability. Trespass thereafter was the fault of the victim. Thus, there was a duty to protect friends and neighbors who came to one's home or land, but the liability did not include trespassers or guests who entered a fenced pasture with a dangerous bull therein.

Laws of liability are thus *laws of responsibility*. They declare that a man is responsible for his acts, his possessions, and for his failures, negligences, and omissions. To be *responsible* means literally to be *answerable*. Since it is God who gives the law, it means we are answerable to Him for what we do to ourselves and to our fellow men, to our neighbor. Cain was thus answerable to God for his murder of his brother Abel.

*Responsibility* is a religious, a theological, idea. Without the God of Scripture, the idea of responsibilty breaks down. When every man becomes his own god, then man is not responsible, because a god

---

1. George Horowitz: *The Spirit of Jewish Law*, p. 123.

350

answers to no one and to nothing. All things answer to a god.

As a result, under humanism, man assumes that the world owes him all things, because, as the center of life, all things are responsible to him. There is thus a *total liability* to the man-god; in Scripture, man is totally liable to the God who created him, but his responsibility to other men is not total; it is a *legal responsibility*, i.e., one spelled out by God's law and therefore under limits. *Legal liability* in Scripture is a *limited liability*, but not limited in the modern humanistic sense but in the Biblical sense by the word of God, God's law. The great statement of limited liability in Scripture is Exodus 21:23-25:

And if any mischief follow, then thou shalt give life for life,
Eye for eye, tooth for tooth, hand for hand, foot for foot,
Burning for burning, wound for wound, stripe for stripe.

The limitation on liability which God imposes is a restraint on man. Man's desire for vengeance, or man's estimation of his damages, is restrained by God's requirement that the restitution or liability be commensurate with the damages.

Because man sees himself as his own god, he puts an infinite value on himself. Humanistic courts continually award higher and higher damage awards in liability cases because of this fact. This is why Exodus 21:20-27 is so offensive to moderns. Scripture is here discussing slaves (apparently foreigners and unbelievers) and liability. The law here has two assumptions: *first*, the slave is a human being, a creature of God, and a master is accountable to God for his treatment of a slave. The slave is God's creature, and both slave and master are God's property and under God's law. *Second*, the slave is also, in a secondary sense, another man's property. If the slave is injured or maimed by an angry master, he must be granted his freedom. If the slave is murdered by his master, the master must be punished. However, if the slave is struck, lingers a day or two, and then dies, there is no punishment; the master has been punished by the loss of his money invested in the slave.

It must be noted, *first*, that this law functions practically to inhibit brutality towards a slave: injuries resulted in the slave's freedom, and manslaughter or murder in punishment for the master. The master was thus an assured loser if he injured the slave corporally. Such a law inhibited the mistreatment of slaves.

*Second*, it is very obvious that there is a variable principle of liability. The liability for injuring a slave, one's own slave, is different from the liability for a freeman, and the implication is clear that it will differ among freemen. We cannot place the same liability upon, for example, a broken leg for a drunken derelict and for a Christian leader in some area of activity. In either case, there is an *inescapable* liability; both are God's property, and we are accountable in both cases to the Lord. God, however, in His law makes a clear distinction between one man and another in terms of their character and importance. Modern man is at this point schizophrenic; he does not like to admit that there is a difference in the loss of a good private's life, and a good general's life; in theory, he denies the difference on religious (humanistic) grounds; in everyday practice, he affirms it; in weighing his own life against others, modern man emphatically holds to the difference.

*Third*, while there is a difference between men, and hence a variable liability for injuries (but not for murder), there is a common responsibility to God. Any injury to any man means accountability to God. This applies to direct action, i.e., in striking and injuring a man, or in carelessness, as with a parapet, a pit, or an animal. All men and things are God's property, and we are accountable in all things to Him.

*Fourth*, liability is not only for injuries but for loss of time, so that an injured man is not only compensated for the cost of his injuries, but also for the loss of his time, depending on the value of that time (Ex. 21:18-19).

If liability ceases to be a theological concept, it becomes an instrument of social and class warfare. It is then used by the rich to rob the poor, or by the poor to rob the rich. History is full of examples of both.

When liability is theologically grounded, it rests on the priority of God's order and the restoration thereof. Man's liability for his rebellion against God is the death penalty. Christ's atonement means that restitution is made and our restoration effected. We are therefore to live responsibly and to work for a society in which the liability law concept works, not to decapitalize society nor to rend it asunder by injustice and class war, but to prevent troubles and conflicts, and to effect restitution and restoration. *Liability* presupposes damage or potential damage: its purpose must be to limit that damage, effect restitution, and make clear the priority of God's claims and order.

To summarize, humanism, *first* of all, sees man as god. A god is not responsible, i.e., answerable to anyone else; others are responsible to a god. *Second*, the implication of this is that man, as a would-be god, seeks escape from responsibility. His goal is to have no liability. Practically, he gains as a first step limited liability laws which limit his responsibility for his actions. *Third*, because of his claim to be god, the humanist demands unlimited liability from others to himself. In fact, he sees the universe as totally liable to him. He demands all and gives nothing unless compelled to. The consequences of humanism's view of liability are legal and social chaos.

Scripture, on the other hand, declares *first* that God alone is God. There is none other, no other gods beside Him. *Second*, the universe and man are totally responsible to the Lord. This means total and unlimited liability. *Third, all* liability to men is limited by God's law. We cannot set the limits of liability; this God alone can do and does, and Exodus 21:23-25 sets forth the basic principle thereof. *Fourth*, we can therefore make *no* limitation on our due responsibilities; God alone establishes the limits. *Fifth*, God alone establishes not only the limits of liability, but the nature of liability and responsibility. Man's way is injustice.

## 78

## "THOU SHALT NOT DESTROY"

In the laws of warfare, it is stated

> When thou shalt besiege a city a long time, in making war against it to take it, thou shalt not destroy the trees thereof by forcing an axe against them: for thou mayest eat of them, and thou shalt not cut them down (for the tree of the field is man's life) to employ them in the siege:
> Only the trees which thou knowest that they be not trees for meat, thou shalt destroy and cut them down; and thou shalt build bulwarks against the city that maketh war with thee, until it be subdued. (Deut. 20:19-20)

In understanding this law, we must remember that it is case law, i.e., a specific example which illustrates a broad principle. It is necessary then to note, *first*, that the ancient Hebraic interpretation of this law is that it represents a general principle, a prohibition against wanton destruction, in particular of anything protected by God's law and of use to man. This prohibition included not only an enemy's possessions, or a neighbor's, but one's own. This interpretation has continued in Judaism, and it has been greatly stressed through the centuries by the rabbis, as witness R. Ganzfried who declared:

> Just as one must be careful not to destroy one's body, not to impair or injure it... so must one be careful not to destroy, impair or damage one's property. Whoever breaks a utensil, or tears a garment, or destroys food or drink, or filthies them, or throws money away so that it is lost, or who spoils any other thing that is fit for human enjoyment transgresses the command: Thou shalt not destroy.[1]

This statement is correct as to details although humanistic in its emphasis. The test is not "human enjoyment" but God's property rights. God permits the use of non-fruit trees; He does not permit the use of fruit trees to build bulwarks, nor their destruction during war (or in enmity) under any circumstances.

*Second*, the fruit tree represents sown land, cultivated areas, as against the wilderness, and it is therefore protected because it represents an area of dominion, of the subduing of the earth. There is, however, no blanket call for the destruction of wilderness trees: they too are God's property.

---

1. Horowitz: *The Spirit of Jewish Law*, p. 124.

Necessity, whether of war or peace, can lead to their use. However, wanton destruction anywhere is banned. "Thou shalt not destroy" is a basic principle everywhere.

*Third,* total war is prohibited, either against man or against his land. From Calvin to the present, many have rendered what the KJV translates "for the tree of the field is man's life etc." as "Are the trees of the field people, defenders of the city, that you should lay siege to them?" We can declare war against men, but not against the earth, nor against God, without incurring His radical judgment. As far as is known, no similar law has ever existed apart from Biblical law. It is in particular significant that, on the brink of a war to destroy the Canaanites totally, Israel was still prohibited from warring against God's earth.

*Fourth,* even in wartime, God's purpose, the furthering of life for the purposes of godly dominion, must be obeyed. The fruit trees cannot be cut down, because the men can eat the fruit during the siege as well as later. A fruit tree is a continuing wealth and legacy; it is a form of dominion. The earth yields its increase to man through the tree, and therefore any wanton destruction of such a tree is a denial of the priority of God's purpose. Not even so bitter a warfare as that waged against Canaan could justify such a destruction of the earth's wealth. The riches of the ungodly are to enrich the Kingdom of God. Isaiah 61:6 declares, "Ye shall eat the riches of the Gentiles, and in their glory shall ye boast yourselves." The wealth of the world is God's property, and to be our inheritance in Him.

*Fifth,* beyond this there is God's concern for His creation, for animals and birds. His law reminds us to be mindful of them. After the gleaners take their fill, the wild animals are entitled to eat in the sabbath year (Ex. 23:10, 11; Lev. 25:3-7). Even the animal is worthy of his hire and must not be muzzled when treading out the corn (Deut. 25:4; I Tim. 5:18). Domestic animals are entitled to the Sabbath rest (Ex. 20:8-10; Deut. 5:12-14). "A righteous man regardeth the life of his beast" (Prov. 12:10), and "the good shepherd giveth his life for the sheep" (John 10:11). An animal in distress must be aided (Ex. 23:5; Deut. 22:4). Stray animals were to be returned to their owners (Ex. 23:4). The life of a bird specie was protected (Deut. 22:6), and so on.

God's concern is not only with and for man, although man is His appointed vice-gerunt and His image bearer. God is mindful of the sparrows of the field (Matt. 10:29-31).

*Sixth,* man cannot therefore use the earth, its animal creation, *nor himself,* apart from the purposes of God. God has created all things for His purpose and glory, and nothing can legitimately be used or viewed apart from His purpose. Hence, "thou shalt not destroy" means that God's purpose must prevail, and that we use all things and ourselves only in obedience to Him.

*Seventh*, "Thou shalt not destroy" has as its positive form, "Thou shalt plant," or, "Thou shalt build." The garden of Eden, planted by God, is to be the model for all the earth. Man must exercise dominion and subdue the earth. This is not done by the destruction of any good thing, such as fruit trees. However, neither is it done by negation. It is done by obedience to God's creation mandate, by the exercise of dominion. This can mean war against God's enemies, but even in war, the fruit tree, an example of increase and harvest, gains priority over the immediate demands of warfare.

Man too often assumes that mere negation is virtue. Thus Christians too often equate Christian action with fighting vice, immodesty, heresy, and the like. Conservatives equate their faith too often with fighting liberalism, socialism, lawlessness, and the like. Liberals and radicals in turn commonly equate their faith with a war against wealth, against poverty, discrimination, inequality, and so on. However, we can have full possession of a good field and spend fifty years fighting weeds therein, and make little progress. At the first opportunity, the weeds will be there again in full force, or, by that time, the field may be dead and sterile. A more productive course is to plant the field in fruit trees and husband them. The weeds then will be a minor matter in comparison to the task of gaining and developing an increase from the earth.

The requirement that we refrain from destroying even an enemy's fruit trees turns our attention beyond the warfare of the moment to the basic task. When men and nations forget this, God and history pass them by.

There was a time when this law was a very familiar one. Most of us were brought up to regard waste and wanton destruction as sin. For most of us, the Biblical context was gone, although some of us had these words cited to us, "Thou shalt not destroy." Without the God-centered context, however, this once-basic teaching eroded and largely disappeared. Its remnants in the conservation and ecology movements are often essentially suicidal in their concerns, not godly, and hence their unhappy emphases.

## 79

## "THOU SHALT NOT STAND IDLY BY"

The Jewish translation of the Masoretic text (1917) renders Leviticus 19:16 "Thou shalt not go up and down as a talebearer among thy people; neither shalt thou stand idly by the blood of thy neighbour: I am the LORD." The various Christian translators have given the second half of this verse a more active sense than the word "idly" conveys. They have seen it as related to Exodus 23:7, "Keep thee far from a false matter; and the innocent and righteous slay thou not: for I will not justify the wicked." In favor of the Jewish version is the age-old Jewish tradition that non-involvement in a case of an attack upon an innocent man is meant by the text. The first half of the verse, by condemning gossip, suggests an active assault upon a man's reputation, but the nature of gossip, being idle viciousness, can also support the Jewish interpretation. Most clearly, however, Psalm 50:16-22 echoes and expands Leviticus 19:16, speaking of both talebearing and standing by idly (which implies consent) when men are robbed:

> But unto the wicked God saith, What hast thou to do to declare my statutes, or that thou shouldest take my covenant in thy mouth?
> Seeing thou hatest instruction, and castest my words behind thee.
> When thou sawest a thief, then thou consentedst with him, and hast been partaker with adulterers.
> Thou givest thy mouth to evil, and thy tongue frameth deceit.
> Thou sittest and speakest against thy brother; thou slanderest thine own mother's son.
> These things hast thou done, and I kept silence; thou thoughtest that I was altogether such an one as thyself: but I will reprove thee, and set them in order before thine eyes.
> Now consider this, ye that forget God, lest I tear you in pieces, and there be none to deliver.

God here addresses nominal believers who recite God's word, engage in official or formal worship, and claim to be within the covenant fold. When these people saw a thief, they were not only silent about his act but they were drawn to him by an unspoken respect. H. C. Leupold renders verse 18a, "When you saw a thief you liked his company."[1] *God recognizes no neutrality*: to be "non-involved" in stopping a thief or a murderer is to be involved in their crime and to consent to and like their

---

1. H. C. Leupold: *Exposition of the Psalms*, p. 395.

357

person. These false believers have their "portion" or "partaking" with adulterers, i.e., their "participation, common interest, communion."[2] Such people are involved: they slander or "air a blow" against their godly brother rather than speak out about an act of theft or adultery. They may claim to be innocent of the actual acts of theft or adultery, but in God's eyes they are emphatically guilty. With their mouth, they slander the righteous, and with their refusal to act to defend the righteous and God's righteousness, they manifest their essentially evil nature. Tale-bearing is thus linked with theft (of a man's good name) and with murder (of a man's reputation), and the tale-bearer is shown as happiest in the company of thieves and adulterers. Such men recite God's word in worship; in their gossip, and in their partiality to evil men, they manifest their true faith: they stand idly by while God's law is broken. Their mouths are given to evil, and their tongues to deceit (Ps. 51:19), because their lives are in essence evil, and their involvement is therefore with evil.

The Jewish translations thus bring out the seeming non-involvement of men who stand idly by while crimes are committed. The Christian translators stress the lack of neutrality in such acts: non-involvement in the defense of God's law and people is involvement with those who are evil. Both versions of Leviticus 19:16 thus bring out an important aspect of this law.

We need to declare therefore that none can stand idly by, because God recognizes no such thing as non-involvement or neutrality where He and His law are concerned. All men are involved in God's law: they are covenant-keepers or covenant-breakers with God.

Alexander renders verse 22, "Oh consider this, forgetters of God, lest I rend and there be no deliverer."[3] The forgetters of God are those who remember with envious pleasure and thereby active participation the workers of iniquity.

As a consequence of Leviticus 19:16, the Hebraic legal tradition developed the law of pursuer and pursued. It requires every witness to come to the aid of a victim of an assault, theft, or criminal act, and to take action to stop or arrest the criminal. While Talmudic interpretations of the law of pursuer and pursued embroidered the law with a variety of qualifications, the law nonetheless stood. It entered into Western legal traditions, where it has had a similarly checkered history.

In spite of this, Western law, where not too heavily infected by humanism, holds a man responsible within limits for a crime committed by another in his presence. The test of responsibility for such an offense is whether or not he could have rendered aid or prevented the commission of the crime. However, Western law is generally lax in this matter.

---

2. J. A. Alexander, *The Psalms* p. 228.
3. *Ibid.*, p. 229.

Our Lord made clear the meaning of the requirement, "Thou shalt not stand idly by," in the Parable of the Good Samaritan (Luke 10:30-37). In terms of Psalm 50:16-22, He indicts the religious leaders for passing by the victim. Our Lord has in mind both this psalm and the Hebraic interpretation of Leviticus 19:16.

Equally to the point is the fact that this parable is told to a lawyer, an expert in the law, who was trying to "tempt" Jesus (Luke 10:25). Our Lord in return indicts the religious leaders who are experts in the law but stand idly by or pass by while their neighbor is assaulted or in need, and God's law broken.

The priests and Levites whom our Lord indicted were experts in the law and strong for legislation. Like our modernists, neo-evangelicals, and pseudo-Calvinists, they were ready to pass laws and to feel that they had thereby done their duty. The answer is not in legislation; the law already exists, God's law. Humanistic social legislation is pseudo-involvement as a cover for a radical non-involvement. It involves a hatred of both God and man, and its answer is to manage people, not to be a good neighbor. Hence the counsel of our Lord is to do as the Good Samaritan did: "Go, and do thou likewise" (Luke 10:37). Do not stand idly by; social legislation is a mask in most cases for standing idly by.

The roots of this evil of standing by are in false religion. A theology influenced by neo-platonism will pull away from this world and any godly responsibility for it. It will develop false eschatologies which will deny the requirement of godly dominion and reconstruction. Such eschatologies will turn salvation into escape rather than victory, and will regard all standing by and passing by as a virtue.

Indeed, all too many churchmen today on the one hand substitute legislation for action, and, on the other, regard action as a surrender of the Gospel.

Our Lord did not teach us that the Good Samaritan went home to work for better social legislation to control problems of crime, poverty, disease, medical care, or the like. Neither did He teach us that it was a virtue on the part of the priest and Levite to avoid social problems. But many churchmen advocate both these forms of passing by.

**80**

## ONE LAW

Earlier this week, I read an amusing column in the daily paper and found it so delightful I decided to read it at the table to my wife, Dorothy, and to Ed Powell; the three of us usually laugh at the same things. This time, however, they responded as though I had read them a particularly tragic funeral notice. I put down the paper with some disappointment, and remarked "Please don't cry over it." The next day Chalcedon's secretary, Mrs. Arlene Gollnick, picked up the paper and laughed with delight over the column.

God has created us differently. Each of us is unique and separate, having particular aptitudes unlike all others. We are all unequal, because we are all different. Any attempt to equalize men runs counter to the uniqueness of each person, different from all others in all his being. We can neither equalize persons nor races, and we must abandon the mathematical terminology of equal and unequal in dealing with the diversities of mankind. The diversity is of God's ordination, and its purpose is His, and for His kingdom's glory. Wherever men begin to talk the language of humanistic equality, they at the same time bring into focus humanistic inequality, and vice versa. A society which stresses either creates an antithesis which brings that which it condemns into sharp focus as an aspect of basic reality.

The focus in Scripture is not on man but on God and His law. The differences among men are real and are of God's creation. I am not permitted by Scripture to make my sense of humor, my race, my tastes and aptitudes, or any like thing, a criterion whereby men can be judged. On the other hand, I am not permitted to set aside the cross of Christ and the enscriptured word and law of the triune God as the necessary standard of judgment. At this point, all men are equal. None of their unique differences matter as they stand before the Lord. With respect to their salvation, all who have "put on Christ...are all one in Christ Jesus" (Gal. 3:27-28). This oneness is with respect to justification: Christ is our only ground, and all are equal in this respect. Where sanctification and our eternal reward are concerned, we are again different (I Cor. 3:11-15). However, we are again equal in relation to God's law: all men, covenant men and aliens or strangers to the covenant, are equally under God's law. According to Numbers 15:15-16,

One ordinance shall be both for you of the congregation, and also for the stranger that sojourneth with you, an ordinance for ever in your generations: as ye are, so shall the stranger be before the LORD.

One law and one manner shall be for you, and for the stranger that sojourneth with you.

These verses must be read in the context in which they appear, laws of sacrifice (Num. 15:1-14). Their meaning is this: the relationship of Israel to God was one of privilege, the privileges of grace. Israel saw itself as set apart from other nations. In matters of justice, there had to be, indeed, one law for all. However, here the emphasis on one law is given a sharp stress. Even with respect to religious privileges and matters of the covenant, the alien who shared the faith had the same access to the altar as the native-born Israelite. The covenant is a covenant of grace, not of race. The differences among men have no standing before God. "One law shall be to him that is homeborn, and unto the stranger that sojourneth among you" (Ex. 12:49; cf. Num. 15:29). *Where God's grace is operative, human differences are irrelevant; where God's law governs in the whole of creation, no other factor can govern.* The religious privilege of the covenant people is thus not of Abraham nor of Israel, but of God; its origin is not in blood or birth, but in sovereign grace. Therefore the laws of the God of sovereign grace can alone govern men.

This requirement that God's law over-rule all human differences is repeatedly stated:

Ye shall do no unrighteousness in judgment: thou shalt not respect the person of the poor, nor honour the person of the mighty: but in righteousness shalt thou judge thy neighbour. (Lev. 19:15)

Ye shall not respect persons in judgment; but ye shall hear the small as well as the great; ye shall not be afraid of the face of man; for the judgment is God's: and the cause that is too hard for you, bring it unto me, and I will hear it. (Deut. 1:17)

Thou shalt not wrest judgment; thou shalt not respect persons, neither take a gift: for a gift doth blind the eyes of the wise, and pervert the words of the righteous. (Deut. 16:19; cf. Prov. 24:23, 28:21)

This emphasis on one law, however, requires a God-centered society. If the society is to any degree humanistic, it will create an equal-unequal antithesis. It will talk of one law for all, and it will create radical inequalities. Because it makes man the basis for a common ground, it runs into serious problems, because the reality of man evades categorization in terms of either equality or inequality. The very real and great differences among men favor those who stress inequality. The very real and common needs of men for justice favor those who stress equality. Both emphases stretch man out on a Procrustean bed and do him a radical injustice. For a society to stress either equality or inequality is to create an antithesis whereby the dissidents are pushed into the opposing camp. The equalitarian society develops a radical elitism, and the anti-equalitarian society begets a revolutionary equalitarianism. A false problem creates false answers.

A practical example of unequal law in an equalitarian society was apparent in an incident on July 25, 1976, Sunday night at the White House, Washington, D. C. An intruder carrying a three foot section of pipe was shot and killed after climbing a White House fence and failing to heed orders to halt.[1]

The significance of this killing is far-reaching. If any ordinary citizen shot and killed an intruder into his garden, he would be arrested for murder. In one instance, a woman, at home alone, shot and killed an intruder who broke into her house and then into her locked bedroom. Because the man was unarmed (i.e., had no gun, only a knife, something she did not know), she was arrested on a possible murder charge. Apparently, she should have allowed herself to be raped, and asked if he intended to kill her, before pulling the trigger. The point is clear: there is one law for the kings in the White House, another for the people. But if it is right to protect the president's life, it is right to protect the citizens' life in the same way. If it is wrong to protect the citizen's life by killing an intruder, it is wrong to protect the president's life by killing someone who climbs over the fence. Where a difference is made, and it is legal to shoot an intruder into the White House lawns, but not a housebreaker into a citizen's home, we have, not God's law, but tyranny.

Tyranny does not mean oppression necessarily. Tyranny in its root meaning is rule without God's law. Such a rule may have an indulgent purpose. It is, however, evil in essence, and finally oppressive. Tyranny is implicit in all humanism, because it is rule without God's law. Antinomian churches are also instruments of tyranny.

Humanism cannot give justice, because it cannot establish responsibility. Is it heredity or environment? If humanism is inequalitarian, it establishes guilt in terms of race or class; some kinds of people are by nature seen as more irresponsible and hence of a lower breed. If humanism is equalitarian, then it accounts for the condition of slum-dwellers by blaming landlords, capitalism, society, and anything but the slum-dweller, because it must account for the obvious difference between the slum-dweller and the property owner.

Because in both cases God's law is set aside and denied, the *moral* factor in assessing responsibility is either denied or prejudged as belonging to a class of men only.

A God-centered society will recognize that the essential differences

---

1. *Los Angeles Herald-Examiner*, Monday, July 26, 1976. p 1, "White House Guards Kill Intruder."

between men are in terms of God's covenant of grace and His law. God's law alone is truly *moral* law, because good and evil are determined by God's law alone. God's law establishes the grounds or basis of social order, and it is the principle of discrimination.

Scripture gives us one God, one Savior, one word and law, and one way of salvation and sanctification.

## 81

## ONE LORD

On the day of Pentecost, St. Peter, in declaring the resurrection and its meaning to the people of Jerusalem, summed it up thus: "Therefore let all the house of Israel know assuredly, that God hath made that same Jesus, whom ye have crucified, both Lord and Christ" (Acts 2:36). To declare Jesus as the Christ meant to set forth the title of Jesus as the annointed Redeemer-King. But this was not all: Jesus is also the *Lord*. "God hath made that same Jesus...Lord."

The word *Lord* is so freely and unthinkingly used that its meaning is largely lost, and it has become a mere title. The term, however, is central to an understanding of Scripture and of Jesus Christ. St. Paul tells us that, because of the faithfulness of God's Son, Christ or Messiah-King Jesus, and His obedience "unto death, even the death of the cross,"

> Wherefore God also hath highly exalted him, and given him a name which is above every name:
> That at the name of Jesus every knee should bow, of things in heaven, and things in earth, and things under the earth;
> And that every tongue should confess that Jesus Christ is Lord, to the glory of God the Father (Phil. 2:9-11).

Christ is always Lord, in all places and times. But this is not all. *All men*, without exception, shall confess Christ as Lord *before* the end of history. Some will do so in joyful faith, others because the government of all things is in godly hands and all must acknowledge Christ's Lordship. Much of Isaiah's prophecies are given to setting forth this triumph of God, and St. Paul here quotes Isaiah 45:23. Calvin held this lordship to apply to all of history as well as eternity:

> The kingdom of Christ is on such a footing, that it is every day growing and making improvement, while at the same time perfection is not yet attained, nor will be until the final day of reckoning. Thus both things hold true—that all things are now subject to Christ, and that this subjection will, nevertheless, not be complete until the day of resurrection, because that which is now only begun will then be completed. Hence, it is not without reason that this prophecy is applied in different ways at different times, as also all the other prophecies, which speak of the reign of Christ, do not restrict it to one particular time, but describe it in its entire course.[1]

---

1. John Calvin: *Commentaries on the Epistles of Paul the Apostle to the Phillippians, Colossians, and Thessalonians*, p. 62f. Grand Rapids, Michigan: Eerdmans, 1957.

The term *lord, kurios* in the Greek, means having power (*kuros*), or authority. It means not only one who is a God-King, but a conquering God-King, a warrior who is triumphant and certain in His power, authority, and kingdom.

With this in mind, Scott's comments throw great light on St. Paul's words:

> It needs to be remembered that in ancient thought a peculiar value was attached to a name. The person himself was supposed to be somehow present in his name, so that in uttering it one brought oneself under the other's influence. A soldier took his oath in the name of Caesar, and thereby became Caesar's man. A Christian convert was baptized in the name of Jesus, and thus yielded himself to Jesus' will and secured his protection. So Paul assumes that the new name bestowed on Christ carried with it an active power, in virtue of which he had a divine authority....
> (vvs. 10-11)...Here at last he reveals the new name which is above all others. Christ, by way of his humiliation, has won his place as universal *Lord.* Three times in the course of his epistles Paul quotes the formula "Jesus is Lord," and each time with a special solemnity (Rom. 19:9; I Cor. 12:3; and here). There can be little doubt that he repeats the confession which every convert made at his baptism....
> In calling Jesus "Lord" they had acknowledged that he was supreme. A day would come when all things in God's creation would join with the church on earth in submitting to this Lord, *to the glory of God the Father.*[2]

The modern church and the modern Christian cannot confess that "Jesus is Lord" and, at the same time, deny Him His victory and lordship over all things. Ephesians 4:5 speaks of "One Lord, one faith, one baptism." This means that there is only one acceptable way of salvation, only one true faith in every country, place, realm, or sphere of thought, and only one Lord in every realm. Caesar and the devil do not rule in politics, autonomous man in economics, and anarchistic man in the arts. One Lord rules every realm, and He rules them totally. His sovereign purpose governs the rise and fall of His enemies. He allows the tares to ripen for His own purposes, not because He cannot destroy them. He allows the evils implicit in man's rebellion to develop to their logical end and become their own destruction. In all the processes of history, He alone is Lord, and it is His purpose alone which is fulfilled and stands.

To be a Christian means to look at our present problems and distresses, as well as the course of history around us, and to declare, "Jesus is Lord." He alone governs, conquers, and prevails. Not only eternity, but time and history know only *one Lord.*

We become polytheists if we confess Christ as Lord for the future only, or eternity only, and turn over vast areas of history to the devil.

---

2. Ernest F. Scott: "Phillippians," in *The Interpreter's Bible*, vol. 11, p. 50f.

Post-millennialism is implicit in the confession, "Jesus is Lord."

To declare "Jesus is Lord," and to approve of abortion, or to deny the validity of what Scripture says concerning husbands and wives, or to limit Christ's lordship to spiritual things, or to a millennial time or to heaven, is to deny our confession.

His name "is above every name," i.e., it is above them because He alone is *Lord*. To name Jesus *Lord* means to acknowledge no other gods, powers, rulers, or possibilities before Him.

Those in our day who hold that, in terms of their premillennial thinking, they must deny Christ's lordship until the millennium, are more logical than most but they are emphatically not Biblical. The heart of the Christian confession, and the original baptismal creed, is that "Jesus is Lord." Any denial of this is a departure from the faith.

The beginning and end of the Christian faith is the confession, "Jesus is Lord." Without this confession, God's sovereignty is denied. There is then no sovereign grace, no sovereign power, only the demonic forces of a world not really under the control of the triune God. Such a faith is not Christianity.

Whatever its shortcomings in other areas, the early church recognized the significance of declaring "Jesus is Lord." It meant the total kingship and authority of Jesus Christ in and for every sphere of life. It meant for them, despite the cost of their own lives in the battle, the certainty of His triumph. Not Caesar but Christ is Lord. In *The Martyrdom of Polycarp*, we read that the Irenarch Herod and his father Nicetes tried to persuade Polycarp to continue as a Christian but to declare "Caesar is Lord." They asked, "What harm is there in saying, Caesar is Lord, and in sacrificing, with the other ceremonies observed on such occasions, and so make sure of safety?" Later, before his death, the proconsul also attempted to dissuade Polycarp, who declared, "Eighty and six years have I served Him, and He never did me any injury: how can I blaspheme my King and my Saviour?"[3] The confidence of the martyrs was in the lordship of Jesus Christ. The imperial power of Rome quite rightly saw the declaration of Christ's lordship as the potential overthrow of Roman lordship. We should manifest at least as much wisdom as the Romans and declare "Jesus is Lord" in the confidence that, "If God be for us, who can be against us?" (Rom. 8:31). Only such a faith will make us "more than conquerors" (Rom. 8:37) under Christ the Lord.

---

3. "The Martyrdom of Polycarp," chs. VIII, IX, in *Ante-Nicene Christian Library*, vol. I, *The Writings of the Apostolic Fathers*, p. 87f. Edinburgh, Scotland: T. & T. Clark, 1867.

# 82

## THE PATTERN OF GOVERNMENT

We have in Exodus 18:13-26 an interesting account of the origin of Israel's form of civil government.

And it came to pass on the morrow, that Moses sat to judge the people and the people stood by Moses from the morning unto the evening.

And when Moses' father in law saw all that he did to the people, he said, What is this thing that thou doest to the people? why sittest thou thy self alone, and all the people stand by thee from morning unto even?

And Moses said unto his father in law, Because the people come unto me to inquire of God:

When they have a matter, they come unto me; and I judge between one and another, and I do make them know the statutes of God, and his laws.

And Moses' father in law said unto him, The thing that thou doest is not good.

Thou wilt surely wear away, both thou, and this people that is with thee, for this thing is too heavy for thee; thou art not able to perform it thyself alone.

Hearken now unto my voice, I will give thee counsel, and God shall be with thee: Be thou for the people to God-ward, that thou mayest bring the causes unto God:

And thou shalt teach them ordinances and laws, and shalt shew them the way wherein they must walk, and the work that they must do.

Moreover thou shalt provide out of all the people able men, such as fear God, men of truth, hating covetousness; and place such over them, to be rulers of thousands, and rulers of hundreds, rulers of fifties, and rulers of tens:

And let them judge the people at all seasons: and it shall be, that every great matter they shall bring unto thee, but every small matter they shall judge: so shall it be easier for thyself, and they shall bear the burden with thee.

If thou shalt do this thing, and God command thee, so, then thou shalt be able to endure, and all this people shall also go to their place in peace.

So Moses hearkened to the voice of his father in law, and did all that he had said.

And Moses chose able men out of all Israel, and made them heads over the people, rulers of thousands, rulers of hundreds, rulers of fifties, and rulers of tens.

And they judged the people at all seasons: the hard causes they brought unto Moses, but every small matter they judged themselves.

The significance of this pattern of civil government has been discounted by many because the counsel came from Jethro, a Midianite priest, Moses' father-in-law. In appraising this text, however, we must remember, *first*, that Jethro was a faithful priest of God. Not only was Jethro's priesthood acceptable to God, but Jethro was the administering priest in sacrifices and a communion service, presiding over Aaron and the elders of Israel (Gen. 14:18), a survival of the original priesthood after the Flood. Abraham recognized the priority of Melchizedek (Gen. 14:19; Heb. 7:2-9); so Moses and Aaron recognized that of Jethro. Jethro's counsel was thus of the Lord. *Second*, Jethro asked Moses to confirm his counsel with God directly. In verse 19, "and God shall be with thee," can mean either that Jethro declared that his counsel was God's counsel, or, if translated, "that God may be with you," (as suggested by J. Coert Rylaarsdam,) that God's blessing would be with Moses only if he heeded Jethro's counsel. Again, verse 23 means that Moses was to seek God's confirmation of Jethro's counsel before acting. In Deuteronomy 1:3-18, Moses refers to this pattern of civil government without mentioning Jethro; the significant fact about this pattern is not Jethro's part in it but God's requirement.

*Third*, this pattern utilized an already existing family office, the eldership. The elders are mentioned *before* Jethro speaks, in Exodus 18:12. They were heads of families, clans, and tribes. The elders also apparently had a military leadership as well as other authorities prior to Jethro's counsel. At any rate, the basic institution in Scripture is the family, and this pattern of civil government requires the utilization of the family. The office of *elder* in Israel is thus basic to family, church, and state. It is a central part of Scripture's plan of government in several spheres of life.

*Fourth*, in verses 20 and 21 a few summary comments are made about the qualification of these elders of Israel. The judges of later years were probably and almost certainly elders. Elders were normally heads of clans, and they were the source of leadership in every area of life. They were also known as *fathers*, and were thus the Fathers of Israel. Both city and village were ruled by elders. Elders were the pool from whence all officers were drawn. At a later date, elders provided officers for the Sanhedrin and the synagogue. It is significant that St. Paul's counsel concerning the qualifications of an elder are written to Timothy, who was half-Greek, and who was laboring in a Gentile city. For Jewish Christians, such counsel (I Tim. 3:1-13) was not necessary; they already were thoroughly familiar with the meaning of eldership and its qualifications. Moreover, there is no reason to restrict Paul's counsel concerning the election of elders (or bishops) to the institution for worship. Paul's *church* is the Kingdom of God, the assembly of the redeemed. His counsel sets forth the requirements for eldership in every realm, church, state, school, etc.

*Fifth*, the function of Moses, or his successors, is as a supreme court under God. Moses' function was to set forth God's law in difficult cases. There was thus a gradation of courts, from tens, to hundreds, to thousands, and on up to the governing elder.

*Sixth*, at the beginning, Moses chose the elders (Ex. 18:21); later on, apparently other means were used. In I Samuel 8:5, we see the elders with power to set aside government by judges for government by a king. There was apparently some elective power, subject to certain qualifications. What Scripture does stress is the eldership as such. However, the New Testament witnesses to the fact the elections did take place (Acts 6:5) which were also called appointments (Acts 6:3), because the terms of qualification for office were God-given.

*Seventh*, the Bible does not set forth this pattern of rule as a fool-proof system. The history of Israel is one of repeated apostasies and corruption. The eldership and the decimal system of government did not prevent sin from working its will when the people were apostate. What it did do was to tie in rule with the pattern of family life on the one hand, and the very local community on the other. It was a plan of grass-roots government under God. It placed responsibilities for the major part of government on the family and the local community.

Does this system, apart from its divine sanctions, still have a validity? A pragmatic question is sometimes important to raise, because others will raise it.

Numerous instances of its validity can be cited. Police report that the Neighborhood Watch Program, where given even some degree of cooperation, works markedly to eliminate crime and increase local responsibility. Again, neighorhood Jewish groups in New York City have been effective in policing areas and in reducing a variety of problems. David Morris and Karl Hess, in *Neighborhood Power*, discuss a libertarian (or anarchist) attempt to create local self-government in a slum area; although the effort finally collapsed, because they had no remedy for sin, its achievements were all the same notable in setting forth the potentialities inherent in such a plan.

Scripture gives us the basic ingredients for success: the godly family, and the system of elders. The early Christians created new institutions, all aspects of the Kingdom of God: a state within the state, a church within the existing church of Israel (the Temple and synagogues), a welfare system (the diaconate) and much, much more.

Within recent weeks, I have learned of several instances of radically non-Christian persons who, when confronted with a crisis (a runaway wife, a promiscuous husband, etc.) went to a strong Christian acquaintance at work for counsel. They wanted justice, and they looked to a natural eldership for it. One of the reasons for the rapid growth of the early church was precisely the leadership and help it provided in a number of areas. It offered a better kingdom than that of Caesar.

# 83

## THE THRONE OF CRIME

The psalmist, in Psalm 94, speaks of God's superiority to all opposing forces and powers, and the necessary security of God's covenant people in that fact. The evil-doers destroy God's people. "They slay the widow and stranger, and murder the fatherless" (Ps. 94:6). The psalmist, as he stands against these evil rulers, declares,

> Who will rise up for me against the evildoers? or who will stand up for me against the workers of iniquity?
> Unless the LORD had been my help, my soul had almost dwelt in silence.
> When I said, My foot slippeth; thy mercy, O LORD, held me up.
> In the multitude of my thoughts within me thy comforts delight my soul.
> Shall the throne of iniquity have fellowship with thee, which frameth mischief by a law?
> They gather themselves together against the soul of the righteous, and condemn the innocent blood.
> But the LORD is my defence; and my God is the rock of my refuge.
> And he shall bring upon them their own iniquity, and shall cut them off in their own wickedness; yea, the LORD our God shall cut them off. (Ps. 94:16-23)

A key to understanding this psalm is verse 20, and the phrase, "the throne of iniquity." All too often popular interpretation sees this as Satan and thus takes the reference out of history. The meaning is historical. *Iniquity*, according to Alexander, is "more exactly, *crimes.*"[1] The "throne of crimes" which frames or contrives, plots, "mischief by a law" (or, by a statute, according to Leupold),[2] is man's civil and ecclesiastical agencies, as they set aside God's law by their humanistic presuppositions and thereby legalize their evil into law.

This means that every neglect of, and departure from, the law of God involves in some degree a part in framing mischief by law. Mischief, *amal* in the Hebrew, means labor, perverseness, misery. Man's lot is made harder and more laborious, more miserable and perverse, by any and every neglect of the whole word of God.

An example of this is cited by Molnar from a report on a meeting with Senator John V. Tunney, Friday, June 13, 1975, at the Grand Hotel,

---

1. J. A. Alexander: *The Psalms*, p. 393.
2. H. C. Leupold: *Exposition of the Psalms*, p. 674.

*Law and Society*

Anaheim, California. Spokesmen of the Right to Life Society, concerned because of legalized abortion, questioned the senator:

Q. Am I right, Senator: You would not steal?
T. No, I would not.
Q. But it is all right if I do?
T. No, if there is a law against it.
Q. But why should there be a law against it? It is my personal opinion that if there is more money in the other man's pocket than in mine, I can take at least his surplus.
T. Is there a law against it?
Q. There is at the moment but we could repeal it.
T. If you repeal the law then it would not be a crime.
Q. But would you be against it?
T. I think I would certainly be against it. I don't like thievery, but if there were no law against it it would not be a crime.
Q. Would you try to pass one?
T. If there were no law against thievery?
Q. Yes.
T. I think I probably would, yes.
Q. Well, there you are, pointing out to us an instance of your legislating your personal attitude.
T. But if the great majority of people in my state thought that thievery was perfectly all right, I am not sure that I would support such a law.

In such a perspective, truth is what the majority or the state says it is. Truth is then defined by man and is subordinate to man. Such a view is a logical application of the principle of sin, every man his own god, determining for himself what constitutes good and evil (Gen. 3:5). From this perspective of the fall, truth is only what man says it is, and its validity is limited to the occasion. We meet this view in current constitutionalism: a constitution has validity only for the time in which it is framed in the sense in which it is framed. Hence, its meaning must be continuously subject to revision and re-interpretation in terms of the truth of the moment. Man can never be bound, for such people, to a truth outside of himself.

The result of such a view of truth is a high arrogance in man, and in his approach to law. Courts today manifest a hesitation to deal with crime, having no truth concerning the matter, but no hesitation in asserting their own arrogant power. A minor example of this appeared in a Los Angeles, California, episode, according to a news report:

Rebuffed in his bid to gain county supervisor support for additional judicial officers, Los Angeles Municipal Court Presiding Judge Joseph R. Grillo has declared war on the county.

---

3. Thomas Molnar: *Authority and its Enemies*, p. 109f. New York: Arlington House, 1976.

First victim in what is apparently a battle between the power of contempt and the power of the purse is County Auditor Mark Bloodgood's deputy, James B. Czarnecki, who was arrested yesterday and charged with contempt for refusing Grillo's order to issue airline tickets.

The airline tickets were intended for Grillo and Judge James DiGiuseppe to fly to Sacramento Sunday to lobby for a state senate bill that would increase the size of the Los Angeles Municipal Court.

When original transportation requests were denied on advice of County Counsel John Larsen, Grillo prepared a court order, served it on Czarnecki at the auditor's office and arrested him when he refused to comply with it. . . .

"The court can't stand shackled or have to run to the CAO whenever something is needed," Grillo said.

"I have no time for red tape. Under the separation of powers, the court has the inherent power to control its operations; under the California rules, a presiding judge is required to supervise the administration and business of the court."

"When the presiding judge speaks," Grillo continued, "it is the court, and in my opinion the court must be represented in Sacramento Monday. No other opinion counts."

Farell's request that Grillo disqualify himself and assign the contempt issue to another judge was ordered stricken from the record.

"I have no prejudice in this matter," Grillo insisted. "In fact I have more concern and sympathy for this man than his bosses. If they will issue the plane ticket now, then I will dismiss charges."

However, Larsen and Bloodgood said they went to Grillo's chambers and volunteered to take Czarnecki's place.

But Larsen said the judge's only reaction was to order them out of his office for failing to knock before entering. Larsen branded the proceeding "an incredible travesty."

Larsen said he intends to refer the matter to the State Commission on Judicial Qualification, which has power to recommend removal of judges.[4]

Such zeal is rarely shown by judges today in dealing with crime. Significantly, the premise of Judge Grillo's argument is humanism to the core, the claim to radical autonomy. Whether called judicial independence, or academic freedom, the claim to a radical autonomy from responsibility and law is common to one area of life after another today.

Ironically, one of the county supervisors, Baxter Ward, offered a compromise solution to the conflict:

Supervisors Chairman Baxter Ward yesterday wrote a letter to the judge offering a compromise on the situation which would drop all

---

4. "County Employee Faces Jail for Obeying Boss's Orders," in the *Los Angeles Herald-Examiner*, Saturday, August 7, 1976. p. A-3.

action against Czarnecki as well as stop the possible review of the situation by a state judicial panel.

Ward said the judge should seek changes in the law to give jurists independence from budget decisions by the board and added that if the compromise was accepted, he would recommend that the supervisors also drop any plans for an inquiry into Grillo's actions.[5]

The idea of objective law and truth, it seems, must be sacrificed to preserve man's radical autonomy.

None of this should surprise us, however, when the real problem, the studied irrelevance of the churches, is considered. Note, for example, this statement by one organization:

> God made it clear to Paul that he was through with all the customs and ceremonies of the Law. They had all been fulfilled in Jesus Christ. "For Christ is the end of the Law for righteousness to every one that believeth."[6]

The arrest of Paul which followed Paul's presence in the Temple during the discharge of his Nazirite vow is then cited as an instance of compromise which brought trouble to Paul!

The premise of such thinking is false. *First*, in trying to quote Paul against Paul, the writer misinterprets Scripture. What Paul says in Romans 10:1-4 is that all attempts to gain righteousness before God, i.e., to be justified, are invalid. The only acceptable justification is through the atoning sacrifice of Jesus Christ, received by faith. *Second*, St. Paul's Nazirite vow had nothing to do with any attempt by Paul to gain righteousness or justification, nor were his actions in the least governed by a spirit of compromise. *Third*, the compromise is there, however, in this writer against compromise. He compromises and limits God and His word. He denies the validity of the law as the way of sanctification, which means that sanctification becomes then an exercise in self-righteousness.

One champion of sanctification without the law once made the statement to a "retreat" of pastors that "No man is seeking holiness who is not regularly weeping over his sins in hours of agonized prayer. We need weeping, praying pastors. Only then can we have holy congregations." There is nothing in the Bible which tells us that this is the way of sanctification. However, such opinions are commonplace. So important a theologian as Dr. Herman Hoeksema is cited thus in this respect:

> In this connection, I remember a remark which Rev. Hoeksema made from time to time both in his preaching and to us in school:

---

5. "Judge's Jurisdiction Faces Court Hearing," *Los Angeles Herald-Examiner*, Tuesday, August 10, 1976. p. A-3.

6. "The Failure of Compromise," Fundamental Evangelistic Association, Los Angeles, 1976.

"The most important good work which the child of God performs in this life is sorrow for sin."[7]

"The most important good work"! Shades of the Pharisees who fasted "twice in the week" to mourn their sins and were condemned as proud and self-righteous by our Lord (Luke 18:12). While young, I attended a "prayer retreat" for pastors, invited or taken by another pastor, not knowing what I was getting into. I heard more caterwauling about sins by graceless pastors who believed "sorrow for sin" was a good work before God than I believed possible. I realized at once that, under the same name, we belonged to different religions.

The net result of all such religious activity is a retreat from responsibility and a surrender of the world, law, and society to the devil. It is a license to evil-doers, to humanists, to frame "mischief by a law." "The throne of iniquity," or of crimes, with which God cannot have fellowship, includes not only the humanistic law-makers but all churchmen who surrender the realm of law to them. Law-making is the prerogative of God alone. Men can apply His law, administer it, and work out its implications, but they can neither create law, nor give freedom to others to do so, without sin.

Proverbs 25:26 speaks of the evil of compromise. "A righteous man falling down before the wicked is as a troubled fountain, and a corrupt spring." Those who compromise the word of God, or limit it, become corrupted or poisoned springs. They convey death, not life.

---

7. H. Hanko, "Letter to Timothy," in *The Standard Bearer*, vol. LII, no. 19, August 1, 1976.

## 84

## ONE FAITH

One of the familiar passages of Scripture is Ephesians 4:4-6. It is also one which is all too often read with an ecclesiastical perspective. According to St. Paul,

> There is one body, and one Spirit, even as ye are called in one hope of your calling:
> One Lord, one faith, one baptism,
> One God and Father of all, who is above all, and through all, and in you all.

The clergy, with their institutional mentality, have too often taught the laity that the church is spoken of here. Bishop Westcott was wiser: he saw these sentences as a statement of "the unity of the Christian Society."[1] More plainly stated, St. Paul speaks of the Kingdom of God. Baptism is more than ecclesiastical in its implications. Baptism cannot be read as merely entrance into the church: it means fellowship with Jesus Christ. "For as many of you as have been baptized into Christ have put on Christ" (Gal. 3:27). Baptism is into Christ, into the new creation and membership in Christ's Kingdom. It is a mark of citizenship whereby we confess one Lord and one faith.

The one faith the Christian Society proclaims is that "Jesus is Lord."[2] "No man can say that Jesus is the Lord, but by the Holy Ghost" (I Cor. 12:3). To say that Jesus is Lord is to assert His Crown Rights over every domain of life; it means that there is no area or sphere of life and thought which is not under the absolute lordship of Jesus Christ.

*One faith* does not mean therefore that we have a theology for the church but no theology for law, education, politics, economics, the arts and sciences, medicine, and all things else. *One faith* means precisely that the Kingdom of God being total in its sway, the word of God governs all things. Whenever and wherever a theology for every sphere is not developed, then and there we have a denial of the *one faith*. We have then an implicit polytheism.

Polytheism is exactly what most churches, with their eschatologies of defeat, preach to their congregations. They speak of a beautiful but weak

---

1. B. F. Westcott: *Saint Paul's Epistle to the Ephesians*, p. 58. Grand Rapids, Michigan: Eerdmans, (1906) 1952.
2. *Idem.*

Christ who now rules the church but little else; in the "sweet bye and bye," He will rule more, but not now. Man is his own god in all other realms. The universe is an open do-it-yourself realm, where many gods compete, and each carves out a small niche for his own private universe. The church thus preaches not one faith but a world full of faiths as options. There is one faith for the church, another for politics, another for economics, and so on. Not surprisingly, the church *courts* people, courts the little gods to come to Jesus and to honor Him as another god in a private realm. It has no sovereign word of God for every area of life and for every man.

The logical conclusion of such a faith is existential theology. For Karl Barth, Reinhold Niebuhr, and others, Christ is not risen in the world of matter, in historical time, but in the world of faith. Crudely but plainly stated, it means that, if I accept Christ, He is risen for me. This is the logical conclusion of Arminianism and existentialism: the sovereign man "resurrects" Christ at will!

Too commonly, the expectation of the church is that the Christian will be an honest, witnessing man outside of the church. He is thus seen at best as a missionary out in an alien world, summoning people to come into the safe harbor of the convent-church. But the Christian is to be an equipped soldier and conqueror, a man who applies Christ's crown rights to every domain of life as the only valid principle thereof. A man who holds to the one faith will apply that one faith to every sphere of life and will work out its implications rigorously and systematically.

Polytheism abstracts a man from life. The polytheist has only a limited area in which his god and therefore his life is real. This was the premise of the counsellors to the king of Syria who advised him, saying of Israel, "Their gods are gods of the hills; therefore they were stronger than we; but let us fight against them in the plain, and surely we shall be stronger than they" (I Kings 20:23). For all too many today, Christ is real in the church; He has no word for the totality of life, in their thinking. Polytheism thus leads not only to a limited view of reality, but to a museum view. In the museum view of life, the best things must be taken out of the real world, raptured out of it, in a sense, and stored in a safe place. The best things, it is held, do not belong in the living, workaday world. In fact, many people feel guilty about owning anything superior or great unless they stipulate that, when they die, it will go to a museum. Museums perhaps have their place, but, in the modern world, this process of abstraction withdraws the best from life into the pseudo-eternity of the museum.

Thus, *first*, polytheism limits reality to a small sphere of life. *Second*, it abstracts man and things into that small sphere to create a museum of faith, not the power and reality thereof. *Third*, polytheism has only one kind of future, as does all abstraction, a departure from life to the grave. The world and life are God's creation: to depart from the totality of things is to deny life for the grave.

To affirm one faith, on the other hand, is *first*, the logical and necessary consequence of affirming one Lord. God being creator of all things, His lordship is total and unremitting. Because there is one Lord, there can only be one faith and one baptism, one world and life view, and only one way to Jesus Christ the Lord.

*Second*, theism cannot limit our view of life. The Lord being creator of all things, we have a duty to hear His word for every sphere, and serve and glorify Him in all. We cannot limit our world without sin, or without forsaking the one faith.

*Third*, instead of being abstracted from reality, our one faith immerses us therein. We are in it though not of it: we are of the Lord. Christ did not come to take us out of the world but to give us His victory therein.

*Fourth*, the conclusion of our faith is thus not the grave but eternal life. Where death reigns, there man's best hope is a museum. Where Christ reigns, man's certain hope is the new creation. Life leads to more life, the more abundant life.

To affirm "One Lord, one faith, one baptism," is to affirm marching orders for conquest, to say Amen to God's plan of dominion, and to assert the crown rights of Jesus Christ in every domain, and to establish them.

# 85

## COVENANT FREEDOM

According to Jacob Jocz,

Election in the Bible is a basic theological concept and is inseparable from the biblical doctrine of God. It must be understood in terms of responsibility rather than privilege and refers to divine decree as the expression of God's saving will. But in this context, election is only another aspect of the covenant, for it bears witness to God's unfailing grace toward mankind.[1]

He also stresses the fact that law and covenant are inseparably linked. Moreover, "There can be no redemption in history unless personal redemption affects society. Salvation that does not impinge upon the life of the community is not salvation in the Christian sense."[2]

Responsibility is thus basic to election and the covenant. Salvation requires the exercise of dominion and responsibility, and the law of God is essential to covenant life.

Let us now turn to a radically different subject, a bird known in the King James version as a swallow (Ps. 84:3; Prov. 26:2). It is known in the Near East and Europe also as a swift, a black martinet, and, in some parts of France as le Juif, or the Jew. It is high-flying, unwearyable bird of great wing-power and a soaring freedom. The Hebrew word for this swallow is *dror*, which means *freedom*. Elsewhere in the Bible, *dror* (or *deror*) is translated as *liberty*: Leviticus 25:10; Isaiah 61:1; Jeremiah 34:8, 15, 17; Ezekiel 46:17.

Now Leviticus 25:10 declares,

And ye shall hallow the fiftieth year, and proclaim liberty throughout all the land unto all the inhabitants thereof: it shall be a jubilee unto you: and ye shall return every man unto his possessions, and ye shall return every man unto his family.

It is immediately apparent that the Biblical idea of freedom is very different from the concept held by humanists and other pagans. Such people associate freedom with deliverance *from* responsibility, from work, family, worship, and various ties. For them, the more atomistic and unrelated man is to his context, the freer he is. It is as a natural consequence

---

1. Jacob Jocz: *The Covenant A Theology of Human Destiny*, p. 40. Grand Rapids, Michigan: Eerdmans, 1968.
2. *Ibid.*, p. 298.

of this idea of freedom that modern man has a communications problem: he cuts himself off from all other peoples, and he makes any tie between them untenable because he is in principle opposed to any tie. Speech then becomes, not communication, but an attempt to impress and to sell one's person as an important figure. A dwelling place is then not a home: it is furnished to make an impression conducive to our self-image. Restaurants become, not congenial places to eat good food with relaxed and easy conversation, but places that will conform to people's images of themselves as modern, free, avant garde, and prosperous. Everything then is stage-setting for the individual's play-acting. Clothing becomes more and more theatrical, and, as in the theater, quick changes of costume are necessary to conform to changing moods and scenes. All such "freedom" traps a man in the narrow room of his own being.

The jubilee proclamation is radically different. The servant has security, not freedom. He is a responsibility, not a responsible person. The jubilee sets him free for a return to responsibility, a return to his possessions and to his family. He is now a covenant man, an elder in Israel, with a responsibility to exercise headship and dominion over his family, possessions, and calling. This for Scripture, is freedom, *dror*.

St. James speaks of those who are hearers and doers of God's law-word as blessed, or happy: "But whoso looketh into the perfect law of liberty, and continueth therein, he being not a forgetful hearer, but a doer of the work (or, a doer that works), this man is blessed in his deed (or, doing)" (James 1:25). Liberty is here equated with law and work. Quite obviously, when the Bible and modern man both speak of freedom, they speak of two radically opposite things or ideas. The freedom sought by modern man is to be his own god, having aseity, self-being, self-sufficiency, needing nothing and no one, and yet able to command all. The freedom of man in Scripture is the freedom to glorify God and to enjoy Him forever by being His elect, responsible, and working dominion man. Paradise, the Garden of Eden, was created as a place for work, and the curse on man for his rebellion was a curse on his work. Instead of being his arena of joyful and fruitful dominion, it became an area of frustration. For covenant man, however, it is again an area of dominion and joy, of satisfaction and advance.

The jubilee is thus rightly a type of heaven and of the new creation. It means the end of captivity and bondage, and the glorious liberty of the sons of God to serve God freely and without impediment (Rom. 8:21; Rev. 22:3).

We must remember too the very personal and involved nature of jubilee freedom: "ye shall return every man unto his family" (Lev. 25:10). Freedom is into the covenant family and into possessions. Both of these facts are very important. For Scripture, neither family nor possessions, when covenantal, are impediments. When alien to the covenant, they are to be forsaken (Matt. 19:35-37; Luke 14:26, 33), not otherwise. The jubilee freedom thus restores man to the context of responsibility, to family and to possessions, to work and to obligations, and it is this which manifests that he is indeed regenerated and renewed in the image of God.

It is covenantal responsibility which leads to God's blessing and our freedom under God:

> Wherefore ye shall do my statutes, and keep my judgments, and do them; and ye shall dwell in the land in safety.
> And the land shall yield her fruit, and ye shall eat your fill, and dwell therein in safety. (Lev. 25:18-19)

When men believe and obey God, then they have both freedom and security (or safety). Security and freedom are opposites in a humanistic world. In Scripture, they are both products of God's law.

But the jubilee is not only an aspect of God's law: it is the culmination of God's sabbath. A man only keeps God's law if first of all he knows God's sabbath or rest. To know and obey God's sabbath means to take hands off our lives and to commit them to Christ, acknowledging Him to be our Lord and Savior, King of creation. To keep the sabbath means to walk in the assurance that He is Lord and that it is His will, not our's, which shall prevail. It means that we recognize that our work is our freedom under God and our duty to Him, but it is God's ordination which produces the results.

A psalm of Solomon, Psalm 127, stresses this in verse 2: "It is vain for you to rise up early, to sit up late, to eat the bread of sorrows: for so he giveth his beloved sleep." Anxiety can rob us of rest and peace: it cannot give us what we long for. Solomon's name was also Jedidiah, the beloved of the Lord (II Sam. 12:25). Moreover, in a dream, God promised the sleeping Solomon wisdom, honor, and prosperity (I Kings 3:5-15). God rewards and blesses us, not for anxieties, but for our trusting, working faith. The jubilee is thus a sabbath: before it can give its bounty to the released and the releasers, there must be that faith which lives in Sabbath peace and rest under God.

Sabbath-keeping is thus much more than a keeping of a church day. It is a working faith in every area of life.

## 86

## THE THEOLOGY OF TAXATION

To affirm one Lord means to proclaim the sovereignty of God for every sphere of life and thought. It means therefore that all things are theological concerns, and to exempt any area of life from the government of God is to deny God. It is thus important to assert a theology of taxation.

Taxation is an exercise of sovereignty and an attribute and power of God. The right to exact whatsoever He wills from all that He creates, and to do as He wills, is an aspect of sovereignty. St. Paul declared, with respect to predestination, "Nay but, O man, who are thou that repliest (or, disputest) against God? Shall the thing formed say to him that formed it, Why hast thou made me thus?" (Rom. 9:20). This principle applies to every area: what God declares, man must accept; what God claims, man must yield.

In origin, we are told, taxation was of two kinds, *first*, by the gods, gradually exercised for them by divine rulers, and *second*, by brigands, who demanded protection money on threat of physical harm. This second form of taxation still continues as a criminal activity, as various criminal syndicates take over control of various areas of urban life. This form of taxation is also common to revolutionary movements. Thus, in Ethiopia, before its revolution, a day-time tax, by the civil government, and a night-time tax, by the revolutionists, co-existed and placed people in many areas under a double tax.

According to Seligman's theory of the development of taxation, state taxation by monarchs developed gradually and by indirection:

> As civilization gradually advances, private property develops, and the primitive equality slowly disappears. The interchange of commodities takes place on a larger scale. The old revenues are no longer adequate, and it becomes necessary for the monarch to supplement them by broadening the field of these compulsory contributions of service. In other words, the need of taxation arises. But a direct tax is still out of the question. Public opinion will not yet admit its necessity. The taxation of property is scarcely less impossible than the taxation of the person. It is regarded as a badge of disgrace for the freeman—a *nota captivitatis*, as the Romans first called it—because only conquered enemies have to pay its arbitrary impost. The king, therefore, must endeavor to effect his object covertly. He must go to work in a roundabout way, and hide the tax in a variety of disguises.

He either gradually extends his lucrative prerogatives, or alleges that the charges are simple returns for governmental services. He grants protection or privileges to individuals, and requires some payment in return. Thus begins the period of fees and charges, which the individuals are willing to pay and which gradually reconcile the public to the idea of governmental charges.

Before long, however, the monarch feels able to throw off all disguises, and limits the amount of his exactions only by the degree of his rapacity. Thus the fees and tolls change into taxes on exchange and transportation; thus the people become accustomed to the "customs"; thus the "evil duties" and the excises grow apace; thus the payments become veritable "impositions." In other words, the community enters upon the state of indirect taxation.

This explains why it is so difficult for the idea of direct taxation to force its way into popular favor. The earliest manifestations of the taxing power are generally merciless and brutal.[1]

Seligman's reconstruction is evolutionary and humanistic. It ignores the religious aspects of taxation entirely. The reason for the indirection of taxation in antiquity and in Rome was because those cultures were polytheistic. The gods of polytheism are not sovereign: their jurisdiction is both limited and local. The pagan going to the temple of Castor and Pollux, for example, did not pay them a tithe or tax: they were not sovereign over him. He bought protection from them for a safe journey at sea and was thus voluntarily paying for insurance. A polytheistic culture cannot have a true concept of sovereignty.

As a result, the original terms for *tax* (from the Latin *tangere*, touch) were words meaning in essence *gift*. Seligman notes this fact tellingly, without seeing its theological implications:

The original idea was that of gift. The individual made a present to the government. We see this in the mediaeval Latin term *donum* and in the English *benevolence*, which was used far into the middle ages. The second stage was reached when the government humbly implored or prayed the people for support. This is the meaning of the Latin *precarium*, used for many centuries on the continent, as well as of the German *Bede* (from *beten*, to pray). The *Landbede* was the term applied to the land tax in the German states until quite recently. With the third stage we come to the idea of assistance to the state. The individual felt that, if not making a gift, he was at least doing the government a favor. This idea is expressed in the Latin *adjutorium*, the English *aid* and the French *aide*, which was at one time used for all kinds of taxes. The same idea is discernible in the English *subsidy* and *contribution*. It has survived in the German term for a tax, *Steuer* (steuern, to help), and in the Scandinavian *hjelp*. In France *contribution* is even today commonly used as synonymous with tax.

---

1. Edwin R. A. Seligman: *Essays in Taxation*, p. 3f. (1913 edition) New York: Macmillan, 1921.

The fourth stage of development brings out the idea of sacrifice by the individual in the interest of the state. He now surrenders something for the public good. This is seen in the old French *gabelle,* in the modern German *Abgade,* and in the familiar Italian *dazio.* In each case the citizen gives or sacrifices something. With the fifth stage the feeling of obligation develops in the taxpayer. The English *duty* was not originally restricted to its present narrow meaning in the United States. Here it is usually applied to import taxes and sometimes to the internal revenue tax. But even today in England the term includes some of the most important so-called direct taxes, like the inheritance tax and the income tax. It is not until the sixth stage is reached that we meet the idea of compulsion on the part of the state. We see this in our *impost* and *imposition,* as well as in the French *impot* and the Italian *imposta.* Although we limit the term to a certain kind of tax, the French use it as the generic epithet *par excellence.* The same idea is seen in the German *Auflage* (something "laid on") and *Aufschlag* (something "clapped on"), frequently used at present for certain indirect charges on commodities.

With the seventh and final stage we reach the idea of a rate or assessment, fixed or estimated by the government without any reference to the volition of the taxpayer. We see this in the mediaeval English *scot* (to be "at scot and lot") which is nothing but the German *Schoss* or the Scandinavian *skatt.* It is seen in the German *Schatzung* (or estimate), which was used until about a century ago. Above all, it is recognized in our *tax* (*taxare,* to fix, to estimate), the French *taxe,* the Italian *tassa,* and the English *rate.* It is worthy of note that in the middle ages "tax" always meant a direct tax, for which a regular assessment list or schedule was made.[2]

Seligman saw progress in this development, and, indeed, it was, of an ironic kind. Rome's problem was that, although a polytheistic social order in origin and structure, it was trying to become monotheistic. Its fundamental political thesis was, "Caesar is lord," a monotheistic claim. As a result, Roman emperors took powers, control over coinage and economics, and authority over religions, which Greece never fully dared claim. Greece was polytheistic to the core; as a result, its religion and politics were sharply limited to the citizens of the city-state. No one else had any rights or freedom, and anyone of alien or mixed blood was disposable at the will of the state. Thus, in Pericles day, Athens' law concerning aliens was put into force: 5,000 persons not of pure Athenian blood, who had managed to gain a place on the registers, were banished or sold as slaves. In Athens, there was no god, no law, and no rights for them. The Bible, however, as a theistic polity, declares that the Lord "loveth the stranger" (Deut. 10:18), and "The stranger that dwelleth with you shall be unto you as one born among you, and thou shalt love him as thyself" (Lev. 19:34).

Caesar as lord finally made all his subjects citizens as a part of the

---

2. *Ibid.,* p. 5f.

logic of Roman faith, but, at the same time, faith in Caesar as lord declined, and the empire had no valid theology. It recognized Christianity finally, but it never re-organized itself in terms of Biblical theology.

Modern taxation is a bastard product of brigandage and Christian theism. The background of Christendom has provided the idea of unity whereby total power is concentrated in the god of a society. Polytheism had its totalitarian orders also, divine-human monarchs and states, but they were limited states. The dream of a world state, and the acceptance of the idea of a necessary unity, are products of Christianity. As a result, with these borrowed premises, the modern state exercises total power with a *developed* ease. Whatever the divine rights which monarchs of an earlier era claimed, when it came to taxes, they were still hesitant.

This hesitation was due to the widely assumed priority of God's tax as claimed by the church. It was many generations after the state gained ascendency over the church before it dared to claim the sovereignty implicit in taxation. The belief in God's sovereignty was still too widespread.

The modern totalitarian states have in many cases taken another step: they deny the right of the church or any other agency to claim God's tithe. It is recognized that this means a divided sovereignty.

Thus, the rise of statist taxation is a rejection of God by people and state. This is clearly set forth in I Samuel 8:7. God declares to Samuel, "They have not rejected thee, but they have rejected me, that I should not reign over them." The consequence, God declares, will be another kind of taxation than the tithe and the poll tax (I Sam. 8:11-18).

The Christian solution to the problem of taxation cannot be rebellion. We are commanded in Romans 13:7 to pay the tribute required of us. In Matthew 22:15-22 (cf. Mark 12:13-17; Luke 20:20-26), we see that the Pharisees attempted to trap Jesus on the issue of taxation. Would Jesus deny the validity of any tax other than the tithe and head tax, in terms of God's law, or would he compromise with Rome? Their question was thus, "Is it *lawful* to give tribute to Caesar, or not?" Our Lord called attention to the coinage of the land: it was Caesar's. Caesar was their lord and provided their coinage, law, and order. Hence, "Render unto Caesar the things that are Caesar's, and unto God the things that are God's." If we do not confess the triune God as our total lord in every area of life and thought, then we have confessed another lord. Judea might not like Caesar, but their unacknowledged confession was that some kind of Caesar (Jewish, of course) had to be lord. They were thus rendering unto Caesar in all their being. But all things are God's. If we render unto God the things which are God's, we will soon have no Caesar over us. This will come to pass, not by tax revolts or any form of revolution, but because God's order will steadily supplant Caesar's.

For those who worship Caesar, it is lawful to pay taxes to Caesar. Those who worship the triune God will pay Caesar what he requires because God commands order, but they will soon establish God's order in place of Caesar's. For the Christian, God's tithe and the head tax are alone lawful. The tax to Caesar, however, is paid because God commands it: His Kingdom comes not by revolution and disobedience but by regeneration and the obedience of faith to the law of God.

The survival of the Jews through the centuries has been due to the centrality of the family and also to its perpetuation of a taxation outside the state. While such taxation has become humanistic, its strength has been phenomenal in not only preserving but advancing Jewish faith and culture. Many people, bitter about Jewish power, fail to recognize that it rests on this form of taxation. To cite two examples, Jewish immigrants in New York City, numbering 1.5 million by 1915, had created 3,637 institutions and agencies to administer charity, social welfare, educational enterprises, and the like. Again, during the Six Day War a few years ago, at one luncheon alone, $1 million a minute was pledged for 15 minutes; the total American Jewish giving to that war effort was $230 million. The Puritans, and Americans of some years back, have alone rivalled the Jews in this respect.

But the best and only valid plan is God's, the tithe and the head tax as the lawful forms of taxation. The tithe takes most of government out of the hands of the state and gives it the theocentric focus God requires of government. The head tax limits the state, and the fact that one tenth of the tithe goes to the church (except for the additional support for music), also limits the church. It is Christian society which then flourishes, and the Kingdom of God.

# 87

## THE THEOLOGY OF THE FAMILY

The centrality of the family in the Bible is clear-cut; the centrality of the family in all history is equally evident. Carle C. Zimmerman, in *Family and Civilization* (1947), and Zimmerman and Lucius F. Cervantes in *Marriage and the Family* (1956), make clear how civilizations rise and fall in terms of the nature of their family life and structure.

This does not mean, however, that a strong family in any society is of necessity congenial to Scripture. Far from it. Pagan family life is rife with presuppositions which are radically alien to the Bible. Community is basic to both the pagan and the Biblical family, but the pagan family makes itself ultimate rather than God. Ancestor worship is the logical conclusion of pagan family life.

Pagan family life places central emphasis on an impersonal aspect of its existence, fertility. Having made its own life ultimate, the pagan family regards the lack of fertility, the absence of children, as the ultimate curse. The religious power of the family was seen as sexual power. Although modern humanistic paganism no longer values progeny as was once done, it still regards sexuality as primary. Thus, Dr. Eugene Scheimann, M. D., sees "liberated" sexual activity as "the key" to life and health and agrees with Dr. Frank G. Slaughter that "too much immorality" is better for us than "too much morality."[1] For Scheimann, "Liberated" sex is salvation. Contemporary man regards experience, and sexual experience in particular, as liberation and life.

In whatever form humanism approaches the family, it becomes destructive to man because it subordinates man to some aspect of his being or to a goal or desire. It thus makes man serve something lesser than himself, whereas Scripture has man serve something greater than all creation, the sovereign God.

To illustrate this, let us look at polyandry, as in Tibet. To create a stable and unchanging social order and to keep property intact and unbroken, pre-communist Tibet required all brothers to have a common wife, so that the land might remain undivided. The result was social stability but human misery as one woman doled out sexual favors at her will to several brothers. The lack of change, because social stability was

---

1. Eugene Scheimann: *Sex Can Save Your Heart and Life,* pp. xiii, 6. New York: Bantam Books, (1970) 1975.

gained by arresting development, destroyed initiative and personal growth. The lack of cleanliness was legendary. There was no incentive to to be clean: the polyandrous wife had her captive husbands, and the brothers had a captive wife. A humanistic concern for property and stability led to the degeneration of man.

Old China also sought and developed an "ideal" humanistic "solution." Ancestor worship made the family tight and cohesive. Boys to carry on that family worship were favored, and unwanted girls readily abandoned. The excessive pampering of boys led to a high death rate, so that the boy-girl ratio was equalized. In well-to-do families, the male child was provided with an older peasant girl as a bride, to be his nurse and then his sexual trainer until marriage to a dowered bride took place. This "ideal" humanistic solution produced spoiled men who were readily dominated by their sexual mates and who readily tyrannized over them. What they were not normally capable of was a mature relationship.

The modern solutions are no better. The "key" to marriage is now sex. Where sex is over-valued, it produces less pleasure and becomes a driving frustration. The world of "sexual freedom" is thus a world of neuroses, frustrations, lack of communication, and an unceasing restlessness. It is also the world of abortion and euthenasia. In his abortion decision, Justice Blackmun, of the U. S. Supreme Court who wrote the majority opinion, made paganism his theological guide. He declared, "We need not resolve the question of when life begins." As Dr. Koop noted,

> Indeed need we not! Where does this lead? It leads to infanticide and eventually to euthanasia. If the law will not protect the life of a normal unborn child, what chance does a newborn infant have after birth, if in the eyes of Justice Blackmun, he might be less than normal. Obviously because the Supreme Court acted in such a way as to ignore the rights of the unborn child, this lack of right continues when the unborn child has been *delivered* by the procedure known as hysterotomy.[2]

A theology of the family must begin, *first,* by stressing the fact that man is created in the image of God (Gen. 1:26). This has far-reaching implications. God is a person, totally self-conscious and without any unconscious element in His being. While man in this life, and in his fallen and, where redeemed, not fully sanctified estate, is not fully self-conscious, nor ever infinite in his being as God is, as man grows in grace, he grows in epistemological self-consciousness. He is more clearly and fully a person.

Because the family-life is so close and personal, the family is the place

---

2. C. Everett Koop, M. D., Sc. D.: *The Right to Live; The Right to Die,* p. 39. Wheaton, Illinois: Tyndale House, 1976.

where man's personality is best nurtured, and where it best develops. The intimacy of marriage enhances the growth of personality: we become more self-consciously personal as we are happily married.

*Second,* the family is a community, the central community, and its relationship is patterned after the relationship of Jesus Christ to the *ecclesia,* the assembly or congregation, i.e., to the Kingdom of God (Eph. 5:1-33). The family is the Kingdom of God in miniature when it is a godly family, and the more faithfully it serves the triune God, the more clearly it becomes an embassy of the Kingdom.

*Third,* husband and wife are "one flesh" (Gen. 2:24), they are a community of life, physically and spiritually one. Adam said of Eve, "This is now bone of my bones, and flesh of my flesh" (Gen. 2:23). Their life had a common "bone," framework, or structure, and a common "flesh," a common life and blood animating them. In Adam's case, this was true before marriage; in our case, the physical union is precisely that, a union to a degree not appreciated by science. It is this fact that St. Paul has in mind, when he says, of illicit sex,

> Know ye not that your bodies are the members of Christ? shall I then take the members of Christ, and make them the members of an harlot? God forbid.
> What? Know ye not that he which is joined to an harlot is one body? for two, saith he, shall be one flesh.
> But he that is joined unto the Lord is one spirit.
> Flee fornication. Every sin that a man doeth is without the body; but he that committeth fornication sinneth against his own body. (I Cor. 6:15-18)

Very clearly, sexual union establishes a vital and consequential relationship and union. Our regeneration establishes a union with the Lord. Our every sexual act is an essential step which makes us a member of the other person.

Marriage is an essential community, theologically linked to the relationship of Christ to His Kingdom. It is also a limited community, in that it is for one man and one woman.

*Fourth,* this community, which is the basic soil of personality, is the central institution of society and its basic law unit. The office of elder is first of all a family office, and a test of his qualification is his ability to rule his own house (I Tim. 3:4). Biblical law is personal law, the expression of a personal God to His creation, and to be administered through elders who are heads of households and obedient to their Lord.

*Fifth,* while the law is personal, it is without respect of persons (Lev. 19:15, Deut. 1:17). The elders who rule cannot allow the wealth nor the poverty of the man before them, nor his closeness to them, nor any enmity, to cloud their judgment. The training ground for this is the family. Deuteronomy 21:18-21 requires parents to view their son, not in terms of their relationship to him, but in terms of how God judges their son. This makes clear why the test of an elder requires his ability to rule his household in terms of God's word. This places him beyond respect of persons in the key area of his life.

The theology of the family makes clear why government is in essence personal, while without respect of persons. Humanism's sociological approach to government depersonalizes everything. Crime and criminals are analyzed, not in terms of persons and sins, but in terms of heredity, environment, cultural deprivation, educational opportunity, and so on. The consequence is that the fact that it is persons who commit crimes and are responsible for them is blurred in a fog of social factors. Man is depersonalized and responsibility undercut.

Bibical faith affirms an ultimate personal government, God, in whom law, love, and grace coincide, and in whom alone true community exists. Van Der Leeuw wrote of the old Germanic tribal culture:

> There was therefore no community without some centre of power which might be either a sacrum, a certain specific god or a person, while the power subsisting in the tribal community was guaranteed by the lord, the king or the nobility. Thus life is valid only when it is potent life; but it possesses power, again, only within the community; "mere separation from family and country sufficed to bring life into peril" (Gronbech), and he who was expelled from the Germanic community was as good as dead.[3]

In such a culture, the present world is made ultimate; excommunication is from man. The family, tribe, or nation is the source of law, and true communion is with such an agency.

Because for Scripture, our essential and primary communion is with the triune God, every area of life has a necessary God-centered law and pattern. Man is dead, not when he is separated from his human community, but when he is separated from God the Lord. It is a question of lordship. Our God establishes our community, law, and society.

In His grace and mercy, He makes us members of His family by adoption, and we are privileged to call Him "Our Father." The theology of the family is thus rooted in our relationship to the triune God, and the law of God has its motive in a fatherly care of His own.

---

3. Gerardus Van Der Leeuw: *Religion in Essence and Manifestation,* p. 251. New York: Macmillan, 1928.

# 88

## THEOLOGY OF OWNERSHIP

Some years ago, Versteeg wrote, "You can define stewardship only when you can define Christ or God!"[1] Kublai Khan some centuries ago saw the meaning of property and stewardship when he prohibited all gambling in his realm, not a popular step, since the Chinese were intensely addicted to gambling. Marco Polo reported:

> The present grand khan has prohibited all species of gambling and other modes of cheating, to which the people of this country are addicted more than any others upon earth; and as an argument for deterring them from the practice, he says to them (in his edict), "I subdued you by the power of my sword, and consequently whatever you possess belongs of right to me: if you gamble, therefore, you are sporting with my property." He does not, however, take anything arbitrarily in virtue of this right.[2]

Kublai Khan had a good grasp of the meaning of sovereignty. If man is sovereign, or if a state is sovereign, then that sovereign has total claims on all that we are and possess. Thus, the idea of civil sovereignty, once alien to the United States, is now claimed by the Federal Government and all its constituent units. As a result, we are held to be the possessions of the state. Our lives, families, and properties belong to the state. If the tax collector allows us to keep any part of our income, it is called an "exemption," which means that, as an act of grace, the state allows us to keep a given amount of our income. Whoever claims sovereignty claims total ownership.

Thus, in objecting to gambling because it meant "sporting with my property," Kublai Khan showed a firm grasp of the meaning of sovereignty. Kublai Khan, however, was not God; his sovereignty was not a legitimate one; it was, as he stated, "by the power of my sword," and a stronger sword could take it from him. Thus, it was necessary for him to legislate coercively to establish his claim to sovereignty.

The triune God of Scripture is sovereign over all creation. He does not *claim* sovereignty; rather, it is an incommunicable attribute of Almighty God. The Scripture therefore does not speak, as Kublai Khan had to, against gambling. It is basic to Scripture that "The earth is the LORD'S and the fulness thereof; the world, and they that dwell therein"

1. John M. Versteeg: *Save Money!* p. 61. New York; Abingdon Press, 1939.
2. *The Travels of Marco Polo,* Bk. II, ch. 26; p. 170. New York: The Orion Press.

(Ps. 24:1). We are thus God's property, and all our possessions belong to Him. We are only stewards of whatever we possess. God need not say, as Kublai Khan did, "whatever you possess belongs of right to me: if you gamble, therefore, you are sporting with my property." This is implicit in all that He is, and all that we are. I will be prone to treat with evasion any man's, or any state's claims to my possessions, but if I am in another man's house as a guest or temporary caretaker, I dare not use his property for my own satisfaction, vices, or alien purposes. This should be even more true with God the Lord.

As Versteeg stated, *"Stewardship is the economic result of the Christian experience."*[3] Moreover,

> The Christian experience reveals that property is in the purpose of God. It must be directed Godward. Stewardship creates tensions between those who place property at the service of God and those whose one thought it is to take advantage for themselves out of it.[4]

Thus, because of the theological nature of stewardship and property, we cannot allow any acceptance of socialism as valid. "Private property," however, while seemingly in conformity to the Biblical doctrine, has this weakness. Socialism places sovereignty in the state, private ownership in the individual. The individual, however, is not a sovereign: he is a steward.

What does it mean to be a steward of property? We cannot permit in terms of Scripture the *personal* nature of property and stewardship to be overlooked. A man's property is a part of his life, an aspect of his work and dominion. The depersonalization of property is the depersonalization of man. Stewards in Bible history were often slaves, members of the household, with a personal stake therein. They were guardians and managers for their lord.

Moreover, ownership in the Bible is *historical,* i.e., while personal, it has reference to more than the individual. The *family* is involved. Even apart from the issue of the Biblical land-law (no sale of land), Naboth's attitude has reference to a continuity of faith and inheritance. Ahab offered to give Naboth "a better vineyard" at another location, or its value in money (I Kings 21:2). Thus, from the modern economic point of view, the proposition made by Ahab to Naboth was a good offer. Naboth's answer was non-economic: "The LORD forbid it me, that I should give the inheritance of my fathers unto thee" (I Kings 22:3). Naboth saw the land as a stewardship handed down from his forefathers, and to be handed down to the generations to come. He reacted, not in terms of modern economics, but Biblical economics, namely, in terms of stewardship.

Thus, libertarian economics, which holds strictly to totally private

---

3. Versteeg, *op. cit.* p. 57.
4. *Ibid.*, p. 89.

property, leaves property as rootless as does socialist economics: it divorces it from the past and the future. Property then becomes existential: its meaning is limited to the meaning the existentialist individual gives to it, and no more. Socialism, and also existentialism, ties property to the existence of the state.

The Biblical doctrine of property is thus *covenantal*. It begins with God's covenant, and it is concerned with the continuity of that covenant in history and is concerned with its prosperity. The blessings and curses of the covenant have to do with life and property (Deut. 28). The point of Zechariah 1:6, and of Malachi 3:8-12, as well as all the prophets, is that life and property without stewardship to God plainly lead to God's radical judgment.

The basic aspect of property is *ownership*. While the earth is clearly the Lord's (Ps. 24:1), the land is also man's to own as an inheritance in the Lord (Deut. 26:1). Our modern idea of inheritance presupposes death. Someone *must* die before we can inherit. This is *not* a necessity to the Biblical doctrine. A father's faithful sons have an inheritance while alive; thus, Isaac was the heir and possessor together with Abraham while Abraham lived. Because property in Scripture is a *family* possession, it is such during the life-time of fathers, children, and grandparents. This appears clearly in the parable of the prodigal son, who in the life-time of the father, took his portion and departed. The circumstances are unusual, i.e., the father agreeing to the request, but not unheard of, and hence the point of the parable was telling to its hearers: an inheritance did not require death.

The heir who gained the double portion was the real heir, however, in terms of the continuing and central property of the family. The covenant man, God's Israel, is thus required to support the father. The tithe, the firstfruits, and all gifts to the Lord, thus are in agreement with family law. The living father turns over the property to the heir, who is then a steward of that property to the father and to the future generations of the family.

This sets the context of tithes and offerings. In Deuteronomy 26:1-11, the firstfruits are given to the Lord, because it is the due of the Head of the covenant family. Man's *inheritance* (Deut. 26:1, 3, 9-11) requires the recognition of the Father's sovereign right. The *first*fruit stresses the *first* place of the Father in all that our inheritance produces. The *tithes* stress the necessity of separating to the Father's purpose a portion of our increase.

These are not *gifts* to the Father; only what we give above the required amount constitutes a gift. The necessary tax stresses rather the fact that we are heirs. We did not come into a barren world, and we must leave it the richer for our coming. The purpose of the Father requires, *first,* that we exercise dominion over our property and, by means of work, produce an increase. The Kingdom of God must be strengthened and developed by our family life and by our vocation. We are therefore duty bound to produce an increase, as the parable of the talents makes clear (Matt. 25:14-30).

*Second,* the Father plans that through our increase, our tithes and offerings bring about the increase of His Kingdom beyond our own limited area of action. Thus, these taxes serve to fuel Kingdom causes in missions, education, reconstruction, worship, music, and so on. As stewards, we have a duty beyond our walls. The whole earth being the Lord's, He requires us to reconquer every area of life and thought for Him.

*Third,* our gifts and taxes minister to God's poor, and to emergency needs outside His fold.

The chosen people of God are called His firstborn (Hosea 11:1). God declared to pharaoh, "Israel is my son, my firstborn" (Ex. 4:22). The Hebrew term for firstborn is *bekhor,* and the Hebrew term for firstfruits is *bikkurim,* derived from the same root.

The firstborn, the redeemed of God, the heirs of His Kingdom, give to the Lord His firstfruits and of the substance of their possessions and increase. Proverbs 3:9-10 make clear that this is the prerequisite to all material blessings:

> Honour the LORD with thy substance, and with the firstfruits of all thine increase:
> So shall thy barns be filled with plenty, and thy presses shall burst out with new wine.

These verses teach, as Fritsch makes clear, that "This is a spiritual law," and it means that "Obedience to God's law brings material reward."[5]

In our time, there is a marked tendency to avoid the material promises of Scripture and to spiritualize them. This means a doubting of God's sovereignty over the material realm, a distrust in His word, and therefore as ready a distrust in any "spiritual" promises. This was made clear by Charles Bridges:

> There is no presumption, or enthusiasm in looking for the literal fulfilment of the promise. If we doubt the temporal, should we not suspect our assumed confidence in the spiritual, engagements? For if the Lord's word be insufficient security for our *substance;* much more must it be for the infinitely weightier deposit of our soul![6]

But more is implied in failing to give, and in mistrusting God's promise: it means that we do not feel the family relationship to God is a

---

5. Charles T. Fritsch, "Proverbs," in *The Interpreter's Bible,* IV, 801.

6. Charles Bridges: *Exposition of the Book of Proverbs,* p. 27. Grand Rapids, Michigan: Zondervan, (1846) 1959.

real one, and hence we have no sense of gratitude and family responsibility. We therefore treat our possessions as our own, not as a stewardship. We then feel that neither we nor our children are God's family, and we do feel that our possessions are self-created. Our theology of ownership then has implicit to it a belief that we are gods, not the Lord. We then manifest a humanistic theology of ownership.

How we give also determines our theology. If we give to ourselves and to our family, we give without stinting. To a landlord, we give only what is his due, not a penny more. If we give in a like manner to God, we give as to a landlord, not as to our Father.

## 89

## OWNERSHIP AND SONSHIP

Our relationship to God as our creator, redeemer, owner, and Father is totally a personal one, but not individualistic nor private. There is a difference between what is personal and that which is private. The *private* can be something impersonal, such as a bedroom, and it is also usually something separate from the law. The *private* can be personal, but not necessarily so. That which is truly private has no public or social aspect. The sexual act is normally private in its setting but thoroughly social in its context and implications. (The modern sexual revolutionaries deny the social implication of sex, i.e., its moral character; they insist that morality is a private concern, which is another way of denying morality. At the same time, they deny the need for a private setting for the sexual act.)

It can be questioned whether anything in God's universe can be called in any true sense private. All things are under God's government and law. Men, however, like to reduce things to an antinomian status by regarding them as private and purely individual in their relevance. We are told that acts between consenting adults are private and of no concern to the law. For humanistic law, such boundaries are possible, but there are no boundaries to God's government and hence no private areas outside His jurisdiction and law.

The individualistic bias thus seeks to reduce the world of relevance to only those who are immediately involved, or to men who may become involved as a by-product. God's law has no such limitations: it is at all times involved, because God is totally the Lord.

All this is especially relevant to the doctrine of The Fatherhood of God. We are commonly told that there is a progression in the doctrine of the Fatherhood of God from the Old to the New Testament. In the Old Testament, the doctrine has reference, we are told, only to collective Israel, whereas in the New, it is personal and individualistic for all believers.[1]

The Fatherhood of God is cited in the Old Testament in Exodus 4:22; Deuteronomy 1:31; 8:5; 32:6; Hosea 11:1; Isaiah 1:2; 63:16; Jeremiah

---

1. Geerhardus Vos: *Biblical Theology, Old and New Testaments,* pp. 391-395, Grand Rapids, MI: Eerdmans, 1948, discusses some of the common beliefs about the supposed differences.

3:19; Malachi 1:6; etc. Oehler, in summing up the meaning of the Fatherhood of God in the Old Testament made clear, *first,* that it is not a physical but an ethical or moral fatherhood. "It denotes the relationship of love and moral communion in which Jehovah has placed Israel to Himself." *Second,* this relationship is with the chosen people alone, not with all men and nations. When in Deuteronomy 32:6 God speaks of creating Israel, His words do not "indicate the creation of the people in the same sense that all men are made by God, but signify those divine acts by which Israel is established and prepared as the people of God's possession and covenant, and so simply denote its election."[2]

*Third,* the Fatherhood of God is covenantal. He is the Father of a covenant people. This is a personal relationship by the adoption of grace to every covenant man, but it is not private nor limited to the individual. God is the covenant man's Father in the context of a family, and in terms of a *moral* relationship, i.e., obedience to His law. It is also a *religious* relationship: God's Fatherhood is inseparable from the fact that He is the creator who also makes atonement and separates a people unto Himself. Of godly widows and orphans Psalm 68:5 declares, "A father of the fatherless, and a judge of the widows, is God in his holy habitation," i.e., in His tabernacle, the place of covenant atonement. Psalm 103:13 states, "Like as a father pitieth his children, so the LORD pitieth them that fear him," and verse 18 makes clear who these are: "To such as keep his covenant, and to those that remember his commandments to do them."[3]

When we turn to the New Testament, we do not find, contrary to common opinion, this pattern altered. *First* of all, it is still an ethical, not physical, sonship. We are not sons by nature, but by the adoption of grace (Gal. 4:6, 7; I John 3:1). It is a moral fact, which reveals itself in that we are then led by the Holy Spirit, and we overcome in Christ. "For as many as are led by the Spirit of God, they are the sons of God" (Rom. 8:14). "He that overcometh shall inherit all things; and I will be his God and he shall be my son" (Rev. 21:7).

*Second,* these above cited verses make clear that sonship is by adoption into the covenant of grace and is a covenant, not private, fact. It is not an individualistic sonship, although fully personal, but covenantal.

*Third,* just as our sonship is covenantal, so is God's Fatherhood. Hence it is under law because a covenant without law is impossible. Our Lord distinguishes between His Sonship and ours: "Go to my brethren and say unto them, I ascend unto my Father and your Father; and to my

---

2. Gustav Francis Oehler: *Theology of the Old Testament,* p. 178. Grand Rapids, MI: Zondervan.

3. Ernest Gordon: *Notes From a Layman's Greek Testament,* p. 244. Boston, MA: W. A. Wilde Co., 1941.

God and your God" (John 20:17). His relationship to the Father is one
of a common being and a physical fact; ours is not. His relationship to
God the Father as God is radically different from ours. As a result, Jesus
separates His Sonship from ours very clearly.

Because our relationship to God as Father is covenantal, we *cannot*
legitimately or without sin pray to Him as "My Father," but only as
"our Father." In prayer, we always approach Him in the name of Jesus,
i.e., through the intercession of God the Son, and, even in our most
solitary prayer, always as a member of the covenant people or family.

As Calvin saw, this has implications for prayer:

> XXXVIII. But since we are not instructed, that every individual
> should appropriate him to himself exclusively as his Father, but
> rather than we should all in common call him Our Father, we are
> thereby admonished how strong a fraternal affection ought to
> prevail among us, who, by the same privilege of mercy and free
> grace, are equally the children of such a Father.... Let a Christian,
> then, regulate his prayers by this rule, that they be common, and
> comprehend all who are his brethren in Christ; and not only those
> whom he at present sees and knows to be such, but all men in the
> world; respecting whom, what God has determined is beyond our
> knowledge; only that to wish and hope the best concerning them, is
> equally the dictate of piety and of humanity. It becomes us, how-
> ever, to exercise a peculiar and superior affection "unto them who
> are of the household of faith;" whom the apostle has in every case
> recommended to our particular regards. In a word, all our prayers
> ought to be such, as to respect that community which our Lord has
> established in his kingdom and in his family.
>
> XXXIX. Yet this is no objection to the lawfulness of particular
> prayers, both for ourselves and for other certain individuals; provided
> that our mind be not withdrawn from a regard to this community,
> nor even diverted from it, but refer every thing to this point.[4]

On sonship is as members of a community, and our prayers are as
members of that community. The community is, as Calvin said, "His
Kingdom." Our prayers are to be fully personal and fully covenantal.

But this is not all. Deuteronomy 14:2 declares

> For thou art an holy people unto the LORD thy God, and the LORD
> hath chosen thee to be a peculiar people unto himself, above all the
> nations that are upon the earth.

Phillips, commenting on Deuteronomy 7:6, says of *holy:* "anything *holy*
is that which has been separated off for God's exclusive use. Such was
Israel, for it was through her that God had chosen to manifest himself to
the world (cg. Ex. 19:5f.)."[5] The phrase "to be a peculiar people unto

---

4. John Calvin: *Institutes of the Christian Religion,* Book III, Chapt. XX; vol. II, p.
148f. Philadelphia, PA: Presbyterian Board of Publications, 1936.

5. Anthony Phillips: *Deuteronomy,* p. 61. Cambridge, England: Cambridge University
Press, 1973.

himself" can be more clearly rendered, "to be a people of property unto Himself."[6] God never allows us to forget His property right in us: it is the ground of our election and calling. Having made us, He can do as He chooses with us. "Shall the thing formed say to him that formed it, Why hast thou made me thus?" (Rom. 9:20). We are persons because He has chosen to make us so, and our total personality and possessions are thus to be at His command. We are His creation, and thus we are never private individuals. We can never separate ourselves from God's universe and law, so that His word or law is basic to life as persons and inseparable from us. "For in him we live, and move, and have our being" (Acts 17:28). Just as our fall into sin was a moral fall, so our sonship by grace manifests itself in a moral consequence: we bear fruit in terms of His word and calling (Matt. 7:16-20). Psalm 37:31 says of the righteous, "The law of his God is in his heart; none of his steps shall slide." Again, Psalm 40:8 tells us, "I delight to do thy will, O my God: yea, thy law is within my heart."

Because we are a people who are the property of God, His law regulates our lives exactly as He chooses. Thus, Deuteronomy 14:1 and 3 declare

> Ye are the children of the LORD your God: ye shall not cut yourselves, nor make any baldness between your eyes for the dead. Thou shalt not eat any abominable thing.

We are covenant *children* of the Lord, but not in any human physical sense whereby we can also grow up and go our own way. We are children by the adoption of grace who are also God's personal property: this never changes. As a result, what we do to our body is entirely under God's jurisdiction, and the same is true of all that we eat. What God calls "abominable," many men have often called appetizing food. The holiness of the sons requires that God's law govern us.

In Scripture thus, the theology of ownership rests in the doctrine of the covenant and God's property right over all men; men of the covenant are doubly His possession: He created them, redeems them at a great price (I Cor. 6:20), and thus makes them doubly His own. In giving men the adoption of sonship, God does not separate them from His ownership and law: these are aspects of His relationship to us, and they must be our confidence in Him.

---

6. Oehler, *op. cit.*, p. 179.

## 90

## ONE BAPTISM

When St. Paul speaks of "one baptism" (Eph. 4:5), the usual reaction of clergy and laity is to think of the mode of baptism and the rite. This is the same as associating a library with the alphabet rather than with learning.

Baptism is indeed a rite, and it has a form which involves the use of water. Similarly, the Bible is indeed a book, and it involves the use of the alphabet, but the meaning of the Bible, and its purpose, can no more be reduced to the alphabet than the meaning and purpose of baptism can be reduced to the form and rite.

I Peter 3:21, according to some, means that the experience of Noah and his family was a type of spiritual death, burial, and resurrection, an *antitupon,* in the Greek text, a corresponding type, or a like figure. Others would argue with this. What is clear, however, is that Noah and his family went from a doomed world to one marked by God's covenant rainbow (Gen. 9:12-16). Whatever else then that baptism means, it means the passage from one kind of life and world to another.

It also means *the responsibilities* of that new creation, *royal responsibilities.* This appears clearly in Matthew 20:20-28:

> Then came to him the mother of Zebedee's children with her sons, worshipping him, and desiring a certain thing of him.
> And he saith unto her, What wilt thou? She saith unto him, Grant that these my sons may sit, the one on thy right hand, and the other on the left, in thy kingdom.
> But Jesus answered and said, Ye know not what ye ask. Are ye able to drink of the cup that I shall drink of, and to be baptized with the baptism that I am baptized with? They say unto him, We are able.
> And he saith unto them, Ye shall drink indeed of my cup, and be baptized with the baptism that I am baptized with: but to sit on my right hand, and on my left, is not mine to give, but it shall be given to them for whom it is prepared of my Father.
> And when the ten heard it, they were moved with indignation against the two brethren.
> But Jesus called them unto him, and said, Ye know that the princes of the Gentiles exercise dominion over them, and they that are great exercise authority upon them.
> But it shall not be so among you: but whosoever will be great among you, let him be your minister;
> And whosoever will be chief among you, let him be your servant:

Even as the Son of man came not to be ministered unto, but to minister, and to give his life a ransom for many.

It is possible to say that the use of the words *baptized* and *baptism* are here merely figurative and have no essential reference to the rite itself, but verses 22 and 23 have an insistent use of the word, not a casual one; then verses 25-28 give us the kind of life and responsibility this baptism involves. It is a life in terms of the requirements of the Kingdom, and it is emphatically different from the life of pagan princes and rulers, although it is a life of princely rule. It means a godly service and ministry to Christ's Kingdom and its peoples.

Matthew 28:19 reinforces this: baptism is literally "into the Name of the Father, and of the Son, and of the Holy Ghost." "The baptized was closely bound to, or became the property of, the one into whose Name he was baptized."[1]

It would thus appear that baptism means 1) a new creation, with 2) new and great responsibilities, which involve service; 3) these are royal responsibilities, princely services rendered by the princes of grace, but they also manifest a sense of ministry and humility; 4) baptism is a mark of ownership; we are owned by Christ the Lord and are His property, and we are therefore at His command.

*One Lord* thus means that Christ's Kingship is over every area of life and thought; Jesus Christ is absolute lord over all things, because "All things were made by him; and without him was not any thing made that was made" (John 1:3). We cannot surrender the crown rights of the King in any realm without denying His Lordship.

*One faith* means that the word of God is the basic faith and presupposition in terms of which all things must be understood. We understand all things only when we begin with the sovereign and triune God and His creation of them, His eternal counsel and decree. According to I John 2:20, "But ye have an unction from the Holy One, and ye know all things." Our knowledge of all things is not in detail but in principle, in terms of epistemology. We have the key in terms of which all knowledge can be known. To deny the God of Scripture is to deny total meaning to the universe, and thereby to render knowledge untenable. Our *one faith* thus is the key to every area of life and thought.

One baptism means that the manifestation of our belief in "one lord," "one faith," is a reality, because, as the property of the Lord, we are responsibly active in His service and according to His word.

John the Baptist tells us more about the meaning of this "one baptism":

I indeed baptize you with water unto repentance: but he that cometh after me is mightier than I, whose shoes I am not worthy to bear:

---

1. W. E. Vine: *Expository Dictionary of New Testament Words,* I, 97.

he shall baptize you with the Holy Ghost, and with fire:
Whose fan is in his hand, and he will throughly purge his floor, and
gather his wheat into the garner; but he will burn up the chaff with
unquenchable fire. (Matt. 3:11-12)

In Acts 1:5, our Lord speaks of the baptism of the Holy Ghost at the Day
of Pentecost, soon to come to the disciples. We are told that this usage in
Matthew 3:11 and Acts 1:5 is metaphorical, but, even if we grant this, the
fact is still clear that baptism is comparable to a major transition from
one conditon to another, i.e., from a usual estate to being filled with the
Holy Ghost on the one hand, to the radical and total judgment which
destroyed Jerusalem in the war of 66-70 A. D. on the other. Clearly,
therefore, baptism is a metaphor for a drastic and radical change because
baptism when valid is precisely such a change in the life, thought, and
activity of a man.

Westcott wrote, on Ephesians 4:5,

> This historical foundation of the Christian Society also witnesses to
> its unity. It is established by the acknowledgment of *one Lord* as sov-
> ereign over all life: it confesses *one faith* in proclaiming that 'Jesus is
> Lord' (I Cor. xii. 3): it is entered by *one Baptism,* in which the
> believer is brought into fellowship with Christ Jesus (Gal. iii 27).[2]

Our confession of *one faith* and our participation in the *one baptism* are
acts of God in essence; our role is to respond to His sovereign and irresistible grace. Lenski has written:

> Baptism is the washing of regeneration and is thus never a mere sym-
> bol. Nor is it an act of ours by which we merely confess; it is an act
> upon us by which God bestows the treasures of salvation upon us.[3]

Those who truly confess "One Lord, one faith, one baptism" manifest
thereby God's ownership in and over them. It means that they have indeed been baptized "into the Name" and manifest the life and works of
their new creation.

2. B. F. Westcott: *St. Paul's Epistle to the Ephesians,* p. 58.
3. R. C. H. Lenski: *The Interpretation of St. Paul's Epistles to the Galatians, to the Ephesians, and to the Philippians,* p. 513. Columbus, Ohio: The Wartburg Press, (1937) 1946.

## 91

## THE THEOLOGY OF THE DIACONATE

The word *minister* in Scripture is *diakonos,* which is also translated as *deacon. Diakonos* refers to one who is a servant; it can mean either one doing servile work, or a man rendering voluntary service out of faith and love. The word probably comes from the verb *dioko,* to hasten after, run after, or pursue. It is used for domestic servants (John 2:5, 9), civil rulers (Rom. 13:4), Christ Himself (Rom. 15:8; Gal. 2:17), the followers of the Lord in their relationship to Him (John 12:26; Eph. 6:21; Col. 1:7; 4:7), the followers of Christ in their relationship to one another (Matt. 20:26; 23:11; Mark 9:35; 10:43), the work of preaching and teaching by Christ's servants (I Cor. 3:5; II Cor. 3:6; 6:4; 11:23; Eph. 3:7; Col. 1:23, 25; I Thess. 3:2; I Tim. 4:6); those who serve in the churches (Rom. 16:1; Phil. 1:1; I Tim. 3:8, 12), and of false prophets who are servants of Satan (II Cor. 11:15).[1] In its verb form, the word is *diakoneo,* to serve, minister. We have a telling usage of both noun and verb in Matthew 20:25-28:

> But Jesus called them unto him, and said, Ye know that the princes of the Gentiles exercise dominion over them, and they that are great exercise authority upon them.
> But it shall not be so among you: but whosoever will be great among you, let him be your minister;
> And whosoever will be chief among you, let him be your servant.
> Even as the Son of man came not to be ministered unto but to minister, and to give his life a ransom for many.

The chain of references linking these words to the Old Testament are so many that only a few can be cited here. *First* of all, there is the matter of dominion. The Fall brought about a perversion of man's calling to exercise dominion. Genesis 1:26-28 makes clear that dominion is to be exercised over the earth, not over man. The reference to "every living thing" is to animal life. Man the sinner seeks to gain dominion over other men and to assert authority and power over men. Such a dominion is the prerogative of God, not of man. To exercise God's dominion means to deny Him and to make war aganst Him. For Christians to seek such power is godless.

*Second,* the goal of pagan efforts to exercise dominion is to make others servants, whereas the goal of Christian efforts is to become a

---

1. Vine, *An Expository Dictionary of N. T. Words,* I, 272f.: III, 72f.

servant in Christ and of Christ to other men, unto Christ's people in particular. This is stated repeatedly, as in I Peter 5:2, 3.

> Feed the flock of God which is among you, taking the oversight thereof, not by constraint, but willingly; not for filthy lucre, but of a ready mind;
> Neither as being lords over God's heritage, but being ensamples to the flock.

In spite of the commonplace abuse of the term, civil officers are still called "public servants" because Romans 13:4 so describes them: they are ministers, deacons, or servants. It is the Christian heritage which leads to this usage. The goal of "the princes of the Gentiles," of unregenerate society, is to exercise dominion over men and to make servants of other men. This leads to *a society of vultures,* all men seeking to prey on other men. It leads to radical conflicts, disorders, and stresses. On the other hand, a diaconal theology sees Christ the King giving His life as a ransom for many, and as one who came to minister, not to be ministered unto. It is therefore the duty of every Christian to manifest the same diaconate in his own life. *A diaconal society* is one of mutual interdependence and service, a society in which men seek to meet needs in Christ's name. A vulture-society will self-destruct; a diaconal society will prosper and flourish.

The Old Testament is full of laws regarding our duty to our neighbor, laws of charity, laws involving a concern for strangers, widows, orphans, and much more. This led, in subsequent developments to "the law of neighbors," whereby a man was required to be thoughtful of his neighbors: no undue noise, no intrusion designed to harm a community, no self-assertion in violation of other's property rights, and so on.

*Third,* the emphatic duty to minister is stated by our Lord in telling words: "But it shall not be so among you." Those who desire to be great in His Kingdom must be ministers to others, and he who desires to be chief, he must be a slave, for the word translated as "servant" is literally *doulos,* slave, bond-servant. The implication is clear: *we are not our own;* we have been bought with a price (I Cor. 6:19-20), and we must therefore do that which our Lord and owner requires us to do, to minister in His name. Because our ministry or service is as servants of Christ and in His name as well as according to His word, we cannot be the servants of men. We are Christ's *freemen* as well as His servants (I Cor. 7:22). "Ye are bought with a price: be not ye the servants of men (or slaves, under man's direction)" (I Cor. 7:23).

*Fourth,* this duty of ministry applies not only to the redeemed man but also to his institutions. Church and state must both be diaconal in their nature and ministry. The state as lord, exercising dominion, claiming the power of eminent domain, and treating citizens as subjects, is pagan. It becomes a vulture state, not a diaconate. The same is true of the church.

*Fifth,* the heart of any theology of the diaconate being Christ's ministry and atoning death, it follows that the diaconate is a ministry of justice and grace. God's absolute justice was upheld by Christ and made the means of opening up grace to fallen man. The diaconate thus is grounded in the reality of justice and grace, and it can never despise either. It is an extension of the government and jurisdiction of grace, and it moves in terms of God's law, the essence of which stresses the diaconal community.

*Sixth,* because the diaconate establishes community in Christ's name among His people, and witnesses to that community to those outside the Kingdom, communion is basic to the diaconal community. *Communion* is a fact which means more than a ritual: it is mutual service as members of Christ and as members of one another. Church life today is in violation of this. People seek their own kind, socially and intellectually. Instead of communion, we have division and snobbery. The church celebrates communion in a rite and denies it in practice. The line of division between a vulture society and a diaconal society is thereby blurred and slighted.

Modern vulture societies, because of their Christian past, seek to maintain the facade of communion and service, but it is transferred from the realm of the person's daily life to the impersonal agencies of state, which handle charity and welfare. This impersonality is a further shove outside of society to the recipient: it is a witness to unconcern. It says in effect, we are paying you well to stay out of sight and to become no nuisance to us. The vulture society has no heart, only a dole of money. When the money runs out, the vulture nature will appear very clearly.

Unlike the vulture society, the diaconal society is not created from the top down, but from the bottom up. It appears wherever any believer ministers in Christ's name and in terms of His word: "Freely ye have received, freely give" (Matt. 10:8). Its essence is communion in deed, not merely in rite. A society without communion will explode into violence. *The choice is between communion and revolution.* Fallen man drifts into revolution, because he is capable of nothing else. The social explosion in a vulture society need not be, and usually is not, ideological. It self-destructs, because every man, as his own god, is at war with every other man. Any supposedly Christian group which reduces communion only to a rite is aiding and abetting the forces of disintegration. It is salt without savor, fit only "to be trodden under foot of men" (Matt. 5:13).

History will see, Revelation 19 makes clear, the destruction of the society of vultures, devoured by the vultures of the heavens (Rev. 19:17-18), whereas the diaconal society is summoned to enjoy "the marriage supper of the Lamb" (Rev. 19:9). A wedding banquet means rejoicing, dancing, drinking, happiness unbounded. It is a symbol of the fulness of communion, whereas the humanistic vulture society is a cannibalistic conclusion to the Kingdom of Man.

## 92

## THE THEOLOGY OF SIMPLICITY

William Carroll Bark, in writing of the basic causes of failure of the Roman Empire, cites as one the yearning for a simple life. The Romans, he states, "yearned for an ancient time of small independent yeomen, of black bread, earthen pottery, and plain customs. In so doing, they confused simplicity with strength, as if one could exist without the other."[1] They sought to revive the customs but not the virtues of the past. Because the same yearning for simplicity is so great in our day, it is important to understand its meaning.

Our Lord said, with respect to salvation, "With men this is impossible; but with God all things are possible" (Matt. 19:26). Men cannot save themselves, but God is able to do all things, not only with respect to salvation, but with reference to all problems. Nothing exists apart from His eternal decree and will, so that there are no problems for God. As God Himself declares, "Is any thing too hard for the Lord?" (Gen. 18:14). Problems exist for man: they are aspects of the fall, of man's rebellion against God and His law-word. But even in an unfallen world, man would have problems, although sin-free ones. If man were the god he claims to be, there would be no problems for him. In fact, the claim of humanism is that man will in time solve all problems, eliminate poverty, sickness, tensions, crimes, and death itself. Man will thereby establish his claim to be god and forever cast off the claims of the God of Scripture on him.

There are no problems for a god, because all things are simplicity itself for him; a god rules without rivalry, without any possibility existing outside of his will and being unless he creates it, and thus without a shadow or cloud on his will and act. Of the true and living God of Scripture it is said:

> Neither is there any creature that is not manifest in his sight: but all things are naked and opened unto the eyes of him with whom we have to do. (Heb. 4:13)

James 1:7 says of God that there is "no variableness, neither shadow of turning" in Him. We are subject to circumstances, and to our own weakness and changes of feelings, but with God there is no variation or

---

1. William Carroll Bark: *Origins of the Medieval World,* p. 144. Garden City, NY: Doubleday Anchor Books, (1958) 1960.

alteration of nature. All things are more than simple for God: they are His handiwork.

The more nakedly and self-consciously men claim to be god, the more clearly they will profess to have an omnicompetence and the power to circumscribe every realm with their wisdom. In the highly epistemological awareness of humanistic socialism, the planners feel that problems are too complex for the masses, but thoroughly simple for themselves. All they need is the fulness of power to save all men. I recall vividly, in an academic setting, hearing a prominent federal administrator declare with intense feeling, how *all* social problems could be solved with simplicity, provided we trusted the "responsible" experts and gave them a free hand. In effect, he was saying, let us be gods, and we can deliver all things to you, and nothing shall be impossible for us.

The grasping for simplicity is thus a claim to be as God. The yearning for a simple life is a desire for self-sufficiency which is impossible for man. The "good old days" are a myth. No man can be his own butcher, farmer, shoemaker, garment manufacturer, tool-maker, and so on without disaster. Some of us have varied talents, and it is a pleasure to apply them. But the hippie-urge to return to a "natural" life of self-sufficiency always courts disaster. Men need one another. Our varieties of calling supplement one another. Specialization and the division of labor is a mark of progress. It frees us from a variety of chores to do our work, to fulfill our calling, with freedom. It is *only* as we have specialization that we can have some of the things which mark "the good life" which many of us yearn for or are enjoying. The kind of flower and vegetable gardening, as well as animal husbandry, which mark the lives of many active and retired people alike is a mark of a complex society. In a primitive society, no one has the time for too much activity or interest beyond bare survival. In a sense, the more complex the world becomes, the simpler and better our lives become.

Thus a necessary pre-condition to the good life and to progress is the recognition that the problem-free life belongs to God, but that our good life comes from dealing with problems in terms of God's law-word. Instead of yearning for simplicity, we strive to obey God's word in faith and thereby to develop even further the particularization and specialization of human action.

Because of the complex technology of our time, our lives have become, in the material sphere, more simple. Washing machines, electricity, central heating, automobiles, trains, planes, and other technological advances have given us more freedom. To renounce this complexity is to complicate, not simplify, our lives. It means a reversion to a life requiring more effort by us or by servants to make living conditions tenable.

In the world of the mind, the same is true. If a man seeks to overthrow the "simple solution" which some call God, then simplicity is supposedly transferred to the human scene. But man cannot be God; the result is tyranny and death.

Only as the complexity of life is recognized, honored, and made an accepted premise of human action can man begin to move with simplicity in that vast complex of causes and effects. He then moves as a man under God, not as a would-be god.

It is this that Moses has in mind in Deuteronomy 29:29, declaring,

> The secret things belong unto the Lord our God: but those things which are revealed belong unto us and to our children for ever, that we may do all the words of this law.

According to Wright, "the secret things," which belong to God has reference to the future.[2] Keil and Delitzsch stated

> That which is revealed includes the law with its promises and threats; consequently that which is hidden can only refer to the mode in which God will carry out in the future His counsel and will, which He has revealed in the law, and complete His work of salvation notwithstanding the apostasy of the people.[3]

Von Rad sees this as a statement of "the limits of all human wisdom," a clearer perception of the text's meaning. The text thus reads in its meaning: "Yahweh's will expressed in the law is manifest; it is this which belongs to Israel for all time, and for which it is accountable; all else lies in God's hand."[4]

Von Rad makes clear the meaning of the text and its covenantal nature. *First,* Moses says that "those things which are revealed belong unto us and to our children for ever." The ungodly deny God's law: it is no revelation to them but rather an offense. They seek to master the secret things and to command the future and to mold it in terms of their decree and will. The realm of simplicity and the life which is beyond problems replaces God. Man's dream is now made totally lord and creator, and this divinity is transferred to man, future man, but he is still present man in process of becoming god. Covenant man alone sees the revelation of God's law-word as his means to problem-solving. It is a revelation which simplifies his life because it gives it meaning and declares,

> Ye shall observe to do therefore as the Lord your God hath commanded you, that ye may live: ye shall not turn aside to the right hand or to the left.
> Ye shall walk in all the ways which the Lord your God hath commanded you, that ye may live, and that it may be well with you, and

---

2. G. Ernest Wright, "Deuteronomy," in *The Interpreter's Bible,* II, 507.

3. C. F. Keil and F. Delitzsch: *Biblical Commentary on the Old Testament,* vol. III, *The Pentateuch,* p. 451. Grand Rapids, MI: Eerdmans, 1949.

4. Gerhard Von Rad: *Deuteronomy,* p. 181. Philadelphia, PA: The Westminster Press, 1956.

that ye may prolong your days in the land which ye shall possess. (Deut. 5:32-33)

Only be thou strong and very courageous, that thou mayest observe to do according to all the law, which Moses my servant commanded thee: turn not from it to the right hand or to the left, that thou mayest prosper whithersoever thou goest.

This book of the law shall not depart out of thy mouth; but thou shalt meditate therein day and night, that thou mayest observe to do according to all that is written therein: for then thou shalt make thy way prosperous, and then thou shalt have good success. (Joshua 1:7-8)

Thus, it is also the means to God's blessing and His prospering grace to His covenant people.

*Second,* Moses declares not only that God's law belongs to us as the key which opens up the world to us as our area of dominion, but that we are required to "do all the words of this law" because God so declares it. The law of God is man's only true means to dominion and prosperity, but, whatever the results, it is our duty to obey God. In times which are evil, to obey God has penalties. Nonetheless, we are told,

Let us hear the conclusion of the whole matter: Fear God, and keep his commandments: for this is the whole duty of man.

For God shall bring every work into judgment, with every secret thing, whether it be good, or whether it be evil. (Eccles. 12:13-14)

*Third,* there is a limit to human wisdom. To understand the mind of God and His works we would have to be a god ourselves. The universe is totally rational and yet incomprehensible to the mind of man, because its vast complexity is beyond him. This is even more true of God. We cannot fathom the depths of the meaning of the Trinity, of predestination, creation, grace, and much more, but by faith we can understand them in the sense that we know that God is faithful. There is no inconsistency but rather perfect harmony between His every revealed word and Himself, and between His revelation of Himself in Jesus Christ, and His eternal Godhead and mystery.

To say that "the secret things belong unto the Lord our God" is to say that God is God and we are His creatures. It means that the complexity and simplicity of life are alike from God, and the key to understanding is faith and the obedience of faith.

# 93

## SOCIAL SUICIDE

We are rarely told how seriously the early colonists in America regarded Biblical law, nor in what detail. It was not easy to espouse Biblical law, because it often meant a break with English royal law, and pressure from England often led to revision or suppression. Thus, the missionary to the Indians, John Eliot, sought to establish civil government among Christian Indians entirely in terms of the Biblical eldership and decimal system. Elders over ten families, a council of elders for hundreds, and again for thousands, was planned by Eliot. Eliot saw Christ as the only true King and wrote, "Much is spoken of the rightful heir of the crown of England, and the injustice of casting out the right heir; but Christ is the only right heir of the crown of England and all other nations also."[1] After the Restoration, the Massachusetts General Court found it necessary to suppress Eliot's book.

Massachusetts, however, bought little peace by this act. Its own charter was soon under attack by the crown. For our purposes, what is significant is the theological principle whereby the popular party opposed the surrender of the charter. The sixth commandment, "Thou shalt not kill," forbad the surrender of the charter, it was held. "Men may not destroy their political lives any more than their natural lives."[2] The sixth commandment forbids murder. Since we are not our own, for us to commit suicide is murder, a violation of God's law and an offense against God's property. Since the earth is the Lord's, and since all institutions and orders in society are required to be in conformity to God's word, anything which harms, endangers, or kills God's order is a violation of the sixth commandment.

Was this simply an imaginative over-extension of the application of the law, or was it a valid interpretation? Deut. 30:11-20 makes clear that the interpretation was a sound one:

> For this commandment which I command thee this day, it is not hidden from thee, neither is it far off.
> It is not in heaven, that thou shouldest say, Who shall go up for us to heaven, and bring it unto us, that we may hear it, and do it?
> Neither is it beyond the sea, that thou shouldest say, Who shall go over the sea for us, and bring it unto us, that we may hear it and do it?

1. Larzer Ziff: *Puritanism in America,* p. 174. New York: The Viking Press, 1973.
2. *Ibid.,* p. 221.

But the word is very nigh unto thee, in thy mouth, and in thy heart, that thou mayest do it.

See, I have set before thee this day life and good, and death and evil; In that I command thee this day to love the Lord thy God, to walk in his ways, and to keep his commandments and his statutes and his judgments, that thou mayest live and multiply: and the Lord thy God shall bless thee in the land whither thou goest to possess it.

But if thine heart turn away, so that thou wilt not hear, but shalt be drawn away, and worship other gods, and serve them;

I denounce unto you this day, that ye shall surely perish, and that ye shall not prolong your days upon the land, whither thou passest over Jordan to go to possess it.

I call heaven and earth to record this day against you, that I have set before you life and death, blessing and cursing: therefore choose life, that both thou and thy seed may live:

That thou mayest love the Lord thy God, and that thou mayest obey his voice, and that thou mayest cleave unto him: for he is thy life, and the length of thy days: that thou mayest dwell in the land which the Lord sware unto thy fathers, to Abraham, to Isaac, and to Jacob, to give them.

*First,* it must be noted that some hold that Romans 10:4-10 is a cancellation of Deuteronomy 30:11-20, because Paul contrasts the righteousness which is of the law with the righteousness which is of faith. Calvin, in citing Paul's words here against all doctrines of salvation by works, declares that the law was not given by Moses "in order to detain them (Israel) in a dependence on works, but, on the contrary, to lead them to Christ... By the teaching of the law itself he confirms the righteousness of faith."[3] It is equally an error to hold on the one hand that all Scripture teaches a works-salvation, and, on the other, that it teaches two plans of salvation, first a works-salvation and then a grace-salvation. God's covenant is always a covenant of grace.

When Moses says of the Lord, "He is thy life, and the length of thy days (Deut. 30:20), he is stating the same thing that our Lord declares in John 11:25, 26 of Himself: "I am the resurrection and the life. He that believeth in me, though he were dead, yet shall he live; and whosoever liveth and believeth in me shall never die." The relationship between these two statements has long been recognized.

*Second,* Moses is declaring to Israel that their future is determined by their faith, by either faith in God or faith in idols, false gods. "The way of the former led to blessing: the latter could only result in curse."[4] But faith is not empty belief. Faith has consequences in obedience, either to the law-word of God or to the law of idols. The issue as declared by

---

3. John Calvin: *Commentaries on the Epistle of Paul the Apostle to the Romans,* p. 385f. Grand Rapids, MI: Eerdmans, 1948.

4. Anthony Phillips: *Deuteronomy,* p. 202. Cambridge, England: Cambridge University Press, 1973.

Moses is faith and the obedience of faith: the consequence is either blessings or curses.

*Third,* the covenant people are not being asked to do anything difficult. They are not asked to search the heavens physically or intellectually. God's law-word has been revealed: it is as near as hearing and seeing, and it is plainer, because it is written in every atom of their being, so that it is in their mouth and heart. The law of God is a more constituent part of my being than I am, or my personality. Therefore, when I depart from God's word, I choose death. Theologians have stressed too heavily the difficulty of obeying God's law. What Scripture says is that, for those who are *dead* in sins and trespasses, it is impossible, because death is the end of possibility with respect to life. The law is inseparable from life, because God's law is the way for the life of grace. Moses declares that to believe and obey God is life. Obedience to the law of God is simply living. The living are able to act, and the law of God is life in action.

*Fourth,* as G. Ernest Wright has written,

> The viewpoint here is typically biblical, and one which has made Christianity a truly "democratic" faith in the sense that it can be laid hold of with power by the simplest and the most humble. We are surrounded by mystery, and ultimate knowledge is beyond our grasp. Yet God has brought himself (Deut. 4:7) and his word to us. We can have life by faith and by loyal obedience to his covenant, even though our knowledge is limited by our finitude. One need not wait to comprehend the universe in order to obtain the promised salvation. It is freely offered in the covenant now.[5]

There is nothing occult or esoteric about Biblical faith: "it is the power of God unto salvation to *every one* that believeth; to the Jew first, and also to the Greek" (Rom. 1:16).

*Fifth,* Scripture is clear throughout that *sin is death.* From Moses through Paul and John, this is stressed. The Puritan view is therefore faithful to Scripture: "Men may not destroy their political lives any more than their natural lives" without violating the law, "Thou shalt not kill." Anything which harms or destroys our political, ecclesiastical, vocational, or family life is a violation of this law of God. The commandment is emphatic: "therefore choose life." To avoid social suicide, we must obey God's law.

---

5. G. Ernest Wright, "Deuteronomy," in *The Interpreter's Bible,* II, 509.

## 94

## MEN AS DICE

One of the more striking images used by St. Paul is one in which immature and childish people are compared to dice, rolled around and tossed about by crafty men as though they were merely something to be used. St. Paul speaks of the work of the ministry as "the perfecting of the saints" (Eph. 4:12), the goal being that all be edified and instructed

> Till we all come in the unity of the faith, and of the knowledge of the Son of God, unto a perfect man, unto the measure of the stature of the fulness of Christ:
> That we henceforth be no more children, tossed to and fro, and carried about with every wind of doctrine, by the sleight of men, and cunning craftiness, whereby they lie in wait to deceive;
> But speaking the truth in love, may grow up into him in all things, which is the head, even Christ,
> From whom the whole body fitly joined together and compacted by that which every joint supplieth, according to the effectual working in the measure of every part, maketh increase of the body unto the edifying of itself in love. (Eph. 4:13-16)

There are some striking contrasts in this text. *First,* childish immaturity is alien to true faith. It is our duty to grow, to "be no more children" in the faith. Children are easily misled and are not mature workmen. The Kingdom of God requires us to be dominion men, furthering God's purpose in every area of life and thought. We are to be *perfect* or mature men, and only such can effectually serve their Lord.

*Second,* if we remain children, we are tossed here and there, and carried about with every drifting wind of doctrine and opinion, like a rudderless ship, because evil men are readily and cunningly using us by sleight. The word sleight is literally "as by dice playing," so that the immature believers are compared to the loaded, tossed dice of a gambling game.

We have here a dramatic figure which summons men to be determined by the will and word of God rather than the controls and doctrines of men. The dice suggest chance; God's determination of us is predestination. Paul is not denying that God's predestination governs the mature and the childish alike. What he is suggesting is that the more mature and the more self-determined we are as Christians, the more clearly too God's Spirit and decree are manifest in us. On the other hand, the more childish and the less responsible we are, the more we become pawns of the will of evil men, and the less our faith manifests itself.

*Third,* the stronger and the more responsible the Christian individual is, the stronger also his corporate sense, and his unity with Christ and with the covenant people of Christ. Christian maturity is not in isolation; it is not a virtue of retreat from the world, but of community in the faith within the world. It is not formal or institutional unity which is spoken of, but "the unity of the faith." Francis W. Beare notes that we have here an equation "of *the unity of the faith* with the attainment of *mature manhood,* and this again with the attainment to *the measure of the stature of the fulness of Christ.*"[1] The immature Christian is acting like the ungodly and is ungodly if he remains immature, adding his disarmed condition to immaturity to make himself a pawn, like dice, to be tossed about and used. The person who professes Christianity and remains immature is not a Christian. To be a Christian means life and growth.

*Fourth,* the Christian's duty is "speaking the truth in love." The word speaking has in Greek a broader meaning than in English, so that it includes "apprehending the truth," "living by the truth," and "being true."[2] To be in Christ means "participation in a dynamic, growing life."[3]

*Fifth,* John says of Jesus, "All things were made by him; and without him was not any thing made that was made"(John 1:3). St. Paul repeatedly stresses the cosmic power, government, and authority of Christ. The "church" or Kingdom is Christ's new creation, and, as in Colossians 2:19, in Ephesians 4:16, St. Paul stresses that the true and proper working, the life of this new creation is Jesus Christ. When we are a working part of that body, then we are stable, strong, and assured. We are no longer dice tossed by cunning men but members of Jesus Christ.

Basic to this declaration by Paul is the emphatic fact that man is a theological creature. He can only truly live by the every word of God (Matt. 4:4). Unless man is firmly grounded in the knowledge that he is God's creation and creature, totally created by God for His own sovereign use and glory, he is a dice in the hands of evil men.

Today, man does not see himself as a theological but as a *biological man,* a product of chance variations in a long, evolutionary history. The name of his game is survival. As a result, one scientist declares, "What moral imperative is higher than that of survival?" Michael A. Faia thus holds that duplicity is essential to survival, and both students and professors need to play the game of cheating.[4]

Because modern man sees himself as biological man, (and then as

1. Francis W. Beare, "Ephesians," in *The Interpreter's Bible,* X, 693.
2. *Ibid.,* X, 694.
3. *Idem.*
4. "An Apple for the Student," in *Human Behavior,* vol. 5, no. 11, November 1976, p. 52.

economic or political man, i.e., a product in every area, not a king in Christ), the scientist is his new priest. As Richard Currier notes, "modern science has taken over the role—once performed by traditional religions—of answering fundamental questions about the nature of the universe in general and the human species in particular...The questions we once asked of priests, we now ask of our new religion."[5] As biological man views himself, he has a choice of basically two options, heredity or environment as the determining factor, genetic determinism or behaviorism, two rival deterministic faiths. In either case, man is a product of forces which toss him about like dice, and make of him what they will. The result is a growing personal and social immaturity. Biological man is a product of meaningless and blind forces, and he is thus himself truly "beyond freedom and dignity," as B. F. Skinner sees it.

If the Christian is mature, not a human dice, he can, as dominion man, readily subdue the earth under God. Biological man has no such capacity nor power: he is a pawn.

---

5. Richard Currier, "The New Heresy," in *ibid.,* p. 20.

## 95

## INHERITANCE AND ESCHATOLOGY

A young couple I know face an insoluble problem: it is their hunger and passion to own a ranch. Both of them were brought up on a ranch. At the small rural house they now rent, they have perhaps an acre of ground, and every inch of it is utilized for animals, goats, chickens, and other farm animals. The young man's parents owned a sizable ranch; their son was running it for them; the parents in turn had inherited it. But it was sold. The parents decided that a good life, with the opportunity to travel and to enjoy "the finer things of life," was better than living on a modest ranch while their son worked it. In effect, they denied their own inheritance, disinherited their son, and cut themselves off from the past, present, future, and God. Instead of gaining "the finer things of life," they are actually out of touch with life.

A godly perspective on inheritance puts us in touch with past, present, and future. *Touch,* both physical and historical, is important to life. Babies who are deprived of the needed touch can grow up physically and mentally retarded. *Touch* is basic to health and to healing, a fact professional healers use and exploit. As a pastor, I found that many sick or dying persons reached out for my hand as I prayed for them. *Touch* is basic to love; a touchless marriage is a loveless marriage. The touchless nature of rock and roll dancing is a symptom of a radical breakdown in man. For youth, normally so hungry for the touch of a loved one, to dance unseeing and untouchingly with a "partner," is evidence of existentialist isolation and inner death. This absence of touch is also Manichaean in its implications and spells schizophrenia for a culture.

I recall one lovely woman, once part of a famous professional dance group, who had long vaguely believed in God but without any certainty at any point of doctrine. On becoming a Christian, and accepting the doctrines of creation, the incarnation, and providence, she remarked how *close* God was now, within touching distance.

In my travels, I have often heard men tell of their family's past with pride: my grandfather shook hands with John Adams; my grandfather shook hands with Robert E. Lee, or Jefferson Davis, and so on. They touched the past.

Touching is life. It establishes a relationship. We are emphatically told that sexual relations make a couple *one flesh,* or *one body* (I Cor. 6:16).

417

Sexual relations are therefore to be limited to marriage, because it is God's will that only husband and wife become one flesh (Gen. 2:24). We know that, with certain poisons, even touching any empty can will kill a man, because the slightest residue is absorbed into the skin. The absorbing powers of the skin are one of many facts of the meaning of touching. The Bible has many laws which forbid touching the unclean thing. We are also told of our Lord that, "as many as touched were made perfectly whole" (Matt. 14:36).

But this is not all. We are told that our bodies are "the members of Christ," and hence it is a fearful evil to "take the members of Christ, and make them the members of an harlot" (I Cor. 6:15). Believers are called the body of Christ's Kingdom and Kingship. They are therefore members of Christ. Again, the culminating privilege of which St. John speaks, in terms of his association with the Lord, is touch: "That which was from the beginning, which we have heard, which we have seen with our eyes, which we have looked upon, *and our hands have handled,* of the Word of life,...declare we unto you" (I John 1:1, 3).

The purpose of a godly inheritance is to maintain a sense of touch with past, present, and future in terms of God's sovereign purpose. Inheritance and eschatology are thus very closely related. God's purpose with regard to history requires that our lives be directed towards that end. If that purpose is the triumph of evil, or if it be our rapture out of this world, then indeed the subject of inheritance is irrelevant. If, however, God's purpose is the triumph of His Kingdom and its rule over all things, then inheritance is an important concern, as indeed it is in all of Scripture. We are spoken of as *heirs* with Christ of all things (Rom. 8:17). We are told very plainly that it is a mark of the good man that he leaves an inheritance to his children's children. According to Proverbs 13:22,

> A good man leaveth an inheritance to his children's children: and the wealth of the sinner is laid up for the just.

This is an eschatological statement: it tells us that it is the nature of history as God has ordained it that the wealth of the sinner become the inheritance of God's righteous men. Isaiah 61:6 (as well as many other texts) makes this same point: "ye shall eat the riches of the Gentiles, and in their glory shall ye boast yourselves." On the other hand, it is an aspect of the righteousness of the good man that he works to leave an inheritance, however humble, to his children's children.

The essence of a godly inheritance is its eschatological perspective: it is being mindful of God's purpose for history, and it means work and care in terms of that future. Having been touched by God's grace, we are in touch with our inheritance as children of Abraham in Christ, and we transmit that faith and our worldly goods in terms of that calling. We touch the beginning and the end by faith.

Medieval foundations, and then later Puritan foundations, were established in terms of this principle. Inheritance is an eschatological concept. How we view inheritance will manifest our eschatology.

Calvin, though childless, was able to answer those who mocked him at this point, that Europe was peopled with his sons. His eschatology gave him a godly perspective, and he was more in touch with the future than those with money and sons but no real faith, because he was in touch with life and the principle of life, the triune God.

One of the most beautiful and radiant deaths I ever saw was of a girl dying of syphillis, who had learned of her desperate condition within days after her conversion. Her hope of now having a good life and children was replaced by the certainty of death. Her reaction, after the first shock, was to recognize that she was now closer to true life and to her Lord than ever before, and to accept and rejoice in that fact: for the first time in her life, she had a future.

With faith, we all have a future, in time and in eternity. We are in touch with history, past, present, and future. We have an inheritance, and a duty to add to that inheritance. The world was not empty when we came into it, and it should not be emptier because we have been here. We are heirs, rich heirs, and we must leave our heirs still richer. Otherwise, we are *out of touch,* and what we have will be taken from us and given to another (Matt. 25:14-30).

## 96

## TOUCH AND LAW

A very interesting aspect of the doctrine of the divine right of kings was *the king's touch.* The kings of England, for example, could supposedly heal scrofula by their touch. Queen Elizabeth often "healed" people. Charles I on Midsummer Day, 1633, "cured" one hundred people in the Holyrood chapel royal, and Charles II, during his reign, is said to have touched close to a hundred thousand persons.

A king's person could not be lightly touched: he was a species of divinity, and his person was inviolable. His touch was a favor, an act of grace, and it thus had a healing potential.

However false this faith with respect to kings, it is sound with respect to God. The healing touch of Jesus is often cited in the gospels. In the story of the woman "who had an issue of blood twelve years" who came behind our Lord and "touched the border of his garment," her reasoning was, "If I do but touch his garment, I shall be made whole" (or, saved) (Matt. 9:20). The Greek word for *touch* is *hapto,* to fasten or cling to, lay hold of, to have fellowship and association with (II Cor. 6:17). In I John 5:18 we are told that "he that is begotten of God keepeth himself, and that wicked one toucheth him not." Satan's touch communicates his evil; Christ's touch communicates His grace and power. *Touch* is thus not only physical touch but is also used for fellowship and communion. When the woman touched the hem of Jesus' garment by faith, she was made whole. We are told that Jesus perceived "in himself that the power proceeding from him had gone forth" (Mark 5:30).

In a humanistic and existentialist framework, there is no God to touch, or to have fellowship with and neither are there any people. Every man is his own private universe and god. Wilson Bryan Key calls modern teenage dancing the "loneliest scene in town. . . . No touching is permitted, not even with the eyes."[1]

On the intellectual scene, we have had several generations of contempt for small-town, neighborly life, because it involves too great an intimacy, too close a fellowship between peoples. The preference has been for the anonymity of the big modern city, New York in particular, where there is no closeness and no responsibility for other people.[2]

---

1. Wilson Bryan Key: *Media Sexploitation,* p. 142f. Englewood Cliffs, NJ: Prentice-Hall, 1976.
2. Nicholas Lemann, "Going Home," in *The Washington Monthly,* November, 1974, vol. VIII, no. 9, pp.8-18.

The result of all this has been isolation and sterility for man and modern urban culture has a tinsel flash and cheapness because of its basic lack of touch with God and man. Men now suffer, as they pass their teens and twenties, from this isolation, and the result is the substitution of the superficial touch for reality. Man is out of touch with God, out of communion with his Lord, and hence out of touch or communion with himself and his fellow men. He looks for his substitute in a new king's touch. In "group grope" therapy, people touch and handle one another for ostensible therapy, each as a divine king touching and supposedly healing both himself and the other. In this modern mockery of our Lord's healing touch, each egocentric person trades touches with another, and each remains a stranger to God, man and self.

Another aspect of this modern view of touch is the "groupie," the girl who is anxious and eager to have sexual relations with every important or famous person they can way-lay. This impetus is also very strong among the wealthy and the famous: each seeks power, and the touch of power, by seeking sex promiscuously with "important people." Thus, F. D. Roosevelt, to cite one example among many, delighted in commanding the millionaire granddaughter of a famous banker; it gave him a sense of power to control her. She in turn, while finding him a boring and superficial man, saw him as a "sun-god" because of his political power and never refused him. Her husband encouraged the relationship, which gave him a second-hand touch with the world's most powerful man.[3] Such activity is commonplace today: it gives blacks a sense of power to touch and copulate with a white, and the white feels the same about sex with a black. Sleeping with a Jewish girl gives renegade Catholics and Protestants a perverse delight, and Jewish men get a similar pleasure in taking a girl from the ranks of Gentiles. The same perverse impulse is true of women who seek extra-marital sex. The goal is to gain power over the other, and the point of touch is to dominate, despoil, and possess, not to establish community. Sex is reduced to a power game devoid of love.

Arthur Koestler, in his novel *The Call Girls,* satirizes the international academic community which regularly meets in conferences to present "solutions" to all the world's problems. He calls them "call girls," prostitutes of the intellectual world who are interested in power and who disguise their degeneracy with high-sounding professions of humanitarianism. Their basic philosophy is that "Democracy is too serious a matter to be left to the electorate."[4] Their answer to world problems includes full self-expression:

---

3. Jeffry Potter: *Men, Money and Magic, The Story of Dorothy Schiff.* New York: Coward, McCann & Geophegan, 1976.

4. Arthur Koestler: *The Call Girls,* p. 149. New York: Random House, 1973. While the characters of this book are fictitious, the authors, publications and experiments quoted by them are authentic.

Never be reasonable about anything. Get rid of your irritations. Don't keep your feelings corked up, any more than you would your stomach. Yelling gets the knot out of your gut. Remember, they that spit shall inherit the earth.[5]

All of this only puts people more out of touch with one another. The wealthy Dorothy Schiff had her first husband tell her, when she appeared beautifully gowned for breakfast on the morning after their wedding, " 'I never could stand women in the morning,' and that was our last breakfast together."[6] Her fourth husband was a wealthy man, and she a wealthy woman. "Even when we were married, he wanted to go fifty-fifty on the hotel bill, and I said, 'Goddamnit, on our honeymoon *you* can pay. After that, I'll go fifty-fifty.' "[7] Her life, while full of physical touch, was out of touch with the reality of life, God and His creation and law.

Isolation and sterility are the marks of man and culture when God is not central to all things. Man hungers for the healing touch of power and grace. He will seek the touch of power and grace where he believes it to exist. The lust for the touch of power, contact with the wealthy and the famous, is evidence of faith that these people are the source of power. Dorothy Schiff's life witnesses to the fact that the intellectuals, the politicians, and the wealthy are often in a frenzied search for power in the touch of one another. All are empty, and all seek power in another man, because their faith is in man.

Of Jesus we are told, that the people "pressed (or, rushed) upon him for to touch him, as many as had plagues" (Mark 3:10). Nowadays, the pressing or rushing to touch is centered on famous people, because man's hope is in man. Reforms thus will accomplish nothing as long as man hungers for the healing, cleansing touch from man. Only when men see their need for God's royal touch, the true King's touch, will politics, wealth, and intellectual culture recede to their rightful and limited place in society. Men will not be out of touch with their fellow men when they are touched by God.

Law is a form of touch, a hold, a principle of fellowship and association between God and man, and among men. In a humanistic society, men naturally seek humanistic laws. The humanistic law, touch, or fellowship moves in terms of the pre-eminence of man, hence its insistence upon democracy, and equality. However, because humanistic faith locates law in man, it also destroys the democracy and equality it professes. If power is in man, then some men will obviously and empirically demonstrate that they have more power than others, by

---

5. *Ibid.,* p. 91.
6. Jeffrey Potter, *op. cit.,* p. 60f.
7. *Ibid.,* p. 237.

political, economic, sexual, or some other means. Humanism thus enthrones the charismatic leader, the person whose being radiates power and whose touch is hence desired. Other people then press or rush upon him, to touch him and to gain power thereby. For such people, law is of necessity humanistic, because for them power proceeds from man. The cry is "Power from the people, and, Power to the people." It was Hitler who held, "All power issues from the people." Like Stalin, he became the voice of that people and the totality of its power.

The Berkeley Version renders I John 5:18 thus: "he whose birth is from God retains hold on him and the wicked one does not get a grip on him." If we are in touch with God, we are in touch with His life, grace, and law. If we are in touch with the Evil One, we are under his dominion and law, the law of antinomianism and anarchy, every man his own god. We cannot eliminate the lawlessness of our time unless we hearken to Isaiah: "Cease ye from man, whose breath is in his nostrils: for wherein is he to be accounted of?" (Isa. 2:22).

## 97

## INHERITANCE AND POWER

Psalm 62:11 declares that "power belongeth unto God," who is the only souce of power. God's power is manifested in the creation of (Ps. 148:5-8) and the sustaining of the world (Ps. 65:5-13). God has delegated power to man (Gen. 1:26-28), and the regenerate are in particular confirmed and strengthened in their right, privilege, and power as the sons of God by the adoption of grace (John 1:12).

The word translated as power in John 1:12 is the Greek *exousia* (*dynamis* is used also in the New Testament), and it means a derived or conferred authority, right, privilege or power.

All man's powers are thus from God, either from creation, shared by all men but perverted and weakened by the fall, or from regeneration, whereby man is confirmed in his creation gift of power and dominion. "As many as received him, to them gave he power to become the sons of God, even to them that believe on his name" (John 1:12). This is the power, *first* to accept Christ, because God's grace is operative in them, and, *second,* the power to manifest their sonship by the obedience of faith and the exercise of dominion.

Those who by God's power are made a creation are also made *heirs* of God and joint-heirs with Christ (Rom. 8:17). Thus, in any consideration of the laws of inheritance, it is essential that we consider at least some aspects of our inheritance from the Lord.

*First,* it is obvious that we are heirs of the earth, which must be made over into God's Kingdom. The blessed meek, the tamed of God, shall inherit the earth (Matt. 5:5). It is essential, therefore, that the heirs actively work to claim every area of life and thought, and every area of the earth, as their inheritance in Christ. All is to be claimed and also developed in terms of His law. This is a clear mandate to *work,* but it involves more than work. Work can be performed by slaves, time-servers, and the unregenerate. Godly work has as its end the glory of God and the extension of dominion under Him. It cannot be for our own glory or ambition.

*Second,* a neglected area of our inheritance is the Sabbath. The church has converted the Sabbath into a church-oriented day. The Sabbath is both God-centered and man-centered. Our Lord declared,

> The sabbath was made for man, and not man for the sabbath. Therefore the Son of man is Lord also of the sabbath. (Mark 2:27-28)

Alexander's comment on these verses is very important:

Passing over the two arguments preserved by Matthew, one derived from the labours of the priests in the temple (12:5, 6), and the other from Hosea's declaration of God's preference of human welfare even to required observances (Hos. 6:6; Matt. 12, 7). Mark records an answer, found in neither of the others, though involved in the citation from Hosea, and perhaps originally uttered as a kind of paraphrase or commentary on it. If God chooses mercy, i.e. kind regard to human happiness, and not (i.e. rather than) sacrifice (or other ceremonial service), we might well conclude, though it were not recorded, that the Sabbath is an institution meant for human benefit, and therefore to be set aside when inconsistent with it, not a necessary or inexorable law, to which the interests of man must yield, whenever they are brought into collision. And if this was true even of the Sabbath as a purely divine institution, how much more of its corruptions and unauthorized additions. If the holy rest commanded on the seventh day might lawfully be broken for the sake of saving life or even mitigating its distresses, how much more must such emergencies dispense with an extravagant and uncommanded abstinence from active labour....

.... *Therefore,* or more exactly, so that (as a necessary consequence), *the Son of man is lord* (not only of all other things affecting human happiness, but) *also* (or *even*) of *the Sabbath,* which you might suppose to be exempt from his control.... The meaning of the sentence therefore must be, that the Sabbath having been ordained for man, not for any individual, but for the whole race, it must needs be subject to the Son of Man, who is its head and representative, its sovereign and redeemer. This implies that though the Sabbath, in its essence, is perpetual, the right of modifying and controlling it belongs to Christ, and can be exercised only under his authority.[1]

The man-centered emphasis is thus clear. The sabbath has man's rest in mind. It is not intended to be a strait-jacket or a burden but a joy and rest. The God-centered emphasis is also clear: man can only rest and enjoy the sabbath when he knows that it is God's ordination which settles the issues of life. As the psalmist declares, "It is vain for you to rise up early, to sit up late, to eat the bread of sorrows: for so he giveth his beloved sleep" (Ps. 127:2). Keeping the Sabbath means faith in the Lord: it means that we realize that the determination of things is from the Lord, and, having done our duty, we leave the results in the Lord's hands. Instead of fretful work, endless worrying over the results, we trust the Lord to care for His Kingdom, in His time, and in His appointed way.

The Sabbath is thus an inheritance: it gives us one day in seven to delight in God's sovereign grace and government, one year in seven to rest, and an extra year in fifty to rejoice before the Lord. The sabbatical

1. J. A. Alexander: *Commentary on the Gospel of Mark,* p. 54f. Grand Rapids, MI: Zonderan, (1854) reprint.

years should be the goal of godly reconstruction: they will limit debt and eliminate inflation; they will require providence and will enhance both godly production and godly consumption, because the Sabbath years will compel providential planning as well as recreational pleasure.

It requires true faith to *rest* in the Lord, "casting all your care upon him; for he careth for you" (I Peter 5:7). The Sabbath is thus an inheritance: those who truly *rest* in the Lord can set aside their work because they know that a life in the Lord, which is given over to one-seventh of its weekly time in Sabbaths, and, in a lifetime, to a yet higher percentage when the sabbaths of years are reckoned in, is more productive than a fretful, driving life outside of Christ. The heirs of God in Christ claim the Sabbath. It is not the church but man who is the lord of the Sabbath in Christ.

*Third,* we have the inheritance of the keys of the kingdom (Matt. 16:19; 18:18; John 20: 22, 23). The power of the keys is the power of knowing, interpreting, and *applying* the word of God. We bind or loose men (and ourselves) by means of the word: it declares the law of God. It shows the way of salvation and of sanctification. It sets forth the conditions of blessings and curses. It is the means whereby dominion is exercised. "Every man," says St. Paul, speaking of the redeemed, "shall receive his own reward according to his own labour" (I Cor. 3:8). Not all labor leads to dominion, nor can all the labor of the godly add up to the same degree of dominion. The extent of our faithful obedience to God's law will determine the extent of our reward. We are assured that, when we abound in the work of the Lord we have the assurance that our "labour is not in vain in the Lord" (I Cor. 15:58). The principle of increase, productivity, or "abounding" is labor or work which is in faithful obedience and conformity to God's law.

*Fourth,* an aspect of our inheritance which is also a means to power is the law. The law is *death* to the unregenerate sinner (Rom. 8:2; Col. 2:14, etc.), but, to the regenerate people of Christ, it is "the perfect law of liberty" (James 1:25; 2:12). The law is no longer a death penalty to us, and an enemy, because we are no longer dead in sins and trespasses; we are a new creation, and the law is now written on the tables of our hearts (Jer. 31:33; Heb. 10:16), so that our hearts, instead of being in rebellion against the law, echo the law. The law is now not alien to us but is our new nature, and we say with Christ, "Lo, I come to do thy will, O God" (Heb. 10:9). To be antinomian is to be unregenerate: it means that the law, not being a joyful part of the new life in us, cannot be accepted as the infallible word of God, given unto us as an inheritance, to bless us. God speaks of the law as a gift to His covenant people:

> Wherefore I caused them to go forth out of the land of Egypt, and brought them into the wilderness.

And I gave them my statutes, and shewed (or, made them to know) my judgments, which if a man do, he shall even live in them. Moreover also I gave them my sabbaths, to be a sign between me and them, that they might know that I am the LORD that sanctify them. (Ezek. 20:10-12)

God sees no warfare between grace and law. The Sabbath and the law are both spoken of as a sign and gift of grace and an evidence of the covenant of salvation. Fairbairn, in comparing these verses with Deuteronomy 30:16, observed

But neither Moses nor Ezekiel, it is obvious, meant that the life spoken of, which comprehends whatever is really excellent and good, was to be *acquired* by means of such conformity to the enactments of Heaven; for life in that sense was already theirs, freely given and secured for the goodness of God in the covenant of promise. What they meant was, that only thus could the children of Israel retain possession of what was given, or attain to the secure and continued enjoyment of it.[2]

Thus, we are reborn rich in Christ, with a great inheritance, if we claim it and develop it. If we are sons, we do.

---

2. Patrick Fairbairn: *An Exposition of Ezekiel,* Evansville, IN: Sovereign Grace Publishers, 1960 reprint.

## 98

## ISRAEL AND DOMINION

The origin of the name *Israel* comes from Jacob's wrestling with the Angel of the Lord at Peniel. Genesis 32:28 defines the name for us:

> And he said, thy name shall be called no more Jacob, but Israel: for as a prince hast thou power with God and with men, and hast prevailed.

What God here declares to Jacob is that he has *striven (sarita)* with God and with men, and has prevailed. Sarita comes from sara, strive. This is the same root as in the original name of Sarah, princess (Gen. 17:15). *Sarai,* Jah is prince. Israel means ruling with God, and also God rules. It can also be rendered as Rudolf Smend does,

> Israel means *El fights,* and Yahweh was the fighting El after whom the people named itself. The war camp was the cradle of the nation, it was also the oldest sanctuary. Israel was there and Yahweh was there.[1]

How do we get from *striving* and *fighting* to *ruling?* And where do *prince* and *princess* come in? The gap is a great one to us only because the modern mind sees *rulership* in abstraction. The modern idea sees courts, courtiers, banquets, endless servants and wealth, as the meaning of ruling. There are several words in the Old and New Testament for *rule,* and all convey a sense of action and dominion. One of these words is *sarar,* to be a prince. In Isaiah 32:1, we read, "Behold, a king shall reign in righteousness, and princes shall rule in judgment." The successful enforcement of justice means ruling. In Proverbs 8:15, 16, Wisdom declares that it is only by Wisdom that "princes decree justice. By me princes rule, and nobles, even all the judges of the earth." True government and rule presuppose the sway of justice. An amusing instance of the use of the same word is in Esther 1:22, when Ahasuerus, after his problem with Queen Vashti, "sent letters into all the king's provinces, into every province according to the writing thereof, and to every people after their language, that every man should bear *rule* in his own house...."

The presupposition of the word *rule, sarar,* is thus of triumphant and confident struggle to victory. *Rule* presupposes opposition, but also a clear-cut and full success.

---

1. Rudolf Smend: *Yahweh War & Tribal Confederation,* p. 27. Nashville, TN: Abingdon Press, (1963) 1970.

For Jacob to be called *Israel* was thus a witness to his triumphant struggles which marked him as a prince with God, because God was also present in those struggles, accomplishing His own purposes. God ruled in Jacob's ruling.

Thus, when the covenant people in the Old and then in the New Testament (Gal. 6:16) are called the Israel of God, it means that they are princes with God, princes of grace, friends of God (John 15:13-15), and also a people over whom God rules. The name Israel also means that God fights, wages war successfully, in and through the people of God.

St. Paul makes clear that the name Israel cannot belong to an apostate and defeated people. It is the name of those who are the called of God, over whom God rules:

> . . . . For they are not all Israel, which are of Israel:
> Neither, because they are the seed of Abraham, are they all children: but, In Isaac shall thy seed be called.
> That is, They which are the children of the flesh, these are not the children of God: but the children of the promise are counted for the seed. (Rom. 9:6-8)

St. Paul says, *first,* that there are two Israels, the outward entity, the nation, which claims, despite its rejection of God the Son, to be still Israel. There is, on the other hand, God's true Israel, the *ecclesia,* the Kingdom of God. *Second,* membership in God's Israel is not nor ever was by birth. It is always and only by God's grace, received by faith. Only those who share in Abraham's faith are members of Christ, the chosen seed. *Third,* those with a hereditary claim to the covenant by blood or birth, the Jews and church members, are the children of the flesh of unredeemed human nature, not the regenerate children of God. "The children of the promise" are alone counted as the true seed in Christ, who is the seed of Abraham. *Fourth,* in Romans 11 Paul makes clear that, whereas the true Israel of God shall be saved, blessed, and triumphant, the Israel which is Israel by name only shall be cut off until it becomes the regenerate Israel of God.

Thus, on the one hand we have judgment, on the other, blessing. The true Israel of God is *a ruling people.* This is also the point of I Corinthians 6:1-20. The saints are to *judge* or to rule the world. They must therefore learn to rule themselves, conquer their sins, obey God's law, resolve their conflicts, and maintain, in every area of life, their struggle to dominion.

As we have seen, the name *Israel* has in it not only the word *El,* God, but also *sarar,* strive. St. Paul echoes this meaning in the Greek text of I Corinthians 9:25, where the Greek word is *agonizomai,* to strive or contest:

> And every man that striveth for the mastery is temperate in all things. Now they do it to obtain a corruptible crown; but we are incorruptible.

The imagery here is in part athletic, but also in part royal, in that the goal is mastery and rule, not simply a race ended but an eternal rule in Christ.

Thus, to be the Israel of God means to be a people exercising dominion in the name of the Lord, and also a people over whom Christ rules. By our redemption, we are made "kings and priests unto God and his Father; to him be glory and dominion for ever and ever. Amen." (Rev. 1:6). This same principle is set forth in Exodus 19:6; the covenant people are called to be a Kingdom of Priests (cf. I Peter 2:19).

The Hebrew word for *king* is *melek,* which seems to be related to ancient root words meaning *possess,* and *counsellor.* This would indicate that the true king is not only the source of wise counsel but also is the one who possesses the realm. For us to be God's Israel means that we, who are the source in history of God's counsel, His decree, word, and law, are also the heirs of God and possessors of this world as His Kingdom.

There is thus *an eschatology* of victory implicit in the name Israel. The premillennialists, while wrong in their eschatology, are sound in associating the name Israel with God's triumphant Kingdom; they confuse that triumphant Israel with the children of the flesh rather than identifying it with the covenant of grace. In every age, the true Israel of God and the covenant of grace are identical.

If we deny the striving and warring, we deny our kingship, God's Kingdom, and Christ our King.

## 99

## GOD'S SON, ISRAEL

In Hosea 11:1, we read God's affirmation, "When Israel was a child, then I loved him and called my son out of Egypt." Earlier, God had declared to Pharaoh, "Israel is my son, even my firstborn: And I say unto thee, Let my son go, that he may serve me: and if thou refuse to let him go, behold, I will slay thy son, even thy firstborn" (Ex. 4:22-23). The covenant people are called "the Israel of God" in both Old and New Testaments (Gal. 6:16).

They are, however, the Israel of God only insofar as they are in the Lord their Redeemer. The true Israel is God's Son, Jesus Christ. Hence, in Matthew 2:15, Hosea 11:1 is seen as more than historical statement: it is prophecy which is fulfilled or enacted when the Christ-child returns from the Egyptian sojourn. Just as historical Israel was called out of bondage and slavery in Egypt, so the Christ of God leads His covenant people in every age out of the captivity of sin and death into the glorious liberty of the sons of God (Rom. 8:21). They are made a new creation, no longer members of a world sentenced to death and destruction more drastic than the world before the Flood, but members and citizens of the Kingdom of God. They are joint-heirs with Jesus Christ (Rom. 8:17) and thus are princes with God. They are friends and princes (John 15:13-15) because they keep God's commandments, and God rules and wars in and through them.

Christ the Lord is declared King, the one in whom and through whom the triune God rules, in Isaiah 33:22: "For the LORD is our judge, the LORD is our lawgiver, the LORD is our king; he will save us." The angel Gabriel told Mary that her son would be the Great King predicted from of old and promised by God:

> And the angel said unto her, Fear not, Mary: for thou hast found favour with God.
> And, behold, thou shalt conceive in thy womb, and bring forth a son, and shalt call his name JESUS.
> He shall be great, and shall be called the Son of the Highest: and the Lord God shall give unto him the throne of his father David.
> And he shall reign over the house of Jacob for ever; and of his kingdom there shall be no end. (Luke 1:30-33)

We have Isaiah 9:6-7 echoed here: "The Mighty God, The Everlasting Father, The Prince of Peace" is He of whom it is said, "Of the increase of his government and peace, there shall be no end." Jesus came as the heir to David's throne (Matt. 2:1-6, Luke 1:30-33, John 19:19-21). Paul declares Jesus to be "the blessed and only Potentate, the King of kings, and Lord of lords (I Tim. 6:15), and history will in God's time manifest this fact (Rev. 19:11-16).

This God-King shall rule, and shall wage war through His covenant people, Israel, and all rival gods and forces shall perish and disappear:

> But the LORD is the true God (God of truth), he is the living God, and an everlasting king: at his wrath the earth shall tremble, and the nations shall not be able to abide his indignation.
> Thus shall ye say unto them, The gods that have not made the heavens and the earth, even they shall perish from the earth, and from under the heavens.
> He that made the earth by his power, he hath established the world by his wisdom, and hath stretched out the heavens by his discretion.
> When he uttereth his voice, there is a multitude of waters in the heavens, and he causeth the vapours to ascend from the ends of the earth; he maketh lightnings with rain, and bringeth forth the wind out of his treasures.
> Every man is brutish in his knowledge: every founder is confounded by the graven image: for his molten image is falsehood, and there is no breath in them.
> They are vanity, and the work of errors: in the time of their visitation they shall perish.
> The portion of Jacob is not like them: for he is the former of all things (Berkeley Version, for He is the Creator of all things): and Israel is the rod of his inheritance: The LORD of hosts is his name. (Jer. 10:10-16)

The Scriptures are so full of such declarations of God's Kingship, power, and victory, that it requires wilful blindness for churchmen to retreat into neoplatonic pietism and a dispensational denial of Christ's Kingship.

Jesus Christ is the true Israel, God as King, God at war victoriously. In Him God has called His sons of grace, the children of adoption, out of Egypt, out of bondage to sin and death. He has set their feet on the road to the Promised Land, and He goes before and behind them, a pillar of fire and a cloud, to protect and defend them. He is their assurance of victory, and their confidence. As long as the covenant people move by faith, and in obedience to Him , God rules over them and through them, and God wars in and through them. They are God's Israel, His visible Kingdom and army. Christ is God's true Israel, and we as members of Christ are the Israel of God. He is King of the nations and King of the earth (Ps. 2), and all nations shall submit to Christ the King and His law:

> All the ends of the world shall remember and turn unto the LORD: and all the kindreds of the nations shall worship before thee.
> For the kingdom is the LORD'S: and he is the governor among the nations. (Ps. 22:27-28)

Psalm 47 celebrates the universal Kingship of God: "he is a great King over all the earth. He shall subdue the people under us, and the nations under our feet" (Ps. 47:2-3). Of Christ's Kingdom we are told "And the LORD shall be king over all the earth: in that day shall there be one LORD, and his name one" (Zech. 14:9), i.e., there will be only one God worshipped. Christ's reign shall be as King of peace (Heb. 7:2; Isa. 9:7), but first His enemies must be made His footstool by His willing people (Ps. 110:1-7).

> He shall judge among the heathen, he shall fill the places with dead bodies; he shall wound the heads over many countries.
> He shall drink of the brook in the way: therefore shall he lift up the head. (Ps. 110:6-7)

So assured is He of victory that He drinks readily and without fear from any stream he has to cross: this is a picture of assurance and certainty in victory. Then the Lord raises His head and standard and "charges forward triumphing" (James Moffatt).

Christ is God's Israel, His covenant King and man. Through Christ, the true Israel of God, God rules and God wars, and none can stand before Him. We are either the people of His Kingdom, members of Israel by faith and ruled by His statutes and laws, or we are among those against whom He wages war. He is God's Son, Israel. There are no noncombatants in His war.

## 100

# THE SABBATH AS INHERITANCE

The Book of Hebrews gives us an account of the Sabbath as a "promise" or inheritance from God to the covenant people. The *rest* promised by God was denied to the faithless and disobedient generation which perished in the desert after leaving Egypt (Heb. 3:7-19). This *rest* promised by God is set forth in the Sabbath and in the Promised Land, but its fulness is Jesus Christ and life in Him (Heb. 4:1-16). The fulness of our Sabbath is thus our full and perfect life in Christ in the new creation.

It is important for us therefore to understand the meaning of the Sabbath. Its meaning is not worship, which should be a daily fact, but *rest. Rest,* however, is more than a holiday or inactivity. Thus, in the United States, July 4 is a national holiday; no one works, but it is by no means a Sabbath. Too often, churchmen have equated Sabbath observance with inactivity. What then constitutes the Sabbath rest?

We have an insight into the meaning of the Sabbath and of rest in Ruth 3:1. *Rest* is here equated with marriage. Ruth's rest is marriage with Boaz. Now it is obvious to any woman that marriage is neither a holiday nor inactivity. It often involves more work for a woman, and less work for the man, but it is called a *rest* for the woman, not the man. It is essential for us to understand *why* this is so. In a godly marriage, the woman is under the authority of her husband. *To be under authority is to have power, to the degree of the authority over us.* The woman's hair is to be long as a sign of this. "For this cause ought the woman to have power on her head because of the angels" (I Cor. 15:10). If I am directly under the authority of a great person, and at his right hand, I then am a person with power. A man is called to be under God's authority in Christ. If he is faithful to his calling to be under authority, he is then a power in Christ. If he is faithless, he is then powerless, and his wife is even more powerless and frustrated. The apostasy of men becomes a ground for women's liberation movements from impotent men. The Lord declares, "But the wicked are like the troubled sea, when it cannot rest, whose waters cast up mire and dirt. There is no peace, saith my God, to the wicked" (Isa. 57:20-21).

To be at rest thus means to be faithfully under authority, and to trust in that authority. There is a suggestion of this meaning of rest in our Lord's statement concerning children: "Whosoever shall not receive the kingdom of God as a little child, he shall not enter therein" (Mark 10:15). The child trusts that his parents will care for him and rests in that fact with unquestioning faith. To rest in the Lord means to take hands off our lives in the confidence that the Lord is able to do all that we have committed unto Him. As St. Paul declared, "for I know whom I have believed (or, trusted), and am persuaded that he is able to keep that which I have committed unto him against that day" (II Tim. 1:12).

The Sabbath, according to Hebrews 4, is an eschatological fact and symbol. We celebrate both creation and re-creation, the beginning and the end. We work towards a purpose, knowing that our labor is not in vain in the Lord (I Cor. 15:58). On our Sabbaths, we celebrate our assured victory and the new life which is already ours.

We are told that neither the weekly Sabbath nor the Promised Land give us the fulness of the meaning of the Sabbath;

> There remaineth therefore a rest (or, keeping of a sabbath) to the people of God.
> For he that is entered into his rest, he also hath ceased from his own works, as God did from his.
> Let us labour therefore to enter into that rest, lest any man fall after the same example of unbelief (or disobedience).
> For the word of God is quick, and powerful, and sharper than any two-edged sword, piercing even to the dividing asunder of soul and spirit, and of the joints and marrow, and is a discerner of the thoughts and intents of the heart.
> Neither is there any creature that is not manifest in his sight: but all things are naked and opened unto the eyes of him with whom we have to do. (Heb. 4:9-13)

Unbelief is disobedience, and it deprives us of the reality of the Sabbath now and in the world to come. The opposite of disobedience is faith, and faith is obedience: it is living response to the Lord. As Westcott noted, "unbelief (iii. 12) is here seen in its practical issue," i.e., disobedience. Those who believe are those who obey, and those who obey are those whose lives are so transformed and permeated by the word of God that they are in their innermost lives more alive to God's word than anything else. As Westcott said, of Hebrews 4:12,

> The main thought in the description of 'the word of God' is not that of punishment, as it is taken by Chrysostom, but of its essential nature as it enters into, permeates, transforms, every element in man. There is no question of an external rest apart from the harmony of the believer with God or, in the figure of vs. 2, apart from the vital union of the hearer with the word. The rest is the consummation of that divine fellowship of which the life in Canaan was a type.[1]

This pervading power of the word of God has behind it "the universal

---

1. Brooke Foss Westcott: *The Epistle to the Hebrews,* p. 100. Grand Rapids, MI: Eerdmans, (1892) 1952.

Providence of God with regard to all created things,'' according to verse 13.[2] The word translated as "unbelief" (or, disobedience) is *apeitheia,* meaning unpersuadable, meaning the deliberate rejection of the word of God.

Hebrew and Jewish thought has seen, as did Augustine in the conclusion of his *Confessions,* the Sabbath as a type of the end, as an eschatalogical celebration, and rightly so. The true observance of the Sabbath means a thorough trust in the absolute authority of the triune God, that, what He has declared, He will accomplish. It means that we are under authority, and we celebrate that authority and the confident rest it gives us.

Modern man has no Sabbath; he cannot rest, because he is not under authority. Men and women are alike fretful and restless, because they reject authority. If we are passengers in an automobile whose driver we mistrust, we cannot rest. If we trust the driver, we can relax, rest, and even sleep with confidence, because we trust the driver. The same applies to the Sabbath. If our faith is Humanism, or if we are Arminians, or only nominally adhere to God's sovereignty, we can be idle on the Sabbath, but we will not rest. We cannot take hands off our lives, nor keep from trying to run the universe. We will be fretful at God's government. We can be idle on the Sabbath, and worship morning and night, but we will not rest.

The Sabbath is an inheritance for covenant man. It is an inheritance claimed by faith and obedience, and it means living under authority in a confident rest therein.

---

2. *Ibid., p. 104.*

# 101

## INHERITANCE AND TRUSTEESHIP

In a novel based upon her parent's lives, Thyra Ferre Bjorn describes the marriage of her mother, a young housemaid, to her father, an older man and a pastor. The social gap between them was a real one. After their marriage, they returned to his pastorate in the old country, in Swedish Lapland. The question in the young bride's mind on the first Sunday morning was a real one: long-standing custom required the husband, normally head of the household, to serve his wife breakfast in bed on Sunday morning. She may have laid out everything the night before, including coffee measured out in the pot, and a serving tray made ready, but his service thereof was symbolic and important. When Maria was served her breakfast in bed, she declared, "You are a real husband now, Pontus."[1] This simple tradition echoes the Biblical requirement that authority be a service and ministry (Eph. 5:25-26; Matt. 20:25-28). It illustrates the fact that in Scripture authority is a trusteeship, and the family is a trustee of an authority and an inheritance.

Carle C. Zimmerman has pointed out that there are three types of families in history: the trustee, the domestic, and the atomistic families. The trustee family has central authority in a society: it is the basic power and institution, and most government is in its hands. The trustee family sees its possessions and its work as an inheritance from the past to be transmitted to the future. The family wealth is thus not for private use but for the family's on-going life.

The domestic family is a weakening of the family's powers, with the state as gainer. It is a transition stage to the atomistic family, when the totalitarian state is the on-going life and power, the main heir and the controller of inheritance, and the source of direction for society.[2]

The family in Scripture is a trustee type family, and Biblical law is geared to the family as trustee. This means that authority in the family, i.e., the authority of the husband and the wife, is *not personal but theological*. This appears very clearly in Ephesians 5:21-33. The matter of family authority is theological. The husband's headship is established by God as a ministry through the family. His authority, while resting in his person, is not personal; it is religious and theological. His authority is

---

1. Thyra Ferre Bjorn: *Papa's Wife*, p. 23. New York: Bantam Books, (1953) 1970.
2. Carle C. Zimmerman: *Family and Civilization*. New York, NY: Harper & Brothers, 1947.

valid thus only insofar as he is faithful to the word of God; when he departs from it, God will confound his authority. Women and children will then rule over men and be their oppressors (Isa. 3:4, 12).

All authority on the human scene, in the family, church, state, and school, as well as the vocations, is ministerial (Eph. 6:5-9) and theological rather than personal. The personal exercise of authority for the sake of power is the mark of the Gentiles, i.e., of unbelief (Matt. 20:25-29; Mark 10:35-45).

Since Biblical authority is a trusteeship from the Lord, it is basic to that authority that it must be exercised in the name of the Lord for His Kingdom. What we are and have belongs neither to us, to the family, the church, or the state, but to the Lord and His Kingdom. We must thus protect ourselves and our possessions from the attempts by an ungodly heir, or by the state, to gain possession over them as if the right of inheritance were a personal fact. Inheritance, however, is a theological principle, with an eschatological framework. It must serve the purposes of God and His Kingdom, and its goal is the new creation, and all the glory of the earth made an inheritance of God's Kingdom.

We are, *first,* in our totality God's handiwork, so that there is nothing in us that is inherently or essentially of us. We are not creators or originators: we are a creation, vessels of the Great Potter, and for His sovereign purposes, not ours. St. Paul makes this very clear:

> Nay but, O man, who art thou that repliest (or, disputest) against God? Shall the thing formed say to him that formed it, Why hast thou made me thus?
> Hath not the potter power over the clay, of the same lump to make one vessel unto honour, and another unto dishonour? (Rom. 9:20-21)
> For who maketh thee to differ from another? and what hast thou that thou didst not receive? now if thou didst receive it, why dost thou glory, as if thou hadst not received it? (I Cor. 4:7)

Humanism regards man as the repository of authority. It affirms the sovereignty of man as against the sovereignty of God. Wherever sovereignty is placed on the historical scene, whether in man, the state, the church, reason, or science, the result is a bloody contest between men and institutions to appropriate that sovereign power. History is the story of that struggle. Sovereign power in man's hands is the foundation of tyranny and of revolution.

Thus, for men to claim that power and authority are inherent in men, in a status or rank, or in an institution, means an illegitimate doctrine of sovereignty.

*Second,* since authority is a ministry (Mark 10: 35-45) and a trusteeship, it cannot be surrendered where Scripture does not permit it.

The husband, father, civil ruler, pastor, or employer has no authority apart from God's word, but where God's word requires it, he cannot surrender it. Both democracy and monarchy have been illegitimate forms of government: both treat authority as an inherently human power, an inherited power, whereas what we inherit is not power but a trusteeship.

Thus, whether our position be that of a husband, wife, pastor, civil official, or as heir of some given amount of wealth, we are trustees before God of the authority that position and/or wealth gives us.

*Third,* while this trusteeship is in touch with the past and future, we cannot speak of it as simply future-oriented without adding that it is governed by the word of God. Marxism is, up to a point, future oriented, but it is governed by totally humanistic concerns. Our concern is theological: authority is not of us, but from the Lord. Thus, the husband who served his ex-maid turned wife breakfast in bed was witnessing to the fact that, however much both his older years, his superior social position, and his status as a husband gave him precedence over his young wife, his authority was ministerial. He was God's servant and agent in a limited realm, and no more. As such, it was his duty to be a minister and a servant in Christ's name (Mark 10:35-45).

Serving his wife breakfast in bed was a ritual. Rites or rituals are faiths and meanings acted out. Our disagreement should not be with rituals as such but with their meanings. Without meaning, a rite either collapses or becomes an empty tradition. True ritual is a continuing witness to a faith. Christianity today is bereft of ritual because it is bereft of faith. Some churches, as Rome, and the Church of England, are in the midst of radical changes in their rites because their faith has changed radically. Other churches have dropped ritual entirely, because their perspective, in the name of purity, is in essence humanism. Thus, in several "nonliturgical" churches I have encountered bitter arguments on the location of the American flag: this is a ritual concern and testifies to a strong faith in America. In other cases, there are controversies over the relationships of pastors and lay officers, over church order, and so on, all man-centered concerns and also ritual concerns. Most churches today are careless about doctrine, but they are intensely concerned that Robert's Rules of Order, church polity and practice, and all the by-laws be strictly adhered to; this is a ritual concern, and it is a manifestation of a particular faith. A non-ritual church does not exist. Our problem is that most of our ritual represents humanistic meanings and concerns rather than the word of God.

## 102

## MUSIC AND THE TITHE

One of the aspects of modern Christian life and worship which best reveals its distance and departure from Scripture is the place of music. The role of music is now peripheral and supplemental, whereas in the Bible it is central and basic. In no other society than that of faithful Israel, and the various branches of the church through the middle ages, has music been so important. The decline of music is a consequence of the rationalism first introduced by Abelard. By identifying increasingly man in terms of reason rather than faith, the modern world has seen the progressive relegation of music to the background. In fact, this became precisely the role of music in the Enlightenment: the composers provided background music for the royal courts. Since then, the music of Humanism has taken two directions. On the one hand, we have a highly contrived, rationalistic music which explores musical possibilities and techniques. On the other hand, popular music, from jazz to rock and roll, explores emotionalism for the sake of pure experience. In either case, music represents, even at its best, a fragmented man and a world view which is emphatically non-catholic or non-universal but is rather private and limited.

The Bible sees music as a mandatory fact in the life of faith. It is a necessary aspect of worship and to be supported by the tithe. In Numbers 18:26-28, we see that the tithe was paid to the Levites, who then gave a tenth of the tithe to the priests. The priests thus received one percent of the tither's income. The Levites had charge of the care of the tabernacle and temple, not too great a charge, the task of education (Deut. 33:10), and much else. One of their duties was to provide the music of worship.

In I Chronicles 15:16-24, and 24:1-31, we get a glimpse of what this duty involved. David organized the Levitical chorus and musicians. As James Millar observed, "The whole of the choristers and players were divided into 24 classes, and are said to have been 4000 in number, with 288 leaders. Even the name of the director of the choral recitals is given."[1] One aspect of Josiah's reform was the restoration of music (II Chron. 29:25-28, 30). While the continuing form of temple music was reshaped by David, it existed from the beginning, and music was closely

---

1. James Millar, "Music," in James Hastings, ed.: *A Dictionary of the Bible,* III, p. 457. New York, NY: Charles Scribner's Sons (1900) 1919.

tied to prophetic utterances (I Sam. 10:5; II Kings 3:15). The Bible refers specifically to nineteen musical instruments, besides mentioning other instruments generally (Dan. 3:5).[2] Peter Lorimer, in analyzing and comparing the date of I Chronicles 23:5 and I Chronicles 24 with I Chronicles 15:17, concluded that David "appointed four thousand Levites—being a fourth of their whole tribe—to be singers and musicians in the two tabernacles of Gideon and Mount Zion, dividing them into twenty-four classes under the leadership of Asaph, Heman, and Ethan-Jeduthum."[3] David, in stating that he appointed 4000 musicians, adds that he created new instruments for religious use (I Chron. 23:5).

We have not yet mentioned a most important point. A central book of the Bible, the Psalms, is a book of music: it gives us the sacred songs inspired of God, which were used for worship. The *command* to sing is a common one in Scripture: "Sing unto the LORD; for he hath done excellent things: this is known in all the earth" (Isa. 12:5). God Himself describes creation singing with joy when God laid the foundations of the earth, and the sons of God, the angelic hosts, shouting for joy (Job 38:7). David declares that, when God comes in judgment during history's course, the very trees respond with music: "Then shall the trees of the wood sing out at the presence of the LORD, because he cometh to judge the earth" (I Chron. 16:33). We cannot regard this as merely beautiful imagery: God having created all things, all things find their truest being and nature when God's presence, judgment, and grace are most manifest. Just as our hearts sing within us, and we feel marvellously alive at joyful news, so too all creation responds to its Maker. In the New Testament, such statements as Ephesians 5:19 and Colossians 3:16 make clear the centrality of music not merely to worship but to faith.

Moreover, music is to be not only an expression of joy but of faith. "Sing unto the LORD, O ye saints of his, and give thanks at the remembrance of his holiness" (Ps. 30:4). A faith with poor or little music is likely also to be a faith with a weak memory for God's grace, mercy, and blessings.

Instrumental music is also important, and regularly referred to in Scripture as witness Psalm 33:1-5:

> Rejoice in the LORD, O ye righteous: for praise is comely for the upright.
> Praise the LORD with harp: sing unto him with the psaltery and an instrument of ten strings.
> Sing unto him with a new song; play skilfully with a loud noise.
> For the word of the LORD is right; and all his works are done in truth.

---

2. Bathja Bayer, "Music," in *Encyclopaedia Judaica* vol. XII, p. 562ff.
3. Peter Lorimer, "Music," in Patrick Fairbairn, ed.: *Fairbairn's Imperial Standard Bible Encyclopedia,* vol. IV, p. 307. Grand Rapids, MI: Zondervan, (1891) 1957.

He loveth righteousness and judgment: the earth is full of the goodness (or, mercy) of the LORD.

We are to praise God by song and instrument because God is, and because the whole earth is under His government and witnesses to His mercy and judgment. The reason for music is thus transferred from man's mood to God's being and grace. While the subjective aspect of music, our experience of God's grace, our griefs, sorrows, and burdens, is very much present in the psalms, it is the objective fact of God's being and majesty which must be the central fact of our music. Music is here called *praise,* and it is comely or befitting for the upright to praise God. To withhold praise is to separate ourselves from the Lord. Our music is to be "with a loud noise," with jubilation, "for the word of the LORD is right." It is the exact and total word: it speaks to our every need and answers our every problem. It is grace, and it is law. It is truth and knowledge. Hence, our music is to be skillful and rich instrumentally and vocally.

The church has beggared itself musically, not only in its worship, but in its education, family life, and private life. My maternal grandfather was killed by Turks in Armenia while on a pilgrimage, as he walked singing on his way to an ancient church. It is difficult to imagine someone doing that now, which is also why it is difficult for most to see any Christian victory in the future, or any victory for anyone. Music on the whole has left the modern age, except for its schizophrenic manifestations. There is good music, but it is entertainment, not life and worship.

Because music has become peripheral to worship, worship has become peripheral to man. Faith today is a warped, minimal thing. Especially with Arminianism, it is saying, "Yes, I accept Jesus as my personal Savior." This is the mind saying yes, with sometimes emotion added to it. About the only time modern man puts his whole being into anything is when he is radically frightened or terrified. For the modern man, even sex, or perhaps especially sex, is divorced from love, faith, and reason. As a result, it is a shallow and ephemeral thing. In terror, modern man functions as a whole man. He therefore courts an induced terror by going to films like *Rosemary's Baby, Jaws,* and the like. Then, briefly, he is alive until the next time he has an opportunity to terrify himself. Again, modern man is able to be a whole man in *hatred.* As a result, he loves to hate. He will use love as an excuse for hating, i.e., he will claim that it is his love of a minority group, of the natural environment, or some such thing, that leads him to hate most men so passionately. In any case, he is most alive when he is filled with hatred. In the 1960's, we saw normally apathetic and emotionally callous college youth become totally involved in hatred. Almost anything sufficed to excite their hatred, and anyone not sharing their intense will to hate was in their eyes hardly alive.

Modern man cannot be whole except in terms of evil. This is especially true of the ungodly, but it is reflected also in Christians, because their lawlessness has led to despising the tithe, God's law, and hence music. When men will not see the tithe as mandatory, as God's law, it means that they choose to retain in their own hands the initiative in approaching God. It is practical, living Arminianism. The idea of supporting musicians and composers is then alien and repellant. Man then chooses to approach God in his own way, and at his own discretion. The songs he then sings are expressive of his feelings rather than the glory of God. Song too is then dead in his heart.

We have a telling bit of evidence of the closeness of music to life in ancient Israel in Numbers 21:16-18. Moffatt's rendering best conveys a hint of the nature of the song:

> Then they pushed on to Beer (Welltown), the Beer where the Eternal said to Moses, "Gather the people and I will give them water"; and Israel sang this song,
>
> > Spring up, O well—
> > Ah, sing to the well
> > That chieftains dug,
> > That captains delved
> > wielding their wands
> > wielding their staves!

Music, from its simplest to its more complex forms, was basic to man's life because it was, like life, God-centered. The point of Psalm 33:1-5 is that we sing to the Lord because His word is right, all His works are done in truth, and His government, justice, mercy, and grace are so gloriously right and perfect that song is the covenant man's ever new response.

## 103

## HEART, LAW, AND LIFE

Proverbs 4:20-23 declares

My son, attend to my words; incline thine ear unto my sayings.
Let them not depart from thine eyes; keep them in the midst of thine heart.
For they are life unto those that find them, and health (or, medicine) to all their flesh.
Keep thine heart with all diligence (or, above all keeping); for out of it are the issues of life.

It is necessary to understand the meaning of *heart* in Scripture in order to grasp the meaning here and elsewhere of Biblical references to the *heart*. For us, the heart is a physical organ which is the life and blood center of man's body. For the Bible, the *heart,* which can be rendered soul (and often is in the King James version) or *mind,* is the *center* of man's being and its unifying factor. C. Ryder Smith has suggested that "The First great Commandment probably means 'Thou shalt love (*agapan*) the Lord thy God with all thy heart—that is with all thy soul and with all thy mind and with all thy strength' (e.g. Mark xii. 30, 33)."[1]

The heart is the religious center of man. Man is what his heart is; a man's life is his faith in action. For the fallen man, this means that, since "every imagination of the thoughts of his heart (is) only evil continually" (Gen. 6:5), man's actions will reveal the nature of his heart, his life's center.

Paganism has always denied this unity of man. It has insisted that, in some form or another, man is a dual or a tripartite being, whose actions do not necessarily reveal his nature. A man intellectually or religiously can be one thing, according to paganism, but his actions can be another. This pagan perspective can be summed up in the old proverb, "You can't judge the heart." The man may be a murderer, adulterer, thief, liar, and a covetous man, but, we are told, we cannot judge his heart. The atheistic humanist tells us that such a man is still pure in heart. The pietistic pseudo-Christian tells us that such a man, in his heart, may be a Christian.

Religiously, this doctrine is called the carnal Christian doctrine. Bill Bright of Campus Crusade, in his booklet *Have You Made the Wonderful*

---

1. B. W. Banwell, "Heart," in J. D. Douglas, ed.: *The New Bible Dictionary,* p. 510.

*Discovery of the Spirit-Filled Life?*, p. 6,

represents three classes of people, natural, carnal and spiritual, by diagrams. The diagram that represents the "carnal Christian" is identical to the diagram that represents the natural man, with the exception that the cross is inside the circle of the diagram of the "carnal Christian" (showing that he has made a decision for Christ). Also the sins listed for both diagrams are the same. According to (Dr. Lewis Sperry Chafer) Chafer and Bright, therefore, the "carnal Christian" is no different from the unregenerate in life and conduct.[2]

This view renders our Lord's declaration that a man is known by his fruits or actions untenable (Matt. 7:16-20). Our Lord then should have said that a man *cannot* be known by his actions, nor a tree by its fruits!

Those who hold to this doctrine of the carnal Christian (which makes as much sense as Christian atheism) have either a dualistic or tripartite doctrine of man. Man is for them not a unity. He can believe one thing and act out another faith. Man then is not a sinner but a victim of his divided being. He can thus be two mutually exclusive things at once. I have been told that a man can be a homosexual and a Christian, a woman can be a prostitute and a Christian, and so on.

Such views are common to our culture. Thus, *Book Digest Magazine* in January, 1977, reprinted portions of James Roosevelt's (with Bill Libby) book, *My Parents, A Differing View.* James Roosevelt describes his father's fornications and adulteries, and at least one continuing adulterous relationship maintained by his mother. Sara Roosevelt, Franklin Delano Roosevelt's mother, financed F. D. R. almost all his life, paying for his home, his marriage, his babies, hobbies, and more. Martin L. Gross, editor of *Book Digest,* insists (with James Roosevelt) that we cannot judge F. D. Roosevelt's presidency, nor John F. Kennedy's, in terms of their sexual life or other like problems. If we do, we are guilty of failure!

> It is inevitable that such material should surface. But one senses that we are all involved in a failure of perspective—as if our public leaders are to be judged by their domestic tranquility, or conversely by expertise in extramarital affairs.
>
> The reality of leadership is that none of this information should be significant in judging performance in high office.[3]

Roosevelt, in his private life, was financially irresponsible and incompetent; can we indeed believe that this had no relationship to the irresponsibility of his national financial policies? In his marital life, Roosevelt

---

2. Arend J. ten Pas: *The Lordship of Christ,* p. 15 (1972). Revised edition. Vallecito, CA: Ross House Books, 1978.
3. Martin L. Gross, "The Editor's Column," in *Book Digest Magazine,* vol. 4, no.1, January, 1977, p. 6.

was a covenant-breaker; can we believe that this was unrelated to his faithlessness to his campaign promises and to the U. S. Constitution? To believe this is to reduce the world to a realm of causelessness and accident. It posits a moral impossibility.

This divided view of man leads to antinomianism and falsely dividing Scripture (II Tim. 2:15) into law and grace, seeing two patterns of salvation and two plans (or more) on God's part. It is radically destructive of theology. It leads to Barthianism and its doctrine of the freedom of God, so that God tomorrow may be what the devil is today, and vice versa.

In such a doctrine, we cannot judge any man, nor can God, because every man is two or three things rather than one. The total man then cannot be judged, only his body perhaps, or some local aspect of his being.

Scripture, however, is emphatic. Man's being has a *heart,* a center. His total being is governed by that center or heart. "Out of it are the issues of life," or, according to the Berkeley Version, "the sources of life." Unless our heart be governed by Wisdom, by the word of God in its "every word" (Matt. 4:4), we are governed by original sin, the desire to be our own god and the source of all law (Gen. 3:1-5). The words of Wisdom are "life unto those that find them, and health (or, medicine) to all their flesh." The medicine which heals all the ailments of our being, our moral, theological, and intellectual problems and more, is the word of Wisdom, God's word. Moffatt rendered Proverbs 4:22, "to those who find them, they are life, and health to all their being."

The idea of carnal Christianity is a denial of this. Instead of a governing, healing, and determining word and power, God's word is simply an *insurance* word, i.e., an insurance policy. This, of course, is the gospel according to R. B. Theime, who, in *Apes and Peacocks,* declares, "You can even become an atheist; but if you once accepted Christ as your Savior, you can't lose your salvation."[4]

Chafer held that it was wrong to preach the Lordship of Jesus Christ to the unsaved. The content of preaching should only be saving grace; "in all gospel preaching every reference to the life to be lived beyond regeneration should be avoided as far as possible," he held. For Chafer, thus, pure gospel preaching was only a call to be saved. No connection between faith and life could be asserted.[5] Chafer hoped, of course, that, after being "converted," such persons as received this gospel would begin to manifest a Christian life. However, having separated Christ's lordship from His role as Savior, Chafer and others have logically separated the law from the gospel. As a result, they proclaim an antinomian gospel and an antinomian righteousness, a radical contradiction in

---

4. Cited by Arend J. ten Pas, *op. cit.,* p. 19.
5. Lewis Sperry Chafer: *Systematic Theology,* vol. III, p. 387. Dallas, TX: Dallas Seminary Press, 1948.

terms. Arend ten Pas notes that

> The great soul-winner George Truett observed that 80% of profes-sing Christians had never been born again. Evangelist Ron Comfort concluded after ten years of evangelism that 50% of the people in Fundamentalist churches had never experienced the new birth.[6]

If anything, these estimates over-state the number of Christians. Wherever the relationship between the heart and life, between faith and action, between grace and law, and between life and faith is severed, there we have, not Biblical faith but paganism. Socrates could calmly discourse about truth and justice while indulging in homosexuality; for him, there was no necessary connection between his mind and his body. To hold that Roosevelt's moral character was unrelated to his political character, or that grace and law are unrelated, is paganism, not Christianity. Those who champion such a dissociation will manifest neither grace nor law in their lives but rather a contentious spirit. The Greek word for *contentious, philoneikos,* means *loving strife.* St. Paul describes those who are lawless with respect to woman's place and hair as *contentious,* as hostile to God's law order (I Cor. 11:16). Again, in Romans 2:8, Paul sees a contentious spirit as going hand in hand with disobedience to the truth. God's *every word* is a law word and a grace word. To deny it is to "obey unrighteousness"; indignation and wrath is their reward from God as a result. To keep our hearts with all diligence means that with all our heart we love and obey God, because we believe Him to be God, and we bow before His sovereignty in gratitude for His saving grace.

---

6. Arend J. ten Pas, *op. cit.,* p. 19.

## 104

## IDOLATRY

Over the years, I have repeatedly encountered the following complaint, or variations of it, among couples having marital conflicts. The husband will say, "I come home after a hard day's work, and it never occurs to her to greet me with a kiss or to show any pleasure in seeing me." The wife will say, "He comes home day after day and never thinks of giving me a kiss; all he brings home is his tiredness and grumpiness." The obvious answer is to say that each should take the first step in being loving, or in greeting the other happily and with a kiss. Such an answer does not register, however. The quick answer is that the situation is too complicated for such a simple solution, and this is, of course, true. What is involved is idolatry, and man's basic and most passionately worshipped idol is himself. The essence of original sin is this idolatry. The tempter's plan was that every man should be his own god, determining what constitutes good and evil for himself (Gen. 3:5).

Idolatry has many facets, and the basic aspect is our worship of ourselves and our own will. In the New Testament, hypocrisy is closely related to idolatry. The Septuagint twice uses the Greek *hypokrites* to translate *godless*. Christ called attention to hypocrisy in the Pharisees as a

blindness to their faults (Mt. vii.5), to God's workings (Lk. xii. 56), to a true sense of values (Lk. xiii. 15), an over-valuation of human tradition (Mt. xv. 7), (Mk. vii 6), sheer ignorance of God's demands (Mt. xxiii.14, 15, 25, 29), and love of display (Mt. vi. 2, 5, 16)[1]

Because we are all born in Adam, hypocrisy is a fault common to all of us. We cannot begin to understand what our Lord has to say if we direct His words to hypocrites to the Pharisees only, and exclude ourselves from their thrust. In particular, we cannot understand what our Lord has to say on judgment apart from understanding this fact. Our Lord does not forbid judgment. In fact, He requires it: "judge righteous judgment" (John 7:24). In Matthew 7:1-5, hypocritical judgment is plainly and sharply condemned:

Judge not, that ye be not judged.
For with what judgment ye judge, ye shall be judged: and with what measure ye mete, it shall be measured to you again.
And why beholdest thou the mote that is in thy brother's eye, but

---

1. H. L. Ellison, "Hypocrite," in J. D. Douglas, ed.: *The New Bible Dictionary*, p. 550.

considerest not the beam that is in thine own eye? Or how wilt thou say to thy brother, Let me pull out the mote out of thine eye; and behold, a beam is in thine own eye? Thou hypocrite, first cast out the beam out of thine own eye; and then shalt thou see clearly to cast out the mote out of thy brother's eye.

Several things are immediately apparent in this text. *First,* our Lord makes clear that he is addressing hypocrites and is describing hypocrisy. It is very convenient for people to say that this passage is about judging as wrong, when, in fact, it is about hypocrisy and the hypocrite's judgment. *Second,* our Lord never says the hypocrite is a liar. The mote is there in the brother's eye. There is a need for us to see "clearly to cast the mote out of (our) brother's eye." The subject of our Lord's condemnation here is clearly not a case of false witness: it is hypocritical judgment. *Third,* the hypocrite talks; he "shoots off his mouth." He sees faults, often clearly, sharply, and intelligently. The hypocrite does not falsify the evidence. We have today many scholars who defend the Pharisees and feel that their reputation for hypocrisy is undeserved. Clearly, the Pharisees were in very many ways superior men; their observations on their times were incisive and highly moral. *The problem, however, with all hypocrisy is that it is critical talk, not godly action.* Our Lord makes clear that the mote in the brother's eye needs removing. The hypocrite sees the motes everywhere, and his answer is to condemn and withdraw. *Fourth,* both in Matthew and Luke, our Lord stresses love as the counterpart to hypocritical judgment. Thus, in Luke 6:31-36 we are told, immediately preceding the comments on judgment, of the love which grace manifests, and then, in verses 37-45, the meaning of a non-hypocritical life is set forth:

And as ye would that men should do to you, do ye also to them likewise.
For if ye love them which love you, what thank have ye? for sinners also love those that love them.
And if ye do good to them which do good to you, what thank have ye? for sinners also do even the same.
And if ye lend to them of whom ye hope to receive, what thank have ye? for sinners also lend to sinners, to receive as much again.
But love ye your enemies, and do good, and lend, hoping for nothing again; and your reward shall be great, and ye shall be the children of the Highest: for he is kind unto the unthankful and to the evil.
Be ye therefore merciful, as your Father also is merciful.
Judge not, and ye shall not be judged: condemn not, and ye shall not be condemned: forgive, and ye shall be forgiven:
Give, and it shall be given unto you; good measure, pressed down and shaken together, and running over, shall men give into your bosom. For with the same measure that ye mete withal it shall be measured to you again.

And he spake a parable unto them, Can the blind lead the blind? shall they not both fall into the ditch?

The disciple is not above his master: but every one that is perfect shall be as his master.

And why beholdest thou the mote that is in thy brother's eye, but perceivest not the beam that is in thine own eye?

Either how canst thou say to thy brother, Brother, let me pull out the mote that is in thine eye, when thou thyself beholdest not the beam that is in thine own eye? Thou hypocrite, cast out first the beam out of thine own eye, and then shalt thou see clearly to pull out the mote that is in thy brother's eye.

For a good tree bringeth not forth corrupt fruit; neither doth a corrupt tree bring forth good fruit.

For every tree is known by his own fruit. For of thorns men do not gather figs, nor of a bramble bush gather they grapes.

A good man out of the good treasure of his heart bringeth forth that which is good; and an evil man out of the evil treasure of his heart bringeth forth that which is evil: for of the abundance of the heart his mouth speaketh.

This passage is a favorite one with antinomians, who isolate it from the rest of Scripture in order to give it their particular meaning. Also, it involves a mistranslation in verse 35, which reproduces the Vulgate rather than the Greek. "Lend, hoping for nothing again." should be rendered, as Goodspeed did, "lend to them, never despairing."[2]

To understand what our Lord here says, it is necessary to realize, *first,* reciprocity ethics is clearly not enough. The perversion of the Golden Rule is condemned; some would read it as "Do unto others as they have done unto you," i.e., on a quid pro quo basis. In some cultures, wedding presents are assessed and valued at the door, so that, later, an exactly equivalent gift can be returned. In verses 32-34, reciprocity ethics is denied by the citation of three examples. Our Lord drives home His condemnation of reciprocity ethics by declaring in verse 35, "Love your enemies, do good, and lend, hoping for (or, expecting) nothing again (or, in return)." Our Lord is not requiring a policy of foolishness on our part, nor setting down the guidelines for the Spiritual Franciscans. He is sharply condemning reciprocity ethics. Just as the rich young man was told to sell all he had, not because this was a requirement for believers, but to bring him face to face with his basic faith and loyalty, in himself and his riches (Mark 10:17-22), so our Lord confronts all who hold to reciprocity ethics with the requirement that they forsake themselves for Christ the Lord.

*Second,* the hypocrite holds to reciprocity ethics because he sees himself as central, not the Lord. Our reward is not from men but from the Father, and, when done unto him, our "reward shall be great"

---

2. See S. MacLean Gilmour, "Luke," in *The Interpreter's Bible,* vol. VIII, 121f.

(vs. 35). If we expect a reward from men, we will judge them for their failures, and we will see ourselves as central: they have failed us, taken advantage of us, or been thoughtless toward us. If we are servants of the Lord, we expect our thanks and reward from Him, because we have done it for His sake, not man's.

*Third,* the hypocrite tells the truth, i.e., he describes men accurately, but he judges as though he were God. God is on the judgment throne, not man. We are not to usurp God's judgment. The meaning of verse 37 is, "Judge not, so that God may not judge you." One who never misses a chance to cite the failures and sins of others and to judge them will have God citing their every sin and judging them. Theirs is not *righteous* judgment, however correct, but censorious judgment, *hypocritical* judgment. It does not seek the removal of our brother's mote, i.e., the fault of a fellow believer, but to condemn him for it. It manifests neither love, patience, nor forbearance, but distaste and distance.

*Fourth,* we are not only told that our Father will reward us, but, when we fulfil the Lord's requirement of obedient and brotherly love, men shall give unto us: "Good measure, pressed down, and shaken together, and running over, shall men give into your bosom" (vs. 38). Instead of a reciprocity ethics, we have an ethics of *godly generosity.* Reciprocity ethics puts a sour distance between men, and between man and God; the ethics of godly generosity brings God and man together, and it brings men closer to one another, not because it "saves" or "changes" the sinner, but because it accomplishes God's purpose and thus fits in to God's purposes for our lives and theirs.

Hypocrisy is thus an aspect of idolatry, because the hypocrite warps reality by judging men in relation to himself, not himself and men together in relation to the Lord. Hypocritical judgment is personal, not theological. It is personal even when it cites moral faults only, i.e., motes in the other person's eye, because its principle in judgment is our irritation and annoyance with them, not our struggle to heal ourselves and them also of our mutual infirmities. St. Paul states it plainly:

> I therefore, the prisoner of the Lord, beseech you that ye walk worthy of the vocation wherewith ye are called,
> With all lowliness and meekness, with longsuffering, forbearing one another in love;
> Endeavouring to keep the unity of the Spirit in the bond of peace.

Having said these things, it is necessary to add, lest Scripture be misinterpreted, that we cannot use these passages to justify overlooking heresies, being indulgent of their errors, or of any attempt to forestall a judgment of their errors. We are strictly forbidden such conduct (II John 9-11). It is never our kindly disposition which is the criterion: it is the Lord and His word. To elevate our kindliness or love in any form to a position of priority is idolatry. Judging and condemning come very easily to some; being indulgent and tolerant comes very readily to others. Neither course is godly: both are ruled by man's disposition rather than the word of God. This constitutes idolatry.

The first two commandments forbid idolatry. To assume that idolatry is to be restricted to the literal use of idols is to misunderstand the Bible. We should remember that St. Paul identifies covetousness among other things, as idolatry (Gal. 3:5).

## 105

## COVETOUSNESS AS IDOLATRY

The New Testament speaks of covetousness as idolatry. St. Paul tells us

For this ye know, that no whoremonger, nor unclean person, nor covetous man, who is an idolater, hath any inheritance in the kingdom of Christ and of God. (Eph. 5:5)

Mortify therefore your members which are upon the earth; fornication, uncleanness, inordinate affection, evil concupiscence, and covetousness, which is idolatry. (Col. 3:5)

All sin is idolatry, because all actual sin is a product of original sin, Satan's temptation whereby every man made himself his own god and idol (Gen. 3:5). Sin is the moral consequence of idolatry.

Covetousness in particular is singled out as exemplifying idolatry. In analyzing why this is so, it is necessary, *first,* to note that, while the Stoics regarded covetousness as the fountainhead of all evil, their motive in so doing was radically anti-theistic. The Stoic goal was self-sufficiency and passionlessness. Covetousness was a denial of the god-like freedom from all things which the Stoic sought, and hence it was regarded as the key sin. Stoic virtue was thus a form of idolatry and original sin, the desire to be a god and to gain aseity. The Biblical condemnation has radically different grounds. *Second,* there is a difference in the meanings of the Old Testament Hebrew word *betsa,* and the New Testament Greek word *pleonexia,* although both are translated as *covetousness.* The Old Testament word means "dishonest gain"; hence, the Tenth Commandment forbids all fraudulent gain. The New Testament word means "the wish to have more" and is the opposite of godly contentment (I Tim. 6:6).

*Third,* both in Ephesians 5:5 and Colossians 3:5 covetousness is closely associated with sexual sins as well as with idolatry. The idolatry of seeking to be god means the imperialistic urge to have more and more, to extend our power over other men and properties, and also to the sexual urge to power. Sexual immorality has in it, among other things, the will to violate God's law, and pleasure therein, and the desire to use other people. A common problem in our time is an early impotence in legitimate, marital relations: sin only excites and appeals to the sinner. Again, a major pleasure in sexual immorality is that it is irresponsible: other people are used for pleasure and without any continuing responsibility. It is the essence of paganism, and commonplace in the myths of

453

their gods, that creaturely responsibility is a burden and the amoral freedom of the gods is bliss. Covetousness wishes to have more, and with less responsibility.

This desire can be masked in a facade of godliness and often is. I recall some twenty years ago a churchman who built up his store from a modest venture to the leading one in his small city; he saw the forthcoming inflation and capitalized on it. A highly covetous man, he sacrificed his family and friends to an all-out concentration on work. He justified it by giving very generously to his church and declaring that he wanted to succeed in order to support the Lord's work better. His family, associates, and employees found him anything but Christian, and he was in essence an irresponsible man, given to hurting others brutally, but emphatic that he was serving the Lord. Sin is often disguised as virtue in our thinking; we find it easier to sin if we convince ourselves that we are really being virtuous.

*Fourth,* still another Hebrew word (*chamad*) defines covetousness as the desire for our neighbor's possessions. This appears in the Tenth Commandment (Ex. 20:18). It also appears in Micah 2:1-2:

> Woe to them that devise iniquity, and work evil upon their beds! when the morning is light, they practise it, because it is in the power of their hand.
> And they covet fields, and take them by violence; and houses, and take them away: so they oppress (or, defraud) a man and his house, even a man and his heritage. (Micah 2:1-2)

It involves desire and fraudulent action to fulfil that desire. It has at its roots the imagination which desires and plans to increase itself at the cost of one's neighbor. Degrading and surpassing the neighbor is basic to this kind of coveting. Achan was guilty of such covetousness (Joshua 7:21). Still another word in Proverbs 21:26 speaks of the wicked and slothful man coveting "greedily all the day long." Crime and revolution are behind such covetousness. Men who will not work believe that, because in their imagination they are as gods, they are entitled to seize that which belongs to others.

We have thus in covetousness much of the social legislation of our times. The greedy rich pass laws to eliminate competition and to gain subsidies, and the greedy slothful men legislate to rob others of their wealth. Covetousness is not limited to any class: it is an aspect of fallen man, and it appears in strength wherever godliness is replaced by idolatry.

Moreover, the sinner seeks to give the status of virtue and respectability to covetousness. It is regarded as a desire for one's "rights," for social justice, and for "real community." It is disguised in others as ambition, a desire to get ahead and improve one's lot, and as a "natural" reaction to injustice.

It is however, simply the worship of the self. Covetousness or greediness is the insatiable desire for more because we see no limits to what we are "entitled" to own. When we reach our supposed goal, we are not satisfied or grateful: we immediately want more, and we want it passionately and aggressively.

J. Marsh has defined contentment thus:

> The acceptance of "things as they are" as the wise and loving providence of a God who knows what is good for us, who so loves us as always to seek our good, and whose power is adequate to his love.[1]

Covetousness is the direct opposite of this. It involves a radical discontent with God's purpose in our lives, a distrust of His love and providence, and a pervasive restlessness and impatience with God and man.

The Ten Commandments are both law and a declaration of inheritance and promise. The covenant people of God are those who forsake all forms of idolatry to believe and obey the true and living God. They are promised an inheritance of long life and land for their faith and obedience. They must, however, love God and their neighbor, and they must not covet or seek to deprive any man of that which the Lord gives to them. The Tenth Commandment thus forbids those covetous or fraudulent acts which are the results of discontent with God. In the New Testament, those insatiable desires which are behind these greedy acts, legal or illegal, are condemned, and their root is declared to be idolatry. Thus

> in the NT covetousness is considered a hindrance to true worship and faith in God. Where a man's treasure is, there is his heart; he who loves material possessions cannot truly love God (Mark 7:22; Luke 12:15; cf. Rom. 1:20). Thus in some passages covetousness is identified with idolatry (Eph. 5:3,5; Col. 3:5); recognition of this fact helps in interpreting the difficult text of Isa. 57:17.[2]

The law of God strongly condemns and forbids idolatry. Covetousness is the hidden and veiled return of idolatry into the mind, heart, and life of man. Like all idolatry, it is destructive of man's life and of society.

---

1. J. Marsh, "Contentment," in *The Interpreter's Dictionary of the Bible,* vol. I, p. 677.
2. E. R. Achtemeier, "Covetousness," in *ibid.,* I, 724.

## 106

## IDOLATRY AND THE SABBATH

Because our modern perspective is evolutionary, we tend to view idolatry as the practice of a primitive rather than a rebellious and sinful mind. Idolatry was not limited to graven or molten images. It included pillars, groves of trees, the sun, moon, and much else. Moreover, where idols were involved, we miss a basic aspect of idolatry when we fail to realize that many idols had their hands extended in supplication towards man. Man was at the center in idolatry.

In idolatry man views the world, not as it is, but as he would like it to be, or as he believes it to be. The world then is commonly seen as an evil and frightening place. Because the idolater knows, without acknowledging it, the anarchy and evil in his own heart, he sees the universe as made in his own image. Thus, it is a dark and evil cosmos, and a dangerous place. Again, because the idolater moves in terms of power plays, bribery, and self-interest, his approach to the spirits and powers within this chaotic cosmos or multiverse is the kind of approach he wants made to himself, bribery. Pagan religion is not worship: it is the bribery of a supernatural Mafia in order to gain protection for oneself, or to buy power to use against someone else. The idolater prefers a Mafia-type world: he knows his way around better in such a world, and everything is then on a trustworthy cash and carry basis. An ugly world is most to the taste of ugly souls.

In Exodus 23:13, we have an especially interesting law with respect to idolatry:

> And in all things that I have said unto you be circumspect: and make no mention of the name of other gods, neither let it be heard out of thy mouth.

The Berkeley Version renders the first half of this verse, "Pay strict attention to everything I have told you." Cole observes of this verse, "It is probably a reference to swearing by another god's name instead of by the name of YHWH: this would of course indicate lack of faith in YHWH. Paul seems to refer to this verse in Ephesians 5:3."[1] According to Rawlinson, while Jewish commentators understood this to mean swearing by the name of other gods, the text goes far beyond such a limitation. He added,

> They were not to be spoken of, unless by preachers in the way of warning, or historians when the facts of history could not otherwise

---

1. R. Alan Cole: *Exodus, An Introduction and Commentary.* p. 179. Downers Grove, IL: Inter-Varsity Press, 1973.

be set forth. Moses himself mentions Baal (Num. xxii. 41), Baal-peor (ib. xxv. 3, 5), Chemosh (ib. xxi. 29), and Moloch (Levit. xx. 2-5, xxiii.21).[2]

All this is very true, but the commentators neglect an important aspect of this law. *First,* it appears in the midst of an important statement of Sabbath law. Moffatt found this so incongruous that he arbitrarily re-arranged the chapter to place verse 13 after verse 19, as though it were a separate law and no part of Exodus 23:10-19, the laws of the Sabbath year, the seventh year, and of the three great annual feasts or Sabbaths. However, if we take Scripture at face value, we must say that this law is somehow either a part of or connected with the Sabbath laws.

To name a god in any sense other than the historical and homiletical senses is to invoke his power, whether by faith or blasphemously. What is involved in the naming of other gods? The obvious answer is that all other gods represent a sabbathless world without true rest.

In the world of the gods, everything has its price, an antinomian price. A man bought the favor of Castor and Pollux, Venus, Zeus, and all others. These gods were deified men, powerful men and women on earth who, after death, became powers in the spirit world. In God's world, God's law and grace give us assured guidelines; because it is God's world, and because He absolutely governs it, we can rest at His com-mand in the confidence that we are in His hands. In the world of the gods, there is no such certainty or confidence, because, beyond the gods of all the nations is a blind and inexorable Fate to which even the gods are subject.

Modern man's faith is close to that of ancient paganism. With human-istic evolutionary thought denying the God of Scripture, the powers which have emerged are the stars (astrology), spirits (occultism), and demonic forces (Satanism and magic). Modern man has an abundance of leisure time but no true rest, no Sabbath, because his world lacks God's law and grace. It is a Mafia-like universe, and modern man is most at home in a Mafia world where protection is a cash transaction. The Mafia only demands money to deliver protection; the God of Scripture com-mands every atom of our being. Fallen man prefers the Mafia to God: he sees more hope for himself with the Mafia.

*Second,* this law is set in the center of laws which stress the life of the community in the Sabbath. The produce in the fields during the Sabbath year must be left for the poor and for the beasts of the field. The animals as well as the servants shall rest on the weekly Sabbath. The three great festivals are for all the males of Israel, and the firstfruits must be brought to the Lord, who gives the increase (Ex. 23:10-13, 15-19).

Man never approaches God alone. We approach God only through

---

2. George Rawlinson, in "Exodus," in Ellicott, *op. cit.,* I, 274.

Jesus Christ, the mediator, and are in Christ as members of the covenant people, Israel. Our Sabbath rest is thus a community rest that points in its fulness to a cosmic rest, all things made new and all things manifesting the full glory of God.

The law thus enjoins us as individuals and as a community to be totally separated from idolatry in any form. Our lives, families, churches, schools, states, and vocations, as well as all things else, must be totally dedicated to God and free of idolatry, from man's self-worship in any form.

*Third,* basic to the Sabbath law is the fact that the earth is the Lord's (Ex. 9:29; Deut. 10:14; Ps. 14:1; I Cor. 10:26). It is because the earth is the Lord's, and because He gives it to His covenant people (Lev. 25:27), that the law of the Lord must be observed on earth, and the name of no other god even named. There is only one power and one Lord, the God of Scripture. Hence, "Thou shalt have no other gods before me" (Ex. 20:3). In Exodus 23:20-33, the Lord goes on to declare that the Angel of the Lord shall go before His people to overthrow their enemies and to protect His people. Therefore, there can be no allegiance to any other god, nor any covenant or treaty with a godless people. "Thou shalt make no covenant with them, nor with their gods" (Ex. 23:32). To do so is to deny the Sabbath, to deny that the Lord is our sufficiency and that we can rest in His salvation, providence, and government.

If we are without the Sabbath faith, we will not only be restless and impatient with God, but we will continually rely on a false god or idol, usually ourselves, to our own confusion.

Zechariah 13:2 declares, of the Messianic era, "And it shall come to pass, saith the LORD of hosts, that I will cut off the names of the idols out of the land, and they shall no more be remembered: and also I will cause the prophets and the unclean spirit to pass out of the land." With the triumph of God's covenant grace and people, the very memory of idolatry will disappear: "For I will take away the names of Baalim out of her mouth, and they shall no more be remembered by their name" (Hosea 2:17). The true Sabbath rest means also the disappearance of idolatry.

*Fourth,* and finally, related to this law against naming other gods is the emphatic condemnation of any study of evil powers, i.e., the attention to them as though they rule the world. All such study of conspiracies falls under this ban of Revelation 2:24, where the study of the deep things of Satan, or knowing the depths of Satan, is condemned in the Thyatiran Church. It is idolatry. To assume, as students of conspiracy do, that evil powers plan and govern the world is to deny the absolute sovereignty and predestination of God. It means believing and delving into the forbidden; it involves a misplaced and false faith. Such people lack a true Sabbath rest.

# 107

## THE IDOLATRY OF TESTING GOD

In Deuteronomy 6:10-19, the covenant people are commanded not to "go after other gods, of the gods of the people which are round about you," and such apostasy is described as tempting or testing God, and as a disobedience to the whole body of His law.

The life of the covenant man and people, *first,* is described thus: "Thou shalt fear the LORD thy God, and serve him, and shalt swear by his name" (Deut. 6:13). Three words sum up the duty of man: "fear, serve, swear."[1] To fear God means to believe that He is the absolute Lord and only Savior, He with whom we must reckon in every thought, act, moment, and place in our lives. To *fear* God means to be unafraid of all men and idols, for the more we fear God, the less we will fear man. To *serve* God means to obey His law and to work in terms of His calling with our whole heart, mind, and being. To "swear by his name" means to place our whole life before Him as grounded in His word and truth, so that our every word and action is in effect under oath to God. This is the confession of faith.

*Second,* we are to "beware lest thou forget the LORD, which brought thee forth out of the land of Egypt, from the house of bondage" (Deut. 6:12). Idolatry is a temptation, because it makes us sovereign, whereas the Lord as sovereign makes a total claim upon us. To "forget the LORD" thus means to neglect and by-pass His absolute claim to sovereignty. God is forgotten where His sovereignty is denied, however much He may be named. Thus, all too many talk endlessly about Jesus Christ as Savior who have wilfully forgotten that He is the Lord.

Idolatry can use the name of the Lord, as did Jeroboam, the great apostate, who took and had made two bull-calves of gold, established a new sanctuary, and told Israel, "behold thy gods, O Israel, which brought thee up out of the land of Egypt" (I Kings 12:28). In name, the worship of Israel for most of its history was Jehovah worship; in actuality, it was idolatry because it was selective in its approach to God's revelation. Hence, the judgment of Israel was more severe than of Judea, whose apostasy was usually an abandonment of Jehovah worship. If we defend those who deny God's sovereignty in predestination and salvation, those who are antinomian, and those who by-pass man's total

---

1. G. Ernest Wright, "Deuteronomy," in *The Interpreter's Bible,* II, 375f.

depravity, we are vindicating Jeroboam's course of action and defending idolatry. The god of the Arminians is the god of their imagination, not the God of Scripture. The fact that many of them are "good, moral people" no more alters the fact of their idolatry than does Jeroboam's obvious ability and character negate his sin.

*Third,* it is idolatry to tempt or test God. To doubt God's sovereignty and His grace is to demand that God prove Himself in some way to satisfy us. We are then refusing to live by faith and are demanding that God meet our requirements. Testing God is a way of declaring our own sovereignty, and God's answer is judgment (Deut. 6:15-16). In testing God, we deny His absolute claims over us and insist that we have some claims upon Him. The reference to Massah is in Exodus 17:1-7. Testing God means denying His claims over us and is an insistence that we have earned some claims over Him, or that our will is prior to His will and can command Him. All who try to test God are in effect declaring that it is their will and their idea of right and wrong which should govern the universe.

*Fourth,* in Deuteronomy 6:10-11 we have what von Rad describes as "the stereotyped list of 'real estate'.... (cf. Josh. 24:13; Neh. 9:24f.). Its form is derived historically from the legally binding list, like a land-register, contained in... ancient Near Eastern treaties."[2] God declares emphatically that the Promised Land belongs to the covenant people. The blessed meek are told they will inherit the whole earth (Matt. 5:5). The question is not, will the Lord keep His promises, but will man keep God's covenant and enter into the covenant promises?

*Fifth,* testing God is closely related to the basic idolatry of Genesis 3:5. We should remember at all times that neither Satan nor his devils are atheists. As James 2:19 declares, "Thou believest that there is one God; thou doest well: the devils also believe, and tremble." If mere belief is sufficient for salvation, as many tell us, Satan and his devils then have a claim on heaven; none of them are atheists. But Satan is the great Arminian: he believes in the freedom and the sovereignty of the creature. It is not an accident that Satan is called the Tempter (Matt. 4:3; I Thess. 3:5), i.e., the Prover. His demand is that man put God to the test: Is it the chief end of God to glorify man and to enjoy him forever? Only such a God is worthy of man, in Satan's eyes.

Moreover, the whole of Satan's program in the temptation of our Lord (Matt. 4:1-11) is that Jesus demonstrate that he is indeed man's Savior by submitting Himself, and therefore God, to a series of tests satisfying to man. We are told of the medieval church,

The two holies of the Gnostics and NeoPlatonists, Sophia and

---

2. Gerhard von Rad: *Deuteronomy, A Commentary,* p. 64. Philadelphia, PA: Westminster Press, (1964) 1966.

Eirene—Wisdom and Peace—were adopted as saints in the calendar of Constantinople. Dionysius, the god of the mysteries, reappears as St. Denys in France, St. Liberius, St. Eleutherius, and St. Bacchus; there is also a St. Mithra; and even Satan, prince of shadows, is revered as St. Satur and St. Swithin. Their relics are in keeping.[3]

This is a milder evil than that which confronts us on all sides today, declaring, "Give Jesus a chance." A chance to do what? The answer is, to prove Himself. This is a theology which says in effect, "Try it. You'll like it. Here is a God who knocks on the door and begs for your heart and the privilege of saving and serving you." This is blasphemy in the name of Jesus. It is the religion of the Tempter or Tester, not of the Lord and Savior who declares:

> Ye have not chosen me, but I have chosen you, and ordained you, that ye should go and bring forth fruit, and that your fruit should remain: that whatsoever ye shall ask of the Father in my name, he may give it you. (John 15:16)

The condition of receiving is acknowledging the Lord's sovereign grace, bearing fruit to Him, fruit that lasts or remains, and hence, by His grace, being privileged to ask and to receive from the Father.

As against this, the Tempter's plan of salvation calls for turning stones into bread, i.e., offering man cradle to grave security; miracles on demand, i.e., testing God at will; and bowing down and worshipping Satan, i.e., recognizing the rightness of his plan of salvation, which gives freedom to man to choose God if God meets man's testing.

Satan does not for a moment doubt God's existence. His plan of salvation by idolatry calls instead for God to recognize man's free will and sovereignty, and to allow man to test God at will. Place the name of any theology or church over this, and it still remains idolatry. The law of God condemns it.

---

3. Cited from Westropp and Wake, *Ancient Symbol Worship,* by Abram Herbert Lewis: *Paganism Surviving in Christianity,* p. 27f. New York: G. P. Putnam's Sons, 1892.

## 108

## IDOLATRY AND AUTHORITY

A remarkable passage, related to idolatry and testing, is Deuteronomy 13:1-5:

> If there arise among you a prophet, or a dreamer of dreams, and giveth thee a sign or a wonder,
> And the sign or the wonder come to pass, whereof he spake unto thee, saying, Let us go after other gods, which thou hast not known, and let us serve them;
> Thou shalt not hearken unto the words of that prophet, or that dreamer of dreams: for the LORD your God proveth you, to know whether ye love the LORD your God with all your heart and with all your soul.
> Ye shall walk after the LORD your God, and fear him, and keep his commandments, and obey his voice, and ye shall serve him, and cleave unto him.
> And that prophet, or that dreamer of dreams, shall be put to death; because he hath spoken to turn you away from the LORD your God, which brought you up out of the land of Egypt, and redeemed you out of the house of bondage, to thrust thee out of the way which the LORD thy God commanded thee to walk in. So shalt thou put the evil away from the midst of thee.

The *first* thing to note here is that the prophet or seer is not an open idolater or pagan. He is not called a false prophet, but a prophet who arises from among the covenant people, an ostensible spokesman for the word of God. The man in question is thus not a spokesman for Baal or Moloch: he is an ostensible prophet of the Lord. Open idolatry, the religion of the peoples round about Israel, is dealt with in Deuteronomy 13:6-11. In Deuteronomy 13:1-5 we have idolatry masked as the faithful proclamation of the word of the Lord.

*Second,* this religious leader may perform signs and wonders. He may seem to be indeed mightily endowed of the Lord. He has every indication, in the power he manifests, of being another great and true prophet of the Lord.

*Third,* this religious leader or prophet will use his power to lead people into another faith. He will introduce innovation into the covenant faith and will seek to create another religion out of the existing one. He is a covenant preacher outwardly, coming from among the covenant people, and he seems signally blessed of the Lord. The true intent of his ministry, however, is to say, "Let us go after other gods, which thou hast not known, and let us serve them." This will be done, however, under the facade of the covenant.

*Fourth,* the Lord states that He Himself is responsible for this. He is proving or testing His covenant people. They must discern and choose between the form of the faith and the reality thereof. Their *love* of God, their faithful *walk,* their *fear* of Him and their *obedience* and *service* to Him will be made manifest and stronger by this test, and they will *cleave* to the Lord.

*Fifth,* this religious leader is a traitor to the covenant people, and is to be executed. Treason in the Bible is religious, not political. This is no less true today: treason is defined now in terms of humanistic religion; it is treason to the state rather than to God.

*Sixth,* testing is the prerogative of the Lord, not of man. Man has no right to test God, but God has every right to test man. Idolatry requires exposure, and the idolatry latent in the covenant people is tested and sifted out.

*Seventh,* the key in the discernment of any religious leader who is a covert spokesman of idolatry is not signs and wonders but covenant faithfulness. We cannot use experience and miracles as a standard, but only the word of God, the covenant word. It is the law-covenant of God which binds us to our Lord, not signs and wonders. To shift the covenant-bond from its law-grace focus to a miraculous one is to say that what God does for us is the test. This is humanism and idolatry. The logical consequence is for a people in such a faith to say, "What has God done for me lately?" This was in effect the cry of the people at Massah, and it remains as a symbol of apostasy (Ex. 17:1-7; Deut. 6:16; 9:22; 33:8). Those who follow signs and wonders will forsake the Lord for idolatry, for self-worship.

*Eighth,* there is a question here of authority. Von Rad says of the prophet or dreamer spoken of in this text, "What is evident is merely that these are persons whose words have an authoritative influence by virtue of a special commission."[1] Their authority plus their performance of a sign or a wonder gave them a semblance of divine commission which should over-rule the doubts of the covenant people. The men of the covenant are told, however, that the test is not the authority of men nor their display of power but the authority of God. Simply to trust in the authority of any man is to have another god before the Lord.

Moreover, it is easy for men in authoritative positions to vindicate their steps with sometimes a persuasive or even dazzling display of logic and data. Thus, in 1923, when Germany was at the height of a brutal inflation, the monetary economists, whose false thinking had helped create

---

1. G. von Rad: *Deuteronomy,* p. 96.

that inflation, were producing statistical data to prove that there was no real inflation at all; quite the contrary! In Hazlitt's telling summary,

> Viewed in retrospect, one of the most disheartening things about the inflation is that no matter how appalling its consequences became, they failed to educate the German monetary economists, or cause them to re-examine their previous sophisms. The very fact that the paper marks began to depreciate faster than they were printed (because everybody feared still further inflation) led these economists to argue that there was no monetary or credit inflation in Germany at all! They admitted that the stamped value of the paper money issued was enormous, but the "real" value—that is, the gold value according to the exchange rate—was far lower than the total money circulating in Germany before the war.
>
> This argument was expounded by Karl Kelfferich in official testimony in June 1923. In the summer of 1922 Professor Julius Wolf wrote: "In proportion to the need, less money circulates in Germany now than before the war. This statement may cause surprise, but it is correct. The circulation is now 15-20 times that of pre-war days, while prices have risen 40-50 times." Another economist, Karl Elster, in his book on the German mark, declared: "However enormous may be the apparent rise in the circulation in 1922, actually the figures show a decline!"[2]

Since then, our self-worshipping experts have only grown worse. This should not surprise us. The true God needs no education: He is omniscient. False gods refuse to be educated, because it involves a denial of their claims to be god. Thus, they will add data to their store, but not wisdom.

*Ninth,* we have seen that the Sabbath, true rest, is only possible for man when he is under God's authority. Paganism has no Sabbath, because it cannot give rest. The gods of idolatry are themselves subject to Fate, to the cycles of a meaningless cosmic recurrence, and hence neither the gods nor the worshippers in idolatry have any rest. False religions can give delusions, but not rest. There is less capacity for work in the non-Christian world becaue it can give neither a valid motive for life and work, nor the capacity for rest. No false god has power, omnipotence, and omniscience, and hence no false god can generate true trust and rest.

The restlessness of unbelief manifests itself in mental and physical ways as well as in religious forms. The world of idolatry is a sleepless world in a very real sense. Jean-Paul Sartre was a logical existentialist in denying the doctrine of the unconscious.[3] The true existentialist must in some sense be at all times totally conscious, because he is a being whose passion it is to be God, who never slumbers nor sleeps (Ps. 121:3-4).

---

2. Henry Hazlitt, "Lessons of the German Inflation," in *The Freeman,* vol. 26, no. 12, December, 1976, p. 723.

3. Jean-Paul Sartre: *Being and Nothingness,* pp. 50ff. New York: Philosophical Library, 1956.

Hence, the existentialist cannot rest under the authority of the Lord. *Sleep* is an aspect of faith and trust. David declares, "I will both lay me down in peace, and sleep: for thou, LORD, only makest me dwell in safety" (Ps. 4:8). The more an age is infected with idolatry, the more restless and sleepless it will be. If we distrust the authority over us, divine and human, we are less able to rest.

False preaching thus leads not only to idolatry but to the restless, Sabbathless world of unbelief.

Scripture is emphatic about requiring rest, but rest is joined to confidence in God's authority and government. God sends the traitorous religious leaders, not to undermine the principle of authority, but to strengthen it. We are to be under human authority for conscience's sake, in obedience to God, but not blindly so. We must obey without a surrender of personal responsibility and without disobedience to God. Human authorities can neither be absolutized nor set aside. The responsibility of the people is to judge all human authorities in terms of God's unchanging word.

## 109

## IDOLATRY AND THE LAW

Deuteronomy 13 is not a popular chapter of Scripture. Several ministers have expressed to me their hostility to Biblical law by citing Deuteronomy 13; or 17: 2-7 (or, Ex. 22:20); going back to Biblical law, they declare, means going back to burning heretics. Do I want that? Others have made clear that the church's task of defending Scripture as retaining the plan of salvation is difficult enough without the added complication of Biblical law, with its death penalties.

It is important for us to face this issue squarely. Either the whole of Scripture is defensible, or it is not. Moreover, defending Scripture from false criticism is not to be confused with defending either the medieval church or the Reformation churches.

Moreover, as we have seen, no law structure can be enforced more than relatively for a short time unless almost everyone accepts it as the necessary law order. A small fraction of militant dissidents can destroy any law order. In the earlier middle ages, only the law structure of Christendom offered any hope; therefore, virtually all men assented to it, whether believing it or not. At that time, there was no Inquisition, and yet the actual percentage of the truly faithful may have been less than it was during the Inquisition. The difference was that the old law order no longer satisfied an increasing number of people, who saw no alternatives in Humanism or in other ideas of Christian order.

Communism today is the Humanist Inquisition in action. In every humanistic state, there are strong indications of dissent and even disintegration. The modern world is in process of inner decay and break-up. Moreover, since the modern age has, since 1914, seen a higher percentage of mankind killed by war, revolution, prison camps, torture, mass executions, and famine than ever before in history, it is hardly in a position of validity in casting stones at the Bible.

Deuteronomy 13 gives us three instances of "enticement" to idolatry, (1) by a prophet or preacher (vvs. 1-5); (2) by a relative (vvs. 6-11); or (3) by a city (vvs. 17-18).

In analyzing these verses, it is important to note, *first,* that it is not heresy which is condemned but idolatry. There is an important difference. Heresy is wrong thinking about the word of God, but it is not idolatry. To illustrate, an orthodox Seventh Day Adventist and an

466

orthodox member of the Church of England can each regard the other as a heretic, but not as an idolater. The Bible requires us to separate ourselves from a heretic (Titus 3:10; cf. Acts 24:14; I Cor. 11:19; Gal. 5:20; II Peter 2:1), but it does not go beyond that. Moreover, heresies or sects are seen as having a purpose in God's plan of sharpening the truth for us who resist them, so that our faith becomes more clearly manifest in all its implications (I Cor. 11:19); (this verse is rendered by Moffatt thus: "there must be parties among you, if genuine Christians are to be recognized").

*Second,* this commandment simply expands what was given in the first two of the Ten Commandments, and stated also in Exodus 22:20. Moreover, the condemnation of idolatry is so basic to the whole Bible, including the New Testament (e.g., Gal. 5:19, 20; Eph. 5:5; Col. 3:5; I Cor. 5:11; I John 5:19-21), that it is impossible to soft-pedal or eliminate the force of Deuteronomy 13. The declaration of the Lord is sharp and clear-cut: "I am the LORD: that is my name: and my glory will I not give to another, neither my praise to graven images" (Isa. 42:8). And, as von Rad notes, "This exclusive attitude towards all alien cults is part of the most essential character of the faith of Yahweh and stretches right back to its origins."[1]

*Third,* it is important for us to understand what is forbidden by the law of Deuteronomy 13. What specifically is meant by idolatry? In verses 2, 6, and 13 we are told that it is this sin: "Let us go and serve other gods." To grasp the meaning of this means to recognize that this is covenant law. God's people in *every* age are in covenant with Him; the bond of that covenant is the atoning blood of the Lamb. In Jesus Christ, the covenant made at the very beginning, with Adam, Noah, Abraham, Isaac, Jacob, Moses and others is fully and openly ratified by the triune God and set into force, i.e., fulfilled, put into operation. *There is no covenant, and hence no salvation, without covenant law.* We have seen that all law is in essence totally religious; every legal structure is a religious establishment. Every law system is an attempt to establish ultimate and essential moral and basic order as the foundation and structure of a society. Thus, the summons, "Let us go and serve other gods" is a demand for another kind of law system. This has always been true, but it was much more obviously the case in Bible history. Israel's demand for a king was thus plainly seen by God as a rejection of Him and of covenant law (I Sam. 8). The prohibition of all heathen alliances was a prohibition of all foreign treaties, because treaties, as a form of law, involve an agreement and compromise between two law systems. God's covenant (or law), however, cannot be compromised: it is either obeyed or broken. Exodus 23:31-33; Deuteronomy 7:1-4; and Exodus 34:12-16,

---

1. G. von Rad: *Deuteronomy,* p. 98.

all stress the fact that foreign alliances are denials of the covenant and law of God. Hence, the prophets always opposed all foreign alliances as a great sin. Similarly, mixed marriages are condemned as a violation of God's covenant or law, because marriage is a law system among other things, and to marry outside God's covenant is to marry idolatrously (Deut. 7:3-4). To marry idolatrously means to obey another law than God's covenant law.

The implications of this are clear: All who are content with a humanistic law system and do not strive to replace it with Biblical law are guilty of idolatry. They have forsaken the covenant of their God, and they are asking us to serve other gods. They are thus idolaters, and are, in our generation, when our world is idolatrous and our states also, to be objects of missionary activity. They must be called out of their idolatry into the service of the living God.

*Fourth,* every law system has a doctrine of treason, humanism no less than any other. Thus, in communist countries, where humanism is more fully developed, all dissent is counter-revolutionary and potentially punishable by the slave-labor camp and death. In the humanistic democracies, the definition of treason is still less explicit though state-centered. It is, however, moving in the same direction as communism. The death penalty in terms of God's law is in process of being dropped. It is gradually being replaced by a new doctrine of capital punishment: death for the murder of prison guards, policemen, presidents, and other public officials. In other words, life has meaning if it is state life, and the capital offenses are against the state, not against God's law. The logical development of this is to say that all crimes against the state merit death. Treason becomes then a refusal to commit idolatry.

Two systems of treason are thus in conflict, God's system and man's. We cannot avoid this conflict, nor can we avoid defining treason, either in terms of Scripture, or in terms of humanism.

What then must Christians do? Some ask, are we to work for the execution of all idolaters in our midst today? The question presupposes either stupidity, or malice, or both. It is our duty to evangelize, to work for the conversion of men and nations to Christ as Lord and Savior. At the same time, as part of our evangelism, we witness to the meaning of covenant law, and, in our own personal dealings, we live by it: we practice the tithe, restitution, debt-free living, and much, much more. Only as God's law is made the practice of men can it become the practice of nations. Only those laws are enforceable which virtually all men are already enforcing in their own lives. so that the state's law affects a minuscule minority.

The reality of the modern world is that it is idolatrous. The reality of the modern church is that it is idolatrous. Our law structure thus has long been in gradual process of conversion, and now in rapid process, from Biblical law to humanistic law. Because most Americans are to some degree humanistic, as are most people everywhere, humanism is butchering millions of babies annually through abortion. This is murder. Not all the evils of heresy trials and the injustices of some witchcraft trials are equal to this, in their brutality and carnage. It is arrogance of a fearful sort to believe that ours is an enlightened age, and earlier ones darker. Moreover, Scripture emphatically requires us to reject both the earlier and the present law systems in favor of a rigorously Biblical, covenantal law structure. To deny covenant law is to deny that there is a covenant: it is to reject the salvation plan offered by God in Christ.

# 110

## IDOLATRY AND THE INVISIBLE GOD

In Deuteronomy 4:15-28, we have still another emphasis on the relationship of idolatry and law. Von Rad, who does not see the verses on idolatry (vvs. 15-20, 23-24) as part of "the original form" of this text, still recognizes that the text moves "along a double tract." On the one hand, we have the declaration that the true law is the revelation and covenant of Yahweh, and, on the other, the prohibition of all idolatry.[1] But, von Rad to the contrary, the two are essentially related. To obey the covenant law of the Lord is to avoid strictly all false gods and their covenant laws. There is, moreover, an important stress in this particular declaration.

*First,* the invisibility of the covenant God is strongly declared (Deut. 4:5). Unlike all other nations, Israel had no visible symbols of its God. For this reason, both the Jews, and, later, the Christians, were sometimes described by the pagans as atheists.[2] It is important for us to treat this charge of atheism seriously. It is naive to assume that other peoples were ignorant of the details of Biblical faith. The Old Testament writings were widely read by other peoples, and the New Testament history very widely known. Moreover, in view of the centrality of Jesus Christ to the church, it would have been easier for the pagans to say, with justice and truth, that Christians worshipped Jesus Christ. To accuse the Christians of atheism introduced a subtlety of description into the attack. Here was Jesus Christ, and here were the Christians: why was this atheism? Why was it not a "theism" comparable to "Zeus-worship" or "emperor-worship?"

The answer lies in the deliberate and principled avoidance by the Christians of all visible forms as symbols in worship. The emphasis on the *invisible* God and Savior was a denial also of the immanent-and-temporal nature of God. The idols, the gods of the nations, are either aspects of nature or are products of man's history and creation. All such gods are involved and totally involved in the historical process. They may be in ostensible advance over or superior to man in that process, but they are all the same equally a part of that same process. There is an emphatic denial of any god beyond time and history in favor of a god or gods who are partners with man in time and history.

---

1. G. von Rad: *Deuteronomy,* p. 49.
2. C. H. Waller, "Deuteronomy, in Ellicott, II, 20.

*Second,* the law of a God beyond history will differ very radically from the law of a god in history. The supernatural and eternal God will declare a law over time and history in terms of His sovereign purpose and nature. A god within the temporal process and a part of it will instead always have a law conditioned by the temporal process, and hence by the dominant force therein, man. Existentialism and situation ethics are logical consequences of such a religion. Moreover, for all such temporal and naturalistic religions, because the world is a closed system and self-defining, any recourse to the God beyond the world is a denial of their religion and their god, and hence is atheism.

*Third,* the issue between God and Pharaoh was the freedom of Israel to obey its covenant God and His law. In Deuteronomy 13:2, 6, and 13, the sin of idolatry is the summons, "Let us go and serve other gods." In Exodus 8:1, God's demand of Pharaoh is similar: "Let my people go, that they may serve me." The way of service is declared later at Sinai in the law. The greatness of Moses was that "he endured, as seeing him who is invisible" (Heb. 11:27). Although a prince of Egypt by adoption, he forsook Egypt, its gods and law, for the covenant God and His law; he forsook the mighty visible power of a great empire for the invisible power of the covenant God. This same issue, the Lord declares in Deuteronomy 4:15-28, confronts all men at all times: they must think and act "as seeing him who is invisible."

*Fourth,* in verse 20, God declares that He redeemed Israel (and, in the New Testament, the same point is made repeatedly) to be His *inheritance* or His *possession.* The covenant people are thus God's property, not only by creation but also by redemption. It is the essence of idolatry and its humanistic law that man denies God's ownership to make himself a creature of time and space. As such a product of nature, he is free from God and free to dominate the world that produced him as god over that world. God's law is law for man, God's property, to use in governing God's Kingdom or property as God's agent or vice-gerunt. The covenant law is emphatic that man is God's possession or inheritance: to deny that law is to deny God's ownership and deity in favor of idolatry.

*Fifth,* because we are God's possession, God is jealous of our unfaithfulness and idolatry. He is a jealous God, and a consuming fire (Deut. 4:24; Heb. 12:29). To turn away from the true God is national suicide (Deut. 4:15-27). Idolatry thus cannot be treated lightly, either in ourselves or in others. It is always and invariably an evil which brings drastic judgment, and, when unrepented, can lead to the death of a people.

Therefore, God declares, "learn to fear me" (Deut. 4:10), a phrase repeated in Deuteronomy 14:23; 17:19; and 31:13, and a holy fear is enjoined also in Deuteronomy 6:24; 8:6; 10:12 and 28:58. Again, Moses speaks ten times of God speaking "out of the midst of the fire" (Deut. 4:12, 15, 33, 36; 5:4, 22, 24, 26; 9:10; 10:4; cf. 32:22)[3]

*Sixth,* God declares that the very universe which men use to further their idolatrous separation from God will be His witnesses against them (Deut. 4:26). Later, God declares through Moses that these witnesses, heaven and earth, will be in judgment against them, when rain and fertility are withheld from them by God's judgment (Deut. 28:23-24).

*Seventh,* God has given idolatry, the worship of the creature, to all the covenant-breaking nations (Deut. 4:19). It is an aspect of their judicial blinding by God (Isa. 6:9-10) and a prelude to their judgment and destruction. Those nations which immerse themselves in history are drowned by it; to deify the temporal realm is to be the victim of history, because it is the triumph of meaninglessness and despair. History of itself can give neither meaning nor law, and those who seek gods from within history are doomed to find only the empty moment. To deny the God over and beyond time and history means the affirmation of time and history as our god and law, and hence of the moment, the only reality. This means existentialism, the commitment to the moment. We become our own gods, denying any ties of past or future, from God or from eternity, over us. But to be lord of the moment is to be in bondage to its changes. As Keniston has recognized, in studying alienated youth,

> The patterns of life and the values to which we commit ourselves today may soon become outmoded; and those who sense this—as most young men and women do—accordingly must make their commitments tentative, and often are forced to prefer "role-playing" to deep devotion.[4]

Life then having no reality becomes a pretense, role-playing, and fads, trends, and caprices govern man and the moment. The end of idolatry is self-destruction.

---

3. See G. T. Manley, "Deuteronomy" in F. Davidson, A. M. Stibbs, E. F. Kevan, eds.: *The New Bible Commentary,* p. 202. Grand Rapids, MI: Eerdmans, 1953.

4. Kenneth Keniston: *The Uncommitted, Alienated Youth in American Society,* p. 235f. New York, NY: Harcourt, Brace & World, (1960) 1965.

# 111

## IDOLATRY AND THE COVENANT

In time and history, nothing stands still. All things are in transition, and their inherent implications eventually become omnipresent actualities. Thus, whether we are dealing with ourselves or with someone else, we can never allow the moment alone to determine our judgment. Our assessment must always be in terms of God's law and in terms of what the moment is and will become. A murderer's mother once said of her son, "He was always such a sweet child, a bit wilful at times, but always so sweet and appealing." I am told that she never saw him as anything other than that baby who still lived in her mind's eye. Her inability to see what her son's wilfulness could become, or to apply God's standard to her child's life and her own, made her incompetent as a mother and unable to recognize and cope with reality. She never saw the brutal, ungovernable man her son had become.

The Bible, however, in dealing with children, does not dwell on their appealing ways: it is concerned with the heart of man, and it therefore declares, "Foolishness is bound in the heart of a child; but the rod of correction shall drive it far from him" (Prov. 22:15).

The same is true of idolatry. The unregenerate man and the fool insist on looking at idolatry in its most harmless form, where it is restrained by the impact of Christianity and is a well-laundered tourist attraction. Moreover, we regularly get a partial and hence distorted view from modern writers. Thus, in reading about one people whose passion for homosexuality and bestiality is celebrated by their own men, and whose women skin captives alive and urinate and defecate over their faces, I have found that most writers present them in well-laundered terms as symbols of ancient virtues! Some publications, such as *The National Geographic Magazine,* while accurate in what they say, are always sure to omit untidy and ugly facts.

The Bible indulges in no such evasions. It tells us that idolatry is evil: it murders, and it glorifies its evils. It is degeneracy, and it has no extenuating aspect.

Let us examine some of the laws in this respect:

> Take heed to thyself, lest thou make a covenant with the inhabitants of the land whither thou goest, lest it be for a snare in the midst of thee: But ye shall destroy their altars, break their images, and cut down their groves:

473

For thou shalt worship no other god: for the LORD, whose name is Jealous, is a jealous God:

Lest thou make a covenant with the inhabitants of the land, and they go a whoring after their gods, and do sacrifice unto their gods, and one call thee, and thou eat of his sacrifice;

And take of their daughters unto thy sons, and their daughters go a whoring after their gods, and make thy sons go a whoring after their gods.

Thou shalt make thee no molten gods. (Ex. 34:12-27)

When the LORD thy God shall bring thee into the land whither thou goest to possess it, and hath cast out many nations before thee, the Hittites, and the Girgashites, and the Amorites, and the Canaanites, and the Perizzites, and the Hivites, and the Jebusites, seven nations greater and mightier than thou;

And when the LORD thy God shall deliver them before thee; thou shalt smite them, and utterly destroy them; thou shalt make no covenant with them, nor shew mercy unto them:

Neither shalt thou make marriages with them; thy daughter thou shalt not give unto his son, nor his daughter shalt thou take unto thy son.

For they will turn away thy son from following me, that they may serve other gods: so will the anger of the LORD be kindled against you, and destroy thee suddenly.

But thus shall ye deal with them; ye shall destroy their altars, and break down their images, and cut down their groves, and burn their graven images with fire. (Deut. 7:1-5)

When the LORD thy God shall cut off the nations from before thee, whither thou goest to possess them, and thou succeedest them, and dwellest in their land;

Take heed to thyself that thou be not snared by following them, after that they be destroyed from before thee; and that thou enquire not after their gods saying, How did these nations serve their gods? even so will I do likewise.

Thou shalt not do so unto the LORD thy God: for every abomination to the LORD, which he hateth, have they done unto their gods; for even their sons and their daughters have they burnt in the fire to their gods.

What thing soever I command you, observe to do it: thou shalt not add thereto, nor diminish from it. (Deut. 12:29-32)

In analyzing these texts, which are only a few of many on the subject of idolatry, it is obvious, *first,* that idolatry is an extremely serious offense in the sight of God. It is so frequently and strongly condemned in the law and the prophets, as well as in the New Testament, that it is, at the least, presumptuous to neglect the subject or to relegate the subject to a past age or dispensation. For us to evade something so clearly important in God's sight means to evade God's word and to create a new and imaginary word out of scattered texts from His book.

*Second,* a dramatic fact in all these laws against idolatry is that God manifests by these laws a concern for man's welfare. "Take heed to thyself," we are told more than once. Idolatry will not only destroy man's relationship to the Lord but also his own household. Its 'insane' practices include child sacrifice and all kinds of perversions or abominations practiced as a part of temple ritual and sacrifice. Idolatry, while the triumph of humanism, is also at the same time the suicide of man. Hence, "Take heed to thyself."

*Third,* the Lord makes clear that we cannot live at peace with evil. We must separate ourselves from it. This means no mixed marriages. It means, where the Conquest of Canaan was involved, warfare to the death. For us, it means no compromise, active evangelization, and, with the world-wide conquest by Christ's Kingdom, the abolition of all idolatry. All Biblical separation means warfare in some sense. We are at war with all aspects of godlessness, injustice, and fraud; evil is something we cannot compromise with, and accept as part of the landscape.

*Fourth,* man's life is covenantal. If he is in covenant with anything or anyone, his life is enmeshed therein, and there is then a reshaping of his life in terms of that covenant and faith. Marriage is declared by God to be a covenantal life. Therefore, to make a mixed marriage is to deny the covenant of the living God in favor of an idolatrous covenant. Paganism is syncretistic, inclusivistic; the Bible is exclusivistic in its demands on man. The one true God demands the total life of redeemed man. Idolatry undercuts and destroys God's covenant. No more than good and evil can be made one can the worship of God and idolatry be made one. To make a covenant with idolatrous man is to make a covenant with idolatry, whether that covenant be in the form of marriage or some kind of community life and fellowship. "Can two walk together, except they be agreed?" (Amos 3:3). In the sight of God, there is no more fellowship possible with idolatry than there is with murder. Idolatry is murderous in God's sight: it demands in its ultimate implications the sacrifice of man, the life of children "burnt in the fire" of idolatrous sacrifice. This is why mixed marriages are impossible, or any kind of yoking together with unbelief. St. Paul summarizes the covenant doctrine thus:

> Be ye not unequally yoked together with unbelievers: for what fellowship hath righteousness with unrighteousness? and what communion hath light with darkness?
> And what concord hath Christ with Belial? or what part hath he that believeth with an infidel?
> And what agreement hath the temple of God with idols? for ye are the temple of the living God; as God hath said, I will dwell in them, and walk in them; and I will be their God, and they shall be my people.
> Wherefore come out from among them, and be ye separate, saith the Lord, and touch not the unclean thing; and I will receive you,
> And will be a Father unto you, and ye shall be my sons and daughters, saith the Lord Almighty. (II Cor. 6:14-18)

*Fifth,* idolatry and the idolatrous nations were placed under the *ban* when Israel entered the Promised Land, *i.e.,* they were judicially sentenced to death by God and Israel was commanded to execute them. We are hereby to know how serious idolatry is in the sight of God. It is the destruction of His covenant, because it is its antithesis. The reason why Moses broke the two tables of the covenant when he saw Israel's idolatry was not anger but a judicial declaration that Israel, instead of being in covenant with God, was under the ban and thus under sentence of death. About three thousand were killed that day in judgment (Ex. 32:1-35; Deut. 9:7-29). Idolatry is thus a breaking of the covenant bond; it places the violators thereof directly under the ban of God, who, by His providential government, brings judgment upon them.

The comment of Gershon Bacon on idolatry sums up the Biblical law clearly:

> .... The Bible conceives idolatry not merely as the worshipping of images but as worshipping of anything, real or imaginary, other than God Himself. This is implicit in the second commandment (Ex. 20:3). ... The Bible attacks idolatry on two independent grounds: it violates the Covenant, and it is useless. Since idolatry is specifically forbidden (cf. Ex. 20: 4ff.), its practice constitutes the violation of the Covenant (Deut. 31:16, 20; Jer. 11:10). This is grounded on the belief that the worship of God is to be determined by Him alone. Accordingly, any form of worship not specifically prescribed by Him is an affront to His absolute sovereignty and omnipotence. The second argument can be properly understood in light of the pagan belief that natural phenomena such as fertility, rain, health, and so on may be controlled by idolatry. Since, according to the Bible, God is in control of all nature, idolatry is useless (cf. Isa. 41:23-24; 44:6-21; Jer. 10:1-5). Furthermore, as Maimonides observed (*Guide* 3:30), the Bible emphasizes that since idolatry is a violation of the Covenant, it produces negative results; as a punishment God will turn nature against the idolaters (cf. Deut. 11:13-18; 28)[1]

At this point, Jewish thought has had a sounder perspective than the church has had. We can neither ignore these laws against idolatry nor assume that they give the church the right to play god. That too becomes idolatry. The church confused idolatry with heresy. As a result, it attacked dissent. Idolatry, however, is not dissent. It is another faith entirely: it is a revolution against the faith and its law order. It is treason, and it is warfare against the law structure of society and the faith structure which informs it. When a humanistic society becomes plainly and openly humanistic, it must of necessity legislate against Christianity as a dangerous and revolutionary force, as some nations already do, and others are in process of doing, step by step. The logic of their faith requires it. No social order can permit its own destruction. When, however, the hostile

---

1. Gershon Bacon, "Idolatry," in *Encyclopaedia Judaica,* VIII, 1231.

faith is so strong that massive reprisals and executions are necessary, the situation is too far gone for repression. Basic evangelism is then necessary. This is the situation in the Soviet Union. Repression is futile, and educational evangelism is failing, and the people are showing increasingly a hunger for a Christian social order, apparently. In most of the world, the situation is too far gone into dissolution for either Christians or humanists to suppress one another. The need is for basic evangelism on both sides. Successful laws are those which rarely need enforcing. Laws which are not religiously grounded in the lives of the people soon erode into brutal repression or empty and dead relics.

# 112

## ON FEEDING A HUNGRY TIGER

One of the Buddhist sects has a story about a Bodhisattva, *i.e.,* one whose essence is perfect knowledge. This Bodhisattva manifested that perfect love which is the ideal of much non-Biblical thought. On seeing a hungry mother tiger with unfed and hungry cubs, this Bodhisattva threw himself down the cliff to provide food for the hungry tigers below. In this story, we have in logical form the end result of the modern doctrine of love.

We are asked to show undiscriminating love to everyone and for everything. In fact, if there is any element of discrimination, it must be for the undeserving and the unlovable, and the more it costs us, the better.

Have you fed any hungry tigers lately? The answer is that we all have. Ours is the politics, economics, education, and religion of feeding hungry tigers.

This religion of feeding hungry tigers regularly presents itself as true Christianity. For example, the Rev. Richard Bennink, Christian Reformed Church chaplain at their Bethesda Hospital, a mental health hospital, reports a like story from India, which he in turn gets from a Dutch priest, Henri J. M. Nouwen, writing in the March 13, 1976, issue of *America.* An old holy man, meditating on the banks of the Ganges River, noticed a scorpion floating helplessly in the river's strong current. Time and again, the old Hindu ascetic reached out to rescue the scorpion, but each time "the scorpion stung him so badly with its poisonous tail that his hands became swollen and bloody and his face distorted with pain." Benninck continues,

> A younger passer-by, seeing the old man stretched out on the roots of the tree, struggling with the scorpion, called to him: "Hey, stupid old man. What's wrong with you? Only a fool would risk his life for the sake of an ugly, useless spider. Don't you know that you may kill yourself trying to save that ungrateful creature?"
>
> Slowly the old man turned his head. Looking calmly at the stranger he said: "Friend, because it is the scorpion's nature to sting, why should I give up my nature to care?"
>
> This story graphically illustrates the Christian concept of mercy. The Bible presents a message of God's continued reaching out to ungrateful human beings. This serves as a model of mercy for all believers.... We feel stung by an ungrateful response.... But that is not how God responds. He keeps trying.[1]

---

1. Rev. Richard Bennink, "A Ministry of Mercy," in *Bethesda Bulletin,* vol. 52, no. 3, Fall, 1976, p. 8f.

Bennink derives his idea of Christian conduct from a Hindu tale which sets forth Hindu morality! There is nothing in his account of a helpless God who "keeps trying" to reach a sovereign and hostile man of the sovereign God of Scripture, of salvation by God's sovereign grace, or of a Biblical doctrine of mercy. Instead, we have the morality of feeding ourselves to hungry tigers.

This kind of theology is also apparent in the comments of the murderer, Gary Gilmore, who declared to the press that love is the answer to all our problems, that "we are all God," and that "All souls are headed for the same place, the land of no darkness. Some call it heaven."[2]

The practice of feeding a hungry tiger is common to our courts of law. In a California Supreme Court decision, the case was of a woman who had been in a six-year sexual relationship with a prominent actor. There was no intent to marry. The woman subsequently went to court seeking division of one million dollars of the actor's assets along community property lines. She alleged an oral agreement to share like a legally married couple. The California State Supreme Court ruled in her favor:

> The state court, however, went beyond the issue of written or oral non-marital contracts and mandated the trial courts to consider whether the couple's actions demonstrated an implied contract.

> "In the absence of an expressed contract," the court held, "the court should inquire into the conduct of the parties to determine whether that conduct demonstrates an implied contract, agreement of partnership, joint venture or some other tacit understanding between them."[3]

Justice William P. Clark, Jr. in the lone dissenting opinion, while unwilling to condemn all non-marital sexual contracts, still felt the decision granted too much:

> .... He accused his colleagues of going too far in the decision and attempting to "determine all anticipated rights and duties and remedies within every meretricious relationship in vague terms."

> "By judicial overreach," he said, "a majority (of the court) performs a unc pro tunc (backdated) marriage, dissolves it and distributes its property on terms never contemplated by the parties, case law or the legislature."

He warned that the decision could place "meretricious spouses in a

---

2. Various interviews with Gary Gilmore, reported in the *Salt Lake Tribune* and elsewhere in the early days of December, 1976, made clear that he was a dedicated exponent of such religious ideas. Gilmore, in a letter of Nov. 27, 1976, to 12 year-old Lisa La Rochelle, of Holyoke, Mass., expects "eventually" to "meet God." Cited in the *Salt Lake Tribune,* Saturday, Dec. 4, 1976. p. A3.

3. Edd Clark, "The Future of Marriage. Marvin Divorce Case Rocks Institution," in the *Los Angeles Herald-Examiner,* Thursday, December 30, 1976, p. A6.

better position than lawful spouses; violate the Family Law Act intent to eliminate bitterness and acrimony from marital break-ups, and reimpose the 'unmanageable burden' of arbitrating domestic disputes on the state's trial courts.''[4]

This decision was the climax of several throughout the Western world. All were aimed against Biblical law and the legal reforms of the Empress Theodora in the Code of Justinian, whereby the only legal form of sexual relationship is marriage, and all non-marital sexual relations and contracts are illegal and invalid.

To set aside Biblical family law and sexual regulations means the destruction of the family as we know it. It is ironic that feminists hailed the California Supreme Court decision as a major step in women's liberations.[5] In actuality, the decision means that the protection the law once gave to the legitimate, monogamous family is now gone. Prior to Theodora's insistence that civil law regulate sex in terms of Biblical law, the wife and children of a man could find themselves stripped of all their inheritance because of a non-marital sexual contract made by the man.

The effect of the decision is thus far-reaching. The Biblical control over property and inheritance by the legitimate family is denied. In Scripture, the family is a corporation holding property in trust for its legitimate and godly members. This corporation has now been breached in two ways. *First,* the state, by controlling and taxing property and inheritance, has declared itself to be the primary member and beneficiary of the family corporation. *Second,* in various recent legal precedents, the state through its courts has given illegitimate children and mistresses some claim on community property and inheritances.

The law now, in every kind of situation, tends to favor feeding the hungry tiger and the greedy whore. The idea of *sinners* is increasingly being supplanted with the concept of *victims.* The criminal, the mistress, the liar, the adulterer, the offender in any realm, is now a victim, not a sinner.

Biblical law makes clear the priority of justice over humanistic considerations. In Exodus 23:1-9, we read

> Thou shalt not raise a false report: put not thine hand with the wicked to be an unrighteous witness.
> Thou shalt not follow a multitude to do evil; neither shalt thou speak in a cause to decline after many to wrest judgment:
> Neither shalt thou countenance a poor man in his cause.
> If thou meet thine enemy's ox or his ass going astray, thou shalt surely bring it back to him again.
> If thou see the ass of him that hateth thee lying under his burden, and wouldest forbear to help him, thou shalt surely help with him.

---

4. *Idem.*
5. Linda Bernier, "Marvin Ruling Sparks Controversy. Marital law," in the *Los Angeles Herald-Examiner,* Thursday, December 30, 1976, p. A-6.

Thou shalt not wrest the judgment of thy poor in his cause.
Keep thee far from a false matter; and the innocent and righteous slay thou not: for I will not justify the wicked.
And thou shalt take no gift: for the gift blinded the wise (or, judge), and perverteth the words of the righteous.
Also thou shalt not oppress a stranger: for ye know the heart of a stranger, seeing ye were strangers in the land of Egypt.

We have here, *first,* a very obvious concern for the poor, the helpless, and the alien, but this concern must always be in terms of God's law and God's determined order as expressed in His law. Priority clearly belongs to God's order. We are neither to favor the poor because they are poor, nor be unjust to them because they are poor and helpless. Primacy cannot be given to man or to the human condition without destroying justice. The requirement of justice is that it be impartial with respect to man and partial rather to God's law.

*Second,* the greatest defense of the poor, the helpless, and the stranger is God's law, not man's antinomian pity and favor. God's law requires a concern in terms of justice for even the ass of our enemy, and our enemy who is in trouble. This concern must be godly concern: we do not feed hungry tigers; we do care for the needy in terms of God's law. Exodus 23:10-12 goes on to cite the Sabbath year's gleaning by the poor, and the weekly Sabbath rest.

*Third,* the morality of feeding hungry tigers rests on an antinomian religion of love and an implicit or explicit pantheism. No differences between good and evil have any ultimate validity, and all men share a common divinity (or a common nothingness); in such paganism, we must feed hungry tigers as a means to witnessing to the death of good and evil. We declare that we are living beyond good and evil in terms of this antinomian love. Where man lives beyond good and evil, he also lives beyond justice. Thus, in those countries where this tale of feeding hungry tigers is popular, there has long been a common unconcern for justice. The effect of this same morality in the Western world is to promote injustice in the name of this antinomian love. This idea of love is not really love but a tolerance for evil. We give the mistress legal claims on property by denying them to the legitimate family. Where we are unjust to favor the poor, we have, by denying the priority of justice, made possible tomorrow a radical injustice to the poor in favor of the rich, or in favor of the state.

*Fourth,* we can neither act nor speak ("Thou shalt not raise a false report") in terms of human needs and priorities, nor can we allow the will of the majority or minority ("a multitude") to determine our conduct. Not hungry tigers nor hungry men but the word of God is our standard. The morality of feeding hungry tigers is a dangerous one for all men: the men who today are the hungry tigers to whom men are fed may tomorrow themselves be fed to hungrier tigers than themselves. The Scripture is clear: "Keep thee far from a false matter."

## 113

## THE RELIGION OF THE HEART

The word *heart* in Scripture has reference to the religious center of man, to his mind, soul, or life. It is not one aspect of man among many, nor is it to be seen as simply physical or spiritual. It is both and more. It is man at his core.

It is easy to see then how far we have departed from Biblical usage. Thus, in some pietistic circles, it is common to speak of heart religion as opposed to head religion. Heart religion refers to feelings, head religion to intellectual grasp and theological formulation, and heart religion is supposedly real religion, and head religion is only the form of it and not true or converted religion. Such usage rests on a false doctrine of man, a dualistic or tripartite view. In pietism, heart religion, or emotional experience, is made basic to faith, and the result has been a loss of doctrinal clarity, antinomianism, and anti-creedalism.

The evangelical pietists believe in an emotional heart experience as true religion; this heart experience is with respect to Jesus as savior, not as lord. The modernistic pietists likewise believe in a heart experience as true religion, except that the focus is not on Jesus but on the "victims" of capitalism, or minority groups, and the like. The one sings, "O, how I love Jesus" as evidence of true religion, and the other in effect sings, O, how I love anybody who is down-trodden, poor, or oppressed. *Love* has come to replace faith and knowledge; it has also become the new law. Christian grace and growth are not manifested in obedience to God's law but in the expression of love, or in the belief that one's heart is filled with *pure love.*

Let us look at the formulation of this in John Wesley's doctrine of Christian perfection. In answer to the question, What is Christian perfection, Wesley wrote

> The loving God with all our heart, mind, soul, and strength. This implies that no wrong temper, none contrary to love, remains in the soul; and that all the thoughts, words, and actions, are governed by pure love.
>
> *Question,* Do you affirm, that this perfection excludes all infirmities, ignorance, and mistake?
>
> *Answer.* I continually affirm quite the contrary, and always have done so.
>
> *Q.* But how can every thought, word, and work, be governed by pure

love, and the man be subject at the same time to ignorance and mistake?

*A.* I see no contradiction here: "A man may be filled with pure love, and still be liable to mistake." Indeed I do not expect to be freed from actual mistakes, till this mortal puts on immortality. I believe this to be a natural consequence of the soul's dwelling in flesh and blood. For we cannot now think at all, but by the mediation of those bodily organs which have suffered equally with the rest of our frame. And hence we cannot avoid sometimes thinking wrong, till this corruptible shall have put on incorruption. . . .

*Q.* What was the judgment of all our brethren who met at Bristol in August, 1758, on this head?

*A.* It was expressed in these words: (1) Every one may mistake as long as he lives. (2) A mistake in opinion may occasion a mistake in practice. (3) Every such mistake is a transgression of the perfect law. Therefore, (4) Every such mistake, were it not for the blood of the atonement, would expose to eternal damnation. (5) It follows, that the most perfect have continual need of the merits of Christ, even for their actual transgressions, and may say for themselves, as well as for their brethren, "Forgive us our trespasses."

This easily accounts for what might otherwise seem to be utterly unaccountable; namely, that those who are not offended when we speak of the highest degree of love, yet will not hear of living without sin. The reason is, they know all men are liable to mistake, and that in practice as well as in judgment. But they do not know, or do not observe, that this is not sin, if love is the sole principle of action.

*Q.* But still, if they live without sin, is it not plain that they stand no longer in need of Christ in his priestly office?

*A.* Far from it. None feel their need of Christ like these; none so entirely depend upon him. For Christ does not give life to the soul separate from, but in and with, himself. Hence his words are equally true of all men, in whatsoever state of grace they are: "As the branch cannot bear fruit of itself, except it abide in the vine; no more can ye, except ye abide in me."

In every state we need Christ in the following respects. (1) Whatever grace we receive, it is a free gift from him. (2) We receive it as his purchase, merely in consideration of the price he paid. (3) We have this grace, not only from Christ, but in him. For our perfection is not like that of a tree, which flourishes by the shape derived from its own root, but like that of a branch which, united to the vine, bears fruit; but, severed from it, is dried up and withered. (4) All our blessings, temporal, spiritual, and eternal, depend on his intercession for us, which is one branch of his priestly office, whereof therefore we have always equal need. (5) The best of men still need Christ in his priestly office, to atone for their omissions, their shortcomings (as some not improperly speak), their mistakes in judgment and practice, and their defects of various kinds. For these are all deviations from the perfect law, and consequently need an atonement. . . .

To explain myself a little farther on this head: (1) Not only sin, properly so called, (that is, a voluntary transgression of a known law), but sin, improperly so called, (that is, an involuntary transgression of a divine law, known or unknown), needs the atoning blood. (2) I believe there is no such perfection in this life as excludes these involuntary transgressions which I apprehend to be naturally consequent on the ignorance and mistakes inseparable from mortality. (3) Therefore sinless perfection is a phrase I never use, lest I should seem to contradict myself. (4) I believe, a person filled with the love of God is still liable to these involuntary transgressions. (5) Such transgressions you may call sins, if you please: I do not.

*Q.* How shall we avoid setting perfection too high or too low?

*A.* By keeping to the Bible, and setting it just as high as the Scripture does. It is nothing higher and nothing lower than this—the loving God with all our heart and soul, and our neighbour as ourselves. It is love governing the heart and life, running through all our tempers, words, and actions.[1]

Wesley's thinking here rests on a Greek foundation, a mind-body dualism, and his idea of perfection has a neoplatonic heritage. The regenerate aspect of man is his "soul," Wesley assumes, and hence "if love is the sole principle of action," then man is perfect. The sins he then commits from ignorance, in mistake, or by "involuntary transgression," do not represent the loving soul, which is pure, but the corruptible body. (When later Wesleyans applied the atonement to the body, they held to healing as being part of the atonement.) For Wesley, Christ gives "life to the soul." The sins of the flesh thus represent the fact that the corruptible in man is still active, whereas pure love ruling in the soul assures perfection in the redeemed soul. Such is pietism, or heart religion. Its test of grace is the heart and its love, or the emotional life of man and its pious gush. The law is set aside in effect. We must recognize that, in early Methodism, the law had its place as in all other churches, and its social impact was very real. However, as the pietistic heart religion followed its logical implications, it became antinomian.

When we turn to Scripture, we do not find the opposition of law and love which marks pietism. Rather, they are seen in essence as one, different aspects of the same thing. This is clearly apparent in Romans 13:8-10:

> Owe no man any thing, but to love one another: for he that loveth another hath fulfilled the law.
> For this Thou shalt not commit adultery, Thou shalt not kill, Thou shalt not steal, Thou shalt not bear false witness, Thou shalt not covet; and if there be any other commandment, it is briefly comprehended in the saying, namely, Thou shalt love thy neighbour as thyself.

---

1. *The Words of John Wesley*, XI, pp. 394-397, cited in *The Wesleyan Advocate*, vol. 135, no. 1, January 3, 1977, p. 1f.

Love worketh no ill to his neighbour: therefore love is the fulfilling of the law.

We are not told that love replaces the law, but that love fulfills the law, *i.e.,* puts the law into force. Love will not work ill, *i.e.,* acts of lawlessness to a neighbor.

The same point appears with telling force in three other verses:

Circumcision is nothing, and uncircumcision is nothing, but the keeping of the commandments of God (I Cor. 7:19)

For in Jesus Christ neither circumcision availeth any thing, nor uncircumcision; but faith which worketh by love. (Gal. 5:6)

For in Christ Jesus neither circumcision availeth any thing, nor uncircumcision, but a new creature. (Gal. 6:15; cf. Rom. 2:25-31)

These are three virtually identical statements; more, they are in St. Paul's mind identical. He is in each case affirming the same thing, a true and living faith which is the totality of a man's being, as against an emphasis on externalism and ritual compliance. He thus uses three things to express this core religion, the faith which is from the heart, from the center and totality of a man's being. *First,* there is "the keeping of the commandments of God." *Second,* there is "faith which worketh by love." *third,* there is the fact that in Christ we are "a new creature," or, as Moffatt rendered it, "For what counts is neither circumcision nor uncircumcision, it is the new creation." These three things are in essence the same: the new creation means faith working by love, which means keeping the commandments of God. This is what the Biblical doctrine of man involves: it is a unity of life, thought and action.

To be "double minded" (or, literally, two-souled, or two-minded) means to be "unstable in all (our) ways" (James 1:8); it means an inability to function, and it prevents us from receiving anything from the Lord (James 1:7). The double-minded man is one who halts between two opinions, who wants the advantages of both but the liabilities of neither. The problem with the double-minded is not that he has two substances, mind and body, making up his being, but that he is unwilling to commit himself openly to either one or the other of two moral decisions. He wants sin without the consequences of sin, and virtue without the responsibilities of virtue. Double-mindedness is a moral, not a metaphysical, fact.

## 114

## CRIME: IRRATIONAL OR IMMORAL?

Biblical law allows no room for a plea very dear to the heart of humanistic man, fallen man, namely, not guilty by reason of insanity. Such a plea strikes at responsibility: it destroys the concept of sin or the possibility of coping with crime. The end result of allowing such a plea is the argument increasingly heard in our day, that *all crime is irrational,* and hence no criminal is responsible or guilty.

The fallacy in such an argument is, that it sees rationality as the key to man, not his heart, his faith, his moral character. If a man is determined by his level of rationality rather than by his faith, then university professors should be our finest men, and orthodox Christians very sorry characters, if we define rationality as the modern world does. Crime would then decrease with "secular education," as Horace Mann argued that it would. However, this clearly has not been the case.

Moreover, crime is not *irrational;* rather, it is *immoral.* Crime often represents a highly rational attempt to achieve a sinful goal. Street crime does not represent more than a street level reason, but the often unpunished crimes of politicians, labor and business leaders, and academicians goes hand in hand with a high level of sophisticated reasoning. The key in all cases is moral character, not reason or unreason. Not reason but faith is the determinative aspect of man. It is humanism to view man rationalistically rather than religiously. Man is essentially a religious rather than a rational creature. His reason is one aspect of his being among many which is put to the service of his faith. Man as a unity, being totally God's creation, acts in all his being in terms of his faith. There is a basic direction to his life. He may lag behind, be somewhat incompetent, and often fall short, but his life has a direction. He moves either in terms of his Creator and Redeemer, in faith and in obedience serving the Lord of life, or he moves in terms of rebellion, apostasy, and death.

In either case, he is responsible, and the nature of man's responsibility is determined by his faith and character. Anyone who has encountered more than a few morons and idiots knows quickly enough that there is a vast difference between those who have a real faith, and those who do not. It is a very tragic and rationalistic assumption all too common today that no one can be regenerate unless he has a certain level of intelligence. This is a denial of sovereign grace and predestination.

When we lessen moral responsibility by making sin and crime the products of rationality rather than a war against God and His law, we both destroy causality in the world and also develop a passivity towards evil. If sin or crime is irrational and not a product of moral revolt, then there is no causal relationship between faith and life, between a man and his acts. We become environmentalists. Then too we become resigned towards evils: they are finally beyond man, because man's ability to remake his environment is limited, and man becomes a product of nature, not God's dominion man called to subdue and develop it.

When evil is transferred from man to the world, it means that evil is metaphysical, not moral. It means that evil is basic to the nature of reality rather than a moral blight on the face of an essentially good reality (Gen. 1:31).

If evil is metaphysical, then it follows, *first,* that life is evil. All things, either material or spiritual, or both, are either evil, or an illusion and not good. *Second,* the necessary goal of life and religion then becomes deliverance from life and the world. *Third,* man must therefore seek the means of release. These three factors are the main elements of Hindu religious thought.[1]

Because Western thought has denied the Biblical doctrine of man and religious responsibility, it has increasingly gravitated towards Hinduism and other Far Eastern religions of like character. The consequences of such a religious perspective are very far-reaching and are destructive of human initiative and activity. Hinduism produces passivity and resignation in the face of evil. Not involvement but separation from life becomes the motive force. If evil be moral, it can be overcome; if metaphysical, it must be lived with.

This note of passivity and withdrawal is very clear in the Bhagavad-Gita, which is basic to any understanding of Hinduism. Krishna declared,

> The truly wise grieve neither for the dead, nor yet for the living. Just as the brave man feareth neither Death nor Life, so doth the wise man avoid grief over either, though the half-wise grieve over either or both, according to mood and circumstance. . . .
>
> As the soul, wearing this material body, experienceth the stages of infancy, youth, manhood, and old age, even so shall it, in due time, pass on to another body, and in other incarnations shall it again live, and move and play its part. Those who have attained the wisdom of the Inner Doctrine, know these things, and fail to be moved by aught that cometh to pass in this world of change; to such Life and Death are but words, and both are but the surface aspects of the deeper Being. . . .

---

1. T. Walter Wallbank: *India in the New Era,* p. 31. Chicago, IL: Scott, Foresman & Co., 1951.

These bodies, which act as enveloping coverings for the souls occupying them, are but finite things of the moment—and not the Real Man at all. They perish as all finite things perish. Let them perish. Up, O Prince of Pandu, knowing these things, prepare to fight!

He who in his ignorance thinketh: 'I slay,' or 'I am slain,' babbleth like an infant lacking knowledge. Of a truth, none can slay—none can be slain.[2]

We are told not to be moved by anything that happens in this world, in effect to be callous to human problems and sufferings. We are told that killing or being killed is a matter of indifference, because reality lies beyond time and matter. Hence, all these temporal things are irrelevant to reality, and we must separate ourselves from undue concern over them.

How did Hinduism get to this place of indifference to man's problems and a contempt for time and matter? It began with a total concern for precisely those things, a radical humanism which opposed taking the life of animals, including rats, flies, and mosquitos. Vegetarianism became a religious concern, and even today Hindu scientists tell us how much vegetables suffer when we harvest and cook them. When morality is removed as the basic factor and replaced with metaphysics, *all life* becomes equally valid, equally prized, but also equally meaningless. We can thus be told to avoid killing even a mosquito but also counselled that killing and being killed is of no consequence. If all things are equal, then there is no standard nor criterion left, and all things then can go their hellish way without interference. We then have regard for rats, but no more regard for a lower caste or an outcast. Let all live, and be oblivious to all.

Indifference to moral issues and moral character is thus the prelude to a basic indifference to life itself: it begins by destroying the basic moral differences between peoples.

A classic and telling example of this is a series of photographs of New Orleans' prostitutes made by photographer E. J. Bellocq circa 1912. Johnny Wiggs, a New Orleans cornetist who knew the prostitutes and the photographer, says of the portraits that "these are really the only pretty whores that I've seen in my life." In real life these girls Bellocq photographed were definitely not pretty. In fact, "something that I never ran across in my life, was a pretty whore."[3] However, to Wiggs amazement, these girls were sometimes beautiful in Bellocq's pictures. Even

---

2. Yogi Ramacharaka, ed.: *The Bhagavad Gita,* pp. 28-30. Chicago, IL: The Yogi Publication Society, (1907) 1935. Note the imitation of Biblical (i.e., King James) language in this translation; it is typical of the imitations of Scripture, by a variety of means, in various pagan religions.

3. Lee Friedlander: *E. J. Bellocq: Storyville Portraits,* p. 15. New York, NY: The Museum of Modern Art, 1970.

more, all of them look *innocent!* When they are shown in a whorish mood, it is with a child-like innocence, play-acting at evil and doing it poorly. Some pictures give us a sense of tragic pensiveness and *the whore as a madonna, as one whose suffering is the passion of humanity.* The photographer's own sense of self-pity catches the self-pity which is basic to all sinners, and prostitutes especially. Modern literature stresses this note of self-pity to an intense degree.

To be filled with self-pity and to be merciless go hand in hand. Self-pity makes a man oblivious to others: his being is too wrapped up in his own concerns. However, self-pity commonly masks itself in a supposed concern for humanity in order to avoid self-exposure. But a concern for humanity *cannot* begin with self-pity: it must begin with the love of God. When our Lord was asked which is "the great" or greatest command-ment, He declared, "Thou shalt love the Lord thy God with all thy heart, and with all thy soul, and with all thy mind." He then added that a second similar commandment exists: "Thou shalt love thy neighbour as thyself" (Matt. 22:35-40).

We are to love God with the totality of our being, and to love God means to keep His commandments (John 14:15). Only such a person can love himself and his neighbor.

Moreover, such a love is not antinomian nor irresponsible. The love of God and therefore the love of our neighbor is the love of a regenerate man who keeps God's commandments. His love and obedience is not a product of rational conclusions nor of critical analysis. It is the moral act of a regenerate man. A child not old enough yet to talk can know what pleases his or her mother; the child will beam with delight at a sight of the mother or father, and will seek to please them. This is a moral response, not an intellectual one in the modern sense. So too people of diminished mental capacities can and do respond in terms of their nature, regenerate or unregenerate. The sovereign God whose grace is effectual unto salva-tion from a mother's womb is equally effectual in the mind of a retarded or senile person. While moral perfection belongs to none of us in this life, we are all of us endowed with moral character, regenerate or unregenerate, and without exception. Mental defects do not place us out-side of God's universe.

## 115

## THE LAW AS INHERITANCE

Law is an inescapable aspect of all life. It is the principle of order and authority, as well as the rule of truth and faith, applied to life. When men deny the law of God, it is not because they are planning to live with no law, but because they substitute their own will as law. The choice is not law or no law, but God's law or man's law. In the sight of God, however, man's law is not law but anti-law, *anomia*. Man cannot live without law. If he replaces God's law with humanistic law, then his social order soon begins to crumble, because he has built on a rotten foundation, on an idea of law which in reality is anti-law.

We can thus understand how fearful is the offense of those who, like Hal Lindsey declare, "seeking to live for God by the principle of the law—is the first and worst doctrine of demons."[1] Such men should heed the warning of Matthew 18:6. Lindsey attempts to justify his position by citing Romans 7, where we are told, not that the law is dead, but that the redeemed man is dead to the law as a death penalty, but alive to it as the righteousness of God and the way of sanctification (Rom. 8:4). Lindsey believes that sin did not exist before the giving of the Ten Commandments, which plainly contradicts all that Genesis teaches. "Before the law was given, if a man had a weakness for sleeping with other men's wives and his conscience didn't bother him, then it wasn't sin."[2] Lindsey does not see the law of God as a constituent part of God's creation, as Romans 1:18f. makes clear it is. Moreover, in Romans 7, Paul is telling us that the law makes clear to us how far-reaching sin is. Paul cites the Tenth Commandment; he always knew that defrauding others is a sin, but the law made clear to him that even in the absence of any *act* violating the Tenth Commandment, all ideas, or desires, or concupiscence towards that end constitute sin. In brief, St. Paul, then a Pharisee, saw that his attempt to justify himself by an outward obedience to the law was a failure: the law cannot justify. But the law remains as the way of holiness. Paul cites the law repeatedly, as witness I Corinthians 7:39; 9:8f.; 14:21, 34; etc. The law is the possession of God's heirs (Deut. 33:4; Ps. 119:11), and the mark of an heir is that he obeys his Father (Matt. 21:28-32).

---

1. Hal Lindsey with C. C. Carlson: *Satan is Alive and Well on Planet Earth,* p. 154. New York, NY: Bantam Books, (1972) 1974.
2. *Ibid.,* p. 157.

The early church was far from the ideal thing some imagine it to be. It had its share of heretics, its problems, and its blindness. Like any mission field church, its converts brought in many problems with them. All the same, the early church evidences strongly the rule of God's law.

The law requires government by elders (or, presbyters, or bishops), and, very plainly, they exist in the New Testament church without explanation (Acts 6:3, 5; I Tim. 3:1ff.). They do not appear as something new, but as an old office, and Paul declares, citing an old proverb, which has Talmudic parallels, "This is a true saying, If a man desire the office of a bishop, he desireth a good work." These bishops or overseers are men who labor in the ministry of the word and government of the church in terms of God's law (I Tim. 5:17). The term *elder* has reference to the requirement that God's people be ruled by elders in households, elders over tens, over hundreds, and over thousands (Ex. 18:13-26; Deut. 1:3-18). (The identity of the terms *presbyter* and *bishop* appears in Titus 1:5, 7).

There was *no need* for the New Testament to explain this office. The new covenant people were the true Israel of God, with the Twelve Apostles continuing as the rightful heirs of the Twelve Sons of Jacob or Israel. The office and the form of government were taken over without discussion or comment by the new Israel of God. So closely did the church pattern itself after the old Israel that, as late as the 16th century, papal decree set the number of cardinals in the College of Cardinals at seventy members, with the pope as the seventy-first. As Goldberg notes,

> This arrangement parallels that of the Great Sanhedrin, which consisted of seventy judges plus the High Priest, who presided over it. The position of Pope parallels the Temple High Priest, Judaism's highest religious office. The triple crown of the Pope was derived from the High Priest's golden diadem and turban.[3]

This is not all. The Temple had a pneumatic pipe-organ, worked by twin bellows. In the earliest days of church use of organs, some church fathers were hostile to its use for fear that this Jewish instrument would seduce some Christians into Judaism. Some churches nowadays oppose all musical instruments; this too comes from Judaism. After the fall of Jerusalem, the rabbis banned musical instruments from the synagogues as a sign of mourning.[4]

The ark-like ship-like shape of the synagogue was also transferred into the church, coming into its own with the Armenian and Gothic architecture. However, very early, we find *The Apostolic Constitutions* comparing the church to a ship. The overseer, presbyter, or bishop is instructed:

---

3. M. Hirsh Goldberg: *The Jewish Connection,* p. 67. New York, NY: Stein and Day, 1976.
4. *Ibid.,* p. 68.

When thou callest an assembly of the church as one that is the com-
mander of a great ship, appoint the assemblies to be made with all
possible skill, charging the deacons as mariners to prepare places for
the brethren as for passengers, with all due care and decency. And
first, let the building be long, with its head to the east, with its
vestries on both sides at the east end, and so it will be like a ship. In
the middle let the bishop's throne be placed, and on each side of him
let the presbytery sit down; and let the deacons stand near at hand, in
close and small girt garments, for they are like the mariners and
managers of the ship: with regard to these, let the laity sit on the
other side, with all quietness and good order. And let the women sit
by themselves, they also keeping silence. In the middle, let the reader
stand upon some high place: let him read the books of Moses, of
Joshua the son of Nun, of the Judges, and of the Kings and of the
Chronicles, and those written after the return from the captivity; and
besides these, the books of Job and of Solomon, and of the sixteen
prophets. But when there have been two lessons severally read, let
some other person sing the hymns of David, and let the people join
at the conclusions of the verses. Afterwards let our acts be read, and
the Epistles of Paul our fellow-worker, which he sent to the churches
under the conduct of the Holy Spirit; and afterwards let a deacon or a
presbyter read the Gospels. . . . And while the Gospel is read, let all the
presbyters and deacons, and all the people, stand up in great silence;
for it is written: "Be silent, and hear, O Israel" (Deut. xxvii. 9).[5]

The resemblances to the synagogue are many, from the bishop's throne
to the segregation of the women. Moreover, the eastern wall was the
position of honor in the synagogue. In the church,

After this, let all rise up with one consent, and looking toward the
east, after the catechumens and penitents are gone out, pray to God
eastward, who ascended up to the heaven of heavens to the east;
remembering also the ancient situation of paradise in the east, from
whence the first man, when he had yielded to the persuasion of the
serpent, and disobeyed the command of God, was expelled.[6]

With a different rationale, the eastern orientation remains. The continuity
with Israel, and with the priestly functions thereof, is also evident:

After this let the deacon pray for the whole church, for the whole
world, and the several parts of it, and the fruits of it; for the priests
and the rulers, for the high priest and the king, and the peace of the
universe. After this let the high priest pray for peace upon the people, and bless them, as Moses commanded the priests to bless the
people, in these words: "The Lord bless thee, and keep thee: the
Lord make His face to shine upon thee, and give thee peace" (Num.
vi. 24). Let the bishop pray for the people, and say, "Save Thy people, O Lord, and bless Thine inheritance, which thou has obtained
with the precious blood of Thy Christ, and hast called a royal

---

5. "The Apostolic Constitutions, Book II, Sec. VII, in *Ante-Nicene Christian Library,*
vol. XVII, *The Clementine Homilies, The Apostolical Constitutions,* p. 83f. Edinburgh:
T. & T. Clark, 1870.

6. *Ibid.,* p. 85.

priesthood, and an holy nation" (Ps. xxviii. 8; Acts xx. 28; I Pet. i. 19, ii. 9).[7]

Jewish law forbad recourse to non-Jewish courts.[8] The system of elders of tens, hundreds, and thousands provided a graded system of courts. St. Paul assumes this same system, and the obligatory recourse to such courts, in I Corinthians 6:1, "Dare any of you, having a matter against another, go to law before the unjust, and not before the saints?" The idea is especially offensive to Paul, and his language assumes the validity of the same structure of government by elders.

A Castilian Jewish Synod of 1432 made it mandatory for ten Jewish families settling together to establish a synagogue.[9] Any ten men can establish a synagogue, with or without a rabbi, because the eldership can then function. In Puritan New England, something analogous prevailed, in that colonizing in unsettled areas had to be by groups of families, not lone individuals or families, so that a church could be established wherever Christians settled.

In the synagogue, it was a requirement that members feed and lodge needy Jews for at least three days on orders from the synagogue beadle.[10] If an interest-free loan were needed by a penniless Jew, this too was required of members on direction from a synagogue leader.[11]

In the New Testament, the requirement of hospitality is plainly stated (I Tim. 3:2; Titus 1:8; I Peter 4:9), with this difference: the elder or bishop does not merely require it of others. He sets an example in his own home (I Tim. 3:2; Titus 1:8). The charitable loan to needy fellow believers is required in Matthew 5:42 and Luke 6:30 in terms of Deuteronomy 15:7-8.

The *Didache* (IV, 8) makes the same requirement of the early church:

> Do not turn away the needy man, but share everything with your brother, and do not claim that anything is exclusively your own; For if you are sharers in the immortal, how much more in the mortal things?[12]

Barnabas has a similar statement: "Do not hesitate to give nor grumble when you give, for you know who is the good paymaster of the reward."[13]

The Old Testament word, *priest,* the Hebrew *gohen,* is not the same as our English word, priest, which is simply the word *presbyter* or elder

---

7. *Ibid.,* p. 85f.
8. Uri Kaploun: *The Synagogue,* p. 13. New York, NY: Leon Amiel, 1973.
9. *Ibid.,* p. 14.
10. *Ibid.,* p. 11.
11. *Ibid.,* p. 11f.
12. Robert A. Kraft, translator, ed.: *The Apostolic Fathers,* vol. 3, *Barnabas and the Didache,* p. 152. New York, NY: Thomas Nelson & Sons, 1965.
13. *Idem.*

shortened to *priest.* In the early church, the whole people, as a royal priesthood (I Peter 2:9), offer up Christ as their own and only sacrifice and propitiation for sin, so that, in this sense, the Old Testament sense of priesthood was retained for the people, the priesthood of all believers, and for the elder, presbyter, or bishop, who was called the high priest of the congregation, and the prophet who spoke for God, and to whom the first-fruits were faithfully given, as the Law required. We see this usage of the term "high priest" and "prophet" in the *Didache's* statement (13:1-7) concerning first-fruits:

> And every true prophet who wishes to settle among you deserves his food. Similarly, a true teacher also deserves, like the laborer, his food (cf. Matt. 10:10b). Take, therefore, every first fruit—of the produce of wine press and threshing floor, and of cattle and sheep—and give it to the prophets. For they are your high priests. But if you have no prophet, give to the poor. If you make a batch of dough, take the "first fruit" and give it in accord with the commandment. Similarly with a jug of wine or of oil, take the "first fruit" and give to the prophets. And so with money, and clothing, and give it in accord with the commandment.[14]

The extent to which the Old Testament and its law is seen as fully valid for Christians appears also in *Barnabas* 3:3, 5b, which speaks of true fasting to the Lord as not mere self-humiliation but rather obedience to the Lord's requirement of mercy, charity, and brotherliness:

> Loose every bond of injustice, untie the knots of forcibly extracted agreements. Release the downtrodden with forgiveness, and tear up every unjust contract. Distribute your food to the hungry, and if you see someone naked, clothe him. Bring the homeless into your home, and if you see someone of lowly estate, do not despise him, nor (despise) anyone of your own household... give your food to the hungry without hypocrisy, and have mercy on the person of lowly estate (Isa. 58:6-10a).[15]

This echoes also the Gospels and James clearly.

Enough has been said to make clear that the law was important to the church: it was the law of the covenant and the mark of heirship. To be God's people, to be His heirs, means to be the people of the law. This is clear in Deuteronomy 33:4-5:

> Moses commanded us a law, even the inheritance of the congregation of Jacob.
> And he was king in Jeshurun, when the heads of the people and the tribes of Israel were gathered together.

We are told here, *first,* that God gathered His people together, i.e., He made a covenant with them. It was by virtue of God's gathering that

---

14. *Ibid.,* p. 172.
15. *Ibid.,* p. 86f.

Israel became Israel, God's covenant people.

*Second,* God became King over His covenant people. He gathered them and created them into a covenant people, a kingdom of priests whose calling now became the service of the Lord.

*Third,* God, the covenant King, gave to His priestly and royal people His law for their possession and as an inheritance.

*Fourth,* the mark of God's covenant people is thus twofold, on the one hand, God's gathering, His sovereign grace unto salvation, and, on the other, their possession of and obedience to God's covenant law as their privilege and inheritance.

When St. Paul indicts the Pharisees, the keepers of the law, he indicts them for the misuse of it. The Pharisees, *first,* made obedience to the law the means of gathering, not God's sovereign grace. They turned the law from the sign of covenant holiness and obedience to man's way of salvation. *Second,* they set aside God's law for the traditions of men, their own rules and regulations. *Third,* Phariseeism made the law a purely external matter. Hence, our Lord called them "whited sepulchres, which indeed appear beautiful outward, but are within full of dead bones, and of all uncleanness" (Matt. 23:27). Paul saw that any outward restraint from acts of covetousness or fraud did not constitute obedience, when a man's heart burns with covetousness (Rom. 7:7-12). When, before God's salvation came to Paul, the Spirit (and "the law is spiritual" *i.e.,* of the Holy Spirit, Rom. 7:14) came to him and began His work in Paul's heart, it made clear the power of sin in Paul's heart, "and the commandment, which was ordained to life, I found to be unto death" (Rom. 7:10). Paul saw that the law condemned him to death as an unregenerate sinner, although the law, as the inheritance of the covenant people, was "ordained to life," ordained to give life and power to God's congregation. Phariseeism had converted the law into a yoke of bondage, not the way of life, by their interpretation of it "in the oldness of the letter," or letter-oldness. Does "letter-oldness" refer to the law? Paul makes clear that it does not: "Do we then make void the law through faith? God forbid: yea, we establish the law" (Rom. 3:31). By "letter-oldness" Paul does not refer to the ever-fresh and living word of God but to the false interpretations thereof, to the *traditions of the rabbis.* Tradition compels by the oldness of the letter, to the age and continuity of a practice, but we are rather called to "serve in the newness of the spirit," i.e., in spirit-newness (Rom. 7:6). When the redeemed of God read God's law-word, they read it in the newness of the Spirit, not as having the authority of tradition but rather the authority of God the Father, attested by God the Spirit.

All of God's word is law, because His every word is authoritative and binding. All of God's word speaks in the newness of the Spirit to His covenant people, because it is their inheritance. Those who deny the law thereby deny their inheritance and the covenant. By denying God's law, they deny God the King.

The idea of setting aside God's law is very offensive to St. Paul. Hence his strong language: "Dare any of you," *i.e.,* how can you even consider so ungodly a recourse as to go outside of God's law-ordained way?

The fact that Christians long kept the law meant problems in their relations to the Jews. No one has studied the extent to which Jews became Christians through the centuries, and Churchmen (*i.e.,* members) became Jews, but the hints indicate that there was some traffic back and forth. The similarities sometimes made for friendliness to the Jews, and sometimes hostilities. Each claimed to be the true Israel of God, the people of God's inheritance. As time passed, the waywardness of both also grew. The Jews, having rejected God's Messiah, moved further and further away from His word. The church, as it became Hellenized in its philosophy, became also antinomian, and it sought in neoplatonic pietism a substitute way of holiness. In so doing, it began to worship a god of its imagination.

## 116

## OATH AND TREASON

The word *treason* means literally to give up or betray, i.e., a trust, a vow, or an oath. It is in essence a religious concept and has at its center an actual or implied oath which is violated or betrayed. The oath, moreover, is one having to do with a Biblically ordained duty. Thus, early in the middle ages it was held to be treason to betray a king, or for a wife to kill her husband, a servant his master, or a priest his bishop. The counterpart to treason is *faithfulness.*

It is thus important for us to begin our study of treason by examining *the background* of the oath. Violation of an oath is treason; keeping an oath is good faith or faithfulness. The penalty for the violation of an oath is a *curse;* the return for faithfulness is a *blessing.* An oath is a sign of a *covenantal relationship.* There is a treaty between the two parties and mutual obligations which are summed up in a *law.* Every oath thus rests on a covenant and covenant law.

The king provides the social order, and the subject renders obedience to the law of that order and its officers. Each is under the curse of God for breach of covenant, and each is under the blessing of God for faithfulness to the covenant. For the king to turn wolf and destroy his subjects in contempt of God's law meant a betrayal of his oath. On this ground, medieval and Reformation thinkers held, magistrates had the legal right to prosecute and execute the monarch.

The same was true of priest and bishop, servant and master, and husband and wife. Their oath or implied oath placed them under a covenant, God's covenant since God was invoked in the oath. They were therefore under God's law, not their own will.

In Deuteronomy 27 and 28, we have the oath and law of God's covenant summarized, together with its curses and blessings. Originally, the oath of office in the United States was taken on an open Bible, with these two chapters being the ones on which the oath-taker placed his hand and his life.

If there be no common faith and covenant between two persons, groups, or nations, it follows that there can be no common law, no oath, no union, and no treason. The Bible thus forbids treaties between nations of differing faiths (Ex. 23:31-33; Deut. 7:14; Ex. 34:12, 13, 15, 16). Covenants with unbelievers are forbidden, because they are an evil;

either they involve dishonesty, or the surrender of one faith to the other. "Can two walk together, except they be agreed?" (Amos 3:3). Similarly, mixed marriages are forbidden (Deut. 7:1-3; Ex. 34:12, 15, 16; Num. 25:6-8; Neh. 13:23-27; Ezra 9:2, etc.).

The oath therefore presupposes a common faith and law. Where a common faith and law do not exist, there is no treason, because there is no giving up or betraying a common bond.

It becomes apparent by this why treason in the modern world is an increasing problem, and more and more difficult to define. Without the background of a common faith and law, there is no treason. Since World War II, it has become less and less possible to define treason because of the increasing disintegration of the Christian foundations of law.

For many, such a statement is nonsense. After all, the U. S. Constitution, Article III, Section 3, defines treason thus:

> Treason against the United States, shall consist only in levying war against them or in adhering to their enemies, giving them aid and comfort. No person shall be convicted of treason unless on the testimony of two witnesses to the same overt act, or on confession in open court. The congress shall have power to declare the punishment of treason, but no attainder of treason shall work corruption of blood, or forfeiture except during the life of the person attainted.

The trouble with this definition is its innocence. It was written when virtually all men in the U. S. believed thc Bible to be the infallible word of God and had a common opinion of what constitutes right and wrong.

The situation now is very different. Who is the enemy that one adheres to, or gives aid and comfort to? Some men were tried during the war who believed that the enemy, the communist conspiracy, was controlling the United States. Their trials represented no small confusion. After the war, and through the Viet Nam war, many had come to believe that the United States was the enemy because it was, in their opinion, a fascist state. Both these groups of supposed traitors manifested an intense conviction on differing humanistic premises, that their position was not treason but faithfulness to truth. The confusion has been compounded by the fact that no common definition of freedom exists, again because of differing faiths, and the courts have had their own confusion in defining freedom and treason.

In such a situation, the idea of treason is blurred, because there is behind it no common law, no common covenant and covenant oath and law.

The oath thus is basic to any understanding of treason. The actual or implied oath thus must be examined. Perhaps the best way to understand the oath is to examine an actual oath in Biblical law, one given in the law of the trial of jealousy, whereby, in a case unique in Biblical law, judgment is left to the supernatural action of God. According to Numbers 5:16-22,

And the priest shall bring her near, and set her before the LORD:
And the priest shall take holy water in an earthen vessel; and of the
dust that is in the floor of the tabernacle the priest shall take, and put
it into the water:
And the priest shall set the woman before the LORD, and uncover
the woman's head, and put the offering of memorial in her hands,
which is the jealousy offering: and the priest shall have in his hand
the bitter water that causeth the curse:
And the priest shall charge her by an oath, and say unto the woman,
If no man have lain with thee, and if thou hast not gone aside to
uncleanness with another instead of thy husband, be thou free from
this bitter water that causeth the curse:
But if thou hast gone aside to another instead of thy husband, and if
thou be defiled, and some man have lain with thee besides thine
husband:
Then the priest shall charge the woman with an oath of cursing, and
the priest shall say unto the woman, the LORD make thee a curse
and an oath among thy people, when the LORD doth make thy thigh
to rot, and thy belly to swell;
And this water that causeth the curse shall go into thy bowels, to
make thy belly to swell, and thy thigh to rot: And the woman shall
say, Amen, amen.

If the woman were guilty, the curse ensued; if innocent, she was blessed
with conception (Num. 5:28) and her husband lost the power to divorce
her (Deut. 22:19)[1]

In analyzing this oath, we should note, *first*, that the *amen* constitutes
an oath. The Hebrew word *amen* means surely, so be it, and comes from
a root meaning trustworthy and is cognate to truth, and faithfulness in
the Hebrew. In essence, an oath is saying *amen* to God and to His law.
Whether in marriage, in civil office or daily life, or in ecclesiastical courts
and functions, the oath, while taken in the presence of men, is to God.
All those present have an implied oath to that same law, and faithfulness
to the same God. Every prayer is thus an implied oath, because it expresses faith in God and His power, and says *amen* to it, whatever God's
answer to us may be. In marriage, the first vow of the bride and groom is
directly to God, and the second, while made to one another, is again to
God. The oath thus says *amen* to God's law and God's judgments. The
oath is a confession of faith.

*Second,* the word for oath here used is *shebuah* (Num. 5:21), virtually
the same word in Hebrew as *seven*. Oath and covenant are related ideas.
Oaths confirm a covenant and declare adherence to its law. God Himself
binds His actions to the covenant by an oath of faithfulness (Gen.
22:16-18). *Seven* means the number of fulness, the fulness of sacrifice, of

---

1. See on this matter R. J. Rushdoony: *Institutes of Biblical Law,* pp. 606-611, 617;
R. J. Rushdoony: *Politics of Guilt and Pity,* p. 100f.; R. J. Rushdoony: *The Biblical Philosophy of History,* pp. 77-86; R. J. Rushdoony: *The Mythology of Science,* pp. 96-98.`

curses or blessings, and the fulness of witnesses. This might involve seven actual sacrifices and seven witnesses to the oath. Normally, it meant an unreserved and total commitment to the thing sworn. Thus, in marriage, it means forsaking all others and supporting one another in sickness and in health, for better or worse, until parted by death or by God's law.

*Third,* the oath affirms faith in God's justice as basic and as man's life and hope. God's blessing on faithfulness and his curse on lawlessness are man's assurance of justice in every age, and by his oath man declares his faith in that law. In Zechariah 5:1-4 we have an exciting declaration of God's judgment or curse on treason to His law:

> Then I turned, and lifted up mine eyes, and looked, and behold a flying roll.
> And he said unto me, What seest thou? And I answered, I see a flying roll; the length thereof is twenty cubits, and the breadth thereof ten cubits.
> Then said he unto me, this is the curse that goeth forth over the face of the whole earth: for every one that stealeth shall be cut off as on this side according to it; and every one that sweareth shall be cut off on that side according to it.
> I will bring it forth, saith the LORD of hosts, and it shall enter into the house of the thief, and into the house of him that sweareth falsely by my name: and it shall remain in the midst of his house, and shall consume it with the timber thereof and the stones thereof.

So powerful is the law of God that it will destroy the violators thereof, and the very stones of their houses.

This vision of Zechariah portrays the scroll or roll of parchment of the law or judgment as 30 by 15 feet, the exact dimensions of the temple porch (I Kings 6:3) from whence the law was read, and of the Holy Place of the Tabernacle (Ex. 26:8). It flies, reaching every transgressor, and descends upon them to envelop them in judgment. Each side represents one table of the law, perjury the first table, and theft the second, "and both united in every case where a thief took the oath of expurgation to acquit himself of the charge of theft."[2]

*Fourth,* the purpose of the curse of the law upon oath-breakers is to *cut off,* or, more literally, *to cleanse by purging* (Zech. 5:3). The word comes from a root that means "to be clean."[3] The purpose of judgment is the cleansing of God's earth, and the oath invokes that cleansing.

*Fifth,* because God created man and placed him on earth to exercise dominion and to subdue the earth (Gen. 1:26-28), He thereby placed man under His word, law, and judgment and thus under an implied oath. The command of God in Genesis 2:16-17, to obey Him and to avoid the

---

2. T. V. Moore: *A Commentary on Zechariah,* p. 79. London: The Banner of Truth Trust, (1856) 1958.

3. H. C. Leupold: *Exposition of Zechariah,* p. 102. Columbus, OH: The Wartburg Press, 1956.

tree of the knowledge of good and evil required thus an assent from Adam, an amen, an implied oath. Hence, all men are then covenant-breakers in Adam, under a curse, even as all men in Christ are covenant-keepers and under God's blessing. Treason thus is sin in essence. Every definition of treason is a definition of sin. Each religion will thus define sin and treason differently, and every civil order will relate its doctrine of treason to its basic faith.

## 117

## TREASON AND RELIGION

As we have seen, treason is an essentially religious act: it is the violation of a covenant, and its law and oath. The poet Dante was in many respects a heretic and a statist and quickly earned condemnation for *The Divine Comedy* because of its many departures from the faith.[1] However, in his view of treason, strong elements of an older view are apparent. The lowest circle of hell for Dante is the 'realm' of traitors. The first of the four circles of this area of hell is reserved for those who have done violence to their own kin, like Cain. The second is for those who have betrayed their native land. The third circlet is for those who violate the laws of hospitality, and the fourth and lowest circles of hell is for those who betray their master and benefactor. Here we find Judas Iscariot, Brutus, Cassius, and, at the very bottom and center, Satan. Thus, while Dante gives us political treason in this circlet, it takes its name from Judas and has as its essential person, Satan. Moreover, Dante's reason for placing political traitors in this lowest circle is also religious: for him the state, in particular the emperor and the dream of the world state or monarchy, constituted man's truest religious hope and salvation.

Treason was in origin openly theological. Loyalty was to the god or gods of a state or city-state, and a traitor turned from one god to a more powerful one, and hence from one state to a greater one. The rulers and their states represented the gods, or were the gods, so that treason was also apostasy.

A political order is a law order which represents a religious faith. That faith may be theistic or humanistic, but it is a religious faith. To cut a man off by excommunication from his faith was thus also a separation from the state, and vice versa. In the modern world, this close relationship is not as explicit, but it is still there and is becoming more explicit as the various modern states become more and more openly humanistic.

David saw the meaning of his expulsion from Israel. His enemies, recognizing in David a man who in some sense had the Lord's blessing or anointing, were trying to destroy David's position before the Lord by driving him out of Israel and thereby saying, "Go, serve other gods"

---

1. See R. J. Rushdoony: *The One and The Many,* pp. 212-224. Fairfax, VA: Thoburn Press, (1971) 1978.

(I Sam. 26:19). Their purpose, as David saw, was to make David an enemy of God's covenant law and order and to place him thereby under God's curse. David, however, was insistent upon protecting Saul, the king in that covenant order, in order to prove himself a member of it. Twice (I Sam. 24 and 26) David spared the life of Saul, who was seeking to kill him, in order to demonstrate thereby that he was a defender of the covenant and its king. But this is not all. When David began his flight, he went with his men, hungry, to Ahimelech, the priest, for charity. Having nothing on hand, Ahimelech could have honestly refused David or given him some silver to procure food elsewhere. Instead, Ahimelech gave David and his men the hallowed shewbread loaves from the altar, which were to be eaten only by the priests. By this act, Ahimelech did two things: *first,* he made clear the priority of charity to ritual correctness, an aspect of the faith stressed by our Lord (Matt. 12:1-4; Mark 2:25-26). The form of the law cannot be used to deny its meaning. *Second,* Ahimelech placed David emphatically in the covenant and its care, and he gave to David the sword of Goliath from behind the ephod, to indicate that David was not an outlaw to the covenant but a covenant man (I Sam. 21:1-9). Even as in defeating Goliath he had been a champion of the covenant, so now in his flight and seemingly outlaw status, David was still the man of God's covenant.

Has politics replaced religion in the definition of treason? Rebecca West held that, when men lost faith in the God of Scripture, they turned to politics and political leaders for salvation. The salvation which theology had once offered, economics, as administered by a political order and its leader, now held forth as man's salvation.[2] Just as Biblical theology affirms the sinlessness of Jesus Christ, so too do the new scientific planners and would-be planners of society, affirm the same sinlessness for themselves.[3]

Margret Boveri is equally clear about the religious nature of treason. Even more clearly, she sees to a degree its relationship to the oath and its faith. The oath to God has the clarity of the written word of God, spelling out God's law and purpose. The modern state, however, as Romano Guardini has pointed out, "draws all authority from the people," so that the oath has no unchanging meaning.[4]

As Boveri noted, "Treason is closely tied to the question of oaths."[5] Earlier, "It had been a religious principle which was the focus of loyalty" in Europe.[6] Now politics was proving to be a poor substitute as

---

2. Rebecca West: *The New Meaning of Treason,* p. 119f. New York, NY: The Viking Press, 1964.
3. *Ibid.,* p. 173.
4. Margret Boveri: *Treason in the Twentieth Century,* pp. 29-40; 297-310. New York, NY: G. P. Putnam's Sons (1961) 1963.
5. *Ibid.,* p. 303.
6. *Ibid.,* p. 348.

a religion, and loyalty to a political leader or to a state very different from a loyalty to the triune God and to duly constituted authorities in terms of God's word.

The crisis created by this difference is a real one everywhere. Thus, Paul Borchardt, a German General Staff officer of ability and stature, held to a Biblical view of oaths. He had worked on the plans for the African Campaign and was familiar with more. Because he was half-Jewish, in 1938 he was dismissed from the General Staff. In 1942, he refused to reveal the General Staff plans to U. S. Army intelligence and chose instead a 40 year prison sentence in faithfulness to his oath as an officer. At the same time, he became a traitor in the eyes of the Jewish community because of his obedience to his oath. For him, an oath was unconditionally binding.[7]

At the same time, Colonel-General Ludwig Beck came, after much agonizing, to another religious conclusion concerning his oath. He told General Kortzfleisch, who cited his oath to Beck, "You have the nerve to talk of oaths. Hitler has broken his oath to the constitution and people a hundred times and you uphold oaths to such an oathbreaker."[8] Beck escaped Gestapo torture and execution for his part in an anti-Hitler plot by committing suicide, July 20, 1944. Beck like Borchardt thus held to a Biblical view of oaths while recognizing that, in an oath, it is God who is the unchanging and the absolute, not man.

In the eyes of the Nazis, men like Beck were traitors and to be executed. For Beck and others, the Nazis were traitors to God and to Germany; their faith and loyalty had not changed, but Germany and its official and actual faith had. Who then was the real traitor? Are the words of a political court the final word, or the judgment of God?

Let us turn again to Ahimelech. Doeg the Edomite, an alien, betrayed Ahimelech to Saul for aiding David. As a result, Saul sentenced Ahimelech, his family, and his community to death. By this act against the priest and sanctuary of the Lord, Saul, already an alien to the covenant, placed himself further outside of it and more clearly under the judgment of its law. The traitor in the situation was not Ahimelech but Saul.

In the world today, many men place themselves in opposition to the existing order for a variety of reasons, Christian reasons at times, and humanistic ones in other cases. What the state calls treason, these men call their moral duty.

The evasiveness of many courts, or their undue attention to the purely formal aspects of the law, rests on their inability to come to grips with the meaning of treason. A clear definition of treason means that a faith or a

---

7. *Ibid.,* p. 34f.
8. *Ibid.,* p. 229.

trust which certain acts violate is either explicitly or implicitly defined. Slowly, but all the same clearly, a definition of treason is taking shape behind the masses of words in legal decisions. As usual, the courts are echoing what is shouted in the streets and manifested in war, revolution, and rioting. Since World War II, we have been seeing a new definition of treason taking shape. It is an expression of the religion of humanity, the faith of statist education.

## 118

## TREASON AS THE CRIME AGAINST HUMANITY

One of the central legal events of the 20th century was the war crimes trials of Nazi leaders after World War II. The trials are an embarrassment to many scholars, who tend to skip over them hastily, or, as with the *Larousse Encyclopedia of Modern History from 1500 to the Present Day* (1964), to omit all mention of the Nürnberg trials.

The origin of the trials was at the Teheran Conference. At that time, Stalin (called "Uncle Joe" by Elliott Roosevelt) proposed the mass execution by firing squads of at least 50,000 Germans at the end of the war. Churchill at once protested against this as injustice. President F. D. Roosevelt suggested, as though the matter were a joke, a compromise of 49,500 executions.[1]

The final decision was to execute some leaders of Nazi Germany by means of a formal trial. Others, far more than the 50,000 stipulated by Stalin, were summarily executed while the British and Americans looked the other way. Thus, Churchill's request for legal procedure was met, and the Stalinist demand for vengeance satisfied.[2] What Stalin had done earlier to the Poles in the Katyn Forest Massacre was again repeated, but this time a portion of it was given the facade of legality.

An agency was created by the victors, called the International Military Tribunal, and a schedule attached, called "The Charter." This agreement was made by Russia, the United States, Great Britain, and the so-called Free French Government. Article 6 of the Charter created two new crimes against international law, "Crimes against peace," defined as "planning, preparing or waging a war of aggression or a war in violation of international treaties." The second crime, "Crimes against humanity," was defined as "inhumane acts against any civilian population before or during the war and persecutions on political, racial or religious grounds."[3] Under these terms, the leaders of Britain and the United States could have been tried and executed for the brutal bombing of Dresden.[4] Dresden had been registered with the Red Cross as a

---

1. Elliott Roosevelt: *As He Saw It*, pp. 188-191. New York, NY: Duell, Sloan and Pearce, 1946.
2. F. J. P. Veale: *Advance to Barbarism*, p. 142f. Appleton, WI: C. C. Nelson, 1953.
3. *Ibid.*, p. 155.
4. See on the bombing, David Irving: *The Destruction of Dresden*. New York, NY: Holt, Rinehart and Winston, 1963.

hospital city. More destruction and death were wrought there than in Hiroshima and Nagasaki.

The Russians were fully aware of the fact that the trials were a farce. To embarrass their "allies," who knew full well that the Russians were guilty of the mass-murder of Polish officers, about 15,000 of them, in the Katyn Forest, the Russians charged the Germans with the Katyn Forest Massacre. These charges made obvious to the Germans on trial, and thoughtful Germans everywhere, what a monstrous hoax the claims of the court were. Much time was spent on the Katyn Forest Massacres at Nürnberg, but the embarrassed allies eliminated all mention of it in the final verdicts. While the murder of 50 Allied officers in Germany was investigated, and judgment rendered, the death of 4,443 to 4,800 Allied officers and men, and the disappearance of 10,000 more, in the Soviet Union was ignored, as were other Soviet offenses, not to mention British and American ones.[5]

The Nürnberg war crimes trials were a brutal, barbarian travesty on justice. They demonstrated how far indeed humanism had gone in its march into barbarism. Legally, they were without justification. Beck had more justification for his anti-Hitler activities: Hitler had broken his oath to uphold the German Constitution.

On the other hand, the Nürnberg war crimes trials did meet a very major religious function, and it anticipated a new kind of morality and thinking, one which would soon begin to penetrate regular legal circles, *the crime against humanity.*

At the heart of David's awareness of his sin is his cry, "Against thee, thee only, have I sinned, and done this evil in thy sight" (Ps. 51:4). David was a war criminal: he had used the occasion of a war to kill off Uriah, in order to cover his adultery with Uriah's wife, Bathsheba, who was pregnant with David's child. David, however, does not speak of his crime against humanity, society, or man. Rather, he declares that he has sinned *only* against God, because, however much men were affected, the law was God's law, the people were God's creation and servants, and David himself another servant and creature of the Most High God, the only sovereign and law-giver. Crime is against a sovereign and the sovereign's law. Hence, to this day in England, whatever the offense, a criminal is charged with offenses against Her Majesty, the Queen, because it is believed that the monarch is sovereign, and the law is royal law.

In terms of Christian legal tradition, crime is against God, and against God's law, God's peace, and God's justice. Hence, at one time all courts began by invoking the Trinity, the source of all law, and university

---

5. J. K. Zawodny: *Death in the Forest, The Story of the Katyn Forest Massacre,* pp. 59-76. Notre Dame, IN: University of Notre Dame Press, 1962.

classes began with the same invocation, since all instruction comes from the word of the Triune God. This kind of order is possible when theology is the queen of the sciences, and theology is not speculative but Biblical theology.

Humanism, the religion of humanity, has a new definition of crime, because it has a new sovereign, man, collective man, *humanity*. Crime is thus *against humanity* and against, not the Peace of God, but *the peace of man*.

Since World War II, this view of crime has been increasingly in evidence. In France, Pierre Laval, trying to save France from absorption into German hands, worked shrewdly as prime minister of Vichy France. He was able, although incurring the bitter hatred of Hitler, to save half of France's Jewish population and several hundred thousand Frenchmen from deportation. For all of this, he was executed.[6] His crime was his nationalism. The French Resistance killed more Frenchmen than did the Nazis, but they were international socialists, rather than national socialists, and their murders were thus seen as justice. Many other lesser men than Laval, such as Quisling, were similarly tried. After 1917, the world began to view affairs from an internationalistic rather than a nationalistic perspective, under the influence of the Russian Revolution. Earlier, humanism had racial and national overtones; now it had become internationalistic and crime was defined as *against humanity*.

But the result was also confusion, and moral chaos. Raymond Aron, a French scholar, commenting on the Frenchmen who joined a Hitler Legion during the war, raised the question:

> If they were not traitors, who is a traitor? If they were traitors, why are the Frenchmen who collaborated with the Americans and the British not traitors? Why are the Communists, who may someday collaborate with a Russian army, not traitors? On the day on which each party has chosen its ideology, there is no longer a national entity, and with the same stroke of the clock there are no more traitors. There are just clusters of foreign parties accusing each other of treachery.[7]

Indeed, in such a situation either all are traitors, or none are.

The issue came up again after World War II in the 1950s and early 1960s in various trials of scientists guilty of passing on important secret data to the Soviet Union. On two counts, there was massive resistance and public pressure from intellectuals, students, and radicals to these trials. Alger Hiss is still viewed as a martyr by many, and Ethel and Julius Rosenberg, who were executed, are still subjects of books reflecting the humanistic addiction to hagiography. We still live in a world of

---

6. See Hubert Cole: *Laval, A Biography*. London: Heineman, 1963.
7. Boveri, *Treason in the Twentieth Century*, p. 48.

saints' legends; only the saints have changed to humanistic ones, and the legends have become even more unbelievable.

*First,* the offenses of these various spies and traitors were regarded as no offense at all, because they were working for an international socialist movement which, for all its faults, was ostensibly dedicated to the cause of humanity. Hence, these traitors and spies became heroes and saints to millions. They were noble souls who were dedicated to humanity. Most of these traitors believed this of themselves.

*Second,* some were scientists who saw themselves, both politically and scientifically, as members of an international community and hence dedicated to the cause of humanity rather than the country of their citizenship. They were thus above the law of the state because they represented the order of humanity.

The student movements of the 1960s also, among other things, took up the cause of humanity and viewed all things it disliked as crimes against humanity. Racism, inequality, colonialism, and much else, all aspects of the older humanism, were now condemned by the newer internationalistic humanism as crimes against humanity.

The idea of crimes against humanity is a very dangerous one, however. *First,* a crime against humanity can mean almost anything a mob, an elite, or a majority can choose to make it mean. It is thus destructive of law rather than supportive.

*Second,* the concept enthrones as sovereign and law-giver a non-existent entity, a collective noun. *Humanity* includes Christians and non-Christians, who cannot be agreed. It includes very alien racial and national traditions. In practice, therefore, the sovereign is not humanity but the greatest immediate power, and the nearest gun.

*Third,* since humanity includes all men, who then is the criminal? Of course, it is not humanity as such which is meant. Various international agencies have refused to date to see any crimes against humanity, for example, in Idi Amin and Uganda's brutal massacres of Christians and dissidents, but they do see crimes against humanity in Rhodesia's and South Africa's white regimes. The key, of course, is that Uganda has a socialist, black regime, whereas South Africa has a white regime which is widely held to be conservative although it is economically also socialist. *Humanity* thus means the idea of humanity and world order as espoused by the newer humanism. Older humanism and Christianity are alike under condemnation in terms of this concept.

Thus, treason has a new definition in terms of the new religion. Treason is now increasingly viewed as a crime against humanity. More and more, not merely treason, but other crimes are being defined in relation, not to the God of Scripture, but humanity.

## 119

## TREASON AS A BREACH OF FAITH

In 1769, Sir William Blackstone defined treason in his *Commentaries on the Laws of England* (Book IV, Ch. 6) in these terms:

Treason, *proditio,* in its very name (which is borrowed from the French) imports a betraying, treachery, or breach of faith. It therefore only happens between allies...; for treason is indeed a general appelation made use of by the law to denote not only offenses against the King and Government, but also that accumulation of guilt which arises whenever a superior reposes a confidence in a subject or inferior, between whom and himself there subsists a natural, a civil, or even a spiritual relation; and the inferior so abuses that confidence, so forgets the obligation of duty, subjection, and allegiance as to destroy the life of any such lord or superior.

Treason is thus a breach of faith between allies or between those having duties or obligations one to another. The echo of the doctrine of original sin, man's violation of his covenant with God, is clearly in the background here.

It is understandable too why the middle ages, and Europe up to as late as 1828, regarded as "petit" treason the murder of a husband by a wife, or a master by a servant, or of a bishop by his priest.

In England, the Treason Act of 1351 spelled out the various aspects of treason, and five classifications are still valid in English law today. These are, *first,* composing or imagining the death of the king, queen, or of their eldest son and heir. *Second,* violating the King's Consort, the wife of his eldest son and heir, or his eldest unmarried daughter. Queen Anne Boleyn was convicted of treason on this ground as a supposed party to her alleged violation. *Third,* levying war against the King in his realm. *Fourth,* adhering to the King's enemies, in terms of which Sir Roger Casement in 1916, and William Joyce in 1946, were convicted and executed. Joyce was legally an American citizen, but, having received the King's protection and peace as a resident of England for some years, he was therefore guilty of a breach of faith. *Fifth,* slaying the Chancellor, Treasurer, or the King's Justices while in their places doing their office.[1]

The law, however, was silent about offenses on one side of the two parties, the King's side. Sir Matthew Hale, in the *History of the Pleas of*

---

1. "Treason," in Geoffrey Grigson and Charles Harvard Gibbs-Smith, general eds.; *Ideas,* p. 400 New York, NY: Hawthorn Books, 1957.

*the Crown,* in the 17th century, wrote, "Because as the subject hath his protection from the King and his laws, so on the other side the subject is bound by his allegiance to be true and faithful to the king."[2] Although there was no legal *precedent* for it, Charles I was tried and condemned in effect as a traitor, for waging war against the laws and people of England rather than protecting them. It was precisely a *breach of faith* that Charles was rightly charged with. This breach of faith was not mere human fallibility but deliberate and radical. After the Restoration, which Hale worked for, the "regicides" were charged with treason on the ground that "the King was supreme Governor, subject to none but God, and could do no wrong, and that if he could do no wrong he could not be punished for any wrong."[3]

It is interesting to note that, while the trial of Charles I has many critics, the trial of the "regicides" has few. The trial of Charles I undercut statist absolutism, while the trial of the "regicides" upheld that same absolutism.

Breach of faith, thus, has largely been defined in one direction. Neither Charles I nor Hitler, nor Stalin for that matter, are condemned for breach of faith, but on other grounds, the latter two, in varying degrees, for crimes against humanity. The "regicides" and the German officers, however, were executed as traitors.

In the Western world, and elsewhere, treason is thus seen as a one-way street. A strong current from the Old Testament prophets through medieval and Reformation writers has seen it as a two-way street, although some have differed on the punishment of the ruler, whether by God, by magistrates, or by any man.

The theological roots of this lie in the Bible, and the doctrine of the covenant. God's covenant of grace with man was indeed pure grace. Yet out of pure grace, God bound Himself to fulfil certain promises to covenant man. Moreover, in a re-statement of the covenant to Abraham, God binds Himself by an oath to Himself to be faithful to the covenant (Gen. 22:16-18). Not only so, but in pure grace God undertakes to provide the victim for man's treason, as well as the perfect covenant-keeper, in the person of Jesus Christ, God incarnate. By this means, God underscores the mutuality of the covenant and the necessity of faithfulness on both sides.

Attempts have been made to introduce mutuality into the new religion. Humanity has a duty, we are told, to its unfortunate members, to the savages, those discriminated against, whether minority groups or sexual deviates, towards criminals, and so on. Statist action is commonplace

---

2. West, *The New Meaning of Treason,* p. 13.
3. Patrick Morrah: *1660, The Year of Restoration,* p. 184. Boston, MA: Beacon Press, 1960.

towards providing this help. However, it is not mutuality, in that no responsibility is laid upon these groups. The homosexuals and the abortionists are not asked to meet a standard other than their own. Thus, the mutuality of the religion of humanity is not mutuality at all: it is the subsidy of some by others, and the surrender of one faith and law to another.

Is there a breach of faith where there is no common faith or alliance, and is there treason where no protection and peace are provided? When and where a state has explicitly or implicitly declared war on a segment of society, is it treason to resist, or is it self-defense and survival?

Thus, in 1946, the Attorney General of England, Sir Hartley Shawcross, M. P., declared, "Parliament is sovereign; it may make *any* laws. It could ordain that all blue-eyed babies be destroyed at birth."[4] It should be remembered that Shawcross was chief British prosecutor at the Nürnberg war trials. He held that those trials were free of politics and laid down great and valid legal principles![5] Lord Shawcross, who was knighted in 1945 and made a life peer in 1959, was the prosecutor as a matter of duty of Dr. Alan Nunn May, a scientist found guilty of treason, and Rebecca West tells us that Shawcross "showed that he was heavy-hearted under the necessity of making the prosecuting speech, and he waited for the sentence with an apprehension rarely shown even by a defending counsel."[6] Shawcross was also the prosecutor in the Dr. Klaus Emil Fuchs atom spy case. A Labour Party member and an internationalist in his humanism, Shawcross still demonstrated in these latter two cases that, whatever his sympathies, the state has neither friends nor constraints. All blue-eyed babies, or anyone the state proscribes, Nazis, Communists, and all others are subject to the will of the state and its disposal. In practice, thus, the particular state is the sovereign, and it speaks as sovereign man, and as the reigning god. It speaks in terms of its own interests, and particular men are expendable.

The state, however, sees itself increasingly as the voice of humanity. Thus, the U. S. feels a world responsibility to all men, and a moral obligation to interfere in Viet Nam and Rhodesia, but no obligation to unborn babies. In the name of humanity, the modern state can proscribe any group within humanity, because it recognizes no law beyond this world and no god other than itself.

A Jacobin edict issued in the French Revolution in the name of man declared, "All is permitted those who act in the Revolutionary direction."[7] In terms of the newer humanism, the humanitarian state is that revolutionary agency.

---

4, Clarence Manion: *The Key to Peace,* p. 91. Chicago, IL: Heritage Foundation, 1951.

5. Veale, *Advance to Barbarism,* p. 245.

6. West, *op. cit.,* p. 157.

7. Otto J. Scott: *Robespierre, The Voice of Virtue,* p. 205. New York: Mason & Lipscomb, 1974.

As a result, the definition of treason is blurred. All sin against God is treason to God, but, in terms of human society, God has varying degrees of offenses and corresponding requirements for restitution. The principle is summarized in the case law with respect to abortion, which concludes.

> And if any mischief follow, then thou shalt give life for life,
> Eye for eye, tooth for tooth, hand for hand, foot for foot,
> Burning for burning, wound for wound, stripe for stripe (Ex. 21:23-25)

Restitution in proportion to the offense is mandatory.

If, however, treason is against humanity, then at every point we are guilty if we offend an unwritten and a changing "law." In my travels onto college and university communities, I often find startling examples of this crime, e.g., "All ethnic jokes are a crime against humanity." Is this ludicrous and extreme as an example? I would have thought so prior to 1976, when an extensive outcry forced the resignation of Secretary of Agriculture Butz from President Ford's cabinet because he told a totally tasteless and vulgar joke to a couple of associates. The man's previous equally tasteless public humor over a papal pronouncement brought a lesser outcry and no dismissal. The pope, clearly, is not humanity in this view, merely someone with a following. A clerical joke can be bad politics and poor public relations; an ethnic joke is a major sin.

It is no wonder that the idea of treason is breaking down. There is no covenant behind the new meaning of treason, and no clear-cut and principled law. High treason and "petit" treason are now eroding concepts, because the very idea of law is in erosion. Where the rule of law is uncertain, treason becomes a dangerous and vague concept.

## 120

## TREASON AND THE RULE OF LAW

The term, the rule of law, has had a long history and a variety of definitions, although a precise definition was made in a series of lectures in 1885 by Albert Venn Dicey (1835-1922), professor of Common Law at Oxford. In origin, it goes back to Exodus 12:48-49, God's command to Moses and Aaron with respect to the ordinance of the Passover:

And when a stranger shall sojourn with thee, and will keep the passover to the LORD, let all his males be circumcised, and then let him come near and keep it; and he shall be as one that is born in the land; for no uncircumcised person shall eat thereof.

One law shall be to him that is homeborn, and unto the stranger that sojourneth among you.

This means, *first,* as Rylaarsdam points out, that all who are in Israel, like Israel itself, belong to the Lord. Slaves must therefore be circumcised, because God's claim on them supersedes all human claims. Foreigners, slave and free, can also voluntarily become members of Israel by faith.[1] *Second,* because God's ownership of all things and all men is the essential and basic fact, the principle of life and citizenship is not Israel, nor race and blood, but God and His law. *Third,* the principle of government, rule, and authority is thus not in man nor in the state but in the rule of law, God's law. There is thus one law, God's law, for all men, without exception.

The idea of the rule of law thus militates against concepts of royal law, national law, folk law, positive law, or any other like humanistic concept. The rule of law presupposes that both man and the state are under a common law, and that ruler and ruled are equally subject to that law. The idea of royal or state absolutism, or of democracy, *vox populi vox dei,* is hostile to the rule of law.

Dicey, in his lectures and studies of the British constitution, analyzed the idea of the rule of law into three basic aspects. *First* of all, the rule of law means the absolute supremacy of regular law as against arbitrary power. It excludes executive privilege and prerogatives as well as administrative and bureaucratic fiats and regulations. In terms of the rule of law concept, a man can only be ruled by the law alone, and punished by the law alone, and for and by nothing else.

---

1. J. Coert Rylaarsdam, "Exodus," *The Interpreter's Bible,* I, 921.

This aspect has in the years since World War I been eroded by administrative agencies which have been given, in one country after another, broad legal powers and thus function as police and courts alike. For the most part, men are today governed by statist agencies which violate this aspect of the rule of law concept.

*Second,* the rule of law means the even and equal subjection of all classes to the law, and it excludes the exemption of any and all officials from the duty of obedience to the law.

This aspect was generally subject to the exemption of foreign diplomats, and the protection of judges, while exercising their legal functions, from actions for libel and slander. This exemption has been broadened over the years. Labor unions now have exemptions, and, in some countries, public officials have a growing area of exemptions.

*Third,* the rule of law concept sees the rights and immunities of individuals as derived, not from the constitution, the state, or the courts, but from the nature of things, i.e., from God's creation and law, although this theological aspect is not usually openly stated. The state and its laws and courts, as well as its constitution, *recognize* these rights and immunities; they do not *grant* them. Their source is beyond the state. The state thus does not create law nor create rights and offenses: it has no such power. It simply recognizes them. The state has no arbitrary power.

This last aspect, which is basic, was least clearly formulated in recent years, and is the key to the decline of the rule of law. The rule of law is only tenable as a working principle if law is theological in a Biblical sense, God-ordained and God-created. If this be denied, as it has been in the 20th century, the result is the decline of the rule of law in favor of the rule of the state.

Biblical law deals with law which is basic to reality, because it is the law of the creator of all reality. It is thus inescapable law, because it meets us in the very constitution of the universe and history. Arbitrary humanistic law has no such necessity in it: the necessity comes from statist compulsion. Statist law has forbad the use of gold coins as legal tender, the buying and selling of wine, and much, much more which has only the stamp of statist arbitrariness behind it.

In the past century, the growth of legal positivism has increasingly made the state the source of law. Law is what the state says it is, and beyond the state there is no law. It was the rise of such a legal philosophy which made Nazi legal theory possible.[2]

With such a changed view of law, the idea of the rule of law also changed. Clark and Sohn thus saw United Nations Law as the rule of law

---

2. John H. Hallowell: *The Decline of Liberalism as an Ideology.* Berkeley, CA: The University of California Press, 1943.

because it was declared to be the alternative to force, war, or the threat of it as the means of settling international disputes.[3] The rule of law now means the rule of the state.

How is the rule of law related to treason? The relationship becomes clear when we look at Dorr's Rebellion. Thomas Wilson Dorr was a lawyer and a popular figure in Rhode Island, the leader of a people's party. Rhode Island in 1840 still kept the form of government set up under royal charter. The right to vote was sharply limited by that charter. Dorr, finding the normal constitutional channels too slow and reluctant, proceeded in terms of *justice.* The Dorr people held a state-wide election of their own contriving to select a People's Convention for constitutional revision. In 1841, the convention submitted a new constitution to the same extra-legal vote. In December, 1841, this constitution was adopted by a claimed vote of 13,944, a clear majority of the 23,000 adult male citizens of Rhode Island. Moreover, although about 9,000 legally qualified voters alone could vote under the old charter, the Dorr people claimed that 4,960 of the 13,944 favorable votes had been cast by legally registered voters.

Instead of using this majority to work through the existing legal framework, Dorr and his party held another extra-legal election under their constitution. Dorr was elected "governor," and a new "legislature" was also elected. Both sides armed for battle, but Dorr's party was broken up in a skirmish. Dorr was convicted of treason and imprisoned for life. One aspect of Dorr's Rebellion went to the U. S. Supreme Court, an action of trespass as a result of the activity of the state militia. The court opinion in *Luther* v. *Borden* held that the legitimacy of a state government was a political and not a justiciable issue.[4]

In 1842, a constitutional convention did in fact revise Rhode Island's charter, and Dorr was released after a year in prison, a physically broken man.

By this appeal to an extra-legal process when they apparently had the legal power to affect a change, the Dorr party associated the rule of law with their will and with whatever expedients they chose to hasten their reforms. They identified the higher law with themselves in a manner characteristic of humanism. They were thus in line with those who identified, in the next century, treason with crimes against humanity. Abolitionists were soon to take a similar stand.

On the other hand, the state and the courts were unwilling to see any

---

3. Grenville Clark and Louis B. Sohn: *World Peace Through World Law,* pp. 40, 335. Second Edition, Revised. Cambridge, MA: Harvard University Press, 1960.

4. James Willard Hurst: *The Growth of American Law, The Law Makers,* p. 206. Boston, MA: Little, Brown, and Company, 1950.

law beyond statute law and were equally humanistic. Their position was not unlike those who justified slavery on the grounds that it was legal. This is an attitude which has since flourished, as witness Senator John Tunney's equation of morality with legality: Abortion is moral because it is legal, and theft will be moral if and when it is legalized.

In such a situation, the idea of the rule of law perishes. Law, when it is God's law, controls both man and the state, and it judges both. Judges are then ministers of God whose robes indicate a holy office. Treason then is related to the rule of law, not the fiats of the state and the current "needs" of humanity. Without the rule of true law, God's law, treason becomes, not an act of individuals guilty of a breach of faith, but of classes, races, and religious groups, churches, and schools who resist the tyranny of the humanistic state and its theological claims for itself in the name of humanity.

# 121

## JUSTICE AND THE RULE OF LAW

On February 15, 1965, an International Commission of Jurists met in Bangkok, Thailand, and issued a report on *The Dynamic Aspects of the Rule of Law in the Modern Age.* By common consent, it was held that evils such as hunger, poverty, feudal land tenures, and dictatorships militate against the proper application of the Rule of Law. As Sean MacBride summarized it,

> At Delhi it was declared that the Rule of Law is a dynamic concept for the expansion and fulfilment of which jurists are primarily responsible, and which should be employed not only to safeguard and advance the civil and political rights of the individual in a free society but also to establish social, economic, educational and cultural conditions under which his legitimate aspirations and dignity may be realized. . . .

> It is a quest for answers to the questions posed in this theme which inevitably leads to the realization that political, economic and social factors are closely linked to the proper application of the Rule of Law. In other words, such evils as hunger, poverty, dictatorships, feudal land tenures, corruption, inefficient administration, inadequate educational provisions and an inadequate Bar and Bench are all factors which militate against the proper application of the Rule of Law and which in some areas reduce the respect which the Rule of Law should command from the ordinary man in the street. It is in this sense that we regard the eradication of these evils as forming a vital part of the responsibility of lawyers and as coming within the framework of the dynamic aspect of the Rule of Law in the modern age.[1]

The Rule of Law thus requires "Social Justice." This means "updating the concept of property" in view of "the relative shortage of land." It means re-examining the concept of "just compensation," and net profits. It means asking who is entitled to unearned increments, and limitations to rights of succession.[2] The Commission held that "the best safeguard for the protection and respect of personal liberty is an enlightened democracy." It admitted at the same time that all modern states, from communistic states, dictatorships by the military or a party,

---

1. International Commission of Jurists: *The Dynamic Aspects of the Rule of Law in the Modern Age,* p. 108. Report on the Proceedings of the South-East Asian and Pacific Conference of Jurists, Bangkok, Thailand, February 15-19, 1965. Geneva, Switzerland.
2. *Ibid.,* p. 128f.

on through "Western democracies," claim to be democratic.[3] All the same, the Commission held that democracy and free elections are *fundamental* to the Rule of Law and concluded, "There are no basic factors in the South-East Asia and Pacific areas which prevent the maintenance and promotion of the Rule of Law."[4] This statement is, of course, sufficiently broad to mean anything. The Commission, while clearly socialistic, held that communism "both in practice and theory is hostile to the Rule of Law."[5]

Every system of thought is at heart religious and begins with a religious, ultimate principle which is the source of power and authority. This source is plainly stated by the Commission in its statement on "Free Elections."

> The purpose of an election is twofold: to enable the people to choose the policy to be pursued by the government and to choose a government to implement that policy.

> The Universal Declaration of Human Rights sets out the essential requirements of free elections and government authority in the following terms:

>> The will of the people shall be the basis of the authority of government; this will shall be expressed in periodic and genuine elections which shall be by universal and equal suffrage and shall be held by secret vote or by equivalent free voting
procedures. [6]

This is clearly an expression of humanistic faith, a faith in man. The Rule of Law is thus associated with the will of the people and a democratic idea of social justice rather than with any objective and absolute standard of law. The laws demanded by the Commission, and its idea of the Rule of Law, are religious expressions, as is all law. Law is in essence a theological concern: failure to recognize this and to deal with it as such leaves law wide open to abuse, decay, and collapse.

In the West, law became secularized when the Hellenic concept of natural law was confused with God's revealed law, and God's creation law, *i.e.,* the laws whereby God rules in creation. For the Greeks, natural law is an abstract universal which is *not* a part of creation, the world of matter, but of the world of ideas, or reason, mind. Natural law thus becomes an expression of the mind of the rational elite, as in Plato's *Republic* and Aristotle's *Politics* and *Ethics. History* therefore best expresses nature, and the dialectical process of Hegel and Marx, as well as Dewey's Great Community, becomes the concrete expressions of natural law. The elite planners are thus voices of natural law and reason.

---

3. *Ibid.,* p. 39, 17-20.
4. *Ibid.,* p. 50.
5. *Ibid.,* p. 146.
6. *Ibid.,* p. 44f.

When Christendom confused God's law with natural law, it made possible the abandonment of Biblical law for a humanistic, rationalistic idea of law. In the new theology of law, therefore, it is the will of the people which is basic to the Rule of Law, not the word of God, or Biblical law.

When law becomes humanistic, it then responds to varying impulses. To cite a specific example, from Bronx County, New York, a black youth, an honor student in high school, was on his way home and was stabbed to death by a total stranger, a white youth. The killer was an 18 year old who came from a fine and devout Italian immigrant family. The young man, a good student, was in rebellion against the strict morality of his parents and intensely anxious to win the approval of his peers, and hence the murder. The parents of both youths were overwhelmed; the black parents were bitter, and the younger brother of the murdered youth began in bitterness to neglect his studies and finally wound up indicted for armed robbery. The defense lawyer too was bitter: the murderer could not be helped by a prison sentence, and his record up until then was good. In prison, he would be gang-raped by homosexuals as a soft, good-looking youth and would end up as the "wife" of some strong inmate in order to survive. The prosecutor tried to leave the decision up to the judge, who returned the decision to the prosecutor, since the evidence made guilt obvious, and the plea was "guilty." The murderer was finally sentenced to 15 years in state prison, and will be eligible for parole in three years. His father suffered a stroke and is now an invalid. The question raised by the prosecuting attorney was in essence this: how could justice have been served in any way which would be fair to all? His conclusion was, "Whether or not I did the right thing I shall never know."[7] The title of his account raises the right question, "Justice for Whom?" From a humanistic perspective, the question is impossible to answer. Justice in such thinking is related to man, to humanistic society. Crime was not reduced in the Bronx, Phillips notes, nor was either family satisfied with the justice rendered. One youth was dead, his brother's life warped, another is in prison being debauched by degenerates. The fact that this youth is a vicious murderer does not justify what the prison system is doing to him. Both families are blasted, and the prosecutor feels heart-sick. Where justice has reference to man, it can never satisfy. The question then is indeed, "Justice for Whom?" None are satisfied, and all are losers. Justice which is related to so general and diverse a thing as humanity has too many demands to satisfy and none that it can then fill.

From the perspective of Biblical law, restitution is basic. This means

---

7. Steven Phillips, "Justice for Whom?" in *Psychology Today,* vol. 10, no. 10. March, 1977, p. 88.

also no prison system, and, in this case, death. Moreover, we then have no attempt by the law to satisfy conflicting human needs and demands but rather the satisfaction of God's law. What prevails then is a principle of order independent of the parties involved. But this is precisely what the International Commission of Jurists, in their 1965 Bangkok meeting, were setting aside. For them, a *dynamic* Rule of Law meant a principle of order and justice radically dependent upon all the peoples involved. Not only do they redefine the Rule of Law but of justice also. Justice for them has reference, not to the supremacy of law over the human context but rather to the supremacy of the human context in and through law. It is not man who must meet a standard, but a standard which must provide for man the satisfaction of his wants and needs.

We are told, in Scripture,

> That which is altogether just shalt thou follow, that thou mayest live, and inherit the land which the LORD thy God giveth thee. (Deut. 16:20)

> To do justice and judgment is more acceptable to the LORD than sacrifice. (Prov. 21:3)

Deuteronomy 16:20 begins, literally, "Justice, only justice, shalt thou follow." Life and prosperity on earth are dependent upon justice. Justice does not follow man's needs, but man follows justice. Justice is God-centered, not man-centered. Modern law is not in touch with reality, because it seeks to be man-centered and defines the Rule of Law in terms of man and the will of man. Such a view of law is treason to God's covenant and the suicide of man.

Again, it is made clear by Scripture that the practice of justice and righteousness is more important to the Lord than formal worship. This does not mean that the practice of worship is decried, but, rather, that worship without justice and righteousness is not acceptable to the Lord. Practically, this means that for Christians to be unconcerned about law is to manifest an unconcern about worship in any valid sense. Their worship becomes then an empty rite. It is not only the Christian School for children which is basic to Christian reconstruction but the law school as well. Justice, only justice, must we follow, and it is not of man, but from the Lord and in His law, not man's.

## 122

### OATH AND COVENANT

The question of oaths is an important but neglected one. Oaths are repeatedly referred to in Scripture. In Psalm 24:4, we are told that a false or deceitful oath bars us from God's presence. In the law we read

Thou shalt not take the name of the LORD in vain; for the LORD will not hold him guiltless that taketh his name in vain. (Ex. 29:7)

And ye shall not swear by my name falsely, neither shalt thou profane the name of thy God: I am the LORD. (Lev. 19:12)

In Deuteronomy 23:23, reference is made to personal oaths. Exodus 20:7 and Leviticus 19:12 have reference to religious oaths and to courts of law. In Deuteronomy 23:23, the context is still religious, but the reference is to free-will offerings:

That which is gone out of thy lips thou shalt keep and perform; even a free-will offering, according as thou hast vowed unto the LORD thy God, which thou hast promised with thy mouth.

In the Sermon on the Mount, Matthew 5:33-37, our Lord refers to all such oaths with respect to free-will offerings and declares, "Swear not at all;" rather, our every word should be our bond, and, as God's covenant people, the blessed heirs of the Kingdom of God, we should be constantly before God in our total life and speech. As "the salt of the earth" and "the light of the world" (Matt. 5:13-16), God's heirs cannot have two kinds of speech, one for important vows, another for getting by with as little truth as possible. Our Lord did not thereby abolish the legal use of oaths. He did make clear that, because all our speech and thought (Matt. 5:22-28) is before God, from whom nothing is hidden, there is no need for our private religious pledges to the Lord. Man's every word binds him before God. Swearing by the name of the Lord is used by Scripture as a synonym for adhering to Him. In Psalm 63:11, we read, "Every one that sweareth by him shall glory: but the mouth of them that speak lies shall be stopped." We have on the one hand the reprobation of all false witness, of all liars, and, on the other, the glorification of all who speak the truth, *i.e.,* who swear by the Lord. Again, Isaiah, in looking to the future, the Messianic era, declares, "In that day shall five cities of Egypt speak the language of Canaan, and swear to the LORD of hosts; one shall be called, The city of destruction" (Isa. 19:18). Even in the stronghold of God's once bitter enemies, five out of six will speak the language of faith and be as men under oath to God, whereas only one-sixth will be reprobate. This equation of faith with being under oath to the Lord appears also in Jeremiah 44:26 and Zephaniah 1:5. On the other hand, apostasy is described as swearing by other gods in Joshua 23:7, Amos 8:14, Jeremiah 5:7 and 12:16 (cf. Ex. 23:13).

Again, the kind of oath or vow referred to in Deuteronomy 23:23, and by our Lord in Matthew 5:33-37, is described more fully in Numbers 30:1-16. According to Numbers 30:2,

> If a man vow a vow unto the LORD, or swear an oath to bind his soul with a bond; he shall not break (or, profane) his word, he shall do according to all that proceedeth out of his mouth.

This law goes on to state that a daughter or a wife can have their vow disallowed or cancelled by their father or husband at the time it was made, because they are under his authority and cannot bind themselves even to God apart from God's duly constituted authority over them. It was all such vows and oaths that our Lord set aside.

Judaism, not accepting Christ as Lord, retained the continuing validity of this private religious vow. The result was serious problems. Let us suppose that a devout Jew in the early middle ages vowed to give the Lord a thousand gold pieces because of some particular blessing. Subsequently, disaster struck him and destroyed his fortune, leaving him unable to pay ten, let alone a thousand gold pieces. In an unstable society, such seemingly simple vows can suddenly become major problems. The result was a religious problem. The answer was the *Kol Nidrei,* a ritual declaration of the annulment of vows made at the beginning of the evening service which officially opened the Day of Atonement in the synagogue. The *Kol Nidrei* has nothing to do with oaths made in a court of law or with business contracts with Gentiles. It applies only to personal religious vows to the Lord.[1] The *Kol Nidrei* was resisted by many religious leaders, and, with the rise of Jewish modernism, was dropped in such circles simply because the entire subject was not now deemed important.

The adoption of the *Kol Nidrei* was a very important theological step. It was the cancellation of man's religious will devotion.[2] It was an admission of the weakness and impotence of man's efforts to serve God, and it in effect looked to God for a sabbath from man's own will and word.

The Biblical Sabbath decrees one day's rest in seven, for man and his animals, one year in seven for man and the earth, and a jubilee year after the forty-ninth year to mark a double sabbath. The *Kol Nidrei* added a sabbath for man's vows each year and is in effect a confession of the failure of Judaism. Man cannot save himself, and man cannot keep his

---

1. Naphtali Winter: *The High Holy Days,* p. 73. New York, NY: Leon Amiel, 1973.

2. Eugene Rosenstock-Huessy, ed.; *Judaism Despite Christianity,* p. 190. University of Alabama Press, 1969.

own vow to the Lord, the most important of vows.

Man being sinful, limited, and fallible, has thus a limited ability at keeping his own word. But, as even Balaam recognized,

> God is not a man, that he should lie; neither the son of man, that he should repent: hath he said, and shall he not do it? or hath he spoken, and shall he not make it good? (Num. 23:19)

Paul speaks of God as the one who "cannot lie" (Titus 1:2). Hence it is that God's word is alone the infallible and binding word. His covenant rests not only on His word but also His confirming oath and is hence particularly compelling in its assured promises (Heb. 6:13-20).

Thus, the significance of our Lord's declaration concerning Deuteronomy 23:23 is, *first,* all speech is placed before God, and the total life of the covenant man must be in conformity to the word of God and as a vow before Him. *Second,* it makes clear that our word, however truthful it must be in obedience to the Lord, can never be an assured and certain word. Hence, vows are to be avoided except where legal procedures require them.

There is, however, a *third* factor. As we have seen previously, our membership in Christ's covenant is an actual or an implied oath. Baptism is in fact a vow between man and God. The individual vows to be God's man, and God vows to make him one of His people, and to bless him for obedience. With infants, parents, having received the child from the Lord, vow to give the child to the Lord and to rear the child as the Lord's own (cf. I Sam. 1:27-28). Every baptized person is thus under a vow, and the vows of Deuteronomy 23:23 are thus redundant. Our whole life is under oath, and a separate oath in relation to a promise to God is thus unnecessary. A court of law, however, is not God: it does not know our hearts nor the validity of our profession of faith. The court thus places us under oath in order to bind us publicly to our word and to invoke more particularly our attention to the judgment of God and man for false swearing.

The oath thus was a covenant sign, and, with baptism, a covenant fact which conditioned all of life. It is significant that, from early years, Israel developed certain legal principles concerning the oath. One of these, which finds repeated reference in the Talmud, is that the oath must not be administered to suspected liars or to gamblers, usurers, criminals, or to any who have once perjured themselves. The oath is the privilege of the covenant man of good repute. Legal testimony was thus under oath or without oath, so that evidence could be assessed in terms of its source. This principle was carried over into Western courts but has been nullified in recent years.

In certain cases, it was possible that neither defendant nor plaintiff could be placed under oath. Since it was the plaintiff's duty to provide the proof, this placed a burden on the plaintiff, but a necessary one.

At any rate, our Lord does not abrogate Deuteronomy 23:23; His declaration in effect confirms the full validity of covenantalism. A covenant requires an oath and rests on an oath. Covenant man is thus already under oath, and hence need not swear at all, but must speak and act under the law, which is the perfect law of liberty (James 2:12; cf. 5:12).

# 123

## THE MYTH OF PIECEMEAL RELIGION

It is essential for us to see again a major problem for modern man, and a central source of error and confusion. The modern mind is horrified by such legislation as Deuteronomy 13:1-16, which calls for the death penalty for idolatry. Why, the modern man demands, should a simple act of bowing down to an idol call for death? The idol, after all, represents a superstition; the faith in question is an error. Why then death? Even more, such a person will immediately cite the witchcraft trials as an example of what such legislation can produce. Do you want this?, he demands. It can, of course, be answered that modern humanism has produced the greatest tyrannies in history, but we cannot justify one error by citing a greater one.

It is not our purpose to justify the witchcraft trials. Certainly, they were often at fault in their judicial process, and far from infallible. We should remember, however, that what we are usually told about those trials is at best partial history and often anti-Christian propaganda. A liberal historian, Jeffrey Burton Russell, after discounting as much of the trial proceedings, hearing, evidence, and documentation as possible, still found clear evidence that the witchcraft trials were dealing with an organized movement which practiced murder, human sacrifice, and cannibalism, as well as other offenses against law.[1] In effect, what some critics are saying, with De Sade, is that these offenses are preferable to Christianity.

But our concern is not with the details of history but with principles. The problem with the ignorant critics is their belief in *piecemeal religion*. The Bible knows of no such thing. A man did not simply bow down to an idol and then go about living as good a life as his covenant keeping Israelite neighbor. Idol worship, *i.e.,* Moloch worship, for example, was a part of a total world and life view. It meant the sovereignty, not of God, but of the king or state, because Moloch (or Molech, Melek, Melik, Milcolm, or Malcolm) means *king.* It meant that the earth was the king's, or state's, not the Lord's. It meant state taxing power rather than God's tithe and head tax. It meant state ownership of the children rather than God's ownership, and hence the passing of the children through

---

1. Jeffrey Burton Russell: *Witchcraft in the Middle Ages,* 67, 69f., 81, 88ff., 125, 239f., 251, 263, etc. Ithaca, NY: Cornell University Press, 1972.

the fire, and on rare occasions, their actual sacrifice, rather than circumcision and now baptism. It meant the sexual revolution rather than Biblical sexual ethics. It meant fiat law rather than Biblical law, and so on. It meant, simply, total revolution, as did the late medieval revolution, of which the witches' covens were an expression.

Modern man seems to believe in piecemeal religion; he thinks it is possible to profess Biblical faith on the Lord's Day, repeating the Apostle's creed. On Monday, he sends his children to a state school which teaches humanism. He works in terms of non-Biblical economics in a humanistic state, and he sees no contradiction. Our Lord, however, was emphatic: piecemeal religion is an impossibility:

> No man can serve two masters: for either he will hate the one, and love the other; or else he will hold to the one, and despise the other. Ye cannot serve God and mammon. (Matt. 6:24)

Our Lord here, *first* of all, is clearly dealing with religion, not two jobs. Hence the alternative is religious, God or mammon. The key phrase is, "No man can serve two masters," or, literally, "No man can be the slave of two masters." To be a slave is to be under the direction of someone, and our Lord makes clear that we are to be under the total direction of God as Lord and see ourselves as His property. Religion is a total thing; a man may try to serve two masters, or to live in terms of two differing religious principles, but it is an impossibility. Modern man holds to piecemeal religion, *i.e.,* to serving two masters, but such an attempt only disguises the fact that a departure from one faith is in process. Our culture has been for some time in process of departing from and hating God and adhering to and loving humanism. Because it is unwilling to acknowledge this fact, it indulges in viciously unfair arguments, *e.g.,* Do you want to kill a man for *nothing more* than bowing before an idol? Are you in favor of executing witches for *nothing more* than a harmless superstition? Such statements are radically dishonest. They deny the unity of life and faith. We can ask in return, Do you believe in arresting and trying someone for *nothing more* than conspiring to kill the president, or to kill you? Are you in favor of allowing them to kill you and the president before they are apprehended?

Whether in sophisticated or unsophisticated forms, witchcraft, among ancients and savages and with medieval and modern man, has consequences. Cannibalism, incest, homosexuality, and other practices have accompanied the modern revival of witchcraft. Moreover, as Gary North has pointed out, witchcraft is humanism come to flower, humanism in its logical implications.[2]

Humanism is another master, with another law, education, sexual

---

2. Gary North: *None Dare Call it Witchcraft.* New Rochelle, NY: Arlington House, 1976.

standard, another view of property and taxation, and so on, than Biblical faith holds to, and it is total revolution against, and treason to, a Christian order. Similarly, Christianity is total treason to a humanistic order, and Rome recognized this, and acted accordingly. The persecution of the Christians was, from the perspective of the legal foundations of Rome, a sound one, although, from God's perspective, its culminating offense.

*Second,* although man's sin is his attempt to be a god (Gen. 3:5), man is a creature, and, even in his sin, he remains a creature. Thus, as Lenski notes,

> The thought that underlies this word of Jesus is the fact that no man is his own master; it is ingrained in our very nature that our heart, will, and work be governed by another. The only question is who this other shall be.[3]

Man may pretend to be a god, but even in that pretense, and, more, especially in that pretense, he becomes most of all a slave, and most in bondage. To be a creature under God in Christ is man's true freedom. Every attempt at freedom from God means slavery for man, first of all to his own sin, then to death, and then to things and people because his slavery to sin makes him prone to slavery in every area. Our Lord declares, "Whosoever committeth sin is the servant (or, slave) of sin" (John 8:34).

*Third,* the choice is between God and things which are not really gods. Mammon is a Syriac word for money, wealth, or riches. As Thomas noted, "It is a fact, that whatever object we love *most,* is our monarch; it governs our thoughts, feelings, and purposes."[4] Those who rebel against God end up deifying some aspect of creation as a god. They change the truth of God into a lie, and worship and serve a creature rather than the Creator (Rom. 1:25). They then re-organize the whole of their lives in terms of that lie. The whole point of Matthew 6:1-23 is that life is a unity; hypocrisy cannot cover the fact that a man serves his master, *one* master, and, in terms of that love and service, he *hates* all other masters.

This means, *fourth,* that the service of God means the hatred of all that is anti-God, just as the service of humanism means the hatred of all that is of God. Piecemeal religion, whether it calls itself Christianity or humanism, seeks to deny the validity of the antithesis made by our Lord. It attempts to isolate and thereby neutralize acts. Thus, professing Jesus Christ is held by many to be unrelated to our views on politics,

---

3. R. C. H. Lenski: *The Interpretation of St. Matthew's Gospel,* p. 279. Columbus, OH: The Wartburg Press, 1943.
4. David Thomas: *The Gospel of St. Matthew,* p. 60. Grand Rapids, MI: Baker Book House, (1873) 1956.

education, taxation, or abortion. The humanist takes a similar stance. What both imply is that a vast realm of factuality constitutes a realm of neutrality unrelated to God and to faith. But religion is, as Tillich saw, ultimate concern, and hence it is total concern. Our principle of ultimacy governs all of reality. If our faith is in the God of Scripture, then no area of life, reality, or time is outside His government, law, and jurisdiction. There are no neutral realms. Any attempt to isolate any area from God is an attempt to unseat God and is a principle of revolution. It is premised on another faith and on another world and life view.

Modern man holds to piecemeal religion because to think otherwise is to think systematically and hence *responsibly*. It is of the nature of sin and treason to think irresponsibly and to deny consequences. Adam and Eve each denied responsibility for their sin (Gen. 3:9-13). Agur, the son of Jakeh, tells us,

> Such is the way of an adulterous woman; she eateth, and wipeth her mouth, and saith, I have done no wickedness. (Prov. 30:20)

For the adulteress, her sin is as unremarkable as a routine meal, as Derek Kidner has pointed out. She sees it as a natural and brute fact, *i.e.*, unrelated to any moral principle or concern. It is an isolated and piecemeal fact.

Piecemeal religion thus presupposes a piecemeal universe or multiverse of brute or unrelated facts. Things have no relationships; causality does not exist, and to insist, personally and legally, on causality, consequences, and responsibility is held to be illegitimate and offensive.

An old and familiar illustration says that to shout fire in a crowded theater is not a harmless but a criminal act. This illustration is an especially telling one. In using it since the early 1960s, I find that objections are readily raised, and these objections have as their premise *motivation*. "It can be only a joke," it is now commonly said. This statement is all the more interesting, because humanistic psychologists themselves tell us that all jokes have serious meanings behind them. Clearly, shouting fire as a joke has a murderous meaning and intent. It is also asked, What if no one were hurt? We can in turn ask, can a man be immune to arrest as long as his efforts to murder a man fail?

Witchcraft and other forms of idolatry may be fads, as we are sometimes told, but these are still fads with meaning. They indicate a major revolution in process, and its goals are not harmless.

The ancient world knew of no piecemeal religion. Hence, every state was intensely concerned over religious practices within its realm. The modern world has a pervasive faith in the possibility and validity of piecemeal religion; it also believes in evolution, flying saucers, and political saviors. This does not give reality or truth to any of these myths, nor does it lessen their evils.

Moreover, however much the humanists may try to get Christians to slumber and sleep away their power and freedom under the myth of piecemeal religion, the leaders of humanism know better. Thus, the Tennessee constitution until recently declared that Christian ministers and priests are ineligible to serve in the state legislature.[5] The priests of humanism are its politicians and educators: they are established by law, and neither Tennessee nor any other modern state is moving in any other direction, whatever its facade, than that of a systematic and rigorous humanism as the legal establishment. The logical outcome of this is the suppression of Christian Schools, churches, and their adherents. To believe in the possibility of piecemeal religion is suicidal.

---

5. *The United States Law Week,* vol. 45, no. 37, March 29, 1977, Section 2, 45, LW 2445.

## 124

## THE FAILURE OF PIECEMEAL RELIGION

The world of piecemeal religion is a nightmare realm in which the most unwelcome of all things is reality. Men reject the fact of consequences. They refuse to believe that certain things follow inevitably when men commit themselves to certain courses of action. They insist on believing that the road to Babylon will not take them to Babylon but to Eden.

Consider, for example, Walter Kaufmann's *Without Guilt and Justice*. Kaufmann rightly recognizes that guilt and justice, like good and evil, truth and error, and right and wrong, are theological doctrines. They presuppose the existence of the God of Scripture. Having abandoned that God, he holds that we must abandon the doctrines of guilt and justice in favor of autonomy. He finds the paradigm for autonomy in the tempter's plan as presented in Genesis 3:1-5.[1] He rejects also the ideas of a good and bad conscience.[2] On the other hand, he illogically believes that morality, integrity, and honesty are possible without God and in terms of autonomy.[3] He believes that standards of honesty have been raised in the 20th century, apparently because of philosophers and scientists like himself![4] He adds, in radical contradiction to all that he affirms, that "autonomy is not enough."[5]

The Marquis de Sade was more consistent. His premises were the same as Kaufmann's, but his conclusions were in conformity with his premises. Perhaps we should not expect too much from Kaufmann, since he is a man who, in 1942, found Hegel to be honeymoon reading![6] On the other hand, since every man is created in God's image, we have the right to require more of them than this. In any case, ideas do have consequences, and they are inescapable. Our Lord makes this clear in Matthew 7:24-27:

> Therefore whosoever heareth these sayings of mine, and doeth them, I will liken him unto a wise man, which built his house upon a rock: And the rain descended, and the floods came, and the winds

---

1. Walter Kaufmann: *Without Guilt and Justice*, p. 237. New York, NY: Peter H. Wyden, 1973.
2. *Ibid.*, p. 125ff.
3. *Ibid.*, pp. 140ff., 174ff.
4. *Ibid.*, p. 197.
5. *Ibid.*, p. 186.
6. Walter Kaufmann: *Hegel: Reinterpretation, Texts and Commentary*, p. 10. Garden City, NY: Doubleday, 1965.

blew, and beat upon that house; and it fell not: for it was founded upon a rock. And every one that heareth these sayings of mine, and doeth them not, shall be likened unto a foolish man, which built his house upon the sand:
And the rain descended, and the floods came, and the winds blew, and beat upon that house; and it fell: and great was the fall of it.

*First* of all, while a man's faith has immediate consequences, those consequences are not necessarily apparent at once. Thus, a man who builds without a foundation has at once endangered his life's structure, but that collapse will become apparent only with a storm. People who try to establish their lives and their children's lives on a character without faith, on morality without roots, have thereby destroyed their future. The fact that the damage may only become apparent years later does not nullify the causal relationship.

Men who take the first step into a false faith are at the same time moving into blindness: they refuse to see the consequences of their religious commitment. Arend J. ten Pas, in *The Lordship of Christ* (1976), has shown the results of false theology. The carnal Christian doctrine produces men who are neither Christian nor moral but who fail to see their blindness and nakedness. The state schools, with their emphasis on equality and integration, are totally humanistic in their plan of salvation. The more vigorously they apply their salvation dogma, the less willing they are to see its failure. A U.C.L.A. psychiatrist, Dr. Alfred Bloch, reported a growth in violence against teachers. His accounts of brutal violence against teachers was at once discounted by school officials, who insisted that such incidents were minor, and exaggerated.[7] Teachers reported that Dr. Bloch scarcely knew a fraction of the problem. One teacher, in a better junior high school, reported that, on one usual day, students broke a hole in a hall wall to enter a classroom, started a fire, ripped up tile to clog a toilet, and, by the hundreds, smoked marijuana in the halls. Assaults on teachers are common. Attempts to inform the vice-principal in charge of discipline are futile. She is a woman, hired because of her sex, and afraid of her job; when a teacher comes with a problem (now only serious things like assaults), she hides in her closet until the teacher leaves. Earlier, a vice-principal who wanted to discipline was forbidden to do so! Why the inability to face up to these facts? The *facts* of humanism are such that these incidents are increasingly dismissed as irrelevant, as products of racism, bigotry, sexism, and the like. A faith either equips us to deal with problems, or it disarms us. Kaufmann's faith both blinds and disarms him, and the same is true of state school officers and officials.

*Second,* it is the mark of the foolish man that he has a piecemeal

---

7. Lyn Nabers, "The Bottom Line: Teachers Alone in Fear," in the *Los Angeles Herald-Examiner,* p. 1, 2, Thursday, May 5, 1977.

religion. The fool hears the Lord's words; he may profess to believe them, and he may reject them as an unbeliever by open profession. In either case, he "doeth them not." He rejects God's statement of causality and consequence. Instead, he affirms that it is his will that determines consequences. He decrees that he will build without the Lord, beyond good and evil, and without guilt or justice, and his building shall stand. The rejection of God's causal order means an insistence that man's piecemeal order can stand because man so decrees it. Man takes bits and pieces of God's world at his own choosing, i.e., integrity and honesty, as Kaufmann does, and declares that his own autonomous will can give them meaning. The house built on sand is a structure built on an inconsequential plan, on a design whose permanence rests on man's will rather than God's universe of law and consequence. When subjected to stress, it collapses.

*Third,* the fool's premise is that he himself is god and therefore the determiner of consequence. A man lives without, or in indifference to, God because he believes in his own autonomy, self-sufficiency, and godhood. For him, the real world is the world of his imagination. The world of the imagination is a piecemeal world, and hence is devoid of true consequence. A Walter Mitty can, lacking all training, imagine himself an aviator, a ship's captain, or an industrial magnate. He can see himself as a great swordsman, lover, horseman, or anything else, without cost, because the word of dreams is not the real world. When men see themselves as autonomous, they live in a dream world; they are comparable to impotent men who in their dreams keep a harem larger than Solomon's aquiver with delight and satisfaction. For such men, the world of the Bible is a very harsh world, because the Bible declares plainly that idolatry has consequences. The man whose world is the world of imagination isolates the act of bowing down and worshipping an idol from faith, morality, and world and life view which is basic to that simple act. He isolates events from causes and consequences, because he admits the existence of no other world.

*Fourth,* the man who hears the Lord's words and obeys them is the man who lives in terms of God's reality. Consequences are real to him, because actions are not autonomous nor isolated. All thoughts, acts, and words occur in God's universe, and all have their consequences in terms of the world of God's law. Nothing exists in autonomy or isolation from God and His law world. Every moment, thought, and event is inextricably linked to God's total world and is inseparable from it. To be godly means in part recognizing that we are *creatures* of God, His creation and for His purpose and glory, and in seeing our lives in their totality as a part of that purpose. Then, instead of piecemeal religion, we have a Biblical faith.

## 125

## GOD'S PROPERTY RIGHTS

The Biblical doctrine of real property is summed up in several verses in the Psalms:

> The earth is the LORD'S, and the fulness thereof; the world, and they that dwell therein. (Ps. 24:1)

> For the LORD most high is terrible: he is a great King over all the earth. . . .
> For God is King of all the earth; sing ye praises with understanding. God reigneth over the heathen: God sitteth upon the throne of his holiness. (Ps. 47:2, 7-8)

> The heaven, even the heavens, are the LORD'S: but the earth hath he given to the children of men. (Ps. 115:16)

Very briefly, we are told, *first,* that God, who is the creator of all things, is therefore the Lord and ruler over all things. We are told repeatedly in Scripture that God regards men as the sheep of His pasture (Ps. 95:7; 100:3, etc.), His creatures, and therefore totally subject to His law and government. Neither an atom nor a moment of creation is ever outside His government and law.

*Second,* God has reserved heaven as His throne place, despite His temporary tabernacling in the most holy place of the sanctuary. The earth He has given "to the children of men" to be used only under His direction and law.

*Third,* this kingly government of God is over covenant-keepers and covenant-breakers alike. No man can ever step outside God's absolute government.

The implications of this are spelled out in the law. Sovereignty means taxing power: hence the tithe. Sovereignty means absolute jurisdiction: thus man can use the earth and his own being only subject to God's law. Sovereignty means property rights: the Bible thus affirms the absolute ownership of the earth by God, and its possession as a steward by man under God. The private possession of property is God's purpose, but it is at all times subject to God's law and taxation.

For a state to claim ownership over land means thus a direct assault on God's prerogative. State taxation of property, income, and inheritance is therefore in its essence anti-God. The claim to have the power to tax is the claim of ownership. This is a fact not commonly recognized. Many taxpayers complain that, in effect, they are merely renters from the state because of their high taxes. They do not recognize that this is in effect as well as in fact the case. Title to property is title to its use, subject to past, present, and future restrictions, claims, and appropriations by the state. The land, its water resources, and other assets are owned by the state. Hughes has observed,

> It would surprise most American landowners today, as it often does those who cannot meet their property taxes, to learn that the state owns the land outright.[1]

The origins of this state ownership are in English law, from the middle ages, when the king was "the only absolute (allodial) owner of land" under feudalism.[2] This concept was later an aspect of the open avowal of the divine right of kings, the origins of which are pagan. The early settlers began with royal charters which assumed this royal ownership, although the emphasis of Biblical law was increasingly in evidence.

Chancellor James Kent held that these feudal holds on land were gone in his day, although their legal relics survived. In his *Commentaries on American Law* (4 vols., 1826-1830), he stated:

> This idea of tenure pervades, to a considerable degree, the law of real property in this country. The title to land is essentially allodial, and every tenant in fee-simple has an absolute and perfect title, yet, in technical language, his estate is called an estate in fee-simple, and the tenure free and common socage. I presume this technical language is very generally interwoven with the municipal jurisprudence of the several states, even though not a vestige of feudal tenure may remain. In many of the states, there were never any marks of feudal tenure, and in all of them the ownership of land is essentially free and independent. By the statute of New York, of the 20th February, 1787, entitled *An Act concerning Tenures,* the legislature re-enacted the statute of 12 Car. II., c. 24, abolishing the military tenures, and turning all sorts of tenure into free and common socage. Under that statute, all estates of inheritance at common law were held by the tenure of free and common socage; but all lands held under grant of the people of the state, (and which included, of course, all the lands in the western and northern parts of the state which have been granted and settled since the revolution,) were declared to be allodial and feudal, and to be owned in free and pure *allodium.* The *New-York Revised Statutes,* which took effect on the first day of January, 1830, went the entire length of abolishing the existing theory of feudal tenures of every description, with all their incidents, and declaring all lands within the state to be allodial, and that the entire and absolute property was vested in the owners, according to the nature of their respective estates, subject only to the liability of escheat. But through the distinction, in this country, between feudal

1. Jonathan R. T. Hughes: *The Government Habit,* p. 15f. New York, NY: Basic Books, 1977.
2. *Idem.*

and allodial estates, either does not exist at all, or has become merely nominal, it will be impossible for the student to understand clearly and accurately the doctrine of real property, and the learning which illustrates it, without bestowing some attention to the history and character of feudal tenures.[3]

Free and common socage was at the beginning the only kind of land tenure which the British crown allowed in the colonies. This form of tenure permitted the owner to inherit, will, lease, rent, or sell the land or portions or assets thereof, but the land was at all times subject to whatever levies, assessments, or taxes the crown might make against the owner or the land. Failure to pay meant that the socman (or tenant) lost his land to the "donor," the crown. Because the essential religious principle had become political, socmanry (or tenant ownership of land from the crown) had become the legal fact. Instead of the doctrine, "The earth is the Lord's," the reality in politics was, "The earth is the human king's."

Kent is right that in America this concept of tenancy under the crown had disappeared or become a mere legal relic without meaning. However, the legal precedent was there, in the background, and, as statism or centralism began to develop, courts and legislatures quickly seized on that precedent. *First,* this meant the taxation of land, which more and more states adopted. The taxation of real property today, and of all forms of property, has made socmanry again a reality. We do not own our property: we rent it from the state for a very high fee. *Second,* the power of the crown set the precedent for the regulation of commerce. It was at first the states that assumed this power. In Illinois, the state in 1871 passed a law setting rates to control grain storage at public elevators and grain properties. Munn and Scott, owners of a grain elevator, refused to take out a license. The lawsuit, *Munn* v. *Illinois,* went to the U. S. Supreme Court, and in March, 1877, Chief Justice Waite delivered the majority opinion. He held that the rights of the crown, which were exercised by Parliament, had devolved upon the American states, and the medieval and earlier powers to regulate commerce, to set prices for goods sold, and to establish wages, now belonged to the states. Waite cited the existing statutes, either relics or actual regulations, as evidences of this continuing power.[4] Subsequently, of course, the powers claimed in the Munn case by the states were assumed by the U. S. Federal Government.

The extent to which this pagan doctrine has been developed, and is in process of being enhanced, has been especially in evidence of late in the case of Mel Fisher. Fisher, a treasure hunter and sea diver, located a sunken Spanish galleon, a treasure ship with gold and silver, outside the

---

3. James Kent: *Commentaries on American Law,* vol. III, p. 487f. Sixth edition. New York, NY: James Kent, 1848.
4. Hughes, *op. cit.,* p. 110.

waters of the U.S. As a hydraulic engineer, Fisher was successful in coping with the problems involved in raising the treasure, piece by piece, but another problem began. *First,* Florida claimed 75%, then 25%. The Supreme Court soon ruled that the galleon *Atocha* was not in Florida's offshore boundaries. This only set the stage for a federal claim. As Colin Leinster reported it,

> A flurry of suits and counter-suits followed. The U. S. position was that the Department of the Interior inherited George III's "sovereign prerogative" over the treasure because it lies on the continental shelf, and that the Antiquities Act of 1906—which gives ownership of artifacts to the government—also applied. The U. S. additionally claimed that it had "control" over what its citizens, like Mel Fisher, found—whether or not they found it within U. S. territory. The last argument, of course, flaunts the Hague Convention.[5]

The origin of all these legal premises is, of course, in the tempter's claims in Genesis 3:1-5, that God is not truly God, but that man is a god. It is a claim to sovereignty, and sovereignty is a theological concept. The exclusion of the word *sovereignty* from the U. S. Constitution has behind it a religious premise, as does the express powers doctrine, which was intended to bar the type of claim made by an ostensibly sovereign power. True, almost at once, implied powers were claimed, but the fact of their exclusion from the Constitution is still true, and the 10th Amendment was designed to emphasize the limitations of powers.

The problem is that today the sovereignty of God is an abstract concept even to those in the Reformed tradition who most profess it: it does not occur to these people that the sovereignty of God has implications with respect to all things, including property, taxation, and the state. Taxation is a prerogative of sovereignty. Modern man has a sovereign, and it is the state. While modern man may complain about the applications of that sovereignty, e.g., a tax rate, or a condemnation proceedings, he does not very often complain about or challenge the principle of state sovereignty. The few who do are anarchists, who hold to the sovereignty of man, so that it becomes with them a family disagreement with fellow humanists. To regard the sovereignty of God as an abstract concept means regarding God as an abstraction rather than a reality. If we limit God's sovereignty to heaven and the spiritual realm, we are not Christians but Manichaeans. It is a denial of Scripture, and of God's emphatic declaration:

> I am the LORD: that is my name: and my glory will I not give to another, neither my praise to graven images. (Isa. 42:8)

For mine own sake, even for mine own sake, will I do it: for how

---

5. Colin Leinster, "The Pirating of Mel Fisher's Gold," in *Free Enterprise,* vol. 6, no. 3, June, 1976, p. 33.

should my name be polluted? and I will not give my glory unto another. (Isa. 48:11)

The prayer of Asaph and of all saints is that all who in any way, by word or deed, deny God's sovereignty be confounded:

> Make their nobles like Oreb, and like Zeeb; yea, all their princes as Zebah, and as Zalmunna:
> Who said, Let us take to ourselves the houses of God in possession.
> O my God, make them like a wheel; as the stubble before the wind.
> As the fire burneth a wood, and as the flame setteth the mountains on fire;
> So persecute them with thy tempest, and make them afraid with thy storm.
> Fill their faces with shame; that they may seek thy name, O LORD.
> Let them be confounded and troubled for ever; yea, let them be put to shame and perish:
> That men may know that thou, whose name alone is Jehovah, art the most high over all the earth. (Ps. 83:11-18)

Oreb and Zebah were Midianite kings who raided Israel in Gideon's day. Gideon captured and killed Zebah and Zalmunna and destroyed Oreb's power (Judges 8:1-21). All who attempt to attack God's people and property rights are compared to Oreb, Zebah, and Zalmunna. Their transgressions are against God the Lord: they are attempts to possess God's property. All the nations and all the earth are the Lord's: He is the Lord their Maker, and they are as nothing "and less than nothing" in His sight (Isa. 40:12-17). All God's judgments throughout history, culminating in the Last Judgment, are expressions of His sovereignty, His Kingship, and His property rights.

The beginning of a Biblical doctrine of property is to see God's absolute property rights over us, and over our income, vocation, family, and total life. *What belongs to God cannot be surrendered to another.* Our sin begins with a claim that we are our own property, and it ends with our enslavement by a tyrant state.

The first step to freedom is to acknowledge that God is the Lord, and that beside Him there is none else (Isa. 45:22). It means confessing and declaring,

> O LORD our God, other lords beside thee have had dominion over us; but by thee only will we make mention of thy name. (Isa. 26:13)

It is only the name and sovereignty of God that we will celebrate, obey, and acknowledge as our absolute Lord. Only then can we begin to recapture our freedom from humanistic tyrants and to restore God's property rights and our own freedom under God. There is no other way.

## 126

## THE GOVERNMENT OF PROPERTY

Unregenerate man on the whole tries to evade epistemological self-consciousness. He refuses to stand clearly in terms of his unbelief *and* to follow the implications thereof logically. As a result, he asks for atheism *plus* God's world and order. The result in history is a variety of mixed systems. Regenerate man too is often unwilling to stand clearly in terms of the faith, and he is thus also congenial to mixed systems.

To illustrate, the Soviet Union believes in a completely planned economy; this is logical for all Marxists. However, a completely planned economy spells disaster, and, as a result, the illegal black market is allowed to exist under Soviet supervision. The pricing of goods on the black market makes it possible for the planners to determine what foods are in abundant or short supply and to establish their plans and policies. The black market makes socialism null and void and reveals its radical incapacity to function and even to plan apart from the freedom of the black market. Are the Soviet planners thereby convinced that their Marxist theory is false? No. Not believing in God's absolutes, nothing is necessarily so in their world of thought *except* their theories!

Similarly, in the relatively free United States, it is abundantly clear from 20th century history alone that freedom is productive, and controls create economic shortages and chaos. This has only led to more controls, however, because of the blind faith that a *mixed* economic system is the most successful and productive! The more the mixed system fails, the more emphatically the demand for a more radical mixture increases. The fact that the demand calls for an impossibility and a contradiction is not commonly recognized.

The same is true in the history of property. On the whole, in the history of Christendom, a mixed system has usually prevailed. From pagan antiquity, we have inherited the belief in the deity of rulers or the social order. Divinity was in paganism associated either with (1) the ruler, or (2) the office rather than the person who ruled, or (3) the state, tribe, clan, or social order. Thus, the basic confession demanded of Christians by Rome was that "Caesar is Lord," i.e., that Caesar is the god and owner of all things within his realm. The word *lord,* or in Greek *kyrios,* denotes power and authority. "It was used basically to denote the owner of property and slaves, one who has the right to do as he wishes with his property."[1] The lordship of Christ was an impossible concept for Roman political theology to tolerate. It meant that Caesar was the slave and property of Jesus Christ. Rome demanded that the church confess instead to the lordship of Caesar over Christ. It was especially offensive to Rome that a man legally executed for treason by Rome should be held to be lord over Rome. All who held so dangerous and "insane" a faith were thus liable to execution, because the welfare of Rome required the extirpation of this faith which challenged its every foundation.

On the other hand, the church had in its Bible the clear and repeated declaration of the Lordship of Jesus Christ, who is "the blessed and only Potentate, the King of kings, and Lord of lords" (I Tim. 6:15). The church moved in the confidence of God's challenge to the nations in Psalm 2:7-12:

> I will declare the decree: the LORD hath said unto me, Thou art my Son: this day have I begotten thee.
> Ask of me, and I shall give thee the heathen for thine inheritance, and the uttermost parts of the earth for thy possession.
> Thou shalt break them with a rod of iron; thou shalt dash them in pieces like a potter's vessel.
> Be wise now therefore, O ye kings: be instructed, ye judges of the earth.
> Serve the LORD with fear, and rejoice with trembling.
> Kiss the Son, lest he be angry, and ye perish from the way, when his wrath is kindled but a little. Blessed are all they that put their trust in him.

These and many many like verses were in common use in the early church. Anyone who assumes that Rome was not aware of what the Bible taught, and how the Christians used it, is not thinking historically. Consider, for that matter, how Rome would react to the common and widespread Christian use of Psalm 110: it was in their eyes part of a pattern of subversive activity of a dangerously insane nature: it speaks of a "willing" people obeying their Lord Christ: it speaks of Christ's rule over His enemies, and of filling the places with their dead bodies. Rome understood clearly that this new faith was a total religion concerned with the conquest of every area of life and thought to Jesus Christ. In their eyes, whether this Jesus were dead or alive made no great difference: His religion was an extremely dangerous matter.

Because Christianity is so radical in its implications, the collapse of its enemy, Rome, and all its enemies, is similarly radical. Hence the collapse of Rome. But even then the mixed system had its appeal and began to operate. The medieval history of land gives us a conflicting story: feudalism was at this point pagan. It held to a feudal lordship over land

---

1. I. Howard Marshall: *The Origins of New Testament Christology*, p. 97. Downers Grove, IL: InterVarsity Press, 1976.

and to a degree over men. Hence the feudal lord, ultimately the king, had an ownership over men, over their lives (military service at his will), their land as absolute owner, their income and the power to tax it, their inheritance, and the power to govern or appropriate it, their families and the power to order or prohibit marriages, and so on.

In the providence of God, these and all other aberrations have been used. Thus, the feudal tenure of land in American colonies prevented its possession by a landed aristocracy and ensured the break-up of holdings.[2]

In America, the colonists sought to establish God's law, insofar as permissible. Royal law was in sharp contradiction to Biblical law, having pagan roots and a divine right theory basic to it. As a result, a mixed system prevailed. Land tenure was in terms of royal law, and criminal law to a considerable degree in terms of Biblical law. This statement must be seriously qualified to indicate that in both areas a mixed system prevailed. Thus, in New England, Pennsylvania, and elsewhere the Biblical requirement of the double portion to the eldest (deserving) sons was made a matter of law. By 1830, both the Biblical and pagan aspects of property law had been extensively eliminated, and *the people* became lords over their own lands. The relics of feudal legal terminology later became the foundation for the revival of state ownership of land and people as sovereign lord.

Thus, man's tenure on his land today is subject at every point to his sovereign, the state. This is necessary and logical; since modern man looks to the state for both law and salvation, he must in practice acknowledge the state as his lord. This means the power to tax, regulate, and confiscate. Man's person, income, inheritance, and property are possessions of the state and are held by grace and the obedience of law by the citizenry. The state can dispossess any man subject to laws of its own making.

The question for man is thus a choice of lords, because God also claims sovereign rights over man and his possessions. The difference is that God has by covenant bound Himself to be faithful to man and to protect man, subject to man's faithfulness to God's law, the law of the covenant. The state too often makes a covenant, or a charter, constitution, or what you will. This state covenant is neither absolute nor infallible and is subject to changing interpretations by the state courts, as well as revision and amendment.

God's law, however, is fixed and established. Man's tenure on the earth, on God's land, is an enduring one when man is faithful to the covenant. As David pointed out,

---

2. J. R. T. Hughes: *Social Control in the Colonial Economy,* p. 24. Charlottesville, VA: University Press of Virginia, 1976.

For evildoers shall be cut off: but those that wait upon the LORD,
they shall inherit the earth.
For yet a little while, and the wicked shall not be: yea, thou shalt
diligently consider his place, and it shall not be.
But the meek shall inherit the earth; and shall delight themselves in
the abundance of peace. (Ps. 37:9-11)

At this point, many will agree, *provided* that, in some deistic fashion,
God has left the practical jurisdiction of the earth in the hands of man or
the state. In the mixed system of Deism, God as the first cause provided
all things and then retired, leaving mankind in full control. In terms of
the deistic tradition, man and man's law governs all things; God's role is
that of the original cause. The immediate cause and law is from man.
Most evangelical and reformed Christianity is in essence deistic, as is
Roman Catholicism, in this respect. In William Paley, we have a classical
formulation of this, as witness his comments on property:

The real foundation of our right is THE LAW OF THE LAND.

It is the intention of God, that the produce of the earth be applied to
the use of man; this intention cannot be fulfilled without establishing
property; it is consistent therefore with his will, that property be
established. The land cannot be divided into separate property without leaving it to the law of the country to regulate that division; it is
consistent therefore with the same will, that the law should regulate
that division; and, consequently, "consistent with the will of God,"
or "right," that I should possess that share which these regulations
assign me.

By whatever circuitous train of reasoning you attempt to serve this
right, it must terminate at last in the will of God; and the straightest,
therefore, and shortest way of coming at this will, is the best.[3]

Paley goes on to say, and rightly so, that a man's right to his estate does
not depend on the manner or justice of the original acquisition some centuries earlier. Because English property was seized from the earlier
Britons by Saxons, and then by Normans, with many acts of fraud and
violence, does not negate a present title. His reason is that "the right of
property depends upon the law of the land."[4] In a sense, Paley's position
is sound: we cannot undo the past. The "original" inhabitants of Britain
are long since gone or absorbed, and they themselves may not have been
the first. The reality of the present is one of legal and morally valid
possession by purchase or inheritance. But is state law the determiner?
State law can be communistic; is its law then valid? Paley's God is not as
important as the state, and the supposed laws of nature. To illustrate,
Paley wrote, concerning incest,

---

3. William Paley: *The Principles of Moral and Political Philosophy,* p. 89f. Reprint of
11th American edition. Houston, TX: St. Thomas Press, 1977.
4. *Ibid.,* p. 90.

In order to preserve chastity in families, and between persons of different sexes, brought up and living together in a state of unreserved intimacy, it is necessary by every method possible to inculcate an abhorrence of incestuous conjunctions; which abhorrence can only be upheld by the absolute reprobation of *all* commerce of the sexes between near relations. Upon this principle, the *marriage,* as well as other cohabitations of brothers and sisters, of lineal kindred, and of all who usually live in the same family, may be said to be forbidden by the law of nature.[5]

Paley's reasoning here was humanistic: not the holiness and righteousness of God but the preservation of family chastity is his basic principle. True, he cites in passing "The Levitical law," but he also cites other historical legislation on both sides of the subject. His essential justification for the prohibition of incest is not God's law but the human consequences. In the 1970s, those who defended homosexuality and incest argued, like Paley, in terms of human consequences; they liked the results, whereas Paley did not. Who judges between them, if God's law is not absolute and binding on all? The whole point of Biblical law is that man and the state are alike under and bound by the law of God. Property laws and all laws are thus to be derived from God's law, and both man and the state have a duty to enforce them. Every man must enforce the law in his own life, in his family, vocation, and general jurisdiction. Church, state, school, and other institutions similarly must apply and enforce God's law within their jurisdictions.

Hughes is right: "Social control over property rights in land is fundamental to the coherence of any community."[6] The anarchistic idea is a myth; man can never function as a universe. Collective man, *i.e.,* the state, can arrogate such controls to itself, but the result is inescapably tyranny. In the historical process, state claims only increase into absolutism unless altered by a theocratic faith. But the state cannot be under God's law if man is not governed by it.

Milton Friedman has rightly observed,

Government is necessary to preserve our freedom, it is an instrument through which we can exercise our freedom; yet by concentrating power in political hands, it is also a threat to freedom.[7]

It is not enough, however, to say that "the scope of government must be limited," and "government power must be dispersed."[8] Much more is needed. If this sufficed, then passing legislative cures should eliminate all our problems. The real problem is man, his sin, his desire to be his own

---

5. *Ibid.,* p. 196.
6. Hughes, *Social Control in the Colonial Economy,* p. 23.
7. Milton Friedman: *Capitalism and Freedom,* p. 2. Chicago, IL: The University of Chicago Press, (1962) 1963.
8. *Ibid.,* p. 2f.

god and law (Gen. 3:5). There is no remedy for this other than God's regenerating power and the obedience of man to the law of God.

The law of God is not remote: it is omnipresent and total. All of history is governed by it, men, nations, natural processes, time, events, and the totality of all creation. All things move in terms of God's ordained purpose and to His appointed end. Psalm 37:9-11 makes clear, *first,* that "evildoers shall be cut off." More, "the wicked shall not be." God moves to eliminate them from His property. Clearly, property is either used in terms of God's law, or men and nations are under God's curse, as Deuteronomy 28 makes very clear. Although

> The wicked plotteth against the just, and gnasheth upon him with his teeth.
> The LORD shall laugh at him: for he seeth that his day is coming. (Ps. 37:12-13)

This is the holy confidence the faithful must manifest. *Second,* "the meek shall inherit the earth; and shall delight themselves in the abundance of peace." The Greek word *praus,* "meek," in the New Testament, is in origin the taming of wild animals, or breaking a horse to harness and usefulness. It means here that the blessed meek, those who are made useful to God by being harnessed to his law in faith, shall inherit the earth.

*Third,* as Deuteronomy 28, and all the law and the prophets makes clear, God's possession of the earth means that God's laws of tenure and tenancy prevail. Possession and inheritance requires that we believe and obey God. We must keep His sabbaths, pay His tithes, enforce His laws, and in all things acknowledge that *He is the Lord.* If we fail to do these things, we are subject to His *judgments.* If the judgments of the Almighty do not arouse us from our abuse of His property, ourselves and the earth, *dispossession* follows.

The government of all God's property, ourselves and the earth, must be by God's law. "Shall the thing formed say to him that formed it, Why hast thou made me thus?" (Rom. 9:20), or, worse, 'let my law govern God, myself and the earth.' The issue in property is that, not man, but God is the Lord.

127

## FANTASY AS LAW

The age of humanism has been marked by a pronounced *will to fiction,* a desire to live in a dream world. To a degree unequalled in all history, modern man immerses himself in fantasy and fiction; in novels, films, television, and daily fantasies, he lives in a realm of fantasy. But this is not all. Politics is converted into efforts to try to enact dreams into reality by legislative fiat. In the realm of economics, the same is also true, as in education and other areas.

Of late, a rash of books and articles have stressed the supposed value and importance of fantasy in sex. It would appear from these writings that the only possible way modern man can realize himself sexually is to indulge in wild fantasies. The more bizarre and lawless the fantasy, the greater the stimulation and the greater the sexual experience. The essence of the fantasy is sin, lawlessness, and reality must match the fantasy. Thus, basic to the sexual revolution, if the magazines which are its voice are to be believed, are two factors. *First,* sex must be "free," which really means that it must be lawless, sinful. It means freedom from morality for the purpose of sinning. *Second,* even in the exercise of that freedom to sin, the fact of lawless sex is not enough: there must be added to it the ingredient of fantasy in order to make the experience "valid."

Is this an over-statement? Two sociologists, writing in the *American Journal of Psychiatry,* reported a singular lack of interest in marital sex by young married couples. The situation was serious enough for *Oui* to ask, "Is there sex after marriage?" and to answer, "Sometimes." A third of the couples had stopped all sexual activity for periods averaging eight months. Of the non-abstaining couples, ages 18 to 24, the average was only three times a week.[1] The letters printed in such periodicals as *Penthouse* are strong on fantasy and probably low in reality. *Oui's* "Sex Tape Letters" are revelatory of this will to fantasy. One Milwaukee secretary wrote, "I spend most of my day typing for an office of lawyers, and the only thing that saves me from mindless boredom is my sexual fantasies."[2]

Now to examine fantasy in a radically different realm, let us consider briefly the implications of James Nathan Miller's article on America's

---

1. "Abstinence Makes Sociologists Ponder," in *Oui,* vol. 6, no. 6, June, 1977, p. 20.
2. "Sex Tape Letter," in *ibid.,* p. 28.

federal dams. The collapse of the Teton Dam in Idaho, June 5, 1976, took 14 lives and damaged or destroyed property to a value of $400 million. The dam was built on a faulty site, in an earthquake region, without strain gauges, with a too-rapid fill, and with other instances of neglect, or faulty construction. Morever, since 1950, it is admitted that 37 other large dams have been built without various necessary strain gauges. Moreover, serious questions have been raised about many other federal dams. Why? The federal agency responsible "felt that nothing could happen inside those dams that would require instruments to detect."[3] That trained engineers and geologists would be guilty of such careless construction indicates more than corruption; they live in a dream world without consequences. Hegel expressed it clearly: "the rational is the real." What modern man, in his fantasies, decides is reasonable for his purposes becomes for him reality.

To illustrate from still another area, it has become increasingly apparent that much of contemporary scientific experimentation is fraudulent. Dr Richard W. Roberts, director of the National Bureau of Standards, has estimated that *at least* "half of the results in all published scientific papers are unusable, because there is no evidence that the data used were reliable." Dr. Leroy Wolins, an Iowa State University psychologist, found even more serious deficiencies:

> Dr. Wolins authorized one of his students to write to 37 authors of recent scientific reports in psychology journals and to ask for the raw data upon which the reports' authors had based their conclusion.
>
> *Of the 32 scientists who replied to the request, 21 said that their data either had been lost or accidentally destroyed.*
>
> But nine researchers did send copies of their data. Dr. Wolins, an expert in statistics, analyzed seven of the nine submissions. And he found that three of the seven contained errors invalidating what had been published as "fact."[4]

Moreover, "the most common consequence of a discovered fraud was—nothing. In many cases, the person perpetrating the fraud was actually promoted." In a famous case, Sir Cyril Burt apparently fabricated theories of inherited intelligence differences which affected the educational and legal systems of England for the past 30 years, and influenced the world course of psychology.[5]

These and other examples of like conduct in other areas clearly involve fraud, but basic to that fraud is fantasy. When men forsake God, fantasy replaces reality. In Genesis 6:5, we are told

---

3. James Nathan Miller, "The Awful Truth About Our Federal Dams," in *Readers Digest,* June, 1977, pp. 92-96.

4. "An Unscientific Phenomenon: Fraud Grows in Laboratories," in *Science Digest,* vol. 81, no. 6, June, 1977, p. 38.

5. *Ibid.,* p. 39.

And God saw that the wickedness of man was great in the earth, and that every imagination of the thoughts of his heart was only evil continually.

*Imagination* here includes rational thought which is apostate and hence guilty of fantasy because it begins with man rather than God, and also all frauds by man, whereby man acts on the belief that sin can succeed and that God can be mocked. It included also the dangerous realm of fantasizing and reshaping the world after our imagination, which is what all sin attempts to do.

The denial of God is the denial of reality, which is His creation, and is the affirmation of fantasy. With the denial of God, fantasy politics, economics, education, religion, and all things else become preferred to God's reality. Consider the implications of fantasy sex. To judge by the sexual revolution magazines, men and women can only have sexual relations, in or out of marriage, by resorting to fantasy. Sexual stimulation is thus essentially from the fantasy rather than the living partner. This means that an imagined person is better than the real person, that *the creation of our minds is more to our liking than God's creation.* In brief, it means that men arrogate to themselves the role of creator, because God's world cannot please them in and of itself. It follows thus that sex, religion, politics, economics, science (as witness evolution), and all things else must be turned into areas where man's fiat governs, and man's fantasy is declared to be reality. "The rational is the real" for all such men.

Law too becomes fiat law, fantasy law, because it is basic to sin to play god and to fantasize about a new world created by the mind of man. It is no longer necessary to go to an amusement park or to Disneyland to enter into a world of fantasy: this can be done far more systematically and rigorously in most courts of law.

The love of fantasy is important in understanding the war against property. Property means responsibility; it means accountability, work, and stewardship. Men who want a fiat world refuse to accept the world of property, because it is a world of consequences and work, of time, of yesterday, today, and tomorrow, and duties in terms of time. The love of fantasy involves a desire for detachment from such a gross reality as property. Hence, the fantasizers declare in various ways that property must be destroyed.

But the only real world is God's world, and the only possible life is not that created by fantasy but that which God ordains. *Hence, the love of fantasy is the love of death, because it means a rejection of life and the world as God orders it.* As Wisdom declares, "But he that sinneth against me wrongeth his own soul: all they that hate me love death" (Prov. 8:36).

Meanwhile, in the world of Hegel, in the mind of modern man, the source of law is fantasy, and hence the crisis of the modern age. The Christian cannot be indifferent to this. As St. Paul tells us, in II Corinthians 10:4-6,

> (For the weapons of our warfare are not carnal, but mighty through God to the pulling down of strong holds;)
> Casting down imaginations, and every high thing that exalteth itself against the knowledge of God, and bringing into captivity every thought to the obedience of Christ;
> And having in a readiness to revenge all disobedience, when your obedience is fulfilled.

Paul says, *first,* that our weapons, our instruments in defending and propagating our faith, are not human weapons. Our reliance is not on human resources but on the power of the Almighty and sovereign God. *Second,* our weapons in the Lord are powerful and effectual. They can tear down fortresses of the mind and destroy the world of fantasy. All who set their minds against the truth of God are destroyed by God's power. *Third,* every thought or *mind* is brought into captivity to Christ. Both human reason and the products of human reason are to be captured by the faithful for Christ. *Fourth,* God's truth and justice must be maintained and enforced over the world of fantasy, to shatter and to subjugate it. Thus, all disobedience, all vain imaginations, will be avenged by God, and all obedience blessed.

The goal of fantasy is *to make fantasy law. Fantasy as law* is what modern man is attempting to realize. As a result, when humanists talk about the rule of law, they are to a great degree talking about the rule of fantasy.

Christians cannot be indifferent to this. Either they stand in terms of Biblical law, or they shall become the subjects of fantasy law. To stand in terms of Christian faith *requires* the "casting down" of imaginations, of every stronghold of modern humanistic man's world of fantasy.

# 128

## COERCION

One of the common characteristics of churchmen in the 20th century is their professed horror for coercion. The roots of this perspective are tangled ones. As a student, I was amazed to hear professors and churchmen view with horror the medieval inquisition and at the same time praise the policies of Stalin, and justify them. Their condemnation of coercion was obviously a tainted and hypocritical one.

In recent years, one facet of this professed horror for coercion is the renewed interest in and approval of the Anabaptist movement. The 16th century world had three major religious groupings: Roman Catholic churches, Reformation churches (Lutheran, Calvinist, and Anglican), and Anabaptist. Much of the interest in Anabaptism is governed by its renunciation of coercion, or, at least, its supposed renunciation. There was a time when Anabaptism meant to most people revolution, polygamy, and tyranny. However, if we eliminate such groups as the Muntzerites, we do have, in Anabaptism, groups stressing separation and even pacifism.

One of the problems of the day was that, earlier, church reform from within had been strangled by the Vatican. Previously, reforming orders had regularly arisen to cleanse and renew Christendom, but the consolidation of power and control in the Vatican closed this door to reform. Two of the major hopes thereafter for the reform of the church were, *first,* a general council of the church, and, *second,* Christian princes. The conciliar movement had its high point in the Council of Constance, 1414-1418. Its work was notable and important. It did unify the church, but its ability to reform was limited. An occasional council or synod cannot cope with the power of an on-going central administration. Basic to this conciliar hope was the faith that the church was the answer to Europe's inner decay.[1] After Constance, men began to look to the princes to reform the church and Europe. The result was the Reformation and the Counter-Reformation, both the work of civil rulers, or princes. It was, we must remember, the emperor who was responsible for the calling of the Council of Trent. George Huntston Williams has called

---

1. See Louise Roper Loomis, translator, John Hine Mundy and Kennerly M. Woody, eds.: *The Council of Constance,* New York, NY: Columbia University Press, 1961.

the Protestant aspect "the *magisterial* Reformation."[2] As Kingdon summarizes it, "Basic to the Magisterial Reformation is the conviction that the instrument of reform should be the civic power, whether the 'godly prince' as in Luther's Germany or the city council as in Calvin's Geneva."[3] It should be noted that this did not necessarily mean, and with the Calvinists emphatically did not mean, the continuing power of the magistrate in the church once the reform was instituted.

At the same time, a growing sentiment in Europe saw no hope in church reform, and, in many cases, wanted no part of it. The institution of the future, and the means of unifying society, was not the church for these men but the secular and humanistic state. It took some generations for this position to become open and vocal, but, in spite of this, it is clear that very early the state was seen as the answer to man's problems. We are now living in the last days of that hope. Like the earlier faith, it is collapsing, and far more dramatically.

It is important for us to understand the Anabaptist hope as it developed after the disasters of revolutionary regimes. *First,* the Anabaptist writings strongly stress "spiritual" religion. There are echoes of Joachin of Flora's Third Age of the Spirit in such an emphasis.[4] Moreover, the Anabaptists tended to a Manichaean division of material things as evil and the spiritual as good. The Bible is clear that *all* things are created by God and created *good;* all things in their fallen estate are evil, not by nature, but as a consequence of a fall on man's part.

*Second,* the Anabaptist doctrine of separation was seriously in error. In Scripture, separation is from sin and from close associations with sinful men, as in marriage (Num. 16:26; Ezra 10:11; Prov. 9:6; Isa. 52:11; II Cor. 6:17; 7:1; Rev. 18:4, etc.). Anabaptist separation is from the state, from science, from the vocations and professions which minister to people at large (i.e., medicine, dentistry, etc.) and so on. It is a withdrawal which surrenders the major part of the world to the devil. According to Melchior Hofmann, in "The Ordinance of God" (1530), the true Christian is called to separate himself into "heavenly bands."

> These accordingly, go out now from the world and from the kingdom of Satan and from all which is still of the old Adam and thereupon enter into Christ Jesus in order to walk in the eternal living word of God, yea, and to do the whole will of God and of the Lord Jesus Christ.[5]

2. George Huntston Williams, and Angel M. Mergal, eds.: *Spiritual and Anabaptist Writers,* p. 21. The Library of Christian Classics, vol. XXV. Philadelphia, PA: The Westminster Press, 1957.

3. David Kingdon, "Church Discipline Among the Anabaptists," in Herbert Carson, etc.: *The Way Ahead, Papers Read at the Carey Conference,* p. 80. Sussex, England: Carey Publications, 1975.

4. See Williams, *op. cit.,* p. 189n.

5. *Ibid.,* p. 197.

Of course, these "heavenly bands" cannot survive, for example, in the Soviet Union; only in a Christian realm are they free to exist. In any case, the major part of life is closed off to the believer: separation is thus less from sin and sinners and more and more from anything other than the holy community. In the United States, Christian neighbors of the Amish and Mennonites not only frequently find themselves repulsed in attempts to be helpful and neighborly but often cheated. A Christian neighbor may know his Bible better, and read it and pray more conscientiously, but he is repulsed by one and all as an "outsider." The separation, being based on a false principle, readily leads to Phariseeism.

*Third,* the doctrinal basis of Anabaptist faith is thin, strong on free will, weak on original sin, and given more to emphasizing the unique community rather than the faith. Since the Quakers are so highly regarded by modern man, it is well to examine their thinking in its most "orthodox" form, Robert Barclay's *A Catechism and Confession of Faith, Approved of and Agreed to by the General Assembly of the Patriarchs, Prophets, and Apostles, Christ Himself Chief Speaker in and Among Them* (1673).

The *Catechism and Confession* speaks of the universal love and grace of God to all, and the universal inner light; it is perfectionist and antinomian. Quaking or trembling is held to be necessary to salvation, and there is no article on original sin. Moreover, pacifism is emphatically affirmed, even with respect to defensive warfare.[6] Two aspects and premises of the Westminster Confession are strongly attacked:

First, *That God has committed his will now wholly to writing.* Secondly, *That the former ways of God's revealing his will, as by immediate revelation, are now ceased.*[7]

Not surprisingly, the Anabaptists are widely favored by modernists, who use these men as means of attacking the Reformation and all forms of orthodoxy.

*Fourth,* the Anabaptists were on the whole antinomian. They denied the validity of Biblical law and held that the Gospel era had ended the legitimacy of warfare and the taking of human life. Conrad Grebel, for example, wrote against such activities:

True Christians use neither worldly sword nor engage in war, since among them taking human life has ceased entirely, for we are no longer under the Old Covenant.... The Gospel and those who accept it are not to be protected with the sword, neither should they thus protect themselves.[8]

6. Robert Barclay: *A Catechism and Confession of Faith,* p. 63f. Philadelphia: Friends' Book Store, n.d.
7. *Ibid.,* p. 97.
8. Kingdon, in Carson, etc. *op. cit.,* p. 86.

However, no man can live without law. If God's law is denied, man's law takes over. The coercive power of Anabaptist church law, then and now, is very great. Kingdon cites examples of this, *i.e.,* use of the ban and of shunning:

> There are even instances where the elders, or those commissioned by them, entered the house of an adulterous husband by night and forcibly removed his protesting wife and screaming children in enforcement of the ban.[9]

The punishment is in some groups economic as well. The Anabaptists took pride from the beginning in their supposedly voluntary basis. This was in part their opposition to infant baptism: faith was entirely a voluntary act of man's free will. However, whether in ostensible Christians or open humanists, voluntarism is commonly the foundation of the greatest coercion, because it separates man from the absolute law of God and His sovereign grace and concentrates electing power in man's hands. A man excommunicated from Anabaptist groups was, and in some cases still is, seen as a reprobate man. The only redeemed world is within the Anabaptist church: outside of it there is no salvation. No other church has had a more coercive power over its members than the Anabaptist churches. Coercion is denied to the state but not the church, and the church is now the world and the state for the Anabaptist. In the 1930s, a weeping excommunicated Mennonite told a neighbor that it would have been more merciful if they had killed him: he had been stripped and cast out. Anabaptist hypocrisy here is comparable to those Buddhists, who, being too holy to shed blood, strangle men instead.

For this reason, their pacifism is not an honest one, and, despite their claims to it, it must be denied them. True, very early pacifism was emphasized: Conrad Grebel wrote,

> Moreover, the gospel and its adherents are not to be protected by the sword, nor are they thus to protect themselves, which, as we learn from our brother, is thy opinion and practice. True Christian believers are sheep among wolves, sheep for the slaughter; they must be baptized in anguish and affliction, tribulation, persecution, suffering, and death; they must be tried with fire, and must reach the fatherland of eternal rest, not by killing their bodily, but by mortifying their spiritual, enemies. Neither do they use worldly sword or war, since all killing has ceased with them—unless, indeed, we would still be of the old law. And even there (in the Old Testament), so far as we recall, war was a misfortune after they had once conquered the Promised Land. No more of this.[10]

The Anabaptists may avoid formal weapons of war, but this is not enough to qualify a man as a pacifist when he applies coercion to keep

---

9. *Ibid.,* p. 89.
10. Conrad Grebel, "Letters to Thomas Muntzer," in Williams *op.cit.,* p. 80.

his fellow churchmen in line, and is apt at defrauding his non-Anabaptist neighbors. Anabaptism emphatically believes in coercion of a selective sort but seeks credit as a pacifist movement.

Moreover, coercion is *not* avoided even by the most rigorous pacifist. If I become a pacifist, I cannot thereby avoid civil or ecclesiastical coercion. Rather, pacifism *condones* coercion by its withdrawal. Coercion in some form is inescapable. If we deny the God-appointed forms of coercion, we will favor ungodly forms. If we resist a thief, a murderer, or an invader, we do not thereby *advocate* coercion as such; rather, we *deny* ungodly coercion its legitimacy. We deny evil its claim to sovereignty.

To deny coercion and to reject capital punishment is to deny and reject God, and to be under His judgment. In Genesis 9:5-6, we are told,

> And surely your blood of your lives will I require; at the hand of every beast will I require it, and at the hand of man; at the hand of every man's brother will I require the life of man.
> Whoso sheddeth man's blood, by man shall his blood be shed: for in the image of God made he man.

H. C. Leupold renders *I will require it* as *I shall demand an account.*

Clearly, *first* of all, the foundation of this law is that man is created in the image of God, and to respect that image is to respect the Lord. Because man is a creature, moreover, *the only law* which can legitimately govern his being is God's law. Church law, state law, or any other law must be grounded unswervingly on God's law.

*Second,* the enforcement of God's law means civil government, which God's law provides for and ordains. To the civil order is given the power to enforce justice and to take human life where God's law requires it, and nowhere else. Any other execution by the state is murder.

*Third,* God declares that He makes a strict accounting of all things, no less murder. If we kill, we must account for it and be killed by God's requirement. If we are silent, cowardly, or pacifistic in the presence of murder, we also shall be held accountable (Ps. 50:18-20). There can be no pacifism with respect to God's law. "At the hand of every man's brother will I require the life of man."

*Fourth,* if animals are guilty of murder, and must be executed when they kill a man, how much more clearly is this true of guilty men? God's law thus places a protective hedge about the life (and family, property, and reputation) of man. When man diminishes that hedge, he is held accountable by God.

The law thus gives us, and the Great Commission underscores it, a world responsibility. We must preach the Gospel to every creature, and we must bring every area and sphere of life under the law of God. The Anabaptists have withdrawn from every aspect of that calling, by and large. Can this be godly? They have substituted an ungodly coercion for godly coercion. Anabaptism cannot be justified by reference to Luther and his tracts against them. It must be justified in terms of the word of God, and here it falls far behind both Protestants and Catholics.

Why is the subject of the validity of Anabaptism important today? The reason is that both Protestant and Catholic pietism has moved strongly into a neo-Anabaptist theology. In liberal and conservative circles alike, the Anabaptists are widely held up as an example of spiritual and brotherly religion. But Anabaptist brotherhood is really ecclesiastical coercion: it masks greed and fraud with its coercive structure. An Anabaptist pastor, who left his tightly disciplined church for another denomination of vaguely Reformed lineage, told me that the beginning of his doubts about his church came when he realized that his supposedly holy people were, in church after church, guilty of more fornication than were neighboring churches, and that pregnant brides, a rarity in neighboring churches, were common in his. Whenever men have sought to escape from the world and from God's law, their little retreat begins to resemble hell rather than heaven.

Man is God's property. He cannot escape that fact. As God's property, man is "bound" by God's law, and God's law is the principle of freedom to the regenerate, and condemnation to the ungodly.

As God's property, man must apply God's law to the total world of life and thought, beginning with himself, and he has no right to withdraw from that task. Coercion in and of itself is not ungodly. Coercion can be intensely evil, and it can also be just and righteous. The Anabaptist rejection of all coercion, while not truly held, is still a deadly opinion, and its essential influence is alien and hostile to the Kingdom of God.

## 129

# THE QUEST FOR TIME OUTSIDE OF GOD

Basic to any understanding of the social and legal revolutions of the modern world is an awareness of the importance to these upheavals of the idea of *leisure*. The word *leisure* comes from the Latin *licire,* to be permitted, and has a long history en route. It has a foreign sound in English, and class connotations, and rightly so. The idea of leisure is deeply imbedded in the modern mentality, and yet it has a foreign implication, and with reason: it is radically alien and hostile to Christian faith and culture. *Leisure is an anti-Sabbath faith in all its implications and meaning. Leisure presupposes a war against God.*

Lest this seem an over-statement, let us glance at some sociological definitions of *leisure*. According to Joffre Dumazedier, "Leisure is not all time which is free from work. It occupies only a part—that part which does not involve any legal or moral obligation."[1] According to Marrus, leisure is "free activity which the individual engages in for his own purposes, whatever these may be." It is an act of autonomy "made basically by autonomous individuals free from the long arm of traditional authority." It is not to be confused with group activities resting on group relationships but is a manifestation of autonomy.[2]

Leisure did not come in to relieve the drudgery and toil of medieval and Reformation man. Christian man did not lack rest and play. Not only did work then have its diversions, but, according to Marrus, in England, medieval man may have had a regular working year of 44 weeks. In addition, there were work breaks for baptisms, confirmation, marriages, funerals, pilgrimages, and so on, so that "one could well arrive at an estimation of one-third of the year being 'leisure.' " It was, of course, not leisure in the modern sense, because it was a religious rest.

Shorter found the turn to leisure, in his studies of Bavaria, to be marked by a new and different spirit. Dancing and sexuality, with a marked rise of premarital sex, and illegitimacy, began to prevail. A proverb expressed the new hedonism and sexual revolution of Bavaria, 1800-1850: "We'll have no masters."[4]

---

1. Joffre Dumazedier and Nicole Latouche, "Work and Leisure in French Sociology," in Michael R. Marrus, ed.: *The Emergence of Leisure,* p. 128. New York, NY: Harper & Row, 1974.
2. Michael R. Marrus, "Introduction," in *ibid.,* p. 4.
3. *Ibid.,* p. 5.
4. Edward Shorter, "Toward a History of La Vie Intime: The Evidence of Cultural Criticism in Nineteenth-Century Bavaria," in *ibid.,* p. 61.

Lawlessness was thus basic to the rise of leisure. Autonomous man first expressed his freedom from God's law in play, in non-working activities. Work is a necessity for survival: however man may dream of a work-free world, and work towards that end, he is still tied to work. As a result, his immediate act of separation from God's law is leisure, autonomous activity apart from God. During the 1960s, one of the basic demands of the student movement was for education not for work or war, but for equality *and* leisure. The insistence on leisure very quickly took the form of the sexual revolution. In the early days of the Berkeley movement and the Ad Hoc Committee's demands concerning the Triple Revolution, the emphasis on leisure in general was more pronounced. However, the revolt was a revolt against authority, including parental authority. The leisure of parents, activity outside of God, meant travel abroad or to resorts, the theatre, and entertainment of various sorts. The students rejected these parental *forms*. Travel thus was retained, but by bumming rides, not by plush jet-planes. The theatre came to be a theatre of protest and warfare against the Establishment, and so on. The goal was still leisure, play activity outside of God, but a new note, always implicit in the past, now came to the forefront: *leisure now meant lawless play with reference to the laws of God and man.* The result was the sexual, political, educational, and drug "revolutions." Sex meant lawless sex, defiant of God and man. Politics meant the politics of destruction, of dismantlement of all order and structure. Education means the "free universities" of the 1960s, which often taught the same basic humanism of the universities, and the same radicalism, but with a fierce desire to be somehow independent, different, and outside the established order. Drugs meant a departure from orderly mental processes, and a defiance of laws. Many students who disliked marijuana, for example, felt it was necessary to sample "pot" occasionally in order to maintain status with their fellow students.

Leisure is thus an attempt to escape from God's world of law and grace. It is an attempt to ground man in his supposed autonomy. Leisure activity becomes more and more imaginative in its lawlessness, and man seeks to build his Great Community around the principle of man's freedom from the Kingdom of Necessity, *i.e.,* from God's world of law. Man's dream of rest is thus total leisure, totally free and autonomous activity outside of God, with a world of slave-machinery doing all the work. Perfect automation and perfect leisure is the goal.

The Sabbath principle is anti-autonomous and anti-leisure. The church is by and large anti-Sabbath in that it orients the Sabbath to the church and worship rather than to God and His sovereign purposes concerning the Sabbath. Hebrews 4:4-10 make clear what the Biblical faith declares:

For he spake in a certain place of the seventh day on this wise, *And*

*God did rest the seventh day from all his works.*
And in this place again, *If they shall enter into my rest* (*they shall never enter my Rest.* Moffatt).
Seeing therefore it remaineth that some must enter therein, and they to whom it was first preached entered not in because of unbelief;
Again, he limiteth a certain day, saying in David, *To day,* after so long a time; as it is said, *To day if ye will hear his voice, harden not your hearts.*
For if Jesus (Joshua) had given them rest, then would he not afterward have spoken of another day.
There remaineth therefore a rest to the people of God.
For he that is entered into his rest, he also hath ceased from his own works, as God did from his.

It is apparent, *first,* that the Sabbath, which means *rest,* has reference to two things, rest and time, and the two are inseparable. If we concentrate only on the aspect of rest, we lose the meaning of the Sabbath. It has reference to *sevens,* the number of fulness: the seventh day, the seventh year, seven sevens of years and then the jubilee. Thus, the Sabbath contemplates the fulness of God's work. It commemorates the completion of the work of creation, and also the work of redemption. The Sabbath marks the end of the creation work. It also marks the deliverance of Israel from Egypt, and the resurrection of Jesus Christ and His victory over sin and death. The Sabbath thus is a foretaste of the fulness of God's work and the new creation. It rejoices in the first creation and its regeneration and glorious calling in Christ.

*Second,* we are to rest from our works, "as God did from his." God's creative work was ended, and it was all "very good" (Gen. 1:31). We are to rejoice at what He did in creation, and in the history of redemption as it culminates in the First and the Second Coming. It is all a finished work in God's eternal decree, and we are to rest in it, and to rejoice over it. There is therefore a cessation of work: we rest from our labors, knowing that he has already ordained and accomplished all things. "Known unto God are all his works from the beginning of the world" (Acts 15:18). Thus, on the Sabbath, we not only do *not* work, but we also do *not* plan: we rest in God's predestined plan. We become aware of and confident in the past, present, and future under God, because we are mindful of eternity and God's eternal decree of predestination. We rest in that by faith. The future is not in our hands, but the Lord's. We cease from our work and our planning, because it is God's plan we contemplate.

*Third,* the Sabbath thus is not destructive but instructive. Our Lord, in terms of Exodus 23:4, 5 and Deuternomy 22:4, and their known meaning, declares:

And behold, there was a man which had his hand withered. And they asked him, saying, Is it lawful to heal on the sabbath days? that they might accuse him.

And he said unto them, What man shall there be among you, that shall have one sheep, and if it fall into a pit on the sabbath day, will he not lay hold on it, and lift it out?
How much then is a man better than a sheep? Wherefore it is lawful to do well on the sabbath days.
Then saith he to the man, Stretch forth thine hand. And he stretched it forth; and it was restored whole, like as the other. (Matt. 12:10-13)

As we rejoice in past, present, and future under God, we do not destroy that past nor limit the future. We rejoice in God's providence in our past, and we maintain it by rescuing the calf or sheep. We perform works of necessity, such as power plants, hospital work, and the like. We do not work or plan for tomorrow on the Sabbath. We do honor and maintain the past and the present by works of mercy and necessity. We do feed hungry animals on the Sabbath, but we do not plan for their tomorrows nor ours. We cannot use the Sabbath as an excuse to decapitalize or destroy. Our works of mercy and necessity are instructive in purpose rather than constructive, because they make us mindful of how blessed we are, and how much there is in the Lord's provision for us.

*Fourth,* the emphasis on *time* in the Sabbath makes us mindful that all time comes from God's hand. The Sabbath rest is a way of declaring to the Lord, with David, "My times are in thy hand" (Ps. 31:15). All time is holy time, because all time is from God, totally governed by His decree, and to be lived in terms of His calling. In Sabbath time, we rejoice that time is from God and is totally controlled by Him. Leisure time is thus an impossibility: there is no autonomous time, no time outside of God. Hence, all attempts at leisure represent efforts to escape from God and to create in that leisure time a center of autonomy from whence the world can be made autonomous.

Leisure time in the modern world is increasingly evidencing its inner link to the old Saturnalia. In the Saturnalia, man sought to renew himself by total chaos, by a radical autonomy from God's world of law.

Macrobius, writing on Saturnalia, held that, according to "natural science. . . at first all was chaos."[5] The Saturnalia was a celebration of time, like the Sabbath, but it saw the rejuvenation and regeneration of time and history in acts of chaos, lawlessness and autonomy. Saturn or Cronus is Time, Macrobius wrote.[6] The god Time or Saturn-Cronus was assaulted and castrated by his sons and thereby the world became fertile. The war against God and time is thus the key to pagan regeneration: it means ritual adultery, incest, homosexuality, and total lawlessness. When the peoples of Bavaria in the first half of the 19th century danced and then copulated, affirming, "We'll have no masters," they were setting forth the ancient creed of Saturnalia. The goals of leisure time have ancient roots.

---

5. Macrobius: *The Saturnalia,* p. 123. Translated with introduction and notes by Percival Vaughan Davies. New York, NY: Columbia University Press, 1969.
6. *Ibid.,* p. 64f.

## 130

## SABBATH AND PROPERTY

Sabbatarianism within the church holds to a very defective view of the Sabbath as simply a church day. The focus of the Sabbath is thus made the church, whereas in Scripture it is God's total purpose with respect to His Kingdom. The church has tended to observe the *shadow* of the Sabbath rather than *the body,* which is of Christ (Col. 2:16-17).

Before going directly into this matter, let us summarize the Biblical laws with respect to the Sabbath.[1] Four reasons are given for its observance: *First,* it is the day of rest (Gen. 2:2-3; Ex. 20:11). No work is allowed (Ex. 20:10; Lev. 23:3; Mark 16:1; Luke 23:54-56). No burden is to be carried (Neh. 13:19; Jer. 17:21). No purchases are allowed (Neh. 10:31; 13:15-17). Works and acts of necessity are permitted (Matt. 12:1; Luke 13:15; 14:1). *Second,* the Sabbath is a time of grace and mercy. Hence, servants and animals must rest (Ex. 20:10; Deut. 5:14). Works of mercy and grace are lawful (Matt. 12:12; Luke 13:16; John 9:14). The Sabbath is to be a blessing and a benefit to man (Mark 2:27-28). *Third,* the Sabbath is a memorial of redemption. For old Israel, this meant redemption from Egypt (Deut. 5:15; Jer. 17:21-22). For the new Israel of God, it meant the day of Christ's resurrection (Rev. 1:10; Matt. 28:1; Mark 16:9; Luke 14:1-3; John 20:1-2; Acts 20:7; I Cor. 11: 18-26; 16:2). *Fourth,* the Sabbath is a holy day (Ex. 16:23; 20:8; 31:14-17; 35:2-3; Deut. 5:12-14; Neh. 9:14; Isa. 58:13-14; Ezek. 44:24). Scripture is read (Acts 13:27; 15:21), and the word of God preached (Acts 13:14, 15, 44; 17:2; 18:4), as well as religious instruction given on the Sabbath (Mark 6:2; Luke 4:16, 31; 6:6; 13:10; Acts 13:14, 42, 44; 15:21; 17:2; 18:4). Religious works are lawful on the Sabbath (Num. 28:9; Matt. 12:5; John 7:23). Vain and hypocritical observances as well as disregard are not holiness but an abomination to the Lord (Isa. 1:13; 20:13-24; 22:8, 26; 23:38).

Up to this point, church Sabbatarians will agree, with minor differences. The fact is, however, by leaving out most of the Sabbaths they have made the Sabbath a church day rather than a basic factor in the whole of life. Other Sabbaths are

1. the first and seventh day of the feast of the passover and of

---

1. This summary is taken from Harold E. Monser, editor: *Monser's Topical Index and Digest of the Bible,* p. 539f. Grand Rapids, MI: Baker Book House, 1960.

unleavened bread (Lev. 23:7, 8);
2. the day of the first fruits (Lev. 23:21);
3. the feast of trumpets (Lev. 23:24,25);
4. the day of atonement (Lev. 23:32);
5. the feast of tabernacles, first and eighth day (Lev. 25:39);
6. every seventh year a sabbatical year (Lev. 23:1-4);
7. and every fiftieth year a sabbatical year (Lev. 25:8-13).

Certain aspects of these Sabbaths, like the weekly Sabbaths, are shadows, and hence gone. But what of the body which remains, and is Christ's?

As we have seen, work was forbidden on the Sabbath. Keil and Delitzsch noted:

> On the Sabbath and the day of atonement every kind of civil work was prohibited, even to the kindling of fire for the purpose of cooking (Lev. 23:3, 30, 31, cf. Ex. 20:10, 31:14, 35:2, 3; Deut. 5:14 and Lev. 16:29; Num. 29:7); on the other feast days with a holy convocation, only servile work (Lev. 23:7, 8, 21, 35, 36, cf. Ex. 12:16).[2]

Servile work was "ordinary handicraft," the daily duties of one's calling.[3]

However, if we stop here, as churchmen do, we miss the meaning of the Sabbath. The Sabbath years also called for
1. the release of slaves (Lev. 25:39-43);
2. the release of mortgaged lands (Lev. 25:23-34);
3. the release of debts (Lev. 25:13-17); and
4. rest for the land (Lev. 25:1-7).

Clearly, we have something more than "shadows" here. If we drop these aspects of Sabbath law, we have abandoned both rest and salvation in anything other than a neoplatonic and spiritual sense.

Our world today has abandoned the doctrines of salvation and rest in their Biblical meanings. To understand what has happened, let us turn our attention to the work of John Law (1671-1729), the father of modern banking and of modern monetary policies. He is thus a father of both modern commerce and of the modern state. Although not a Christian, Law should perhaps be called also a father of the modern church, because he has so radically altered the idea of rest.

Law developed the modern use of paper money, in particular, a paper currency unbacked by either gold or silver. We hear it commonly said today that the American dollar is sound, because it has behind it the wealth and productivity of America. This is simply a statement of Law's doctrine that money should be established upon the evidences of commercial

---

2. C. F. Keil and F. Delitzsch: *Biblical Commentary on the Old Testament;* vol. II, *The Pentateuch,* p. 439. Grand Rapids, MI: Eerdmans, 1949.

wealth, actual or potential, upon land and its potential, or upon the potentials of industrial productivity. This means a non-convertible currency; it also means a restless society. Such a view of money means that society must forever boom or face collapse. The economics of Law is inflationary: it requires a continual boom, and any abatement thereof leads to a bust or collapse. Because of the inflation of the money (*i.e.,* of a paper assurance of potential production), the economy moves forward rapidly. But the paper money assumes a *potential production;* it produces, however, an *actual consumption,* so that it creates a consuming rather than a producing economy. It decapitalizes instead of capitalizing. Its end is destruction.

In the process, it destroys *rest.* It becomes impossible to relax and enjoy one's wealth, or to rejoice in accomplished goals, because a consuming, inflationary economy eats up capital accumulated from the past. Man is, economically and emotionally, on a hopeless treadmill. An inflationary economy, or, more broadly, a paper-money economy, is marked by emotional and mental instability among the people. It begins with a false religious premise, namely, that man as god can create something out of nothing. It ends with man making nothing out of something and turning himself into a mental, emotional, and moral shambles in the process. As Isaiah makes clear,

> But the wicked are like the troubled sea, when it cannot rest, whose waters cast up mire and dirt.
> There is no peace, saith my God, to the wicked. (Isa. 57:20-21)

Law's iniquitous system has been "improved," however. For Law, paper money was an evidence of commercial and agricultural potentials in wealth. Law's great Mississippi Bubble thus rested on the potential development and wealth of the Louisiana Territory. The wealth and potential Law imagined was actually there, but it required countless generations to develop it. Law was assuming that a future wealth, a potentiality, could be converted into an actuality, a present wealth, by a piece of paper. This was as logical as assuming that the food California produces fifty years from now can be used today; the possibility of that food is very great; in *actuality,* it is non-existent, and will feed no one today.

Law thus banked on *the future.* The modern monetary system banks on *the past.* It assumes that the food we ate ten years ago can fuel us today. Paper money thus is no longer an evidence of potential wealth but of past debt. The more debts we have, the more money. Each year, the modern state monetizes its debts, and it encourages debt living among its subjects. Money now represents not potential *production* but past *consumption.*

This places man on an even worse treadmill. He needs more of this new money, and hence more inflation and new debt, to pay on his old debts. He must accelerate his pace. Up to a point, in industry, production can be speeded up, but not in agriculture. It still takes a year to produce one harvest of apricots, and nothing can hasten this process. After a point, services are more profitable, because more quickly rendered, than production, and shortages appear.

Even more, however, in the debt economy man's inner life is shackled, because the treadmill moves backwards. His debts rivet him to the past. He cannot rest in the present, because his past faces him today and tomorrow with demands for a reckoning, a payment. Debt is perhaps the major immediate cause of problems in marriages. A mental instability and an inability to have peace of mind marks modern man. He has no salvation and no rest. He is a Sabbathless man.

The Sabbath in any true and full sense is a national fact. This is why it is fruitless to argue as to whether or not a Sabbath observance existed before Moses and the Red Sea crossing. The patriarchs, as redeemed men, rested in the Lord. But the Sabbath as the law envisions it, is a social fact, a Kingdom fact, and it requires the establishment of the visible structure of the Kingdom. It is rest in God's salvation and law. It means debt-free living, or at the most, short-term and very limited debt. It means rest for man and his servants, for animals and for the land. It means the confidence of salvation and God's providential care. It means a people whose future is not mortgaged by either past sins or past debts, so that they are a free people in Jesus Christ (I Cor. 7:23; Prov. 22:7). This is why the first Sabbath we find in Scripture is in God's Kingdom, Israel, after their deliverance from slavery to Egypt, and with the giving of manna, the sign of God's providential care:

> And it came to pass, that on the sixth day they gathered twice as much bread, two omers for one man; and all the rulers of the congregation came and told Moses.
> And he said unto them, This is that which the LORD hath said, To morrow is the rest of the holy sabbath unto the LORD; bake that which ye will bake to day, and seethe that ye will seethe; and that which remaineth over lay up for you to be kept until the morning,
> And they laid it up till the morning, as Moses bade: and it did not stink, neither was there any worm therein.
> And Moses said, Eat that to day; for to day is a sabbath unto the LORD; to day ye shall not find it in the field.
> Six days ye shall gather it; but on the seventh day, which is the sabbath, in it there shall be none.
> And it came to pass, that there went out some of the people on the seventh day for to gather, and they found none.
> And the LORD said unto Moses, How long refuse ye to keep my commandments and my laws?
> See, for that the LORD hath given you the sabbath, therefore he giveth you on the sixth day the bread of two days; abide ye every

man in his place, let no man go out of his place on the seventh day. So the people rested on the seventh day. (Ex. 16:22-30)

*First,* as Keil and Delitzsch noted, "It is perfectly clear from this event, that the Israelites were not acquainted with any sabbatical observances at that time, but that, whilst the way was practically opened, it was through the decalogue that it was raised into a legal institution."[4] The Israelites had been a slave people in Egypt, under an alien lordship, and there had been no Sabbaths for them.

*Second,* the Sabbath comes with deliverance from Egypt and with the giving of manna. Israel rests in God's redemption and providence. The foundation of the Sabbath is God's salvation *and* His law (Ex. 23:28). Like His law, the Sabbath is the sign of God's government. To substitute another law and to refuse to rest means to distrust or deny the sufficiency of God's government. This is the meaning of the death penalty for Sabbath breaking (Ex. 31:13-15). The Sabbath was declared to be the covenant "sign," the evidence of treaty-faithfulness by man to God. The covenant or treaty was with Israel; i.e., it is between God and His Kingdom-people. It has reference to a civil order which recognizes, obeys, and enforces God's law. The Sabbath, *in all its ramifications,* is the treaty sign between God and man, *i.e.,* man organized into a nation under God. There was in the New Testament, and there is today, no national covenant with God. Hence, the nations are under God's judgment.

*Third,* the Sabbath is a gift of grace: "the LORD hath given you the Sabbath." It is a witness to the fact that God will care for His redeemed people. To keep the Sabbath means to *trust* in that care. To keep the Sabbath means, not only one day in seven for rest, but debt-free living, or no more than a six-year debt. It means, having received *rest* and mercy from God, we give it to others. It means that we work towards a universal Sabbath, *i.e.,* a society living debt-free in its economic and monetary life, and manifesting grace, charity, and mercy one towards another.

*Fourth,* it means that our labor is in vain when it is not in the Lord. "Today ye shall not find it in the field." When we substitute our word and will for God's, our labors are fruitless, and our efforts futility.

Thus, we cannot claim to be faithful Sabbatarians when we follow a false economic and monetary policy, as individuals and as a nation. We are violating the Sabbath when we are uncharitable and unscripturally in debt. We may still be attending church every Sunday without fail, but we have no true rest, because our rest is humanistic and ecclesiastical, not holy unto the Lord.

The Sabbath rests in God's property rights over us, and it therefore has a very necessary requirement that it makes with respect to our use of property, animals, and persons. The Sabbath principle must go to the

---

4. *Ibid.,* II, p. 68f.

heart of a man, his family, society, social and civil order, or it is not kept. God is totally God, and His law is a total law. This is no less true of His Sabbath law. God's property rights are over us, our possessions, and our time. *This Sabbath is co-extensive with His sovereignty.*

## 131

### THE SABBATH AS A PRINCIPLE OF LIFE

In analyzing the Sabbath as a principle of life, it is important to remember the fact that church history is a development in awareness. This can be seen, first, by answering the question, Were Christians previously aware of the implications of the Sabbath as a principle of life? The answer is both yes and no. To understand what such an answer means it is helpful to turn our attention to another aspect of Scripture, the doctrine of infallibility and inerrancy. Not until the Westminster Standards do we have a clear statement of this doctrine, and only in this century have its implications come to the forefront. Does this mean that for sixteen centuries the church and its theologians did not believe in this doctrine? Clearly, they did, but, since infallibility was not *directly* under attack, they did not develop its implications. It has been the modern era which has forced the church to think through this doctrine and to develop it. Previously, it was taken for granted. The same has been true of the Sabbath. Men took for granted the necessity for short-term debts, a contentment in God's providence, and more. Relatively little attention was given to the doctrine, because the laws of the Sabbath and its practice generally prevailed. Our era is compelling us to give a deeper attention to the Sabbath, and to Biblical law generally.

*Second,* men in every age seek to practice a minimal religion, and hence there is generally an unwillingness to develop the implications of doctrines. Such people are content to call themselves believers and boast of their holiness to the faithful, whom they regard as less holy, while being offensive to God, because they are ready to compromise with paganism and call it faith (Isa. 65:1-5). Every age has such a vein of antinomianism, and ours especially.

Thus, the understanding of the Sabbath as a principle of life has been latent and implicit in the past, rather than explicit and developed. The key to an understanding of this meaning of the Sabbath is in Ezekiel 20:10-12, 18-22, although the whole chapter is relevant:

> Wherefore I caused them to go forth out of the land of Egypt, and brought them into the wilderness.
> And I gave them my statutes, and shewed them my judgments, which if a man do, he shall even live in them.
> Moreover also I gave them my sabbaths, to be a sign between me and them, that they might know that I am the LORD that sanctifieth them.

565

But I said unto their children in the wilderness, Walk ye not in the statutes of your fathers, neither observe their judgments, nor defile yourselves with their idols:
I am the LORD your God; walk in my statutes, and keep my judgments, and do them;
And hallow my sabbaths; and they shall be a sign between me and you, that ye may know that I am the LORD your God.
Notwithstanding the children rebelled against me; they walked not in my statutes, neither kept my judgments to do them, which if a man do, he shall even live in them; they polluted my sabbaths: then I said, I would pour out my fury upon them, to accomplish my anger against them in the wilderness.
Nevertheless I withdrew mine hand, and wrought for my name's sake, that it should not be polluted in the sight of the heathen, in whose sight I brought them forth. (Ezekiel 20:10-12, 18-22)

*First,* it should be noted that God says He "gave them my sabbaths" *after* the deliverance of Israel from Egypt. The Sabbath is a covenant and national fact. It requires personal *and* social obedience and observance. Ellison's comment here is very good:

In spite of strong arguments to the contrary, it seems conclusive from this chapter and Neh. 9:14 that the Sabbath is part of the Sinai revelation and does not date from Eden. Certainly all efforts to find traces of a weekly rest-day elsewhere in the ancient world have conspicuously failed. It is easy enough to keep the Sabbath in a legalistic way, but once it is correctly understood, it becomes a very real test of a man's faith. Only where the Lord is recognized as controller over the great powers of nature can one go beyond a legalistic cessation of work and turn heart and mind away from all the clamant claims of the world.[1]

*Second,* Ezekiel makes clear that the law is given to the covenant people. It speaks to the faithful, and it is declared to be *the way of life* for the faithful, the means of sanctification, "which if a man do, he shall even live in them."

*Third,* the Sabbath is declared to be *a sign.* Ezekiel 20:12, 20, simply echo Exodus 31:12, 13,

And the LORD spake unto Moses, saying,
Speak thou also unto the children of Israel, saying, Verily my sabbaths ye shall keep: for it is a sign between me and you through your generations; that ye may know that I am the LORD that doth sanctify you.

Here we come to the heart of the matter. We cannot understand the Sabbath unless we see it as *a sign.* Signs are basic to Scripture, and two of the central signs are the rainbow and circumcision. A sign "is used throughout the Bible of any symbol or token, but more especially of

---

1. H. L. Ellison: *Ezekiel: The Man and His Message,* p. 80f. Grand Rapids, MI: Eerdmans, 1956.

such as mark the relation of man to God and the providential care which God lavishes upon men."[2] The rainbow (Gen. 9:12) marks God's miraculous deliverance of His own in a time of judgment. The same is true of the plagues on Egypt (Ex. 10:2): as signs, they meant grace and deliverance to the covenant people, and death and judgment to the ungodly. Circumcision (Gen. 17:11; Rom. 4:11), and baptism, are signs of God's covenant and His grace, mercy, and providential care, but a sign despised means judgment. The prophets made their predictions often as signs (Isa. 7:14; 38:7; Jer. 44:29; Ezek. 14:8). John speaks of Christ's miracles as signs (John 3:2; 4:54; etc.). The apostolic miracles were signs (Mark 16:20; Acts 4:16; 6:8; 8:6, 13; II Cor. 12:12, etc.).

The supreme sign, however, is the sabbath. It is the mark of faith, and of judgment. We either rest in the Lord, or we are restless and without peace. It is both a personal and a social sign. We can observe a weekly Sabbath and have no rest. We can be fretful, easily annoyed, and readily complaining, because we seek our rest apart from the Lord. We can seek it in the society of men, or in isolation from men, but, in either case, we have no Sabbath. We remain restless and fretful. The true Sabbath means a trust in God's providential care, so that we take hands off our lives and commit them into His care. James 5:8 requires us to be patient, and to fortify our hearts. A few of the very many texts calling for such a faith are these:

Rejoice in the Lord always: and again I say, Rejoice.
Let your moderation be known unto all men. The Lord is at hand.
Be careful for nothing; but in every thing by prayer and supplication with thanksgiving let your requests be made known unto God.
And the peace of God, which passeth all understanding, shall keep your hearts and minds through Christ Jesus. (Phil. 4:4-7)

Cast thy burden upon the LORD, and he shall sustain thee: he shall never suffer the righteous to be moved. (Ps. 55:22)

Commit thy works unto the LORD, and thy thoughts shall be established. (Prov. 16:3)

Therefore I say unto you, Take no thought for your life, what ye shall eat, or what ye shall drink; nor yet for your body, what ye shall put on. Is not the life more than meat, and the body than raiment? (Matt. 6:25)

Casting all your care upon him; for he careth for you. (I Peter 5:7)

Peace I leave with you, my peace I give unto you: not as the world giveth, give I unto you. Let not your heart be troubled, neither let it be afraid. (John 14:27)

Therefore being justified by faith, we have peace with God through our Lord Jesus Christ. (Rom. 5:1)

---

2. J. H. Bernard, "Sign" in James Hastings, ed.: *A Dictionary of the Bible,* vol. IV, p. 512. New York: Charles Scribner's Sons, (1902) 1919.

And let the peace of God rule in your hearts, to the which also ye are called in one body; and be ye thankful. (Col. 3:15)

Many, many more such verses can be cited. They abound from one end of the Bible to the other. These texts tell us what the Sabbath is about: it is a law, but more. It is a principle of life. It means, *first,* resting in the Lord outwardly, knowing that it is not our work which accomplishes God's purpose and ours, but His sovereign decree. His work is a finished and perfect work, and we rest in the glory of His perfect plan. We manifest our faith by keeping His Sabbaths in all their fulness, and this includes the laws concerning debt.

*Second,* the outward observance is meaningless if we are inwardly restless and fretful with God. We *cannot* plead that our disposition makes us so. God *requires* us to be content, and in *everything* to give thanks. What we call our disposition, or our weariness, is simply a form of rebellion, and it is *sin.* The psychological distresses of our age are manifestations of unbelief, or at least a distrust of God; they mean that we resent God's plan and demand that our own plan prevail.

No Sabbath is possible for modern man. Having taken the government of all things on his shoulders, modern man can never rest. Everything always depends on him, and he can never vacate his worrisome throne for even a moment. The Psalmist declares of the Lord,

My help cometh from the LORD, which made heaven and earth.
He will not suffer thy foot to be moved: he that keepeth thee will not slumber.
Behold, he that keepeth Israel shall neither slumber nor sleep.
(Ps. 121:2-4)

It is an attribute of God that He never sleeps, and all men who play at being a god will be fretful and discontented by day, and sleepless by night. Their answer is not better circumstances but *faith.*

To be thankless and discontented is to indict God and to distrust His government. It means inviting either His judgment or even greater burdens until we learn to be trustful and contented. Our Lord in Matthew 6:25 does *not* counsel heedlessness: what He requires is that, having obeyed and served our Lord faithfully, and in obedience to His law (Matt. 6:24; 5:17-20), we are to "take no thought" for our lives, because we are His own, and He cares for us. To be "content" without the law is to be content with evil. We can never care for ourselves with the wisdom and the omnipotence which marks the triune God, and hence to nurse our cares, or indulge our disposition, is a sign of rebellion and unbelief. We must believe, obey, and rest in the Lord.

It should be apparent now what the Sabbath as *a sign* means: it is a principle of life. More than the rainbow, circumcision, and baptism, it is a sign of God's covenant grace. Its observance is both inward and outward. The Pharisees were strong sabbatarians outwardly, but unbelievers inwardly, and they have many followers today. To be restless, fretful, and sleepless is to deny the Lord and the meaning of His Sabbath. David stated the matter very clearly:

> I will both lay me down in peace, and sleep: for thou, LORD, only makest me to dwell in safety. (Ps. 4:8)

## 132

## CREDIT AND PROPERTY

If it were possible to speak of words falling from grace, we would have to say this is the case with the word *credit*. It comes from the Latin *credo,* I believe, and its essential meaning once was to believe, to accept as true. To credit something or someone was to regard them as believable or true. A man of credit was once a man of character, marked by trustworthiness and reliability. In the financial world, credit meant in bookkeeping an amount in one's favor. These meanings are now in the background. *Credit* now means essentially debt. When in 1971 I sought to buy a house, I had serious problems; I was told that I had "no credit," meaning "no debt." Several other persons have reported similar experiences to me. Let us now examine the significance of the newer meaning of credit.

We have noted the implications of John Law's view of money, and the "improvements" made on Law. Groseclose has stated the matter tellingly:

> Law attempted to build a money system based upon evidences of commercial wealth; modern banking attempts to build a money system upon evidences of debt. Law sought by the Midas touch of banking to convert tangible wealth, produced and above ground, into money; modern banking seeks to convert our debts, our lack of wealth, our promises to pay from proceeds of wealth which is still unproduced and still in the future, into money.[1]

Consider the *moral revolution* modern money involves. Debt is now the basis of, and behind, all money, so that debt is now an asset, and credit means the ability to contract debt because of a record of debt. This is a more basic revolution than the sexual revolution, and we can with justice say that, behind the religious and moral revolutions of this humanistic era stands the basic error which is epitomized in the modern idea of money as debt.

It follows logically that, if debt is an asset, as the modern view of money sees it, then sin too is a social asset to modern man.

St. Paul had to deal with a like attitude, although milder in form, in his letter to the Romans:

> For if the truth of God hath more abounded through my lie unto his glory; why yet am I also judged as a sinner?

1. Elgin Groseclose: *Money and Man,* p. 144. Fourth edition, revised. Norman, OK: University of Oklahoma Press, (1934) 1976.

And not rather, (as we be slanderously reported, and as some affirm that we say,) Let us do evil, that good may come? whose damnation is just. (Rom. 3:7-8)

What shall we say then? Shall we continue in sin, that grace may abound? (Rom. 6:1)

Because St. Paul denied the validity of self-righteousness in man's salvation and affirmed sovereign grace, there were those who held that sin was an asset, and the more man sinned, the greater the good which would follow. They were twisting St. Paul's words to make him espouse evil as the means to grace. What St. Paul means, when he says, "where sin abounded, grace did much more abound" (Rom. 5:20), is *not* that sin causes grace to flow, but that sovereign grace is more powerful than sin. Where sin flourishes, grace is more powerful still and overcomes the powers of darkness to make all things new. Paul does not affirm antinomianism. He specifically denies this: "Do we then make void the law through faith? God forbid: yea, we establish the law" (Rom. 3:31).

But apostate man believes that, unless the law represents his works, his own righteousness, and his own decree of law, there is no law. Antinomianism says the only tenable law is man's own work.

Paul's critics were charging him with making an asset out of sin. Paul turns this charge back on them: they are the ones "whose damnation is just," because they refuse to recognize their own total depravity (Rom. 3:7-18), or that God's indictment makes "all the world guilty before God" (Rom. 3:18). It is only God's grace through Christ which redeems man (Rom. 3:23-25).

Paul's critics were thus trying to establish their own fiat righteousness as law, and they tried to villify Paul by calling him what they themselves were with respect to God's law, an antinomian. Isaiah says of self-righteous man, of man in apostasy,

But we are all as an unclean thing, and all our righteousnesses are as filthy rags; and we all do fade as a leaf: and our iniquities, like the wind, have taken us away. (Isa. 64:6)

Of those who are His redeemed ones, who move in His grace, power, protection, and blessing, the Lord declares:

No weapon that is formed against thee shall prosper; and every tongue that shall rise against thee in judgment, thou shalt condemn. This is the heritage of the servants of the LORD, and their righteousness is of me, saith the LORD. (Isa. 54:17)

"Their righteousness is of Me, saith the LORD." The modern world does not state the matter in the same language, but it does say in effect, Let us sin that grace may abound. Grace for modern men is freedom from God and His law. All too frequently I hear of young women who leave their husbands and good homes to become sexual tramps. What is their reason? The phrases commonly heard are "I want to be free," and "I want to be me" ("I wanna be free, I wanna be me"). This for them is the blessed life, because they see sin as an asset.

The earlier manifestations of this appeared in the 1920s, when a study by Dr. G. V. Hamilton made clear that most cases of adultery by women were motivated by the desire to exercise "freedom." It was not problems in the marriage but a belief that they would be missing out on life if they did not engage in adultery.[2] Since then, male and female adults, young, and even children have been pursuing the same illusion. Sin is seen as a social asset.

This view is an aspect of a faith in credit as the ability to contract debt, and debt as the foundation of money.

This same moral revolution expresses itself in law. The psalmist sings of those evil forces, described as "the throne of iniquity," "which frameth mischief (or, perverseness) by a law" (Ps. 94:20). Framing here means contriving, plotting.[3] "The throne of iniquity" means the throne or civil power which is based on wickedness.[4] This civil power acts as though it were God or allied with God, as though God Himself gave consent to perversity and evil. Much modern civil government operates on this premise, and sin is made into law. This was the basis of "the gay rights" ordinance in Dade County, Florida, in 1977, repealed by community efforts headed by Anita Bryant.

> The ordinance mandated that all employers, including private, religious schools, could not refuse to hire someone because he was a homosexual. Nor could employers fire anyone because of his sexual preference. Those who did "discriminate" were subject to a $500 fine and/or 60 days in jail. The ordinance, in fact, would seem to have applied to flaunting homosexual as well as "closet" gays.
>
> Under this ordinance, private schools—both religious and secular—would have been forced to hire or keep on homosexual activists, even though the schools and the parents who sent their children to those schools held the deepest conviction that homosexuality was not just an "alternate lifestyle," but a perversion that should neither be sanctioned nor propagated.[5]

On the federal level, similar measures were introduced by several congressmen.

Such efforts, and many existing laws, seek to make sin a social asset and bulwark. The defense of sin becomes important, and this means an assault on righteousness.

---

2. Lewis Joseph Sherrill: *Family and Church,* p. 116f. New York, NY: Abingdon Press, 1937.

3. Joseph Addison Alexander: *The Psalms,* p. 393.

4. H. C. Leupold: *Exposition of The Psalms,* p. 674.

5. "Homosexuality Still A Live Issue," in *Human Events,* July 9, 1977, p. 5f.

When money becomes debt, then real wealth is rapidly eroded, because the economy becomes inflationary and unstable. Wealth is transferred by inflation to debtors, and the biggest debtor is civil government. The result is the erosion of wealth and property in any Biblical sense.

Similarly, when sin becomes a social asset, protected by law (and one modern European state now protects incest), then all righteousness is under attack and at odds with the law.

The word *property,* like the word *proper,* comes from the Latin *proprius,* meaning one's own, belonging to the natural or essential constitution. Something of this meaning is conveyed in the term as used in Shakespeare, "My proper son," *i.e.,* my true son, who is mine by blood and nature. The word *property* also refers to the nature and characteristics of a thing or person, as in the expression, "the properties of gold." The properties of gold are inseparable from the nature of gold, and gold cannot be described apart from its property.

Because man is a fallen creature, the properties of his fallen estate are essentially sin and death. As a result, fallen man will frame perversity by a law, and he will seek to make an asset out of debt as well as sin. He is manifesting his properties.

The properties of the redeemed man, having been regenerated in the image of God, are righteousness, holiness, knowledge, and dominion (Gen. 1:26-28; Col. 3:10; Eph. 4:14; Ps. 8:2-8). As man grows in his sanctification, he will increase his properties in these areas, and their implications will be material as well as spiritual. His dominion will manifest itself materially and intellectually. He will be a man of property in the broadest sense of the word, so that religiously he will abound. This will manifest itself culturally, in his arts and sciences as well as in his physical possessions.

Those who feel that grace and prosperity will abound when sin abounds are destroying themselves and decapitalizing their culture. Only where men see not debt but faith and obedience as the basic expression of *credit,* only where credit rests on *credo,* I believe, and in the fruits or works of that faith, will there also be property, prosperity, and growth in the Biblical sense of the meaning of life and culture. Apart from that *credo,* credit, as in the modern sense, is the love of death (Prov. 8:36).

## 133

## THE PRINCIPLE OF LIFE

And the LORD spake unto Moses saying,
Speak unto all the congregation of the children of Israel, and say
unto them, Ye shall be holy: for I the LORD your God am holy.
Ye shall fear every man his mother, and his father, and keep my sab-
baths: I am the LORD your God.
Turn ye not unto idols, nor make to yourselves molten gods: I am the
LORD your God. (Lev. 19:1-4)

In this remarkable passage, the word for idols, *elelim,* is *nothings,* God's
description of all other gods. In contrast, He is *Elohim,* God. Thus, man
is confronted with the alternatives, either to establish his life upon
nothings, or upon the living God. To establish our lives upon God's
redemption and to be governed by His law is to be holy, because He is
holy. To despise God's redemption and law is to be reprobate, and
nothing. If our life is founded upon nothing, we are nothing.

Robert Nathan titled a brief poem, "Sum, Ergo Sum."[1] "I am, there-
fore I am." For God's "I AM," Nathan substituted his own. But
Nathan's "I am" was a product of the void and evolution, a cosmic emp-
tiness, and it meant finally only death, "The terror that soaks my sheets,
The fear that crawls in my belly" and "Is more than I can abide."[1]
Man's every idol, including himself, is finally only *nothing.*

As the alternative to reprobation, death, nothingness, and hell, God
offers *holiness,* His law, and makes clear that His laws, the laws of
holiness, are the way of life and the principle of life to all His covenant
people, whose lives are grounded, not on nothings, but on the Lord.

The sabbaths are again cited as basic to this principle of life. We
should note well that the Lord does not here limit the Sabbath to one,
*i.e.,* to the weekly Sabbath, but included all His Sabbaths.

Coupled with this is the commandment: "Ye shall fear every man his
mother, and his father, and keep my sabbaths." The word for *fear* is
*yare,* which means reverential fear. C. D. Ginsburg's comment is
especially good:

The first means to attain to the holiness which is to make the Israelite
reflect the holiness of God, is uniformly to reverence his parents.

1. Robert Nathan: *Evening Songs Selected Poems,* 1950-1973, p. 30. San Francisco, CA:
Capra Press, 1973.
2. *Ibid.,* p. 26; cf. 31.

Thus the group of precepts contained in this chapter opens with the first commandment in the Decalogue (Ex. xx. 12), or, as the Apostle calls it, the first commandment with promise (Eph. vi. 2). During the second Temple, already the spiritual authorities called attention to the singular fact that this is one of the three instances in the Scriptures where, contrary to the usual practice, the mother is mentioned before the father; the other two being Genesis xliv. 20 and Lev. xxi.2. As children ordinarily fear the father and love the mother, hence they say precedence is here given to the mother in order to inculcate the duty of fearing them both alike. The expression "fear," however, they take to include the following: (1) Not to stand or sit in the place set apart for the parents; (2) not to carp at or oppose their statements; and (3) not to call them by their proper names, but either to call them father or mother, or my master, my lady. Whilst the expression "honour" which is used in the parallel passage in Exodus xx. 12, they understood to include (1) to provide them with food and raiment, and (2) to escort them. The parents, they urge, are God's representatives upon earth; hence as God is both to be "honoured" with our substance (Prov. iii. 9), and He is to be "feared" (Deut. vi. 13), so our parents are both to be "honoured" (Exod. xx. 12) and "feared" (Lev. xix. 3); and as he who blasphemes the name of God is stoned (Lev. xxiv. 16), so he who curses his father or mother is stoned (Lev. xx. 9).[3]

The fifth commandment, in requiring that parents be honored, adds, "that thy days may be long upon the land which the LORD thy God giveth thee" (Ex. 20:12; Deut. 5:16). Here again obedience to God's law means life. Clearly, Deuteronomy 28 establishes, as does all of Scripture, that the obedience of faith to the law means life and blessing. However, certain areas are in particular singled out as areas of concentrated promise and blessing, areas incorporating in particular the principle of life.

The *first* of these is obviously the Sabbath, man's rest of trust, faith, contentment, and thanksgiving in the Lord. Such a rest means a trust in God's authority and government.

A *second* is clearly the requirement that we honor our parents, the first commandment with the promise of life. Here again, it means respect and honor given to God's ordained authority in the family, our parents. Any down-grading of the family by church, state, and school is a violation of this commandment. This law thus has a social and a personal aspect. It is not enough for us to render a personal honor to our parents, important and necessary though this is. Many a man who is exemplary as a son will socially favor policies in church, state, and school which are destructive of this commandment's claims. If we contribute in any way to the diminishing of the family's power, authority, and position as declared by Scripture, we have broken this law. The reverse is also true: if we champion the family socially but negate its place personally, we have broken the law.

---

3. C. D. Ginsburg, "Leviticus," in Ellicott, I, 421f.

A *third* area spoken of as incorporating the principle of life is marriage. St. Peter declares,

> Likewise, ye wives, be in subjection to your own husbands; that, if any obey not the word, they also may without the word be won by the conversation of the wives:
> While they behold your chaste conversation coupled with fear.
> Whose adorning let it not be that outward adorning of plaiting the hair, and of wearing of gold, or of putting on of apparel;
> But let it be the hidden man of the heart, in that which is not corruptible, even the ornament of a meek and quiet spirit, which is in the sight of God of great price.
> For after this manner in the old time the holy women also, who trusted in God, adorned themselves, being in subjection unto their own husbands;
> Even as Sarah obeyed Abraham, calling him lord; whose daughters ye are, as long as ye do well, and are not afraid with any amazement.
> Likewise ye husbands, dwell with them according to knowledge, giving honour unto the wife, as unto the weaker vessel, and as being heirs together of the grace of life; that your prayers be not hindered.
> (I Peter 3:1-7)

Note especially the phrase, "heirs together (or, joint-heirs) of the grace of life." The property of life outside of Christ is sin and death. The property of life in Christ is grace, so that our life manifests righteousness, knowledge, holiness, and dominion.

The *knowledge* required of husbands in dwelling with their wives is not a knowledge of feminine psychology, but of the word of God. Here too the principle of life is associated with the government and authority of God and our rest therein. Most men today cannot rule in the Lord because they are unwilling themselves to submit to God's rule and to rest in Him. They are either tyrants, ruling according to their word, or they are hen-pecked and ruled by their wives. No man has any authority in and of himself over any woman, or anything. All authority is from God and must be exercised according to His word. Too many men assume it is godly to rule a woman for their convenience. They forget that the Biblical standard of authority is ruling to serve (John 13:1-17; Luke 22:17; Matt. 20:28, etc.). Too many husbands are tyrants, not godly heads of households. Clearly, Ephesians 5:21-23 requires that the husband rule with the same self-sacrificing spirit as Christ the church. He must serve the Lord, and meet his wife's needs in the Lord. If not, the grace of life is denied.

Similarly, the wife must serve her husband as he serves the Lord. To rebel against his obedience to the Lord is to rebel against God Himself and manifest a reprobate heart.

A major problem in our time is such rebellion by wives and husbands. To illustrate, a very considerable percentage of married seminarians have major problems with their wives, who refuse to agree to their calling and show it by rejecting the conditions of their husband's calling. They refuse to go to the mission field, or to a city church, or a country church, or away from family and friends. In the name and under the cover of objecting to the terms of their husband's calling, they are denying God in a disguised but real warfare. It is their goal to break their husband and laugh at their victory over God. A reprobate heart produces reprobate courses of action.

The same is true in other areas. Many doctors have wives who enjoy the prestige of their position but wage war on the terms of their husband's calling, and on their husband. Again and again, the man is put to shame because his calling does make heavy demands on his time. Policemen face a similar problem.

To cite one more illustration, many women marry prospective forest rangers, knowing their calling, and then proceed to wage war against it until they break the man and cause him to quit, a defeated man.

All such women are manifesting a reprobate nature, and they can never be dealt with until this is recognized. Men who submit to such wives become castaways, useless to God because they are unfaithful to Him. Peter is clearcut: the prayers of all such couples are not heard by God, and they are denied the grace of life. God's principle of life rests on His authority and government, and our rest therein. Parents are required to rule according to God's law and themselves to be under Him and His law. Husband and wife, in their relationship one to another, must likewise be in submission to the Lord, resting in Him, content and giving thanks, or else they will fall prey to a "root of bitterness" (Heb. 12:15) which will destroy them.

Notice the association: God, the Sabbath, parents, and husband and wife. Life flows from them into all of society. God is the Creator; the family, man and wife, are the human area of fertility. If rest in God and His government and authority are denied, then the principle of life is denied, and human fertility or conception, instead of being a joy, becomes a sorrow (Gen. 3:16), and the earth's fertility becomes "thorns also and thistles" (Gen. 3:18). Then sin and death prevail, and man's life is a burden and futility.

No minister, doctor, forest ranger, or any other man, by changing his calling, spending more time with his wife or children, or any other such means, can satisfy the Lord or rest in Him. As St. Augustine declared at the beginning of his *Confessions,* "Our hearts are restless until they rest in Thee." It is not the hours nor conditions of work which produce weariness as much as a rebellious and discontented heart. The observance of an outward Sabbath is necessary and required, but it alone cannot give rest. Our rest comes from trusting in the Lord and relying on His word and government. Paul's words are to be taken very literally:

> Perverse disputings of men of corrupt minds, and destitute of the truth, supposing that gain is godliness; from such withdraw thyself.
> But godliness with contentment is great gain.
> For we brought nothing into this world, and it is certain we can carry nothing out.
> And having food and raiment let us be therewith content. (I Timothy 6:5-8)

This contentment comes, however, only with obedience to God's law, never with disobedience. There is no contentment in sin or in surrender to sin. Submission to evil is not obedience to the Lord. Solomon is right:

> Let us hear the conclusion of the whole matter: Fear God, and keep his commandments: for this is the whole duty of man. (Eccl. 12:13)

The consequences of obeying God will commonly produce human conflicts, but they will also produce peace with God and peace in Him. To refuse conflicts with men in the name of peace is to choose conflict with God.

## 134

## PAUL'S WAR ON THE ANTINOMIANS

In discussing "Fantasy as Law," we have seen something of the implications of II Corinthians 10:4-6. Let us examine now this same text as translated by Gerrit Verkuyl (in the Berkeley Version) and by James Moffatt:

> I do live in the flesh, but I do not make war as the flesh does; the weapons of my warfare are not weapons of the flesh, but divinely strong to demolish fortresses—I demolish theories and any rampart thrown up to resist the knowledge of God, I take every project prisoner to make it obey Christ, I am prepared to court-martial anyone who remains insubordinate, once your submission is complete. (II Cor. 10:3-6, Moffatt)

> For while we spend our life in a body of flesh, we do not war with carnal weapons. For the weapons of our warfare are not physical, but they are powerful with God's help for the tearing down of fortresses, inasmuch as we tear down calculations and every height that is raised against the knowledge of God. And every mental perception we lead into subjection to Christ. We are prepared also to administer justice upon all disobedience, when your obedience is fully shown. (II Cor. 10:3-6, Verkuyl)

St. Paul makes clear that he is engaged in a total war, but that, while engaged in this war as a man, he is not "warring with human weapons, relying on human resources."[1] Paul has directly in mind those in Corinth who are resisting God's law and are living in defiance of it, but he plainly generalized to include *every* fortress, theory, height, calculation, and imagination which is opposed to God.

The problem in Corinth was antinomianism, a disobedience to God's law, in particular, sexual and marital law. What Paul demands is *obedience to Christ,* whose word is the every word of Scripture. The case of incest in Corinth had to do with laws in Leviticus; Paul sees it as disobedience to Christ, whose work the whole of Scripture is. Paul's goal is thus "the obedience of Christ."

His weapons in enforcing obedience in Corinth and in all the world, *wherever* these vain imaginations and strongholds of rebellion against God exist, are "mighty through God." Thus, just as Deuteronomy 28:1-14 promise blessing on all who obey God's law, so Paul declares

---

1. Charles Hodge: *An Exposition of the Second Epistle of the Corinthians,* p. 233. Grand Rapids, MI: Eerdmans, 1950.

that all who work to enforce God's law are powerful with God's help. Those in authority have a duty to revenge or to administer justice upon all disobedience. Obedience and disobedience have reference to God's law. The power of the redeemed in their enforcement of God's law is plainly post-millennial in its meaning. In verse 5, Paul speaks with confidence of his ability to overthrow all the ideas and intellectual evasions of those who oppose the truth of God; he does not say that his reason will convert them, but that it will confound them and cast them down. In verse 6, he goes beyond the realm of ideas. Ideas have consequences, and Corinth's antinomianism led to flagrant sin. Paul declares that not only will these ideas be overthrown, but the sinning persons will be judged and punished. Paul does not want the Corinthians to think that Paul's triumph over their sin is an accident: rather, in God's order, *all* disobedience will be avenged, so that there is no escaping God's judgment in time and eternity.

Let us now examine the implications of antinomianism. Whether in Paul's day or ours, it is the same in its import. In an interview, Andrew Jackson Young, U. S. Ambassador to the United Nations and an ordained minister, defined morality as "thinking clearly through the alternatives and making a decision that is best for the largest number of people." The interviewer stated that this was not morality but Kissinger's *Realpolitik.* Young agreed, but said his concern for people was broader based than Kissinger's, since he had learned his theology from Reinhold Niebuhr, Paul Tillich, and Dietrich Bonhoeffer.

> My understanding of Jesus Christ is that he came to fulfill the law. And you're trying to talk in terms of a moral law. And I don't believe in it.[2]

Young is a modernist. Now let us examine the conduct of a professing fundamentalistic antinomian, an associate justice of the Texas Supreme Court and former counsel to a national evangelistic organization. He was indicted for perjury and for helping a man forge an auto title. The state bar prepared to add charges of soliciting a murder and obstructing justice to a long list of offenses as it sought disbarment and removal. The judge had a simpler answer to his problems:

> Last week a misty-eyed Yarbrough called reporters to his judicial chambers to confess his "sins" and "wrongdoings." Said he, "I have asked my God through the power of Jesus Christ to forgive me and I know in a very glorious way that He has forgiven me." The justice refused, however, to answer any questions about the details of his "sins."[3]

---

2. Peter Ross Range, "Playboy Interview: Andrew Young," in *Playboy,* vol. 24, no. 7, July, 1977, p. 82.
3. "The Sins of Justice Yarbrough," in *Time,* vol. 110, no. 3, July 18, 1977, p. 44.

Is this an unusual situation? It is, only with respect to the publicity given to it, but not in its nature. Anyone who has been a pastor in varied situations will encounter, in lesser virulence, similar cases. The antinomian is normally at ease with sin, as with the case with the adulteress described by Agur:

> Such is the way of an adulterous woman; she eateth, and wipeth her mouth, and saith, I have done no wickedness. (Prov. 30:20)

This is a picture of moral indifference to sinful *actions*. Such persons can on occasion weep and wail over the consequences, over the judgment that confronts them. Then we get a pseudo-repentence, *no* restitution, only regrets at the consequences. Antinomianism fails to see sin as sin, because it fails to see God as the Lord. It reserves lordship to man.

Andrew Young is emphatic about rejecting all of God's moral law in favor of the greatest good for the greatest number of people. Man will determine what that greatest good is, and Ambassador Young and President Carter seem to be sure that they know what it is. The antinomians, whatever they call it, are in effect giving us another revelation, from another god, and they are that god.

Paul in II Corinthians 10:3-6 is speaking about God's vengeance on the antinomians of Corinth and upon all antinomians. He makes war against them in the name and power of God, because he recognizes that they are enemies of Christ. They take sin lightly and even boast of their freedom from the law, so that their sin, instead of making them ashamed, leaves them "puffed up" (I Cor. 5:12). They take sin lightly, because they take God lightly; and, because they take God lightly, they take his law lightly. They sin, see it as harmless as eating, wipe their mouth, and say, "I have done no wickedness."

In the same issue of *Playboy* as that carrying the Rev. Andrew Young's denunciation of God's law, the nude "playmate" is a girl not yet 21. She had been a Bible School teacher in a Lutheran Church not too long before. Now she is *Playboy* publisher Hugh Hefner's "current steady date," and interviewer Carol King observed, "she looks every inch of what saying 'yes' can do for a girl." The girl observes that, if her friends really love her, "they'll not judge me."

> Regarding her church, she said: "All of a sudden I couldn't stand the way they viewed the world. The negative attitudes. I still believe in God, but not what they drilled into me about sinners."[4]

Of course, denying what Scripture says about sin, she denies God's law, and God Himself. Her "God" is simply her ideas about life given a name: it is not the living God of Scripture, with whom all antinomians some day must reckon as their judge.

---

4. Carol Soucek King, "Playmate Sondra Theodore, Throwing a Curve," In the *Los Angeles Herald-Examiner,* Friday, June 24, 1977, p. C-1.

Paul declares that he is *at war* against every rampart which is thrown up to resist the knowledge of God. This resistance to the knowledge of God at Corinth was the knowledge of God's holiness and righteousness as manifested in His law. To know God is to know Him in His self-revelation, in His infallible word, and to believe and obey Him. James is emphatic that faith is not simply belief; "the devils also believe and tremble" (James 2:19). It is faith, which means saying Amen to God, and living and working on that basis (James 2:20-26). Paul makes the same point in Romans 1:17-20. "The just shall live by faith," but faith is more than mere belief. *All men* know the truth of God, and "the invisible things of him from the creation of the world," but they "hold (or keep down, suppress) the truth in unrighteousness." All men know, whether or not they confess it, that God is, but they refuse to say Amen to Him, *i.e.,* to act on that belief, to manifest faith and its works.

To declare that "the just shall live by faith" means thus that the covenant man, saying Amen to God, has thereby the principle of life in him. Habakkuk tells us that, in the midst of judgment and disaster, "the just shall live by his faith" (Hab. 2:4); he has the principle of life. The world disaster is the handiwork of his covenant God, moving against the enemies of God and His people.

Antinomians deny that the just shall live by faith; rather, they hold that the just shall live by his beliefs. If this be true, then the devils in hell are redeemed and have the principle of life in them. They are, however, the living dead. "Faith without works is dead" (James 2:20). It is, in fact, then not faith, which is a living thing, but mere belief. "He that hath the Son hath life" (I John 5:12), and life means growth and development. The churches are full of lifeless members who cannot grow: they have no faith, only beliefs, no life, no growth.

Belief is necessary. James, in 2:19, declares, "Thou believest that there is one God; *thou doest well:* the devils also believe, and tremble." It is good to believe; we are repeatedly summoned to *believe* in Jesus Christ, but, just as clearly, the Scriptures make clear that, "as the body without the spirit is dead, so faith without works is dead also" (James 2:26). Where belief is a living faith, there also we find God's "effectual working" (I Thess. 2:13) in the salvation and sanctification of that man.

Paul did not content himself, in dealing with the Corinthians, with mere verbal professions of faith. He summoned them to obey God's word, declaring, "I am prepared to court-martial anyone who remains insubordinate" (II Cor. 10:6, Moffatt). To have the Son is to have *life,* but no man has the Son who will not hear His every word, and strive to obey it.

Paul thus is clearly at war with easy believism and antinomianism. If every man, as Romans 1:17-20 makes clear, inescapably has the knowledge of God written in all his being, then *faith* and *belief* in the Bible obviously do *not* mean what modern churchmen claim they do. The Bible plainly does not ask us to accept as true what it sets forth concerning God and salvation. Because we are all God's creation, this knowledge is inescapable for all men. Man's problem is not lack of knowledge: it is sin. Man suppresses the truth of God out of unrighteousness. He holds the truth in all his being, but he will not acknowledge that truth because he chooses to be his own god. Even the Death of God school did not deny the existence of God; rather, it declared, God is dead *for us;* they did not choose to recognize Him.

Every apologetic system which seeks to "prove" God to unbelievers is sinning thereby. It is conceding to the sinner that his false statement of his problem is true. The doctrine of creation is basic to Scripture, and it means that all things were made by the triune God, and all things are revelational of Him. The knowledge of God is thus inescapable knowledge. It is the only true knowledge, and God's law is the only true law. Man is a covenant-breaker if he tries to assume that believing that God is real is his problem, and man is a covenant-breaker if he acts in terms of any other law than God's law. Scholastic thought, with its rationalistic efforts to "prove" God, speaks of a god unknown to Scripture. Fundamentalistic apologetics and preaching which try to convince men that there is a God is blasphemy.

To have faith and to believe in the Biblical sense is not to assent to a proposition as true but to say Amen to it, to rely on it, and to act on it: in the Biblical sense, faith without works is not faith. They cannot be separated.

Some years ago, standing before a frozen stream, I was told by an Indian friend that it was strong enough to hold a team of horses. I believed him, and I crossed over. Faith acts; it is never mere assent. When God speaks, in His word, and in every man's being, all men know that His word is truth, but not all men act on that knowledge. Many deny God as God in favor of themselves as gods potentially (Gen. 3:5). Those who believe in God as God, act on His word and obey His law. Nothing else can be called faith in any Biblical sense. Thus, current preaching about faith is all too commonly unbiblical and false.

## 135

### JUSTICE AND RIGHTEOUSNESS

Girdlestone very clearly called attention in the past century to the essential identity of the words *justice* and *righteousness* in the Bible:

> The renderings righteous and just usually stand for some form of the word *tsadak,* which originally signified to be stiff or straight, and whence the names compounded with *Zedek* are derived. It is rendered lawful in Isaiah 49:24; moderately in Joel 2:23; and right in several passages. It is unfortunate that the English language should have grafted the Latin word *justice,* which is used in somewhat of a forensic sense, into a vocabulary which was already possessed of the good word *righteousness,* as it tends to create a distinction which has no existence in Scripture. This quality indeed may be viewed, according to Scripture, in two lights. In its relative aspect it implies conformity with the line or rule of God's law; in its absolute aspect it is the exhibition of love to God and to one's neighbour, because love is the fulfilling of the law; but in neither of these senses does the word convey what we usually mean by justice. No distinction between the claims of justice and the claims of love is recognized in Scripture; to act in opposition to the principles of love to God and one's neighbour is to commit an injustice, because it is a departure from the course marked out by God in His law.[1]

*Mishpat,* often rendered *justice,* means the godly administration of judgment, the application of God's righteousness.

Because our culture is so deeply infected by various forms of dialectical thought, from the Greeks to modern philosophy, it holds radically to the theory of *the conflict of interests* rather than to *the harmony of interests.* If God created and governs the world, then a harmony of interests is basic to all things because of His absolute decree of predestination (Rom. 8:28). If all things are a product of chaos and evolution, then the conflict of interests is basic, and love must be opposed to law and justice, righteousness to mercy, grace to judgment, and more. This however, is clearly contrary to Scripture.

In the Bible, the godly society is of necessity the righteous or just society, and therefore the loving society. Man's love, justice, mercy, and law are inevitably in conflict, because they have no ground in being. Not so with the Lord. As Deborah declares, "the stars in their courses fought

---

1. Robert Baker Girdlestone: *Synonyms of the Old Testament, Their Bearing on Christian Doctrine,* p. 101. Grand Rapids, MI: Eerdmans, (1897) 1976.

against Sisera" (Judges 5:20). God's righteousness is so basic to all things that to war against God's people is to war against the sun, moon, and stars also. As Zvi H. Szubin notes, "Righteous action results in social stability and ultimately in peace: 'And the work of righteousness shall be peace' (Isa. 32:17; cf. Hos. 10:12...)."[2]

The Bible knows only one kind of justice or righteousness, God's justice as set forth in His law. Thus, whether justice or righteousness in Scripture is ascribed to God, or to man and man's dealings, the reference is to the same fact. Man is righteous when he is in obedience to God's law. This righteousness is made possible by grace alone. God's grace in Christ, who fulfilled the judgment of the law against us as our sin-bearer, gives us a juridical righteousness before God. Through the obedience of faith, we grow in grace and in righteousness as we obey God's law.

God's justice or righteousness is synonymous with His holiness (Isa. 5:16), and is paired with his mercy or grace (*hesed*) repeatedly (Ps. 103:17ff., Isa. 45:19), and holiness, righteousness, grace, and mercy are inseparable in man, because they are inseparably one in God.

But this is not all. Pagan righteousness is an abstract concept, because the universe is abstract, impersonal, and essentially meaningless. As a result, when the pagan, ancient or modern, talks about justice, he cannot relate it to anything except man. Humanistic justice is abstract from all being *and* from all supernatural or transcendent law and is personal and concrete *only* with reference to man. This appears very clearly in Plato, who cited Socrates as declaring,

> It can no more be the function of goodness to do harm than of heat to cool or of drought to produce moisture. So if the just man is good, the business of harming people, whether friends or not, must belong to his opposite, the unjust.
>
> I think that is perfectly true, Socrates.
>
> So it was not a wise saying that justice is giving every man his due, if that means that harm is due from the just man to his enemies, as well as help to his friends. This is not true; because we have found that it is never right to harm anyone.[3]

Then and now, this is the faith of homosexuals and humanists. If they harm no man, they have done no injustice, and they themselves are the judges as to what constitutes harm.

Moreover, even in this form, the humanistic doctrine of justice or righteousness remains abstract. It is impersonal with reference to all the universe, and personal with reference to man, but still abstract. There is no catalogue of concrete acts which constitute injustice, other than

---

2. Zvi H. Szubin, "Righteousness," in *Encyclopaedia Judaica,* vol. 14, p. 179.
3. Francis MacDonald Cornford, translator: *The Republic of Plato,* p. 14. New York, NY: Oxford University Press, 1945.

occasional and varying ones. Racism is justice in one era, and injustice in another. "Do no harm" can be variously defined from age to age, and sometimes from decade to decade.

The Bible, on the other hand, has no definition of justice or righteousness other than the many detailed laws which govern every area of life. Judicial or justifying righteousness or justice is in Christ's atonement, a specific and particular death and atonement. Sanctification or growth in holiness, sanctifying righteousness, is in obedience to God's laws with respect to our relationship to Him (the first table of the law, the tithe, Sabbath, faith and obedience, etc.), to our neighbor (the second table of the law), to our family, to the world around us, to ourselves (the laws of diet, etc.), and so on.

Justice or righteousness in the Bible is never abstract: it involves a multitude of specific acts and attitudes that cover all of life.

This is why the modern view, which abstracts law from sanctification and makes the concept vague, "spiritual," or more accurately, *abstract,* has deeper roots in paganism than in Scripture. In Greek paganism, both salvation and sanctification meant *enthusiasm* or *mania.* It meant God-possession culminating in ecstatic experiences akin to madness and involving charismatic experiences. The Phrygian and Lydian cults in particular stressed the charismatic and extreme emotional experiences.

In most of these cults and mystery religions, if not all, antinomianism was the rule. Experience, not faith and obedience, was the emphasis, and as a result both doctrine and law were peripheral. Because of this combination of the experiential and the antinomian emphases, the sexual and erotic element in the mystery religions was often pronounced.

It is apparent, in any close contact with various antinomian and experiential groups in our day, that the same proneness to the sexual is still present. In some cults, it becomes prominent. Thus, it is alleged that one cult leader trains girls to be Happy Hookers for Jesus, and a school trains girls in the art of seduction. One leader in the cult, a European duchess, declared, "There is nothing wrong with a sexy conversion. We believe sex is a human necessity, and in certain cases we may go to bed with someone to show people God's love."[4]

Where righteousness or justice is separated from the specifics of God's law and Christ's atonement and related instead to ecstasy, experience, and enthusiasm, the result is not Christianity but the revival of paganism.

Righteousness or justice is conformity to the law of God. The law of God is an expression of God's being. For man to deny that law and seek righteousness on his own terms is to deny God.

Enthusiastic or spiritual righteousness is not righteousness or justice

---

4. "Tracking the Children of God," in *Time,* August 22, 1977, p. 48.

but sin. The same is true of *social justice,* which, unlike divine justice, derives its law or righteousness from man and man's needs, not from God. For social justice, righteousness is the freedom and fulfilment of man. But man is a sinner, and, whether great or small, rich or poor, black or white, needs condemnation, not fulfilment. His only hope is condemnation and deliverance through Christ's atoning death as his vicarious sacrifice and substitute, and obedience to God's law as the way of holiness and righteousness in Christ.

Because faith is more than mere belief, it requires, and is part and parcel of, righteousness. Our justification is by God's sovereign grace; it manifests itself in us by faith. Faith without works is dead. The man of faith is the man of righteousness, the man of justice. Antinomianism is antichristianity.

## 136

## KENOSIS, LAW, AND HOLINESS

A text without a context is a pretext or worse. Clearly, this is true of the often cited words, "Resist not evil" (Matt. 5:39). The context is the Sermon on the Mount. Our Lord speaks concerning the true meaning of the law: He has not come to destroy it but to put it into force (Matt. 5:17-20). He corrects the pharisaic perversions of the law in Matthew 5:21-37, and continues to do so in verse 38ff., commenting on Exodus 21:23-25. We *cannot* understand "Resist not evil" apart from this context, nor can we understand the verses which follow (Matt. 5:40-48) except in terms of this same context.

Thus we have, *first,* a commentary on Exodus 21:23-25, which, like the preceding comments (Matt. 5:16-37), upholds the full letter of the law and requires obedience from the heart. It is not enough to avoid physical adultery; our heart and mind must be free from adulterous thinking. To refrain from murder while harboring murderous hatred is a violation of the law, and so on. This is the *textual context.*

*Second,* we have the historical context. Judea was moving towards the total war against Rome which subsequently destroyed the people and the land. Their course was a sinful one, and its consequence was death, not freedom. They were concerned with resisting evil, not establishing righteousness. Their course of resistance was a denial of God's way. Freedom for them came, not through God's ordained way, as a product of righteousness, but through military means. While the Bible makes godly warfare legitimate, it never makes war against evil a substitute for righteousness. For a Hitler to war against Stalin did not make Hitler righteous, nor was Stalin righteous because he warred against Hitler. Similarly, none of the Allies could claim any righteousness for their part in the war. It is phariseeism to war against another man's evil and not our own. A selective war against evil is itself evil and phariseeism. True and total war against evil begins, for the redeemed man, who alone can wage it, with the full application of God's law. What we have here, thus, is not pacifism but the requirement of holy war, beginning with the application of God's law to all of society, first of all to our hearts and minds, and then the steady conquest through God's ordained ways.

There is much more to these verses, but the beginning of their understanding is an awareness of the textual and historical contexts.

In the history of the church, however, these verses and others have been read in a non-Biblical context, in the context of platonic thought.

Their impact in this sense is clearly seen in our time. To illustrate, one of the most influential of all 19th century British preachers was a man, married to the daughter of a notable man, whose wife was no better than a whore. Night after night, he searched for her in the streets, where she picked up men voraciously, and having found her, tenderly took her home, cleaned her up, and put her to bed. For this, he was widely regarded as eminently Christian and saintly. When I was younger, and before psychiatric ideas made such behavior less saintly, this preacher and his treatment of his whorish wife made for choice sermonic illustrations for evangelicals, Calvinists, and modernists. He was seen as an example of true love.

Such antinomianism rests, not only on a contempt for God's law, but on platonism and neoplatonism. This British churchman was a student of Plato, and his modern admirers are equally platonic in their ideas, if more ignorant of their sources.

What is the source of such an abomination? Why did it never occur to the British churchman or to his admirers that the whorish wife deserved to die, and that she should have been cast out? Why this surrender to evil? Matthew 5:39ff. deals with compulsory service by a conqueror; the modern intrepretation means the surrender by rulers to the ruled and to evil, a faith basic to modern politics.

The roots of this perspective are deep in neoplatonism and also in various other non-Christian beliefs. In their modern form, they are summed up in the doctrine of Kenosis, an ugly blight in church history. The Kenosis doctrine, in its more radical forms, holds that God the Son emptied Himself of His divinity in order to become man, or functioned in virtual abdication of His deity for the duration of His earthly stay. This is followed by the belief that the true Christian likewise empties himself of power and authority to emulate the Kenotic Christ in a pacifistic role towards all men. This doctrine, with respect to Christ, has a defective view of the incarnation; somehow God is not fully God in the union, and man also is an emptied man, devoid of the dominion aspect of his image. The doctrine of Kenosis has been strongest in Russian Orthodox and Lutheran circles, but it has spread far and wide throughout Christendom. This idea seeks its Biblical validation chiefly in Phillipians 2:6-8, which speaks of Christ's incarnation. Very early, the Gnostics made use of this text for their purposes, as did the Docetists. However, what Paul says in Phillipians 2:6-8 is simply that God the Son left the glory of heaven for the burden of His calling in a literal incarnation. When our Lord speaks of Himself and His followers becoming servants one to another, He does not call for a divestiture of all power but the use of power and authority responsibly and for the service of His Kingdom rather than self glorification. Kenotic theory and spirituality places a radically alien view on these texts. It calls for a flight from power, authority, and the world, rather than their godly use. Kenotic theory and spirituality are radically antinomian and implicitly ascetic.

As a result, we have the widespread idea that we are to allow evil to prevail. A godly husband or a godly wife is required by the Kenotics to submit to every evil and degradation as though such submission were sanctification. But sanctification or holiness (for the two words are the same) is growth in righteousness or justice, in the application of and faithfulness to God's law. God's law does not ask us ever to live with adultery, and serve it, as an act of holiness. It is blasphemy to hold so. It regards condoning rebellion and lawlessness as itself a form of rebellion and lawlessness against God. The British churchman was more evil than his wife; she had one goal: to satisfy her lust. Her husband was equally lawless, but, what was worse, he called it holiness. Kenosis is in some respects at the opposite end of the spectrum from phariseeism, but, at heart, it is the same doctrine, in that it substitutes man's way for God's way, and man-made laws for God's law, and, in both cases, the end product is called the way of holiness. Our Lord declares, however,

> Whosoever therefore shall break one of these least commandments, and shall teach men so, he shall be called the least in the kingdom of heaven: but whosoever shall do and teach them, the same shall be called great in the kingdom of heaven.
> For I say unto you, That except your righteousness shall exceed the righteousness of the scribes and Pharisees, ye shall in no case enter into the kingdom of heaven. (Matt. 5:19-20)

These words are addressed to all who teach. Any and all who "break" or "relax" (RSV) the slightest commandment of God "shall be called the least in the kingdom of heaven." Because man is a sinner, he searches the Scriptures for loopholes when he reads it; hence, every verse which can be interpreted to set aside the law is exploited to that end. Consider, for example, I Corinthians 7:18-19:

> Is any man called being circumcised? let him not become uncircumcised. Is any called in uncircumcision? let him not become circumcised. Circumcision is nothing, and uncircumcision is nothing, but the keeping of the commandments of God.

In the context, Paul is speaking against breaking up marriages when one partner becomes converted, and the other remains in unbelief. Only if the unbeliever breaks up the marriage is it properly ended, no other violations of God's law being present. In verse 20, Paul is to the point: "Let every man abide in the same calling wherein he was called." Paul is not condemning *circumcision;* he uses the term to denote the Jewish believer, and *uncircumcision,* the Gentile believer. Neither is asked to divest himself of his heritage. The Gentile cannot be asked to become a

Jew before becoming a Christian, and the Jew cannot be told to divest himself of his heritage. Both stand before God in Christ and in Christ alone, not in Jewishness nor in Gentileness, *i.e.,* in circumcision or in uncircumcision. Both are nothing before God; their standing is in Christ, and then their holiness is in "the keeping of the commandments of God" in Christ. Thus, Scripture cannot be used to undermine Scripture.

Hence, those who relax God's law are least in His Kingdom, and if, in the process, their faith is the self-righteousness and humanism of the Pharisees, then they shall not enter into God's Kingdom. The Pharisees turned the law into a means of justification. In the Mishnah, *Aboth* 3:16, a man's salvation and stature in the world to come is said to be determined by the balance of good deeds in his ledger: "The store is open and the storekeeper allows credit, but the ledger is open and the hand writes."[1] Although set in the context of legalism, *Aboth* 2:1 is better counsel when it declares, "And be thou careful with a light precept as with a grave one."[2]

Thus Phariseeism, like Kenosis, undercuts and denies God's righteousness in favor of a man-made righteousness. It is against resisting evil in God's appointed way, the way of faith in Christ and obedience to God's law, because it is in resistance to the Lord, not to evil.

St. Paul gives us one aspect of the meaning of our Lord's words, "Resist not evil," in his commentary thereon in Romans 12:17-21:

> Recompense to no man evil for evil. Provide things honest in the sight of all men.
> If it be possible, as much as lieth in you, live peaceably with all men.
> Dearly beloved, avenge not yourselves, but rather give place unto wrath: for it is written, Vengeance is mine; I will repay, saith the Lord.
> Therefore if thine enemy hunger, feed him; if he thirst, give him drink: for in so doing thou shalt heap coals of fire on his head.
> Be not overcome of evil, but overcome evil with good.

God's declaration of sovereignty is affirmed by these words, something the pacifist, Kenotic, and pharisaic interpretations deny. *First,* God reserves vengeance against evil to Himself and to those God-ordained agencies of justice appointed in His word. We do not deny justice; we affirm God's sovereignty by making His appointed instruments fully faithful and effective.

*Second,* we can only overcome evil in God's appointed way, with good. To return evil for evil is forbidden: it is an attack on God's sovereignty. It means saying that evil is more powerful and effective than God and His law.

*Third,* to return good for evil means, socially, to enforce God's justice

---

1. *Aboth* 3:16, in *The Babylonian Talmud,* Seder Nezikin, IV, p. 39.
2. *Ibid.,* IV, 11.

in and through the courts, and, personally, to be honest in all relationships to men, to manifest grace and charity towards our enemies, and to live as peaceably as is possible.

This is not Kenosis. It is the righteousness of God manifested in our lives. Faith means the application of our knowledge of and reliance on God and His word. It is righteousness in action, God's power and word manifested in and through us. Kenosis regards holiness as a surrender to evil, as pacifism, inaction, and withdrawal, and faith is seen as a mere assent to concepts. It is not a theology of incarnation. As the Word of God, God the Son, became flesh, so His law-word for us must become flesh in our lives. We must become God's ambassadors, workers, priests, prophets, and kings on earth, manifesting, incarnating, and setting forth God's sovereign purpose, His creation mandate, His law, and His calling, in all our being. This is holiness.

## 137

## COVENANT AND LAW

One of the more remarkable yet unappreciated texts of Scripture is II Samuel 5:1-3:

> Then came all the tribes of Israel to David unto Hebron, and spake, saying, Behold, we are thy bone and thy flesh.
> Also in time past, when Saul was king over us, thou wast he that leddest out and broughtest in Israel: and the LORD said to thee, Thou shalt feed my people Israel, and thou shalt be a captain over Israel.
> So all the elders of Israel came to the king to Hebron; and king David made a league with them in Hebron before the LORD; and they anointed David king over Israel.

The civil war was over, and the nation was united under David *by covenant.* A "league" was made "before the LORD." The word *league* is here in Hebrew *berith,* an eating, covenant, or league. We are reminded of the Last Supper, and Christ's institution of the renewed covenant, where He declares that the elements are His body and blood (Matt. 26:26-28). The elders of Israel declare themselves to be the body of David because of the Lord's ordination; the church is declared to be the body of Christ (Col. 1:18).

But this is not our first encounter with this language. In Genesis 2:23, we read that Adam declares Eve to be "bone of my bone, and flesh of my flesh." She is this, because she was created out of him and in the image of God as reflected in Adam (I Cor. 11:7-8). They are one humanity, created in terms of God's calling to Adam to subdue the earth and to exercise dominion over it (Gen. 1:26-28). Headship belongs to man, and therefore the woman is created in terms of man, *i.e.,* in terms of man's purpose and calling under God (I Cor. 11:9-12).

But this is not all. The unity of Adam and Eve is the unity of all men in Adam, and the headship of Adam is his headship over all men born of Adam (I Cor. 15:21-23, 47-50). In the Fall, Adam surrendered the active exercise of this headship to Eve, whose direction and leadership he followed, and she to the tempter (Gen. 3:1-6). The tempter and his apostate principle that every man is his own god, knowing or determining good and evil for himself, thus came to dominate humanity. Man is a unity in the fall, but because mankind is now in its heart given over to a false principle, its unity is only in sin, and its every attempt to unify results in murder, coercion, and confusion (Gen. 4:19-24, 6:1-5; 11:1-9).

God therefore ordained the coming of a new principle of unity for the new humanity (Gen. 3:15). A new seed would be the victory of man and the beginning of a new humanity (I Cor. 15:21-22, 45-49). In between, as a part of His league or covenant of redemption, God gave to men anointed leaders who were the forerunners of the new Adam, and who were to rule the covenant people in terms of covenant law.

The plain assumption of Scripture denies the modern doctrine of man's radical individualism and autonomy. Man is not autonomous. He has no autonomy from God, and no autonomy from man. He is at all times a member of a body of humanity, either the old and fallen humanity at war with God, or the new humanity created in Jesus Christ and at peace with God through His atonement.

The myth of autonomy denies this unity of man in either Adam or in Christ which Scripture plainly sets forth. Moreover, history and experience make clear that man is inseparably bound to his fellow men and responds to impulses, emotions, and mass hysterias as a part of his invisible unity.

Man, however, rejects this *inescapable* unity, which is of God's creation, and seeks to replace it by a humanistic unity of man's creation. Various forms of man-made unity have been attempted. Notable in the 20th century are two attempts, *by blood and by law.* National Socialist Germany attempted, as have others, to create a natural unity in terms of a fragment of humanity and in terms of race. Whereas the unity in Adam is in apostasy, sin, and death, National Socialism sought to ground their idea of unity in a racially governed state. On the other hand, others have attempted to create unity by fiat law, by the establishment of a humanistic state grounded on man-made laws. Both concepts of unity are arbitrary and fallacious.

In Jesus Christ, the new humanity is inclusive of all the redeemed "out of every kindred, and tongue, and people, and nation" (Rev. 5:9). The unity of the new humanity is through the atoning blood of Jesus Christ, and the new humanity is under the law of God (Rev. 5:9; Luke 16:17).

The elders of Israel thus acknowledged the necessity of becoming one body in and under David as a part of being one body in covenant before the Lord. Authority was in terms of the covenant and its law. They were "a kingdom of priests" (Ex. 19:6), but priests function, not autonomously, but in terms of the Lord and His ordained authorities and laws. As a result, the confirmation of David's kingship was by a covenant, a covenant meal, and a covenant affirmation of being one body in his headship. This covenant did not exalt David to a divine statue; rather, it placed David and the people alike under God's authority and covenant law. God's judgment would now govern both. The covenant declared God to be the Lord over David and the people, the witness to the covenant, its lord and judge, and the only law-giver thereof. Laban had said at Mizpah to Jacob, "The LORD watch between me and thee, when we are absent one from another" (Gen. 31:49). Laban and Jacob would not see each other again, but God would provide the unifying government and judgment.

The essence of the principle of the Fall, Genesis 3:5, is, legally, that man, as his own god, is also his own autonomous law. Thus, any social order which does not begin and end with the covenant of God and God's law will be always destined to run into anarchy. Its basic principle will manifest itself, and the result will be social decay and collapse.

The premise of God's regeneration and the creation of a covenant people in Christ is that man is not his own creature, but the Lord's (I Cor. 6:20; 7:23). The law of his life, society, family, church, state, school, and calling must therefore be the law of the Lord. Covenant man can have no autonomous or fiat law: he is under God in Christ, in covenant to Him, and hence under God's law.

Because covenant man is a man of faith, his way of life is the law of the Lord. He relies on God's every word and places his whole being on the truth and power of that word. For covenant man, his own law-word is anathema; the horror and grief in his life are results of his own word and way, and hence the direction of his life is to bring himself more and more into obedience and conformity to the word, law, and rule of God. It is the word of power.

Our Lord declares, "If any man will come after me, let him deny himself, and take up his cross and follow me" (Matt. 16:24). To follow Jesus Christ means that we deny, reject, and repudiate ourselves as gods, as the source of the governing law-word (Gen. 3:5); this man does by the grace of God unto salvation. His faith comes by hearing the word of God (Rom. 10:17), and faith means relying on and obeying that word with all our being. To hear and believe God's word means to deny and repudiate our own word. Because we are not perfectly sanctified in this life, this means crucifying our way, law, and word, daily sentencing to death our word in favor of God's word.

Covenant man is the man of faith. To be in the covenant means to be in a relationship of grace and law with the triune God through Jesus Christ. If there is no faith, there is no covenant. Thus, every attempt to give the covenant some validity in the Kingdom of God apart from faith is illegitimate and unsound. However, the blessings of the covenant can accrue or fall upon those who are unbelieving, as with an unbelieving spouse (I Cor. 7:14). Their relationship to the godly gives them a position of privilege, not because they are of the covenant, but because they stand within the community of privilege. The fall-out of blessings all such receive gives them no place or status of membership in the covenant. Paul makes clear that the friendly and unbelieving spouse of a Christian is separated by virtue of his or her marriage, but this does not make them members of the covenant nor of the church.

## 138

## GOD'S SON, ISRAEL: THE TYPOLOGY

St. Matthew tells us, of the visit of the wise men to the Christ child,

> And when they were departed, behold, the angel of the LORD appeareth to Joseph in a dream, saying, Arise, and take the young child and his mother, and flee into Egypt, and be thou there until I bring thee word: for Herod will seek the young child to destroy him.
> When he arose, he took the young child and his mother by night and departed into Egypt:
> And was there until the death of Herod: that it might be fulfilled which was spoken of the Lord by the prophet, saying, Out of Egypt have I called my son. (Matt. 2:13-15)

The quotation in verse 15 is from Hosea 11:1, "When Israel was a child, then I loved him, and called my son out of Egypt." What we have here is *typology;* typology is much more than symbolism. In symbolism, we have a representation, an emblem standing for something else. Thus the owl of Minerva is symbolic of wisdom; this does not mean that an owl is itself wise, but merely that it is suggestive of wisdom and is used to symbolize or represent wisdom. There is a great deal of symbolism in the Bible, but it is not to be confused with typology, which is God's predestined and developing pattern in history. To reduce typology to symbolism is to reduce much of Scripture to neoplatonism, and to convert reality into symbols. In typology, all the factors are real and historical; they represent necessary stages in the unfolding of God's revelation and His plan in history. To reduce certain stages of typology to mere symbols is to destroy the meaning of God's revelation and to convert it from history to neoplatonic emblems, to shadows on the wall of Plato's cave.

Thus, *first,* as we examine the typology of Christ as Israel, we must recognize the totally valid and historical meaning of Hosea 11:1. Its meaning is that God adopted Israel when Israel was a child. Moreover, at the time of its adoption, which was an act of sovereign grace, Israel was in bondage, in slavery to Egypt. God's election of Israel as His chosen people, His Son, was an act of grace. This grace was manifested in love and instruction, in law and protection, but Israel proved itself a prodigal and wayward son. The whole of the Old Testament is God's record of His grace, mercy, and judgment to His chosen people, Israel. We cannot under-rate the importance of Israel's election as God's son by adoption. Israel was much more than a symbol or emblem of the Son to come:

Israel was God's son by adoption.

*Second,* Jesus Christ came as the natural Son of God, supernatural in birth as very God of very God and very man of very man. Like Israel of old, He too went into Egypt for a time, to be protected, but without bondage. His bondage was the burden of being the new Adam, called to redeem His people from the world-wide Egypt of sin, of the fall. God called His adopted son Israel out of Egypt, but Israel carried Egypt with it into the promised land (Ezek. 20:6-9). Israel was incapable of overcoming the consequences of the fall; sin and death marked its life emphatically. Jesus Christ, as the sinless Son and the new Adam (I Cor. 15:45-47), destroyed the power of sin and death. The adoption of old Israel was spectacular: Egypt was confounded and shattered in a series of plagues of miraculous character. The birth of Jesus Christ, the natural Israel of God, was miraculous also, the ultimate and unique miracle of the incarnation.

The *third* phase of this typology is our own adoption into Christ as sons of God. St. Paul declares, in Galations 4:4-7,

> But when the fulness of the time was come, God sent forth his Son, made of a woman, made under the law,
> To redeem them that were under the law, that we might receive the adoption of sons.
> And because ye are sons, God hath sent forth the Spirit of his Son into your hearts, crying, Abba, Father.
> Wherefore thou art no more a servant, but a son; and if a son, then an heir of God through Christ.

Old Israel was heir to the promised land, Canaan. Jesus Christ is "appointed heir of all things, by whom also he (God) made the worlds" (Heb. 1:2). The New Israel, the elect people in Christ, is also an heir, but the heirship, being in Christ, is to "all things," and it is attended by the atonement (Heb. 1:2). Old Israel's atonement, while real, was subordinate to Christ and a type of His work. New Israel's atonement rests on the accomplished work of Christ, who "when he had himself purged our sins, sat down on the right hand of the Majesty on high" (Heb. 1:3).

*Because* of the typology, there is a continuity between the three Sons, Old Israel as an adopted son, Christ as the natural and virgin-born Son, and New Israel as the son adopted by grace in Christ. This means a continuity of both law and grace throughout the Bible. To deny grace is to deny salvation; to deny the law is to deny heirship.

But this is precisely what the antinomians do. Thus, Cornelius R. Stam writes on the "impossibility" of obeying the Great Commission of Matthew 28:18-20. His reasons for this are that Israel has been set aside (but Israel continues in Christ and His people, who are "the Israel of God," Gal. 6:16); and that it "would bring in the fulfillment of Isaiah 2:1-3, not the forming of the Body of Christ" if the Great Commission stands (which is the point of all Scripture). Again, Stam holds that "If this were our commission it would, as we have shown, put us and our hearers under the law of Moses," to which, we must answer, we are, for our sanctification, never for our justification. We are free from the law as an indictment and a death penalty, and we deny the pharisaic use of it for supposed justification, but never its necessity for our sanctification. Baptism is apparently rejected by Stam, because, he holds, "This would take us back under a dispensation when, as we have seen, water baptism was required *for the remission of sins.* This would indeed make the cross of Christ 'of none effect.' " Apparently Stam believes the cross was "of none effect" during the years of apostolic baptizing! Moreover, baptism never remitted sins: it set forth the fact of Christ's remission of our sins, received by grace. Stam writes further,

> *"Preach the gospel...."*
>
> To ascertain the content of this gospel we may not anticipate revelation and find answer in the Acts or Paul's epistles. These were not yet written. The term "the gospel" denotes *prior reference,* therefore we must consider *the preceding context* and ask ourselves what "gospel" they *had been* preaching. When we do this the answer is simple. They had been preaching *"the gospel of the kingdom"* (Matt. 4:23; 9:35; 24:14; Mark 1:14, 15; Luke 4:43; 8:1; 9:2, 60), and our Lord was now sending them forth to preach this same gospel, for the King who had been crucified and was alive; raised from the dead to sit on the throne of David. And this is in fact what Peter preached under this commission (Acts 2:29, 30; 3:10-21). The gospel of the grace of God was not revealed until years later.
>
> We cannot preach the "gospel" of Mark 16 today, for the risen King was again rejected by His own nation and is a royal Exile. Our message, unlike theirs, is *an offer of reconciliation* to Jews and Gentiles who have been alienated from God (II Cor. 5:13-21).[1]

This is a denial of typology; Christ and the New Israel of God are reduced to pale ghosts of the Old Israel, whose fulfilment alone provides the goal of history. Moreover, Stam demands a radical break in history and a new revelation during the apostolic age, the most staggering of all breaks. Yet nowhere are we told that this great and dramatic change has taken place. Such a change should be the most obvious fact of Scripture, whereas it only appears in Scofield's ungodly notes. Finally, Stam has no sovereign God, only a defeated Christ, and it is not surprising that this school of antinomian heresy and blasphemy emphatically denies the Lordship of Christ, whom Scripture declares emphatically is Lord (Rom. 10:9; I Cor. 12:3; Rev. 19:17; etc.).

---

1. Cornelius R. Stam, "The Impossibility of Obeying the So-called 'Great Commission' Today," in *The Berean Searchlight,* vol. XXVV, no. 9, December, 1974, pp. 262f.. 265, 266f.

The coming of the King does not end in the defeat and the retreat of the King. Israel's rejection of Christ was not, Stam to the contrary, the "Exile" of the King, but the destruction and *exile* of the Old Israel.

When God declares, "Out of Egypt have I called my son" (Matt. 2:15), He declares that Christ, as the Greater Moses, shall lead His people out of bondage into world conquest, so that, as heirs of all things in Christ, they shall reign with Him. The birth of our Lord is thus a joyful word of victory; it declares the ordained continuity of grace and law, and of God's Israel by adoption. We who were strangers are grafted into the chosen tree, and some of the old branches are broken off (Rom. 11:17), so that God's continuity and purpose be upheld.

Having been called out of Egypt in Christ, to remain in Egypt means to deny Christ and to be no member of the adoption of grace.

## 139

## THE MAGNIFICAT

With good reason, one of the favored passages of Scripture for centuries has been Luke 1:46-55, the Virgin Mary's Magnificat. It is an eschatological declaration: it declares that the birth of the Messiah is the sign of victory. The King, God incarnate, comes to claim His Kingdom, to dethrone all His enemies, reverse all the priorities of men to establish in their stead His priorities and will, and to rule in strength, mercy, and grace. Mary put together the various promises of the Old Testament in a joyful hymn of triumph.

The Magnificat shows an intensive study on the part of the Virgin Mary of the whole of the Old Testament, and an imaginative and perceptive fusion of its prophecies into a faithful and unified summary. Mary, very obviously, had, after the annunciation, spent some time in re-studying all of the Old Testament as it related to her and the miraculous conception of the Christ child. She echoes the Song of Hannah (I Sam. 2:1), the Psalms, Malachi (3:12), Genesis (17:7), the whole spirit of the Torah, Isaiah, and much more.

However, she sees the meaning of these prophecies, not in terms of herself, or in terms of her Son as such, but in terms of the world and its history: a mighty reversal of all things is marked by the birth of her Son. She sees the whole of Christ's future accomplishment, the finished historical work, in a joyful summing up of its implications.

Moreover, not for a moment is she thinking in her song about heaven, or the new creation *after* the Last Judgment. Her attention is entirely focused on history, on what shall happen before the end of history because her child is born. It is not that she doubted the reality of heaven, but heaven was already heaven, whereas the world, created to be God's paradise for man, was now a wilderness of sin. It was in this wilderness of sin that the Messiah was to work, making it once again into God's paradise of righteousness and obedience.

God would accomplish this through his incarnate Son. *First,* "his mercy is on them that fear him from generation to generation" (Luke 1:50). Some of the verses Mary here echoes are the following:

> And I will establish my covenant between me and thee and thy seed after thee in their generations, for an everlasting covenant, to be a God unto thee and to thy seed after thee. (Gen. 17:7)

> And showing mercy unto thousands of them that love me, and keep
> my commandments. (Ex. 20:6)

> But the mercy of the LORD is from everlasting to everlasting upon
> them that fear him, and his righteousness unto children's children;
> To such as keep his covenant, and to those that remember his com-
> mandments to do them. (Ps. 103:17, 18)

God, in terms of His covenant mercy and promises, brings forth His
salvation in the person of His Son, born to redeem man from the consequences of the Fall, from the power of sin and death. The emphatic emphasis of the covenant is on God's grace and mercy. In contrasting His
judgment with His mercy, God declares, in the Ten Commandments,

> Thou shalt not bow down thyself unto them, nor serve them: for I
> the LORD thy God am a jealous God, visiting the iniquity of the
> fathers upon the children unto the third and fourth generation of
> them that hate me,
> And shewing mercy unto thousands of them that love me and keep
> my commandments. (Deut. 5:9-10)

According to Rawlinson, "thousands" should be rendered *"to the
thousandth generation,* as is distinctly expressed in Deuteronomy 7:9.
God's mercy infinitely transcends His righteous anger. Sin is visited on
three, or at most four generations. Righteousness is remembered, and
advantages descendants, for ever."[1] Deuteronomy 7:9-11 makes this emphatically clear:

> Know therefore that the LORD thy God, he is God, the faithful
> God, which keepeth covenant and mercy with them that love him
> and keep his commandments to a thousand generations,
> And repayeth them that hate him to their face, to destroy them: he
> will not be slack to him that hateth him, he will repay him to his face.
> Thou shalt therefore keep the commandments, and the statutes, and
> the judgments, which I command thee this day, to do them.

The election of grace is here set forth, God's faithfulness to His covenant
people despite their sins, and His promptness as well in punishing all
violations of His covenant by covenant-breakers. Loving God is keeping
His commandments; breaking God's law means to hate God. This emphatic stress on God's electing grace marks the Magnificat from start to
finish.

*Second,* Mary begins the Magnificat by praising God for His electing
grace with reference to herself: "My soul doth magnify the Lord, And
my spirit hath rejoiced in God my Saviour" (Luke 1:46-47). God has
"regarded the low estate of his handmaiden" (Luke 1:48). Like Joseph,
Mary was of the House of David, the royal line, now sunk very low and
of no consequence in the life of the nation. Its last ruler was many centuries in the past, and its status even then was indeed a "low estate."

---

1. George Rawlinson, "Exodus," in Ellicott, I, 261.

However, "behold, from henceforth all generations shall call me blessed" (Luke 1:48). Mary had just been called "blessed" by Elizabeth, her cousin (Luke 1:36, 42) so that, in predicting that *all* generations would call her blessed, Mary was beginning with a present fact, one which came from the Holy Ghost speaking through Elizabeth (Luke 1:41).

*Third,* while the premise of this blessedness is the fact that the Messiah was to be born through Mary, she does no more than cite it as the starting-point and foundation of a world-wide change. "For he that is mighty hath done to me great things; and holy is his name" (Luke 1:49). She was blessed indeed, and to be called such, but we cannot isolate the blessing to Mary: Mary declares that *all* generations will call her blessed because *all* generations shall know the grace and mercy of God through her Son. Thus, Mary, in her own life, experiences the supreme act of electing grace, and she recognizes that, because she has been blessed, the whole world is to be redeemed and blessed through her son. All those who experience that grace will call her blessed.

*Fourth,* the consequences of the blessing of Mary are the over-turning of all things by her Son, in fulfilment of Ezekiel 21:27, "I will overturn, overturn, overturn it: and it shall be no more, until he come whose right it is; and I will give it him." The world of politics, social orders, and the realms of thought ("the imagination of their hearts"), will all be included in this radical overturning:

> He hath shewed strength with his arm; he hath scattered the proud in the imagination of their hearts.
> He hath put down the mighty from their seats, and exalted them of low degree.
> He hath filled the hungry with good things; and the rich he hath sent empty away.
> He hath holpen his servant Israel, in remembrance of his mercy;
> As he spake to our fathers, to Abraham, and to his seed for ever.
> (Luke 1:51-55)

The blessed Virgin Mary clearly echoed Hannah's prayer on the birth of Samuel. Hannah saw her deliverance from the contempt of Peninnah and from barrenness as one aspect of a world-wide salvation and restoration planned by God. A comparison of the Son of Hannah with the Magnificat makes clear that Mary saw the meaning of her pregnancy in terms of Hannah's prophecy:

> And Hannah prayed, and said, My heart rejoiceth in the LORD, mine horn is exalted in the LORD: my mouth is enlarged over mine enemies; because I rejoice in thy salvation.
> There is none holy as the LORD: for there is none beside thee: neither is there any rock like our God.
> Talk no more so exceeding proudly; let not arrogancy come out of your mouth: for the LORD is a God of knowledge, and by him actions are weighed.

The bows of the mighty men are broken, and they that stumble are girded with strength.

They that were full have hired out themselves for bread; and they that were hungry ceased: so that the barren hath born seven; and she that hath many children is waxed feeble.

The LORD killeth, and maketh alive: he bringeth down to the grave, and bringeth up.

The LORD maketh poor, and maketh rich: he bringeth low, and lifteth up.

He raiseth up the poor out of the dust, and lifteth up the beggar from the dunghill, to set them among princes, and to make them inherit the throne of glory: for the pillars of the earth are the LORD'S, and he hath set the world upon them.

He will keep the feet of his saints, and the wicked shall be silent in darkness; for by strength shall no man prevail.

The adversaries of the LORD shall be broken to pieces; out of heaven shall he thunder upon them: the LORD shall judge the ends of the earth; and he shall give strength unto his king, and exalt the horn of his anointed. (I Sam. 2:1-10)

In the birth of her child, given to God before birth to be a Nazirite from birth, Hannah saw a type of the birth of the Messiah, and the great overturning to be inaugurated by Him. She predicts total victory: "The adversaries of the LORD shall be broken to pieces," and Mary sang of the glorious beginning of this world-wide victory in her womb.

A medieval poem, found only in a single manuscript, heralds this same victory. Mankind, or Adam, lay bound in the chains of sin and death for four thousand years, but the end result of Eve's sin is the glorious birth of an everlasting freedom and glory in Christ, born of Mary. Hence, the Fall made possible the glory of our salvation, enabling us to stand by grace, and not of ourselves or our works:

> Adam lay i-bounden
> > bounden in a bond.
> Four thousand winters
> > thought he not too long;
> And all was for an apple
> > an apple that he took
> As clerks finden written
> > in their book.
> Ne had the apple taken been,
> > the apple taken been
> Ne had never our lady
> > a been heaven's queen.
> Blessed be the time
> > that apple taken was!
> Therefore we may singen
> > Deo Gracias.[2]

---

2. Frances M. M. Comper, ed.: *Spiritual Songs, From English Mss. of Fourteenth to Sixteenth Centuries,* p. 3. London: Society for Promoting Christian Knowledge, (1936). *Ne* expresses negation—neither, nor.

All who share in that victory must indeed call the Virgin Mary "blessed," because she witnesses, *first,* to the greatness of electing grace in her own person, and *second,* because through her came He who is accomplishing the mighty reversal of all things, and God's work of restoration.

To have a part in the life of the Son is to have a part in the work of restoration.

## 140

## PENTECOST

The harvest feast or festival of Israel, described in Leviticus 23:15-22, is known in the Bible, and in ancient Israel, by several names. In Exodus 23:16 and Numbers 28:26, it is called the feast of *harvest,* the feast of *first-fruits,* and also the *day of first-fruits.* Since it fell, according to the unanimous testimony of Hebrew sources, fifty days after the giving of the law on Mt. Sinai, it was also called the feast of Pentecost, its most common name in the New Testament era.

Because the feast was also a thanksgiving, the two loaves for the offering *had* to be leavened (Lev.23:17). The offering of atonement, representing God's gift and sacrifice, had to be unblemished and incorruptible. Man's response to God is his service, which passes away. The buildings we build to God's glory and the work we do, while never in vain, are not eternal, and hence they must be typified by leaven, a symbol of that which is temporal and corruptible. All thank-offerings of loaves had to be leavened.

There was thus a sequential character to Pentecost. It observed by its name the passing of time from the giving of the law. The giving of the law, and obedience thereto, in terms of Deuteronomy 28, meant a harvest of blessings as the result. For Christians, the Day of Pentecost was indeed the feast of the first-fruits of the church, and a witness to the necessity of recognizing that the church lives in the time of harvest. The Great Commission of the church thus is a *harvest* commission:

> All power is given unto me in heaven and in earth.
> Go ye therefore and teach all nations, baptizing them in the name of the Father, and of the Son, and of the Holy Ghost:
> Teaching them to observe all things whatsoever I have commanded you: and, lo, I am with you alway, even unto the end of the world. Amen (Matt. 28:18-20)

*Because* the earth is the Lord's, and the harvest thereof, He, having all power, commands that we reap His harvest. Christ, as the perfect lawgiver, commands the people of grace to obey "all things whatsoever I have commanded you" as the means to this harvest of victory.

Deuteronomy 28 makes clear God's curse on disobedience and his blessing on obedience. Disobedience is sin and unbelief, and obedience is faith and righteousness in action. The curse of the fall had as its outcome

Babel, and the confusion of tongues, the dispersing of mankind, and the loss of communication. As has been so often pointed out, Pentecost was the reversal of the curse of Babel. It meant that the people of the Great Commission, the harvest commission, had an assured victory in terms of faith and obedience. Christ, having all power in heaven and in earth, would prosper His election of grace in terms of their faithful obedience to Him.

The harvest festival has implicit in it an eschatology of victory. It is the clear implication that, when the people of grace seek a harvest in terms of God's law-word, they are given a great out-pouring of blessings.

The feast of the first-fruits looked back, in terms of its nature, to the day of redemption and the giving of the law. As the harvest festival, it looked ahead to the great and final ingathering.

The repeated use of the term "first-fruits" in the New Testament (Rom. 8:23; 11:16; I Cor. 15:20, 23) has reference largely to this feast.

This harvest festival was also a time of thanksgiving to the Lord as the source of rain and agricultural fertility. Failure to recognize this fact is cited as a sin by Jeremiah 5:24:

> Neither say they in their heart, Let us now fear the LORD our God, that giveth rain, both the former and the latter, in his season: he reserveth unto us the appointed weeks of the harvest.

The recognition by Israel of the typical meaning of the harvest festival is apparent in the psalms of victory which were sung, and in the celebrations at its conclusion. According to Rylaarsdam,

> All males attending the ceremonies assisted by dancing an "altar dance," during which they sang the Hallel (Ps. 113-118). The feast was brought to a conclusion by the eating of communal meals to which the poor, the stranger, and the Levite were invited. Thus a basically agricultural rite honored the God of Israel and also recognized the fraternal bond of responsibility uniting the community bound by his covenant.[1]

The feast of weeks or harvest marked the wheat harvest, and *the feast of tabernacles* or booths, or *the feast of ingathering* (Lev. 23:33-43), marked the completion of the harvest of fruit, oil, and wine. It celebrated the pilgrimage in the desert and God's provision during their wilderness journey; it celebrated also the stranger and pilgrim spirit of God's people, and it anticipated the great ingathering in the general resurrection at the end of the world, of which Christ's resurrection was the first-fruit (I Cor. 15:20).

The one harvest feast points to the other. Their eschatological framework is the confidence that all nations shall indeed proclaim Christ as King, and every knee shall bow to Him.

---

1. J. D. Rylaarsdam, "Weeks, Feast of," in *The Interpreter's Dictionary of the Bible,* R-Z, p. 828. New York: Abingdon, 1962.

The essence of *thanksgiving* in any era must be the same confidence in Christ's victory. Instead of a gratitude for a successful retreat from the enemy, it must be a joyful celebration of the certainty of victory.

It is noteworthy that, when thanksgiving was first celebrated in America, the Biblical pattern was observed, and the Indians, as the strangers near them, were invited to the feast. All men are summoned to the restoration. Those who will not come choose judgment.

## 141

## DISCRETIONARY POWER?

Faith means, as we have seen, more than mere belief: it means relying on the every word of God. It means placing our entire life under the authority of God and His word.

Paul, in Romans 1:17-32, speaks of God's judgment on those who, while knowing God and His law, *as all men do,* live instead by their own word. Paul singles out the homosexual and the lesbian as examples of the radical insistence of man on his own word and law. They are representative of ultimate apostasy. For God's law and God's order, they substitute their own. The result is radical *disorder* in the sexual sphere, in the family sphere, and in the general social sphere, a revolt against all God-given authority and against all God-ordained human ties (Rom. 1:28-31). The judgment of God upon all such is death (Rom. 1:32).

Then Paul continues, citing all men and setting forth their depravity in Adam (Rom. 2:1-3; 3:1). There is "none righteous, no, not one" (Rom. 3:10). *None,* no man, in himself is righteous or just. No man has in and of himself anything in him to commend him to God; no man can dare to instruct or correct God, because all men are, apart from the grace of God unto salvation, fallen and corrupt. They stand only *by* the grace of God, and they can only stand in terms of the whole word of God. What does this mean, says Paul? It means this: "Do we then make void the law through faith? God forbid: yea, we establish the law" (Rom. 3:31).

To grasp what Paul is saying, it is important to see that, in Romans 2, he is clearly denouncing the faith of old Israel and defining the true Jew as one who is such from the heart, whose faith is not merely a formal assent but the *works* which the faith and the law require (Rom. 2:13, 29). Phariseeism by and large was respectful of God's word, as much and often more so than the church today. The Talmud is evidence of this; the law of God was to govern man's total life. In practice, however, Phariseeism undercut this principle. In effect, it said what many modern churchmen say, namely, that· many current problems are unique and unforeseen by God. As a result, discretionary powers are needed in applying God's law. Restitution may not always be necessary, and God's requirement for the death penalty need not always apply. God, after all, did not apply the death penalty against Cain for murder, against David for murder and adultery, and against the woman taken in adultery.

God's "exceptions" to His own laws, whether in the natural realm as miracles, or in the moral realm as *sovereign grace,* constitute, in either case, exercises of sovereignty. Man is nowhere given such a sovereign power to amend or make an exception to God's law. It is a power which belongs to God alone.

Today, however, this claim to *discretionary power* over the law is claimed by the civil courts, the church courts, and all men. Such men will declare, "I uphold the law," but they deny it when they claim discretionary powers. Such a power is not in man: it is in implication and explication a claim to sovereignty over God. It is a declaration that a higher justice comes from man and his discretionary power. Paul declares, however, that there is *none* just, no, not one. The discretionary power is not in man. Paul in Romans 2 indicts all such false teachers of the law, who can confidently disobey the law, because, by means of their claim to discretionary power, they have placed themselves *above the law.*

When I was a seminary student, a class sermon I gave cited the case of a man named Morgan, convicted of murder in Puritan New England. The judge called upon the clergy to witness to and instruct in the word of God the condemned man. The result was his conversion. At the place of execution, he gave an eloquent witness, expressed his gratitude, and was hung. The class was outraged: the man should have been forgiven! The man indeed had theological forgiveness, but God's law *required* his death all the same.

To set aside the death penalty where God requires it will give us exactly what we have today, a lawless society. *The exercise of discretionary power means the collapse of law. It means God's law and judgment are replaced by man's law and judgment.*

In Judea, at the time of our Lord's birth, the requirements of God's law had been made inoperative both by the people, their rulers and teachers, and the Roman overlords. The death penalty for adultery was thus set aside; divorce replaced it, but even then divorce was not mandatory. Joseph, however, when he learned that Mary was pregnant, "*being a just* (or, righteous) man" decided to divorce her, although it was his decision to do so as quietly as possible (Matt. 1:19). It should be noted that Joseph is described as being a just man *because* he was determined that ostensible adultery be judged. Commentators and translators too often attempt to equate Joseph's justice with his desire to avoid publicity! Calvin's comment is closer to the truth:

> Some commentators explain this to mean, that Joseph, *because* he was a just man, determined to spare his wife: taking *justice* to be only another name for humanity, or, a gentle and merciful disposition. But others more correctly read the two clauses as contrasted with each other: That Joseph *was a just man,* but yet he was anxious about the reputation of his wife. That justice, on which a commen-

dation is here bestowed, consisted in hatred and abhorrence of crime. Suspecting his wife of adultery, and even convinced that she was an adulterer, he was unwilling to hold out the encouragement of lenity to such a crime. And certainly he is but a pander to his wife, who connives at her unchastity. Not only is such wickedness regarded with abhorrence by good and honourable minds, but that winking at crime which I have mentioned is marked by the laws with infamy.

Joseph, therefore, moved by an ardent love of *justice,* condemned the crime of which he supposed his wife to have been guilty; while the gentleness of his disposition prevented him from going to the utmost rigour of law. It was a moderate and calmer method to depart privately, and remove to a distant place. Hence we infer, that he was not of so soft and effeminate a disposition, as to screen and promote uncleanness under the pretense of merciful dealing: he only made some abatement from stern justice, so as not to expose his wife to evil report. Nor ought we to have any hesitation in believing, that his mind was restrained by a secret inspiration of the Spirit. We know how weak jealousy is, and to what violence it hurries its possessor. Though Joseph did not proceed to rash and headlong conduct, yet he was wonderfully preserved from many imminent dangers, which would have sprung out of his resolution to depart.[1]

Thus, Calvin sees Joseph's righteousness as his desire to see God's law enforced as far as was possible; forgiving adultery was not his prerogative. Joseph's mercy Calvin sees as the restraint of the Spirit until the truth was made known to Joseph by revelation.

The disastrous fact today, however, is that discretionary power is seen by churchmen as *a higher way* than God's law. Man's wisdom is seen as more full of grace than God's law-word, a startling conclusion. The fact that verses are used from Scripture to justify discretionary power does not alter the matter. These verses deal with forgiveness. Forgiveness is theological, not humanistic. It is granted in terms of God's word, not man's. It means that charges are dropped and restoration is effected because God's law is put into force. Man's forgiveness and man's discretionary powers only compound the offense. Instead of forgiving sin, they meet sin with greater sin.

Men cannot say that they were not warned. This question of discretionary power is an age-old one. Thornwell, in the middle of the 19th century, warred against Charles Hodge because of his implicit "theory of the liberty of discretion."[2] Thornwell raised the issue on a debate on aspects of church government and wrote, with respect to his critics,

The other illusion is, that our doctrine reduces the Church to something like Jewish bondage. Dr. Hodge affirms that "it makes

---

1. John Calvin: *Commentary on a Harmony of the Evangelists, Matthew, Mark, and Luke,* vol. I., p. 94f. Grand Rapids, MI: Eerdmans, 1949.
2. *The Collected Writings of James Henley Thornwell,* IV, 255, on "Boards and Presbyterianism." Edinburgh, Scotland: The Banner of Truth Trust, 1974 (reprint).

the Gospel dispensation, designed for the whole world, more restricted and slavish than the Jewish, although it was designed for only one nation, and for a limited period.'' Other speakers in the Assembly indulged in the same idle declamation. The simple question is, What was the bondage of the Jewish dispensation? Did it consist in the subjection of the people to the Divine will? Was that their grievous and intolerable burden, that they were bound in all things to regulate their worship by the Divine Word? Is God's authority a yoke so heavy that we sigh until we can throw it off?[3]

This is the heart of the matter. Is God's law bondage, and is God's authority a yoke to be thrown off by the spiritually advanced? This is another way of asking who is the lord, God or man?

---

3. *Ibid.*, p. 253f. The debate in question took place in 1859-1860.

## 142

## "NO CONDEMNATION"

Some twenty years ago, I knew as pastor a woman, her husband and children, whose father was a church officer in a nearby community, in a "Bible-believing" church. Every Sunday afternoon and evening, after worship services, this man grieved over his sins. He had never fornicated, committed adultery, smoked, drank, cheated, bore false witness, and so on, and had been an exemplary husband and father. Every pastor he had known had only two kinds of messages, however; first, there were sermons with a John 3:16 theme, the call to be converted, and, second, those with an indictment of the faithful for their sins, and a call to repentance.

Now both are great and basic themes of Scripture. They involve the basics of the faith. But both themes, *as presented today,* are perverted grossly. Our concern here is with sin and repentance. When I was in the church pastorate, one officer regularly demanded that I preach such sermons because Jane Doe smokes, John Blank sometimes yawns through Sunday School, and so on. No man needed repentance and conversion more than the man who asked that I preach at people. (He later left the church, with some promptings.)

Again, I regularly hear of pastors preaching sermons at their congregations for a variety of highly refined reasons, often subtle or open efforts to create guilt feelings rather than godly action. The old man whose daughter I knew grieved because he could not pray five minutes without becoming bored and wordless; somehow, this made him very unspiritual. You can talk by the hour with your friends, his pastor declared, with thumps, but you can't talk ten minutes with God! The old man, with such preaching, felt permanently guilty. He never had instruction in living all day with the Lord, his mind ever open to God in sentence prayers.

All such sin and repentance preaching is pagan. This paganism runs deep in Reformed and Arminian circles, in pietism and Catholicism, in medievalism, and, finally, in ancient pagan cults. In each and every form, it adds up to one evil: *no absolution.* If you convince people that they are sinners for non-Biblical reasons, such as being bored with your preaching, or for not praying thirty minutes, an hour, or two hours daily, then you cut them off permanently from one of the most glorious facts of Scripture: *absolution.* Paul declares emphatically:

> There is therefore now no condemnation to them which are in Christ
> Jesus, who walk not after the flesh, but after the Spirit. (Rom. 8:1)

*No condemnation!* How can men dare to condemn where God does not
condemn?

Now let us probe deeper. These same men who in effect preach *no absolution* to men who are bored with their preaching, or cannot, like the
Pharisees, pray by the hour, yard, or mile (Matt. 6:5), *demand absolution* where God does not permit. Forgive, they say, forgive the thief,
adulterer, or murderer; to ask for the application of God's law is
legalism, whereas to forgive or grant absolution is a higher way.

What follows from this? God and His law are undermined, whereas
man and man's law and institution are built up and magnified. This
perverted kind of sin and repentance preaching led to a guilt-ridden
medieval man, and a powerful church. In the modern world, it creates
powerful pastors and churches, who, while claiming to believe the Bible,
exalt the lordship of the pastor and the church, not the Lord Jesus
Christ, and yet rant against "Romanism." The state uses similar guilt to
exalt itself. There is no satisfying of the state's claims over us: they are
perpetual. We can live in peace with God and His law, but there is never
any peace with man and his ever-expanding law.

But this is not all. Guilt-ridden men are impotent men. They cannot
work effectively. Christian reconstruction is *impossible* with guilt-ridden
men. The glorious declaration of absolution, *"no condemnation,"* is a
charter of freedom. Perverted sin and repentance preaching is a summons to enslavement: it is the language of slavery.

Men who are free from condemnation "walk...after the Spirit." This
means that "the righteousness of the law" is "fulfilled" or put into force
in them (Rom. 8:4). Where the righteousness or justice of the law
governs, there inescapable blessings follow. Deuteronomy 28:1-2 is very
clear on this:

> And it shall come to pass, if thou shalt hearken diligently unto the
> voice of the LORD thy God, to observe and to do all his command-
> ments which I command thee this day, that the LORD thy God will
> set thee on high above all nations of the earth:
> And all these blessings shall come on thee, and overtake thee, if thou
> shalt hearken unto the voice of the LORD thy God.

The Bible speaks of a sovereign, predestinating God, and of His
sovereign grace. It affirms that our salvation means *no condemnation.* It
declares that the obedience of faith brings irresistible blessings, so that
both our salvation and our sanctification are marked by sovereign grace
and irresistible consequences. Obviously, this irresistible blessing means
that the only tenable eschatology is an eschatology of victory, post-
millennialism.

To preach no absolution is to preach that there is no saving power of God. Man must remain hopelessly guilt-ridden and without peace. It means scolding, nagging preaching, and cowed, sullen, guilt-ridden congregations. *If there is no absolution, there is no gospel.* Then there is also no saving Lord.

*All* who are in Christ Jesus *of necessity,* because of that fact and status, will "walk not after the flesh, but after the Spirit." They will thus walk in freedom. They are *without condemnation* unless they violate the plain word of God, as declared in Scripture. Even then, although the law may require the death of their body, they stand before God on repentance, without condemnation. If they are the Lord's, they will repent.

False preaching creates sins which are unreal. Because they are unreal, there is no effectual repentance, and hence no absolution. The consequence is perpetual condemnation, without escape. False preaching is marked *by perpetual condemnation,* because it rests, not on the word of God, but on another word. Such preaching has in effect *another word,* and, in some cases, as with Savanarola, special revelation is hinted at. In any case, it is implicit in all such preaching. A new canon of church-related, church-created offenses replaces the plain law of God.

The false preachers condemned in Romans 2 added to the law their own interpretations, and they separated faith and works (Rom. 2:13). The false preachers of today more openly set forth another law: their "higher spirituality" is simply a greater disobedience.

Jesus Christ died on the cross that our sins might be forgiven: we have thus the glorious freedom of *no condemnation;* our sins are forgiven. The brigade of evil preachers rant on about sins that are beyond absolution. In effect, they damn their congregations for creatureliness. Are you bored after 45 minutes of stupid preaching? O wicked man, such boredom proves your depravity! Does your mind wander after a brief time of prayer? Such creaturely limitations are called damnable, or at least sinful! The result? No absolution! How can we ever be absolved of creatureliness, or from a natural boredom with stupidity? When God Almighty declares Himself wearied with man's wordiness (Mal. 2:17), can we expect other men to be less weary? Let us say instead to the brigades of evil preachers, No absolution, unless you repent!

## 143

## THE THEORY OF THE LIBERTY OF DISCRETION

The problem of what Thornwell called the theory of the liberty of discretion was not a new one to the faith. It was a basic part of the conflict of our Lord with the scribes and Pharisees. According to Matthew 15:1-9,

> Then came to Jesus scribes and Pharisees, which were of Jerusalem saying,
> Why do thy disciples transgress the tradition of the elders? For they wash not their hands when they eat bread.
> But he answered and said unto them, Why do ye also transgress the commandment of God by your tradition?
> For God commanded, saying, Honour thy father and mother; and He that curseth father or mother, let him die the death.
> But ye say, Whosoever shall say to his father or his mother, It is a gift, by whatsoever thou mightest be profited by me;
> And honour not his father or his mother, he shall be free. Thus have ye made the commandment of God of none effect by your tradition.
> Ye hypocrites, well did Esaias prophesy of you, saying,
> This people draweth nigh unto me with their mouth, and honoureth me with their lips: but their heart is far from me.
> But in vain they do worship me, teaching for doctrines the commandments of men.

"The tradition of the elders" sought to uphold and honor the law of God in theory. In practice, it sought to replace the canon with its more humanizing rules, to bring as it were common sense and forgiveness to the law, as well as a sense of priorities. It is especially important to note the example of this liberty of discretion chosen by our Lord. He could have cited cases of forgiveness for adultery and homosexuality, but he chose what would appear to be the most defensible case of the use of a discretionary power. More than a few devout men, eager to give more than their due to God's work, found it oppressive to support, as the law required, their parents. Let us remember that these men were not trying to increase their own share of their income; they were tying to increase their giving to the Temple, or to some missionary agency of the Pharisees, who were very missionary minded (Matt. 23:15). Their parents were sometimes ignorant and only casually concerned about Israel's God. Was it not better, they reasoned, to give all that money due to their parents to the Lord? The religious leaders, exercising discretionary power, said *yes. Of all the exercises of discretionary power, the Pharisees no doubt felt that this would be most pleasing to God.* Thus, our Lord's use of this particular example is all the more telling as a radical indictment of the entire use of discretionary power.

But this is not all. *First,* our Lord declares this interpretation to be a violation of the fifth commandment, "Honour thy father and thy mother" (Ex. 20:12; Deut. 5:16; Lev. 19:3; Prov. 23:22; Eph. 6:2-3). *Second,* He declares it to be a clear violation of Exodus 21:17, "And he that curseth his father, or his mother, shall surely be put to death," a law echoed in Leviticus 20:9, Deuteronomy 27:16, Proverbs 20:20 and 30:17. *Third,* by citing Exodus 21:17, our Lord declares that this discretionary power leads to a violation of God's law which calls for the death penalty. To give even to God the money belonging to one's parents as their rightful support from their child calls for the death penalty! No more telling denial of discretionary power is imaginable.

How do our modern Pharisees of the pulpit evade the force of this text? They persuade themselves that somehow fraud is at work. What the Pharisees did was done by bad men; when *they* exercise discretionary powers with respect to God's law, *they* bring a higher spirituality to it! Thus, the traditions of our modern elders and presbyters is held to be good because they are good men!

Because many Pharisees entered the church, as well as Greek and Roman philosophers and lawyers who were accustomed to exercising discretionary power, there was very early a problem in the church at this point. All the same, although churches could not themselves impose the death penalty for such things as idolatry, murder, and adultery, many churches regarded such offenders as the living dead. The sinner could repent, but, while continuing to worship, he was in effect a dead man, and more than a few churches never permitted reconciliation or communion to any such offenders, even when dying.[1]

This use of discretionary power flourished in the later middle ages and was sharply criticized by the Reformation, although most of them immediately began their own exercise of it. The Lutheran approach was and is that whatever is not strictly forbidden is permitted. The Calvinistic approach was that only the specific work of God can warrant any practice. Again, however, this was quickly set aside, and the division in American Presbyterianism between Charles Hodge and J. H. Thornwell was with respect to discretionary power. The particular issue at stake was church polity. By and large, the position of Hodge has governed orthodox and modernist branches of Presbyterian and Reformed Churches. Thus, in

---

1. See Von Espen's comment, in Henry R. Percival, ed.: *The Seven Ecumenical Councils,* p. 416. *Nicene and Post-Nicene Fathers,* Second Series, vol. XIV. Grand Rapids, MI: Eerdmans, 1956.

essence, what Protestantism has objected to in Rome is the Catholic *use* of discretionary power, *not to discretionary power per se, in itself.*

The essence of tradition, whether with respect to Phariseeism, the Roman Catholic Church, Eastern Orthodox Churches, and Protestant churches, is "the liberty of discretionary power." The question is simply this: Does man have the right to use discretionary powers with respect to the law of God?

Our Lord is emphatic. The use of discretionary powers makes "the commandment of God of none effect." Moreover, he declares that those who exercise it are "hypocrites." They are hypocrites because they profess with their lips to honor God, "but their heart is far from me. But in vain they do worship me, teaching for doctrines the commandments of men." Need we wonder then at the impotence of the modern church?

Sherman E. Johnson, in *The Interpreter's Bible,* tells us that verses 3 and 9 are beside the point. He concludes

> Jesus seems to hold that it is the spirit of the law, or God's purpose in giving it, that counts, and not its literal interpretation. But instead of using legal methods to resolve a conflict of laws, he appeals to the average layman's conscience, which is capable of discerning right and wrong (Luke 12:57).[2]

But Johnson is a modernist, and such a wayward interpretation should not surprise us. He begins with the premise that Scripture is to be judged and assessed by man.

Let us turn to a 19th century commentator who is still in print and is favored by the orthodox, David Thomas. Thomas summarized the rabbinic view of tradition thus:

> The criminality, in the judgment of the Scribes and Pharisees, of transgressing any precept of the elders, may be estimated from these sentences in their writings:—'The words of the Scribes are lovely above the words of the law, for the words of the law are weighty and light, but the words of the Scribes are all weighty.' 'The words of the elders are weightier than the words of the prophets.' 'The written law is narrow, but the traditional is longer than the earth and broader than the sea.' The Jews compared the Bible to water, the Mishna to wine, and the Gemara to hippocras.[3]

Thomas continued in this vein. Protestants are very able critics of the Pharisees and Catholics, but not of themselves! He wrote, with respect to the Pharisees, of "their hideous character, as unmasked by their Judge."[4] We would expect him to turn the searchlight of the word upon

---

2. Sherman E. Johnson, "Matthew," in *The Interpreter's Bible,* vol. 7. p. 438. New York, NY: Abingdon Press, 1951.

3. David Thomas: *The Gospel of Matthew,* p. 270. Grand Rapids, MI: Baker Book House,(1873) 1956.

4. *Ibid.,* p. 273.

his own camp, or to tell us clearly that "no prophecy of Scripture is of any private interpretation" (I Peter 1:20), and that, as our Lord makes clear, "the scripture cannot be broken" (John 10:35). Instead, Thomas by-passed the fact of law and the plain meaning of the text to issue a pietistic appeal as the true meaning of Matthew 15:1-9. Using "heart" in the pietistic rather than Biblical sense, Thomas concluded thus:

> Brother, "in vain" is thy theological creed, however scriptural its basis and philosophical its structure; "in vain" is thy ecclesiastical polity, however it may accord with the principles of the New Testament, and be adapted to church edification and order; "in vain" are thy forms of devotion—thy hymns may breathe seraphic piety, thy liturgies may be inspired, thy prayers may be fashioned after the great model prayer; "in vain" is the punctuality with which thou attendest to religious services, and the propriety with which thou dost join in the exercise of the great congregation,—in vain all, and for ever in vain, if "thy heart is far from God." In all thy religious engagements thou art only sowing the wind, and thou wilt reap the whirlwind.[5]

Such writing and preaching is the essence of hypocrisy and dishonesty, not because its comments are false, but because they are unrelated to the text and they obscure it. Thomas made the commandment of God of none effect by his writing. From a very specific and precise text he brought forth unrelated generalities.

Christians thus have paid too little attention to the meaning of Matthew 15:1-9. Ironically, the Scribes and Pharisees recognized their radical vulnerability at this point. Our Lord's account of the perversion of the fifth commandment by their tradition led, not to an abandonment of tradition or discretionary power as such, but to its application in this particular case. By the end of the century, the rabbis and lawyers ruled that no husband or wife could deprive the other of his rights by means of a vow, nor any children deny their parents of what God requires of children by means of a vow.[6] The principle of discretionary power continued to govern them, but, at this point, they recognized their vulnerability.

Thus, in both Judaism and in Christianity, the doctrine of the liberty of discretion prevails, "teaching for doctrines the commandments of men." Our Lord's judgment stands: "their heart is far from me."

---

5. *Ibid.*, p. 275.
6. Nedarim, chapts. II and IX, 16a and 64a, in *The Babylonian Talmud, Seder Nashim,* III, pp. 42, 204. London: The Soncino Press, 1936.

## 144

## THE HERESY OF PERFECT JUSTICE

An important Biblical word which today has a very different meaning is *perfect*. In Scripture, it means complete, mature, clear, having integrity, fitted, or whole. In modern usage, it has the implication of *sinlessness,* a very different meaning. When Scripture speaks of Noah (Gen. 6:9) and Job (Job 1:1, 8; 2:3) as "perfect" it does not mean sinless but complete, plain (*i.e.,* clear in faith and life), and whole. David gives us an indication of the meaning of the word in Psalm 37:37, "Mark the perfect man, and behold the upright: for the end of that man is peace." Moffatt rendered *perfect* in this verse as *integrity;* David sees it as identical with *upright.* The end of that man is godly peace, since he is the blessed meek, rather than the disorder and turmoil brought about by the wicked. This is so, because "The steps of a good man are ordered by the LORD; and he delighteth in his way" (Ps. 37:23).

The way of perfection, in the Biblical sense, is the law of God. It provides the framework and the necessary means for the mature and complete life. God's law gives wholeness to covenant man, and it gives light to his eyes. In the words of David again, in Psalm 19:7-11,

> The law of the LORD is perfect, converting the soul; the testimony of the LORD is sure, making wise the simple.
> The statutes of the LORD are right, rejoicing the heart: the commandment of the LORD is pure, enlightening the eyes.
> The fear of the LORD is clean, enduring for ever: the judgments of the LORD are true and righteous altogether.
> More to be desired are they than gold, yea, than much fine gold: sweeter also than honey and the honeycomb.
> Moreover by them is thy servant warned: and in keeping of them there is great reward.

There is clearly a very great difference between *sinless perfection* and *Biblical perfection.* The one has to do with an essentially individualistic quest for a sinless life; it can mean a withdrawal from the world of action as polluting, but, in any case, it is a quest of the soul for a condition which is in essence a negative one, *i.e.,* to be sin*less,* whereas the Biblical doctrine of perfection is in essence positive and active: "Ye shall be holy: for I the LORD your God am holy" (Lev. 19:2), and the way of holiness and perfection is the law of the Lord.

Thus, the Biblical doctrine is not only more activistic, but it has an unchanging standard which is separate from man and is of the Lord. This puts a brake on man's quietism, but also on his activism. A central problem in human activism is the lust for perfect justice *now.* One of the most damaging aspects of our time and of history as a whole is the demand *for perfect justice now.* Such a demand creates radical injustice and a contempt for law, because it is the essence of man's courts that they are, at their best, slow, painstaking, and fallible.

To illustrate, twice in my life I have seen situations where it was obvious that a man had been murdered, and the murderer was known by the authorities. In neither case was anything said or done, because no evidence existed which could stand up in court. As a result, there was no prosecution, and not even a word to tie the murderer to his crime. Biblical law requires a witness to a crime to testify (Lev. 5:1). It also requires two witnesses to convict (Deut. 19:15); these witnesses can be persons and/or circumstantial evidence, but two are required. Clearly, this law means that some guilty men escape judgment, but it makes clear the limitations of human justice. Men are not God; they cannot administer sinless justice, nor can they always ensure full justice. The *need* for full justice must be recognized, and Deuteronomy 21:1-9 makes clear that unpunished murder must be atoned for; restitution must be made. Thus, the law, *first,* insists on the full restoration of God's order, and nothing short of God's justice is right before God. *Second,* the law also recognizes that man is incapable of this perfect justice. The laws of witness bar man from attempting to do more than a required prosecution. Man cannot presume, in seeking perfect justice, to gain it by lawless means. *Third,* the legal requirement for restitution for all crime still enables man to effect the necessary restitution even where judgment is impossible.

God thus places a limitation on man's ability to prosecute, while retaining the requirement for restitution. Let us see what this means practically. One of the most trying of pastoral and criminal cases it that of the unreasoning demand for justice in cases where no proof exists. A pastor will be confronted by people who are vehement in insisting, I *know* that my husband, wife, or that church member is guilty of such and such an offense, even though I can't prove it in terms of your requirements. The police or the district attorney will get like statements. These are sometimes imaginary charges, and sometimes valid ones. In either case, the accuser is insistent that *their* knowledge or charge must be the ground for prosecution. The basis for prosecution, however, is *God's law,* not the offense we have suffered. The false idea of the liberty of discretion transfers initiative with respect to the law from God to man. It declares that man can forgive where God requires judgment, and it declares that man can demand prosecution where God's law forbids it.

Let us be specific by way of illustration. A woman charges her husband, a church officer, with adultery; he denies it firmly. She insists it is true, begins to talk against her husband throughout the church, although not a trace of evidence can be produced. No charge should be filed against her husband, because a charge requires evidence. She must be charged in terms of Leviticus 19:16, as a talebearer and false witness. Her conduct is ground for divorce; she has deserted her husband by her conduct and despised God's law in favor of her demands, and is thus to be excommunicated.

In another case, a church officer is guilty of adultery, but the wife suppresses the evidence and silences the witness "to preserve her home" and her meal-ticket. As a result, an ugly situation festers in the life of the church until the church officer becomes involved with a high school girl in a youth group, and the matter becomes "a public scandal." The husband is guilty of adultery, and the wife is a party to it (Ps. 50:18).

We can neither set aside the law, nor insist on its enforcement on our terms, without sin.

Man's idea of perfect justice is one which costs him nothing and profits him at every turn. The processes of justice, however, cannot move on man's terms but on God's. Justice and righteousness are one and the same thing. They cannot be separated. Righteousness must mark not only the law but its process: this is the meaning of the law of witnesses.

## 145

## THE PRINCIPLE OF DONATISM

In the third and fourth centuries, three groups or movements within the church created major conflicts as a result of their stands. These were the Novatians, the Donatists, and the Meletians; the origin of the Novatians was in Rome, that of the Donatists and Meletians in North Africa. The Donatists towards the close of the fourth century were so strong that they had some 400 bishops in Africa. It is often popular with Protestants to make a case for these men, because their opposition was at times too heavily involved, as in the time of the Donatists and Meletians, with the Constantinian view of the church. However, the fact that some of their opponents wanted peace at sometimes great cost, and sometimes tended to equate baptism per se with church membership, irrespective of conduct, should not blind us to the serious errors in these groups.

The basic problem was the status of *the lapsed*. During times of persecution, when faced with prison or death, some church members and officers surrendered the Scriptures on demand, and sometimes offered sacrifices to the emperors and saved their lives. In some cases, the lapsed suffered imprisonment before compromising at some point or other.

These three movements refused to restore the lapsed clergy and/or laity to the church. They grounded their position on Hebrews 6:4-6:

> For it is impossible for those who were once enlightened, and have tasted of the heavenly gift, and were made partakers of the Holy Ghost,
> And have tasted the good word of God, and the powers of the world to come,
> If they shall fall away, to renew them again unto repentance; seeing they crucify to themselves the Son of God afresh, and put him to an open shame.

Before going further, it is necessary to state that our concern with these movements is not historical but theological. Historically, both sides had their problems. The separatist groups had their share of hypocrites who used harshness as a means of setting forth their claim to purity. The Catholics had some whose thinking developed later into the equation of church and state as different aspects of the body politic. It came to mean that an Englishman or a Spaniard was automatically in the state and in the church. It would be unfair to blame Constantine for this; he wanted unity in the church, but the roots of the problem preceded him.

The key was Hebrews 6:4-6. To what extent did it govern the problem of the lapsed? Churchmen held to several varying positions on this matter. *First,* it was held that the lapsed could not be received back in the church. *Second,* it was held that they could be received back on rebaptism, a position held by some Eastern and African churches. *Third,* it was held that the lapsed could be received back into the church on repentance but could not be rebaptized. *Fourth,* the lapsed could be received back into the church on repentance and penance.

Paul, in Hebrews 6:4-6, makes clear the impossibility of a second repentance. To repent in Scripture means to change directions; it has reference not to words but to a way of life. The man who repents is the man whose life is changed from one way of living to another. This means that the Christian is a new creature or a new creation (II Cor. 5:17). He is no longer guilty of lawlessness, *anomia,* but of *hamartia,* sin, offenses which fall short of the standard. The unpardonable sin is the deliberate and wilful rejection of the faith; it involves calling good evil, and evil good. It is a sin which places man beyond repentance and forgiveness (I John 5:16-17; Mark 3:29). It means that no real change ever occurred, only hypocrisy.

Thus, with this in mind, it is clear that what Paul has in mind could include some of the lapsed, but does not of necessity characterize them all. What Paul has in mind is seen more clearly in the next two verses, Hebrews 6:7-8:

> For the earth which drinketh in the rain that cometh oft upon it, and bringeth forth herbs meet for them by whom it is dressed, receiveth blessing from God:
> But that which beareth thorns and briers is rejected, and is nigh unto cursing; whose end is to be burned.

The imagery here is clearly taken from the parable of the sower and the seed (Matt. 13:1-43), and from Matthew 7:16-20, our Lord's declaration that men shall be known by their fruits. The act of lapsing thus had to be assessed in the context of a man's life, faith, and works. Was it simply an application of re-admission, or was it actual repentance over sin? Was the lapse a weakness or falling short in an otherwise faithful man, or was it part of a pattern of practical apostasy?

The Catholic party tended to equate mere opinion with faith. The separatists tended to equate the church and the faith with man's "holiness" rather than Jesus Christ. The separatists tended to regard all baptisms and acts of the lapsing clergy as invalid. This placed the Kingdom in man rather than the Lord. The power of communicating grace through the sacraments was thus placed in the clergy's hands: the efficacy was not in Christ's work, and in the faithfulness to the trinitarian form of baptism, but in the clergy.

Let us recognize at once that some thinkers in the Catholic fold were already placing discretionary powers in the hands of the clergy. The separatists did this to a far, far greater degree. The demand for the re-baptism of all who had been under a lapsed clergy made the clergy the effectual mediators of grace. The Catholic thinkers denied this. The separatist position seemed to be the holier and purer one. In reality it represented, not righteousness, but self-righteousness, and it exalted the clergy to a startling degree. It made man the necessary mediator between Christ and His church, so that more than discretionary power was placed in man's hands: it was now a controlling power. It meant, moreover, that no man could be assured of the validity of his baptism unless the baptizing priest died quite obviously in the faith.

This emphasis on self-righteousness led some Donatists to invite martyrdom as a means of establishing holiness and righteousness. This was true of the Meletians also. Meletius held that Peter, the Patriarch of Alexandria, was not fit to rule because he was ready to receive some of the lapsed back into the church. The cause of Bishop Meletius of Lycopolis received a set-back when Peter was arrested and beheaded in December of 311. Since the issue was at root self-righteousness, Peter's public image as a martyr gave his arguments status among the separatists whom he opposed!

With this emphasis on man, it should not surprise us that Arius, the founder of Arianism, was an admirer of Meletius and other separatists. Much later, the Meletians and Arians merged together. In Arius, humanism was more explicit than in the Donatists and Meletians, but it was present in all of them. Man's discretionary power leads to man's self-righteousness and to humanism.

We can understand the separatist mentality of these early movements by examining in passing a like temper in the church today. The separatists said that the lapsed were in effect outside the church and forever barred to some degree. In the church today, many pastors bar the divorced unconditionally: it makes matters easier and keeps the church supposedly purer. They refuse to examine the guilt or innocence of either party. The separatists at least began with an actual sin. The modern pastor presumes that sin is always involved in divorce, and that no innocent party exists. In both cases a discretionary power is exercised which violates the meaning of Scripture.

What does such an attitude lead to? It creates in the church a priority of church law and mores over the word of God.

But Donatism functions in the state as well. The more the state forsakes Biblical law, the more weight it will give to itself and to its own rules and regulations. The more serious crimes become those which transgress some statist regulation. Small businessmen regularly find themselves guilty nowadays of violating some act of state which they never knew existed, for a practice no one would imagine was a civil wrong or a criminal act. Just as in the churches most "disciplinary measures" have nothing to do with morals and doctrine, and everything to do with church-made rules, so too in the Donatist state purity means compliance with statist rules, not God's law.

## 146

## WISDOM

One of the interesting words in the Hebrew of the Old Testament is *shalom,* which appears also as a name, *Salem.* Shalom means not only peace, but also wholeness, completion, and perfection. It also means finished, recompense, restitution, prospered, restored, and rewarded. Girdlestone quite rightly saw this word as an example of "the moral relationship existing between ideas" that we meet in Scripture.[1] When Isaiah says, "Thou wilt keep him in perfect *peace,* whose mind is stayed on thee, because he trusteth in thee" (Isa. 26:3), he means thereby that this peace of God is also man's reward, his prosperity, his restoration, and his recompense and restitution. Solomon declares, using the same word, *shalom,* "Behold, the righteous shall be *recompensed* in the earth: much more the wicked and the sinner" (Prov. 11:31). The righteous are the just, those who believe in God and put God's law into practice. The peace, recompense, and reward they receive is in time and in eternity. No more than we can postpone living can we postpone the consequences of living, and God declares that these consequences are inevitable (Deut. 28). The fact of benediction and blessing presupposes the fact that the consequences of God's favor are temporal as well as eternal.

Moreover, the peace and perfection which the rule of the Messiah brings in is depicted in Isaiah 11:7-11 as so great that the wolf shall dwell in peace with the lamb, and the leopard with the kid. When "the earth shall be full of the knowledge of the LORD, as the waters cover the sea" (Isa. 11:9), then these things will inevitably follow.

But this is not all. This peace is the work of the Messiah, on whom the Spirit of God rests, and the Spirit is the source of wisdom and understanding, counsel and might, of knowledge and the fear of the LORD (Isa. 19:2). Christ identifies Himself as Wisdom (Matt. 11:19, 25-30), and St. Paul declares Jesus to be "the power of God and the wisdom of God" (I Cor. 1:24).

The triune God is the source of all wisdom. For man to be wise means to believe in God, to obey His every word, and to develop the implications of God's law-word in his total life. There is no wisdom apart from God, "For the LORD giveth wisdom: out of his mouth cometh knowl-

---

1. Robert B. Girdlestone: *Synonyms of the Old Testament,* p. 94. Grand Rapids, MI: Eerdmans, (1897) 1976.

edge and understanding" (Prov. 2:6). The word of God, His law, is wisdom and light (Ps. 119). To sin against wisdom or the Lord is to wrong one's own soul; to hate wisdom is death (Prov. 8:36). With God is wisdom, strength, counsel, and understanding (Job 12:13). Lack of faith in and disobedience to God and His word is folly: it is the fool who hath said in his heart, There is no God (Ps. 14:1). The fool is marked first of all by sin: he is wilfully ignorant, because he is wilfully sinful. He rejects God in favor of himself.

When men seek wisdom apart from God, their so-called wisdom is the denial of God's word, law, and order. Isaiah describes them thus:

> Woe unto them that call evil good, and good evil; that put darkness for light, and light for darkness: that put bitter for sweet, and sweet for bitter!
> Woe unto them that are wise in their own eyes, and prudent in their own sight! (Isa. 5:20-21)

Man's idea of wisdom is in essence the tempter's program as set forth in Genesis 3:5, every man his own god, determining for himself what constitutes good and evil. Because the knowledge of God is inescapable, unbelief is not ignorance but sin; it is the wilful refusal to admit the truth of God and to obey Him. The opposite of faith is thus sin. Therefore, disbelief is not ignorance but sin; disbelief is a rejection of faith in God for faith in man. It is an idea of wisdom aimed at supplanting the wisdom of God with the wisdom of man. Lindblom has noted,

> Isaiah speaks of these who are wise in their own eyes, and prudent in their own sight (5:21). He does not think here of 'the wise' as a special group in the nation. People wise in their own eyes are all those who have rejected the guidance of Yahweh and his words through the prophet and acted according to their own plans. Such an attitude was characteristic of the leaders of the people.[2]

Man's way and wisdom is the story of the fall, and the history of mankind thereafter. The choice is always God's wisdom and life, and man's wisdom (or sin) and death. Moses therefore summons Israel to obey God's every word, declaring, "I call heaven and earth to record this day against you, that I have set before you life and death, blessing and cursing: therefore choose life, that both thou and thy seed may live" (Deut. 30:19). To live means to love God, to obey Him, and to cleave unto him, "for he is thy life and thy length of days" (Deut. 30:20).

Isaiah describes the consequences of man's wisdom, his faith in himself:

> Therefore my people are gone into captivity, because they have no

---

knowledge: and their honourable men are famished, and their multitude dried up with thirst.

Therefore hell hath enlarged herself, and opened her mouth without measure: and their glory, and their multitude, and their pomp, and he that rejoiceth, shall descend into it.

And the mean man shall be brought down, and the mighty man shall be humbled, and the eyes of the lofty shall be humbled:

But the LORD of hosts shall be exalted in judgment, and God that is holy shall be sanctified in righteousness. (Isa. 5:13-16)

Isaiah declares that the humbling of man is the exaltation of God, because man has exalted himself and his pretended wisdom against God. A state of war exists, and man aims at the death of God and the universal freedom of man from God's law and necessity. Marxism sees man's salvation as a transition from the kingdom of necessity to the kingdom of freedom. Although Marxism usually defines necessity in economic terms, behind the economic terminology stands a fully developed theology of man. Peace and wisdom are seen in humanistic terms; they are the consequence of human efforts to gain freedom from God's ordained order and necessity. Peace and restitution for humanism mean a God-free universe, purged of every relic of the triune God and made into a domain for man's independent and creative dominion. Man asserts a total liberty of discretion. Wisdom is equated with man's discretionary powers, and love is separated from God and His grace and law to mean again man's exercise of discretion. Liberty of discretion is thus not wisdom. It is man's attempt to gain the last word over God, and to reassert the principle of the fall.

## 147

## THE MINISTRY OF OBEDIENCE

The emperor Constantine the Great was a man whose life lends itself readily to criticism. Such criticism, however, is dangerous, since our knowledge of many of the controversial events of his life is so fragmentary. It can be readily granted that his faults were many, but, unhappily, his very important contributions are too seldom mentioned nowadays. It has become too popular to blame the ills of the church on Constantine.

*First* of all, Constantine came to Christianity as a ruler. Rome faced collapse: its salvation required a new foundation, a religious foundation, and Constantine felt that Christianity alone could save Rome and civilization. His interest in the faith was thus intensely practical.

*Second,* Rome's decay was total: in every area of Roman life, decay and decline had set in. Roman law had given way, in essence, to anarchy and to military rule. The Roman state was increasingly effective only in two ways, in controlling people and the economy, and in taxing. Constantine saw the need for a new and religious basis for society and for law. That foundation he found in Christianity and the Bible. For Constantine, the Bible was, from first to last, God's word and hence God's law. Constantine's word was law, and, therefore, how much more so was God's word law. In 324, writing to Arius and to Alexander, to rebuke them for theological disturbances, Constantine referred to Proverbs 8:22 ("The LORD possessed me in the beginning of his way, before his works of old") as "a certain passage in the law."[1]

Such a view is clearly Biblical. The New Testament often uses the term *law* to describe the whole of the Old Testament. What God says is always law.

*Third,* Constantine opposed forced conversions, declaring, "it is one thing voluntarily to take up the fight for eternal life, it is quite another to compel others to do so from fear of punishment."[2]

A *fourth* point is our main concern here. However sinful and weak Constantine was in other respects, his grasp of the implications of his office as emperor was clear-cut. He saw himself as the bishop of those outside the church.[3]

1. John Howland Smith: *Constantine the Great,* p. 192. New York, NY: Charles Scribner's Sons, 1971.
2. *Ibid.,* p. 183.
3. *Ibid.,* p. 116.

Let us consider the implications of this carefully. According to Romans 13:1-10, the church is the ministry of grace, and the state, the ministry of justice. The church ministers to those within the covenant: it declares God's word to God's covenant people.

The state too has a ministerial function; one can call it an episcopal function, using Constantine's language, or a presbyterian function, or, in Paul's terminology, a diaconate.

The province of this diaconate or service by the state is "the ordinance of God" (Rom. 13:2). *Ordinance* (*diatage*) can also be rendered as *institute;* Moffatt translates the Greek of "the ordinance of God" as "the divine order," and the New English Bible, as "a divine institution." The word *diatage* is closely related to edict and law. The state thus is instituted by God as an aspect of His law order. It is an aspect of God's government over the world. God's law and the state thus have a common and inseparable function: to maintain and further God's order and law.

The state is an authority of power under God and for His purpose. It is a serious misreading of Paul to see his words as an underwriting of Caesar. Rather, Paul places Caesar under Christ as a servant having a given authority, circumscribed by a given and authoritative word. The state has no independent existence: it is the creature of the triune God and must serve Him. "There is no power (or, no authority) but of God: the powers that be are ordained of God" (Rom. 13:1): this being the case, the state must serve God, and the duty of man is to obey the state.

It is a matter of conscience for the Christian to obey the state (Rom. 13:5). Because it is a matter of conscience, it means that the state, viewed as a ministry, must be grounded in its calling under God: it must know and obey God's word. The believer must be subject to the state "for conscience sake," but the state, by being declared to be a ministry, is also placed under conscience. It must uphold and advance the divine order.

Humanistic man makes the state basic to the idea of human order, a man-made order. Instead of the state as a ministry within the covenant of God, the state as a social contract was very early stressed. From a social contract, the state has moved on to the logical conclusion of social justice, as opposed to God's justice. Man defines the state, law, and justice. The norm becomes what man declares it to be. The result of this is the breakdown of the state, because it ceases to be a ministry under God and becomes an idiot god whose mind is variable, unstable, and constantly subject to change. Humanism leads to the malfunctioning and the breakdown of the state. However pragmatic Constantine's choice of Christianity may have been, (and it was far from merely pragmatic), his realistic grasp of Rome's need for a fundamental faith and law was to the point. The problem was that the solution was much too late in coming.

St. Paul says of the state, "For rulers are not a terror to good works, but to the evil. Wilt thou then not be afraid of the power? do that which is good, and thou shalt have praise of the same" (Rom. 13:3). The survival of the state requires good citizens, men of sound moral character and conduct. Without such a nucleus, the state will crumble, unless, as with various socialist and Marxist regimes today, there is a subsidy from the outside. Such a subsidy only postpones and enlarges the collapse, so that the subsidized and the subsidizer alike collapse. The world, having been created by God, operates successfully on God's law only, and every departure carries with it an inherent judgment. The state thus which renounces the protection of that which is good thereby renounces life. It does not rule: it abdicates rule for suicide.

Humanism, because of its anti-God faith, requires such a course of lawlessness, and it must, to be consistent, subsidize lawlessness rather than godliness. This is "the mystery of iniquity" which is already at work, Paul declares (II Thess. 2:7), and which, in every humanistic era, manifests itself, and is always destroyed by the word of God, and by His coming in judgment in history (II Thess. 2:7-9). When such a view of the state appears, *i.e.,* the state as the principle of lawlessness, of humanism, we have a crisis time. Normally, however, even the humanists draw back from the full implications of their position.

Thus, usually, another situation prevails, even with godless judges, so that, Paul declares of the ruler,

> For he is the minister of God to thee for good. But if thou do that which is evil, be afraid; for he beareth not the sword in vain: for he is the minister of God, a revenger to execute wrath upon him that doeth evil. (Rom. 13:4)

Men must serve God, and, one way or another, they will, because God makes all things work together for good in terms of His purpose (Rom. 8:28). Moreover, God's order is basic to social order, and the humanistic state is never able to disavow God's law entirely. Even the communist states, although established on theft and murder, must be intolerant of theft and murder in their midst. Hence, the robber state will still to a degree administer God's law for its own welfare and survival. This fact gives the believer some degree of security.

The believer's course is thus, *first* of all, subjection for conscience sake to the state (Rom. 13:5). This means, *second,* rendering to all men their due, the state included (Rom. 13:6-7). *Third,* the means to triumph and to godly victory is faithfulness to the Lord and His law. Our debt or obligation to all men, as declared by God, is to manifest that love which is the fulfilment or enforcement of God's law. Hence, we are to avoid dishonesty, rioting, drunkenness, "chambering" or sexual promiscuity, strife, and envy, all of which manifest a hatred for God and man. To love God and man means to keep God's commandments. Therefore,

Owe no man anything, but to love one another: for he that loveth another hath fulfilled the law.

For this, Thou shalt not commit adultery, Thou shalt not kill, Thou shalt not steal, Thou shalt not bear false witness, Thou shalt not covet; and if there be any other commandment, it is briefly comprehended in this saying, namely, Thou shalt love thy neighbour as thyself.

Love worketh no ill to his neighbour: therefore love is the fulfilling of the law.

And that, knowing the time, that now it is high time to awake out of sleep: for now is our salvation nearer than when we believed.

The night is far spent, the day is at hand; let us therefore cast off the works of darkness, and let us put on the armour of light.

Let us walk honestly, as in the day; not in rioting and drunkenness, not in chambering and wantonness, not in strife and envying.

But put ye on the Lord Jesus Christ, and make not provision for the flesh, to fulfill the lusts thereof. (Rom. 13:8-14)

Our armor in this battle is Christ. Our obedience to Him is our strength.

To return now to Constantine: Paul does clearly declare the ministerial function of the state; Constantine called it the episcopal function. The state is a ministry of justice. By enforcing God's law, it witnesses to those outside the church or Kingdom of Christ concerning the nature of God's law and the requirements of godly order.

All men, however, by virtue of their calling in Christ to be priests, prophets, and kings, have a ministry also. The nature of this ministry is to manifest in their lives that order and law which is basic to both the ministry of justice and the ministry of grace. God declares this to be a debt owed by man, and to be paid in full. The payment of this means a love of our neighbor. The justice enforced by the state is an aspect also of God's love, law, and order.

Thus, the "ordinance of God," or the divine order, is inclusive of the state's authority and ministry of justice, and of the believer's ministry of obedience. Clearly, obedience is a ministry and an administration. By obeying God, we administer His law order in our lives, our homes, institutions, and callings. The ministry of obedience can alone revolutionize society. The humanistic ideas of revolution are false: they change nothing, but merely re-arrange the corrupt components of a dying social order. It is the ministry of obedience which is the only radical or root solution to man's problem. It means that regeneration is followed by a necessary ministry which reshapes man and society totally. Anything else is superficial.

The whole of Romans 13 is thus a unit. It speaks about our subjection to God in a ministry of service, a diaconate common to all men and institutions. We are in all things subject to the Lord, and to one another in the Lord. God's absolute property right in and over all men and all creation requires of church, state, and man the ministry of obedience.

The day of God's Kingdom will not dawn until we put on the armor of light, that love which is obedience and faithful action and subjection for conscience sake. The ministry of obedience is the necessary way to God's Kingdom.

**148**

## THE MINISTRY OF HATE

Stanton E. Samenow and Dr. Samuel Yochelson, in a study based on years of experience with criminals, have called attention to the strong and powerful element of hatred in the criminal's make-up. The law-breaker's anger is pervasive; it does not trouble him to injure others, or to break his promises. He lies incessantly out of a necessity to deceive people. According to Samenow, the criminal, "If he's going to the A & P, he'll say he's going to the Safeway."[1]

This radical hatred of the criminal makes it next to impossible for him to have a good relationship with anyone. People are there to be used, deceived, exploited, and, above all, hated. This radical hatred of man has its roots in a total hatred of God. The criminal often professes indifference towards God. If there is a minister, priest, or chaplain around to deceive, he is ready to profess interest. But his hatred of God is basic to his outlook.

The law-abiding humanist has a tendency to be sympathetic towards the criminal, and the 20th century has seen many novels, films, and television stories exalting the criminal as a victim and hence implicitly innocent. Only the increasing menace to the citizen at large has somewhat tempered this sympathy.

The key to this sympathy is a common delight in hatred. The humanist professes to love humanity, but he hates man as he is. His love of man is a love for the idea of man, man in his own image, and hence all men must be either remade in his image or be treated as enemies. The humanist is constantly disappointed in people; they are not, when the heat is on, like unto himself, nor will they bend to his will. The world of humanism is the world of alienation, communication gaps, a flight from man and an exaggerated demand for privacy by people who congregate in masses compulsively.

Paul in Romans 1:22-32 depicts the end result of apostasy as a radical hatred of God and of man by man the sinner. *Man's unbelief or sin is a perversity in man.* The knowledge of God is inescapable knowledge (Rom. 1:17-21); for man to suppress this knowledge is the ultimate act of apostasy and perversity. Out of this religious perversity flows physical

---

1. Patrick Young, "How to Reform Criminals," in *Conservative Digest,* vol. 3, no. 11, November, 1977, p. 18; reproduced from *The National Observer,* July 11, 1977.

and emotional perversities. Homosexuality is the ultimate physical perversity, manifesting itself in the sexual sphere, and the hatred of man, emotional perversity. It should not surprise us that homosexuals (male and female alike) manifest in their personalities a concealed but intense hatred. They are a dangerous people, and the relationship between the criminal mind and the homosexual mind is a close one.

According to one man, previously a jail warden and then executive director of Cook County (Illinois) Department of Correction,

> the majority (some 60 percent) of prisoners in the nation's penal systems are latent or overt homosexuals. I am speaking of the hard-core criminals who cause most of the problems in correctional institutions, who, because they have never been able to sublimate their abnormal sexual desires, continuously foment prison riots, rape fellow prisoners, and kill guards and fellow inmates. . . .

> It may come as a surprise to many to learn that the No. 1 cause of murder in prison is not gambling, as one often reads, but homosexual involvement. This is because practicing homosexuals are basically promiscuous. They are rarely interested in only one partner but are constantly in pursuit of new homosexual relationships and conquests. This frequently leads to love triangles and jealousies that end in violence and murder.[2]

The problem, says Moore, is aggravated by the fact that in recent years homosexuals, in increasing numbers, are joining the staffs of correctional institutions.

The homosexual is marked by a deep-seated hatred of God and man, which, while often concealed, comes readily to expressions. Since crime is anti-social behavior in part, it attracts some homosexuals. In any event, the hatred is basic, and the homosexual is central to the total ministry of hate.

Paul tells us, *first,* that this reprobate mentality is marked by a profession of wisdom, whereas it is in reality folly (Rom. 1:22). The word Paul uses for *fools* means senseless and devoid of understanding. It has a moral as well as mental connotation. The perversity of the fool leads him to exchange the glory of the incorruptible God for a new ultimate, derived from the corruptible creation (Rom. 1:23). Because the fool can never escape from the knowledge of God (Rom. 1:17-21), his choice of a new ultimate is a moral choice and an expression of his perversity. The humanist or fool sees himself as a prisoner of time, and he both deifies time and turns on it with hatred. Time is exalted as against eternity, but time is then regarded with hatred as a limitation on man.

*Second,* Paul tells us that this anti-God mentality further manifests its rebellion and perversity by means of homosexuality and lesbianism

---

2. Winston E. Moore, "How to End Sex Problems in Our Prisons," in *Ebony,* vol. XXII, no. 1, November, 1976. p. 84.

(Rom. 1:24-27): the appeal in sex is not to God-ordained sexuality but to perversity. Marital sex is seen as boring and confining. The appeal is in sin, in the violation of God's law and the contempt for loving and responsible relationships. The end result of this love of perversity is sexual perversion, notably homosexuality and lesbianism.

In terms of God's law, man exercises dominion in every area of life through the ministry of obedience. This desire for dominion is basic to the image of God in man. After the fall, the desire for dominion is sought outside of God's law, not in obedience but in disobedience to God. The consequence and inescapable concomitant of God's law is love: love fulfills the law (Rom. 13:10). The concomitant to the sinful urge for dominion is not love but hate, so that hatred is basic to sin and to lawlessness. The criminal is anti-social. The prostitute hates man. The homosexual is marked by radical hatred. Every sinner justifies his sin by affirming that a moral hatred of some person or thing motivated his behavior. The sinner is not only an injustice collector but a hate-collector. His justification is hatred.

In godly marriage, sex is a form of love and of holy dominion. Children are seen as a blessing and a means of extending God's ordained dominion (Ps. 128).

Ungodly sex is a form of rebellion and evil dominion. Its purpose is to exploit and to humble. With the more naive sinner, it may masquerade as love, but for those who are more epistemologically self-conscious, it is openly a means of asserting power and of toying with other lives. The idea is *to make* the other person one's creature.

Slang is at this point very revealing. The good English word *make* has a variety of slang meanings. It means, among other things, to rob, to defecate, to become successful, and to seduce a member of the opposite sex. The goal is to make another person one's own creature, and then to manifest independence by casting them aside.

*Third,* Paul says that, when men deny God, God abandons them to their lie, and to the consequences of their perversity (Rom. 1:25-26). To exchange the truth of God for a lie is a deliberate act: sin is always in its inception deliberate and pre-meditated. God, however, then gives sin dominion over man (cf. Gen. 4:7). Man seeks to be his own god, and to rule over the earth apart from God. Now he finds himself ruled by his own sin. One of the assurances Paul gives to the believer is that "sin shall not have dominion over you" (Rom. 6:14). The problem which confronts the ungodly at every turn is that sin does have dominion over them. Their perversity is thus self-defeating.

It is inescapably so, because, Paul says, God gives them over to a reprobate mind when they refuse to make God the principle of all their knowledge and action (Rom. 1:28). Their lives collapse into a chain of performances and practices which manifest to them what they are.

*Fourth,* Paul then cites some of the central forms of self-expression in this ministry of hate (Rom. 1:29-31). Such men are filled with all unrighteousness or injustice. They are marked by fornication, depravity, envy, and maliciousness. They are backbiters or slanderers, and haters of God. They are insolent, proud, and boastful, given to inventing new vices, disobedient to parents, lacking understanding, without natural affections, pitiless and merciless towards the holy, and covenant-breakers in all their ways. They may profess, on man's terms, to build a new creation, but theirs is always a ministry of hate. It is marked therefore by a love of death (Prov. 8:36).

*Fifth,* all such men have and cannot escape nor evade the inescapable knowledge of God. They know that God's judgment on themselves and on all who are like them is death. All the same, they not only persist in their way of life and their sins, "but have pleasure in them that do them" (Rom. 1:32). It is well said that misery loves company. Even more, the perverse want all men to join them in their perversity: it is their means of justification. As against the inescapable knowledge of God, they oppose the inescapable perversity of man. They assert that the only reason others do not fornicate nor commit homosexual acts is because of religious misinformation, "hang-ups," and inhibitions. How can they be guilty, when they merely give expressions to the true nature of man? As against man created in the image of God, they posit man as a product of chaos. Instead of God's law, man is ruled, they hold, by the struggle for survival. Aberrant behavior is not sin but a relic of an animal past. Man is alone in the universe, they hold, and hence must battle against a hostile and cold cosmos. The doctrine of evolution is a religious expression of man's pleasure in perversity on a cosmological basis. It is an expression of his ministry of hate. Religion is held to be the opium of the masses, whereas acceptance of a cold and dead universe and a ministry of aggression and hatred is held to be wisdom.

We are told, of the fools who say in their heart, "There is no God," that

> .... They are corrupt, they have done abominable works; there is
> none that doeth good.
> The LORD looked down from heaven upon the children of men, to
> see if there were any that did understand, and seek God.
> They are all gone aside, they are all together become filthy: there is
> none that doeth good, no, not one. (Ps. 14:1-3)

From David's day to our own, the sons of men are no different. Those who are by adoption of grace the sons of God move, not in terms of perversity and the ministry of hate, but in terms of the ministry of obedience.

## 149

## TREASURES AND TRIFLES

In the Sermon on the Mount, our Lord declares,

> Lay not up for yourselves treasures upon earth, where moth and rust doth corrupt, and where thieves break through and steal:
> But lay up for yourselves treasures in heaven, where neither moth nor rust doth corrupt, and where thieves do not break through and steal:
> For where your treasure is, there will your heart be also. (Matt. 6:19-21)

These words have deep roots in Biblical thought and in Hebraic proverbs reflecting that faith. Thus, in the Apocrypha, in Tobit 4:9, and the Psalm of Solomon 9:9, we are told, "He who does righteousness lays up life for himself with the Lord," and, in the Test. Levi 13:5, "Do righteousness, my sons, on earth, that you may have treasure in heaven."[1] When King Monobazos of Adiabene (46-47 A. D.) embraced Judaism, in a time of famine he gave away his inherited wealth, declaring, "My fathers stored in a place where the hand can reach, but I have stored in a place where the hand cannot reach. My fathers gathered for this world, but I have gathered for the future world."[2]

Obviously, the concept of treasure in heaven was a well established one, and common to all teachers in Israel. *Treasure* meant *righteousness,* the obedience of faith to the law of God. It meant the confidence of the regenerate man in the government of God and his security therein, and hence his faith in and obedience to the covenant God. In terms of this new view of the meaning of treasure and security, the redeemed man regards what was once wealth to him as a trifle by comparison to his inheritance in Christ. St. Paul is even more emphatic as he contrasts his previous condition, a very wealthy man who believed in justification by works of the law, to his redemption and justification through the atonement of Jesus Christ:

> But what things were gain to me, those I counted loss for Christ.
> Yea doubtless, and I count all things but loss for the excellency of the knowledge of Christ Jesus my Lord: for whom I have suffered the loss of all things, and do count them but dung, that I may win Christ. (Phil. 3:7-8)

---

1. See Sherman E. Johnson, "Matthew," in *The Interpreter's Bible,* VII, 318.
2. W. F. Albright and C. S. Mann; *The Anchor Bible, Matthew,* p. 79. Garden City, NY: Doubleday, (1971) 1973.

The contrast made by both our Lord and St. Paul rests on the fact that all men have an idea of what constitutes a treasure, and what by contrast is a trifle. Men build their lives on this evaluation. The parable of the hidden treasure illustrates this fact:

> Again, the kingdom of heaven is like unto treasure hid in a field; the which when a man hath found, he hideth, and for joy thereof goeth and selleth all that he hath, and buyeth that field. (Matt. 13:44)

A man's *treasure* thus is the governing faith in his life, the motive force which governs his thoughts, words, and actions.

The same is true of a society or culture. Its treasure is whatever faith governs its life, and its trifles will be those things regarded as either peripheral, irrelevant, or even an impediment to life. Paul regarded his previous treasure as dung after his conversion.

To illustrate this fact on the current world scene, Hedrick Smith points out that, "In Russia, the law means nothing. . . . What matters most is power. The Russian obeys power, not the law."[3] The treasure for Russians is naked power. In the West, power must be disguised with humanitarian and equalitarian trappings, because the treasure or governing faith is more closely linked to a humanism still governed by perversions of Christian compassion.

However, the treasure-principle in Western thought is clearly anti-Christian. Harold O. J. Brown calls attention to one aspect of this treasure-principle:

> There is an old Latin maxim, *de minimis non curat lex:* the law is not concerned with trifles. Turned around, it might say, "Whatever the law is not concerned with, is a trifle of no importance." Where the law claims to be unconcerned with morality, it is educating the public to believe that morality is of trifling importance. And this is the message that comes through in countless aspects of American public life.[4]

Let us examine briefly where the treasure-principle is to be found in modern society. *First,* very clearly, its locale is in man. Man is the treasure, and the cardinal principle in all social action and statist legislation is the welfare of man. Man, moreover, is seen as autonomous, but his autonomy is not from other men but from God. We are told that "people need people," which is quite logical in terms of the religious presupposition. If we believe God to be ultimate, we will recognize that all men need God and that no true life exists apart from Him. On the other hand, if our faith is in man, then the idea of living in isolation from

---

3. Hedrick Smith: *The Russians,* p. 252. New York, NY: Quadrangle, The N. Y. Times Book Company, 1976.

4. Harold O. J. Brown: *The Reconstruction of the Republic,* p. 70. New Rochelle, NY: Arlington House, 1977.

man is anathema: man must be close to other men in order to fulfil his being. Thus, medieval man often withdrew from other men, even abstaining from speech, into conventual life, in order to be closer to God. This was seen, not as a punishment, but as a higher way of life. Now solitary confinement is regarded as one of the worst forms of punishment. Again, Daniel Defoe's *Robinson Crusoe* (1719-1720) reflected the Puritan resourcefulness and independence from men and the strength of reliance on God. On a desert island, Crusoe found communion with God, created a culture, and developed the resources of that island. In the 20th century, the fictional Robinson Crusoes are men who are castaways from God, and their hope is in man. Crusoe through the Bible and prayer established fellowship with God. The modern Crusoes are trying to overcome the communications gap, to end alienation, by establishing communion with themselves and their fellow men.

*Second,* modern law is therefore concerned with man, how to educate, nurse, feed, and employ man, and how to enable man better to glorify and enjoy himself. The moral foundation of the law is thus human welfare, a changing concept in terms of the changing and developing needs of man. Like the ancient Romans, modern man has come to believe that the fundamental legal principle is that the health or welfare of the people is the highest law. To achieve this, whatever sacrifice is necessary must be made, it is held.

*Third,* because man is the basic treasure, because the religion of modern society is humanism, the principle of the equality of man governs modern law. It is a theological and logical necessity that, in any religion, there be an equality in the godhead. Inequality in the principle of ultimacy is an impossibility, a contradiction of terms and ideas. Therefore, if man is ultimate, if man is god, then all men are equal. The equality of men is an historical lie, a scientific fiction, and a factual impossibility, because the concept of equality is an abstraction, and man is not a mathematical abstraction. The concepts of equality and inequality are thus not applicable to something as varied and particular as humanity. Particular men are not the universals of man. Very obviously too, modern man has problems with the idea of his equality and inequality: both concepts trouble him. If either is applied in society, legal problems and very serious social problems ensue. Humanistic man, however, much as he dislikes the problems of equality and inequality, cannot drop the problem, as a Christian can, because his religious principle, his faith in man, requires it. The problem dominates politics, and, whatever course politicians take, whether in Britain, South Africa, or the United States, whether they opt for equality or inequality, the consequences are only trouble, because the premise is in any case a false one.

On the other hand, what modern man and the modern state regard as trifles, not treasures, is equally a problem to society. *First,* God, and faith in the triune God, is regarded as a trifle. It is either peripheral to, left out of, or banned, depending on the country, from the state schools. American philosophers of statist education have been vocal about their faith in man, and equally vocal that something so divisive as Biblical faith should be left out of education as both a danger and yet a trifle, a matter of private option and opinion.

A fundamental declaration of Scripture is that God is a jealous God (Ex. 20:5; Deut. 4:24; Isa. 42:8), who will not share His ultimacy and glory with any other. In terms of this, what modern man regards as a trifle is thus the very ground of his judgment and forthcoming destruction. Because his culture treasures a reprobate principle, modern man is reprobate and doomed.

*Second,* Biblical law is regarded as an alien and obsolete trifle whose only place is in a library as a relic of the past, a museum piece. The idea that law must stem from the God of Scripture rather than the humanistic state is seen as alien and unrealistic. It is unrealistic because the new principle of reality is seen as man. Hence, law must be made by man and governed by human needs, not God, it is believed. *Law gears a society to reality:* if the reality is God, then law comes from God; if the reality is man, then law comes from man.

*Third,* whereas equality (or, in some instances, inequality), is the treasure-principle of humanistic society, for godly man it is knowledge, righteousness, holiness, and dominion. This means knowing God's word, law and world, believing and obeying God's word and law, and applying it to gain dominion under God. Practically, in the realm of law, this means justice in terms of God's law. Justice, however, in this sense is a trifle to modern man, although he still retains the word. Walter Kaufmann, in *Without Guilt and Justice* (1973), has argued that, because the idea of justice is inseparable from the idea of God and His law, and punishment for transgressions against Him and His law, modern man must abandon the concept of justice itself. This is clearly a logical conclusion, and it is only the still strong Christian undercurrents which have prevented the wholesale adoption of this philosopher's logical conclusion.

Clearly, our view of what constitutes treasures and trifles is important and does govern what we are and what we do. Moreover, we must say that modern man regards unreal and dangerous trifles as his treasures. If he continues in this path, the consequences will be deadly.

Our Lord is emphatic: "Man shall not live by bread alone, but by every word that proceedeth out of the mouth of God" (Matt. 4:4). The alternative to "bread alone" is not idealism, nor humanism. It is the *every word* of God. If our heart is there, if our treasure is that every word, then neither our lives, our law, nor our societies will be grounded upon trifles, or, as our Lord stated it, upon sand, upon an unstable foundation (Matt. 7:24-27).

Man's ideas of discretion bring trifles to the law, and it is presumptuous for man to take God's word and add his own to it. To live by God's every word means to forsake our word.

150

## THE RESURRECTION AS ENTHRONEMENT

Kingship and law are inseparable. A king rules by means of his law, and the law of a king is the expression of his will, purpose, and plan for his realm.

The premillennialists do recognize this fact. They therefore believe, in terms of their dispensationalism, that the law of God was valid until Christ died and rose again. The reign of the law of God then ceased and will only become operative when Christ comes again to establish His millennial kingdom on earth. From the standpoint of the Scofield Bible notes, Jesus Christ, in His triumphal entry into Jerusalem on Palm Sunday, did not enter as King but merely offered Himself as King. Because He was rejected, His Kingdom was supposedly deferred until the millennium, when the law will again prevail.

The amillennialists do believe that Christ reigns in heaven, and, to a degree, over His church. However, for them too the law has been set aside, because God's Kingdom has somehow lost its centrality from its status before the cross. Things are now on a more "spiritual" basis, as a prelude to heaven, and hence the role of the law is forever finished.

Similarly, some pietistic post-millennialists, who show evidences also of neoplatonism, find the law now irrelevant, because God's people now live on a more "spiritual" plane than did Abraham, David, Isaiah, and others of the old dispensation. The Kingdom of God is changed into an influence rather than a government, and a pervasive mentality rather than a law.

As a result of these attitudes the major part of the Bible is reduced to irrelevance, and man is given a vague do-it-yourself religion and an ethic of antinomian love. The Scripture, however, is emphatic on the Kingship of Christ and declares very clearly that His enthronement came with His resurrection. According to St. Peter, in Acts 2:29-36,

> Men and brethren, let me freely speak unto you of the patriarch David, that he is both dead and buried, and his sepulchre is with us unto this day.
> Therefore being a prophet, and knowing that God had sworn with an oath to him, that of the fruit of his loins, according to the flesh, he would raise up Christ to sit on his throne;
> He seeing this before spake of the resurrection of Christ, that his soul was not left in hell, neither his flesh did see corruption.
> This Jesus hath God raised up, whereof we all are witnesses.

Therefore being by the right hand of God exalted, and having received of the Father the promise of the Holy Ghost, he hath shed forth this which ye now see and hear.
For David is not ascended into the heavens: but he saith himself, the LORD said unto my Lord, Sit thou on my right hand,
Until I make thy foes thy footstool.
Therefore let all the house of Israel know assuredly, that God hath made that same Jesus, whom ye have crucified, both Lord and Christ.

The resurrection was thus seen by the disciples as the vindication of Christ's Kingship, and the Scripture declares that with His victory over sin and death Christ was enthroned as King. This Kingship is the Davidic, messianic Kingship and in terms of God's law as the foundation of His reign. The idea of a vague, "spiritual" Kingdom did not exist in Israel and is totally alien to everything in Scripture. The modern idea of the kingdom was born into the church rather early as a result of Greco-Roman influences and is really not a formulation of the kingdom concept but of the Hellenic philosophy of ideas or forms. The Kingdom of God is changed from the living reality of the King, His law, and His government, to an idea or a universal. Most churchmen speak of the Kingdom of God as Greeks, not Christians.

Peter declared Christ to be enthroned now on David's throne of power and authority. St. Paul speaks of Christ as reigning now (I Cor. 15:25), and declares that God has put all things under the feet of Christ the King (Eph. 1:22). Our Lord Himself declares the extent of His royal power: "All power is given unto me in heaven and in earth" (Matt. 28:18).

Zechariah had prophesied,

Rejoice greatly, O daughter of Zion: shout, O daughter of Jerusalem: behold, thy King cometh unto thee: he is just, and having salvation; lowly, and riding upon an ass, and upon a colt the foal of an ass. (Zech. 9:9)

Scofield to the contrary, Christ's Kingship did not cease, nor was it postponed, because Israel rejected Him. Rather, because Christ was and is King, Israel ceased to be a nation because it rejected the King. What happened to Israel confronts every man and nation throughout history: all who declare, "We will not have this man to reign over us" (Luke 19:14), face the same overwhelming judgment, for Christ is King. Men who try to judge Him are judged by Him, and none can stay His hand.

The crucifixion and the resurrection mean our salvation. Our sins are remitted, our old nature gives way to a new creation, and we become citizens of the new creation. These glorious facts mark our inheritance and status in Jesus Christ.

We must remember, however, that all these things and more are only possible because the risen Jesus is the King of creation, enthroned as both Christ and Lord. What Adam failed to be, the last Adam, Jesus Christ (I Cor. 15:45), has become, King of creation, God's covenant man. What Adam could not do because of his sin and fall, exercise dominion and subdue the earth under God as God's Kingdom (Gen. 1:26-28), the triumphant King of Kings shall accomplish in and through His people.

The central meaning of the resurrection is thus the enthronement of Christ as King. Moreover, St. Peter makes clear that Christ is the Davidic King, king in terms of the covenant and the covenant law. The covenant king, according to Deuteronomy 17:19, must rule in terms of the covenant law, because God's reign requires God's law. Our Lord's coming was hailed as the coming of God's Kingdom (Matt. 3:2), and our Lord, in the Sermon on the Mount, pronounced the first beatitude with reference to the kingdom (Matt. 5:3). As King, He confirms the royal law, God's law. He has come, not to set aside, as false kings do, but to fulfil it, to put it into force, and not one jot nor tittle shall in any way be set aside but all shall be put into force (Matt. 5:17-20).

Where Adam had been disobedient, Christ had been obedient. Adam had replaced the law of God with his own law, his own autonomous ideas of good and evil (Gen. 3:5). The last Adam had instead declared, "Man shall not live by bread alone, but by every word that proceedeth out of the mouth of God" (Matt. 4:4). Every word of God is law to Christ the King, and it is life.

Because men have viewed Christ's Kingship in Hellenic terms and as a "spiritual" thing, *i.e.,* a universal or an idea, they have abstracted it from the substance of life and history. It is an influence, a religious appeal, but not an actual kingship and rule. But man cannot live without government and law, and, having denied the Lord's Kingdom and reign, men now groan under the modern pharaohs. As Christ's reign and law are spiritualized out of this world, the reign of fallen men, and his autonomous law, become progressively more materialized. History is not a vacuum. It requires rule, government, and law, and, when the Kingship of the last Adam is diminished or denied, the usurped kingship of the fallen Adam takes over.

If we proclaim the resurrection of Jesus Christ without His enthronement, we lie. If we seek salvation from that resurrection without bowing down before the Christ and Lord, the King who rose from the dead, we are trying to be grave-robbers. We want the king's riches, but we declare the King is dead as far as His Kingship is concerned.

To declare that Jesus Christ is risen from the dead means to declare that He is enthroned as King, that we must believe in Him as Christ and Lord, obey His law, and recognize that His holy government and Kingdom shall conquer and prevail. God declares through Isaiah,

I have sworn by myself, the word is gone out of my mouth in righteousness, and shall not return, That unto me every knee shall bow, every tongue shall swear. (Isa. 45:23)

The word of Jesus Christ, the greater Moses, to the pharaohs of the church and the world is clear: "Let my people go, that they may serve me" (Ex. 4:23; 9:1). The word of the risen Christ is law and grace: for the redeemed, no other word can bind man, nor can any word be subtracted from, nor can any other word be added to His word. He is the King.

## 151

# THEATRICALS AND THE LAW

In the philosophy of Plotinus, we have the logical development of the Greek dialectic of mind or idea versus body or matter. All of being has this implicit dualism of two alien substances. The God of Plotinus is the "soul" or mind of the universe. The higher realm is thus the realm of the mind, which is one being with God. Instead of the Biblical division of reality between the uncreated Being of God and the created being of the universe, we have instead the division between mind and body, and we are all partakers of both. The goal of our lives, however, should be freedom from the one, matter, and ascension into the other, mind or spirit. From such a perspective, the true realm or Kingdom of God is entirely a thing of the mind or spirit, a kingdom of the mind, soul, or spirit. The Kingdom of God is then the supreme idea or form, the key universal in the life of man. The true word then comes from the man who sees the idea. To become a citizen of such a kingdom means a separation from the material to the spiritual life and realm. A neoplatonic idea of the Kingdom of God will thus of necessity avoid the things of this world, such as law, family life, commerce, farming, and various other mundane affairs. The result is a view of the Kingdom of God which uses Biblical language to perpetuate Greek philosophy.

The Biblical Kingdom of God does not summon us to forsake the material world for the spiritual in the manner of Plotinus, but *to separate ourselves from sin,* a radically different concern. We cannot, like the Manichaeans, associate the idea of the material with sin, and the spiritual with good. Satan is a spiritual being. Sin begins in the heart of man: its consequences affect both mind and body. The whole man is involved in both sin and redemption. While the Biblical Kingdom of God is not of, or derived from, this world, it is in this world, and over this world. It is therefore a Kingdom with very practical concerns: it governs the total life of man, his work, rest, worship, education, sexual and family life, his community, his church, state, and all things else. This Kingdom is one whose citizenship is made up of all who are a new creation in Christ, the last Adam, but it is a Kingdom whose jurisdiction is total, over all heaven and earth (Matt. 28:18f.). It is a Kingdom of grace, because all who exist therein are created and re-created by the grace of God through Jesus Christ, and it is also a Kingdom of law, because it is governed by the word of God, the King. The Kingdom of God is a very real Kingdom; in the Old Testament, God ruled from the Holy of Holies, through judges, kings, and prophets. In the New Testament era and our times, He rules from eternity, but no less powerfully and totally, and His law is still the basis of His government. God has not decided, since Christ's resurrection, that tithing is obsolete, adultery a joke, homosexuality simply a sad affair and a tragedy rather than a sin, theft something no longer requiring restitution, and so on. It is the law, not of the Medes and Persians which does not pass away nor alter, but the law of God.

The purpose of the Kingdom of God is to govern every area of life and thought to the glory of God. Man, as God's image bearer, is called upon to recognize the meaning of the image he bears and to develop the implications of God's Kingdom and law for the totality of his life and the world. *The law of God is thus inseparable from man's calling.* Antinomian attempts to discharge man's calling under God in reality meet the requirements of the tempter and of original sin, namely, that man, as his own god, determines, knows, or establishes good and evil for himself. Neither Satan nor his hosts are atheists (as James 2:19 makes clear); rather, they are antinomians (Gen. 3:1-6).

When ostensible or professing Christians deny the law and Kingdom for a neoplatonic idea, they drift steadily into an irrelevancy and pietism. They concentrate on spiritual affairs, which means a neglect of this world and its concerns. Since the publication of *The Institutes of Biblical Law,* I have found, in every part of the country, hostility from some of the clergy at its implications. Central in their hostility is (1) the requirement of tithing, (2) the death penalty for adultery (the sexual revolution has made heavy inroads in the church, and a hostility to the idea that *any* sexual act is sinful is a strong under-current), and (3) above all, the death penalty for homosexuality. The idea is very common that God *requires* nothing of us, although many will assert that certain minimal acts of morality do serve to show our gratitude. In brief, there are no legal moral imperatives, according to these men.

For them, the concern of God's Kingdom is salvation from hell-fire, a spiritual life, and a concentration on spiritual causes and concerns. It should not surprise us that the result is impotence and irrelevance.

As a result of this false idea of the kingdom, humanism has prevailed. Of course, the concentration on personal salvation rather than the Kingdom of God is itself a reflection of Greek humanism rather than the God-centered faith of Scripture. These neoplatonic churchmen approach the physical facts of the law, and of the tabernacle and its furnishings, with neoplatonic typology and turn the plain and direct word of God into spiritual junk.

The humanists, having denied God, have affirmed themselves as gods.

As good Greeks, they assert man as the new and true universal. If God is the true universal, then man lives and acts before God. He knows that the triune God of Scripture knows his innermost thoughts, and that he is always before God's eyes (Ps. 139), and so his total life is lived in the awareness that God sees all. The humanist has man for his audience, because man is for him ultimate. There is a difference, however, in the "audiences." God is the creator, the determiner, the redeemer, and the audience as well. Man cannot *act* before God; he cannot play a role convincingly, nor pretend to something. After all, God wrote the script, and there is no evasion nor hiding from God. Man is naked in the eyes of God.

Before man, however, man can put on an act. Indeed, humanism began with that emphasis. Castiglione's *Courtier* and Machiavelli's *Prince* are both actors. Their success depends on their acting. White has called attention to the rise of this fact in the Renaissance. It created a new man, man as actor, an individual "who needs society as a resonance box," because society is his stage. "He is, in a word, tied to his society, to his class."[1]

It should not surprise us, thus, that since the Renaissance modern man has loved the theater, often seen the theater as the supreme art, and has imitated the theater in life. In the modern world, much of life is a cheap imitation of the theater, its drama, its heightened emotionalism, and its concentration on the individual. The very courts of Europe began to imitate opera, or to create palaces as stages for their own drama of rule. In the case of Ludwig II of Bavaria, the perspective on rule and power became so radically theatrical that it passed into insanity or radical irresponsibility.[2] Shakespeare set forth this new view of life in *As You Like It:*

> All the world's a stage,
> And all the men and women merely players. (Act II, Sc. vii)

Men might hate or love the audience, humanity, but they could not avoid putting on an act before it. In the 1960s, the hippies supposedly abandoned society for a freer life; all their actions, dress, and remarks represented instead a dedicated role-playing before society. The audience may be hated, but it is still the audience, and it is played to. In William Faulkner's novel, *The Wild Palms,* Harry Wilbourne is always aware, in his flight from society, of that audience, which is referred to as a new god, capitalized as "They," "Them," and so on. In the modern world, it is not a Christian but a theatrical view of life that most people try to maintain. Dress, speech, and conduct are forms of living theater practiced by most people.

---

1. John S. White: *Renaissance Cavalier,* p. 8. New York, NY: Philosophical Library, 1959.

2. See Wilfrid Blunt: *The Dream King, Ludwig II of Bavaria.* New York, NY: The Viking Press, 1970.

A theatrical view of life has far-reaching implications. When life is viewed Biblically as the creation of God and within the Kingdom of God, then the most important things for man are the grace or favor of God, and the law of God. Grace and law become basic for the total life of man.

However, when instead, because of humanism, life is viewed as theater, then the central emphasis is on plot, dialogue, and action. Such an emphasis is alien to law. The modern age has seen the proliferation of conspiracies of various kinds because of this theatrical emphasis, a belief that consequences in history are, like action in a theater, the results of a staged plot-plan. Add to this the spontaneity sought by the new theater, with impromptu dialogue and action, and you have a further hostility to law and order.

But this is not all. The theater has moved out of Broadway and buildings into the world at large. Feigelson has pointed out that, in the 1960s, the peace movement applied "the techniques of the theater to social protest." The Underground theater was a prelude to this, with its invitation to the audience to join in the stage action, an endeavor to unite the theater of revolution with life.[3] We cannot understand the role of the theater (which includes above all films and television) unless we recognize that it is now seen as life. Viewers judge their lives and needs in terms of the theater. Politics now is also theater. Candidates win or lose on theatrical grounds. Legislation is influenced by the theatricals of demonstrations, sit-ins, marches, protests, and the like.

All of this, of course, leads only to bitterness, because theatricals do not change society, nor are the acts of social legislation created by such theatrical acts capable of changing men and society. As a result, the theater of protest becomes more radical and revolutionary, as though this were the solution.

It would be a very serious mistake, however, to assume that theatricals are limited to students, minority groups, feminists, homosexuals, and other protesting groups. One of the areas of theatricals is the court. The courts of today are very much under the influence of humanism, and, as a result, subject to the influence of that philosophy which views life as lived, not before God, but before man, *i.e.,* life as living theater. The implications of this humanism for the courts are, *first,* an insistence on perfection in staging. In a theater, there is a strong insistence on perfect staging in order to heighten the illusions being performed on the stage. Repeat performances and repeated rehearsals are mandatory for a successful theatrical performance. Originally, in the United States, there was no second trial after a final judgment of conviction. In 1834, Justice Story in *United States* v. *Gilbert* held that the double jeopardy

---

3. Naomi Feigelson: *The Underground Revolution, Hippies, Yippies, and Others,* pp. 11, 29. New York, NY: Funk & Wagnalls, 1970.

clause of the U. S. Constitution prohibited the granting of a new trial after a jury had returned its verdict. This was over-turned by the Supreme Court in 1896. In 1911, California amended the state constitution to provide that no judgment should be set aside, or a new trial granted in any criminal case, unless "the court shall be of the opinion that the error complained of has resulted in a miscarriage of justice." As Fleming notes, "For the phrase *miscarriage of justice* the California courts soon substituted the phrase *prejudicial error,* and the constitutional provision rapidly sank into innocuous desuetude."[4] Today we have multiple trials of the same case, multiple reviews, and almost endless delays in this quest for the proper kind of staging of a trial. *The emphasis is not on justice but on the staging of the trial.* Such a concern on perfect staging leads, in fact, to a contempt for justice.

*Second,* this emphasis on perfection in court procedures is also theatrical because it is an emphasis on externals. Where a man (or a court) lives before the triune God who sees every thought of man from all eternity, there is an emphasis on the heart of man, on the truth, nature, and the reality of things. As man sees God, so he sees himself, *i.e.,* if he sees God as He whose concern is with righteousness, truth, and justice, so he will see himself and judge others also in terms of these things. If, however, externalism prevails, it will govern man's every area. If the god before whom we stand is humanity, and humanity sees simply what we act out, then we will put on an act and judge others by their theatricals also. The modern court, with its excessive attention to staging, emphasizes the externals, not justice. The results are quite often amazing. Today's mail brought me the following items from an attorney, David A. Depew of Alhambra, California:

> The Wisconsin Supreme Court rules that convicted murderers can be paroled without going to jail even though the law says they have to be sentenced to life in prison. The judges said a judge could impose the sentence, then "stay" it, and then order probation. But a person who drives without a license *has* to serve 10 days in jail. This shows what happens when a state goes by man's law rather than God's law.

> A Calif. Court of Appeals rules that children 6, 7, 10 & 13 years of age could be given back to their father who was convicted of murdering their mother. The court even ruled that murder is not a crime which would prove a person was an unfit parent.

> Municipal Court Judge Hugh Goodwin of Fresno, Calif., is being investigated by The State Commission on Judicial Performance because he gave convicted persons (up for probation) several probation choices, one of which was to attend church and Bible classes.

This heavy emphasis on externals has led to what Lord Diplock of the

---

4. Macklin Fleming: *The Price of Perfect Justice,* p. 47. New York, NY: Basic Books, 1974.

British House of Lords described as the American law's implication in criminal cases: "the irrelevance of guilt."[5] The play's the thing, not the justice of the case at hand, it sometimes appears.

*Third,* this emphasis on staging and externals leads, as Fleming notes, to the trivialization of the Constitution and of the law in general.[6] While justice is disregarded, the courts have sometimes busied themselves in recent years by defending the "rights" of school girls to wear slacks, boys to let their hair grow long, soldiers to wear unusual hair styles, and so on. This trivialization of the law is basic to the view of life as theater: the emphasis shifts to externals, and the interest in trifles proliferates.

Because of this externalism of the humanistic view, life becomes theater, and law becomes a matter of externals also. Faith in externalism abounds, because "the play's the thing." The law should seek to remedy injustice, but can the law create brotherhood? Modern legislation becomes an exercise in legislating hypocrisy. Externalism is substituted for godly law and love.

As against this, Scripture declares, in Psalm 19:7-14,

> The law of the LORD is perfect, converting the soul: the testimony of the LORD is sure, making wise the simple.
> The statutes of the LORD are right, rejoicing the heart: the commandment of the LORD is pure, enlightening the eyes.
> The fear of the LORD is clean, enduring for ever: the judgments of the LORD are true and righteous altogether.
> More to be desired are they than gold, yea, than much fine gold: sweeter also than honey and the honeycomb.
> Moreover by them is thy servant warned: and in keeping of them there is great reward.
> Who can understand his errors? cleanse thou me from secret faults.
> Keep back thy servant also from presumptuous sins: let them not have dominion over me: then shall I be upright, and I shall be innocent from the great transgression.
> Let the words of my mouth, and the meditation of my heart, be acceptable in thy sight O LORD, my strength, and my redeemer.

*First,* God's law is spoken of as *perfect, right,* and as *judgments* which are *true and righteous altogether.* God's law is more desirable than gold, and sweeter than honey. Regard for the law means *the fear of the LORD.* The delight of David is in the law of God, because it is the witness of God's holiness, grace, and mercy. The law is *pure,* and as a revelation of God's purity, it is an act of grace towards covenant man. There is no externalism here, nor any room for theatricals. God's total word is law, and it is grace. God's Spirit and power are inseparable from His word, and we are told,

---

5. *Ibid.,* p. 121.
6. *Ibid.,* pp. 129f.

> For the word of God is quick, and powerful, and sharper than any
> two-edged sword, piercing even to the dividing asunder of soul and
> spirit, and of the joints and marrow, and is a discerner of the
> thoughts and intents of the heart.
> Neither is there any creature that is not manifest in his sight: but all
> things are naked and opened unto the eyes of him with whom we
> have to do. (Heb. 4:12-13)

We have here a close association of the word, Scripture as a whole, the
Holy Spirit, and God Himself in His eternal majesty. God does not stand
apart from His word but acts in, with, and through that word. The law
of God, unlike the law of man, is not a matter of externals. He who gave
the law is He who made us, and our total being is attuned to the law-
word of God, so that faithfulness and apostasy have their radical effects
on us.

*Second,* the law of God acts in us in various ways: *converting the soul,
making wise the simple, rejoicing the heart, enlightening the eyes,* warning God's servants, rewarding the faithful, and feeding us in all our being
with the righteousness of God. To make "wise the simple" means to convert the ungodly. Solomon repeatedly uses the word *simple* to describe
unconverted men (Prov. 1:22; 7:7; 9:4; 14:15, etc.). Thus, we are doubly
told of the instrumentality of the law in the conversion of the ungodly, a
telling example of its internality. The law thus provides us with God's answer, His salvation and His law as the way of holiness, to the problems
of man and society. This is the antithesis of humanism and its emphasis
on externalism and theatricals. *In the popular imagination, solutions and
salvation are not by grace and law but by theatricals.* We cannot understand the power of modern fiction, theater, film, and television apart
from this fact. These media regularly present problem solving; they offer
various patterns of salvation for men. These plans of salvation vary: they
can be statist action, revolutions, vigilantes, the courts, politics, humanistic love, and so on, but, in every case, they offer theatricals. Grand
gestures and audience-staged actions are seen as the answer. Modern
man is so audience oriented that, even when he expresses his contempt
for the crowd, mass man, or for the middle classes, he must do so before
that audience: he cannot live without it.

The law which humanism offers society is a law dealing with externals
and trying to coerce man. The fallacy of antinomians is their insistence
on seeing God's law as in effect the same as humanistic law, a matter of
externalism. The righteousness, wisdom, and law which shaped every
fiber of my being is also the same righteousness, wisdom, and law which
speaks in the total word of God, in His law. Inescapably, therefore,
every fiber of my being is inseparable from that law. If I am in rebellion
against that law, I am at war with myself as well as with God. If I am in
obedience to that law by faith, then I am at peace with God and with

myself. The law either cries out against me in every atom of my being, or it sounds a great amen to the Almighty. Our Lord puts it more strongly: He declares that, if His disciples be rebuked or silenced, "the stones would immediately cry out" (Luke 19:40), because the stones, as God's creation, thus must witness to the presence of their Lord. God's law and creating power are stamped in all created being, and all things shall witness to Him who made them.

*Third,* the vital work of cleansing or clearing us from hidden faults is the work of the Lord and is closely related to this inner witness of the law. The words of our mouths and the meditation of our hearts are to be informed by the law of God. Only thus are we free from "much transgression." Alexander commented on verse 12:

> *Errors who shall understand? Clear thou me from hidden ones!* The word translated *errors* is akin to one sometimes used in the Law to denote sins of inadvertence, error, or infirmity, as distinguished from deliberate, wilful, and high-handed sins, such as are deprecated in the next verse. See Lev. iv. 22-27, Num. xv. 27. Against such sins no wisdom or vigilance can wholly guard. The word translated *clear* is also borrowed from the Law, and means not so much to cleanse by renovation of the heart, as to acquit by a judicial sentence. See Exod. xxxiv. 7, Num xiv. 18; such an acquittal, in the case of sinners against God, involves the idea of a free forgiveness.[7]

The will, grace, law, and judicial mercy of God function in our hearts in a way impossible for humanistic law.

In theatricals, a perfection of process is sought, a perfection of staging, so that the court now rehearses the fine details of a hearing endlessly. We must have *perfect* theater. This demand for legal perfection is a religious demand. The god of any system of thought must manifest perfection. Hence, we have in our humanistic courts today what Fleming has called "the ideal of perfectibility." This ideal has clear implications of infallibility, so that Judge Learned Hand felt impelled to observe, "due process of law does not mean infallible process of law."[8]

In Biblical law, the perfection is in God; it becomes religious impertinence and heresy then for men to strive for infallibility. What God requires of us is *justice.*

In the modern perspective, *justice* remains as a word but in fact has given way to theater. Demaris has shown that "terrorism. . . is theater."[9] When one terrorist hijack of a plane failed, one of the arrested terrorists, in addition to asserting the "justice" of their cause, observed of their failure, "That's show biz."[10] The word of man and the justice of man ends up as theater.

---

7. J. S. Alexander: *The Psalms,* p. 91. Grand Rapids, MI: Zondervan, (1864).

8. Fleming, *op. cit.,* p. 21; cf. eff.

9. Ovid Demaris: *Brothers in Blood, The International Terrorist Network,* p. 385. New York, NY: Charles Scribner's Sons, 1977.

10. *Ibid.,* p. 387. "Show biz" is an American term for theater business.

## 152

## ELDERS AND THE COURT OF APPEALS

We have become so accustomed to the idea of a court of appeals, or some other kind of recourse against tyranny that we fail to recognize how lacking the idea is in most cultures. Where the right of appeal existed, as in Rome, it was a very limited one. We must recognize, for example, that Paul's appeal to Caesar in Acts 25:11 does not represent a common act but a privilege accorded only to citizens. Citizens, moreover, were few in the Roman Empire and constituted a very insignificant minority. No such right existed for non-citizens, whether they lived in Rome, Jerusalem, Athens, or elsewhere.

As we know it, the right of appeal is a Biblical inheritance which cannot long exist apart from that faith. The appellate system is described in brief in Deuteronomy 1:15-17:

> So I took the chief of your tribes, wise men, and known, and made them heads over you, captains over thousands, and captains over hundreds, and captains over fifties, and captains over tens, and officers among your tribes.
> And I charged your judges at that time, saying, Hear the causes between your brethren, and judge righteously between every man and his brother, and the stranger that is with him.
> Ye shall not respect persons in judgment; but ye shall hear the small as well as the great; ye shall not be afraid of the face of man; for the judgment is God's: and the cause that is too hard for you, bring it unto me, and I will hear it.

In order to understand the meaning of this institution of government by elders, it is necessary to understand what an elder is in Scripture.

*First* of all, an elder was a man. Not only so, he was a free man, not receiving welfare by being under the care, as a bondservant, of another man. Moreover, an elder was a married man, capable of ruling his own household, and able to govern himself. St. Paul, in I Timothy 3:1-13, in discussing church officers, simply sums up the long-standing requirements for all who held the office of elder on any level. Whatever the grade or kind of eldership, every elder was thus a free man, head of a household, and capable of self-government as well as governing others. The basic government, institutionally speaking, is the home, the family, and here the basic authority and rulership exists. To this day, in Jewish circles, it is not a centralized authority but ten men who can constitute and establish a synagogue, with or without a rabbi.

In the Bible, as in Jeremiah 19:1, sometimes the word for elders is *ancients, zagen,* senior, or "the wise" (Ezek. 7:26; Jer. 18:18). In the Old Testament, the word *nobles* means *freemen,* i.e., elders.

The elders were the governors, each in their particular realm, so that family, church, and state had their rule by elders.

Thus, *second,* we find references to the elders of the priests in II Kings 19:2 and Jeremiah 19:1. There were gradations of authority within the priesthood, some elders presiding over others, and culminating in the high priest, a hereditary office in the sense that a blood line was required, but elective in that one man in that very numerous line was alone chosen.

*Third,* we find references to the elders of the city whose functions are seen in the law in reference to five types of law: (1) blood redemption, (Deut. 19:12); (2) the expiation of murder by an unknown culprit (Deut. 21:3, 6); (3) the judgment of incorrigible delinquents and criminals (Deut. 21:19); (4) cases of defamation of virgins (Deut. 22:15); and (5) laws of the levirate (Deut. 25:9). All of these cases are concerned with the protection of the family and its local, patriarchal interests. The law in each case requires discernment and judgment but does not permit discretion. The elders of the city thus constitute an extension of family government, protection, and defense. Clearly, a very different conception of *the city* is in evidence here. In the Bible, the community is a collection of families with a common faith, and its basic government is one which concerns itself with family life.

*Fourth,* the judges constitute still another form of eldership. The judges and their courts act in connection with disputes (Deut. 19:17-18; 25:1-3). Matters beyond the jurisdiction or solution of the elders of the city are referred to the judges, who sit with a priest, who provides judgment, not on the case at hand, but on the laws of God pertinent to the case (Deut. 17:8-11). These elective judges (Deut. 16:18-20) have a certain amount of investigative power in the court with respect to the testimony of witnesses (Deut. 19:16-19). In the case of an unknown murderer, the judges acted in concert with the elders of the city (Deut. 21:1ff.) and the elders of the country (Deut. 21:2).

*Fifth,* we have the elders of the people or the elders of the country. These elders constituted the general government and made up the national assembly, later known as the Sanhedrin, a council of seventy plus the governor, king, or, under the Romans, the high priest acting as a governor. Their creation is cited in Numbers 11:16; their powers included the declaration of war (I Kings 20:7, 8), negotiations by lesser councils with other tribes of Israel (I Sam. 3:17), and the like. They ratified and made possible a king's rule (II Sam. 5:3), and were the ruling body (II Sam. 17:14-15). We find these elders working with Elisha against the king (II Kings 6:32), and, later, interfering in the trial of Jeremiah (Jer. 26:17-24). Thus, the office retained great power even in the times of monarchy.

The functions of the elders of the people were (1) to represent the people in the covenant and in the proclamation and government of the law of God (Ex. 19:7; 24:1, 9; Deut. 27:1; 29:9; 31:9; Joshua 8:33; 24:1; II Kings 23:1). They were to see to it that God's law governed the land and the people. (2) The elders of the people appointed a leader, governor, or king (I Sam. 8:4; Judges 11:5-11). (3) These elders declared war (Josh. 8:10; II Sam. 17:4-15; I Kings 20:7). (4) They conducted political negotiations and made pacts and agreements (Ex. 3:16, 18; 4:29; Numbers 16:25; II Sam. 3:17; 5:3). (5) They performed some sacred ceremonies, as in the Passover (Ex. 12:21), communion (Ex. 18:12), and in witnessing sacrifices (Lev. 9:1). (6) They acted in times of national crisis as an aid and consenting witness to God's prophet (Ex. 17:5-6), in seeking God's mercy through repentance (Josh. 7:6; I Chron. 21:16). It was the elders of the people or of Israel who met in the city square next to the city gate (Deut. 21:19; 22:15; 25:7; Ruth 4:1ff.; Lam. 5:14). Their deliberations were thereby to be open to both God and man.

*Sixth,* we have also evidences of specialized elderships, as of David's palace and entourage (II Sam. 12:17). We encounter this same royal office in Jeremiah 18:18, where the elder is called "the wise" (cf. Ezek. 7:26). We find also references to elders of a tribe, i.e., a clan office (Deut. 31:28). Clearly, there is no understanding of Biblical government apart from the office of an elder.[1]

It would be difficult to miss the fact that his system of elderships created a decentralized government, with limited jurisdiction in every sphere, and a system of graded courts in each sphere. At first Moses, and then the high priest and the governor and then the king, acted as a supreme court under God.

But this is not all. The prophetic office, i.e., the ministry of the word or preaching, had reference to the law. Modern preaching is so antinomian that we miss this fact. The spirit of all the prophets is summed up in Isaiah's great declaration: "To the law and to the testimony: if they speak not according to this word, it is because there is no light in them" (Isa. 8:20). The words translated as "no light" are literally *no morning.* To depart from the law and the testimony is to have no morning or dawn, *i.e., no future.*

---

1. Although the use I have made of the material differs at points, I am very deeply in debt for all the above to the excellent article by Moshe Weinfeld, Senior Lecturer in Bible, the Hebrew University of Jerusalem, "Elder," in *Encyclopaedia Judaica,* vol. VI, 578-580.

The ideas of decentralization and of courts of appeals were basic to Christendom for centuries, although not without a struggle. Feudalism, a highly decentralized society, was one consequence of this heritage. The totalitarian nature of pagan antiquity, and its centralization, gave way to a social system in which local power was basic. American federalism was created as a Puritan version of medieval feudalism.

Local power can become as arbitrary, however, as centralized power, and Europe saw, with the development of feudalism and its interlocking loyalties right up to the Holy Roman Empire, a system which throttled appeals and made justice a local rather than a God-centered concern. Europe was thus witnessing a Christendom in which Christ's rule was being taken over by local lords and their overlords who controlled land, church, and man. A tremendous legal revolution, one of the key events in history, was the work of Hildebrand, Pope Gregory VII (c. 1020-1085). Gregory VII cut through all the bonds on justice to establish himself, i.e., the office of the papacy, as a final court of appeals for all men in Christendom. Thus, the *first* great step in his reform of Europe was to declare himself and his office to be that court. Hildebrand, as a single-minded man of prickly nature, is an easy man to criticize, but the greatness of his reform is with us yet: he shattered the concentration of legal power which had fallen into limited hands. The church and its clergy had become so enmeshed in feudal loyalties that their loyalty to God and His law had been stifled. The Vatican now became in time a Sanhedrin, with its seventy cardinals and its high priest, acting as a court of appeals. *Second,* the hold of feudal lords over the church and church offices was challenged and, little by little, pushed back, although never entirely broken. *Third,* because the clergy, especially the abbots and bishops, were noblemen in most cases, they were deeply involved in closer ties to their families than to the church. Celibacy was introduced to the regular clergy to break that feudal bond. That the celibacy was also sacerdotal represents a neoplatonic tradition; in this context, it was the legal consequences which were of central importance. As Rosenstock-Huessy has pointed out, "The Papal Revolution of the eleventh century introduced the principle of dualism into the political world. . . . In Western civilization, at least since Gregory VII, two sovereign powers have always balanced each other. This, and this alone, has created European freedom."[2] In 1075, in *Dictatus Papae*, Gregory set forth the principles of his crusade.[3] It is easy to err in reading this document, because we see it, not in its context, but in terms of later papal

---

2. Eugen Rosenstock-Huessy: *Out of Revolution, Autobiography of Western Man*, p. 543. New York, NY: William Morrow and Company, 1938.
3. See B. J. Kidd: *Documents Illustrative of the History of the Church*, III, p. 129f. London: S. P. C. K., 1941.

arrogance. In its day, it was a document of freedom: it gave to Christendom a court of appeals; it meant justice.

Side by side with this, the multiplicity of medieval courts served to keep any court from having too extensive a power and jurisdiction. Different cases required differing courts.

As time passed, however, the power of the papacy became the problem and the source of injustice. The question of appeal now took a new turn: where was the court of appeal against a pope? The result was the conciliar movement, which faced a double problem. The Council of Constance did not prove itself to be a successful instrument of appeal, and a limited instrument of reform. Later, in 1460, Pope Pius II (1405-1464), by his Bull, *Execrabilis* (January 18, 1460), condemned any appeal against a pope.[4] It is interesting to note that this Pius took his name, not from Christian history, but from Virgil's Pius Aeneas. He was in spirit closer to pagan Rome than to Christian Europe, and he made inevitable, a half century later, another legal revolution, which began with Luther's *Ninety-Five Theses* in 1517.

Luther's revolution required every Christian to be a priest, and it restored to the state a religious function and responsibility: the civil servant had a duty to be a minister of God. But, above all, Luther made the Christian scholar the voice of protest and a supreme consulting court. As Rosenstock-Huessy pointed out, "the universities became the heirs of the bishops' chair, the cathedra. The professor's chair was called *'Katheder.'* These Katheders became a church-like institution, like the Commons in England,"[5]

When, however, the German university lost its faith, the state took over; Germany was rapidly united and centralized, and any appeal stifled and destroyed. In one country after another, the triumph of Humanism has resulted in a totalitarian concentration of powers and a decrease or cessation of the right of appeal. In the U. S., the Supreme Court has become more powerful than the papacy ever was, because it denies that God's law exists beyond and over all its deliberations. The modern state has issued its own *Execrabilis* of a more fearful sort: it denies that it is subject to appeal, *and* it denies that God's law must govern the state and its courts, something Pius II never dared say.

The problem of appeals is thus very much with us. The Reformation and the Counter-Reformation (at Trent) offered differing solutions to the problem, but their answers have not eliminated the problem. One branch of Calvinism, the Puritans, developed in the U. S. a modified feudalism, i.e., a decentralization of the state through federalism and of the church through the triumph of local authority, or congregationalism

4. *Ibid.,* III, 222f.
5. Rosenstock-Huessy, *op. cit.,* p. 390.

in varying degrees, with graded courts in both churches and states. The result has been a greater strength than elsewhere, and a greater tenacity of the right of appeal, but no final solution.

A final solution is, of course, an illusion. What Biblical law gives us is the pattern of eldership and of graded courts of appeal. This is the necessary form, but the form does not create nor retain the power nor the meaning. This depends on a faithful and prophetic clergy, now sadly lacking, *and* a faithful people. Over and over again, Scripture gives us the resounding prophetic summons and command: "O earth, earth, earth, hear the word of the LORD" (Jer. 22:29). Only those who hear the word of the Lord, and who obey it, can have an appeal to the Lord. For the only dependable and absolute court of appeals is the Almighty, of whom Isaiah declares:

> The LORD standeth up to plead, and standeth to judge the people. The LORD will enter into judgment with the ancients of his people, and the princes thereof: for ye have eaten (or, burnt) up the vineyard: the spoil of the poor is in your houses.
> What mean ye that ye beat my people to pieces, and grind the faces of the poor? saith the LORD GOD of hosts. (Isa. 3:13-15)

God's judgment in history and beyond history is without appeal: He only is the Lord. Apart from faith in Him, no people have any valid appellate court. When people believe and appeal to God in faith and in truth, they are then also a people who obey Him and His law. Then, by their faith and obedience, they create a godly society in which justice and righteousness flourish and God's prospering grace abounds.

## 153

## COVENANT AND APPEAL

Basic to any understanding of Biblical faith is the doctrine of the covenant. *Covenant* means an obligation, treaty, pact, and relationship between two parties. A relationship is established, not necessarily one of equality by any means, but a relationship which is not only a vital one but also a legal one. A covenant is a binding; it is law. Our modern idea of relationship is emotional and antinomian; the Biblical doctrine is radically legal. Our idea now is that if we trust each other, we need no recourse to law. The Biblical doctrine is that law is the recourse and way of faith and trust. To illustrate this, the sexual revolution of the 1960s on has held that, if two people love each other, then the law, or a legal marriage, is superfluous and wrong. Law, some have even claimed, is the antithesis of love and turns a man-woman relationship into legalized prostitution. From the Biblical perspective, love only exists where there is law, and for anyone to circumvent the law of marriage means to manifest an absence of love.

It follows therefore that the depreciation of Biblical law has been the depreciation and denial of God and His covenant. Because God's covenant is from a superior to an inferior, man, it is a covenant of grace, and thus God's grace manifests itself to man by means of law.

Covenants are established, *first,* between individuals (Gen. 21:32; 31:44; I Sam. 18:3; 23:18). Such covenants were made "before the Lord," because the final judgment in all law is the Lord's. Hence, the declaration, "The LORD watch between me and thee, when we are absent one from another" (Gen. 31:49). Because God is the source of all law, He is the one invoked in oath and covenant, because no law can stand apart from Him. *Second,* covenants can be made between states or their rulers or ambassadors (II Sam. 3:13, 21; I Kings 5:12; 15:19; 20:34). A valid covenant requires a common faith and law, and hence the condemnation in the law of foreign alliances (Ex. 23:31-33; Ex. 34:12, 15, 16; Deut. 7:14). *Third,* a covenant could be made between a king and his subjects (II Sam. 5:3; II Kings 11: 4, 17). In the case of a national crisis, the king bound himself under God to the people, and the people to the king. *Fourth*, marriage in Scripture is a law relationship and a covenant. Marriage is in fact spoken of as a covenant (Prov. 2:17; Ezek. 16:8), and the spouse as "the wife of thy covenant" (Mal. 2:14). Precisely because marriage is a covenant, Biblical law requires the death penalty for adultery since it is treason to the fundamental law of that covenant. *Fifth,* the basic covenant is between God and man. Adam was placed under command from his creation, because he was a covenant creature, and hence in his total being under God's law.

The Hebrew term for making a covenant is to "cut a covenant." The cutting has reference to the sacrifices usually offered (Ex. 24:4ff.; Ps. 50:5; Gen. 15:9ff.; Jer. 34:18ff.), which witnessed to the penalty of death for violations of the covenant law. There was a covenant oath (Gen. 21:22ff.; 26:22ff.; Deut. 29:9ff.; Joshua 9:15-20; II Kings 11:4; Ezek. 16:8; 17:33ff.). Since the covenant or law established a relationship, it was commonly celebrated with a communion meal (Gen. 26:30; 31:54; Ex. 24:11; II Sam. 2:20).

A *sign* to witness to the covenant was common (Gen. 21:30; 31:44-45, 52; Joshua 24:27). The Bible gives us several *signs* of God's covenant, and Israel held to the centrality of three signs: *First,* the Sabbath at the creation (Ex. 31:16-17); *second,* the rainbow after the Flood, as a sign of God's covenant mercy and renewing grace (Gen. 9:1-17); and *third,* circumcision, as the mark of all men, potential elders (Gen. 21:4). This sign was replaced in the renewed covenant in Christ by baptism (Ezek. 36:25-27).

Now the doctrine of the covenant is basic to the Biblical doctrine of appeals, because an appeal in law is an implied appeal to the source of law. Two small children, in any family, will, if in a dispute, appeal to their father or mother to judge between them, because they recognize unconsciously that the law of the family is parental law. Thus, a sustained appeal is to the source of law. If that source is Caesar, then the case is carried on appeal to Caesar. If the source of law is covenantal or Biblical, the appeal is to God, *i.e.,* it is to His law-word and to the patterns of judgment established by Him.

In discussing both judgment and appeal, Moses declares:

> Ye shall not respect persons in judgment: but ye shall hear the small as well as the great; ye shall not be afraid of the face of man: for the judgment is God's: and the cause that is too hard for you, bring it unto me, and I will hear it. (Deut. 1:17)

This establishes, *first,* that the right of appeal rests on the fact that "the judgment is God's." In a Marxist state, there is no appeal against a Party decision, because the Party is ultimate and infallible. *Infallibility and ultimacy go hand in hand.* Whatever we make ultimate, we thereby make infallible. There is no possible appeal against ultimacy. In any system of thought, whatever occupies the place of ultimacy is beyond appeal, because nothing exists in that system whereby it can be judged or criticized. In order to criticize that faith, we must step outside of it and pass judgment on its ultimate principle from the vantage of another principle of ultimacy. Thus, theologies and philosophies which make God an open question, or something to be proven, are already non-Christian: they begin and end with autonomous man as ultimate and as the source of all judgment and proof. If, however, we begin with the Triune God, we prove all things and judge all things in terms of Him. He is the foundation of all rationality, factuality, logic, and proof. Thus, because "the judgment is God's," every decision by man is subject to appeal and/or revision. No finality can be ascribed to any system or judgment devised by man or issued by man, even in the name of the Lord. The idea or appeal is thus in essence a theistic concept: it presupposes the supernatural God of Scripture whose "every word" governs every aspect of creation. If law comes from man, there is no appeal beyond man. Practically, this means that the courts become State courts or Party courts. In the United States, for example, the vast majority of cases on appeal which reach the U. S. Supreme Court represent appeals by agencies of the state against the people, or against some aspect of Biblical law, i.e., against God. The continuation of such a trend means the practical end of the concept of appeals.

*Second,* the command is, "ye shall not be afraid of the face of man." Because "the judgment is God's," the basic and ultimate power is God's also, and hence it is God, not man, who is to be feared in the courts. The counterpart to "no respect of persons" where man is concerned is the respect for the person and law of God Almighty. Where respect for the person of God is gone, there respect for the person of man will prevail. The courts will then favor the rich or the poor, one race or another, bureaucrats or unions, employers or employees, and so on. *The law will always respect the source of law.* The law moves in terms of a basic and absolute respect for its principle of ultimacy.

This *respect* for God in the court is set forth in the legislation of Deuteronomy 17:8-11:

> If there arise a matter too hard for thee in judgment, between blood and blood, between plea and plea, and between stroke and stroke, being matters of controversy within thy gates: then shalt thou arise, and get thee up into the place which the LORD thy God shall choose; And thou shalt come unto the priests the Levites, and unto the judge that shall be in those days, and enquire; and they shall shew thee the sentence of judgment.
> And thou shalt do according to the sentence, which they of that place which the LORD shall choose shall shew thee; and thou shalt observe to do according to all that they inform thee:
> According to the sentence of the law which they shall teach thee, and according to the judgment which they shall tell thee, thou shalt do: thou shalt not decline from the sentence which they shall shew thee, to the right hand, nor to the left.

To understand this law, *first,* it is necessary to recognize that what we have here is a court of appeals, and it is made up of (a) Levitical priests, whose main function was normally teaching, and, in addition (b) lay judges. The judges rendered the decision insofar as the case at hand was involved, *i.e.,* with respect to guilt or innocence, sustaining or reversing the case on appeal. The priests made the decision with respect to the application of God's law to the case on appeal. They determined the law which was at issue, and the lay judges then gave their verdict in terms of that relevant law. An appeal thus had a double aspect: determining the nature of the offense, and then determining the nature of the judgment. Because the law is God's law, the determination of the specifics of the law belongs to those who teach God's law. This double aspect of the appelate court increased the degree of caution and protection in appeals.

*Second,* we are told what kinds of problems will require an appeal to a court of teachers and judges of the law. They are, *e.g.,* cases "between blood and blood." This means cases which require a judgment as to whether manslaughter or premeditated murder is involved. "Between plea and plea" covers a wide variety of cases, i.e., theft, embezzlement, and the like. "Between stroke and stroke" means controversial cases of personal injury. In all these cases, the problem is on the one hand to determine which law covers the case, and, second, once the relevant law is established, to review the case in terms of that law.

*Third,* all violations of God's law are seen as offenses "before God" (Gen. 6:11). Hence, judgment must be in the courts ordained by God, in the presence of judges as ordained by Him, and thus in the place of His choosing. In this sense, "the judgment is God's" (Deut. 1:17), and all judgment is *before the Lord.*

If judgment is not *before the Lord* and in terms of His law, justice will steadily leach out of the law. This is, of course, what is happening in the courts today. Historians and humanists generally are most prone to citing the arrogance of medieval papal claims, when the papacy made itself the final court of appeals and denied appeals against itself. However, no pope ever dared to say what is casually assumed by most judges today, that God would not in turn judge him and subject his every word, thought, and act to total review. The very fact that every pope had his confessor and confessional made him continuously subject to review, something lacking in the modern court. The sometimes flamboyant and arrogant claims of medieval popes are never as dangerous as the cold logic of judges who see no God above and beyond their court, and who judge in terms of a humanistic concept of law which ascribes ultimacy to man. The idea of appeal and reform is so basic to Christendom that we have forgotten that the Protestant Reformation was a Catholic fact and rested on the premise of reviving Christendom and the Catholic Christian faith from a growing humanism and unbelief. The idea of reformation and reconstruction in terms of God's law is a Christian fact. The sad fact is that both Catholics and Protestants have forgotten that it is also a continuous fact, and it is governed, not by ecclesiastical tradition, but God's law.

Modern man's substitute for the Biblical doctrine of law, the right of appeal, and the God who hears all appeals, is violence and revolution. This is appeal by destruction. It is not surprising that Thomas Jefferson, as a humanist, toyed with the idea of the necessity of regularly recurring revolutions. The French and Russian Revolutions have instituted by means of death and terror humanism's appeal against Christendom and have created a new problem, counter-revolution as the only means of appeal for their logical children. These men of revolution lack covenant law. Theirs is fiat humanistic law, and there is no appeal against the ultimate power, whether it be the state, a party, a class, a leader, or an elite minority. Where there is no appeal, the consequence is a built-in disaster course, what the prophet Isaiah called *a covenant with death*. According to Isaiah 28:14-18,

> Wherefore hear the word of the LORD, ye scornful men, that rule this people which is in Jerusalem.
> Because ye have said, We have made a covenant with death, and with hell we are at agreement; when the overflowing scourge shall pass through, it shall not come unto us: for we have made lies our refuge, and under falsehood have we hid ourselves:
> Therefore thus saith the Lord GOD, Behold, I lay in Zion for a foundation a stone, a tried stone, a precious corner stone, a sure foundation: he that believeth shall not make haste.
> Judgment also will I lay to the line, and righteousness to the plummet: and the hail shall sweep away the refuge of lies, and the waters shall overflow the hiding place.
> And your covenant with death shall be disannulled, and your agreement with hell shall not stand; when the overflowing scourge shall pass through, then ye shall be trodden down by it.

The foundation stone of the everlasting covenant is Jesus Christ. Because of Him, the great sign of God's covenant grace and mercy, and of the certainty of God's government and law, men's humanistic covenants with death and hell shall all be disannulled. Only God's law governs God's creation, and He destroys and disannulls all efforts to replace His covenant, His law, and His requirements. Men will either serve Him or be destroyed by Him. No regime, revolution, or court that man can devise can annul or shut the supreme court of appeals, the Lord God Almighty.

The court of Almighty God is the final court of a series ordained by His word. The first and basic court on the human scene is the family. The father as elder must exercise government and rule with justice. The wife is his helpmeet in that government. Children must be reared to rule and to exercise dominion in terms of God's law. The old Hebraic saying, that a man who does not teach his son a trade and the law teaches him to be a thief, makes clear why the Jewish family became a self-governing unit and survival-strong under adversity. The same principal governed early Puritanism and left its mark on the U.S. We can only understand the strength and ability of the godly woman as depicted in Proverbs 31:10-31 in terms of an education to govern in terms of God's law. If there is no sound government, education, and dominion in terms of God's law in the family, there can be none in society. Then too God's judgment, against which there is no appeal, falls on that society.

## 154

## THE EXERCISE OF DISCRETION

A few years ago, before I spoke briefly to the assembled house of a state legislature, the elderly speaker of the house expressed to me his dismay at the legislative process. *First,* he said, the more frequently a state legislature met, the greater the controls and the fewer the freedoms of the people. Most state legislatures once met briefly every second year. The progression to yearly and then year-round sessions was always productive of a destruction of freedom, even with conservative legislatures. The bureaucracy had a year-round opportunity then to demand additional funds, and those groups of citizens demanding subsidies for themselves and controls over others had more time to pressure legislators into meeting their demands. *Second,* the function of legislators is to make laws, he said; any man who gains such office is quickly prone to believe that the solution to man's problems lies in the laws he proposes. As a result, the laws and controls multiply, and the taxes increase.

The speaker had no answer, but he did see the problem. A fact concerning Biblical law which is seldom realized is that God made no provision for a law-making body, because He did not intend that there be one. We cannot understand the Biblical order if we fail to grasp the fact that God alone is the law-maker. Men cannot make laws without sinning, nor can judges add or subtract from the law.

The system of civil government in Scripture calls for rule by elders, in church, state, and family, in terms of the law of God. At the accession of the king, the elders met to make a covenant with the king "before the LORD" (I Chron. 5:3), *i.e.,* to agree together by treaty to be faithful to God and to one another in the Lord in terms of His law, to obey it, to enforce it, and to teach it. The function of all rulers, and elders in particular, was to administer God's law, not to make law.

*The elders of the city, the elders of the priests,* of a *tribe* of the *people,* etc. all had basic governmental functions in terms of God's law. These functions were in essence two: *first,* to teach and administer the law of God, and *second,* to apply God's law to all who transgressed. Faithfulness was mandatory in both, so that the elder could not apply legitimately his justice and forgiveness to a situation, but only the justice and forgiveness of God the Lord.

In Deuteronomy 29:9-20, God declares through Moses that to "enter" or "pass" into covenant with God means to keep "the words of the covenant, and do them, that ye may prosper in all that ye do" (vvs. 9, 12). If man walks in "the imagination" or "stubborness" of his heart, he walks then into evil and idolatry (vvs. 17, 19). The word translated in verse 17 as "idols" is "dungy gods." The word can also be rendered as "dung pellets" or pieces of dung (gillulim), and Ezekiel in particular uses this word very frequently for the pagan gods or idols (Ezek. 6:4, etc.).

The chief of man's "dungy gods" is himself. Man not only idolizes his own thinking but asks God and man to bow down before it. Even in dealing with God's law, he interprets it in such a way as to replace it. He does this in the name of "discretion." It is important to examine more closely the meaning of *discretion*. Five meanings for the word *discretion* are common to legal practice. These are, as variously defined by the courts,

1. The exclusive right to decide as the court pleases; power of free decision; undirected choice not revisable or reviewable by the appellate tribunal.
   Examples:
   Discretion "when applied to public officials is the power conferred on them by law to act officially under circumstances according to dictates of their own judgment and conscience uncontrolled by judgment and conscience of others."
   *Schneider* v. *Hawkins,* 179 Md 21, 16 A2d 861 (1940).

2. A relatively wide latitude of judgment; the latitude of judgment when there is an absence of a "fixed" or "hard and fast" rule.
   Examples:
   "A judicial act is said to lie in 'discretion' when there are no fixed principles by which its correctness may be determined and such determinations are not subject to review on appeal."
   *Palliser* v. *Home Telephone Co.,* 170 Ala 341, 54 So. 499 (1911).

3. The quality of being discreet, prudent, circumspect; exercising sound judgment; not arbitrary.
   Examples:
   "Discretion implies knowledge, prudence and that discernment which enables a person to judge critically of what is correct and proper; it is judgment directed by circumspection."
   *Merritt School Dist. No. 50* v. *Kemm,* 22 Wash2d 887, 157 P2d 989 (1945).

4. The power to make a choice from among two or more legally valid solutions. (See Jaffe, *Judicial Control over Administrative Action,* p. 586 [1965].)
   Example:
   " 'Discretion' in performing an act arises when it may be performed in one, two, or more ways either of which would be lawful and where it is left to the will or judgment of the performer to determine in which way it shall be performed."
   *Texas Indemnity Ins. Co.* v. *Arant,* 171 SW2d 915 (Tex. Civ. App. 1943).

5. The normal and usual process of decision-making, i.e., the process of applying legal precepts or concepts to facts.
Examples:
   (a) "Discretion is the responsible exercise of official conscience on all facts of a particular situation in the light of the purposes for which the power exists."
   *Monahan* v. *Jacobs & Politi,* 66NYS2d 207, 215, 187 Misc 332 (1946).

   (b) The exercise of a trial court's "discretion" means nothing more than the application of statutes and principles to all of the facts of a case.
   *Shopiro* v. *Shopiro,* 153 P2d 62 (Cal App 1944).[1]

Very commonly, these varying meanings are confused. Definitions 4 and 5 are clearly legitimate exercises of judicial authority; facts are related to law by analysis. The same is true of Definition 3, when strictly applied. The problems arise with Definitions 1 and 2; no. 2 represents a common situation in contemporary jurisprudence. Because of the modern stress on statute law, the courts face difficulties when the statute fails to cover every contingency, and hence the need for discretion arises. God's law is given with case laws, and God's law is written into man's being (Rom. 1:17-21), so that there is no absence of "fixed principles." In humanistic law, there are a variety of unfixed principles at work, as well as pragmatism, political self-interest, and sheer blundering. The judge ruling in terms of humanistic law is thus constantly compelled to exercise that wide latitude of judgment which is necessitated by an absence of both principles and rules. It should not surprise us, in such a context, that there should be a widespread complaint about judicial arbitrariness. Humanistic law requires arbitrariness and arbitrary discretion, because it lacks a fixed and transcendental doctrine of law.

The consequence is a proneness to exercise discretion in terms of Definition 1, the "right to decide as the court pleases" and "according to dictates of their own judgment and conscience uncontrolled by judgment and conscience of others." This is precisely the power claimed and offered by the tempter in Genesis 3:5, the "right" to be one's own god, determining, knowing, or establishing for one's own self what constitutes good and evil.

God's law and redemption are directed precisely against this claimed power. For churchmen to re-introduce it into the context of Christian thought, Biblical commentary, and pastoral counselling and preaching is to deny the covenant of God. The covenant of our Lord re-establishes us by sovereign grace into a position of obedience, not "free decision." It replaces ourselves and our "dungy gods" with the clear and unchanging

---

1. *Judicial Review of the Exercise of Discretion,* p. 1f. Mimeographed guide for students, University of Oregon Law School.

word of God. It frees us from the burden of our sin, playing god, and it surrenders judgment to God the Lord.

The world often appears to be an easier place if I forgive where God requires judgment. Adultery and murder call for death, as does homosexuality. "Extenuating circumstances" are always easy to find. The world becomes less frightening for me if God is made less harsh, or so it seems. If I undercut God's judgment, I also undercut His grace. If I tamper with the law, it is because I have no law, and if I have no law, I am faced, not with freedom, but with death. Adam and Eve wanted all of Eden, plus their liberty of discretion, the right to independent verification and judgment. They found instead exile in a fallen world. As long as man claims that right of discretionary judgment, he remains a citizen of the fallen world.

155

## "WHAT DOTH THE LORD REQUIRE OF THEE?"

We live in an era which professes a religion of love but manifests savage hatred. Men endlessly parrot the words, "Judge not," while they judge harshly, backbite, gossip, and slander as readily as they breathe. They talk about grace rather than law, but they show no grace, and they despise God's law in favor of man's. A generation that talks of "grace alone" is also the most litigious in all of history.

This should not surprise us. When men abandon the whole counsel and word of God, they fashion graven images out of the partial word, and they use this partial and deformed word of God as a facade for their own word. Schilder wrote, "The Almighty forbid that any man should outline a specific program which the God of heaven and earth should follow in order to realize the great purpose of all that moves and has being."[1] It is a great temptation of man to use precisely God's partial word to promote his own word, to drop the law, or the atonement, love, grace, justice, or anything else, or, more accurately, to minimize their meanings. We need to remember that Satan himself, in seeking to pervert our Lord from His calling, used the very words of Scripture to do so (Matt. 4:1-11). Satan used, in each of the three temptations, a partial word, perverted into another meaning, in order to promote the kingdom of man as against the Kingdom of God. In each of the three temptations, our Lord responds by citing Scripture, by setting the wholeness of the word against a partial and perverted word.

But this is not all. When we deny any part of God's word to God, we appropriate it to ourselves. We do not abolish that word: we transfer it instead from the Creator to the creature. If we deny grace to God, we give it to man; if we deny atonement from the Lord, we seek atonement from ourselves; if we deny God's law as applicable to us, then we bow our necks to the rivets of man's law, to the bondage of our own sinful word.

This is why we are the most litigious generation in all of history. When the Pharisees implicitly denied God's law in favor of their traditions, they produced the Talmud. When the church forsook God's law, it produced the many reams of church laws and regulations, binding the consciences of men to the church rather than the Lord. When civil govern-

---

1. K. Schilder: *The Suffering Christ*, p. 112. Grand Rapids, MI: Eerdmans, 1950.

ment abandoned the law of God for humanistic law, it created libraries full of laws and regulations, and a generation in which lawless men are forever judging one another.

Our generation demands of all men in all things that they be judges. To illustrate, two friends in the Middle West, both of whom I regard with some respect, have recently quarrelled. Neither has consulted me, nor talked to me of their division, for which I am grateful. However, several friends have written or telephoned asking me to issue a judgment on the matter! I have had to reply patiently that I am not their judge, nor do I have any responsibility to pass judgment. I add further that for me to judge would be a sin, and to do other than dismiss their reports would be to participate in gossip and tale-bearing. None of us are constituted by God to be a court.

To cite a second example: a couple I have known from my youth recently secured a divorce, not too long after their children were grown and gone from the home. Since they were both strong and active Christians, this caused some shock. It was obvious that the step was not taken lightly. Both kept the reasons entirely to themselves, and the church authorities kept their investigation and any "disciplinary" action, if any was taken, to themselves. Many people immediately took sides, basing their judgments on various snatches of partial evidences. Again I was asked where I stood, and again I had to say that I knew next to nothing, had not been asked to judge, nor wanted to be asked, nor did I have any authority as a judge. My contacts with both are nowadays rare, and neither has chosen to confide in me. What right have I to judge?

If a man is convicted by a civil or criminal court, or found guilty by a church court, and, on appeal, his sentence is sustained, I have reasonable grounds to assume that he or she is guilty, although no infallible grounds. Certainly, given the nature of church courts, there is reason even then for some doubt. In brief, while I am required to uphold God's law, and to seek its furtherance and application in every realm, I am not thereby made a judge.

What authority is there for such a position? The authority comes from Christ Himself. According to Luke,

> And one of the company said unto him, Master, speak to my brother, that he divide the inheritance with me.
> And he said unto thcm, Man, who made me a judge or a divider over you? (Luke 12:13-14)

Our Lord does not say that questions of inheritance are not important, although He does condemn covetousness (Luke 12:15). He did not come to set aside the law (Luke 16:17; Matt. 5:17-20), and neither had He come to replace the courts that His word had created. He spoke readily and as the interpreter of the law, but even then as the law-giver from the mount, and not as a scribe (Matt. 5:1; 7:28-29). It would be a serious and pietistic misreading to hold that our Lord did not see the question of inheritance as important: He did not come to contradict or to depreciate the law He gave through Moses. He did refuse to become the judge or divider during His incarnation. He did not come to replace judges and courts but to "make all things new" (Rev. 21:5), the goal of a new creation.

The world today is full of cries similar to that described by Luke: "speak to my brother, (or, to this man or that), that he divide the inheritance with me (or, that he right this or that civil or moral wrong)." Injustice is a very real and ugly fact. How shall we answer that cry? Let us examine two representative cases for purposes of illustration.

*First,* in a litigation between two partners, it was clear that one partner had at the least taken advantage of the other, and probably defrauded him. It became equally clear that the wronged partner had at times taken advantage of the other, and, in this case, had been the loser in a case of mutual sharp-dealing. It is to be hoped that some wise judge will untangle the case and render a just decision, because even sinners must be granted justice. This is a difficult problem for the courts, and no personal judgments can help, resolve, or in any way further the matter or add an ounce of righteousness to the situation. The Lord has provided dividers and judges, and it is best left to them, and those courts can truly judge wisely if they judge in terms of God's law.

*Second,* in a similar case, two partners sought a division of their assets and a dissolution of their partnership, and there were charges and counter-charges. In this case, one man was clearly in the wrong, and the other innocent. The judge ruled in favor of the innocent party but saw no reason to destroy the guilty, and so rendered a division which, while favoring the innocent, enabled the guilty to continue business on an independent basis. The realities of a humanistic court are not altered by indignation, endless comments, nor by independent judgments. The world around us is a consequence of man's faith. Humanistic man creates a humanistic culture, and Christian man creates a Christian culture. We get the kind of dividing and judging our faith calls for.

Jesus did not come to be a divider nor a judge but as our Lord. Those who demand that He be a divider or a judge are interested in a partial and a self-serving word from Jesus Christ. They want God's word to buttress their position, and, whether a covetous position or not, it is still *their* position. Our Lord summons us instead to bow before Him as our absolute Lord and Savior (Ps. 2:10-12). The judges of the earth must bow before Him and be instructed and governed by His word and person: He is the Lord, and He is Judge over all judges. Why should He do the work of His underlings?

And what right do we have to arrogate to ourselves His position as Judge over judges, or to compete with His judges? Presumptuous judgments in the name of the Lord are as anathema as the empty and blasphemous sacrifices Micah condemned:

> Wherewith shall I come before the LORD, and bow myself before the high God? shall I come before him with burnt offerings, with calves of a year old?
> Will the LORD be pleased with thousands of rams, or with ten thousands of rivers of oil? shall I give my firstborn for my transgression, the fruit of my body for the sin of my soul?
> He hath shewed thee, O man, what is good: and what doth the LORD require of thee, but to do justly, and to love mercy, and to walk humbly with thy God? (Micah 6:6-8)

It is not the purpose of Biblical law to make every man his own judge: it is the goal of anarchism to do so. Hence, Paul says,

> Render therefore to all their dues: tribute to whom tribute is due; custom to whom custom; fear to whom fear; honour to whom honour.
> Owe no man any thing, but to love one another: for he that loveth another hath fulfilled the law. (Rom. 13:7-8)

## 156

## "BY HIM ALL THINGS CONSIST"

Zacharias, in his prophecy concerning the coming of the Lord, and salvation through His remission of the sins of His people, declares that Christ's coming means that

....the dayspring from on high hath visited us.
To give light to them that sit in darkness and in the shadow of death, to guide our feet into the way of peace. (Luke 1:78-79)

Previously, God had revealed through His prophets that certain things would come to pass, or He had manifested His power in delivering them, in setting forth the majesty of His word, and so on. Now there was a difference: this revelation was full and complete: "the dayspring from on high hath visited us." John, less poetically, says the same thing:

In the beginning was the Word, and the Word was with God, and the Word was God.
The same was in the beginning with God.
All things were made by him; and without him was not anything made that was made....
And the Word was made flesh, and dwelt among us, (and we beheld his glory, the glory as of the only begotten of the Father,) full of grace and truth. (John 1:1-3, 14)

Again, St. Paul tells us the same thing, declaring,

For by him were all things created, that are in heaven, and that are in earth, visible and invisible, whether they be thrones, or dominions, or principalities, or powers: all things were created by him, and for him:
And he is before all things, and by him all things consist. (Col. 1:16-17)

Our Lord is the Dayspring, the dawn and the new world order in His very person. He is very God of very God, made flesh, incarnate and fully man. And yet He is the creator of all things, and all things were not only created *by* Him but *for* His own glory and purpose. Christ is the very Word of God.

Every heresy in the life of the church has been a limitation of the written or incarnate word. What heretics do is to take a partial word and use its elements as the building blocks for an alien faith or an alien Christ.

What does it mean to tolerate such a "limited" faith? Many churches claim to believe the Bible from cover to cover, and yet they rule out great

676

portions of it as inadmissible for one reason or another. Others give us a beautiful Jesus who is not the same Jesus Christ we meet in Scripture. Are these partial truths, or are they lies?

*First* of all, because this is God's creation, no man can escape the truth. The most depraved of men must still use the materials of God's creation: they cannot abandon God's creation for their own. Their minds and all that they conceive of is confined by the limits and boundaries of God's ordination, so that God's truth continually forms a fence around every lie invented by man. Satan has rightly been called the ape of God; he cannot create, and thus he continually imitates, in a deformed manner.

*Second,* a partial word is not the true word. Every heresy uses a partial word to promote an alien gospel. Satan, in his temptation of our Lord, manifested this practice with particular care. Every one of his temptations was an attempt to use either Scripture or Christ's nature and calling as a means of furthering the Satanic plan of salvation. The law calls for a care for the hungry, and for the subordination of the kingdoms of this world to the Lord; Satan used these goals and others in an alien context to give them another meaning. A partial word is an alien word. Scripture cannot be used as though it were a collection of building blocks out of which we construct our own structures and versions, but rather is a mandatory word, and every jot and tittle thereof can be read only in its intended and declared meaning.

In terms of this, let us examine Colossians 1:16-17. *First,* Paul declares the absolute and unequivocal deity of Jesus Christ. "He is before all things." To say this is to say that He is God, the great *I AM,* who alone can declare, "I am the way, the truth, and the life" (John 14:6). It is He who declares through Isaiah, "I am God, and there is none else" (Isa. 45:22).

*Second,* not only is the deity of Christ declared but His pre-existence. "He is before all things." Jesus makes this clear: "Before Abraham was, I am" (John 8:58). Jesus Christ pre-exists before time and creation; He is also "before all things" in terms of His power, His divine being and authority, and His place as creator.

*Third,* "by him were all things created, that are in heaven, and that are in earth, visible and invisible, whether they be thrones, or dominions, or principalities, or powers: all things were created by him, and for him." Creation is creation: it is not dualistic nor dialectical. Greek and Iranian thought is rejected: reality is not spirit versus matter. Reality is rather God, the uncreated, who, by His sovereign word, created all things out of nothing. Francis W. Beare called attention to the fact that the perfect tense of the Greek tells us that "All things 'stand created' through him and for him." Their origin is in Him and His creating word, and their

goal is in terms of His purpose.[1] The life of the universe is mediated to
the universe through God the Son. Our mechanistic views of the universe
blind us to this fact.[2]

*Fourth,* "by him all things consist." He is the cosmic Christ and King.
Christ "maintains in being what He has brought into being."[3] He is the
creator and preserver of all things. Nothing in creation has an iota of independence from Jesus Christ.

*Fifth,* all this leads up to a great declaration concerning this cosmic
Christ-King and His purpose concerning the whole of creation:

> And he is the head of the body, the church: who is the beginning, the
> firstborn from the dead: that in all things he might have the pre-
> eminence. (Col. 1:18)

We miss the entire point of this text if we think of *the church* as the institution for worship, the Christian synagogue. Rather, it is the *ecclesia,*
the assembly, congregation, or people of God in all their functionings: it
is the Kingdom of God. It is the new creation, fulfilling all of Christ's
purpose in all its scope and glory.

We have been told in Colossians 1:16-17 that He made *all things* for
His purpose; He is before *all things,* and that *all things* consist or cohere
by Him. All things, however, have been affected by the fall. Christ's
work is to re-create all things and to make them a new creation. In His incarnation, He is the beginning of that new creation; in His resurrection,
He, the firstborn from the dead, from the decree of death against the old
humanity, is the beginning of a new humanity. The totality of the new
creation is in mind in verse 18. Our modern usage of the word church
leads to a severe restriction of its meaning and a perversion of the text.
Paul speaks of the King of the new creation, so that the word *church* here
is inclusive not only of the new humanity but of the new creation and all
things therein. The stress is on *all things,* and this is no less true of the
new creation. To read this text in any other sense is to do violence to it.
The creator of all has a purpose in all, and He creates a new creation. By
His incarnation and atonement, He who is the creator becomes also the
last Adam, the federal head of the new creation. The cosmic scope is emphatically in view in verse 18. The unity of creation and redemption is in
Jesus Christ as the great King and Redeemer of all. The goal is "that in
all things he might have the preeminence." His lordship and power are
manifested in both creation and redemption. He is "the Dayspring from
on high," the new world order in His person as creator and redeemer. To
declare that "the Dayspring from on high hath visited us" is to declare

---

1. Francis W. Beare, "Colossians," in *The Interpreter's Bible,* vol. XI, p. 166.
2. *Ibid.,* p. 166f.
3. F. F. Bruce, in E. K. Simpson and F. F. Bruce: *Commentary on the Epistles to the
Ephesians and the Colossians,* p. 200. Grand Rapids, MI: Eerdmans, 1957.

that God the Son is the redeemer, the law-giver, the Lord, and the absolute governor of all creation, and that all things move to fulfil His purpose. "All things were made by him; and without him was not anything made that was made" (John 1:3). Now all things are being re-made by Him, and nothing can be re-made, nor any faith and obedience manifested, apart from His full and sovereign word.

157

## SIN AS MAN'S POSSIBILITY

The role of fantasy and imagination in modern sexuality is a very great one. Magazines, plays, films, and television feed the modern imagination with a steady diet of sexually oriented materials. As Donaldson observes,

> Nudity on the stage is now commonplace, after such icebreakers as the rock musical "Hair" and the sexual anthology "Oh! Calcutta," which moves through such various themes as mass masturbation, rape, wife-swapping and various styles of copulation.[1]

The hunger for vicarious experiences leads many people to tolerate much which in life would frighten them. The pages of sexually oriented magazines are full of materials whose main function is to feed fantasies.

The same is true of like materials dealing with violence. Man delights in vicarious violence as a means of satisfying and feeding his own violent fantasies with fresh materials.

One of the major industries of the modern era is fantasy feeding by means of the press, television, films, night clubs, and other channels. Men will pay readily and well to have their fantasies fed. Another era will regard with amazement the appetite of our era, and its insatiable hunger for new experiences in the realms of the imagination. This is, in fact, perhaps the most amazing aspect of the sexually oriented magazines for men: they are directed towards fantasy creation. A revealing example of this is a featured, illustrated article in *Playboy,* January, 1978, on "Film Directors' Erotic Fantasies: Eight of the World's Greatest Film Makers Portray their Sexual Visions for Playboy." The eight men involved all have a background of extensive sexual adventures apparently, but the interest is not in the reality of their sexual life, but in their erotic fantasies. For example, one film director recalled pictorially an Oriental prostitute who passed by him, and of whom he later fantasized. He concluded, "Years later, the aroma is still fresh" (of her perfume, as she walked by him).

Again, to illustrate further, a man had the opportunity to live closely with a slowly dying hoodlum, aged and infirm, and not long out of prison. He heard the old man's reminiscences. What appealed most to him was the old man's fantasies of what he would like to have done to

---

1. Martin Donaldson, "The Not-So-New Morality," in Norman Hill, ed.: *Free Sex: A Delusion,* p. 15. New York: Popular Library, 1971.

certain people, and his savage imagination during prison years. Why was this more interesting than the real savageries of the man's life?

Let us remember the nature of sin, the desire to be as god, to determine for one's own self what constitutes good and evil (Gen. 3:5). As God declares to the prince of Tyre,

> The word of the LORD came again unto me, saying,
> Son of man, say unto the prince of Tyrus, Thus saith the LORD GOD; Because thine heart is lifted up, and thou hast said, I am a God, I sit in the seat of God, in the midst of the seas; yet thou art a man, and not God, though thou set thine heart as the heart of God:....
> Behold, therefore I will bring strangers upon thee, the terrible of the nations: and they shall draw their swords against the beauty of thy wisdom, and they shall defile thy brightness.
> They shall bring thee down to the pit, and thou shalt die the deaths of them that are slain in the midst of the seas.
> Wilt thou yet say before him that slayeth thee, I am God? but thou shalt be a man, and no God, in the hand of him that slayeth thee.
> Thou shalt die the deaths of the uncircumcised by the hand of strangers: for I have spoken it, saith the Lord GOD. (Ezek. 28:1-2, 7-10)

The essence of original sin is man's desire to be his own god, to create a new world of possibility outside of God. God, however, totally controls the real world, so that, as the prince of Tyre found, his sin had ready judgment. This is the nemesis of sin: it cannot escape God's world. The endlessly repeated and bitter complaint of current sexual revolutionaries is that venereal diseases still exist. If they are not a problem, human relations, guilt feelings, demands, responsibilities, and personal ties create far greater problems. For all of this, they blame the world of Christianity bitterly for creating mental "hang-ups," but, whatever the reason, the problems remain. As a result, the "safe" world of sin is increasingly seen as in the world of imagination, which they try to bar against God's intrusions. As a result, both among men and women, masturbation is now sometimes described as perfect sex because the fantasizing individual has freedom to play god in the sexual realm. The appeal of fictional violence is the same: it is a stimulus to violence in the realm of fantasy.

In the realm of fantasy, consequences and judgment are seemingly bypassed. In the real world, actions have consequences; men fight back, sexual partners can reject one or say no, the law is always there, or other people, and man's will to be god is frustrated and mocked by God's reality. In the world of fantasy, all such impediments seem to be irrelevant and gone, and man creates his own possibilities, ostensibly.

This is the key. Reality has pre-determined possibilities. No man grows younger, more handsome, nor more brutally strong in overwhelming all barriers. Reality gives us God's ordained possibilities, and all our potentialities are pre-determined by God. We may say with William Blake, "Oh, Why was I born with a different face?," *i.e.,* why am I not the person of my imagination, but the reality remains.

Sin is possibility thinking. It is imagining a world of possibilities outside of God and His law. It means that our imagination, not God's decree, establishes the boundaries of possibility.

Sin creates a new religion, a new education, a new politics, science, art, and sexuality in terms of man's own idea of possibility. It attempts then to reconstruct the world in terms of this new doctrine of possibility. Again and again in history we see advanced the same old sin, the doctrine of possibility as determined by man. The attempt is then made to force the world into the new mode of possibility, and the result is disaster. Then there begins a retreat from reality into psychology, into fantasy and imagination, and a lessening hold on the real world.

This is more than a retreat from reason. It is a retreat from reality, and the insistence that fantasy is the new reality.

The end result of all such retreats is hell. Hell in Scripture is *Hinnom* and *Gehenna,* words for the city dump. Hell is a place of burning and corruption, of fire and worms, and a place of meaninglessness. In hell, as in a dump, there are no purposive relationships between things. All things stand together in meaningless juxtaposition. There is no communication in hell, only endless self-absorption, endless fantasizing, with every man his own idiot god and senseless universe.

The road to hell begins whenever or wherever men prefer their own world of fantasy to God's reality. The fantasy word and world take precedence over God's law-word and law-world. To isolate any area of life and thought from the law-word of God is to place that area in the suburbs of hell.

But law and society are inseparable, and not only do actions and ideas have consequences, but fantasies also. The fantasies of the modern age cannot escape from the necessities of God's reality. The alternatives are God's law or chaos, or, more clearly, God's law or hell. But, wherever men define possibility apart from God, they have already chosen death and hell.

## 158

## THE TREE OF LIFE

Man's idea of law is usually radically humanistic. He thinks of law as something arbitrary, an idea conceived in abstraction from life and imposed on life. When man's law-making assemblies legislate, they legislate restraints on man which have no relationship to the nature of being, created or uncreated. Humanistic law is thus an unnecessary imposition which, even when it parallels God's law, as with laws against theft and murder, is alien to the nature of reality, because it springs from another source and an alien purpose.

God's law, however, comes from Him who made all things, and His law is expressive of the health of all things, so that it is not a restraint on life but the valid way of life.

To understand what this means, let us begin by examining Biblical law at what to humanists seems its most arbitrary example, namely, the death penalty for Sabbath defilement in Exodus 31:13-17, and the case of the man gathering sticks on the Sabbath, who was sentenced to death (Num. 15:32-36). What is the relationship of this law to the nature of things?

*First,* the pattern of Sabbath rest comes from the creation rest of God (Ex. 20:8-11; Gen. 2:1-3). God's work has a finished character: it has no open ends, unrealized potentialities and possibilities outside of God's decree, nor any independence from His purpose. As a result, man can have rest and peace in that certain world which is in its every atom and hair circumscribed and determined by the word of God. To believe in God is to believe in the reality of rest and peace; there is no Sabbath apart from God, and to break the Sabbath is to question or challenge God's reality and government.

*Second,* the Sabbath is a sign, a covenant sign, between God and His people. To rest in the Lord means to rest in the covenant, *i.e.,* in God's grace and law as the sustaining and governing force in all things. We cannot deny either grace or the law without denying the Sabbath. The Sabbath is our evidence that we live in God's grace and rest in the care of His law, providence, and government. A works religion denies the Sabbath, and an antinomian faith does also: neither can rest in a world in which God's grace and law are absent.

*Third,* this Sabbath rest is not simply an outward cessation of work and an ecclesiastical routine of meetings and attendance but a rest in

God's work and purpose. As Calvin pointed out, God declares that His Sabbaths are *polluted* when they are reduced to a series of observances. God's purpose in the Sabbath is to "keep His servants altogether free from every care, for the consideration of the beauty, excellence, and fitness of His works."[1] Calvin also said:

> And first of all, that this was a ceremonial precept, Paul clearly teaches, calling it a shadow of these things, the body of which is only Christ. (Col. xi. 17.) But if the outward rest was nothing but a ceremony, the substance of which must be sought in Christ, it now remains to be considered how Christ actually exhibited what was then prefigured; and this the same Apostle declares, when he states that "our old man is crucified with Christ," and that we are buried with Him, that His resurrection may be to us newness of life. (Rom. vi. 4.) It is to be gathered without doubt from many passages, that the keeping of the Sabbath was a serious matter, since God inculcates no other commandment more frequently, nor more strictly requires obedience to any; and again, when He complains that He is despised, and that the Jews have fallen into extreme ungodliness, He simply says that His "Sabbaths are polluted," as if religion principally consisted in their observance. (Jer. xvii. 24; Ez. xx. 21; xxii. 8; xxiii. 38). Moreover, if there had not been some peculiar excellency in the Sabbath, it might have appeared to be an act of atrocious injustice to command a man to be put to death for cutting wood upon it. (Num. xv. 32) Wherefore it must be concluded that the substance of the Sabbath, which Paul declares to be in Christ, must have been no ordinary good thing.[2]

The Sabbath, said Calvin, means our death in Christ to ourselves and our new life in Him. Our good works violate the Sabbath, "so long as we regard them as our own," because it is God's work we rest in, God's work we do, and God's grace we stand in.[3]

The Pharisees sought to kill Jesus in terms of Sabbath "violations," for healing on the Sabbath (John 5:15-18), because their Sabbatarianism stressed man's observances and not God's purpose.

God required the judgment of the man who gathered sticks on the Sabbath, not because God took pleasure in idleness, but because under the type of the Sabbath "was comprehended the whole service of God."[4]

Political scientist Harry V. Jaffa has stated the matter very clearly and tellingly in a response to Keith Mano:

> Mano thinks that "gathering sticks" is a trivial offense. But it is not

---

1. John Calvin: *Commentaries on the Four Last Books of Moses,* vol. II, p. 437. Grand Rapids, MI: Eerdmans, 1950.

2. *Ibid.,* II, 435.

3. *Ibid.,* II, 436.

4. Cited from Calvin's *Sermons upon the fifth book of Moses called Deuternomie,* p. 202, by John H. Primers, "Calvin and the Puritan Sabbath: A Comparative Study," in David E. Holwerda, ed.: *Exploring the Heritage of John Calvin,* p. 67. Grand Rapids, MI: Baker Book House, 1976.

the gathering of the sticks, but the violation of the sabbath, that the laws of Moses treat as such a serious offense. These laws were given to a people wandering in the wilderness, after their miraculous escape from Egypt. The Egyptians had honored other gods than God, and so did all the other peoples with whom the Jews did or might have come into contact. The observance of the sabbath was central to their consciousness of themselves as a people, a people apart from those who knew not God. To violate the sabbath deliberately was to reject the One who had commanded its observance; by implication it meant rejecting all His commandments. Certainly it was an act of sedition—as in the case of the golden calf—if not of treason, and punishable as such offenses always are.[5]

To rest in God's Sabbath is to rest in His government and law. To break that rest is to break with God's government and law in favor of self-government or autonomy. It is sedition and treason.

*Fourth,* does this mean that, in the modern world, Sabbath-breaking is punishable by death, or should be? The answer is, very clearly and emphatically, *no.* The modern state is not in covenant with God but is an enemy of God. Sabbath-breaking has no specific penalty of death, just as there is no death penalty for adultery (Hosea 4:14), because the nations are not in covenant with God and are therefore under sentence of death. Because of this general and central indictment, the lesser offenses have no place. Covenant offenses are one thing, enemy offenses another. A bill of particulars is needed to execute a citizen or subject; an enemy is killed as a part of warfare, as a necessary action towards victory.

The covenant relationship is a vital one; it is a relationship of life and law. A covenant is a treaty between two parties, but God's covenant is more. God is the creator of man, so that He covenants with His creature, whose only ground of life is in terms of God's purpose. Thus, at the very beginning, with the creation of man, at the center of the Garden of Eden and the covenant was the tree of life (Gen. 2:9). This was both a literal tree and a type of Christ, who is the tree of life in the center of the new creation or the New Jerusalem (Rev. 22:1-3). The worship of trees was indeed common to paganism, but there is no connection between the animism of such practices and Biblical faith. The heart of the tradition of Christmas trees comes from Rev. 22:1-3, and originally the decorations were largely fruits and nuts, to symbolize the ever-living and ever-bearing nature of the tree of life.

Our Lord speaks of Himself as a fruit-tree, a grapevine, in John 15:1-6: "I am the vine, ye are the branches." If we do not bear fruit, we are cut off and burned; if we bear fruit, we are pruned and disciplined to represent more fruitfully the life of the tree. Our Lord makes clear that

---

5. Harry V. Jaffa, "On Mano's 'Jews for Jesus': in *National Review,* vol. XXIX, no. 48, December 9, 1977, p. 1433.

we are known by our fruits; if we are rooted in an evil tree, we bear evil fruits and are a part of the life of that tree (Matt. 7:16-20).

Paul tells us that the old Israel was cut off from the tree of life, described in Romans 10:17 as an olive tree, and we, the branches of a wild olive, have been grafted in. God's principle is this: "Every branch in me that beareth not fruit he taketh away" (John 15:2).

A branch cannot exist apart from nor in isolation from its tree and roots. It has no independent life. All its life is derived from the tree. Hence, the branch must respond to the will or law of the tree, or else it is dead and is cut off. When men, for example, speak of being no longer under the law, they are declaring that they have no life from the tree, and no governing, life-giving flow from the tree of life. Grace and law are inseparable; the covenant is a covenant of grace, and the covenant is a law life, a law treaty and relationship.

To favor "spontaneous giving" over the tithe is *not* to stress the Holy Spirit; the Spirit cannot be divorced from the word or law of God. Spontaneous giving is autonomous giving, not Biblical or Spirit-governed giving. Autonomy means self-law literally (*auto,* self; *nomos,* law), and it is the enemy of God and His law. The branches of a tree live the life of the tree; the believers in Christ live the life of Christ and His total word.

Communion means that the branches feed on the tree of life; they confess that they have no independent life but are totally His members and property. They feed on Christ's body and blood: they are one community of life with Him.

The goal is set forth in Revelation 22:1-3: the branches are to bear fruit continually. They are to be *servants* or slaves of Christ, the tree of life, totally His and totally given to His law-word.

Sin is autonomy or self-law. It is also death for the branches, and burning.

Access in the Garden of Eden to the tree of life required faith and obedience. The same is true today. We are not a part of the tree of life unless we believe in and obey God the Son.

Law thus is not an abstraction: it is an aspect of life. To abolish law is to abolish life. Humanistic law can be dispensed with: it is an arbitrary invention where it is most clearly and consistently humanistic. Acts of Congress, legislatures, or parliaments can be repealed, and often man is much the better for it. God's laws can no more be repealed than God can be. They are a part of the constitution of things. God's law is basic to the life of man and society.

## 159

## "LET HIS ENEMIES TREMBLE"

Because of the influence of Greek thought and neoplatonism on the mind of Christendom, very early churchmen began to frown on material concerns in favor of spiritual ones. The world of the flesh was despised in favor of a Greek view of man's spirit. This pagan view was continued by many Protestant thinkers and soon re-infected the church. It was, of course, the inner cancer which destroyed Puritanism. An example of this pagan view appears in John Preston (1587-1628), who wrote:

> ...God is sayd to have made man after his owne Image; he doth not meane his body, for that is not made after the Image of God, neither is it only that holinesse which was created in us and now lost: for then he would not have sayd *Gen.* 9:6. *He that sheds mans bloud, by man shall his bloud be shed, for in the Image of GOD made he man.* The principall intent of that place is (for ought I can see or judge, the Scripture speaking of the natural fashion of things, and not of the supernaturall graces) to express that *God* hath given a soule to man, that carries the Image of God, a likenesse to the Essence of God immateriall, immortally, invisible; for there is a double Image of *God* in the soule, one in the substance of it, which is never lost; another is the supernaturall grace, which is an Image of the knowledge, holinesse, and righteousnesse of *God;* and this is utterly lost. But the soule is the Image of the essence of *God* (as I may so speake) that is, it is a spirit immateriall, immortall, invisible, as he is, hath understanding and will, as he hath; he understands all things, and wils whatsoever he pleaseth. And you see an expression of him in your owne soule, which is an argument of the Deity.
>
> Secondly, besides the immortality of the soule, which argues it came not from any thing here below, but that it hath its originall from *God*. . . .[1]

What such thinking says is that the soul is like God an immortal substance, one which never partakes of the Fall, or, as Preston said, "one in the substance of it, which is never lost." The image of God is thus altered from a moral fact to a metaphysical substance which is unalterable. If this be true, then the only need for man to escape the fall is to become spiritual. But Satan, a fallen creature, is totally evil and estranged from God, and yet totally spiritual. Man in all his being is,

---

1. John Preston, "Natural Theology," in Edward Hindson, ed.: *Introduction to Puritan Theology, A Reader,* p. 38. Grand Rapids, MI: Guardian Press, Baker Book House, 1976.

according to Scripture, a creature, a created being. He is of one substance, created being; the image of God in man is not a metaphysical fact. Man has no being in the uncreated Being of God. To hold so is to retain pagan ideas thinly baptized or sprinkled.

Such paganism, however, early led to asceticism and to a false spirituality, to sacerdotal celibacy, to a despising of meats, and the like, to a spiritual religion which St. Paul calls the "doctrine of devils" (I Tim. 4:1-3). It also led to a contempt for the law as too materialistic and as something reserved for a lower stage in the history of redemption, *i.e.,* for Old Israel and its "inferior" religion. But the Bible from start to finish is concerned about law, and is all law, because God's every word is a binding word: it has authority. The fall is a moral fact, and redemption is a moral fact. The atonement has to do with restitution in terms of the law, and sanctification is growth in terms of obedience to the law. Law or morality is the concern of all Scripture, because it is God's word, and the Creator commands men totally.

This false view of the soul was aggravated by the false eschatology it created. Augustine, one of the great minds of Christendom, was responsible for much both good and evil in the life of the church. He was also the father of amillennialism. Manichaean and neoplatonic thought, and the love of Rome, were strong in his life. For him, history offered no hope. As Baumer summarizes it, "In St. Augustine's view, there was spiritual meaning in history, and divine judgment in history, but no City of God in a temporal sense."[2] God can act in history to judge and destroy, but not to reconstruct and build, because the material realm has no end but destruction. The only meaning in history is "spiritual," and the "spiritual" quickly detaches itself from the Biblical and theological.

What then is the spiritual man to do in history? In terms of this pagan tradition, he separates himself from the material world and history to spiritual concerns. Such a view inevitably builds up the church as an ecclesiastical institution: it becomes man's refuge and fortress against an evil world. If the church can dominate and arrest the world and its way, it can to a degree inhibit its corruption, but no more. As a result, the more spiritual churchmen become, the more irrelevant they are. Men then seek a false set of alternatives: a false spirituality or a false materialism.

Then too God's law is abandoned for "higher life" ways and ideas, and men become more and more antinomian and lawless with respect to God. Humanistic law and faith replace Biblical faith, and the lordship of Christ is replaced with the lordship of man.

The church may become an expert at wailing over men's sins and

---

2. Franklin L. Baumer: *Modern European Thought: Continuity and Change in Ideas, 1600-1950,* p. 120. New York, NY: Macmillan, 1977.

apostasies, and at documenting the way of the world, but its only "remedy" is a flight into pagan spirituality in the name of Christ.

But the Bible is not a devotional manual: it is a battle plan and a prescriptive word, a command word, and therefore a law word. The "spiritual" preachers deserve not even a yawn: they are putting the church into the sleep of death. God's servants will declare, "Thus saith the Lord," and His word covers every aspect of our lives, our work, our family life, our sexuality, politics, economics, farming, business, social and personal lives, and all things else.

We have the Lord: He is Jesus Christ, our Immanuel, God with us. Let His enemies tremble. Our God shall put all things under His feet (I Cor. 15:25). Thus we must say,

> Be wise now therefore, O ye kings: be instructed, ye judges of the earth.
> Serve the LORD with fear, and rejoice with trembling.
> Kiss the Son, lest he be angry, and ye perish from the way, when his wrath is kindled but a little. Blessed are all they that put their trust in him. (Ps. 2:10-12)

## 160

## GOD'S PROPERTY AND POSSESSION

God's law-word is binding upon man because man is God's property. Man has no claims on or against God, any more than the clay can say to the potter, "Why hast thou made me thus?" (Rom. 9:20). We are God's property by virtue of creation, and, because of redemption, we are doubly His, "bought with a price." Hence "we are not (our) own" (I Cor. 6:19-20). We are the Lord's, and His right to use us and to govern us is total. Our creation, and election or reprobation, is of His sovereign counsel and choice, not ours. Thus, we have no basis for any valid objection to anything God does. In the famous case of the man executed for gathering firewood on the Sabbath (Num. 15:32-36), it was God's prerogative to do as He had decreed. We can understand the decision as judgment on a presumptuous sin (Num. 15:30-31); the offender deliberately expressed his contempt for God's law and God's provision. It was an act of defiance and treason. However, whether we understand God's law or not, or whether or not it seems reasonable to us, it is binding upon us, because the reason it rests on is God's, not man's.

Moreover, whenever man sets himself up as the judge over God's word, deciding for himself which law is still useful to him or not, the word of God ceases in practice to be God's word and becomes merely a resource man utilized when he needs it. The *authority* then is man, not God. *Time Magazine,* in commenting on the widespread ecclesiastical toleration and even acceptance of homosexuality, reported on the reaction of many conservatives, noting, "Since the Bible is so explicit, they wonder if the church will have any basis for imposing any restrictions on human behavior if it votes moral acceptance of active homosexuality."[1] Exactly. The new moral basis and authority is the word of man, or the word of the church or state. By such decisions, men, churches, and states declare themselves to be gods walking on earth and delivering the new law for man. By denying the binding nature of the Bible, they are declaring their word to be the higher and more authoritative word. The criterion for action becomes then the word and will of man.

The practical implications of such a perspective on culture appear in an interview with actor James Caan, who confesses that nothing holds his interest very long, except acting, and acting must be fun to hold his

---

1. "Homosexuality and the Clergy," in *Time,* vol. III, no. 5, January 30, 1978, p. 85.

interest. "It's not only my acting, but I don't do anything unless I'm going to enjoy it or feel good about it." Caan dislikes work and responsibility: "When you work, you have to assume the responsibility and have the discipline, but I don't want to have to do anything. The more I have to be somewhere at a certain time or do something, the more I don't want to do it." He admits to guilt feelings but hopes to rid himself of them.[2] Caan expresses with honesty and candor the characteristics of most moderns. When man denies God, he substitutes for God either his own ultimacy or the ultimacy of some institution or agency. If he affirms his own ultimacy, then he denies the validity of any authority over him, and he rebells against authority and discipline.

The breakdown of the authority of God's word begins, however, in the church. It is not only antinomianism which marks most churches but anti-Christianity. It is not only the law which is set aside, but the historicity of Scripture, God's grace, mercy, justice, and love. Everything is re-interpreted by the theologians of surrender to mean as little as possible, to be as little binding as possible, and to be in effect another word, the word of the theologian in question. The fact of creation becomes a nebulous and non-historical fact; revelation becomes a historical process whereby man comes to a new insight into himself and the world; and the resurrection becomes an impossible possibility which has nothing to do with the actual resurrection of the physical body of Jesus Christ. Consider, for example, this conclusion concerning the resurrection by Norman Perrin, in a small book of 85 pages, cited as "a help to pastors who proclaim the resurrection message to discover the unique resurrection accents of each evangelist." The resurrection narratives are to Perrin not history but literary expressions of theological viewpoints. He concludes:

> What actually happened on this first Easter morning, according to the evangelists, is that it became possible to know Jesus as ultimacy in the historicality of the every day (Mark), that it became possible to live the life of a Christian within the church (Matthew), and that it became possible to imitate Jesus in a meaningful life in the world (Luke).[3]

With such a perspective, the church would never have been born, and with such a faith, the churches now holding it will, happily, either soon perish or be changed.

Too often, the modern theologian and churchman goes to the Bible seeking *insight, not orders.* Indeed, I may go to Calvin, Luther,

---

2. Rudy Aversa, "James Caan: A Tough Guy With Some Soft Spots And A Craving For Laughter," in *Los Angeles Herald Examiner California Living,* January 1, 1978, pp. 8-9, 21.

3. Cited by Richard Rodning, in a favorable review of Norman Perrin: *The Resurrection According to Matthew, Mark, and Luke,* (Philadelphia: Fortress Press, 1977) *Book News Letter of Augsburg Publishing House,* number 472, January-February, 1978, p. 5.

Augustine, and others, to scholars Christian and non-Christian, for insights, for data, and for learned studies, but when I go to the Bible I must go to hear God's marching orders for my life. I cannot treat the Bible as a devotional manual designed to give me peace of mind or a "higher plane" of living: it is a command book which can disturb my peace with its orders, and it tells me that I can only find peace in obeying the Almighty. The Bible is not an inspirational book for my personal edification, nor a book of beautiful thoughts and insights for my pleasure. It is the word of the sovereign and Almighty God: I must hear and obey, I must believe and be faithful, *because God requires it.* I am His property, and His absolute possession. There can be nothing better than that. To be my own property and possession in a meaningless world is the ultimate in misery and grief. But when the great and high God, possessor of heaven and earth (Gen. 14:19, 22), makes me His elect possession by the adoption of grace through Jesus Christ, I must answer to His every enscriptured word, "Speak, LORD, for thy servant heareth" (I Sam. 3:9-10). This is God's calling and requirement of me, and it is my privilege to hear and obey, for His word is life, and it is health (Ps. 119).

In terms of God's ownership, we yield ourselves to Him as a living and continual offering and sacrifice (Rom. 12:1). We give our children to Him in baptism from infancy, not because of some mystical meaning, but because we confess thereby God's property rights over us and our children, and we vow to bring up our children as God's possession. We tithe, because God, who owns all of us, requires a percentage for His work. All that we have, and all that we are, our persons, families, possessions, and time, belong to the Lord. The whole meaning of the festivals and of circumcision-baptism, the passover-communion, and all rites and ordinances of the life of worship, simply set forth differing aspects of God's property rights over us, and His gracious covenant to care for His own. When we tithe, baptize our children, and obey God's law, we confess thereby that we are not our own, but that we have been bought back by the Lord at a price, and we are therefore totally His possession. Thus, whether we live, or whether we die, we are the Lord's (I Thess. 5:10), and in all things we are to give thanks, because in all things we have no claim on the Lord, and we are the recipients of His grace and mercy (I Thess. 5:18). Thus, we must be under God's law, not man's, because God is God: He is the LORD.

## APPENDICES

### 1. The Robe of Glory

The parable of the wedding feast (Matt. 22:1-14) is somewhat neglected because of its concluding sentence, "For many are called, but few are chosen." For Arminians, this verse seems to smack too much of predestination to be popular, whereas some misanthropic Calvinists have seized on this verse triumphantly to vindicate an erroneous belief in a limited and small number of elect persons. In both cases, the verse is misunderstood. The point of the parable here is an indictment of Israel and its leaders. They were the bidden or "called" to the wedding who rejected the invitation of God the King to the union of His Son with His bride, the church. As a result, the outsiders, the many Gentiles, are called in and chosen, and few are chosen of the Israel of Christ's day. Of those of Israel who came in, some manifested a pharisaic self-righteousness, like the man who had no wedding garment on, and they were cast out.

The Pharisees understood the meaning of the parable, and Matthew 22:15 tells us that they immediately took counsel to entrap Jesus in his talk. They recognized clearly that Jesus had predicted the judgment of God in the destruction of Jerusalem (Matt. 22:7). They saw also Christ's declaration that the Kingdom of God was being given to the Gentiles of all the world, and Israel was being cut off, its city destroyed, and its "converts" in part at least rejected in the person of the wedding guest without a wedding garment.

Thus, this parable does *not* declare that few are chosen for God's Kingdom, but that few of the people of Israel *in that day* were chosen. The meaning of the parable is distorted and destroyed if this is not recognized.

Next, it is imperative to understand the meaning of the wedding garment. The significance of this in relationship to communion was once widely recognized. One of the Exhortations in the Book of Common Prayer declares,

> My duty is to exhort you, in the mean season to consider the dignity of that holy mystery, and the great peril of the unworthy receiving thereof; and so to search and examine your own consciences, and that not lightly, and after the manner of dissemblers with God; but so that ye may come holy and clean to such a heavenly Feast, in the marriage-garment required by God in holy Scripture, and be received as worthy partakers of that holy Table.

693

The wedding garments typify the righteousness of Jesus Christ, so that we come to God, not in our own righteousness but in the righteousness of Christ and through His person.

The wedding garment symbolism has a long history. The gift of a robe by a king symbolized incorporation into his family and life, and the total acceptance of his authority. When pharaoh clothed Joseph, he thereby invested Joseph with dominion over all Egypt subject only to pharaoh. The robe thus meant being *under authority,* but it also meant *having authority* over the ruler's realm (Gen. 44:37-44). Later, when Joseph clothed his brothers, he thereby brought them under his authority and gave them a share of his power (Gen. 45:22).

To be incorporated into the authority of a person of power by the gift of a garment was thus a great privilege. When Naaman the leper came to the king of Israel and Elisha, he brought "ten changes of raiment" (II Kings 5:5), which Elisha ordered rejected (II Kings 5:15-16), because he and Israel were already under the authority of God the King. When Elisha's servant Gehazi sought the more profitable authority of Naaman by deceit, he gained with it Naaman's leprosy (II Kings 5:20-27). When Mordecai was clothed with Ahasuerus' garments, Haman's family knew that it was the end of Haman, because Mordecai now had the authority of the emperor (Esther 6:7-13). Again, when the mantle of Elijah fell upon Elisha, Elisha thereby inherited Elijah's power and authority (II Kings 2:12-15).

Buckler has written, with respect to the parable of the wedding feast,

> The wedding garment was a robe of honour bestowed directly by the king on his guests—those of his vassals who were permitted to eat and drink at the king's table and so were indeed in the bond of 'friendship.' The wearing of the garment was an overt act of allegiance to the king; the refusal to wear it was an act of treason, because it constituted an overt denial of the king's overlordship and sovereignty. The son had accepted it. I need hardly recall the robe of honour of the Christian kingdom—the Cross of shame. The participation in the Eucharist—the royal feast—implied the wearing of the robe of honour by the member of the feast. In other words, he who would approach the table of his king must first of all have taken up his cross.[1]

Thus, when Jesus declared, "If any man will come after me, let him deny himself, and take up his cross, and follow me" (Matt. 16:24), He meant thereby incorporation into His life. This means, because we become members of His body, that we bear the reproach of Christ (Heb. 13:13) and the enmity directed against Him, and we also bear His authority and power as we confront the world.

---

1. F. W. Buckler: *The Epiphany of the Cross,* p. 77. Cambridge, England: W. Heffer & Sons, 1938.

Citing Buckler again, we see that

> ...the robe of honour is the central symbol of incorporation into the body royal. It is used by the king, as well as by all of his deputies and their deputies, to mark the delegation of the royal functions, to transmit the royal Glory, protection (shadow) and power, and to incorporate into the body of the donor, the recipient of the dress. It is always a garment which the donor has worn and taken off...
>
> The great instance of the cast-off garment in the kingdom of God on earth is the Cross, which had been 'worn' by our Lord and had been 'cast-off.' The Cross of Shame is the Christian's 'robe of honour.' To take up the Cross has the same significance as to accept the robe of honour. Likewise the reverse, to reject the Cross is to declare one's independence.[2]

In the parable of the Prodigal Son, the robe given to the repentant son marked the return to loyalty and obedience. In the parable of the Talents, the man with one talent, in refusing to use it, was refusing to exercise the authority given to him and was manifesting his rejection of the lord. "The *talent* is the counterpart of...allotted or fixed authority."[3]

Incorporation into the King's body means incorporation with all the members thereof. Hence, in the parable of the last judgment, the emphatic verdict of Christ is, "Verily I say unto you, Inasmuch as ye have done it unto one of the least of these my brethren, ye have done it unto me" (Matt. 25:40), and, again, "Verily I say unto you, Inasmuch as ye did it not to one of the least of these, ye did it not to me" (Matt. 25:45).

Thus the robe of glory, the Cross, has some very important implications for the believer. *First,* it means that to accept Christ, to be *chosen* of Him, means to be under His authority and Lordship, totally. We *cannot* have Christ as our Savior if He is not our Lord.

*Second,* it means bearing the reproach of the cross, being "without the camp," and feeling the hatred of the old humanity for Christ the King.

*Third,* it means also exercising dominion and authority in His name. Failure to do so leads to our judgment as "wicked and slothful" and to being cast out, as was the man who did not use the talent (Matt. 25:24-30). To deny the creation mandate is to deny Christ and to be cast out as a wicked servant.

*Fourth,* to bear Christ's cross, our robe of glory, is to be one body with Christ and with all the people of Christ. This means that we *must* care for one another, provide for the needy and infirm, relieve the distressed, and in all things be *a family of God.*

*Fifth,* a basic aspect of our Lord's teaching in this parable was His rejection of the *blood* concept of the covenant, its reduction to the Hebrew race. The Gentiles, outsiders, are, brought in to replace the "called"

---

2. *Ibid.,* p. 6f.
3. *Ibid.,* p. 109.

people, who are rejected. The very word basic to the covenant, God as *Father, "Abba, Father,"* does not imply physical fatherhood but essentially the protector, the nurturer, the authority.[4] Every attempt to reduce it to blood is a denial of the covenant. To cry "Abba, Father" (Gal. 4:6) is to reject blood for faith, the natural tie for the supernatural authority. We cannot put on the robe of glory, if, like the guest who came clothed in his own righteousness, we come expecting blood and inheritance can be substituted for the Cross of Christ, our robe of glory.

## 2. The Head or Poll Tax

The tax of Exodus 30:11-16 is commonly seen as a temple tax and not a tax for the support of the civil order. There is no question that this head or poll tax became a "temple" tax *after* the fall of Jerusalem. The Babylonian Talmud sees it strictly as a tax to provide for worship and gives it very brief attention in one of its shortest tractates, the *Shekalim.* Scholars see an allusion to it in II Kings 12:4 and II Chronicles 24:9, but their reference is too general to be specified as referring to the head tax. Josephus, in his *Antiquities of the Jews* XVIII, ix, speaks of it as the "half shekel which every one, by the custom of our country, offers unto God."

The key reference is in Matthew 17:24-27. The word *tribute (temple-tax* in Moffatt) is in the Greek *kensos,* (Latin, *census*). It was a *census* tax because it was exacted of all males, 20 years old and above.

Our Lord clearly sees it as a *royal* rather than *priestly* tax. Because He is the son of the King, He is exempt from the tax. We cannot judge our Lord's choice of words as accidental: He declares it to be God's tax as King over His realm and people. The association of the tax with the tabernacle and then the temple was due to the fact that the throne of God was once in the Holy of Holies. The tax, however, was for the royal government.

The fact that the head or poll tax was once the basic civil tax in some American colonies is confirmation of the fact that this interpretation is not a novel one. In Virginia, the state taxation was 1) tithables, which supported the Anglican clergy, parish expenses, and the poor; 2) poll taxes, used to erect public buildings, repair roads, and build bridges; and 3) set fees on licenses, land patents, and duties on tobacco, which paid the salaries of some civil officers, others working without pay.[1]

But this is not all. Even the fact that it was called the "temple" tax is an interesting fact. The ordinary Hebrew word for *temple* was *Haical,*

---

4. See F. H. Palmer, "Adoption," in J. D. Douglas, editor: *The New Bible Dictionary,* p. 15. Grand Rapids, MI: Eerdmans, (1962) 1973.

1. Robert A. Rutland, editor: *The Papers of George Mason, 1725-1792,* vol. I, 1774-1778, p. 374f. Chapel Hill, NC: The University of North Carolina Press, 1970.

meaning *palace,* and so translated in I Kings 21:1; II Kings 20:18; Psalms 45:15; Isaiah 13:22; 39:7; 44:28; etc. *Palace* is its meaning in Hosea 8:14. The Temple was God's Palace, and taxes collected for the palace or *temple* were throne taxes, to provide for God's royal government, which was also a priestly one in part.

If indeed the poll tax was the tax to provide for the civil government of Israel, this fact should appear in history. It does, and as late as the 9th century. A Jewish princedom existed from at least 768-900 A.D. in southern France. Its rulers were of the Davidic line. The poll tax had previously been collected by the *Nasi* or prince of the Jews in Palestine or wherever else someone exercised governmental functions, either under Rome earlier, or under later powers. These governmental functions were both civil and religious and were financed by the poll tax. Rome earlier had required this poll tax of all Jews, to be paid to the *Nasi,* and in return the *Nasi* helped collect Rome's fiscal demands from all Jews within the empire.[2]

We have become so used to reading all things in the Bible in ecclesiastical terms that it is hard for most to realize that the Bible does not present itself as an ecclesiastical manual.

### 3. Bribery

Very plainly, Scripture condemns the taking of bribes. The law speaks of this in Exodus 23:8, Deuteronomy 16:19, and 27:25. It is regarded as a very serious offense, since it prevents justice. On the other hand, Biblical law has no penalties for offering bribes. This is a point which troubles many Christians.

The fact is, however, that Scripture sees the problem very realistically. The judge or public official is the person in a position of power. In my travels back and forth across the country, and in my conversations with people from abroad, a clear pattern emerges with respect to bribery.

*First,* the bribe is normally solicited by the official in power. It is the standard means of doing business with him. If contracts are to be issued, none are granted without a pay-off. If a decision is to be rendered, a bribe is a prerequisite to any kind of fair consideration. Granted that many who offer bribes are themselves corrupt, the fact remains that all who offer bribes would, on the whole, prefer to do business with civil authorities, their courts, and their agencies, without the pay off. It adds very substantially to their cost of operation; it leaves them open to legal reprisals, and more people giving them than those receiving them are sentenced for bribery. Recently, even while several manufacturers and pro-

---

2. See Arthur J. Zuckerman: *A Jewish Princedom in Feudal France, 768-900,* p. 3 on the tax, pp. 64, 91, 96, 111, 168, 250, etc. on the Nasi of Marbonne. New York, NY: Columbia University Press, (1965) 1972.

ducers were convicted for giving bribes, other politicians were busily collecting more.

This already makes clear a *second* aspect of bribery. The cost of bribery is born by the one offering it; it is an unpleasant tax on him which he feels he must pay. (More than a few businessmen regard bribes as another form of taxation, and actual rates are fixed as in taxation.) The real profit in bribery is on the side of the receiver. The giver often wants justice, and he resents the partiality involved, and the corruption. If the giver of the bribe has an inferior product and is succeeding only because of his bribery, he is still a creature of the politician, and is sacrificed when necessary. All over the world, bribery is standard operating procedure on the part of civil governments. This corrupt tax leads often to the creation of criminal groups whose function becomes the sale of inferior goods at high prices, with large bribes, to civil authorities at the connivance of those authorities.

In most cases, to punish the one who bribes is somewhat analogous to punishing a rape victim rather than the rapist. True, the briber is not always under a like coercion, but often the coercion is very real, so that bribery comes close to being a form of theft. It involves a monetary theft, and also a theft of justice. One man, who began work for the state and then found that his payments would be withheld, his work condemned, and that he would be wiped out financially, if he did not make a pay-off, said bitterly of bribery: "There's no other way to do business with the government." Bribery must be condemned, but in terms of Scripture.

### 4. Phariseeism and Divorce

Two cases of divorce have come to my attention, both of which led to the departure of the wives involved from their reformed churches, because the pastors ruled against any legitimate divorce.

In the first case, the wife had lived patiently with her husband, who was somewhat prominent in the reformed community, keeping hidden his very ungodly treatment of her within the family. She had brought a moderate though substantial amount of money into the marriage, an inheritance. He appropriated all of it, over the years, for various business ventures. Some failed, others did not. In no case was there any repayment, although promised. In anger one night because of her "nagging" (i.e., her rebuke at his extravagance and general lack of thoughtfulness), he crept into his daughter's room and tried to coax and then force her into incest. The daughter and then the mother prevented this; he blamed his wife for "driving" him to this act, because she had made herself unappealing by her violations of his masculine authority and dominion.

The pastor ruled that no divorce was possible, when the wife consulted him, because no adultery, the only supposedly "valid" ground, had taken place, because successful entrance was not accomplished. It was her duty to return to her husband or else face trial in the church court.

She left the church, secured a divorce, and lost all respect for that church.

In the second case, the husband, a good amateur car mechanic, "prepared" his wife's car for her long week-end rest at their mountain cabin, which was on a narrow, winding, and steep mountain road. Anxious to be rid of his wife, he prepared the car for a brake failure on her return trip. Because the cabin was a mess (friends had occupied it recently), she spent extra time cleaning it before resting and decided to stay longer. Thus, before her downward return trip, the brakes were already gone when she barely started out of the driveway, and she stopped immediately. The sabotage became subsequently apparent, and she also discovered the reason for it, the "other woman." Her husband, being a "good man," had not committed adultery: he wanted the other woman legally and properly.

Hence, the wife was told that she had no ground for divorce! Of such pastors are the Kingdom of Pharisees. The wife left the church and secured a divorce.

### 5. Miscellaneous Notes

#### Public Executions

An interesting comment on capital punishments appears in the life of Churchill by his son:

> Churchill expressed himself in favour of capital punishment. "Is it a great deterrent?" he asked. "I think so. Perhaps it is because the sentence is irrevocable, because the actual penalty is and must remain unknown." He must have been thinking, in the last sentence, of a possible after-life. Referring to the recent substitution of public executions by private executions he added: "No difficulties should be placed in the way of any (in moderate numbers) who may wish to see the sentence carried out. Justice in every form should not shrink from publicity. The last expiation which she exacts from man should not be hidden from the eyes of his fellow creatures." A few years before he died Churchill told his grandson Winston that he was still in favour of capital punishment in public as he thought that instead of being secretly hanged in a hut the murderer or traitor ought to be allowed to address a crowd as in the case of the first Marquess of Montrose.[1]

Churchill's comments on public executions have reference to the fact that, in an earlier era, a restraint on injustice and tyranny was the privilege of the condemned man to address the assembled crowd and

---

1. Randolph S. Churchill: *Winston S. Churchill*, vol. I, *Youth, 1874-1900*, p. 326. Boston: Houghton-Mifflin, 1966.

either take his leave of life and make his peace with God, or indict the tyrant rulers if he were the victim of injustice. The modern tyrant state denies this privilege and keeps executions secret in order to prevent its own indictment.

This is not to say that earlier eras did not see denials of the right to make a public statement before death. Thus, during the Reformation era, the French persecution of Protestants was remarkedly brutal (burning over a slow fire, rather than the usual practice of giving the condemned a bag of gunpowder to hang from their necks for a quick death). Protestants in France were first tortured and then their tongues were cut out, before being taken to the stake, to prevent them from addressing the spectators.[2] The brutalities of the communist states of today mark these older tyrants as amateurs by comparison.

### False Witness and Abiding and Abetting a Crime

According to the law, in cases of perjury, the false witness was to receive the penalty sought for the accused (Deut. 19:16-21). If the penalty were death, then the false witness was to be executed.

In Christian Europe, this principle was logically extended to have other applications. If a man helped a prisoner escape from the jurisdiction of the court, or from its sentence, that same sentence was applied to him. An example of this appears in Columbus' crew on his first voyage to America. The ships had good crews of able seaman. Only four were pardoned criminals, and here there were mitigating circumstances. Although Bartolome de Torres had only accidentally killed a man in a fight, he had been sentenced to death for this manslaughter. Three of his friends had tried to help him escape from prison, but were caught, and also sentenced to death.[3] They were pardoned by the crown and sent to sea with Columbus, and all received full pardon on their return. Two of them sailed with Columbus again, on his second voyage.

### Tithing

A common objection to tithing is that the New Testament supposedly sets a new and voluntary standard, whereby men give as they are able. The supposed authority for this is II Corinthians 8:12, and 9:7. But the statement in its original form is in Deuteronomy 16:17: "Every man shall give as he is able, according to the blessing of the Lord thy God which he hath given unto thee." The law here does not negate tithing: it has reference to the due proportion of our prosperity as something which is due to the Lord who gives it. Tithes *and* gifts are basic to both Testaments.

---

2. Jasper Ridley: *John Knox,* p. 258. New York: Oxford University Press, 1968.
3. Bjorn Landstrom: *Columbus,* p. 51f. New York: Macmillan, 1967.

### 6. Obedience and Health

The law makes emphatically clear that, while death and illness are inescapable in this life, there is still a connection between obedience and health. Sickness and death are products of the Fall; they are not eliminated until after the second coming, when "the last enemy," death (I Cor. 15:26), shall be destroyed. Prior to that time, a large measure of health and longevity, as before the Flood, shall again prevail (Isa. 65:20).

To obey the law means 1) physical health, 2) material prosperity, 3) fertility, 4) victory over our enemies, and 5) the love and blessing of the Lord. This is clearly stated in Deuteronomy 7:12-16:

> Wherefore it shall come to pass, if ye harken to these judgments, and keep, and do them, that the Lord thy God shall keep unto thee the covenant and the mercy which he sware unto thy fathers:
> And he will love thee, and bless thee, and multiply thee: he will also bless the fruit of thy womb, and the fruit of thy land, thy corn, and thy wine, and thine oil, the increase of thy kine, and the flocks of thy sheep, in the land which he sware unto thy fathers to give thee.
> Thou shalt be blessed above all people: there shall not be male or female barren among you, or among your cattle.
> And the Lord will take away from thee all sickness, and will put none of the evil diseases of Egypt, which thou knowest, upon thee; but will lay them upon all them that hate thee.
> And thou shalt consume all the people which the Lord thy God shall deliver thee; thine eye shall have no pity upon them: neither shalt thou serve their gods; for that will be a snare unto thee.

Perfect obedience would lead to perfect health and to perfection in every area; while man is not to achieve this totality of obedience in this life, nonetheless a great measure of health and prosperity is clearly open to him on obedience.

The law, moreover, has its significance in more ways than one. Thus, while circumcision, as a covenant rite, has been replaced by baptism, circumcision was given with both spiritual and material consequences involved, in that God's law is to a unified being and has consequences for all his being. Circumcision, thus, while no longer having a significance as a mark of the covenant, is still important as a God-given means of attaining the life of health God sets forth for His people. Several doctors have commented on various implications of circumcision for health. We will cite only Dr. Henschen, because, without being a Christian, he recognizes to a degree the religious nature of health in this area:

> There are examples, too, of religious precepts and simply hygienic precautions giving protection against cancer, however incredible that may sound. It has been established for quite a long time that Jewesses who marry circumcised men, Jews and non-Jews, very seldom have cancer of the neck of the womb, cervis uteria, an otherwise very common form of cancer which in Sweden also is showing

signs of increasing. This is associated with the Jewish law and custom of forbidding intercourse during menstruation and with circumsion, after which the fatty substance which is excreted in the foreskin, smegna, cannot collect and decompose in the absence of personal hygiene. This freedom from cervix cancer is also found in women who have become nuns in youth. Experience shows that decomposed smegna can lead to cancer of the penis, especially in China according to some reports.[1]

The various dietary laws, laws of separation, and other laws no longer mandatory as covenantal signs, are still valid and mandatory as health requirements in terms of Deuteronomy 7:12-16.

### 7.  Incest and Lot's Daughters

In *The Institutes of Biblical Law* (pp. 368-375), I point out that, prior to Moses, there was no law against incest. Since Adam and his descendants had inherent in them all the genetic possibilities of the human race, his children, in marrying one another, were not as closely related genetically as any two Navaho Indians are today. Abraham married Sarah, possibly a half-sister (Gen. 20:12), and the father of Moses, Amram, married a young aunt, his father's sister, Jochabed (Ex. 6:20).

When God through Moses forbad incest (Lev. 18:7-17; 20:11, 12, 14, 17, 20, 21; Deut. 22:30; 27:20, 22, 23) and required the death penalty for most instances of it, it was, first, a radical break with accepted worldwide practice, and second, established a roadblock to genetic damage which was to appear only many centuries later, as inbreeding began to become more prone to concentrate defective genes.

It is important thus not to read back into early history this subsequent prohibition. The story of Lot and his daughters is an instance of this fallacious and moralistic reading. Almost all commentators show only horror for the daughters' act. R. Payne Smith spoke of "the revolting conduct of these women" and declared, "The utter degradation of Lot and his family is the most painful part of his story, which thus ends in his intense shame."[1] Cuthbert A. Simpson, who regards the narrative as myth, not history, is still closer to the truth when he writes of Genesis 19:31, "There is not a man on earth to come in to us," that it "presupposes that the background of the tale was worldwide disaster, such as the Flood, which had wiped out the human race. The action of the two women was thus in its original setting heroic, and the story was doubtless told with pride by their supposed descendants."[2]

---

1. Dr. Folke Henschen: *The History and Geography of Diseases,* p. 309. Joan Tate, translator. New York: Delacorte Press (1962) 1966.

1. R. Payne Smith, "Genesis," in C. J. Ellicott, editor: Ellicott's *Commentary on the Whole Bible,* vol. I, p. 79. Grand Rapids: Zondervan.

2. Cuthbert A. Simpson, "Genesis," in *The Interpreter's Bible,* vol. I, p. 631. New York: Abingdon Press, 1952.

Clearly, the girls viewed their action as good, and the names they gave their sons indicate only a pride in their action as good. Moab means, "From my father," and Ben-ammi, "Son of my kinsman." Very obviously, they felt that they acted to save the human race from extinction, and that, like Noah and his family, they were its sole survivors.

Something more must be said about Lot's daughters. They left Sodom with their father, and chose not to return with their mother. Their mother's act indicated a lack of faith. She returned, perhaps in an interlude in the destruction, assuming that it was over. Her wealthy home and all its advantages were in Sodom. No doubt Lot had left with horses, camels, or donkeys loaded with food and gold. In the cave (Gen. 19:30ff.), they obviously had food and wine brought with them. What they brought with them seemed trifling compared to what was left behind, and Lot's wife chose to return in some interlude in the general destruction, since it appeared that, despite some damage, Sodom would survive. Clearly, she had no faith in the message of the two strangers. The daughters just as clearly shared Lot's faith, and they chose to stay with their father.

As the destruction continued, it began to appear as a worldwide catastrophe, comparable to the Flood, which to Lot and his daughters was fairly recent history. Although one of the angels or messengers assured them that the small town of Zoar would not be overthrown (Gen. 19:21), in the general rain of fire and brimstone which followed, it seemed to Lot that Zoar would also perish, and he fled from it also, although earlier pleading to stay there, because he feared the disaster would overwhelm him in the open country and the hills (Gen. 19:19, 30). A city with buildings had briefly seemed the best protection of all, but, after the upheaval and destruction began, only a cave seemed protection enough. After the conduct of the men of Sodom (Gen. 19:4-5), it seemed to Lot and his daughters that God's anger, once unleashed, would destroy at least all of Canaan and that part of the world, if not the whole world.

The daughters thus assumed with Lot that they were either the lone survivors on earth, or else, if other areas were spared, they were too far away to be reached. This meant an unstable faith in the declared word, but it was still a faith therein, and with it a desire to perpetuate God's apparently chosen man, Lot. The history of Sodom's fall shows Lot as deeply distressed and indecisive out of horror, but, withal, obedient to God. Lot was hated by the Sodomites, because, as a judge sitting in the gates, he was a lone voice against the evils of the city (Gen. 19:1, 9). Before we condemn Lot, let us remember that in like circumstances, few men would do better. Let us remember too that God declares him to be "just Lot" and speaks of him as "that righteous man" (II Peter 2:7). Let us remember also Lot's exhaustion, having spent the night trying to arouse his married children to the danger.

We must remember too that Lot's daughters are not condemned in the narrative. Incest was not yet under the ban of the law. This does not mean that the girls were guiltless. First, they made their father drunk, thereby taking leadership into their hands. Clearly, they felt with some apparent ground that their father was too grief stricken and ill to make any decisions, and they used this as a justification for taking the initiative. Second, it was fornication, and again an offense against God's law and their father. Depraved, they were not; sinners, they were. They were not unbelievers, and, in a critical situation, they had acted on faith, but their faith was a defective one.

## 8. Seduction

Recently, two similar cases were brought to my attention, one by telephone, by the girl's father, the other through a third party who was asked to consult me. In the first instance, a girl was pregnant, and the young man responsible for it, who was anxious to marry her, was a Protestant of perhaps questionable faith. The girl was an earnest Calvinistic Presbyterian. The boy attended, over a period in the previous few years, youth groups in two or three churches, from modernist to Calvinist, as much interested in "finding a girl" as anything. Was this a mixed marriage, and should the pastor refuse to perform the ceremony? The young man could answer few theological questions intelligently, but he claimed that he believed and was a Christian. What should be done? The pastor was inclined to refuse to perform the marriage service.

In the second instance, the girl, also pregnant, came from a Baptist home, evangelical Arminian in theology; the young man was Catholic, very vague about doctrine but professing to believe the basic doctrines. He was very anxious to marry the girl. In this case, the pastor refused, after some indecision.

In neither example was there any previous sexual involvement by either girl or young man. In both cases, the young men were still clearly guilty of seduction.

Most significant, while in both instances the pastors were trying to be strictly Biblical in their decisions, *in neither case* did they allow their decision to be governed by the wishes of the girls' fathers. *The relevant law (Ex. 22:16-17) plainly places the decision, not in the hands of the clergy, but in the father's hands.* In both cases, the fathers *wanted* marriage, somewhat reluctantly, but still very clearly so. Both fathers felt that they could have had a better son-in-law, but, in spite of that, the boy was "all right" and had some elements of ability and character. Both fathers were strong Christians and had held church office. But in neither case did the pastor feel the father's wishes were to be considered, despite the plain reading of Scripture!

Nothing illustrates more clearly the fact that the church, like the state, is undermining the authority of the family. Both pastors were derelict and in violation of Biblical law. Both pastors saw the sins of the young couple before them, and not their own departure from and disregard of the word of God. Both acted as though parental authority were nothing before the authority and jurisdiction of the church. I found subsequently that both pastors were familiar with Exodus 22:16-17, but the fact of paternal authority had not even registered with them!

## 9. Hospitality

Scripture *commands* hospitality, although there is no civil punishment for failure to grant it. Thus, hospitality, while not a matter of indifference but of *command,* is not a civil law in Scripture. It is, however, so closely related to the law-order of the Kingdom that it must be considered. In I Peter 4:8, 9 we are told:

And above all things have fervent charity among yourselves: for charity shall cover the multitude of sins.
Use hospitality one to another without grudging.

Christians are to have an "intense love" (Berkeley Version) or fervent charity for one another; this involves hospitality one to another.

More than this, Christians are to show hospitality to strangers: "Be not forgetful to entertain strangers: for thereby some have entertained angels unawares" (Heb. 13:2). The reference here is to Genesis 18, and Abraham's faithfulness to the law of hospitality to strangers. The Greek original is stronger than the English: be not neglectful of the love of strangers. *Love of strangers* is one word, *philoxemia*. The same word appears in Romans 12:13, "Distributing to the necessity of saints; given to hospitality" (literally, kindness or love to strangers, *philoxemian,* i.e., by hospitality). It is clear from this latter verse the strangers are not saints. They are unbelievers in need.

However, hospitality to heretics is barred (Titus 3:10, 11). "If there come any unto you, and bring not this doctrine, receive him not into your house, neither bid him God speed: For he that biddeth him God speed is partaker of his evil deeds" (II John 10, 11). This is plainly a commandment, and a church law as well.

Still more, hospitality and charity to those who will not work is forbidden. "For even when we were with you, this we commanded you, that if any would not work, neither should he eat" (II Thess. 3:10). Hospitality cannot be made a subsidy to the wicked, to heretics, or to those who refuse to work.

The state in Scripture is minimal, and mainly restricted to the poll or head tax. The basic source of social financing is the tithe. Above and over the tithe, voluntary giving, which is a test of the sincerity of our love of Christ (II Cor. 8:8), must meet the emergency needs of society.

Men are not asked to be foolishly prodigal in their giving, but neither are they morally justified in seeking their own aggrandizement without thought of others. St. Paul, in calling for help for the famine victims among the saints in Jerusalem, declares:

> For I mean not that other men be eased, and ye burdened:
> But by an equality, that now at this time your abundance may be a supply for their want, that their abundance also may be a supply for your want: that there may be an equality:
> As it is written, He that had gathered much had nothing over; and he that had gathered little had no lack. (II Cor. 8:13-15)

This is an important commandment, all too often completely bypassed by the modern church. It has, however, a long and honorable history in medieval charity, and its practice enabled oppressed Christian Armenians to survive. St. Paul refers to the gathering of manna, specifically to Exodus 16:18, "And when they did mete it with an omer, he that had gathered much had nothing over, and he that had gathered little had no lack; they gathered every man according to his eating." Whatever men gathered, God made it measure out to the same, miraculously, so that, in the necessities of food, God introduced an equality for all that labored. Hodge, in commenting on St. Paul's words, assumed that, in the measuring, an equalizing by authorities took place. He did sum up Paul's statement very clearly:

> The moral lesson taught in Exodus 16:18 is that which the apostle had just inculcated. There it is recorded that the people, by the command of God, gathered of the manna an omer for each person. Those who gathered more retained only the allotted portion, and those who gathered less had their portion increased to the given standard. There was as to the matter of necessity an equality. If any one attempted to hoard his portion, it spoiled in his hands. The lesson therefore taught in Exodus and by Paul is, that, among the people of God, the superabundance of one should be employed in relieving the necessities of others; and that any attempt to countervail this law will result in shame and loss. Property is like manna, it will not bear hoarding.[1]

The law of God very clearly upholds private property and free enterprise. It does not allow men to place restrictions upon our use of our property in terms of humanistic feelings and standards. "Is it not lawful for me to do what I will with mine own? Is thine eye evil because I am good?" (Matt. 20:15); so taught Christ. On the other hand, God can and does place limits on our use of all things. We cannot take His laws which please us, such as private property, and eliminate the requirement of

---

1. Charles Hodge: *An Exposition of the Second Epistle to the Corinthians,* p. 206. Grand Rapids: Eerdmans, 1950.

hospitality and generous charity.

The dimensions of a Christian society begin to emerge. The state is very limited in its powers, and the church has its limited domain. Tithe agencies provide the basic social financing. But, above and over that, the moral requirement is that man avoid amassing wealth in terms of self-aggrandizement, survival, or the accumulation of wealth for its own sake. Property is a stewardship. The goal is a society in which all men work, all are good neighbors one to another, and all work to meet the needs of those in want. This does not forbid wealth; Scripture regards wealth as one kind of blessing. It does indicate that wealth must be put to godly uses. We are not asked to strip ourselves (II Cor. 8:13), but we are clearly told that it is a test of our love of Christ when we respond to needs, are gracious and hospitable, and manifest a fervent or intense love of Christ's people. We are not permitted to be recipients only: we must above all be givers, even as Christ gave Himself for us (II Cor. 8:9).

The anarchist or autarkist believes in a stateless society built upon the natural goodness of man, an illusion. The Christian believes in original sin as a fact in a fallen world; he cannot be an anarchist. He is, however, given a vision in all of Scripture of the triumph of covenant man on earth. This triumph requires the law of God to be obeyed by redeemed men. This means the tithe, and, beyond this, generous giving and hospitality. St. Paul's word, *sufficiency,* recalls the Greek cynics' anarchism, as well as the Stoic ideal. *Sufficiency* is in the Greek *autarkeia* (*auto,* self; *arkeo,* sufficient). We are told emphatically: "God is able to make all grace abound toward you; that ye, always having all sufficiency in all things, may abound to every good work" (II Cor. 9:8). *We* gain sufficiency, *autarkeia,* not by planning for ourselves primarily, but by sowing bountifully, i.e., giving bountifully to the needs of God's people and Kingdom, above and beyond the tithe (II Cor. 9:6). We are called to be *cheerful* (in the Greek, hilarious) givers (II Cor. 9:6) and thereby to gain God's blessing. The state of *autarkeia* comes, not by self-seeking, self-advancement, and self-protection, but by a hilarious or cheerful, joyous service to God and the people of God.

Man the sinner has no capacity for *autarkeia.* The careful, niggardly Christian who finds generosity and hospitality painful and costly, also has no capacity for *autarkeia.* Those who lay up treasures for themselves, and are not rich toward God and His people, are called *fools* by our Lord (Luke 12:13-21). "Take heed, and beware of covetousness: for a man's life consisteth not in the abundance of the things which he possesseth" (Luke 12:15).

*Autarkeia* is gained by men and society as they seek *first* the Kingdom of God and His righteousness. *Then* all the material blessings men seek *shall* be added to them (Matt. 6:31-34). When property is over-valued and made our main source of security, like manna, it will not keep. Our Lord declared:

> Lay not up for yourselves treasures upon earth, where moth and rust doth corrupt, and where thieves break through and steal:
> But lay up for yourselves treasures in heaven, where neither rust doth corrupt, and where thieves do not break through nor steal:
> For where your treasure is, there will your heart be also. (Matt. 6:19-21)

### 10. The Law and the Pharisees

"Strict" churches which pride themselves on being scripturally sound are often the most lawless in their view of the Scripture. Two examples can be cited.

A minister in a denomination which permits divorce on the grounds of adultery stated that he refused always to perform any marriage ceremony where a divorced person was involved. Every congregation he had served had agreed with him in his stand. Divorce, he said, is a dirty business, and there has to be guilt on both sides; it takes two to make a fight, and I am not God, so how can I judge? Behind this seeming humility is the most arrogant pride. It does not take two to make a fight: more than one innocent person has been assaulted over the years. The evil need no excuse to wage war on the righteous. When I asked this minister if he admitted that Scripture permits divorce for adultery, he agreed that it does. The point then, I insisted, was that he was trying to be more holy than God and was tampering with Scripture no less than any modernist. He was depriving God's people their due justice and the freedom God's word grants them.

In another case, a young woman, member of a Reformed church, was deserted by her husband, who began to live adulterously with another woman; this other woman was an heiress whose money he intended to enjoy. He made this statement to me and to his wife. This relationship soon broke up, only to be followed by other such unions in another state. The wife, a particularly fine woman, had been reared to regard divorce as shameful and only reluctantly secured a divorce from her long-gone husband, who had secured a Mexican divorce and remarried. Five years later, after a move into another neighborhood in the same city (none too large), she applied for membership (by transfer) to the church whose pastor is G.

> I thought to join Rev. G's congregation and went for a talk with him late in January. Do you know what he said to me??? He said that a spouse who leaves does so "because he is not *satisfied*." I expressed disagreement, and he said it was "plain horse-sense" to see it as such. When I asked for an explanation he said that "a third party would have to decide" the validity of such desertion. There was more said, but I felt so rotten-dirty upon leaving him; I felt he was blaming me for my ex-husband's sin.

The entire story was more or less known to the minister; he simply had no desire to "get involved" with divorced people in his church. His own reprobate nature was clearly manifest in his reasoning. His idea of motivation was radically anti-Christian. The actions of men for a Christian have their roots in *either sin or grace,* not in the "failure" of someone to "satisfy," clearly not true in this case. The plain fact is that Mrs. B., a godly woman, had acted in a thoroughly Christian manner throughout the marriage and had grown in grace *and* intellectual maturity to a considerable degree as a result of her experiences. For this Reformed Pharisee, her obvious Christian grace was too disquieting to the smooth surface of his hypocrisy. Even as one person among a thousand or two, he wanted no part of either her "problem" (divorce) *or* her obvious grace.

Meanwhile, this man and others like him will tolerate adultery (but not divorce) as long as the appearance of holiness is not disturbed. Of such as in the kingdom of Satan.

## Appendix 11

## The Constitutional Law of Privacy:
## Past, Present and Future

### By Herbert W. Titus, Professor of Law

*Past*

The current outcries for women's rights to state financed abortions, for homosexuals' rights to state protection from discrimination, and for other so-called "privacy" rights have roots deep in America's constitutional past. As early as 1795, four years before Chief Justice John Marshall established judicial review in *Marbury v. Madison,*[1] Justice Samuel Chase asserted, in the case of *Calder v. Bull,* that a legislative act, contrary to "the general principles of law and reason," cannot be considered "law" even if there was nothing expressly written prohibiting that exercise of power in either the state or federal constitutions.[2] Justice Chase claimed that the Court's constitutional authority and duty required it to test any legislative act by "the great principles of the social compact:"

> "The people of the *United States* erected their Constitutions. . . to establish justice, to promote the general welfare, to secure the blessings of liberty; and to protect their *persons* and *property* from violence. The purposes for which men enter into society will determine the *nature* and *terms* of the *social* compact; and as they are the foundation of the legislative power, *they* will decide what are the *proper* objects of it: The *nature* and *ends* of *legislative* power will limit the *exercise* of it." (Emphasis in original.)[3]

In opposition to this loosely stated view of constitutional law, Justice James Iredell asserted that the American constitutional experience reflected a quite different assumption:

> "it has been the policy of all the American states, which have, individually, framed their state constitutions since the revolution, and of the people of the United States, when they framed the Federal Constitution, to define with precision the objects of the legislative power, and to restrain its exercise within marked and settled boundaries."[4]

---

1. 5 U. S. (1 Cranch) 137 (1803).
2. Calder v. Bull, 3 U. S. 305, 3 Dall. 386 (1798).
3. *Id.,* 3 U. S. at 307, 3 Dall. at 388.
4. *Id.,* 3 U. S. at 315-16, 3 Dall. at 398-99.

Calling Chase's views those of a "speculative jurist," Justice Iredell summed up his opposition to any contention that the Court had authority to pronounce a law void because it was contrary to the principles of natural justice:

> "The ideas of natural justice are regulated by no fixed standard; the ablest and the purest men have differed upon the subject; and all that the Court could properly say, in such an event, would be that the Legislature (possessed of an equal right of opinion) had passed an act which, in the opinion of the judges, was inconsistent with the abstract principles of natural justice."[5]

When Chief Justice Marshall wrote *Marbury v. Madison* in justification of the Court's authority to review Congressional enactments under the federal constitution, he sided with Justice Iredell, not Justice Chase. While he recognized the "social compact" as the foundation of the American fabric of government, he did not agree with Chase that the simple exercise of the right of the people to establish a government to promote their own happiness established constitutional legal limits on the powers delegated to a legislative body. Rather, he believed that those limits only came if they were expressly embodied in a written constitution:

> "That the people have an original right to establish, for their future government, such principles as, in their opinion, shall most conduce to their own happiness is the basis on which the whole American fabric has been erected. . . .
>
> "This original and supreme will organizes the government, and assigns to different departments their respective powers. It may either stop here, or establish certain limits not to be transcended by those departments.
>
> "The government of the United States is of the latter description. The powers of the legislature are defined and limited; and that those limits may not be mistaken, or forgotten, the constitution is written."[6]

The Chief Justice's argument was twofold: first, the powers granted to the federal government had been "limited" and second, those limits had been embodied in a written constitution. He stressed the latter point repeatedly and rested his case for the institution of judicial review squarely upon the fact that the constitution had been reduced to writing:

> "Certainly all those who have framed written constitutions contemplate them as forming the fundamental and paramount law of the nation, and, consequently, the theory of every such government must be, that an act of the legislature, repugnant to the constitution, is void.
>
> "This theory is essentially attached to a written constitution, and,

---

5. *Id.,* 3 U. S. at 316, 3 Dall. at 399.
6. Marbury v. Madison, *supra* note 1, at 175-76.

is consequently to be considered, by this court, as one of the fundamental principles of our society.[7]

While Chief Justice Marshall's opinion rested the institution of judicial review on the existence of a written constitution, the "natural justice" philosophy found in Justice Chase's remarks in *Calder v. Bull* has survived 175 years of United States constitutional history. While it has a checkered past and while it appeared dead after its heyday in the "liberty of contract" cases in the late 1800's and early 1900's, the presupposition that the judges have a right to review the constitutionality of legislative acts notwithstanding the absence of an explicit written constitutional restraint has come into the fore once again in the cases establishing the so-called right of privacy.

In 1965 the United States Supreme Court decided the case of *Griswold v. Connecticut.*[8] In that case the executive director of the Planned Parenthood League of Connecticut had been prosecuted and convicted for aiding and abetting married persons in the use of any drug or device "for the purpose of preventing conception" in violation of the laws of Connecticut. In a 6-2 decision, the majority struck down the Connecticut statute as having violated the 14th Amendment's prohibition against state denials of "liberty" without due process of law. While the 6-man majority could not agree on a single opinion, Justice Arthur Goldberg wrote on behalf of two other colleagues the opinion which has since become the foundation of the constitutionally recognized right of privacy. Utilizing the Ninth Amendment as a convenient vehicle for grafting onto the constitution the principle of "natural justice," Justice Goldberg wrote:

> . . .the Ninth Amendment shows a belief of the Constitution's authors that fundamental rights exist that are not expressly enumerated in the first eight amendments and an intent that the list of rights included there not be deemed exhaustive. . . .
>
> "In determining which rights are fundamental, judges are not left at large to decide cases in light of their personal and private notions. Rather, they must look to the 'traditions and [collective] conscience of the people' to determine whether a principle is 'so rooted [there] . . . as to be ranked as fundamental.' The inquiry is whether a right involved 'is of such a character that it cannot be denied without violating those "fundamental principles of liberty and justice which lie at the base of all our civil and political institutions". . . .' "[9]

In his dissenting remarks, reminiscent of his 18th century colleague Iredell, Justice Hugo Black reacted to this revival of the "natural justice" constitutional law thesis:

---

7. *Id.,* 5 U. S. at 176-77.
8. 381 U. S. 479 (1965).
9. *Id.,* 381 U. S. at 492-93.

"My Brother Goldberg has adopted the recent discovery that the Ninth Amendment as well as the Due Process Clause can be used by this Court as authority to strike down all state legislation which this Court thinks violated 'fundamental principles of liberty and justice,' or is contrary to the 'traditions and [collective] conscience of our people.' He also states, without proof satisfactory to me, that in making decisions on this basis judges will not consider 'their personal and private notions.' One may ask how they can avoid considering them. Our Court certainly has no machinery with which to take a Gallup Poll. And the scientific miracles of this age have not yet produced a gadget which the Court can use to determine what traditions are rooted in the '[collective] conscience of our people.' Moreover, one would have to look far beyond the language of the Ninth Amendment to find that the Framers vested in this Court any such awesome veto powers over lawmaking, either by the States or by the Congress."[10]

This conflict in the *Griswold* case did not rise full blown after laying dormant for 167 years. Rather, it has constitutional roots in two earlier episodes of American history: first, the ratification of the Civil War Amendments to the United States Constitution and an 1872 United States Supreme Court decision interpreting those amendments; and second, the rise and fall of constitutional "economic liberty" in the name of due process of law in the United States Supreme Court cases beginning in the early 1900's and extending into the 1930's.

Just two years after the ratification of the Fifteenth Amendment to the United States Constitution, the last of a series of three constitutional changes designed to protect the newly freed slave from hostile action against him, the United States Supreme Court, in the *Slaughter-House* cases, faced its first major task calling for an interpretation of the newly ratified Thirteenth and Fourteenth Amendments.[11] Ironically, the plaintiffs in this case were not members of the newly freed slave class; nor did they claim that they were victims of hostile actions taken against them as a class. Rather, the plaintiffs were independent butchers from New Orleans, Louisiana who contested the constitutionality of a Louisiana state statute granting an exclusive privilege to operate a slaughter-house in New Orleans to a legislatively chartered corporation so that they could no longer butcher animals in any place where they pleased. They claimed that this legislatively conferred economic favor violated the newly created guarantees embodied in the first two Civil War Amendments.

A bare majority of five out of nine justices rejected this claim on the ground that neither the prohibition against involuntary servitude, nor the new guarantees of freedom from state abridgement of federal privileges and immunities, from state denial of due process or from state denial of

---

10. *Id.,* 381 U. S. at 518-19.
11. Slaughter-House Cases, 83 U. S. (16 Wall.) 36 (1872).

equal protection of the laws, had been designed to proscribe a state from granting special economic privileges to any individual or group. The majority, after careful review of the constitutional text, its history and purpose, concluded that if the New Orleans butchers had any constitutional right to be protected from the economic favoritism conferred upon the new Louisiana corporation, that right was to be found in the state constitution, not in the newly enacted Thirteenth and Fourteenth Amendments. Indeed, many state constitutions contained prohibitions against the granting of special economic favors to a privileged few.[12] But the *Slaughter-House* majority refused to transfer those traditional state protections into the newly enacted privileges and immunities, due process and equal protection clauses of the Fourteenth Amendment.

While the majority refused to allow the politically disappointed New Orleans' butchers to enshrine into the Federal Constitution rights that are not there, the dissenters welcomed the opportunity to expand the new privileges and immunities, due process and equal protection clauses to include the claimed "economic freedom." Couched in appropriate legal language respecting the "intent of Congress," one dissenter, Justice Stephen J. Field, drew on the common law of England, various state court decisions under the state constitutions, and natural justice to find a federal constitutionally guaranteed "right to pursue a lawful employment in a lawful manner...."[13] After all, Justice Field, resurrecting Justice Chase's *Calder v. Bull* social compact theory, reasoned that:

"(g)rants of exclusive privileges, such as it (sic) made by the act in question, are opposed to the whole theory of free government, and it requires no aid from any bill of rights to render them void. That only is a free government, in the American sense of the term, under which the inalienable right of every citizen to pursue his happiness is unrestrained, except by just, equal and impartial laws."[14]

While Justice Field's views did not prevail in the *Slaughter-House* cases, thirty-five years later a bare majority of the United States Supreme Court did follow in his footsteps in the case of *Lochner v. New York.*[15] This time the plaintiff, owner of a bakery in the state of New York, claimed that a state labor law which prohibited his hiring an employee to

12. e.g., Article 41, Constitution of Maryland: "That monopolies are odious, contrary to the spirit of a free government and the principles of commerce, and ought not to be suffered." This article has been part of every Maryland Constitution since 1776. Grempler v. Multiple Listing Bureau, 258 Md. 419, 266 A.2d 1 (1970). See, also, Article I, Section 20 of the Oregon Constitution: "No law shall be passed granting to any citizen or class of citizens privileges, or immunities, which, upon the same terms, shall not equally belong to all citizens." The grant of an exclusive right to fish in a navigable stream was held under this section to be a prohibited monopoly. Hume v. Rogue R. Packing Co., 51 Or. 237, 259, 83 P. 391, 92 P. 1065, 96 P. 856 (1908).
13. Slaughter-House Cases, *supra* note 11, at 97.
14. *Id.,* 83 U. S. at 111.
15. 198 U. S. 45 (1905).

work for more than sixty hours in one week denied him his liberty without due process of law. In sustaining the plaintiff's claim, the Court majority made no effort to show that the right claimed was one placed in the Constitution by the post-Civil War Congress, the architect of the Fourteenth Amendment. Rather, it drew simply from a laundry list of "liberty" rights that the Court, eight years earlier, had made in its opinion in *Allgeyer v. Louisiana.*[16] The *Allgeyer* list, almost identical to that rejected in the *Slaughter-House* cases, read as follows:

> "The liberty mentioned in that amendment (the Fourteenth) means not only the right of the citizen to be free from the mere physical restraint of his person, as by incarceration, but the term is deemed to embrace the right of the citizen to be free in the enjoyment of all his faculties; to be free to use them in all lawful ways; to live and work where he will; to earn his livelihood by any lawful calling; to pursue any livelihood or avocation, and for that purpose to enter into all contracts which may be proper, necessary and essential to his carrying out to a successful conclusion the purposes above mentioned."[17]

It was this "right of contract" that the Court elevated into a constitutional privilege in *Lochner,* a right not found anywhere in American constitutional history, whether federal or state, or even in English common law. The Court manufactured the freedom to contract out of whole cloth and, then, proceeded to allow those exceptions with which it agreed and to reject all those exceptions with which it disagreed.[18] In reaction, Mr. Justice Holmes, dissenting in *Lochner,* wrote his famous sentence: "The 14th Amendment does not enact Mr. Herbert Spencer's Social Statics."[19]

Mr. Justice Holmes did not, however, issue a call for the Court to return to the text and historic purposes of that Amendment, rather he simply desired a different result:

> "I think that the word 'liberty' in the 14th Amendment, is perverted when it is held to prevent the natural outcome of a dominant opinion, unless it can be said that a rational and fair man necessarily would admit that the statute proposed would infringe fundamental principles as they have been understood by the traditions of our people and our law."[20]

This desire, a far cry from the one articulated by the constitution's drafters and Chief Justice Marshall, was elevated into constitutional doctrine in the 1930's by the Court as it approved again and again New Deal

---

16. 165 U. S. 578 (1897).
17. *Id.,* 165 U. S. at 589.
18. E.g., Lochner v. New York, *supra* note 15, at 53-54.
19. *Id.,* 198 U. S. at 75.
20. *Id.,* 198 U. S. at 76.

and other economic measures as having a "rational basis."[21] But as the above quoted sentence from Holmes' dissent proves, nothing is "arbitrary" or "irrational" in the abstract. Rather, the benchmark in these cases became whether or not the legislature had violated "fundamental principles as they have been understood by the traditions of our people and our law."

## Present

While it is true that under the new constitutional formulation, the New Deal and successor courts ceased striking down, in the name of the federal constitution, federal and state measures regulating man's economic affairs, this change came about not because the new justices found nothing in the text, history or purposes of the written constitutional guarantees prohibiting such measures. Rather, they consistently reserved the right to pronounce an act unconstitutional if it was found to be "irrational" or "arbitrary." While Justice Field's constitutional philosophy set forth in his dissent in the *Slaughter-House* cases did not provide lasting constitutional victories for the economic interests in this country, his philosophy had not been rejected. It was not until the 1960's and the 1970's, however, that this truth became clear as the Court began to struggle with constitutional claims for the right of privacy.

Only two justices, William O. Douglas and Hugo Black, acknowledged the link between the claimed right of marital privacy in the *Griswold* case and the earlier discredited "economic liberty" cases. Justice Douglas, writing in support of a constitutional marital privacy right, admitted that it could not be found in any specific text of the Constitution. Rather, he concluded that it was contained in the "penumbras formed by emanations from those guarantees" found in the First, Second, Third, Fourth and Fifth Amendments. But the "penumbras" were neither shaped nor contained by reference to constitutional text, history, or purpose; rather, Justice Douglas concluded by openly acknowledging the extra-constitutional origin of the right of marital privacy:

> "We deal with a right of privacy older than the Bill of Rights—older than our political parties, older than our school system. Marriage is a coming together for better or worse hopefully enduring, and intimate to the degree of being sacred. It is an association that promotes a way of life, not causes; a harmony in living, not political faiths; a bilateral loyalty, not commercial or social projects. Yet it is an association for as noble a purpose as any involved in our prior decisions."[22]

---

21. E. G., United States v. Carolene Products Co., 304 U. S. 144 (1938); Williamson v. Lee Optical of Oklahoma, 348 U. S. 483 (1955). Only Justice Hugo Black disagreed. See Lincoln Federal Labor Union v. Northwestern Iron & Metal Co., 335 U. S. 525, 536 (1949) and Ferguson v. Skrupa, 372 U. S. 726, 731-32 (1963).
22. Griswold v. Connecticut, *supra* note 8, at 484.

While Justice Douglas found no constitutional text to support the result he desired to reach, he found a convenient case precedent in *Meyer v. Nebraska,*[23] a 1923 case striking down a Nebraska statute prohibiting the teaching of any language but English in the first eight grades of the public and private schools. In support of its holding the Court in *Meyer* had concluded that a German teacher's liberty to teach was protected from the Nebraska law under the Fourteenth Amendment due process clause and reasoned, in part, as follows:

> "While this court has not attempted to define with exactness the liberty thus guaranteed, the term has received much consideration, and some of the included things have been definitely stated. Without doubt, it denotes not merely freedom from bodily restraint, but also the right of the individual to contract, to engage in any of the common occupations of life, to acquire useful knowledge, to marry, establish a home and bring up children, to worship God according to the dictates of his own conscience, and, generally, to enjoy those privileges long recognized at common law as essential to the orderly pursuit of happiness by free men."[24]

Eleven years later Justice Blackmun relied upon the *Meyer* precedent when he wrote the majority opinion in *Roe v. Wade,*[25] the abortion case which established a constitutional right of privacy "broad enough to encompass a woman's decision whether or not to terminate her pregnancy":

> "The Constitution does not explicitly mention any right of privacy. In a line of decisions, however, going back perhaps as far as . . . (1891), the Court has recognized that a right of personal privacy, or a guarantee of certain areas or zones of privacy, does exist under the Constitution. In varying contexts the Court. . . (has) indeed found at least the roots of that right. . . in the concept of liberty guaranteed in the first section of the Fourteenth Amendment, see Meyer v. Nebraska, 262 U. S. 390, 399 (1923)."[26]

Thus, the right of privacy that has been endorsed today in the abortion and other related cases has roots in a "natural justice" constitutional law methodology that was explicitly rejected by the framers of the Constitution and by the Supreme Court, itself, in the first 100 years of its existence. Today, while there are a few who protest this heresy,[27] most welcome the casting off of the 18th Century written constitutional strait jacket. Not only has the current Supreme Court, both "liberals" and "conservatives," endorsed this way of doing constitutional law,[28] so

---

23. 262 U. S. 390 (1923).
24. *Id.,* 262 U. S. at 399.
25. 410 U. S. 113 (1973).
26. *Id.,* 410 U. S. at 153.
27. E.g., Ely, "The Wages of Crying Wolf: A Comment on Roe v. Wade," 82 Yale L. J. 920 (1973).
28. E.g., Whalen v. Roe,_____U. S._____, 97 S.Ct. 869 (1977).

have most constitutional law scholars. Preeminent among the latter is Harvard Law Professor Laurence H. Tribe, a prolific writer and author of the recently published treatise *American Constitutional Law.* In his preface to that 1174 page volume, Professor Tribe unabashedly endorses the "natural justice" philosophy:

> "(T)he Constitution is an intentionally incomplete, often deliberately indeterminate structure for the participatory evolution of political ideals and governmental practices."[29]

In words that echo Justice Samuel Chase's philosophy stated nearly 200 years earlier, Professor Tribe updates the "social compact" theory of constitutional law.

> "(T)he highest mission of the Supreme Court, in my view, is not to conserve judicial credibility, but in the Constitution's own phrase, 'to form a more perfect union' between right and rights within that charter's necessarily evolutionary design."[30]

Nowhere is this "evolutionary design," one imposed upon the Constitution by Mr. Tribe and not by the framers, more evident than in his chapter on "privacy and personhood."

At times Mr. Tribe's evolutionary perspective gets away from tight control as evidenced by the following passage:

> "Society alters; some say evolves. Values change. Majorities grow more complacent; factions rigidify. Locked into frozen configurations, legislators may either ignore sound opportunities for progress, or opt for novelty without adequate thought of consequences. An unchecked spiral of change ultimately entails the same danger threatened by the most stubborn opposition to change. Either possibility can impart a teleology to positivist lawgiving which may equal legislated perpetual conformity."[31]

But Mr. Tribe does not allow such elegant asides to divert him from defining the major task confronting the Court in the right to privacy cases:

> "Human beings are of course the intended beneficiaries of our constitutional scheme. The Constitution was consecrated to the blessings of liberty for ourselves and our posterity—yet it contains no discussion of the right to be a *human* being; no definition of a person.... The judiciary has thus reached into the Constitution's spirit and structure, and has elaborated from the spare text an idea of the 'human' and a conception of 'being' not merely contemplated but required."[32]

---

29. Laurence H. Tribe, *American Constitutional Law* iii (Mineola, N. Y.: Foundation Press 1978).
30. *Id.,* at iv.
31. *Id.,* at 892.
32. *Id.,* at 893.

So the true task of the Court in today's right of privacy cases is to divine, in the name of the constitution, what it means to be human! One need not look very deep into the Supreme Court privacy decisions before one realizes how accurate Mr. Tribe's analysis is.

In *Roe v. Wade,* the case which established the constitutional right to abortions, the Supreme Court not only decided that an unborn fetus could not be a "person" within the meaning of the Fourteenth Amendment, but that essential to the "personhood" of "womanhood" was the right to terminate an unwanted pregnancy. What was the source of these rulings? It was emphatically not the Constitution. Rather, it was the common law. Unborn fetuses were not recognized as "persons" eligible at common law to sue for damages for tortious wrongs done them; but at the same time a woman was not prohibited by the common law of crimes from procuring an abortion.[33] How did these common law truths become grafted onto the Constitution? The significance of *Meyer v. Nebraska,* that 1923 case relied on in both *Griswold* and *Roe v. Wade,* cannot be overemphasized. While the 1923 Court did not specifically include the right of a woman to choose to terminate her pregnancy in its list of "liberty" guarantees, it had included the general "privileges long recognized at common law as essential to the orderly pursuit of happiness by free men."[34] Thus, the Court in the abortion case engaged in its long historical inquiry into the abortion laws and discovered that, at common law, abortion was not a crime. Had it been a common law crime, then presumably the right to choose to terminate a pregnancy could not have been one of the common law privileges referred to in the *Meyer* case and, therefore, could not have been included in the privacy right rooted in the due process liberty guarantee of the Fourteenth Amendment.

In a recent action taken by the Supreme Court, this limiting language of the *Meyer* precedent may have been taken seriously. In *Doe v. Commonwealth's Attorney*[35] a three judge federal court in Virginia refused in 1975 to grant declaratory or injunctive relief to bar enforcement or threatened enforcement of the state's criminal sodomy statute against male homosexuals. The 2 man majority opinion concluded its decision by noting the consistent history of prohibition against homosexuality and other sexual perversions:

> "Although a questionable law is not removed from question by a lapse of any prescriptive period, the longevity of the Virginia statute does testify to the State's interest and its legitimacy. It is not an upstart notion, it has ancestry going back to Judaic and Christian

---

33. Roe v. Wade, *supra* note 25, at 132-36, 138?41, and 158.
34. Meyer v. Nebraska, *supra* note 23, at 399. See note 24, supra, and accompanying text.
35. 403 F. Supp. 1199 (E. D. Va. 1975), aff'd., 425 U. S. 901 (1976).

law. The immediate parentage may be readily traced to the Code of Virginia of 1792. All the while the law has been kept alive, as evidenced by periodic amendments, the last in the 1968 Acts of the General Assembly of Virginia, c. 427."[36]

The United States Supreme Court summarily affirmed this decision[37] and, by doing so, indicated that the Constitutional right of privacy will not be extended to an activity, however private, that has a long and consistent history of condemnation at common law and in the early history of our country.

Yet one cannot be too certain. Justice William Brennan, in a 1977 opinion striking down a New York law regulating the distribution of contraceptives, observed "that the Court has not definitively answered the difficult question whether and to what extent the Constitution prohibits state statutes regulating... (private consensual sexual) behavior among adults."[38] While Justice Brennan may find such protection "in intrinsic human rights,"[39] constitutional law expert Professor Tribe believes that "natural law" and the common law as sources of the right of privacy "prove inadequate to serve as either the fount or the guardian of privacy or personhood in the modern era."[40] But what will be the "fount" and the "guardian"? Again, the Court's opinion in *Roe v. Wade* has provided the current answer, the wisdom of the nine Supreme Court justices, appropriately advised by counsel and by others.

In the abortion case, the Court allowed that a state could limit a woman's right to terminate her pregnancy in the first trimester by requiring that any abortion be performed by a licensed physician, in the second trimester by requiring any additional medical safeguards designed to protect a mother's health and in the third trimester by imposing any limits designed to protect the life of the "viable fetus." Why these criteria were imposed and not others may be explained in part by the fact that the lawyers for the State of Texas defended its anti-abortion statute solely on the grounds that the law was designed to protect the lives of the mother and of the fetus. The state only lamely suggested that the law was aimed, also, at discouraging immoral sexual conduct. Moreover, the state did not even raise an argument that the anti-abortion law rested on a state legislature's determination that life began at the moment of conception and that its laws were designed to protect that moral judgment. Given

---

36. *Id.,* 403 F. Supp. at 1202-03.

37. 425 U. S. 901 (1976); See, also, Gaylord v. Tacoma School Dist. #10, 88 Wash.2d 286, 559 P.2d 1340 (1977), cert. denied,_____U. S._____,_____S. Ct._____,54 L.ed.2d 160 (1977).

38. Carey v. Population Services International,_____U. S._____,97 S.Ct. 2010, 2021 n. 17 (1977).

39. Smith v. Organization of Foster Families,_____U. S._____, 97 S.Ct. 2094, 2110-11 (1977).

40. Tribe, *supra* note 29, at 894.

the instrumentalist and utilitarian arguments of the state, the Court rendered an instrumentalist and utilitarian decision. As Professor Tribe has put it, the Court has chosen not so much "a decision in favor of abortion" as "a decision in favor of leaving the matter, however it might come out in particular cases, to women rather than to legislative majorities. . . ." After all, the greater threat to life may, in fact, come from a rule allowing a legislative majority to choose a policy to prohibit abortions which necessarily would also allow that majority to compel abortions than from a rule giving that authority over life to the potential mother.[41]

Would it have made any difference if Texas had pressed an argument that it had based its anti-abortion statute on a moral judgment that "human life commences at conception?"[42] Could the state thereby have avoided the result in that case? More important, could a state successfully defend its sodomy laws which prohibit private consensual adult homosexual activity by contending that the state has determined that the moral fibre of the community is threatened by private adult consensual homosexual activities?

Justice Blackmun stated in the abortion case that the Court did not answer the question of when life begins:

> "Texas urges that. . . life begins at conception. . . . We need not resolve the difficult question of when life begins. When those trained in the respective disciplines of medicine, philosophy, and theology are unable to arrive at any consensus, the judiciary, at this point in the development of man's knowledge, is not in a position to speculate as to the answer."[43]

Notwithstanding this disclaimer, the Court proceeded to review the divergent opinions on the question ranging from the stoic belief that life begins at birth and extending through various religious positions to the Catholic endorsement that life begins at conception.[44] Justice Blackmun neatly avoided answering the question of when life begins by labelling the fetus "potential life" and, then, by pronouncing the Court's moral judgment that potential life deserved protection only at the point of viability. This intellectual sleight-of-hand was used to support the remarkable statement that "we do not agree that, by adopting *one theory of life,* Texas may override the rights of the pregnant woman that are at stake." (Emphasis added).[45]

In effect, the Court ruled that no state may adopt an abortion law based upon any absolute moral value about when life begins. In the name of the Constitution, the Court has imposed not only a requirement that a

---

41. *Id.,* at 932-33.
42. See, e.g., Rhode Island Senate Bill 73-5287 Substitute A, March 13, 1973.
43. Roe v. Wade, *supra* 25, 410 U. S. at 159.
44. *Id.,* 410 U. S. at 160-61.
45. *Id.,* 410 U. S. at 162.

state must adopt a relativistic view of life, but that it must endorse only the Supreme Court's relativistic view, namely, that life cannot begin before the point of viability![46]

The Court's constitutional endorsement of moral relativism has not been confined to the issue of life in the abortion cases. In *Planned Parenthood v. Danforth*[47] the Court found invalid a Missouri statute requiring, in the case of a married woman, the consent of the husband before the wife could have an abortion in the first twelve weeks of pregnancy and, in the case of an unmarried woman under the age of 18, the consent of a parent or guardian unless a doctor certified the abortion to be required to save the life of the mother. Recognizing that the state had a legitimate interest in promoting marital and family relationships, the Court nonetheless rejected the state's endorsement of a family structure with the husband or the father as the absolute final moral authority. Instead, the Court, again on behalf of the Constitution, imposed a relativistic moral model on the family.

In the case of the husband and wife, the Court found "it difficult to believe that the goal of fostering mutuality and trust in a marriage, and of strengthening the marital relationship and the marriage institution, will be achieved by giving the husband veto power exercisable for any reason whatever or for no reason at all."[48] It is equally difficult to understand how the Court's constitutional rule *allowing* a wife to obtain an abortion without her husband's consent for any reason whatever or for no reason at all will foster and strengthen mutuality and trust in the marriage relationship. Yet, the *Danforth* opinion requires a state to guarantee the wife's veto over the husband's desires on the decision not to bear the couple's child. This absolute rule, while it might be tempered by a state law requiring the wife to inform and to consult with her husband before procuring an abortion, has been justified by the Court as required because "it is the woman who physically bears the child and who is the more directly and immediately affected by the pregnancy, as between the two, (and) the balance weighs in her favor."[49]

As for the unmarried woman under the age of 18, the Court again

---

46. That view, itself, is subject to change. As another Harvard Law Professor, Archibald Cox, has noted: "... (T)he opinion (in Roe v. Wade)... read(s) like a set of hospital rules and regulations, whose validity is good enough this week but will be destroyed with new statistics upon the medical risks of childbirth and abortion or new advances in providing for the separate existence of a fetus.... Constitutional rights ought not to be created under the Due Process Clause unless they can be stated in principles sufficiently absolute to give them roots throughout the community and continuity over significant periods of time, and to lift them above the level of the pragmatic political judgments of a particular time and place." Archibald Cox, *The Role of the Supreme Court in American Government* 113-114 (New York: Oxford 1976).

47. 428 U. S. 52 (1976).

48. *Id.,* 428 U. S. at 71.

49. *Ibid.*

voiced skepticism that "providing a parent with absolute power to over-rule a determination, made by the physician and his minor patient, to terminate the patient's pregnancy will serve to strengthen the family unit." The Court concluded, also, that the veto power would not "enhance parental authority or control where the minor and the nonconsenting parent are so fundamentally in conflict and the very existence of the pregnancy already has fractured the family structure."[50] Because the Court did not believe in the workability of a family structure headed by a father and mother, it chose to impose on the family a democratic system with power in the child to veto the parents' decision conditioned only upon whether the minor is of sufficient age or maturity to vote!

After the Court's constitutional forays into morality in the abortion area, the lesson is clear: The only moral values that are now clearly constitutionally impermissible for a state to endorse are those resting upon Christian Biblical teachings. A state cannot choose absolutely between life and death, but must structure its criminal laws to reflect a continuum of potential life, life, potential death and death. Likewise, a state cannot endorse a family structure designating the husband or the father as the ultimate decision maker for that family, but must choose a view that accommodates within the family structure "democratic and reasonable" processes.

Given this reading of the abortion cases, the impact of those cases on the claim for homosexual rights is much more significant. The state cannot insist on an absolute ban on private adult consensual homosexual behavior because, by doing so, it would endorse the view that all homosexual activity and all homosexuals engaging in that activity are equally bad. Such an absolute view of sexual perversion and of man will simply not square with current utilitarian notions of societal harm and with current scientific studies of homosexual choice.[51] As for measuring societal harm, any claim that any homosexual activity causes serious spiritual harm not only to the participating, related and neighboring individuals, but also to the state and nation does not even fit into the social scientist's empirical measurement formula. It is difficult to imagine either a state's making such an argument or the Court's taking it seriously. Without overt Biblical support, such as that available in Leviticus Chapter 18 and Romans Chapter 1, a state will be hard pressed to show why an absolute ban on homosexual activity is required. Rather, one can already envision the parade of moral goodies that will be marched into court on behalf of homosexual freedom—the problem of overpopulation, the positive contribution of homosexuals to society, and the

---

50. *Id.,* 428 U. S. at 75.
51. See W. Barnett, *Sexual Freedom and the Constitution* (Albuquerque, University of New Mexico Press: 1973).

absence of any scientific data supporting an absolute ban.

But the homosexual claim does not stop here. Rather, they attack the basic assumption that underlies all criminal prohibitions against private adult consensual homosexual acts, namely, that homosexual behavior is the result of a sexual preference over which the actor has control for which he may be morally blamed. But recent "scientific studies" point to genetic or environmental factors.[52] While these studies do not unanimously endorse the conclusion that a person has virtually "no choice" whether he becomes a homosexual or a heterosexual, they point in a direction away from moral responsibility and toward environmental or genetic determinism. If sexual preferences are largely, if not entirely, determined either before birth or in early childhood, then a state could not constitutionally continue an absolute ban on all homosexual behavior given the Supreme Court's penchant for relativistic moral standards.

But the scientific evidence pointing to genes and environment as the causes of homosexuality cuts an even broader constitutional pathway. It also lays the groundwork for the current claims for "gay rights laws" which would prohibit discrimination against homosexuals in housing, jobs, and in other activities.

In an effort to include homosexuals in the same class as Negroes, women and illegitimate children, Harvard Law Professor Tribe, has argued:

> "Plainly, the history of homosexuality has been largely a history of disapproval and disgrace, indeed, it would not be wholly implausible to suggest, just on this basis, that homosexuals form virtually a discrete and insular minority."[53]

If Professor Tribe's remarks are taken literally, one would have to draw the same parallel between Negroes, women and illegitimates and thieves, rapists, murderers and hosts of other malefactors. All criminal classes have a history of "disapproval and disgrace." Does Professor Tribe suggest that a state could not discriminate against any person who has been convicted of a crime? Of course not. But his argument favoring a constitutional ruling prohibiting discrimination against homosexuals rests upon the psychological studies that attribute homosexual behavior to genes and to environment and not to free choice.[54] The basic presupposition of those studies may be extended to all activities that have been

---

52. See, generally, H. Ellis, *Studies in the Psychology of Sex,* Part IV (New York: Random House 1942); D. Cory, *The Homosexual in America* (New York: Greenberg 1951); J. Marmor, ed., *Sexual Inversion: The Multiple Roots of Homosexuality* (New York: Stein & Day 1966); A. Cooper, "Aetiology of Homosexuality" in J. A. Loraine, *Understanding Homosexuality: Its Biological and Psychological Bases* (New York: Amer. Elsevier Pub. 1974).

53. Tribe, *supra* note 29, at 944.

54. *Id.,* at 944-45, n. 17.

traditionally considered criminal as noted psychiatrist Karl Menninger has long favored.[55] Can this logic be ignored by those claiming constitutional protection against state discriminatory practices against homosexuals? Acceptance of the homosexual claim will inevitably open the door for like claims on behalf of all other historic criminal classes.

That prospect would certainly have been a startling one to the Congress responsible for the drafting of the Thirteenth Amendment to the United States Constitution. That Amendment specifically provides that a person may be placed into slavery or involuntary servitude as punishment for a crime if the party has been duly convicted. If that is true, and if a homosexual could be punished for committing a homosexual act, then there can be no justification under the equal protection guarantee of the Fourteenth Amendment to prohibit any state law discriminating against homosexuals or against any other class of convicted criminals.[56] But this conclusion will follow only if the Court accepts, as constitutionally permissible, a state legislature's decision to adopt a moral, not a behaviorist or other psychological, model for man. The danger of constitutionally imposing a determinist model on the states has been recognized in *Powell v. Texas* where the Supreme Court rejected the contention that a chronic alcoholic could not be held liable for public drunkenness despite the fact that there was "scientific evidence" that such a person "has no choice" but to get drunk.[57] In fact, the whole criminal law system would come tumbling down if the Biblical model of man were abandoned in favor of current scientific theories about criminal behavior.

If the scientific theories about homosexuality are imposed on the states by the Court in the name of the constitutional equal protection, then there can be no legitimate stopping point to extending the same protection to all other criminal classes. The Court could, however, draw an arbitrary line short of this all-inclusive protection. On the other hand, the Court could gradually extend the line to alcoholics, drug users and others who engage in criminal activity. In fact, the United States Attorney General has already included "alcoholics" and "drug users" in the class of "handicapped persons" who are entitled to special government benefits and protection under the Rehabilitation Act of 1973.[58] The ero-

---

55. K. Menninger, *The Crime of Punishment* (New York: Viking 1969).
56. See *Richardson v. Ramirez,* 418 U. S. 24 (1974).
57. *Powell v. Texas,* 392 U. S. 514 (1968).
58. Letter dated April 12, 1977 from Griffin B. Bell, Attorney General to Joseph A. Califano, Secretary of the Department of Health, Education and Welfare. Section 504 of the Rehabilitation Act of 1973 [29 U.S.C. Section 794 (1975 Supp.)] provides that "(n)o otherwise qualified handicapped individual . . . shall, solely by reason of his handicap, be excluded from the participation in, be denied the benefits of, or be subjected to discrimination under any program or activity receiving Federal financial assistance." The term, "handicapped individual" is defined, in part, as "any individual who . . . has a physical or mental disability which for such individual constitutes or results in a substantial handicap

sion away of our traditional assumptions about moral blameworthiness in the areas of sexual preference and drug use will encourage the state to deal with "anti-social behavior" by utilizing behavioristic and other methods that Soviet Russia has found convenient in its war against political dissenters.[59]

## Future

In the right to privacy cases the United States Supreme Court has extended itself into areas uncharted by the Constitution. Powerful forces in government and in academia have been marshalled to support these newly created constitutional rights in "personal autonomy." Moreover, the general public has endorsed the privacy rights as a necessary expansion of individual liberty to protect against an ever growing bureaucratic state. In fact, the constitutional right of privacy cases lay the foundation for the erosion of all liberty because they represent humanistic man's effort to redefine what it means to be human. The traditional model of man as a morally responsible being is to be displaced by the social science model of man as a machine. If a man can be blamed for making a wrong choice, then he is entitled to the freedom to choose right instead of wrong. Liberty is essential to man as a moral being. But if man is only a machine, then liberty is either an illusion or, worse yet, it is a hindrance to the natural evolutionary processes.

The current effort in constitutional law to redefine man is suicidal. In the name of humanity and liberty the Court, unless it alters its course and returns to the historic purposes and written text of the Constitution, will usher in an age of totalitarian manipulation of the human being because he will be characterized solely by his genes and his environment. Only behaviorist B. F. Skinner or sociobiologist Norman Wilson has cause to rejoice. God's people, however, have no cause to despair. Rather, they can no longer be misled by those who claim that a Christian has no right to impose his religious values on others in society. Without the Biblical truths that man is *not* a machine and that God is *not* an evolutionary process, law and liberty are impossible. Armed with these truths the Christian must lead his fellow countrymen back to his true Constitutional inheritance.

---

to employment..." Relying upon current scientific authorities the Attorney General concluded that alcoholism and drug addiction are "diseases" and, therefore, could be characterized as physical or mental disabilities and, if sufficiently serious, could be found to result in a substantial handicap to employment for the individual.

59. See, e.g., Z. Medvedev and R. Medvedev, *A Question of Madness: Repression by Psychiatry in the Soviet Union* (New York: Vintage 1971).

# SCRIPTURE TEXTS

## OLD TESTAMENT

*Genesis*

| | |
|---|---|
| 1:26 | 388 |
| 1:26-28 | 9, 74, 78, 190, 272, 311, 315, 403, 424, 500, 573, 593, 646 |
| 1:28ff | 179 |
| 1:31 | 32, 304, 487, 557 |
| 2:1-3 | 683 |
| 2:2-3 | 8, 559 |
| 2:5, 8-15 | 311 |
| 2:7 | 189, 229 |
| 2:9 | 685 |
| 2:16-17 | 500 |
| 2:17 | 32, 190 |
| 2:19 | 92 |
| 2:23 | 593 |
| 2:23-24 | 389 |
| 2:24 | 198, 418 |
| 3:1-5 | 446, 531 |
| 3:1-6 | 593, 649 |
| 3:4-5 | 161 |
| 3:5 | 29, 85, 104, 166, 236, 290, 306, 372, 448, 528, 544, 583, 595, 646, 670 |
| 3:5, 12-13 | 5 |
| 3:7-19 | 29 |
| 3:8 | 244 |
| 3:9-13 | 529 |
| 3:15 | 32, 594 |
| 3:17 | 315 |
| 3:17-19 | 32, 190, 318, 320 |
| 4:7 | 125, 637 |
| 4:8 | 166 |
| 4:9-12 | 319 |
| 4:10 | 310 |
| 4:11-13 | 318 |
| 4:13 | 311 |
| 4:17, 23-24 | 236 |
| 4:19-24 | 593 |
| 4:23-24 | 166 |
| 6:1-5 | 593 |
| 6:5 | 444, 546 |
| 6:9 | 620 |
| 9:1 | 198 |
| 9:1-17 | 663 |
| 9:5 | 320 |
| 9:5-6 | 553 |
| 9:12 | 567 |
| 9:12-16 | 400 |
| 11:1ff | 195 |
| 11:1-9 | 198, 593 |
| 13:10 | 107 |
| 14:14 | 278 |
| 14:18-19 | 368 |

*Genesis*

| | |
|---|---|
| 14:19, 22 | 692 |
| 15:1 | 125 |
| 15:1-4 | 172 |
| 15:2-3 | 300 |
| 15:9ff | 663 |
| 15:19 | 18 |
| 17:1-9 | 181 |
| 17:7 | 601 |
| 17:11 | 567 |
| 17:13 | 278 |
| 17:15 | 428 |
| 18 | 705 |
| 18:1ff | 247 |
| 18:3 | 25 |
| 18:4 | 407 |
| 19:1, 4-5, 9, 21, 30 | 703 |
| 19:1, 9 | 107 |
| 19:2 | 25 |
| 20:11, 13 | 279 |
| 21:4, 22ff, 30 | 663 |
| 21:32 | 662 |
| 22:16-18 | 499, 511 |
| 22:24 | 190 |
| 24:38 | 17 |
| 24:49 | 279 |
| 26:22ff, 30 | 663 |
| 28:20-21 | 200 |
| 28:20-22 | 121 |
| 31:14-16 | 214 |
| 31:44, 49 | 662 |
| 31:44-55, 52, 54 | 663 |
| 31:49 | 595 |
| 32:28 | 428 |
| 36:11, 15, 42 | 18 |
| 37:29, 34 | 209 |
| 41:1ff | 156 |
| 44:20 | 575 |
| 44:37-44 | 694 |
| 45:22 | 694 |
| 46:31 | 17 |
| 47:23 | 311 |
| 48:5 | 18 |
| 49:1ff | 15 |

*Exodus*

| | |
|---|---|
| 3:5 | 58, 317 |
| 3:16, 18 | 658 |
| 4:22 | 394, 396 |
| 4:22-23 | 172, 191, 198 |
| 4:22-24 | 431 |
| 4:23 | 647 |
| 4:29 | 658 |
| 5:12-15 | 49 |

## NEW TESTAMENT

# INDEX